The Future of America's Death Penalty

THE FUTURE OF AMERICA'S DEATH PENALTY

An Agenda for the Next Generation of Capital Punishment Research

Edited by

Charles S. Lanier

William J. Bowers

James R. Acker

CAROLINA ACADEMIC PRESS
Durham, North Carolina

Copyright © 2009
Charles S. Lanier
William J. Bowers
James R. Acker
All Rights Reserved

Library of Congress Cataloging-in-Publication Data

The future of America's death penalty : an agenda for the next generation of capital punishment research / edited by Charles S. Lanier, William J. Bowers, James R. Acker.
  p. cm.
Includes bibliographical references.
ISBN 978-1-59460-426-3 (alk. paper)
 1. Capital punishment--United States. I. Lanier, Charles S., 1950- II. Bowers, William J. III. Acker, James R., 1951- IV. Title.

KF9227.C2F885 2008
345.73'0773--dc22

2008026810

CAROLINA ACADEMIC PRESS
700 Kent Street
Durham, North Carolina 27701
Telephone (919) 489-7486
Fax (919) 493-5668
www.cap-press.com

Printed in the United States of America

To the late Kermit L. Hall—historian, constitutional scholar, and former President of the University at Albany, whose encouragement and support remain a continuing inspiration for our Capital Punishment Research Initiative.

And ...

To Adriana, Trevor, and Logan Henry, who joined us just two short years ago. And, to Gail, who left us just yesterday.
—CSL

To Deborah, Nina, Anna, Paul, Michael, and Steven, all beloved veterans of my capital punishment research.
—WJB

To Jenny, Elizabeth, and Anna: that we may raise a glass and drink l'chaim.
—JRA

Contents

Foreword
  Ronald J. Tabak   xvii

Acknowledgments   xxix

Chapter 1 · Introduction and Overview—The Future of America's
           Death Penalty: An Agenda for the Next Generation
           of Capital Punishment Research
           Charles S. Lanier, William J. Bowers and James R. Acker   3
  References   8

Section I
General Research Directions and Challenges

Chapter 2 · Death Penalty Research Today and Tomorrow
           Hugo Adam Bedau   13
  A Selective Bibliography: Books on the Death Penalty
    Published 2000 to 2008   15

Chapter 3 · The Role of Constitutional Facts and Social Science
           Research in Capital Litigation: Is "Proof" of Arbitrariness
           or Inaccuracy Relevant to the Constitutional Regulation
           of the American Death Penalty?
           Jordan M. Steiker   23
  Constitutional Facts and the Constitutionalization of the
    Death Penalty: Arbitrariness and the Requirement of Narrowing
    in Capital Statutes   25
  The Rejection of Empirically Based Claims   26
  Renewed Regulation of the American Death Penalty:
    The Contemporary Concerns Surrounding Wrongful Convictions
    and Their Significance to Contemporary Death Penalty Doctrine   37

Conclusion 44
References 44

Chapter 4 · Why the Downturn in Death Sentences?
        William J. Bowers and Scott E. Sundby 47
  Anatomy of the Downturn 48
  Explanations for the Downturn 50
    The Jury and the Decision-Making Threshold 51
    The Professionalization of the Capital Defense Bar 55
    Growing Restraints on Prosecutors 56
  Research Strategy 57
    Trial Transcripts: A Lens on the Downturn 58
    Juror Interviews: Spotlighting the Ultimate Decision-Makers 59
    Strategic Sites: The Case Selection Question 60
  The Downturn Research in Context 63
  References 63

Chapter 5 · The ABA Death Penalty Moratorium Implementation Project: Setting the Stage for Further Research
        Deborah Fleischaker 69
  Methodology 70
  Key Findings: The Death Penalty's Fatal Flaws 72
  Information Exists, and Conclusions Were Drawn, but
    Additional Questions Remain 74
    Proportionality 74
    Defense Lawyering 76
    Racial Disparity 77
    Mental Illness 78
  A Lack of Data: Is Anyone Minding the Store? 78
    Basic Statistics/Information 79
    Prosecutors 81
    Clemency 82
    Law Enforcement 84
    Judicial Independence 85
  Conclusion 87
  References 87

Chapter 6 · The National Death Penalty Archive (NDPA):
"The Greatest Body of Evidence Ever Collected about
the Death Penalty in the United States"
Charles S. Lanier 89
Background and Evolution 90
   History 90
   Journey to a Collection 91
   Contents of the NDPA 92
The Future 94
   A Virtual Archive 95
   Quantitative Data 96
   New Collections 99
Conclusion 100
References 101
Appendix: Selected Holdings of the National Death Penalty Archive 103

Section II
The Process Leading to a Capital Sentence

Chapter 7 · Racial and Ethnic Disparities in Resolving Homicides
Michael L. Radelet and Glenn L. Pierce 113
Introduction 113
Assisting Families of Homicide Victims 116
Research on Homicide Clearance Rates 117
Methodology 119
Findings 120
Conclusion 130
References 132

Chapter 8 · Perspectives, Approaches, and Future Directions
in Death Penalty Proportionality Studies
David Baldus, George Woodworth and Neil Alan Weiner 135
Introduction 135
The Basic Approaches to Capital Charging and Sentencing
   Decisions: Supplemental Homicide Reports and *McCleskey*-Style
   Analyses 138
The Pros and Cons of the Two Basic Approaches 140
Studies That Focus on How Race Impinges on Decision Making
   at Specific Stages in the Process 142

Potential Legal and Policy Implications of Findings	143
The Direction of Future Research	145
References	147

Chapter 9 · Empirical Studies of Race and Geographic Discrimination in the Administration of the Death Penalty: A Primer on the Key Methodological Issues
David Baldus, George Woodworth, David Zuckerman, Neil Alan Weiner and Catherine M. Gross   153

Introduction	153
The Research Team	155
Research Design Issues	156
The Unit of Analysis	157
Defining the Universe	159
SHR-Based Studies	159
McCleskey-Style Studies	160
Sampling Issues	161
The Data Collection Instrument (DCI)/Codebook	162
Data Collection, Coding, and Entry for Machine Analysis	163
Setting the Stage for Substantive Analysis	165
Screening Cases for Factual Death-Eligibility	165
Modeling the Stage-Wise Flow of Cases through the System	166
Unadjusted Race and Geographic Disparities	167
Measures of Race and Ethnicity Disparities: The Basics	167
The Race and Ethnicity Measures	167
Disparity Measures of Practical Significance	170
Measures of Geographic Disparities	173
"Adjusted" Race Disparities Computed with Controls for Legitimate Non-Racial Case Characteristics that Bear on Offender Criminal Culpability	174
Basic Approaches	174
Model-Based Methods	174
Scale-Based Methods	176
Alternative Approaches	178
Propensity Analysis	178
Data Mining without Regard to Legal Relevance and Importance	178
Guidelines for Creating Culpability-Based Scales	179
Scales Based on Counts of Aggravating Circumstances	179
Scales Based on Qualitative Analyses of the Cases	179

Culpability Scales Based on Logistic Regression Models	180
Presenting the Results	182
The Basics	182
Variations	182
An Overview of Adjusted Stage-Wise Disparities	183
An Overview of Race and Culpability Interactions	183
Conclusion	185
Appendix	186
References	193

Chapter 10 · The Capital Jury Experiment of the Supreme Court
William J. Bowers, Thomas W. Brewer and Charles S. Lanier

	199
Evidence of Jurors' Failure to Meet Constitutional Requirements	202
The Capital Jury Project Research Agenda	206
Assessing Receptivity to Mitigation	207
Social Pressures on Individual Decision-Making	209
The Confounding Role of Race	210
Looking Ahead	212
Where Do We Stand?	217
References	218

Section III
The Process Beyond the Sentencing Decision

Chapter 11 · The Future of Innocence
Richard C. Dieter

	225
Introduction	225
The Impact of Innocence	225
Areas of Research	226
Counting the Cases of Innocence	228
Future Research Related to Innocence	231
Innocence Commissions	231
Innocent and Executed	233
Legislation	235
Other Questions	236
Conclusion	237
References	237

CONTENTS

Chapter 12 · Mental Retardation and the Death Penalty
Five Years after *Atkins*
John H. Blume, Sheri Lynn Johnson and Christopher Seeds   241
- Introduction   241
- Issues Arising from State Applications of the Clinical Definitions   243
  - Subaverage Intellectual Functioning   243
  - Adaptive Functioning Deficits   246
  - Onset before the Age of 18   249
  - Additional Requirements Employed by States   250
- Issues Arising from State Procedures for Determining Mental Retardation   251
- Additional Significant Issues   253
  - Race   253
  - Experts   254
- Areas for Future Research   255
- Conclusion   256
- References   257

Chapter 13 · The Effects of AEDPA on Justice
David R. Dow and Eric M. Freedman   261
- Introduction   261
- Getting to 1995   262
- AEDPA and After   265
- The Road Ahead   268
- Appendix: AEDPA Statistics—Total   270
- References   293

Chapter 14 · Toward a New Perspective on Clemency in the Killing State
Austin Sarat   297
- Introduction   297
- Playing Long Odds in the Lottery for Life   298
- Creating an Archive of Injustice   302
- Conclusion   304
- References   305

Section IV
The Utility and Efficacy of the Capital Sanction

Chapter 15 · Death and Deterrence Redux: Science, Law and Causal Reasoning on Capital Punishment	
Jeffrey Fagan and Valerie West	311
The Current Controversy	311
The New Deterrence Literature	315
Social Science Reasoning	317
The Structure of the Data	318
Theory and Specifications	320
Deterrence, Incapacitation and Life without Parole	321
Co-Morbid Epidemics	323
Are All Homicides Deterrable?	324
Measurement and Specification Errors	325
Missing Data	326
Early Cutoffs in Panel Designs	327
Computation and Model Specification Errors	328
Estimation Techniques	329
Deterrence	331
Rationality	333
Knowledge	335
Choice and Preferences	337
Cumulative and Conditional Corrosion	340
Conclusion: A Cautionary Tale	341
References	345
Appendix A	357
Chapter 16 · Researching Future Dangerousness	
Jon Sorensen	359
Introduction	359
Prior Studies	360
Commuted Capital Offenders	360
Inmates under a Sentence of Death	363
Murderers Sentenced to Terms of Imprisonment	364
Methodological Issues	367
Operational Definitions of Future Dangerousness and Their Effect on Base Rates	367
Choice of Comparison or Control Groups	368

Utilizing Agency Records 370
Individualizing Predictions Based on Specific
  Inmate Characteristics 371
Toward the Next Generation of Future Dangerousness Research 373
References 375

Chapter 17 · Capital Punishment and the Families of Victims and Defendants
Margaret Vandiver 379

Introduction 379
A Brief Assessment of Existing Research 380
  Families of Capital Defendants 380
  Families of Homicide Victims 382
The Context of Research on Families and
  Capital Punishment 384
  The Frequency of Homicide and the Rarity of Capital Punishment 384
  Time 386
  The Diffuse Effects of Capital Punishment 386
Potential Directions for Future Research 387
Policy Implications 390
Conclusion 392
References 392

Chapter 18 · The Cost of the Death Penalty in America: Directions for Future Research
Jonathan E. Gradess and Andrew L. B. Davies 397

The Early Bewilderment Period 399
The Study Period (1982–1993) 400
The Political Dissemination Period: 1993–2007 403
Areas for Future Research 406
  Indirect Costs and the Cost of Infrastructure 407
  Cost Savings through Coercion 408
  Diversion of Criminal Justice and Human Service
    Budgetary Resources 409
Conclusions: The One Spigot Period—2007 and Beyond 411
References 413

Section V
Examining the Punishment of Death

Chapter 19 · "Symbolic" and "Instrumental" Aspects of Capital Punishment
David Garland — 421
Introduction — 421
The Meaning and Purpose of the Symbolic/Instrumental Distinction — 425
Capital Punishment and Status Politics — 427
Shifts in the Meaning of the Symbolic/Instrumental Distinction — 435
Conclusion: New Directions for Research — 443
References — 449

Chapter 20 · Alternative Sanctions for Aggravated Murder: Form and Function
James R. Acker — 453
Introduction — 453
Why Punish Murder? — 454
   Denunciation — 454
   Social Protection — 456
   Restoration: Victim-Centered Concerns — 457
Death is Different, and So Are Its Costs — 458
Maximizing Benefits and Minimizing Costs — 458
A "Guillotine Effect"? — 462
Conclusion — 463
References — 464

Chapter 21 · Life under Sentence of Death: Some Research Agendas
Robert Johnson, Sandra McGunigall-Smith, Jocelyn Fontaine and Christopher Dum — 469
Introduction — 469
Future Research Topics — 469
   Conditions on Death Row — 469
   Coping — 471
   Guards — 472
   Executions — 473
      Guards — 473
      Prisoners — 474
   Measuring Quality of Life in Prison — 477
References — 479

Chapter 22 · The Future of Execution Methods
    Deborah W. Denno — 483
The Search for a Medically Humane Execution Method — 488
The Search for Solutions — 490
  In-Depth Study of Lethal Injection — 491
  Increased Transparency of Lethal Injection Procedures — 494
Conclusion — 496
References — 496

Chapter 23 · Conclusion — An Agenda for the Next Generation of Capital Punishment Research
    James R. Acker, William J. Bowers and Charles S. Lanier — 499
Facts, Values and Capital Punishment Policies — 499
The Supreme Court's Reception: *Furman*, *Gregg* and Beyond — 500
Research Challenges — 505
  The Need for Data — 505
  Directions for Future Research — 506
Conclusion: Looking toward the Future — 510
References — 510

About the Authors — 521

Index — 531

Foreword

Ronald J. Tabak

There is a continuing need for concerted research bearing on capital punishment. Such research can be important to courts and legislative bodies in considering challenges to aspects of how the death penalty is implemented and proposed judicial or legislative remedies therefor. It can also be invaluable to those considering public policy issues relating to capital punishment, including whether to reform it in particular ways, to declare a moratorium on executions while the issues are studied comprehensively, or to abolish it completely. And for those elected or would-be elected officials who might be contemplating the political ramifications of voting one way or another on reform, moratorium, or abolition measures, careful research can shed light on whether political "conventional wisdom" remains (if it ever was) valid. Finally, sophisticated research into jury decision making can help inform the judgments of counsel who actually litigate capital cases.

Impact on Court Decisions and Possible Legislative Reforms

Research has played a significant role in past court decisions concerning capital punishment. For example, in holding the death penalty unconstitutional if applied to people with mental retardation, the Supreme Court cited various research studies that show that people with mental retardation "have diminished capacities to understand and process information, to communicate, to abstract from mistakes and learn from experience, to engage in logical reasoning, to control impulses, and to understand the reactions of others," and "often act on impulse rather than pursuant to a premeditated plan, and … in group settings … are followers rather than leaders" (*Atkins v. Virginia* 2002:318 & nn. 23–24). Similarly, the Supreme Court relied on several research studies in concluding that juveniles under age 18 have "general differences" from older offenders such that they cannot be said to have the requisite moral culpability to make them constitutionally eligible for execution (*Roper v. Simmons* 2005:569–70, 573).

Future research could affect court decisions or legislative determinations about the manner in which the death penalty is implemented. These could involve a variety of subjects.

Mental Retardation

One example is mental retardation. Despite *Atkins*, it is extremely likely that some people with mental retardation will continue to be sentenced to death, and executed. To some extent, this may occur due to misconceptions by jurors and judges about mental retardation—which may cause them to be unwilling to find someone retarded who, according to the leading definitions, is indeed retarded (*see* Blume, Johnson, and Seeds, this volume).

Among the misconceptions that many people have are that if someone is mentally retarded, he or she cannot possibly do certain things, such as hold a job, get married, and read. It would be useful to have studies done of actual jurors who have sat on cases in which evidence of mental retardation was presented, as well as of citizens who would be eligible for service in a capital case, to see to what extent these beliefs exist and whether such people would be willing either to reconsider these misconceptions if presented with expert testimony about the nature of mental retardation or to follow court instructions that explain the consensus view among experts in the field.

Another area in which research could be useful concerns the ability to assess retrospectively what in the field is called "adaptive behavior." All leading definitions of mental retardation require not only a showing of low mental intelligence (as typically measured by I.Q. testing) but also some inabilities prior to adulthood to engage in normal behavior. When dealing with anyone who could be executed—which after *Roper* means dealing with an adult—one cannot use the usual assessment protocols to assess adaptive behavior, because those tools presume that one is making a contemporaneous assessment regarding the person's present capabilities. But in capital cases, the adaptive behavior shortcomings at issue are those that may have existed prior to age 18. Thus, a retrospective assessment must be undertaken unless—as is almost never the case—an assessment using the usual protocols was done during childhood.

Accordingly, research is needed into how best to make such an assessment after the fact, sometimes well over a decade after the most significant years of development. Moreover, the research should examine whether such a retrospective assessment—relying both on documents from childhood plus people's recollections about the person's childhood—may legitimately be used as a basis for determining whether a person has mental retardation. Some such work has already been undertaken. But there is a significant need for more well-researched studies on retrospective assessments.

Mental Illness

The American Bar Association, the American Psychological Association, the American Psychiatric Association, and others have adopted in recent years proposed limitations on the extent to which people with severe mental illness can be sentenced to death or executed. To the extent that legislative bodies or courts consider adopting these proposals, research could shed light on some significant factors.

For example, to put this subject in context, it could be useful to analyze situations in which a child's severe mental illness was identified, treatment was sought but was not provided, and the child then grew up and committed one or more capital crimes. Such situations have frequently been documented in death row inmates' post-conviction and habeas corpus filings, as well as clemency petitions—but often not in evidence presented to the jury.

With respect to people who volunteer to be executed (which Johnson *et al.*, this volume, estimate to account for about one in ten executions), it would be useful to research the extent to which death row conditions may lead to inmates' exhibiting aggravated mental illness that may cause them to volunteer to be killed.

Jury Instructions

Past studies by William Bowers and his colleagues, as well as by others, have repeatedly shown that some of the most commonly used jury instructions are not properly understood by jurors, and that this has a disproportionately adverse effect on capital defendants (*see* Bowers, Brewer, and Lanier, this volume). These past studies can have continuing utility in judicial and legislative reform efforts.

In addition, new studies that bear on as-yet unstudied but commonly used jury instructions could also be useful. These could include studies about instructions regarding mental retardation, the mitigating effect of mental illness, the use of certain testimony for limited evidentiary purposes but not on the underlying issue of guilt, the use of certain answers not for the truth of the matter asserted but only for credibility, and the use of victim impact testimony solely for the purpose of showing the harm the victim suffered. A key matter that could be studied would be the extent to which jurors, even if they *do* understand the instructions, are likely to violate them.

Averting Convictions of the Innocent

Additional research would be useful in helping to develop protections against convicting, and even executing, innocent people (*see* Dieter, this volume).

One area that has been the subject of some analysis, but could benefit from further work, involves the factors that have led to convictions of people who were later exonerated—whether by DNA or otherwise. Particularly since DNA is not available in the vast majority of capital cases, it is important to examine the extent to which these same factors—for example, threatening the death penalty as a way to get the suspect to confess or to get an alleged co-conspirator to implicate him—may lead to erroneous convictions in cases in which DNA is not available.

Another matter that could benefit from research is the extent to which special pre-trial questioning in capital cases—designed to weed out all potential jurors who would never be willing to impose capital punishment—may contribute to convictions of innocent people. Previous studies have shown that such pre-trial "*Witherspoon*" questioning (*Witherspoon v. Illinois* 1968) makes it more likely that innocent people will be convicted. These studies show that those unwilling to vote for capital punishment are more likely than other jurors to be skeptical of questionable prosecution testimony in determining whether guilt has been proven beyond a reasonable doubt. It would be useful to undertake studies on cases in which innocent people were sentenced to death, and to focus on the impact in those cases of *Witherspoon* exclusions.

It would also be useful to gain more understanding about the nature of false confessions, particularly ones induced by the police. The December 2007 issue of *The Champion* includes a discussion of some of the emerging research in this area and debunks various myths about the supposed implausibility of any sane person's making a false confession. As an article in that issue notes, some leading manuals still promote the use of interrogation methods that have led to false confessions. And many of these methods continue to be approved by most courts. Additional persuasive studies are likely needed in order to get courts or legislatures to preclude the use of "confessions" secured by techniques with an undue danger of producing false confessions,. These new studies, in addition to the existing research, could also form the basis for expert testimony and improved training of police, counsel, and judges.

Jury studies have shown that even when jurors are told to disregard coercive confessions, the conviction rate is greater than if such confessions were never brought to the jury's attention. This suggests the need either for improved instructions or for completely precluding juries from hearing about such confessions.

Race

Racial disparities in capital punishment continue to be the subject of studies relevant to courts and public policy makers (*see* Baldus *et al.*, this volume).

In early 2008, a Connecticut judge refused to dismiss claims under the state constitution regarding alleged racially disparate implementation of capital punishment after considering, among other things, a study by Yale Law Professor John Donohue and his colleagues. In addition, in 2006 and 2007, numerous studies or mini-studies, as part of American Bar Association assessments of capital punishment in numerous states, found significant racial disparities, most often regarding race-of-the-victim. In addition, there have been press analyses of capital punishment, including a series in 2007 by the Atlanta Journal-Constitution that relied on a leading researcher's study of racial disparities.

It is useful, to the extent possible, for such studies to include not only cases in which defendants were prosecuted for capital crimes (that is, crimes for which the death penalty might be imposed), but also cases in which the factual allegations would have permitted prosecution for capital crimes but in which the defendants were actually charged with less severe crimes. This approach—when data make it feasible—permits a more complete analysis of prosecutorial discretion and its potential racially disparate impacts.

Further studies might also be done in the wake of two recent, innovative studies. One found that among all African-American defendants in potentially capital cases, those with darker skin or other stereotypical Negroid characteristics were considerably more likely to be sentenced to death. The other found that among all people actually sentenced to death, African Americans were considerably more likely to be executed.

Moreover, studies by the Capital Jury Project (such as those described by Bowers *et al.*, this volume) about the differences between African-American and white jurors in their consideration of evidence presented in mitigation might be relevant to legal claims concerning prosecutors' exclusions of African-

American jurors—by showing both a prejudicial effect and a reason why prosecutors would wish to exclude such jurors.

Using the Same Jury for Penalty as for Guilt/Innocence

Liebman and his associates (2002) have shown that in cases returned by courts for resentencing, the new sentencing juries are less likely to impose a death sentence than were the original juries that made both guilt and sentencing decisions. According to Bowers *et al.* (this volume), sitting on a jury during the guilt phase has a coarsening effect with regard to punishment.

If further research were conducted into why this is so, it might provide a reason for having separate juries in the guilt/innocence and punishment phases of capital cases. If this were done, those who would automatically vote against the death penalty could be jurors during the guilt/innocence phase. As discussed above, including such jurors would make erroneous convictions less likely. Moreover, it is possible that people who would automatically vote for capital punishment for anyone found guilty of capital murder would be less likely to end up on penalty phase juries if they were questioned in the context of the defendant's having been found guilty of capital murder. Some such people may, under the current system, evade exclusion because they read into the questions about sentencing the possibility that the defendant may not be found guilty.

Finally, defense counsel, during jury selection, often go to great lengths to express reasons why jurors really should be willing and able to vote for the death penalty. These counsel are hoping to avoid exclusions "for cause" of potential jurors who express qualms about ever being willing to vote for capital punishment. Research could fruitfully explore whether this kind of *voir dire* questioning can itself make convictions more likely, and whether it undercuts defense counsel's credibility when counsel later in the case argue against imposing the death penalty.

Public Policy Arguments on Whether the Death Penalty Should Exist

Further research can also play an important role in shaping public policy arguments as to whether capital punishment should be part of our legal system. Many of the "reform"-related subjects discussed above are relevant to those policy arguments. I now turn to issues that do not have reform implications.

Impact on Crime

On the issue of whether capital punishment is a deterrent, it would be useful to follow up on Professor Bedau's suggestion (this volume) that states with capital punishment be compared to states without capital punishment.

There is also a need for statistically sound analysis of whether capital punishment has been a deterrent in particular states. The studies given considerable press coverage in recent years as supposedly supporting the deterrence argument reach hard-to-believe conclusions, such as that every execution deters a large number of murders. These studies have been attacked by several leading experts in the field (*see* Fagan and West, this volume). But what is really needed is a comprehensive assessment by an expert panel—such as the one appointed by the National Academy of Sciences to assess earlier purported showings of deterrence. That panel concluded in 1978 that the studies on which those claims were based were fatally flawed.

Another useful type of research would bear on arguments that capital punishment—even if it may not prevent murders in general, does incapacitate a convicted murderer from killing again. Professor Sorensen notes (this volume) that there has been a tremendous drop in homicides in prisons, from 54 per 100,000 inmates in 1980 to four per 100,000 inmates in 2002. It would be instructive to analyze potential causes for this huge decrease.

Further relevant work would consider the extent to which people convicted of, or pending trial for, capital murder have committed murders while in prison, have escaped, or have engaged in serious assaults on prison staff. My impression is that past studies indicate that such inmates are considerably less likely than the general prison population to engage in such acts, but updated and more comprehensive study would be useful. It would also be useful to consider whether long-term prisoners given non-death sentences are, on the whole, a positive influence on other prisoners.

An additional area of potential research concerns the impact of an active capital punishment regime on other law enforcement. For example, United States Attorneys' offices have faced great financial strains and been further limited in fighting "regular" federal crimes by having many FBI agents devoted to anti-terrorism work and by having to litigate a huge upsurge in immigration appeals. It would be instructive to study the extent to which the dramatic increase in federal death penalty prosecutions in places like the Eastern District of New York has inhibited federal prosecutors' ability to deal with other crimes.

Impact on Prison Guards

It would be useful to research the impact that executions have had on the retention of high quality prison guards.

A powerful documentary released in 2008, *At the Death House Door*, focuses mostly on the experiences of the former long-time chaplain who provided day-of-execution counseling to Texas death row inmates. It also highlights (among many other things) how the experience of participating in executions led to the departure from the prison system of one of its best guards. There have been many other anecdotal accounts over the years of how highly respected prison guards—particularly those who got to know death row inmates well— have left corrections after some of these inmates were executed. These guards have commented that even if the death penalty may have made sense for the person whom the inmate was at the time of the crime, it made no sense to execute the dramatically better person that the inmate had become.

Victims' Survivors

Increasingly over the last 10 to 15 years, capital punishment has been justified as being the best way to support the survivors of murder victims. Yet, there has been virtually no research bearing on this claim.

To see how many murder victims' survivors might purportedly be helped by the death penalty, it would be useful to consider the incredibly low percentage of homicide cases in which the death penalty is secured, and the even lower percentage in which someone is actually executed. As Professor Vandiver points out (this volume), in a great many cases, there is no prosecution at all. In over 1/3 of the cases, she writes, the killer is either unidentified or dead. As she further notes, of the homicide cases that are prosecuted, there are a great many in which the death penalty is never an option, and a great many more where it can be but is not imposed.

Clearly, even if one were to assume that executing the convicted defendant somehow helps the murdered person's survivors, this purported benefit is only available to extremely few of them. This would be so even if the execution rate were to be increased many times over.

What is the effect on the huge majority of murder victims' survivors of being denied this supposed solution to at least some of their problems? Researchers could usefully study these issues, to see whether, in fact, this phenomenon aggravates the suffering of murder victims' survivors by making them feel like second-class survivors.

Beyond that, the underlying assumption should be studied. That is, there should be analysis of whether in those rare cases in which there is an execution, the entire process in some discernible way benefits the victims' survivors—and whether the impact is different where one or more of those survivors are against the defendant's execution.

Finally, as Professor Vandiver properly states, there is a pressing need to focus on interventions that are far more obviously beneficial to victims' survivors than capital punishment. Research could help identify the most cost-effective of these measures.

Costs

Analyses of whether having the death penalty increases the costs of the criminal justice system played a major role in leading to New Jersey's abolishing the death penalty in 2007 and New York's not having corrected a flaw that has rendered its capital punishment statute inoperative since 2004. While such studies have been done in many states, studies in additional states would add to the overall knowledge on this subject (*see* Gradess and Davies, this volume).

When undertaking such studies, or analyzing their results, it is vital to point out a fallacy in the "common sense" view of costs—namely, that the proper approach is to compare the respective costs of putting a particular defendant to death and of keeping that defendant in prison for life. This completely ignores the fact that for every case in which there is an execution, there are several others in which the death penalty is sought but no one is ever executed. The cost of a system that includes capital punishment includes the extra death penalty-related costs—such as two-phase trials, more complex jury selection, and prosecutorial and defense investigation into penalty phase issues—that are incurred even in cases in which the defendant ends up serving a life sentence, or gets acquitted.

State-Specific Studies

Deborah Fleischaker's chapter in this volume points up examples of states in which much more detailed studies of the death penalty system's functioning are warranted. It is only when such thorough analyses of a state's *actual* death penalty system is undertaken that any rational conclusion can be reached about whether to keep the system as is, to reform it, to impose a moratorium pending reform, or to abolish it.

Public Opinion and Influences Thereon

There are many public opinion analyses that could prove helpful in determining the future of capital punishment.

At the most basic level, it is important to know what the public's views on capital punishment are, especially in particular legislative districts. Such studies should not simply inquire about support for the death penalty in the abstract—as if the alternative were what many falsely believe it to be, namely, incarcerating the defendant for a relatively few years and then paroling him. Rather, they should ask those being surveyed to assume that the alternative is (as it is in almost every capital punishment jurisdiction) life with no possibility of parole.

It is also vital to determine the *intensity* of people's views on capital punishment. In particular, would a candidate's taking a different position than that of the person being surveyed likely change the person's vote? One notable after-the-fact study, done by researchers at Princeton University after New Jersey enacted capital punishment in the 1980s, found that lawmakers grossly overestimated the extent to which voters would have held it against them if the lawmakers had opposed the death penalty's enactment. To the extent that much support for the death penalty may be "a mile wide and an inch deep," that would be important for candidates to know.

The perception that being against the death penalty carries with it a political death sentence has been erroneously supported, in political circles, by the defeats in 1988 of Democratic Presidential candidate Michael Dukakis and in 1994 of New York Governor Mario Cuomo. However, Dukakis's infamous answer to the first question in the final debate was so damaging not because he opposed the death penalty, but rather because he seemed like he would not be emotionally affected at all if (as the hypothetical presupposed) his wife Kitty were to be brutally raped and murdered. And Cuomo, who had won three elections in which the voters were well aware of his opposition to the death penalty, was defeated principally because of relatively low voter turnout in heavily Democratic New York City (where many, particularly people of color, had become disenchanted with him for reasons having nothing to do with the death penalty) and a high voter turnout upstate (where people who felt that Cuomo gave preferential treatment to New York City were inflamed by Cuomo's sending New York City Mayor Rudolph Giuliani upstate to campaign for him).

Also worth studying is what has happened to public opinion after the death penalty has been abolished in such places as Canada and Western Europe. Research may show that while a majority favored the death penalty at the time of abolition, public opposition to capital punishment increased thereafter, at least in some countries. Studying post-abolition changes could also shed light on Professor Garland's discussion (this volume) about symbolic aspects of death penalty support, and whether other symbols can replace capital punishment if it is abolished.

A final aspect of public opinion worthy of further research is the impact of television, radio, movies, plays, art, and other media in influencing attitudes about crime and the death penalty. This would include research into the so-called "CSI Effect," whereby juries now purportedly expect startling scientific proof of guilt before they will convict. But it would also include analysis of the myriad other ways in which our media deals with death penalty-related issues, and in particular the misconceptions that the media creates about how the legal system actually works.

Practice Implications of Studies Regarding Jury Decision Making

As suggested by Professors Bowers and Sundby (this volume), it is important to study the reasons why there have been remarkably fewer death sentences in recent years. Among the possible reasons are media-created changes, such as the supposed "CSI Effect" mentioned above; changes in law, such as North Carolina's now giving prosecutors discretion as to whether to seek the death penalty rather than mandating that they do so, and Texas' enacting life without parole as the alternative to the death penalty; and greater public awareness that our legal system is so fragile that many innocent people have been sentenced to death.

But there could be other reasons. In particular, it could be that certain types of mitigation evidence have been particularly successful, at least when presented in a certain way. Or some defense counsel may be improving the chances of life verdicts by essentially conceding guilt and focusing right from the guilt-phase opening argument on the themes of the penalty phase defense.

Conclusion

As you read this book, please consider carefully not only the wealth of information contained herein, but also the ideas regarding future research that could affect the course, or abolition, of the death penalty.

References

Atkins v. Virginia (2002). 536 U.S. 304.
Baldus, David, George Woodworth, David Zuckerman, Neil Alan Weiner and Catherine M. Grosso. This volume.
Bedau, Hugo Adam. This volume.
Blume, John H., Sheri Lynn Johnson and Christopher Seeds. This volume.
Bowers, William J., Thomas W. Brewer and Charles S. Lanier. This volume.
Bowers, William J. and Scott E. Sundby. This volume.
Dieter, Richard C. This volume.
Fagan, Jeffrey and Valerie West. This volume.
Fleischaker, Deborah. This volume.
Garland, David. This volume.
Gradess, Jonathan E. and Andrew L. B. Davies. This volume.
Johnson, Robert, Sandra McGunigall-Smith, Jocelyn Fontaine and Christopher Dum. This volume.
Liebman, James S., Jeffrey Fagan, Andrew Gelman, Valerie West, Garth Davies, and Alexander Kiss. 2002. *A Broken System, Part II: Why There Is So Much Error in Capital Cases, and What Can Be Done About It.* (http://www2.law.columbia.edu/brokensystem2/index2.html).
Roper v. Simmons (2005). 543 U.S. 551.
Sorensen, Jon. This volume.
Vandiver, Margaret. This volume.
Witherspoon v. Illinois (1968). 391 U.S. 510.

Acknowledgments

We are indebted and grateful to each and every one of the authors who has contributed to this volume, both for their scholarly contributions over the years and for the chapters that make up this book. We owe a heartfelt thanks to Susan Ehrhard and Heather Stroker, who have juggled their work as doctoral students and as Research Assistants with, respectively, the Capital Jury Project and the Capital Punishment Research Initiative, for their cheerful and invaluable assistance in helping us ready this work for publication. We appreciate having the opportunity in October 2006 to host a symposium involving the nation's leading death penalty scholars at the University at Albany. The symposium, offered as part of the University at Albany School of Criminal Justice's Symposium on Crime and Justice series, was sponsored by the School of Criminal Justice, the Capital Punishment Research Initiative, the University at Albany Hindelang Criminal Justice Research Center, Massachusetts Citizens Against the Death Penalty Fund, Inc., and Vincent O'Leary, the former President of the University at Albany and the former Dean of its School of Criminal Justice. We also thank Bob Conrow, Beth Hall, and the many other fine people who work at Carolina Academic Press for unhesitatingly agreeing to publish this volume and for all of their help and encouragement along the way.

The Future of America's Death Penalty

CHAPTER 1

Introduction and Overview—The Future of America's Death Penalty: An Agenda for the Next Generation of Capital Punishment Research

Charles S. Lanier, William J. Bowers and James R. Acker

This book provides a unique look not at what we know, but at what we need to know about the death penalty in America. These essays by leading scholars and researchers seek to delineate the directions research on the death penalty should take at this juncture in the history of capital punishment. The authors were asked to identify the questions in their areas of expertise that are most urgently in need of answers, and to sketch out how best to obtain those answers; that is, we invited them to anticipate the research issues and methodologies that will be most important in helping inform the legal and public policy decisions that will determine the future of capital punishment in this country.

The genesis of this book was a symposium held by the Capital Punishment Research Initiative (CPRI) of the University at Albany School of Criminal Justice in October 2006.[1] The many experts who participated in this event were

---

1. The symposium, which was a part of the Albany Symposium on Crime and Justice series, was entitled "The Next Generation of Death Penalty Research: Priorities, Strategies, and an Agenda," and was held at the University at Albany on October 6–7, 2006. Other supporters of the symposium included the University at Albany's Hindelang Criminal Justice Research Center, Massachusetts Citizens Against the Death Penalty Fund, Inc., and

invited to take stock of the areas and policy issues that promise to be critical in upcoming litigation as well as in legislative and executive decision-making, and to then consider the merits of various directions for future death penalty research. Most of the authors who have contributed to this volume attended the symposium, which featured two days of wide-ranging discourse about the death penalty.

Their contributions come at a potentially critical juncture in this nation's experiment with the modern death penalty. In *Gregg v. Georgia* (1976) and companion cases, the United States Supreme Court approved modern death penalty laws that it presumed would remedy the arbitrariness condemned in *Furman v. Georgia* (1972). However, thirty years of experience and a wellspring of research on the modern death penalty are raising doubts in many quarters about the successfulness of the new legislation in overcoming the problems identified in *Furman* (Acker, Bohm, and Lanier 2003). These and a litany of other concerns may figure in what has become a decisive, decade-long, nationwide downturn in the use of capital punishment (Bowers and Sundby, this volume).

Moreover, legislatures and executive authorities in a number of states have recently scrutinized their death penalty laws and practices. Taking the growing numbers of calls for study commissions to examine the administration of capital punishment as a point of departure (Lanier and Acker 2004),[2] the symposium and the ensuing book were designed to confront issues integral to the present operation and the future of the death penalty in America. This is a propitious time for identifying the research issues and strategies that will help inform future policy decisions about capital punishment.

The deeper roots of this volume can be traced to the formation of the CPRI at the University at Albany in the late 1990s. The CPRI was founded with three principal objectives: "(1) to build and maintain a national archive for historical documents and data on the death penalty; (2) to plan and conduct basic and policy related research on capital punishment; and (3) to encourage scholarship, conduct graduate and undergraduate training, and disseminate scientifically grounded knowledge about the ultimate penal sanction" (School of Criminal Justice 2008a). It seeks to foster collaboration among those working

---

Vincent O'Leary, former President of the University at Albany and the former Dean of the University at Albany School of Criminal Justice.

2. "The business of death penalty commissions or, in their absence, of independent researchers and policymakers should be to carefully map the full roster of issues relevant to the practice of capital punishment, systematically collect reliable information about those issues, and make the resulting information available for use in the policy arena" (Lanier and Acker 2004:604).

on death penalty research and aid in the design of studies, the collection of data, and the dissemination of findings about the administration of capital punishment in the United States. The Advisory Board of the CPRI is comprised of David Baldus, Hugo Adam Bedau, William Bowers, Richard Dieter, Jeffrey Fagan, Eric Freedman, Michael Radelet, and Margaret Vandiver (School of Criminal Justice 2008b), all of whom have contributed to the present volume.

The first of the CPRI's purposes is being served through the establishment and growth of the National Death Penalty Archive (NDPA), housed within the University at Albany's M. E. Grenander Department of Special Collections and Archives. The NDPA contains numerous historical collections and other records available to scholars, policymakers, the legal community, media representatives, and the general public. It includes files documenting centuries of executions in this country dating from colonial times that were painstakingly collected and maintained over a period of some forty years by M. Watt Espy; the papers of leading death penalty scholars such as Hugo Adam Bedau, Michael Mello, and Ernest van den Haag; audio- and video-recorded oral histories conducted with individuals who have played a prominent role in the history of capital punishment in the United States; and many other unique historical records and documents including trial transcripts and clemency petitions in capital cases (for further information, *see* Lanier, this volume; University at Albany 2008).

The CPRI's second goal, of planning, facilitating, and conducting research on the death penalty, is evident on several fronts, including sponsorship of the "The Next Generation of Death Penalty Research: Priorities, Strategies, and an Agenda" symposium, and in the work of the third phase of the Capital Jury Project (CJP),[3] directed by Dr. William Bowers at the CPRI in Albany. The CJP has completed in-depth interviews with some 1,200 people who have served on capital juries in 14 states (School of Criminal Justice 2008c). This research has shed light on the previously impenetrable decision-making processes of capital jurors, often revealing pronounced chasms between constitutional doctrine, statutory rules, trial judges' instructions, and jurors' actual deliberations. The work of the CJP, and particularly the third phase of its research now underway, are described more fully later in these pages (Bowers, Brewer, and Lanier, this volume).

This book is a direct outgrowth of the CPRI's third mission, to disseminate scientifically grounded knowledge and stimulate research about the death penalty. Capital punishment is a vital public policy issue. We firmly believe

---

3. For more details on the earlier phases of the CJP, as well as the voluminous body of research it has spawned, see the Capital Jury Project home page at http://www.albany.edu/scj/CJPhome.htm.

that objective, reliable research evidence is indispensable to informed legal and policy decisions about the death penalty. Such information can help address issues of cost and the allocation of finite resources, the possible conviction and execution of innocent persons, potential unfairness in the death penalty's administration, and myriad others that remain in the shadows clouded by myth, misinformation, and political considerations. Hence, the need for a volume devoted to identifying the methodologies and research issues that can help shed objective, scientifically based light on the administration of the death penalty in America.

We have grouped the contributions to this book into five main sections. Section I includes essays collected under the rubric of "General Research Directions and Challenges." The first selection presents Hugo Adam Bedau's reflections on the dominant research issues in the evolving landscape of capital punishment, as informed by developments in the extensive scholarship devoted to the death penalty. Jordan Steiker next addresses whether and how the findings of empirical research can be expected to influence the Supreme Court's capital punishment jurisprudence. The chapter by William Bowers and Scott Sundby documents the striking recent slowdown in newly imposed death sentences, considers how and why it may have occurred, and sketches a research strategy for determining what accounts for this dramatic reduction in the use of capital punishment. Deborah Fleischaker, the Director of the American Bar Association's Death Penalty Moratorium Implementation Project, describes this ambitious undertaking and reports on the absence of data needed to assess even the most rudimentary workings of death penalty systems in many of the jurisdictions studied. In the final writing in this section, Charles Lanier describes the collections within the University at Albany's National Death Penalty Archive, and discusses how and why these and other historical materials are an important source of data for researchers interested in the future of capital punishment laws and policies.

Writings in the next two sections of the book focus on the administration of the death penalty. Section II contains contributions concerned with "The Process Leading to a Death Sentence." In this context, Michael Radelet and Glenn Pierce illuminate how law enforcement officials' investigation practices in murder cases have continuing ripple effects that permeate arrest, charging, guilt determination, and sentencing decisions. In the next chapter, David Baldus, George Woodworth and Neil Weiner examine racial, social class, and geographical disparities in capital charging and sentencing decisions. Those same authors then team with David Zuckerman and Catherine Grosso to deliver a "primer" that identifies critical methodological issues in investigating racial and geographic disparities in the death penalty's administration. William Bowers, Thomas Brewer, and Charles Lanier then review the research of the Capital Jury Project on how jurors make their life and death sentencing decisions. They identify the kinds of data needed to reveal how well jurors comply with constitutionally mandated standards for capital sentencing, and suggest further directions such research should take to have important ramifications for death penalty law and policies.

In Section III, the focus shifts to "The Process Beyond the Sentencing Decision." Richard Dieter's chapter examines the issue of innocence, discusses the importance of conducting research to learn more about how and why wrongful convictions occur, and identifies the important implications of innocence issues for capital punishment policies and practices. John Blume, Sheri Lynn Johnson and Christopher Seeds explore the many critical issues remaining to be resolved in the wake of the Supreme Court's pronouncement in *Atkins v. Virginia* (2002) that mentally retarded offenders are constitutionally exempt from capital punishment, including the implications of this landmark ruling for other intersections of legal and mental health issues. Next, David Dow and Eric Freedman highlight the significant limitations that Congress has placed on federal court review of state criminal convictions and sentences through the Anti-terrorism and Effective Death Penalty Act of 1996, and advocate rigorous study of the consequences of this enactment to evaluate how it has affected the courts' detection and correction of errors in capital cases. In the final chapter in this section, Austin Sarat assesses the immediate and long-term implications of the clemency decisions made in capital cases, placing particular emphasis on the imprint that such decisions will likely have on the future.

The contributions in Section IV are concerned with "The Utility and Efficacy of the Capital Sanction." The initial chapter, by Jeffrey Fagan and Valerie West, addresses the seemingly timeless controversy over general deterrence. It examines critical methodological issues that affect the ability of research to draw valid conclusions about the relative deterrence value of the death penalty and alternative sanctions such as life imprisonment without parole. Next, Jon Sorensen considers directions for research on the issues of incapacitation and predictions of future dangerousness, with a detailed exposition of the data and methods necessary to support reliable measures of convicted murderers' propensities for violence. Margaret Vandiver then considers research to assess the impact of the capital punishment process on murder victims' survivors as well as on the family members of condemned offenders, and identifies the challenges such research will pose. This section concludes with the contribution of Jonathan Gradess and Andrew Davies, who consider the prospects and challenges of research involving the relative costs of capital punishment and life imprisonment and discuss critical policy questions pertaining to alternative decisions about resource investments.

The chapters in Section V are concerned with "Examining the Punishment of Death." David Garland raises theoretical and methodological issues associated with the "symbolic" and "instrumental" aspects of capital punishment, and considers their significance and associated research implications. This chapter is followed by James Acker's related essay, which postulates that the death penalty has unique symbolic attributes and speculates about whether alternative sanctions, short of death, might be structured to fulfill similar expressive functions. The next chapter, by Robert Johnson, Sandra McGunigall-Smith, Jocelyn Fontaine and Christopher Dum, examines the unique conditions of confinement confronting death-sentenced prisoners, anticipates related consequences, and considers future research issues regarding the death row environment. Deborah Denno addresses lethal injection as a method of execution, focusing particularly on lacunae in collaborations between the legal and medical professions and the empirical questions they raise.

Our concluding chapter seeks to locate these contributions in the context of research on capital punishment in the modern, post-*Furman* era, and to elucidate how their themes and challenges are distinctive to this point in America's history with the death penalty. In keeping with the rationale for the symposium that preceded this volume, we consider how the agenda for future research on capital punishment embodied in the chapters in this book can be promoted and facilitated. We identify common themes in the research that is proposed, and discuss the data needed for such research and the potential for collaborative efforts and communication among death penalty researchers. We anticipate, and sincerely hope, that this volume's focus on the defining issues for the next generation of capital punishment laws and policies will help stimulate research and offer much of value to the courts, to policy makers, and to citizens, whose choices will determine what the future holds for the death penalty in America.

References

Acker, James R., Robert M. Bohm and Charles S. Lanier, eds. 2003. *America's Experiment With Capital Punishment: Reflections On the Past, Present, and Future of the Ultimate Penal Sanction.* 2nd ed. Durham, NC: Carolina Academic Press.

Anti-terrorism and Effective Death Penalty Act of 1996. Pub. L. 104-132, Apr. 24, 1996, 110 Stat. 1214, 28 U.S.C. §§ 2261 *et seq.*

Atkins v. Virginia (2002) 536 U.S. 204.

Bowers, William J., Thomas W. Brewer and Charles S. Lanier. This volume.

Bowers, William J. and Scott E. Sundby. This volume.
Furman v. Georgia (1972). 408 U.S. 238.
Gregg v. Georgia (1976). 428 U.S. 153.
Lanier, Charles S. This volume.
Lanier, Charles S. and James R. Acker. 2004. "Capital Punishment, the Moratorium Movement, and Empirical Questions: Looking Beyond Innocence, Race, and Bad Lawyering in Death Penalty Cases." *Psychology, Public Policy, and Law* 10:577–617.
School of Criminal Justice. 2008a. "CPRI Mission Statement." (http://www.albany.edu/scj/CPRImission.htm).
_____. 2008b. "CPRI Background & Advisory Board." (http://www.albany.edu/scj/CPRIboard.htm).
_____. 2008c. "Capital Jury Project."(http://www.albany.edu/scj/CPRIjuryproj.htm).
University at Albany. 2008. "National Death Penalty Archive." (http://library.albany.edu/speccoll/ndpa.htm).

Section I

General Research Directions and Challenges

CHAPTER 2

DEATH PENALTY RESEARCH TODAY AND TOMORROW

Hugo Adam Bedau

For the first time in our history, we have at our disposal the results of a wealth of research on matters having to do with the death penalty. Especially noteworthy are the many new voices that have come forward not just with articles and essays but with whole books devoted to the topic. The necessarily selective bibliography attached at the end of this essay is, in effect, a celebration of these first-time authors, although familiar names also appear. While acknowledging this stunning array of work, I want to draw attention to a dozen issues, chosen more or less at random, and to offer commentary on some of this new research and what remains to be done.

1. The first issue is precisely that there continue to be new angles to be explored. Evidence can easily be found. Governor Ryan's mass commutation of death sentences in Illinois prompted the authorship and publication of at least two books, Scott Turow's *Ultimate Punishment* (2003) and Bill Kurtis's *The Death Penalty on Trial* (2004). Joan Cheever's study of post-*Furman* recidivism, *Back from the Dead* (2006), and Alan Rogers's monograph on the four centuries of the death penalty in Massachusetts, *Murder and the Death Penalty in Massachusetts* (2008), show that the history of the subject has not yet been fully mined. For sheer variety and volume of new work, Austin Sarat's several books lead this particular parade.

2. This unprecedented literary output provokes a variety of interesting questions. First if not foremost is this: How influential will this veritable library be (never mind the scores of law review articles on capital punishment)? Is this research reaching an audience ripe for persuasion? Or is it falling on barren ground?

3. Consider possible state histories like the one completed by Alan Rogers on Massachusetts. Why has it taken half a century or more for historians to undertake book-length studies of the death penalty in abolitionist and retentionist jurisdictions. State histories of the death penalty are especially impor-

tant, inasmuch as the death penalty is overwhelmingly a state (not a federal) issue. The risk is that such studies might amount to little more than tombstone polishing, but they could provide indispensable evidence of the successes and failures of experiments with abolition.

4. Is there any prospect of meaningfully reassessing 8th amendment analyses of whether the death penalty qualifies as a "cruel and unusual punishment"? I am unaware of any essay (never mind a treatise) on the subject in recent years. Does that mark this argument as a dead end? Are there equally good or better moral foundations for questioning the practice of capital punishment? Does the substantive due process argument, relied on by Justice Brennan in his *Furman* opinion, sketch a better way to evaluate the lawfulness and morality of state executions?

5. What is the current status of racist features of the death penalty as it is actually administered in the trial and appellate courts of the nation? In the prosecutors' offices? On the streets during homicide arrests? Are race-based challenges to capital punishment essentially dead on arrival in post-*McCleskey* jurisprudence?

6. Everyone on both sides of the controversy agrees that the risk of executing the innocent is the most powerful, most easily understood, and most persuasive argument in favor of abolition. Does the record show, contrary to the views of Justice Antonin Scalia, not only that innocent defendants have been arrested, convicted, and sentenced to death, but that some have actually been executed? What kind of argument and evidence are needed to convince the skeptical? Are there other jurisdictions like Illinois where the discovery of innocent capital defendants on death row will inspire a governmental response, or was the situation in Illinois a one-of-a-kind freakish occurrence? Now that we have more than a decade of experience since Michael Radelet, Hugo Bedau, and Constance Putnam published *In Spite of Innocence* (1992), their pioneering work on the innocence issue, what can we say about how well their work has stood up to criticism?

7. What can reasonably be expected from the moratorium movement? Will other jurisdictions copy Illinois and New Jersey in creating moratorium study commissions? Or is the moratorium movement already history and of little future political significance? Think of how little of what the Illinois Commission recommended has been implemented.

8. Will the cost of capital punishment be recognized as the important and influential policy consideration that it ought to be?

9. The deterrence argument in favor of the death penalty, once thought to have been safely buried, has been revived and reanimated in recent years. Is it likely that these latest studies will be repudiated as was done with all the earlier ones, beginning with the research by Isaac Ehrlich in the mid-1970s?

10. What can we learn about LWOP and other long term prison sentences that are alternative to the death penalty from a closer look at the experience with abolition in Michigan, Wisconsin, Minnesota, and other such jurisdictions? Why is it that in a century of empirical research on the death penalty, comparatively scant study has been made of the treatment and behavior of long-term prisoners in abolition jurisdictions—surely the source of some of the most relevant empirical evidence deserving of close attention?

11. How important will international human rights law and relevant features of international experience with capital punishment be to the future of the death penalty in this country? Have we been remiss in failing to devote more attention to studying the abolitionist experience in Canada, in particular? Are international developments likely to figure into court decisions or help shift public opinion?

12. Finally, to round off this set of current and future issues, how much damage has been done to the use of lethal injection as the preferred method of carrying out executions? Is there a better—safer, more effective, less painful—method waiting to be bought forward? Or is the refusal of doctors to administer execution by lethal injection the final word on this method?

* * *

Clearly this is not a definitive list of issues of importance, as the essays in this book demonstrate. In addition, it should be noted that the books listed in the bibliography indicate just how widespread interest and concern about the death penalty in the United States are. Among the authors are lawyers, criminologists, political scientists, historians, philosophers, social activists—to say nothing of those affected most directly by the death penalty system, those who spent time on death row, their families, the families of those actually executed, and the surviving family members of murder victims. In addition to personal testimony, history, theory, advocacy, and policy are brought to bear. Much work has been done; much remains to be done.

A Selective Bibliography: Books on the Death Penalty Published 2000 to 2008

Abbott, Geoffrey. 2005. *Execution: The Guillotine, the Pendulum, the Thousand Cuts, the Spanish Donkey, and 66 Other Ways of Putting Someone to Death.* New York, NY: St. Martin's Press.

Acker, James R., Robert M. Bohm, and Charles S. Lanier, eds. 2003. *America's Experiment with Capital Punishment: Reflections on the Past, Present, and Future of the Ultimate Penal Sanction.* 2nd ed. Durham, NC: Carolina Academic Press.

Acker, James R. and David R. Karp, eds. 2006. *Wounds That Do Not Bind: Victim-Based Perspectives on the Death Penalty.* Durham, NC: Carolina Academic Press.

Amsterdam, Tony. 2003. *America's Death Penalty: Beyond Repair?* Durham, NC: Duke University Press.

Banner, Stuart. 2002. *The Death Penalty: An American History.* Cambridge, MA: Harvard University Press.

Beck, Elizabeth, Sarah Britto, and Arlene Andrews. 2007. *In the Shadow of Death: Restorative Justice and Death Row Families.* New York, NY: Oxford University Press.

Bedau, Hugo. 2004. *Killing as Punishment.* Boston MA: Northeastern University Press.

Bedau, Hugo Adam and Paul G. Cassell, eds. 2004. *Debating the Death Penalty: Should America Have Capital Punishment? The Experts from Both Sides Make Their Case.* New York, NY: Oxford University Press.

Bessler, John D. 2003. *Kiss of Death: America's Love Affair with the Death Penalty.* Boston, MA: Northeastern University Press.

Blaskovich, Dagny A. 2007. *A Comparative Analysis of Capital Punishment: Statutes, Policies, Frequencies, and Public Attitudes the World Over.* Rev. ed. Lanham, MD: Lexington Books.

Blecker, Robert. 2004. *By the Hand of Man: The Case for Capital Punishment.* New York, NY: Perseus Books.

Blom-Cooper, Louis and Terence Morris. 2004. *With Malice Aforethought: A Study of the Crime and Punishment for Homicide.* Portland, OR: Hart Publishing.

Bohm, Robert M. 2007. *Deathquest III: An Introduction to the Theory and Practice of Capital Punishment in the United States.* San Francisco, CA: Matthew Bender & Co.

Brimson, Dougie. 2001. *Capital Punishment.* Terra Alta, WV: Headline Book Publishing.

Burnett, Cathleen. 2002. *Justice Denied: Clemency Appeals in Death Penalty Cases.* Boston, MA: Northeastern University Press.

Carter, Linda E. 2004. *Understanding Capital Punishment Law.* Newark NJ: LexisNexis.

Cheever, Joan M. 2006. *Back from the Dead: One Woman's Search for the Men Who Walked Off America's Death Row.* Chichester, England: John Wiley.

Christianson, Scott. 2004. *Innocent: Inside Wrongful Conviction Cases.* New York, NY: NYU Press.

Cohen, Stanley. 2003. *The Wrong Men: America's Epidemic of Wrongful Death Row Convictions.* New York, NY: Carroll & Graf.

Cohen-Jonathan, Gérard and William Schabas, eds. 2003. *La Peine Capitale et Le Droit International des Droits de l'homme.* Paris: Editions Panthéon-Assas.

Commonwealth Caribbean Human Rights Seminar. 2004. Belize City: Penal Reform International, Simons Muirhead & Burton, Foreign & Commonwealth Office, Attorney General's Ministry (Belize).

Coyne, Randall and Lyn Entzeroth. 2006. *Capital Punishment and the Judicial Process.* 3rd ed. Durham, NC: Carolina Academic Press.

The Death Penalty: Beyond Abolition. 2004. Strasbourg, France: Council of Europe Publishing.

The Death Penalty in the OSCE Area. 2006. Warsaw, Poland: Organization for Security and Co-operation in Europe (OSCE) Office for Democratic Institutions and Human Rights (ODIHR).

del Carmen, Rolando V., Scott Vollum, Kelly Cheeseman, Durant Frantzen, and Claudia San Miguel, eds. 2005. *The Death Penalty: Constitutional Issues, Commentaries and Case Briefs.* San Francisco, CA: Matthew Bender & Co.

Diaz, Joseph D. 2002. *The Execution of a Serial Killer: One Man's Experience Witnessing the Death Penalty.* Morrison, CO: Poncha Press.

Dow, David. 2005. *Executed on a Technicality: Lethal Injustice on America's Death Row.* Boston, MA: Beacon Press.

Dow, David R. and Mark Dow, eds. 2002. *Machinery of Death: The Reality of America's Death Penalty Regime.* New York, NY: Routledge.

Edds, Margaret. 2003. *An Expendable Man: The Near-Execution of Earl Washington Jr.* New York, NY: NYU Press.

Eisenberg, James R. 2004. *Law, Psychology, and Death Litigation.* Sarasota, FL: Professional Resource Press.

Elster, Jean Alicia, ed. 2005. *The Death Penalty.* Detroit, MI: Thomson Gale.

Fleury-Steiner, Benjamin. 2004. *Jurors' Stories of Death: How America's Death Penalty Invests in Inequality.* Ann Arbor, MI: University of Michigan Press.

Foley, Michael. 2003. *Arbitrary and Capricious: The Supreme Court, and Constitution and the Death Penalty.* Westport, CT: Praeger Publishers.

Galliher, John F., Larry W. Koch, David Patrick Keys, and Teresa J. Guess. 2002. *America Without the Death Penalty: States Leading the Way.* Boston, MA: Northeastern University Press.

Garcia, Joseph and Selma Kerren. 2006. *A Cry in the Wilderness: The Raw Confessions of Texas Seven's Joseph Garcia.* Parker, CO: Outskirts Press.

Garvey, Stephen P., ed. 2003. *Beyond Repair? America's Death Penalty.* Durham, NC: Duke University Press.

Gillespie, L. Kay. 2000. *Dancehall Ladies: Executed Women of the 20th Century.* Rev. ed. Lanham, MD: University Press of America.

Gottfried, Ted. 2002. *The Death Game: Justice or Legalized Murder?* Minneapolis, MN: Twenty-First Century Books.

Gray, Mike. 2003. *The Death Game: Capital Punishment and the Luck of the Draw.* Monroe, ME: Common Courage Press.

Hamm, Theodore. 2001. *Rebel and a Cause: Caryl Chessman and the Politics of the Death Penalty in Post-War California,1948–1974.* Berkeley, CA: University of California Press.

Haney, Craig. 2005. *Death by Design: Capital Punishment as a Social Psychological System.* New York, NY: Oxford University Press.

Hanks, Gardner C. 2002. *Capital Punishment and the Bible.* Scottdale, PA: Herald Press.

Hodgkinson, Peter and William A. Schabas, eds. 2004. *Capital Punishment: Strategies for Abolition.* Cambridge: Cambridge University Press.

Hood, Roger. 2002. *The Death Penalty: A Worldwide Perspective.* 3rd ed. New York, NY: Oxford University Press.

International Commission of Jurists. 2000. *The Death Penalty: Condemned.* Châtelaine, Switzerland: International Commission of Jurists (ICJ).

Jackson, Jesse, Bruce Shapiro, and Jesse L. Jackson Jr. 2001. *Legal Lynching: The Death Penalty and America's Future.* New York, NY: The New Press.

Junkin, Tim. 2003. *Bloodsworth: The True Story of the First Death Row Inmate Exonerated by DNA.* Chapel Hill, NC: Algonquin Books.

Kaufman-Osborn,Timothy. 2002. *From Noose to Needle: Capital Punishment in the Late Liberal State.* Ann Arbor, MI: University of Michigan Press.

King, Rachel. 2005. *Capital Consequences: Families of the Condemned Tell Their Stories.* New Brunswick, NJ: Rutgers University Press.

_____. 2003. *Don't Kill in Our Names: Families of Murder Victims Speak Out Against the Death Penalty.* New Brunswick, NJ: Rutgers University Press.

Kurtis, Bill. 2004. *The Death Penalty on Trial: Crisis in American Justice.* New York, NY: PublicAffairs.

Lezin, Katya. 2000. *Finding Life on Death Row: Profiles of Six Inmates.* New ed. New York, NY: Norton.

Lifton, Robert Jay and Greg Mitchell. 2000. *Who Owns Death? Capital Punishment, the American Conscience, and the End of the Death Penalty.* New York, NY: William Morrow.

Linderoff, David. 2003. *Killing Time: An Investigation into the Death Row Case of Mumia Abu-Jamal.* Monroe, ME: Common Courage Press.

Linebaugh, Peter. 2003. *The London Hanged: Crime and Civil Society in the Eighteenth Century.* 2nd ed. London: Verso.

Long, William R. [N.d.]. *A Tortured History: The Story of Capital Punishment in Oregon.* Eugene, OR: Oregon Criminal Defense Lawyers Assoc.

Mandery, Evan J. 2005. *Capital Punishment: A Balanced Examination.* Sudbury, MA: Jones and Bartlett.

Martinez, Michael J., William D. Richardson and D. Brandon Hornsby, eds. 2002. *The Leviathan's Choice: Capital Punishment in the Twenty-first Century.* Lanham, MD: Rowman & Littlefield.

McAllister, Pam. 2003. *Death Defying: Dismantling the Execution Machinery in 21st Century U.S.A.* New York, NY: Continuum.

McFeely, William. 2001. *Proximity to Death.* New York, NY: Norton.

Mello, Michael. 2002. *Deathwork: Defending the Condemned.* Minneapolis, MN: University of Minnesota Press.

Mello, Michael. 2001. *The Wrong Man: A True Story of Innocence on Death Row.* Minneapolis, MN: University of Minnesota Press.

Miller, Karen S. 2006. *Wrongful Capital Convictions and the Legitimacy of the Death Penalty.* New York, NY: LFB Scholarly Publishing.

Moore, Billy Neal. 2005. *I Shall Not Die: 72 Hours on Death Watch.* Bloomington, IN: AuthorHouse.

Moran, Richard. 2002. *Executioners' Current: Thomas Edison, George Westinghouse, and the Invention of the Electric Chair.* New York, NY: Knopf.

Nathanson, Stephen. 2001. *An Eye for an Eye? The Immorality of Punishing by Death.* 2nd ed. Lanham, MD: Rowman & Littlefield.

Nelson, Lane and Burk Foster. 2000. *Death Watch: A Death Penalty Anthology.* Upper Saddle River, NJ: Prentice Hall.

Ogletree, Charles J. Jr. and Austin Sarat, eds. 2006. *From Lynch Mobs to the Killing State: Race and the Death Penalty in America.* New York, NY: NYU Press.

O'Shea, Kathleen. 2000. *Women on the Row: Revelations from Both Sides of the Bars.* Ithaca, NY: Ithaca Firebrand Books.

Owens, Erik, John D. Carlson, and Eric P. Elshtain, eds. 2004. *Religion and the Death Penalty: A Call for Reckoning.* Grand Rapids, MI: Eerdmans.

Palmer, Louis J. Jr. 2001. *Encyclopedia of Capital Punishment in the United States.* Jefferson, NC: McFarlane & Co.

Papadopoulos, Ioannis S. and Jacques-Henri Robert. 2000. *La Peine de Mort: Droit, Histoire, Anthropologie, Philosophie.* Paris: Editions Panthéon-Assas.

Pelke, Bill. 2003. *Journey of Hope ... From Violence to Healing.* Philadelphia, PA: Xlibris.

Pickett, Carroll. 2002. *Within These Walls: Memoirs of a Death House Chaplain.* New York, NY: St. Martin's.

Prejean, Sister Helen. 2005. *The Death of Innocents: An Eyewitness Account of Wrongful Executions.* New York, NY: Random House.

Recinella, Dale S. 2004. *The Biblical Truth about America's Death Penalty.* Boston, MA: Northeastern University Press.

Reid, Don. 2001. *Have a Seat, Please.* Huntsville, TX: Texas Review Press.

Rivkind, Nina and Steven Schatz. 2001. *Cases and Materials on the Death Penalty.* St. Paul, MN: West Group.

Rogers, Alan. 2008. *Murder and the Death Penalty in Massachusetts.* Amherst, MA: University of Massachusetts Press.

Rusher, James Thomas. 2003. *Until He Is Dead: Capital Punishment in Western North Carolina History.* Boone, NC: Parkway Publisher.

Sarat, Austin. 2005. *Mercy on Trial: What it Means to Stop an Execution.* Princeton, NJ: Princeton University Press.

_____. 2001. *When the State Kills: Capital Punishment and the American Condition.* Princeton, NJ: Princeton University Press.

Sarat, Austin and Christian Boulanger. 2005. *The Cultural Lives of Capital Punishment: Comparative Perspectives.* Stanford, CA: Stanford University Press.

Schabas, William A. 2002. *The Abolition of the Death Penalty in International Law.* 2nd ed. Cambridge: Cambridge University Press.

Scheck, Barry, Peter Neufeld, and Jim Dwyer. 2000. *Actual Innocence: Five Days to Execution and Other Dispatches from the Wrongly Convicted.* New York, NY: Doubleday.

Solotaroff, Ivan. 2001. *The Last Face You'll Ever See: The Private Life of the American Death Penalty.* New York, NY: HarperCollins.

Sorenson, Jon and Rocky Leanne Pilgrim. 2006. *Lethal Injection: Capital Punishment in Texas During the Modern Era.* Austin, TX: University of Texas Press.

Stack, Richard A. 2006. *Dead Wrong: Violence, Vengeance, and the Victims of Capital Punishment.* Westport, CT: Greenwood.

Steelwater, Eliza. 2003. *The Hangman's Knot: Lynching, Legal Execution, and America's Struggle with the Death Penalty.* Boulder, CO: Westview Press.

Streib, Victor L. 2005. *Death Penalty in a Nutshell.* 2nd ed. St. Paul, MN: West Group.

Streissguth, Thomas. 2002. *The Death Penalty: Debating Capital Punishment.* Berkeley Heights, NJ: Enslow Publishers.

Turow, Scott. 2003. *Ultimate Punishment: A Lawyer's Reflections on Dealing with the Death Penalty.* New York, NY: Farrar, Straus & Giroux.

Urbina, Martin G. 2003. *Capital Punishment and Latino Offenders: Racial and Ethnic Differences in Death Sentences.* New York, NY: LFB Scholarly Publishing.

Vadas, Agnes and Richard Nields. 2005. *Truth Be Told: Life Lessons from Death Row.* Bloomington, IN: AuthorHouse.

Vandiver, Margaret. 2006. *Lethal Punishment: Lynchings and Legal Executions in the South.* New Brunswick, NJ: Rutgers University Press.

von Drehle, David. 2006. *Among the Lowest of the Dead: The Culture of Capital Punishment.* New ed. Lansing, MI: University of Michigan Press.
Weier, John W. 2006. *Capital Punishment: Cruel and Unusual?* Detroit, MI: Thomson Gale.
Westervelt, Saundra D. and John A. Humphry. 2001. *Wrongly Convicted: Perspectives on Failed Justice.* New Brunswick, NJ: Rutgers University Press.
Williams, Nanon. 2003. *Still Surviving.* Port Townsend, WA: Breakout Publishing.
Zimring, Franklin E. 2003. *The Contradictions of American Capital Punishment.* New York, NY: Oxford University Press.

CHAPTER 3

The Role of Constitutional Facts and Social Science Research in Capital Litigation: Is "Proof" of Arbitrariness or Inaccuracy Relevant to the Constitutional Regulation of the American Death Penalty?

Jordan M. Steiker

One of the great puzzles in constitutional litigation—particularly litigation in the U.S. Supreme Court—concerns the role of constitutional "facts." On the one hand, there are the basic "facts" about which the particular parties often disagree and the empowered factfinder, jury or judge, must resolve in the course of the litigation (*e.g.*, did the interrogator read *Miranda* warnings, did the abortion provider accept public funds, did the school use race as a factor in its admissions decisions?). But there are also facts of a different order that are part of the decision-rule calculus, facts about the broader context in which the controversy occurs: do *Miranda* warnings prevent coercive interrogation, does public financial support for abortion encourage reckless behavior, do racial preferences enhance or undermine the educational success of minorities? As to these latter questions of constitutional fact, the Court rarely has factfindings from the lower courts to which it can defer. The parties might have made factual assertions regarding these questions during the course of the litigation, but often they lack methodologically sound empirical research to support their assertions. Moreover, even in many cases where lower courts have made "findings" regarding these broader questions of constitutional fact, the Court is understandably wary about allowing such findings to control the litigation, given the vagaries of the specific litigation (including the quality of counsel or experts in the trial court and the potential idiosyncrasies of the factfinder). Thus, the Court often must rely on its own assessment of facts in the world as it decides how to implement constitutional guarantees. In some cases, the Court self-consciously and transparently engages the accuracy of its factual premises in its opinion, and in others such premises operate powerfully but discreetly.

In the context of the American death penalty, the justices' perceptions regarding the facts on the ground have been critical to the development of contemporary American death penalty law. Indeed, the modern turn toward federal regulation in the early 1970s was strongly rooted in the Court's assessment of the arbitrariness of death penalty decision-making under prevailing state schemes. The Court's belief that the death penalty operated randomly and perhaps even discriminatorily was central to its holding that the Eighth Amendment requires states to channel sentencer discretion in capital cases. But the Court's willingness to regulate based on the perceived failings of the system did not lead the justices to embrace an empirically based jurisprudence. In several important cases following *Furman*, defendants sought increased federal constitutional regulation based on substantial (though contested) empirical studies highlighting particular inadequacies in the states' administration of the death penalty. In each case, the Court refused to tie federal constitutional rules to empirical demonstrations.

More recently, the Court has increased its scrutiny of the American death penalty, and this development again appears to reflect the justices' concern about facts on the ground. This time, though, the Court's concern relates to the accuracy rather than the general distribution of the American death penalty, mirroring a shift in public and elite opinion in this regard. Indeed, four justices have recently suggested in astonishing and unprecedented terms their view that the potential for wrongful convictions justifies a new level of scrutiny in capital cases. But these concerns are not necessarily shared by the balance of the Court. Justice Scalia rejected both the premises and conclusions of such an argument, insisting that studies do not support the claim of widespread error in capital cases, and that error in any event is an inevitable part of any criminal justice system, including one that implements the death penalty.

Overall, if these trends continue, empirical research will play a powerful, though indirect, role in the federal constitutional regulation of the American death penalty. To the extent empirical researchers are able to document the arbitrariness or inaccuracy of the American death penalty, or the reverse, or perhaps the value of the death penalty as a deterrent to homicide, such demonstrations will likely shift both public opinion and judicial regulation. But contemporary doctrine makes it exceedingly difficult for litigants to seek doctrinal shifts based on the empirical studies themselves, apart from their atmospheric value in shaping perceptions and public opinion about the fairness, accuracy, and utility of the underlying capital system.

Constitutional Facts and the Constitutionalization of the Death Penalty: Arbitrariness and the Requirement of Narrowing in Capital Statutes

About thirty-five years ago, in *Furman v. Georgia* (1972), the United States Supreme Court first embarked on its regulatory efforts in response to three important facts on the ground. First, notwithstanding broad death-eligibility under then-prevailing capital statutes, few defendants were sentenced to death and fewer still were executed (Steiker and Steiker 1995:364–69). Second, polling data suggested that the gap between death eligibility, on the one hand, and death sentencing and executions, on the other, might be attributable to declining popular support for the death penalty (Steiker and Steiker 2005:291). Third, the absence of any guidance in state capital punishment statutes undermined any credible claim that the few offenders selected for death sentences and executions were truly the "worst of the worst offenders."

Death penalty opponents marshaled these facts to support two general critiques of the American death penalty. First, they argued that the administration of prevailing death penalty statutes was at best arbitrary and at worst discriminatory given the absence of any mechanisms to ensure that those selected for death were truly the most deserving. Second, and more fundamentally, they insisted that the declining and marginal use of the death penalty coupled with unprecedented weakening of public support for death as an available punishment revealed that the American death penalty had run its course and was no longer consistent with prevailing standards of decency.

In response to these concerns about the seemingly arbitrary and ambivalent administration of the death penalty, the Court created largely procedural protections to ensure that applications of the death penalty would reflect contemporary views about its appropriate scope. The justices insisted that states refine their capital statutes by narrowing their definitions of capital murder, which most states accomplished through the enumeration of aggravating factors. The Court simultaneously insisted that states preserve a defendant's right to "individualized" consideration, by ensuring that defendants could present, and sentencers could consider, relevant mitigating evidence broadly conceived. Lastly, the Court endorsed an amorphous and quite limited set of procedural protections unique to capital cases under its general "death-is-different" doctrine (Steiker and Steiker 1995:371–403).

The justices rejected the broader critique that prevailing practices reflected an emerging rejection of the death penalty as an available punishment. As a result, the Court refused to craft any broad substantive right against the death penalty as an excessive punishment (*Gregg v. Georgia* 1976). Moreover, over the ensuing two decades, the Court rarely embraced any other proportionality limitations on the death penalty's reach, such as prohibiting the execution of juveniles (*Stanford v. Kentucky* 1989), non-triggermen (*Tison v. Arizona* 1987), or persons with mental retardation (*Penry v. Lynaugh* 1989). Its decisions reflected a wariness regarding the Court's ability to gauge "evolving standards of decency."

The Court's initial intervention into state death penalty practices was thus both significant and limited. It marked the first time in American constitutional history that state death penalty practices were subjected to any meaningful regulation at all. But the justices stopped short of banning a practice that was beginning to come under intense pressure throughout virtually the entire Western world (Steiker 2002). The Court was clearly persuaded that the American system for imposing the death penalty was deeply flawed, based on evidence of its haphazard administration, but the justices were not persuaded, especially in light of the massive state legislative response to *Furman*, that the death penalty had become unacceptable to the American people.

The Rejection of Empirically Based Claims

In the two decades following *Furman*, death-sentenced inmates sought to challenge particular aspects of the American death penalty on the basis of empirical studies and social scientific research. These claims sought to capitalize on the justices' apparent concern, reflected in *Furman*, for the actual administration of the death penalty. But the Court uniformly rejected such claims, emphasizing that *Furman* should be read to regulate *procedures* rather than *outcomes*. For a variety of reasons, the Court appeared unwilling to embrace— and continues to reject—social science as a basis for crafting constitutional doctrine in the death penalty context. The justices' decisions in this regard appear to rest on a number of considerations. First, and foremost, the Court is wary of having constitutional doctrine subject to potentially shifting empirical demonstrations. As in other doctrinal areas, an empirically based jurisprudence would be only as stable as the empirical research available at any given time. Second, the justices appear skeptical of empirical data presented in capital litigation, in part because of their fear that studies might reflect an anti-death penalty bias of the researchers who produce and interpret the data. Lastly, the Court has particular expertise and experience crafting procedural requirements in the criminal context and is reluctant to cede that authority to social scientists, especially if such an approach would require states to achieve some empirically verifiable level of reliability in their criminal systems.

The Court's leading cases rejecting claims based on social scientific evidence reflect these concerns. In one of its foundational death penalty decisions issued before *Furman*, the Court restricted states' efforts to "death qualify" jurors by excluding jurors with any moral reservations about the death penalty (*Witherspoon v. Illinois* 1968). Although the justices did not reject the state interest in death-qualification altogether, they limited the scope of that right to those jurors unalterably opposed to the punishment. Defendants also advanced a related but unresolved claim that death-qualification should occur only after a non-death qualified jury renders a verdict in the guilt-innocence phase, on the ground that death-qualification otherwise skews the guilt-innocence determination (because jurors who support the death penalty without reservation are uncommonly disposed toward finding defendants guilty) (*Witherspoon v. Illinois* 1968:517). There was some empirical support for this claim when it reached the Court in 1968 (*Witherspoon v. Illinois* 1968:517 n. 10); after additional empirical studies appeared to provide further evidence of this dynamic, and the issue returned to the Court in *Lockhart v. McCree* (1986), the Court nonetheless rejected the claim that death-qualification itself impermissibly biases the guilt-innocence phase determination.

In so doing, the majority opinion raised some significant questions about the methodology underlying the studies (*Lockhart v. McCree* 1986:172). But taking a tack that it would repeat in several cases, the Court assumed for purposes of decision that the studies demonstrated what the defendant asserted—"that 'death qualification' in fact produces juries somewhat more 'conviction-prone' than 'non-death-qualified juries'" (p. 173). The Court then defended its conclusion that the Sixth Amendment fair-cross-section requirement does not preclude exclusion at the guilt-innocence phase of persons with some conscientious objections to capital punishment ("*Witherspoon*-excludables"). The majority opinion seemed to suggest that individual defendants are treated fairly so long as impartial jurors are selected in their case, even if systematically the jurors who serve in capital cases are more conviction-prone.[1]

This suggestion is striking, because it essentially embraces systemic skewing of capital juries toward conviction so long as all persons who actually serve on capital juries are free of bias that would *require* them to be struck for cause. In a jurisprudence committed to heightened reliability, the impact of death-qualification on the guilt-innocence phase should be quite troublesome; indeed, death-qualification turns heightened reliability in capital cases on its head, because defendants on trial for their lives will face less sympathetic juries than defendants in non-capital proceedings. The problems posed by death-qualification are exacerbated by the very real concern that the guilt-innocence phase advantages of death qualification might motivate prosecutors to seek death in inappropriate cases, perhaps where the evidence of the underlying crime is relatively weak (or the case for an affirmative defense, such as insanity, is relatively strong) and prosecutors might regard a death-qualified jury as essential to conviction.

But the Court avoided this conclusion by viewing the case exclusively through the lens of the Sixth Amendment fair-cross-section requirement rather than as involving broader Eighth Amendment concerns about the operation of the death penalty. The Court rejected the notion that potential jurors who harbored serious concerns about the death penalty (*Witherspoon*-excludables) constituted a "distinctive" group for Sixth Amendment purposes, because in the Court's view, the Sixth Amendment is primarily concerned with protecting marginalized groups within society, such as groups defined by an immutable characteristic (*e.g.*, race, gender, or ethnic background). By defining the Sixth Amendment in these terms, the justices foreclosed particular challenges based on the over- or under-representation of groups that share particular attitudes toward criminal justice issues, even if such representation will skew the decision-making process. In this respect, the Court cast the defendant's Sixth Amendment right as a more general societal interest in equal access to jury service rather than as a means of balancing the state's and the defendant's chances of obtaining favorable verdicts. The reasoning of the decision also foreclosed any further empirically based challenges that sought to ensure representative juries in terms of criminal justice *attitudes*. The Court made clear that its methodology for applying the fair-cross-section requirement involves

---

1. "McCree characterizes the jury that convicted him as 'slanted' by the process of 'death qualification.' But McCree admits that exactly the same 12 individuals could have ended up on his jury through the 'luck of the draw,' without in any way violating the constitutional guarantee of impartiality" (*Lockhart v. McCree* 1986:178).

a non-empirical assessment of marginalization based on immutable traits, and that this methodology would control future cases.

In another empirically based challenge to a significant aspect of the American death penalty, defendants objected to the use of psychiatric expert testimony in capital cases to support the state's claim of future dangerousness (*Barefoot v. Estelle* 1983). The claim was largely confined to death-sentenced inmates in Texas because, at the time of the decision, Texas was virtually alone among death penalty states in *requiring* the state to prove a defendant's future dangerousness as a prerequisite to obtaining a death sentence. As a result of this feature of the Texas death penalty scheme, prosecutors routinely offered "expert" psychiatric or psychological testimony regarding a defendant's dangerousness. Indeed, because the Sixth Amendment limits the state's use of psychiatric testimony obtained via compulsory interviews with death-eligible defendants (*Estelle v. Smith* 1981), many of these experts testified at capital trials based on "hypothetical" questions—without ever speaking with or observing the defendant about whom they would testify. Many of the state experts testified in dozens of cases, and one notorious expert, Dr. Grigson, routinely expressed his absolute certainty that the defendant before him would commit violent acts in the future.

Defendants sought to disallow such expert testimony, alleging that social scientific evidence demonstrated the inaccuracy of expert opinions of future dangerousness. In *Barefoot v. Estelle* (1983), the defendant presented evidence to the District Court, grounded in contemporary research, that expert predictions of dangerousness were inaccurate at least two-thirds of the time. When the case reached the Supreme Court, the American Psychiatric Association (APA) weighed in on the side of the defendant, asserting that the "unreliability of psychiatric predictions of long-term future dangerousness is by now an established fact within the profession" (*Barefoot v. Estelle* 1983:920, Blackmun, J., dissenting, quoting APA's amicus brief). On the basis of that "fact," the APA urged the Court to prohibit psychiatric experts from testifying to defendants' dangerousness in capital cases.

As in *McCree*'s rejection of the fair-cross-section claim, the Court in *Barefoot* did not attempt to disprove the social scientific support underlying the defendant's claim. Instead, the majority opinion highlighted the longstanding and ubiquitous presence of predictions of dangerousness in the criminal justice system. Such predictions are not confined to capital sentencing, and have long been essential to other determinations, including whether to permit involuntary civil commitments. The Court insisted that the defendant's claim was in this sense asking the justices "to disinvent the wheel" (*Barefoot v. Estelle* 1983:896). The Court also advanced several other considerations for permitting expert testimony on future dangerousness, including the defendant's ability to challenge and cross-examine the state's experts and the oddity of disallowing expert testimony while permitting lay testimony on the issue of dangerousness.[2]

The clear but unstated theme of the Court's opinion is that states must be permitted to decide the appropriate bases for punishment. The real challenge presented by the social scientific evidence in *Barefoot* was the notion that future dangerousness is a reliable basis on which the death penalty decision should rest. It may be true that "expert" predictions of future dangerousness are particularly unreliable, but that fact supports eliminating dangerousness as a death-sentencing criterion altogether, rather than simply leaving the dangerousness prediction in the hands of the lay jury. Even if juries are better able than experts to sort out the dangerous from the non-dangerous, the extraordinarily high error rate of experts gives little reason to believe that lay predictions of dangerousness will meet any reasonable standard of reliability. The reference to "disinventing the wheel" reflects the Court's recognition of the far-reaching implications if the justices were to embrace the apparent social scientific fact that we cannot reliably sort offenders based on their future dangerousness. This recognition would require states—particularly Texas—to limit the role future dangerousness plays in capital sentencing, and thereby constitutionally regulate states' theories of capital murder. States would be required to subordinate incapacitation to other considerations, such as moral desert, and give the Court a much more prominent role in policing state capital statutes.

Barefoot confirms that social science must give way when it directly conflicts with longstanding state criminal practices. The Court is simply unwilling to significantly regulate state death penalty practices based on empirical evidence of poor inputs into the decision-making process. Indeed, *Barefoot* helps to explain why the Court is unlikely to place constitutional limits on the use of eyewitness testimony—in capital or non-capital cases—notwithstand-

---

2. The Court's willingness to indulge the use of questionable expert testimony regarding future dangerousness in capital cases is in some tension with its decision upholding a state's exclusion of defense expert testimony on the issue of mens rea. See *Clark v. Arizona* (2006) (no due process violation in state's decision to restrict expert testimony regarding evidence of mental illness to defendant's claim of insanity and precluding use of such evidence as it relates to defendant's ability to form required mens rea for the offense). The Court in *Clark* relied in part on the difficulties of applying the testimony of mental health experts to non-professional inquiries, exactly the same problem identified in *Barefoot*. "[A] defendant's state of mind at the crucial moment can be elusive no matter how conscientious the enquiry, and the law's categories that set the terms of the capacity judgment are not the categories of psychology that govern the expert's professional thinking" (p. 2735).

ing substantial and growing empirical evidence of the potential unreliability of such testimony, especially in certain contexts (*e.g.,* cross-racial identifications). From the justices' perspective, our adversarial system relies on attorneys to challenge the unreliability of evidence in particular cases rather than the adoption of Court-imposed rules to foster more accurate decision-making.

The most dramatic empirical challenge to the American death penalty was presented in *McCleskey v. Kemp* (1987). An African-American defendant convicted of killing a white police officer challenged his sentence on the ground that race played a significant role in the administration of Georgia's death penalty. In support of his claim, McCleskey offered a sophisticated study of Georgia capital sentencing during the 1970s (the "Baldus study") that examined sentencing decisions in more than 2,000 murder cases. The study, employing multivariate regression techniques, sought to determine the role of race in Georgia's capital sentencing system by controlling for more than 200 nonracial variables. The study concluded that race—particularly the race of the victim—played a powerful role in Georgia's capital sentencing, with a finding that cases involving African-American defendants and white victims were significantly more likely to generate death sentences than any other racial combination; cases involving white victims as a whole were 4.3 times more likely than cases involving African-American victims to result in sentences of death.

McCleskey argued that the Baldus study confirmed what the Court had feared in *Furman*: that the administration of the death penalty was intolerably arbitrary and infected by racial bias. According to McCleskey, the empirically demonstrated role of race in capital sentencing violated both the guarantee of Equal Protection and the requirement of heightened reliability in capital cases under the Eighth Amendment. In rejecting McCleskey's claims, the majority opinion recounted some methodological concerns that had caused the District Court to deny McCleskey relief. But the Court assumed for the basis of its decision that the study was methodologically sound and that it had established at least a "risk" that racial considerations contributed to some capital sentencing decisions in Georgia, including, perhaps, the jury's death verdict in McCleskey's case.

The Court nonetheless denied relief on several grounds. The justices insisted that claims under the Equal Protection Clause generally require *proof* of discrimination in a *particular* case, rather than claims based on statistical showings of differential impact. The Court distinguished the few contexts, such as Title VII litigation and discrimination claims in jury selection, in which it has shifted the burden to the employer or the state after a threshold showing of statistical anomalies. But in so doing, the majority opinion failed to recognize that the statistical evidence in *McCleskey* was actually far stronger than the statistically based disparate impact claims common to Title VII and jury-selection claims. In the latter contexts, the equal protection challenges rely on raw data of disparate impact, whereas the Baldus study sought to control for nonracial variables. If the Court accepted the Baldus study as methodologically sound, it was compelled to conclude that racial considerations in fact played a substantial role in capital sentencing (with the presence of a white victim having as much significance to the sentencing outcome as the existence of a prior murder conviction by the defendant). The crux of McCleskey's claim was thus not "disparate impact" in which racial minorities bore disproportionate hardships as a result of a racially neutral policy, but widespread race-based decision-making in the administration of Georgia's death penalty.

The Court rejected the Eighth Amendment claim on the ground that Georgia had adopted *procedures* calculated to produce rational and proportionate outcomes in capital cases. The Court acknowledged that one of the operative procedures—allowing jurors to consider mitigating aspects of the offender and the offense—confers a level of discretion that opens up the possibility of discriminatory decision-making; but the majority opinion viewed that residual discretion as constitutionally mandated and thus seemed to regard any resulting discrimination—even discrimination on the basis of race—as a regrettable, perhaps even inevitable, consequence of individualized sentencing. The Court also insisted that it could not craft a rule particular to the death penalty, because the Eighth Amendment applies equally to capital and non-capital sentencing; if empirical evidence of racial discrimination in capital sentencing required abandonment of the death penalty, such evidence in the non-capital context might require the end of criminal punishment altogether. Finally, the Court insisted that the risk of racial discrimination established by the Baldus study did not rise to an intolerable level, though it did not explain why the level of salience of race in capital sentencing reflected in the Baldus study fell within an acceptable range.

McCleskey is by any measure a landmark decision. The Court's decision in *Furman* to regulate the American death penalty was rooted in suspicions that arbitrariness and discrimination clouded the capital decision-making process. With the Baldus study, the justices now had significant confirmation of the role race played in the system, even after states had reformed their statutes to conform to *Furman*. Although critics of the Baldus study could quibble with some of the modeling in the research, it was hard to deny that the study offered considerable support for a proposition that most observers already believed: that the death penalty in the South (or in at least in one major Southern state) had a demonstrable caste aspect. Perhaps the most notable finding of the Baldus study was that race played its most significant role on the victim side, with few killers of African-Americans receiving the ultimate punishment; an interesting corollary was that African-American *defendants* might have fared *better* in some respects within the Georgia system, given that most homicides were intraracial, and African-American killers of African-Americans were significantly less likely to receive the death penalty than white killers of whites. The converse, of course, which made problematic the "remedy" of abolition, was that African-American *victims* received less protection because the African-American community was afforded fewer death-penalty "services" (Kennedy 1997:340–45).

The odd conundrum of *McCleskey* is the fact that *suspicions* of arbitrariness could constitutionally require the adoption of *procedural* protections in capital cases, but seeming *proof* of actual discriminatory outcomes did not require further constitutional regulation. The Court could have avoided the conundrum if it had embraced the District Court's decision not to credit the Baldus study; in so doing, the Court also would have avoided the awkwardness of acknowledging the real possibility of racial prejudice in capital decision-making while disclaiming any power to respond to it. Indeed, an early draft of Justice Powell's opinion seemed to embrace this alternative approach, suggesting that a greater showing of discriminatory bias might require relief. But Justice Scalia, writing to his colleagues in response to Justice Powell's draft, emphatically rejected the notion that the problem with McCleskey's claim was the purported inadequacy of the Baldus study. Justice Scalia was prepared to believe—indeed, did believe—that race played a regrettable role in capital sentencing. But more importantly, Justice Scalia maintained that because states cannot eradicate race discrimination in capital cases, the Constitution should not be read to require them to do so. As recounted in Randall Kennedy's excellent book on race and crime, Justice Scalia's memo to his colleagues rejected Justice Powell's effort to put off to another day the decision whether a certain threshold of documented race discrimination renders the death penalty unconstitutional. Justice Scalia indicated that he did not "share the view, implicit in [Powell's draft opinion] that an effect of racial factors upon sentencing, if it could be shown by sufficiently strong statistical evidence, would require reversal." Instead, in light of his view "that the unconscious operation of irrational sympathies, including racial, upon jury [and prosecutorial] decision[s] ... is real, acknowledged by the [cases] of this court, and ineradicable," he declared that "I cannot honestly say that all I need is more proof" (Kennedy 1997:339 n. *, quoting Justice Scalia's internal memorandum to his colleagues (internal quotation marks omitted)).

Justice Scalia's approach appears to prevail in *McCleskey*. The justices are unwilling to tie the constitutionality of the American death penalty to any particular level of reliability in capital sentencing. The ultimate distribution of the death penalty is beyond constitutional regulation if states take appropriate procedural steps—as measured by the Court—to reduce the role of arbitrary or discriminatory factors in capital decision-making. The Court's decision reflects to some degree its concerns about the reliability of the social science offered to support McCleskey's claims. But more fundamentally, the justices are hesitant to embrace the regulation of *outcomes* in the criminal process. Such outcomes are to some unavoidable degree beyond state control, and outcome-based regulation would lead to extraordinary judicial control of states' criminal justice systems. Perhaps the Court could have held that the requirement of heightened reliability in capital cases justified regulating outcomes in the capital context without mandating interference in the non-capital process. Along these lines, the Court might have invalidated Georgia's death penalty while disclaiming any authority to regulate the non-capital system if similar racial disparities were documented in non-capital sentencing. Following Justice Scalia's lead, though, the Court seemed determined to close the door generally to empirically based claims of racially discriminatory sentencing in the criminal justice system, and invoked the prospect of widespread litigation outside of the capital context to justify rejection of McCleskey's attack on the operation of the Georgia death penalty.

To the extent the Court refuses to embrace outcome-based regulation, it obviously diminishes the significance of empirical research to its capital punishment jurisprudence. It makes the constitutionality of state death penalty practices turn on judicial perceptions of the fairness of procedures, rather than on empirically based assessment of the results of those procedures. In this respect, *McCleskey* is consistent with *McCree's* and *Barefoot's* reluctance to make constitutional doctrine dependent on some threshold level of verifiable reliability.

Barefoot and *McCleskey* thus explain why challenges to state capital sentencing schemes based on empirical evidence gathered by the Capital Jury Project (CJP) have had little traction thus far in state or federal courts. The CJP has collected data from more than a thousand jurors who served in capital cases, with the goal of understanding the decision-making process in capital cases. In particular, the CJP has sought to determine whether the intricate state capital schemes adopted post-*Furman* actually reduce arbitrariness in capital sentencing by controlling sentencer discretion. Dozens of scholarly articles have been published based on the CJP data, and much of the research has documented the failure of jurors to understand the guidance embodied in the capital sentencing instructions they receive (see, *e.g.*, Bentele and Bowers 2001; Bowers, Sandys, and Steiner 1998; Bowers and Steiner 1999; Eisenberg and Wells 1993). Armed with the studies, many capital defendants have challenged particular aspects of state capital schemes, but state and federal courts have almost uniformly rejected claims based on such studies. In some cases, the courts express doubts about the findings,[3] but in others the courts simply reject the notion that the constitutionality of state statutes can be challenged on the basis of empirical findings about actual jury behavior. From the courts' perspective, states are required to adopt *procedures* calculated to produce rational capital decision-making, but they cannot be required to achieve any particular level of rationality in capital sentencing, in part because it remains exceedingly difficult to measure the outcomes in capital cases. Hence, most citations to CJP data can be found in dissenting opinions, urging courts to adopt more searching review of state capital practices.[4]

Like the Baldus study reviewed in *McCleskey*, the CJP data represent a radical challenge to prevailing doctrine because they test the fundamental assumption that state schemes can reduce arbitrariness in capital sentencing and ensure a reasoned moral decision as to whether death is the appropriate punishment. By collecting data from numerous jurisdictions, the CJP is able to identify not only idiosyncratic defects in particular state statutes but endemic flaws in jury decision-making, such as the propensity of jurors to decide punishment during the guilt-innocence phase of the trial (Bowers 1995), their frequent misapprehension of the standards governing their consideration of mitigating evidence (see, *e.g.,* Bentele and Bowers 2001:1041, suggesting that mitigating evidence plays a "disturbingly minor role" in jurors' deliberations in capital cases across jurisdictions), and their general moral disengagement from the death penalty decision (see, *e.g.,* Haney 1997, describing how prevailing capital sentencing practices assist jurors in overcoming their resistance to imposing the death penalty in part by diminishing their sense of responsibility for their verdict). In many respects, the CJP data suggest that Justice Harlan might have been right when, a year before *Furman*, he defended the Court's rejection of the challenge to standardless discretion (*McGautha v. California* 1971). Justice Harlan found no violation under the Due Process Clause because he was persuaded that the federal courts could not require states to do the impossi-

---

3. See, *e.g., United States v. Llera Plaza* (2001:450 n. 5) (stating that "the studies do not establish that the concepts of aggravating and mitigating factors as used in the [statute] bear such a degree of intrinsic incomprehensibility as to render them incapable of clarification through adequate jury instructions").

4. See, *e.g., O'Dell v. Netherland* (1997:172 n.7, Stevens, J., dissenting, citing Eisenberg and Wells (1993)); *Ramdass v. Angelone* (2000:198 n. 26) (same); *Summerlin v. Stewart* (2003:1130, Rawlinson, C.J., dissenting) (stating that the "empirically established problems with jury sentencing deliberations calls into question the majority's facile conclusion that transfer of capital sentencing responsibility to a jury will enhance the accuracy of the process").

ble. In his view, it was "beyond present human ability" (p. 204) to tame the death penalty decision via extensive sentencing instructions, and a Court directive to the states to rationalize death-penalty decision-making would be doomed to failure. Of course, Justice Harlan's opinion presupposed that the Constitution could not require a threshold level of rationality in capital sentencing; at most it could require states to adopt procedural safeguards, if available, to improve the sentencing process. Justice Harlan's profound skepticism about taming the death penalty decision thus was an argument *against* federal constitutional regulation rather than an argument, as deployed by defendants relying on the CJP research, *supporting* further regulation.

Constitutional claims based on the CJP data thus encounter an additional obstacle. The Court is likely to view contemporary research documenting the failure of state guided-discretion schemes as something of a "bait and switch." When defendants advanced the standardless discretion claim in *McGautha*, they relied heavily on emerging elite and professional opinion regarding the desirability of standards in capital cases (as well as the need for bifurcation of the guilt-innocence and punishment decisions) (*McGautha v. California* 1971:221, discussing views of the American Law Institute and the National Commission on Reform of Federal Criminal Laws). Justice Harlan was unwilling to constitutionalize the informed opinion of experts who called for radical reform of prevailing death sentencing practices, in part because states were not compelled to adopt the perceived "best" approach to capital sentencing and in part because he was skeptical that the new wisdom counted more than decades of experience. According to Justice Harlan, "the Federal Constitution, which marks the limits of our authority in these cases, does not guarantee trial procedures that are the best of all worlds, or that accord with the most enlightened ideas of students of the infant science of criminology" (p. 221). If Justice Harlan had remained on the Court when *Furman* was decided a year later (he died within nine months of *McGautha*), it is possible that his words for the Court in *McGautha* would have carried the day.

Furman, though, embraced the claim of standardless discretion under the Eighth Amendment and seemed to require states to accept the direction of elite and professional opinion calling for guidance in capital sentencing. The "infant science of criminology" thus appeared to prevail. Now, more than three decades later, it is somewhat disquieting for defendants to attack guided-discretion in capital sentencing on the basis of social scientific evidence suggesting that the required guidance is illusory and in some respects counter-productive. The argument that the current practice violates *Furman* on its own terms naturally invites the response that *Furman* itself rested on a controversial judgment that state capital sentencing practices *could* be improved. Of course, current litigants could argue that the "core" of *Furman* is that state capital practices *must* be improved if the death penalty is to be retained. On this view, "guided discretion" is an attempted remedy for the underlying problem of arbitrariness and discrimination, and the failure of that remedy dooms the death penalty itself. Just such a reading of *Furman* recently led a state trial judge in New Mexico to reject the state capital sentencing statute based on CJP research (*New Mexico v. Dominquez* and *New Mexico v. Good* 2007). But this sort of argument runs into the limits of *Barefoot* and *McCleskey* described above, that the Supreme Court seems reluctant to impose any substantive threshold requirement regarding the non-arbitrary administration of the death penalty. Although the Court seems disposed toward claims that would impose increased "safeguards" in capital schemes, the Court has yet to embrace claims demonstrating the impossibility of safeguards altogether. Thus, to the extent the CJP research is marshaled by defendants to attack the false promise of *Furman*, it runs the risk of destabilizing *Furman* itself rather than the current American death penalty.

Renewed Regulation of the American Death Penalty: The Contemporary Concerns Surrounding Wrongful Convictions and Their Significance to Contemporary Death Penalty Doctrine

McCleskey marked a significant shift in the federal constitutional regulation of the death penalty. At the time *McCleskey* was decided in 1987, only about 100 executions had been carried out nationwide since the resumption of executions in 1977. A large proportion of death sentences were still being overturned in state and federal court, and it was hard to gauge whether the 1976 decisions sustaining the Texas, Georgia, and Florida death penalty schemes would lead to the renewed implementation of a robust death penalty in the United States. *McCleskey*, though, seemed to present the last significant global assault on the death penalty. Had the Court ruled the other way, and granted McCleskey individual relief or suspended the operation of the Georgia death penalty, it seems likely that the American death penalty would have ground to a halt. Instead, executions over the next decade climbed precipitously, and the Court increasingly ruled against capital defendants on a variety of claims. In addition, statutory limitations on the scope of federal habeas corpus, adopted in the wake of the Oklahoma City bombing, accelerated the movement of cases through the federal system. By the end of the 1990s, more than 500 inmates had been executed nationwide, and the death penalty had become a much more significant reality within the nation's criminal justice system.

With the increase in executions, though, came increased concerns about the possibility of wrongful convictions and executions. The discovery of numerous wrongfully convicted death-sentenced inmates in Illinois during the late 1990s led to the most substantial reflection on the American death penalty system since the 1960s and early 1970s. Governor Ryan, Illinois' Republican governor, first declared a moratorium on executions in 2000 and eventually commuted the sentences of all 167 inmates on Illinois' death row in 2003.

The events in Illinois reverberated nationwide. Almost overnight, state legislative agendas shifted from expanding or at least maintaining the prevailing reach of the death penalty to studying its operation and limiting its reach. Unlike the issues of racial and economic disparities, the issue of wrongful convictions had real public and political traction. Of course, the prospect of executing innocents has always lurked as a potential concern for the death penalty, but the apparent breadth of the problem in Illinois, coupled with the increased sophistication of DNA testing as a potential means of identifying innocents, pushed the issue to the social and political fore.

The emerging question in the legal world was whether the concern about wrongful convictions had any jurisprudential significance. Over a decade before, in *Herrera v. Collins* (1993), the Court had not been particularly welcoming of the claim that the Constitution forbids the execution of innocents, so as to require a judicial forum where a defendant can establish his innocence based on new evidence unavailable at the time of conviction. Several justices, led by Chief Justice Rehnquist, insisted that post-conviction proof of innocence did not establish a cognizable claim on federal habeas and that executive clemency has been and should remain the safety valve for convictions or sentences undermined by new evidence. Although the defendant lost that case, a majority of justices suggested that some post-conviction judicial forum must be available in capital cases where a death-sentenced inmate makes a "truly persuasive" showing of actual innocence.

But how else is the prospect of wrongful convictions significant to death penalty law? So far, the courts have said very little. In one notable decision, a federal district judge found that the federal death penalty could not be imposed consistent with due process without additional safeguards because of the excessive risk of error in capital cases, as revealed, among other ways, by DNA exonerations (*United States v. Quinones* 2002a, affirming preliminary injunction against federal death penalty statute). That decision was quickly over-

3 · THE ROLE OF CONSTITUTIONAL FACTS AND SOCIAL SCIENCE

turned (*United States v. Quinones* 2002b), and litigants have made little headway arguing that prevailing death penalty schemes inadequately prevent wrongful convictions. Most of the action is in state legislatures, which have considered (and in some cases adopted) new protections in capital cases designed to prevent wrongful convictions—including alteration of the "beyond a reasonable doubt" standard to a "beyond any doubt" standard, increased funding for capital defense lawyers, and greater access to DNA testing in capital cases.

The first extended discussion of the problem of wrongful convictions recently appeared in the Court's decision in *Kansas v. Marsh* (2006). At first glance the case appears relatively mundane. Kansas's death penalty statute requires imposition of death if the jury finds beyond a reasonable doubt that the "aggravating circumstances [are] not outweighed by any mitigating circumstances." The defendant argued, and managed to persuade the Kansas Supreme Court, that the Constitution forbids requiring the death penalty in cases of "equipoise" where aggravating and mitigating circumstances are evenly balanced. From a doctrinal standpoint, the Kansas Supreme Court's decision was a bit of a stretch, because the U.S. Supreme Court had already sustained Pennsylvania and Arizona provisions that likewise appeared to require the sentencer to impose death without independently determining that death was the appropriate punishment.

That the Supreme Court granted certiorari is somewhat of a puzzle. Kansas is not exactly a death penalty powerhouse (with a death row of eight and no executions in over 40 years, dating back to the era of the murders detailed in Truman Capote's *In Cold Blood* (1965)), and there are few cases in which the Supreme Court has reversed a state high court decision *finding* federal constitutional error within a state death penalty scheme. Indeed, Justices Stevens and Scalia engaged in a lengthy colloquy, with Justice Stevens asserting that no substantial federal interest justifies reviewing state court *over*-enforcement of federal rights, and Justice Scalia maintaining that the Kansas Supreme Court deprived the people of Kansas of their legitimate desire to implement the death penalty in their chosen way.

The majority opinion, by Justice Thomas, seems to miss the boat. The defendant's complaint was that the statute was "mandatory," and the majority concluded that the Court's decisions rejecting the mandatory death penalty did not apply, because the jurors in Kansas were allowed to consider fully and give adequate effect to mitigating evidence. But the real objection is that the statute is mandatory in a different sense. The equipoise provision "mandates" that "ties go to the state" in capital sentencing and that jurors must deliver death verdicts when aggravating and mitigating considerations are of equal strength. This sort of "mandatory" provision dictates a rule of decision (not necessarily a rule of exclusion with respect to mitigating evidence), and such a rule of decision runs counter to the Court's overall effort to ensure that state schemes reliably sort out "the worst of the worst" offenders.

Death sentences remain a notable exception even for death-eligible offenses. The number of capital sentences has dropped precipitously over the past decade, from a national average of greater than 300 in the mid-1990s to an average of less than 150 in the most recent three years for which data are available (2003–2005) (Bowers and Sundby, this volume). As indicated above, the Court's constitutional regulatory enterprise regarding the death penalty was motivated from the start by the vast divide between death-eligibility under state law and states' actual implementation of the death penalty. Given this animating concern and the recent exacerbation of this divide, it seems very odd (if not unconstitutional) for states to permit imposition of the death penalty in what are by definition "close" cases. Given that states have accomplished little in terms of narrowing the reach of the death penalty via statutory definition (most states have been promiscuous in their enumeration of aggravating factors), they should at least require jurors to conclude that the circumstances of the offense and the offender overwhelmingly justify the imposition of the death penalty; at a minimum, capital instructions should directly ask jurors whether the death penalty is appropriate in light of all aggravating and mitigating factors. The problem with the Kansas statute is that it does neither, and permits—in fact requires—jurors to choose death when mitigation and aggravation are in balance.

But the majority opinion is of little interest or significance (even a decision favoring the respondent would have resulted in a slight alteration of the statute so that aggravation would have to outweigh mitigation instead of allowing ties to go to the state). The real action and the true significance can be found in Justice Souter's dissent and Justice Scalia's concurrence. Justice Souter's dissent concludes with something of a Brandeis Brief. He argues that "a new body of fact must be accounted for in deciding what, in practical terms, the Eighth Amendment guarantees should tolerate," and the new body of "fact" to which he refers is the discovery of wrongfully convicted death-sentenced inmates. His dissent discusses the experience in Illinois, exalts the role of DNA in uncovering innocents on death row, and cites statistics about the number of "exonerated" inmates in recent years. Justice Souter concludes by saying that we are in a "period of new empirical argument about how 'death is different,'" and he seems to suggest that death penalty doctrine should take account of the "cautionary lesson of recent experience" with wrongful convictions. Although he disclaims any interest in revisiting the constitutionality of the death penalty as a whole ("it is far too soon for any generalization about the soundness of capital sentencing across the country"), he suggests that we should be chastened by recent experience and reject state death penalty rules, such as the one in Kansas, that might generate additional error in our capital punishment systems.

Justice Souter's opinion is remarkable and far-reaching in its implications. It is joined by three other Justices and it seems to travel the same path, though not as far, as Justice Blackmun's opinion more than a decade before declaring that he will no longer "tinker with the machinery of death" (*Callins v. Collins* 1994:1145, dissenting from denial of certiorari). Instead of adopting Justice Brennan's and Justice Marshall's more general claim that the death penalty is inconsistent with prevailing standards of decency and serves no justifiable penological goal, Justice Souter and his fellow dissenters seem to be setting up the possibility that the death penalty is flawed on the ground in a way that might constitutionally compel courts to cabin its reach. In many respects, this dissent carries forward the same theme of Justice Breyer's concurring opinion in *Ring v. Arizona* (2002:613). In that opinion, Justice Breyer defended the essential role of juries in capital decision-making by detailing the many emerging failures of the American death penalty system. In his view, the jury sentencing right in capital cases emerges not from any general Sixth Amendment interest in juror decision-making, but because doubts about the death penalty's deterrence value, as well as concerns about its arbitrary, discriminatory, and wrongful imposition, require states to preserve the link between the community (via jurors) and resulting death sentences.

Justice Scalia, who had mildly and light-heartedly chastised Justice Breyer in *Ring* for joining the Court's judgment despite his opposition to *Apprendi v. New Jersey* (2000)[5] (suggesting that Justice Breyer "buy a ticket to *Apprendi*-land"), reacts much more vehemently and acerbically to this dissent. First, relying on the work of others, he challenges the empirical claim about the extensiveness of error in capital cases. According to Justice Scalia, the number of "true" exonerations (for "innocent" defendants, as opposed to those later deemed "not guilty," or freed by legal error) is much smaller than Justice Souter's sources claim. Moreover, Justice Scalia views the exoneration of many innocents before execution, coupled with the absence of any demonstrable wrongful execution in the modern era, as indicative of the health rather than the pathology of the current system.

But Justice Scalia's broader concern is that he regards Justice Souter and his fellow dissenters as grandstanding for an international stage. Justice Scalia takes a direct swipe at international opponents of the American death penalty, ac-

---

5. *Apprendi* requires jury findings of fact as to elements of an offense that increase the maximum punishment available.

cusing them of "sanctimonious criticism" because "most of the countries to which these finger-waggers belong had the death penalty themselves until recently—and indeed, many of them would still have it if the democratic will prevailed." Justice Scalia's reaction seems peculiar given that the dissent makes no mention of world opinion or practice. But on the heels of the rejection in *Roper v. Simmons* (2005) of the death penalty for juveniles, in part based on overwhelming international condemnation of the practice, Justice Scalia apparently views the dissenters' criticisms of the operation of state death penalty schemes as essentially designed "to impugn" the American death penalty "before the world." This angle is a new one, and readers of Justice Scalia's opinion might be surprised to find that his comments are a response to a dissent in the *United States Reports* rather than to a speech delivered to the European Union.

His fear of foreign influence aside, Justice Scalia rightly appreciates the significance of Justice Souter's opinion. Like Justice Blackmun's and Justice Breyer's preceding global attacks on the death penalty, this opinion seems to contain a gratuitous assault on the death penalty—gratuitous because of its generality and seeming unrelatedness to the doctrinal issues presented (Justice Scalia accuses the dissent of nailing its complaint to the door of the wrong church because this case involved a challenge to sentencing instructions and not to the guilt-innocence determination). Even Justice Souter's comment that "it is far too soon" to consider the general soundness of American capital punishment, seems self-consciously aimed to raise the possibility of some future global empirical attack on the actual operation of the American death penalty system. When the Court chose to review the Kansas Supreme Court decision, no one would have remotely thought that this technical case about Kansas's statute would call into question the American death penalty system, and yet the four dissenters seem determined to at least raise the prospect.

Justice Scalia's contempt and anger thus stems from his (perhaps justifiable) belief that the dissenters are lying in wait for the opportunity to attack the death penalty as a whole, and his view that the dissenters are motivated or supported by international elites. The real prospect for wrongful convictions affecting death penalty jurisprudence will be if fears about executing innocents shift public opinion at home. Both Justice Souter's and Justice Scalia's opinions are clearly attempting to inform this debate by appealing to facts on the ground (none of which could be in the parties' briefs), and perhaps portend the movement toward a new era of critical attention to death penalty practices and outcomes.

Moreover, Justice Scalia undoubtedly recognizes that the Court has substantially increased its regulation of the American death penalty in the seven or so years since concerns about wrongful convictions surfaced in Illinois and spread nationwide. During those seven years, the Court revisited and overturned its decisions tolerating the execution of juveniles and persons with mental retardation. There had been a substantial, though not overwhelming case, for a significant shift in public and legislative attitudes regarding the execution of persons with mental retardation in the thirteen year interval between *Penry v. Lynaugh* (1989) and *Atkins v. Virginia* (2002)[6] so as to justify a change of course. But the evidence for invalidating the juvenile death penalty was not particularly stronger at the time of *Roper v. Simmons* (2005) than it had been when the Court sustained the juvenile death penalty in *Stanford v. Kentucky* (1989). Instead, the Court's methodology changed, giving greater weight to the views of the twelve abolitionist states within this country in gauging nationwide public opinion surrounding particular death penalty practices, and showing greater solicitude for the views and practices of other countries in assessing the cruelty and unusualness of domestic policies.

Likewise, the Court has substantially increased its regulation of the performance of counsel in capital cases over the past seven years. Before Illinois' wrongful-conviction epidemic came to light, the Court had never actually found—despite numerous opportunities—that a capital defendant was entitled to relief based on trial counsel's ineffective representation at trial. Over the past seven years, though, the Court has reversed three lower court decisions denying ineffective-assistance-of-counsel claims (*Williams v. Taylor* 2000, finding state-court decision ratifying trial representation objectively unreasonable; *Wiggins v. Smith* 2003, same; *Rompilla v. Beard* 2005, same), and has emphasized, to a degree without significant support in its prior cases, the substantial professional obligations of attorneys undertaking capital trial representation. This trilogy of cases reflects a profound shift in the justices' expectations regarding trial representation, and there are numerous indications that state legislatures, state courts, and federal courts have taken notice of the Court's change in this regard.

The recent dramatic shift in the Court's Sixth Amendment jurisprudence cannot be explained by any broader jurisprudential developments within its Sixth Amendment law, as the Court remains extraordinarily deferential in its approach to such claims in the non-capital context. Rather, it seems reasonable to attribute its shift to emerging concerns about the reliability and accuracy of the nation's capital punishment system, as reflected in the developments in Illinois and elsewhere. Together with its decisions prohibiting the death penalty as applied to juveniles and persons with mental retardation, the new Sixth Amendment cases seem to reflect the tacit adoption of the emerging

---

6. *Atkins* invalidated the death penalty for persons with mental retardation.

"heightened reliability" principle called for by Justice Souter's concurrence. The weakening of public support for the death penalty, rooted in growing concerns about wrongful convictions, has made the Court more circumspect about its death penalty jurisprudence over all.

Conclusion

It is far too soon to predict whether the emerging "facts" on the grounds will result in a prolonged period of increasing and extensive regulation of the American death penalty. The replacement of Chief Justice Rehnquist and Justice O'Connor with Chief Justice Roberts and Justice Alito has already shifted the Court to the right on a number of social issues, though it is interesting to note that virtually all of the few "liberal" victories in the recently completed Term came in capital cases (*Abdul-Kabir v. Quarterman* 2007; *Brewer v. Quarterman* 2007; *Panetti v. Quarterman* 2007; *Smith v. Texas* 2007), with Justice Kennedy supplying the crucial fifth vote. If recent experience is any guide, "facts" will continue to matter in the development of capital jurisprudence, but not necessarily the particular facts of the case, and even less likely facts in the form of empirical studies introduced in the lower courts. Rather, the justices' perceptions about the general workability of the capital system, filtered through public and elite opinion, will likely weigh heavily in the Court's future death penalty jurisprudence.

References

Abdul-Kabir v. Quarterman (2007). 127 S. Ct. 1654.
Apprendi v. New Jersey (2000). 530 U.S. 466.
Atkins v. Virginia (2002). 536 U.S. 304.
Barefoot v. Estelle (1983). 463 U.S. 880.
Bentele, Ursula and William J. Bowers. 2001. "How Jurors Decide on Death: Guilt is Overwhelming; Aggravation Requires Death; and Mitigation is No Excuse." *Brooklyn Law Review* 66:1011–1080.
Bowers, William J. 1995. "The Capital Jury Project: Rationale, Design, and Preview of Early Findings." *Indiana Law Journal* 70:1043–1102.
Bowers, William J., Marla Sandys, and Benjamin D. Steiner. 1998. "Foreclosed Impartiality in Capital Sentencing: Jurors' Predispositions, Guilt-Trial Experience, and Premature Decision Making." *Cornell Law Review* 83:1476–1556.

Bowers, William J. and Benjamin D. Steiner. 1999. "Death by Default: An Empirical Demonstration of False and Forced Choices in Capital Sentencing." *Texas Law Review* 77:605–717.

Bowers, William J. and Scott E. Sundby. This Volume. "Why the Downturn in Death Sentences?"

Brewer v. Quarterman (2007). 127 S. Ct. 1706.

Callins v. Collins (1994). 510 U.S. 1141.

Capote, Truman. 1965. *In Cold Blood.* New York, NY: Random House.

Clark v. Arizona (2006). 126 S. Ct. 2709.

Eisenberg, Theodore and Martin T. Wells. 1993. "Deadly Confusion: Juror Instructions in Capital Cases." *Cornell Law Review* 79:1–17.

Estelle v. Smith (1981). 451 U.S. 454.

Furman v. Georgia (1972). 408 U.S. 238.

Gregg v. Georgia (1976). 428 U.S. 153.

Haney, Craig. 1997. "Violence and the Capital Jury: Mechanisms of Moral Disengagement and the Impulse to Condemn to Death." *Stanford Law Review* 49:1447–1486.

Herrera v. Collins (1993). 506 U.S. 390.

Kansas v. Marsh (2006). 547 U.S. 1037.

Kennedy, Randall. 1997. *Race, Crime, and Law.* New York, NY: Pantheon Books.

Lockhart v. McCree (1986). 476 U.S. 162.

McCleskey v. Kemp (1987). 481 U.S. 279.

McGautha v. California (1971). 402 U.S. 183.

New Mexico v. Dominquez and *New Mexico v. Good* (2007). No. D-0101-CR-200400521 and 522, Order, June 8, 2007. (http://capitaldefenseweekly.com/library/TGarciaCJP.pdf).

O'Dell v. Netherland (1997). 521 U.S. 151.

Panetti v. Quarterman (2007). 127 S. Ct. 2842.

Penry v. Lynaugh (1989). 492 U.S. 302.

Ramdass v. Angelone (2000). 530 U.S. 156.

Ring v. Arizona (2002). 536 U.S. 584.

Rompilla v. Beard (2005). 545 U.S. 374.

Roper v. Simmons (2005). 543 U.S. 551.

Smith v. Texas (2007). 127 S. Ct. 1686.

Stanford v. Kentucky (1989). 492 U.S. 361.

Steiker, Carol S. 2002. "Capital Punishment and American Exceptionalism." *Oregon Law Review* 81:97–130.

Steiker, Carol S. and Jordan M. Steiker. 2005. "The Seduction of Innocence: The Attraction and Limitations of the Focus on Innocence in Capital Punishment Law and Advocacy." *Journal of Criminal Law & Criminology* 95:587–624.

_____. 1995. "Sober Second Thoughts: Reflections on Two Decades of Constitutional Regulation of Capital Punishment." *Harvard Law Review* 109:355–438.
Summerlin v. Stewart (2003). 341 F.3d 1082 (9th Cir.).
Tison v. Arizona (1987). 481 U.S. 137.
United States v. Llera Plaza (2001). 179 F. Supp.2d 444 (E.D. Pa.).
United States v. Quinones (2002a). 205 F. Supp.2d 256 (S.D.N.Y.).
United States v. Quinones (2002b). 313 F.3d 49 (2nd Cir.).
Williams v. Taylor (2000). 529 U.S. 362.
Wiggins v. Smith (2003). 539 U.S. 510.
Witherspoon v. Illinois (1968). 391 U.S. 510.

CHAPTER 4

WHY THE DOWNTURN IN DEATH SENTENCES?

William J. Bowers and Scott E. Sundby[1]

There has been a nationwide, decade long decline in death sentences since the mid-1990s. There were 315 death sentences imposed in 1994 and also in 1995; a decade later in 2004, there were 138, and in 2005, 128 (Snell 2006:14, Table 2). Thus, for every ten death sentences in the mid-1990s, only four were returned a decade later. What is the explanation for this downturn? Might we expect it to continue? Does it signal a change in Americans' willingness to use the death penalty? Does it foreshadow the end of capital punishment in America?

Observers have speculated about what lies behind this downturn.[2] They suggest that prosecutors have become less inclined to seek the death penalty because trying capital cases has become too expensive. In particular, where prosecutions are locally funded, the drain on local budgets of capital prosecutions may be seen as too great relative to the foregone benefits of not having the money for other purposes. Another suggestion is that the quality of capital defense services is getting better, that more training and resources are making defense attorneys more effective in capital cases. Still another speculation is that jurors are less likely to decide for death because revelations of innocence and exonerations based on DNA testing have made them more wary about voting for death and because the growing availability of a life sentence without the possibility of parole (LWOP) has made the death penalty less necessary in jurors' eyes. Calls for moratoriums on executions and for state commissions

---

1. The authors thank Susan Ehrhard for her assistance in the preparation of this chapter.

2. Such commentaries, for example, have appeared in the *Baltimore Sun* (McMenamin 2006), *Christian Science Monitor* (Axtman 2001), *The Denver Post* (Knight 2005), *The New York Times* (Liptak 2004; Liptak 2003), *Sacramento Bee* (Bee 2006), and *The Washington Post* (Smith 2004; Masters 2001).

to review the administration of the death penalty by governors such as George Ryan in Illinois also may have heightened the public's misgivings.

Yet this is speculation. There is no clear-cut evidence of how or why this downturn has occurred (Sundby 2006). But it has sparked the interest and captured the imagination of observers because it is a dramatic change from what was mostly a year-to-year increase in death sentences since the mid-1970s, and because it might be setting the stage for more momentous changes. Further consideration of what may be behind this change is needed to appreciate how research can be fashioned to disentangle the myriad influences that may have contributed to this turnaround.

Anatomy of the Downturn

The decline in death sentences is evident across the country, in the Northeast, South, Midwest, and West. Indeed, it is replicated in virtually all states which have imposed two or more death sentences a year over the past 15 years. These trends are documented in Table 1, which shows the distribution of death sentences nationally, regionally, and by state over the period 1991–2005. To facilitate comparisons by state and region, the table shows the percent of the fifteen-year total falling within each of five three-year intervals.

Overall and in each of the four regions, death sentences peak in the three-year interval 1994–1996 and decline thereafter. In absolute numbers of death sentences, the decline is greatest between 1997–1999 and 2000–2002; but relative to the number of death sentences in the preceding three-year interval, the decline between 2000–2002 and 2003–2005 is proportionate to the earlier decline. While there are state by state variations in the magnitude of the decline and the point at which it is most pronounced, the proportionate reduction is greater in the three years following 1997–1999 in 14 states, and in the three years following 2000–2002 in 13 states.

Within states, however, we do not know the extent to which the downturn in death sentences is uniform across the state or concentrated in particular locations. We do know that in the past there were vast disparities in the likelihood of a death sentence by location within some states. For example, in Missouri, St. Louis far outstrips Kansas City in death sentences (Barnes, Sloss, and Thaman 2007). In Texas, Houston had many more death sentences per criminal homicide than Dallas, and both of these locations were well ahead of other Texas jurisdictions; in Pennsylvania, Philadelphia produced many more death sentences than Pittsburgh; and in Georgia, there were virtually no death sentences in Atlanta (Fulton County), compared to Columbus (Muscogee

Table 1. Death Sentences: Nationally, Regionally, and by State, 1991–2005

	Percent of Fifteen Year Total in Each Three Year Interval					
	1991–1993	1994–1996	1997–1999	2000–2002	2003–2005	15-Year Totals
Northeast	26.34	27.23	21.43	14.73	10.27	224
New Jersey	19.05	38.10	23.81	14.29	4.76	21
Pennsylvania	28.57	27.51	19.58	14.29	10.05	189
CT NH NY RI VT*	18.75	6.25	37.5	18.75	18.75	16
Midwest	26.30	29.86	21.09	13.03	9.72	422
Illinois	29.17	33.33	17.50	13.33	6.67	120
Indiana	30.0	26.27	20.0	20.0	3.33	30
Missouri	27.66	29.79	24.47	10.64	7.45	94
Ohio	24.52	30.32	21.94	11.61	11.61	155
KS NE SD	12.0	12.0	20.0	32.0	24.0	25
South	22.71	26.32	24.30	15.69	10.97	2078
Alabama	15.10	31.25	27.08	15.10	11.46	192
Arkansas	24.53	32.08	26.42	9.43	7.55	53
Delaware	37.50	3.13	25.0	21.88	12.50	32
Florida	30.41	27.78	18.42	13.16	10.23	342
Georgia	25.27	20.88	35.16	8.79	9.90	91
Kentucky	24.24	18.18	33.33	18.18	6.06	33
Louisiana	19.81	25.47	29.25	16.98	8.49	106
Maryland	21.05	36.84	15.79	21.05	5.26	19
Mississippi	28.38	22.97	25.68	13.51	9.46	74
North Carolina	25.54	30.94	23.74	14.03	5.76	278
Oklahoma	18.66	32.09	23.13	11.94	14.18	134
South Carolina	18.48	27.17	19.57	19.56	15.22	92
Tennessee	29.58	15.49	23.94	15.49	15.49	71
Texas	17.23	24.06	24.69	20.12	13.69	482
Virginia	23.75	21.25	25.0	18.75	11.25	80
West	24.05	25.22	23.62	15.01	12.10	686
Arizona	31.78	18.69	18.69	14.02	16.82	107
California	22.49	23.21	26.32	16.51	11.48	418
Idaho	35.29	5.88	17.65	17.65	23.53	17
Nevada	14.06	45.31	17.19	14.06	9.38	64
Oregon	33.33	28.21	20.51	5.13	12.82	39
Washington	21.05	26.32	31.58	21.05	0	19
CO MT NM UT WY	22.73	45.45	18.18	4.55	9.09	22
Total	23.62	26.0	23.85	15.65	10.88	3539

* States with fewer than 15 death sentences over this fifteen-year period are grouped and identified by their state abbreviations at the bottom of the list of states within each region.

County) (Steiker 2002). In some locations the death penalty was more common in the surrounding "collar counties" than in the central cities; this pattern holds for Baltimore (Paternoster *et al.* 2004) and for Chicago (Pierce and Radelet 2002). Knowing where turnarounds have been concentrated within states will help in refining and focusing the research.

Explanations for the Downturn

How and why did it occur? The first possibility is that the downturn in death sentences is simply the product of a decline in homicides over this period, that it is a reflection of shrinkage in the supply of death-eligible cases. While there has been a decline in homicides as reported in the FBI's Uniform Crime Reports (UCR) over this period, there are several reasons why this trend is unlikely to account for the observed downturn in death sentences.

One is the fact that the relative decline in death sentences far exceeds the reduction in criminal homicides, and particularly the decline in the incidence of "death-eligible" or capital murders. Using the Supplementary Homicide Reports of the UCR, Fagan, Zimring, and Geller (2006) estimated the number of capital or "death-eligible" murders within the broader category of criminal homicides in death penalty states. They found that this critical group of offenses has declined much less over the relevant period than the number of death sentences. There is a 52% drop in death sentences from the 1994–1996 average to the 2003 value, which is more than twice the 22% fall in death-eligible murders for the corresponding years.

Beyond this, the estimated number of death-eligible murders is 10 to 20 times greater than the number of death sentences since 1991. Although a drop in such murders may have occurred, the decline could not plausibly have depleted the supply of cases where death sentences could be sought. Hence, with the exception of jurisdictions where prosecutors pursue the death penalty whenever possible, there is little downward pressure on death sentences from the reduction in capital murders over this period.

While the reduction in the supply of death-eligible murders may account for only a small fraction of the downturn in death sentences over this period, declining crime rates could influence decision makers in another way. With declining crime rates over the past decade, crime has fallen from the top to near the bottom in Gallup polls as "the most important problem facing this country" (Pastore and Maguire 2006:Table 2.1.). Such a substantial reduction in people's fear of crime, even if the objective risk of death-eligible murder is reduced only marginally, could well influence the thinking and decision-making of participants in the criminal justice processing of capital cases. Let us now turn to those decision makers—jurors, defense attorneys, and prosecutors—

for a broader perspective on what may be behind the downturn in death sentences.

The Jury and the Decision-Making Threshold

In trying to understand why a jury returns a life or a death sentence, it is common to look for factors that would sway all twelve jurors. The reality is, however, that many cases turn on the vote of just one or two jurors. Researchers found that in 53 South Carolina capital cases, the 21 with nine or more jurors whose first vote was for death all ended with a death sentence, and the 21 with seven or fewer whose first vote was for death all ended with a life sentence. The 11 cases with eight first votes for death split seven for death and four for life (Eisenberg, Garvey and Wells 2001:Table 7). Thus, an issue or factor that influences the initial vote of even only one or two individual jurors may serve as a "tipping point" that affects the final jury verdict in a sizable number of cases. Several factors present themselves as possible candidates for being such tipping points.

1. Rising Residual Doubt? An explanation frequently advanced to explain the drop in death sentences is the increased public awareness of the number of inmates on death rows who have been exonerated by DNA evidence (Chalmers 2006). Governor Ryan's high-profile emptying of Illinois's death row, increasing legislative support for moratoriums on executions, and the growing number of commutations based on concerns over innocence have added governmental legitimacy to the concern that innocent persons are at significant risk of being executed. Further, CSI (Crime Scene Investigation) and similar television shows that emphasize DNA testing are calling attention to the risk of mistakes in the criminal justice process. Opinion polls indicate that the lesson has not been lost on the public. In 2003 and 2005 Gallup polls, six to seven out of ten Americans stated that they believed an innocent person had been executed within the previous five years (Jones 2003; 2005).

We know from interviews with capital jurors in the early 1990s[3] that lingering doubt is a powerful mitigating factor for life (Bowers, Sandys, and Steiner 1998:Table 12), but that few capital jurors actually harbored such doubts in their case. One in twenty jurors (5%) accepted the possibility that the de-

---

3. The Capital Jury Project (CJP) conducted interviews with 1198 jurors from 353 capital trials in 14 states. See Bowers (1995) for a description of the research design and methodology; Bowers and Foglia (2003) for a review of the major findings; and Bowers, Brewer, and Lanier (this volume) for an overview of these findings.

fendant "might be altogether innocent, a case of mistaken identity" (Sundby 1998).[4] If, however, the recent rash of exonerations has caused jurors in more current cases to be increasingly worried that the defendant in their case may some day be exonerated, such concerns could be expected to trigger the life sentence tipping point more often. When added to the votes of several other jurors already favoring life, the vote of only one or two additional jurors with residual doubts may be all that it takes to put the jury across the first-ballot threshold for a life outcome. It is also quite possible that where the jury is divided over what the sentence should be, pro-life jurors can use the possibility of a fatal mistake as a wedge argument to persuade pro-death jurors to settle for a sentence of life without parole. And it goes without saying that a heightened appreciation for the risk of mistakes could also bring down the number of death sentences by reducing capital convictions.

2. The Increase of Life Without Parole (LWOP) and Decrease in Fear of Crime. Another commonly cited explanation for the drop in death sentences is the increased availability of life without parole and the fact that jurors in states where LWOP is the alternative to the death penalty must now expressly be told that "life" means "life without parole." Thirty-seven death penalty states and the federal jurisdiction now have LWOP as the death penalty alternative; New Mexico is the only exception. This is a drastic change from the early 1990s, when only 22 states had LWOP as an available death penalty alternative (Dieter 1993), and when jurors were greatly frustrated by not being told unambiguously what the actual alternative was to the death penalty (Lane 1993:376, 379).[5] In the absence of clarity about the alternative, jurors fell prey to a widely prevailing "myth of early release" (Steiner, Bowers, and Sarat 1999).[6] The median release

---

4. Sundby's percentage estimate was based on the responses of California capital jurors, but the same holds for the sample of jurors from all fourteen states where interviews were conducted in the early 1990s; the previously unreported figure for the full sample is 4.8%.

5. Jurors interrupted their deliberations to ask the judge what the death penalty alternative would be in 70 of the first 280 Georgia cases resulting in a death sentence (25%) (see Lane 1993). Jurors complained bitterly that the judge would answer their queries about how long the defendant would spend in prison if not given a death sentence with a statement not to concern themselves with such matters, or by simply saying, "all I can tell you is, life means life and death means death" (p. 379). For examples, see the exchanges between jurors and trial judges in cases reported by Lane (1993) and selectively reprinted in Bowers and Steiner (1999:628–29).

6. The myth of early release appears to have been a culturally imbedded element of "folk knowledge" fostered by the politics of fear (Steiner, Bowers, and Sarat 1999). Not only the public, but legislators as well, vastly underestimated how long convicted capital murderers not sentenced to death would spend in prison (Bowers, Vandiver, and Dugan 1994).

estimates of jurors in all 14 states studied by the CJP were far earlier than when such offenders would actually become eligible for parole consideration.[7]

Fear of crime is the other side of this coin, particularly fear of the defendant in the case at hand. Jurors in the early 1990s indicated that after the facts of the crime, the defendant's dangerousness was the principal consideration in their deliberations and decision-making on punishment (Bentele and Bowers 2001:Table 1; Eisenberg and Wells 1993). Even in California, which offered only a choice of "life without parole" or death, 52% of jurors cited the possibility that the defendant would kill again as a "great" concern (Sundby 1997:1109, 1116, n.119). Moreover, fear of the defendant's future dangerousness comes to the fore especially when jurors appear to be deadlocked on what the punishment should be (Bowers and Steiner 1999).[8] Hence, the myth of early release and the allied fear of the defendant's future dangerousness served in the early 1990s as powerful arguments in the hands of pro-death jurors to break the resistance of jurors who voted for life or who were undecided at the jury's first ballot on punishment.

Does the fact that virtually all death penalty states now have LWOP mean that the public, and especially jurors, are becoming aware that convicted murderers are not getting back on the streets? Are declining crime rates contributing to a reduction in people's fear of crime, and also making jurors less fearful of the defendant in their case? If so, the increased availability of life without parole and the reduced fear of crime may have contributed to the decline in death sentences in various ways. Prosecutors may be more willing to accept a guilty plea and forego death if they can assure the victim's survivors that the defendant will remain in prison for the rest of his life. At trial, life without parole offers the defense a means of assuring jurors that the defendant will not pose a future danger to society. The judge's explicit confirmation that the death penalty alternative is life with no chance of parole should serve jurors' expressed need to know what the death penalty alternative actually is and thus counter what remains of the once widely prevailing myth of early release. And late in jury

---

7. Even in Alabama, California, Missouri, and Pennsylvania, which then had LWOP as the sole alternative to capital punishment, only small minorities of jurors believed that the defendant was apt to spend the rest of his life in prison (Bowers and Steiner 1999:650, 670).

8. Statistical analysis shows that the influence of such beliefs is concentrated in the period between the jurors' first and final votes on punishment, and that it is most pronounced among jurors who were undecided at first punishment vote (Bowers and Steiner 1999:659ff). Jurors' narrative accounts of how they reached their final decisions also make it clear that beliefs about how long the defendant would spend in prison if not sentenced to death were paramount in the final give and take of jury deliberations (*id.*: Part V).

deliberations, the reality of life without parole may now be serving to counter pro-death jurors' claims of the defendant's future dangerousness.

3. *More Representative and Bias-Free Juries.* While venire pools may still underrepresent the minority population, increasing attention to the issue makes it probable that a greater number of capital juries include minority jurors than in the past. The importance of minority representation on capital juries is highlighted by CJP findings about the role of the jury's racial composition in cases involving an African-American defendant accused of killing a white victim (Bowers, Steiner, and Sandys 2001). African-American jurors were more likely than whites to perceive the evidence in a manner supportive of those factors that lead jurors to vote for life sentences: they were more likely to see the defendant as remorseful, to have lingering doubts about the defendant's role in the crime, and to believe that the defendant would not pose a future danger if given a life sentence (*id.*:215–26). While these differences of perspective held regardless of the race of defendant and victim, they were particularly pronounced when an African-American defendant was tried for killing a white victim. In such cases, the seating of a single African-American male dramatically reduced the likelihood of a death sentence. Juries with one African-American male returned death sentences in 42.9% of such cases, compared to 71.9% of the cases where no African-American males were on the jury (*id.*:171, 193–94).

More minority jurors is not the only way in which changing jury composition may have increased the chances that cases will result in a life sentence. In the past, jury selection procedures have failed to purge many jurors who come to capital jury service believing that the death penalty is "the only acceptable punishment" for the kind of aggravated killing they will be considering, contrary to the Supreme Court's "life qualification" holdings in *Wainwright v. Witt* (1985) and *Morgan v. Illinois* (1992). Thus, in the early 1990s, most jurors believed that a death sentence was the "only acceptable" punishment for "a planned premeditated killing," for "the killing of more than one victim," and for "a killing in prison"; almost half held that death was the only acceptable punishment for the killing of a police officer or prison guard and for a drug-related killing (Bowers, Sandys, and Steiner 1998:Table 6). Not surprisingly, many jurors who held these beliefs took a pro-death stand on punishment prior to the sentencing stage of the trial, and most who did so were "absolutely convinced" that the punishment should be death, before hearing mitigating evidence and arguments or the judge's sentencing instructions (*id.*:Table 9). Nor is the influence of such strongly pro-death jurors limited to their own votes. Jurors who tend to believe that the death penalty is the only proper sentence for an intentional killing also tend to be particularly strong and vocal advocates for death within the jury room (Sundby 2005:125–30).

An enhanced understanding of the profile of jurors who are likely to vote for a death sentence, when coupled with the sophisticated use of tools such as questionnaires in jury selection, increases the odds that defense counsel will identify and exclude prospective jurors who are likely to vote for death no matter how strong the defendant's mitigation evidence. The removal of a strongly pro-death juror can tip the balance toward a life sentence even if the replacement juror is inclined to vote for death but will "give effect" to mitigation (*Morgan v. Illinois* 1992). And, of course, if a strongly pro-death-penalty juror is replaced by a juror who is inclined toward a life sentence, chances will be increased that the jury will have a first ballot threshold sufficient for a life sentence.

The Professionalization of the Capital Defense Bar

The years following *Gregg v. Georgia* (1976) saw a number of cases in which the defendant's legal representation was shameful, cases with sleeping lawyers, drunk lawyers, "high" lawyers, and lawyers who failed to do any investigation (Bright 1994). A remarkable number of capital defense lawyers have eventually been disbarred or disciplined after their representation; in North Carolina, for example, more than one in six death row inmates had an attorney who was eventually disciplined or disbarred (North Carolina Coalition for a Moratorium No date). An investigative report based on appellate court records and trial transcripts for 80 defendants sentenced to death since 1997 in Alabama, Georgia, Mississippi, and Virginia found that defense attorneys "routinely missed myriad issues of abuse and mental deficiency, abject poverty and serious psychological problems," and concluded that by failing to investigate or present their clients' histories, these lawyers "fell far short of the 20-year-old professional standards set by the American Bar Association" (Henderson 2007). Nationally, 68% of all death sentences imposed between 1973 and 1995 were overturned upon appeal or later judicial review, and the most common reason given by appellate courts was ineffectiveness of defense counsel (Liebman, Fagan, and West 2000).

Lately, the Supreme Court has become more responsive to the need for adequate defense representation in capital cases. It gave effect to ABA guidelines in its most recent ineffective assistance cases by focusing on defense counsel's failure to do basic mitigation investigation (*Rompilla v. Beard* 2005; *Wiggins v. Smith* 2003; *Williams v. Taylor* 2000). Further, courts appear to be increasingly receptive to an emerging model of capital representation that includes a defense team of investigators and experts, a model to which the Supreme Court's recent ineffective assistance of counsel decisions give added impetus.

The need for a lawyer to be specially trained in capital defense also is now widely recognized. As a result, a professional capital defense bar has begun to emerge. Some states that have had particularly troubling histories with incompetent capital representation, such as Georgia, North Carolina, and Virginia, have created statewide systems specifically devoted to capital representation.[9] While some of these systems are too recent to account for the downturn in death sentences evident in the late 1990s, they were the culmination of standards and best practices that had been implemented by a growing number of sites over the prior decade. In effect, they reflect momentum in the capital defense community that reaches back into the 1990s.

Growing Restraints on Prosecutors

Of all the actors in the criminal justice system, prosecutors can cause the most significant drop in death sentences. Given that the prosecutor controls the initial decision over whether to seek the death penalty and, later, whether to accept or reject a plea that would avoid a capital trial, prosecutors may be pivotal in the death sentence downturn. The cost of capital prosecutions has been increasing. In many states where the county is the sole funding source for such prosecutions, a capital case can cause a county significant financial hardship. Increasingly, the decision to seek the death penalty may subject a prosecutor to political pressure, and the failure to get a death sentence after a considerable outlay may entail political consequences.

The increasing professionalization of a capital defense bar has heightened the costs and risks of capital prosecutions from the prosecutor's perspective. The more vigorous the prosecutor expects the defense to be will increase his or her estimate of the likely cost of the trial and diminish his or her assessment of the chances of getting a capital conviction and a death sentence. A prosecutor faced with a more professionally prepared capital defense may, therefore, find a plea to a sentence of life without parole attractive for a variety of reasons: it avoids the extraordinary costs of a capital trial and the associated appeals; it ensures an outcome that will meet the community's concerns over the defendant's future dangerousness; it avoids a possible "defeat" for the prosecutor if a jury

---

9. See GA. CODE ANN. §17-12-121 (2004) (creating the Office of the Georgia Capital Defender to represent indigent persons charged with a capital felony for which the death penalty is being sought); N.C. GEN. STAT. §7A-498.2 (2005) (establishing the Office of Indigent Defense Services in North Carolina); VA. CODE ANN. §19.2-163.8(A) (2004) (mandating the Virginia Indigent Defense Commission to adopt standards for attorneys who represent capital defendants).

fails to return a sentence of death; and LWOP allows a prosecutor to communicate the desirability of a plea to the victim's survivors in a persuasive way by pointing out that the defendant's attorneys are mounting a skilled defense that may carry a risk of acquittal, the most dreaded outcome from the survivors' viewpoint.

It may also be that as the rate of violent crime has dropped over the past decade and public concern over crime has moved down the list of "hot button" issues, local prosecutors are feeling less community pressure to pursue death sentences in murder cases. This may be especially true in large urban areas where the voting public's perception of a prosecutor's office is not as likely to be driven by its handling of specific murder cases. In less populous areas, on the other hand, where murder cases are relatively rare, the public may be more apt to judge a prosecutor on whether he or she seeks the death sentence on a case-by-case basis.[10]

Research Strategy

The downturn is present in state after state and is evidently the product of changes in decision-making by those who exercise discretion in the processing of capital cases. To understand how and why these changes have occurred, we need data on the exercise of discretion by prosecutors in bringing cases to trial as capital offenses, by defense attorneys in challenging prosecutorial claims and making their case in mitigation, and by capital jurors who must wrestle with the evidence and arguments to make the final sentencing decision. We have considered immediately above how the influences these actors experience may have changed over the past decade. What we need are data that will yield a reliable assessment of the influences we have considered above, and this will entail identifying and selecting sites where the downturn is clearly evident and where the essential data are readily and amply available. In the discussion that follows, we advocate the collection of three kinds of data especially suited for such an investigation: trial transcripts for cases in which the death penalty was sought, interviews with jurors who made the life or death decision, and information on the pretrial exercise of discretion by prosecutors. There will be a premium on sites where these kinds of data can be acquired now and are available a decade earlier, and where collaborating investigators might be found who are familiar with the issues and kinds of data needed in their respective sites.

---

10. Joint Legislative Audit and Review Commission, Draft: Review of Virginia's System of Capital Punishment (2001) (finding that prosecutors in high-density urban areas sought the death penalty 15% less often than those in areas with lower population density).

Trial Transcripts: A Lens on the Downturn

As the official verbatim record of what happened during the trial, trial transcripts provide details of the character and aggravation of the crime as presented by the prosecution's witnesses. They reveal the mitigation as orchestrated by the defense attorney and as advanced by the defense's witnesses. They also cover the *voir dire* questioning and jurors' answers that comprise the give and take of jury selection, and they include defense motions and other evidentiary exhibits. Trial transcripts in capital cases are generally warehoused or archived in court facilities. They are typically voluminous and awkward to work with, but these difficulties are now far more tractable. They may be obtained in electronic form directly from the court reporters who transcribe them, or electronically scanned and converted to a word processing format that makes them searchable, sharable, and economical to obtain.

Carefully drawn samples of trial transcripts in selected jurisdictions from recent death and life cases and a from decade or more ago could be uniquely valuable in understanding why death sentences have experienced this downturn. Death case transcripts alone would reveal two critical things that are indispensable for understanding the downturn. On the one hand, they would show the level of aggravation of cases in which death sentences were imposed then and now, bearing on the argument that prosecutors are presently restricting their charging and trial practices to more serious or depraved crimes. In addition, they would reveal changes in how defense attorneys may be investigating evidence of mitigation and whether they are now presenting it in a more coherent and orchestrated manner. Having life case transcripts from the same jurisdictions and time periods would, of course, serve to confirm and refine the picture of changes in aggravation and mitigation apparent in the death case transcripts. But more critically, they would also afford the possibility of exploring changes in jurors' decision-making over time. The key would be to see how aggravating and mitigating circumstances, as revealed in the death and life transcripts at each point in time, are associated with whether the jury's decision is a life or death sentence.

Comparing the trial transcripts from life and death cases now and earlier, therefore, would permit us to apportion the downturn which has occurred to changes in the aggravation of the cases being tried, the mitigation being presented at trial, and the responsiveness of jurors to particular aggravating and mitigating trial evidence and arguments. And equally important, the absence of such differences will serve to rule out changes in the aggravation and mitigation of the cases over time or in jurors' responses to such aggravation and mitigation as relevant to the explanation of the downturn. While transcripts will leave open questions about the influence of factors other than aggravating and mitigating circumstances, they can establish basic differences in the kinds of crimes being tried as capital offenses, the character of the mitigation evidence being presented to the jury, and the kinds of crimes and defenses for which juries are imposing death, as opposed to life, sentences.

Juror Interviews: Spotlighting the Ultimate Decision-Makers

In the early 1990s, CJP investigators conducted in-depth personal interviews with 1,198 jurors from 353 capital trials in 14 states. These three- to four-hour interviews retrace the stages of the trial and ask about the factors affecting jurors' decision-making throughout the process. They include both carefully worded questions with designated response options and open-ended questions inviting extensive narrative accounts. Both kinds of questions delve into the various influences on the decision-making process, how they affected the thinking of individual jurors, and the decision-making of the jury as a group.

Fortunately, the questions CJP investigators asked jurors in the early 1990s addressed many issues that bear on current speculations about the recent downturn in death sentences. Examples include: (1) whether jurors had "residual doubt" that the defendant might actually be innocent or at least not the one responsible for the killing; (2) what jurors thought the death penalty alternative was and how long they believed the defendant would actually spend in prison if not given the death penalty; (3) how dangerous jurors thought the defendant would be in the future, in or out of prison; and (4) whether jurors held beliefs about the death penalty that predisposed them to vote for death or to take a premature pro-death stand at the guilt stage of the trial. Repeating such interviews with jurors from recent cases would make it possible to see what is different about capital jurors' thinking and decision-making now. For this comparison to be most informative, the cases selected for interviewing now should come, insofar as possible, from the same states and jurisdictions within states as the earlier interviews. The selection of jurisdictions in which to repeat the earlier interviews might give priority to places where the downturn in death sentences has been especially pronounced. Such a focus will aid in specifying the kinds of changes in jurors' decision-making that may have contributed most to the downturn in death sentences.

Moreover, if the data from juror interviews then and now could be linked with data from trial transcripts at the same points in time, that is, by both acquiring trial transcripts and conducting juror interviews in the same cases, the analytic potential of the data would be greatly enhanced. Thus, for example, trial transcripts provide an objective record of the mitigation case presented to the jury, the testimony of each defense witness, the mix or "orchestration" of expert and lay witnesses, the development of themes and sequencing of witnesses, and, of course, the vulnerability of this evidence to internal contradictions and to cross-examination. That is, transcripts provide empirical grounding for assessing jurors' responsiveness to aggravating and mitigating evidence that may be imperfectly or selectively remembered and reported in juror interviews. Juror interviews, on the other hand, will convey jurors' perceptions and interpretations of what transpired and how they reached a decision on the basis of the empirical realities captured in the transcript. The CJP interviews asked, for example, about how well the attorney on each side was prepared for the trial, presented his/her case, communicated with the jury, seemed competent and professional, and fought hard at the guilt and punishment stages of the trial. These subjective evaluations or perceptions, especially when pooled from interviews with several jurors in a given case, will capture aspects of prosecution and defense performance not directly conveyed in the transcript but important for assessing the influence of the prosecution and defense on juror decision-making.

Research presently underway (Bowers, Brewer, and Lanier, this volume) provides for the acquisition of transcripts and the interviewing of jurors in five states. Extending this current effort to include transcripts and interviews in cases from additional states that were covered in the earlier CJP research would ensure comparability over time in a greater number of cases and from a wider variety of places then and now. And, acquiring trial transcripts for cases with juror interviews in the earlier CJP sample that come from the same states or locations within states as those slated for the current data collection effort would greatly enhance the comparability of the data from the two points in time and the analytic power of the two kinds of data at each point in time. Building in this way on the present commitment to acquiring transcripts and interviewing jurors in the same cases would represent a decisive economy of cost and effort in compiling such an analytically powerful database.

Strategic Sites: The Case Selection Question

Changes in the number and kind of murder cases prosecutors bring to trial on capital charges may well have contributed to the downturn in death sentences. If prosecutors are now bringing only the most aggravated murders to trial as capital offenses, trial transcripts could be expected to reflect heightened aggravation levels.[11] Changes in the exercise of prosecutorial discretion for other

---

11. Baldus, Woodworth, and Grosso (forthcoming 2008) observes that there has been a sharp reduction in the rate at which New Jersey prosecutors have advanced death-eligi-

reasons, however, will not be evident in trial transcripts. For example, when prosecutors divert cases for reasons of cost, the availability of LWOP, or the wishes of the victim's family, the aggravation level of crimes tried capital then and now need not change. For an assessment of the extent to which the exercise of prosecutorial discretion may have contributed to the downturn in death sentences, data are needed on cases where death sentences might have been but were not sought. For an understanding of how such reductions have come about, data are needed on cases that will reflect the role of costs, alternative sanctions, the wishes of victims' families, and other factors.

The question of which cases prosecutors bring to trial as capital offenses has been tackled in selected states by various investigators, notably by David Baldus in his landmark study of the role of race in Georgia's processing of potentially capital cases presented in *McCleskey v. Kemp* (1987) (reported in Baldus, Woodworth, and Pulaski 1990). Baldus isolated the charging and sentencing stages of the process and examined them separately for evidence of racial bias. For the charging stage he examined the factors that distinguished defendants who were brought to trial on capital charges and those who were not (see also Nakell and Hardy 1987). Baldus *et al.* (2001; 1998) subsequently conducted a similar investigation in New Jersey and Pennsylvania (reviewed in Baldus, Woodworth, and Grosso forthcoming 2008). The critical issue these studies examined was the role race played in the prosecutorial charging decision, holding many other influences constant. The chief question raised here is, of the many factors that influence charging decisions, including race, what changes have occurred between the 1990s and the 2000s.

For a thoroughgoing assessment of the downturn in death sentences owing to changes in the case selection practices of prosecutors, studies are needed in sites with more refined data on prosecutorial charging and plea bargaining practices. A number of states require prosecutors to file a notice of intent with the court in cases where they wish to pursue the death penalty. When this statement of intent is a part of the official record, it becomes possible to distinguish between death-eligible cases that are and are not initially charged as capital offenses, and of those that are, to distinguish between those that are and are not subsequently brought to trial as capital offenses. Recent studies in South Carolina (Songer and Unah 2006), North Carolina (Unah 2003), Maryland (Paternoster *et al.* 2004), and Missouri (Barnes, Sloss, and Thaman 2007)

---

ble cases to penalty trials. In the 1980s the rate was 53%, in the 1990s it was 20%, and since 1999, it has been 10% (citing Weisburd and Naus 2005: Table 41B.). Correspondingly, they report that the offenses for which defendants have been sentenced to death in recent years appear to have been quite aggravated.

have incorporated such death notices into their analyses of prosecutorial discretion. The South Carolina and North Carolina studies acquired those data for the period 1993–1997, the Maryland study covered the period August 1978 through September 1999, and the Missouri study covered 1997–2001. Replication of these data and analyses for comparable periods since the downturn, and further examination of the data for both points in time, would be invaluable for understanding the role of prosecutorial discretion in the downturn of death sentences. To enhance the national representativeness of the research it would be desirable to include additional states where such data are available. And to trace the influence of factors in addition to prosecutorial discretion on the downturn, it would be desirable to examine states where trial transcripts and juror interviews might also be available at both points in time.[12]

With information regarding which death-eligible cases were and were not initially selected for trial on capital charges, and which cases receiving such notice were and were not subsequently tried as capital cases, interviews with both prosecutors and defense attorneys focusing on those same cases could be especially informative. They could reveal what caused prosecutors to change their minds about seeking a death sentence. Did the availability of LWOP play a role? Did LWOP make it easier for prosecutors to accept a guilty plea or try the defendant on a lesser charge? Did the availability of this alternative sentence make it easier for them to convince the victim's family about the acceptability of the plea arrangement? And, what about the effect of LWOP's availability on defense attorneys and their clients? Did having LWOP as the alternative for a capital conviction make defendants more receptive and their defense attorneys more aggressive in negotiating on behalf of their clients for a plea to a non-capital murder charge? And what about costs? How important is heightened sensitivity to costs on the part of the prosecution? Are defense attorneys now in a stronger position to indicate that their motions and requests for funding will add substantially to the costs of a capital as opposed to a non-capital trial?[13] Interviews hold promise for answering these and a host of related questions about the dynamics of diverting cases from capital prosecution (Ehrhard 2008).

---

12. Missouri, North Carolina, and South Carolina were included in the initial phase of the Capital Jury Project; hence juror interviews conducted in these states in the early 1990s are available. The requisite prosecutorial data might be available in other of the original CJP states.

13. Reliable inferences concerning some of these questions might be drawn from county level statistical analyses that incorporate social, economic, and demographic data on locations where changes in prosecutors' charging practices are available.

The Downturn Research in Context

The first generation of research on America's post-*Furman* experiment with capital punishment has sought foremost to assess the nature and extent of arbitrariness and discrimination in death sentencing. We are now turning attention to the decision makers in the handling of capital cases—namely jurors, prosecutors, and defense attorneys—for an understanding of the factors in addition to racial bias that account for the imposition of death sentences. The first generation of studies were comparative, in demonstrating that the same patterns of racial disparities were replicated in state after state. We wish now to investigate differences in the handling of potentially capital cases over time. We advocate tracing changes over a decade or more in the administration of the death penalty, determining what accounts for such changes, and particularly, what accounts for the declining number of death sentences imposed over this period.

This proposed initiative to learn why the downturn has occurred should be conducted as a collaborative effort involving investigators familiar with research on the processing of capital cases and with an interest in studying the decision-making of jurors, defense attorneys and prosecutors. These investigators will need to work with data that will test the principal explanations advanced for the nationwide downturn in death sentences in sites strategically selected for what they can reveal about how decisions are made in the processing of capital cases. In the hands of a collaborative network of such investigators who jointly craft data collection plans and instruments, and who share and benefit from each other's work, this proposed initiative promises to be a uniquely revealing and rewarding research venture.

References

Axtman, Kris. 2001. "Why State Executions are Dropping." *Christian Science Monitor*, December 19, 2.

Baldus, David, George Woodworth, and Catherine Grosso. Forthcoming 2008. "Race and Proportionality Since *McCleskey v. Kemp (1987)*: Different Actors With Mixed Strategies of Denial and Avoidance." *Columbia Human Rights Law Review* 39.

Baldus, David, George Woodworth, and Charles A. Pulaski, Jr. 1990. *Equal Justice and the Death Penalty: A Legal and Empirical Analysis*. Boston, MA: Northeastern University Press.

Baldus, David C., George Woodworth, David Zuckerman, Neil Alan Weiner, and Barbara Broffitt. 2001. "The Use of Peremptory Challenges in Capital Murder Trials: A Legal and Empirical Analysis." *University of Pennsylvania Journal of Constitutional Law* 3:3–170.

_____. 1998. "Discrimination and the Death Penalty in the Post-Furman Era: An Empirical and Legal Overview, With Recent Findings From Philadelphia." *Cornell Law Review* 83:1638–1770.

Barnes, Katherine, David Sloss, and Stephen Thaman. 2007. Draft: "Life and Death Decisions Prosecutorial Discretion and Capital Punishment in Missouri." Unpublished manuscript.

Bee, Phillip R. 2006. "Fewer are Sent to Death; Experts Divided on Reasons Why Capital Sentences Have Declined Since 2000." *Sacramento Bee*, February 18, A01.

Bentele, Ursula and William J. Bowers. 2001. "How Jurors Decide on Death: Guilt is Overwhelming; Aggravation Requires Death; and Mitigation is No Excuse." *Brooklyn Law Review* 66:1011–1080.

Bowers, William J. 1995. "The Capital Jury Project: Rationale, Design, and Preview of Early Findings." *Indiana Law Journal* 70:1043–1102.

Bowers, William J., Thomas W. Brewer, and Charles S. Lanier. This Volume. "The Capital Jury Experiment of the U.S. Supreme Court."

Bowers, William J. and Foglia, Wanda D. 2003. "Still Singularly Agonizing: Law's Failure to Purge Arbitrariness from Capital Sentencing." *Criminal Law Bulletin* 39:51–86.

Bowers, William J., Marla Sandys, and Benjamin D. Steiner. 1998. "Foreclosed Impartiality in Capital Sentencing: Jurors' Predispositions, Guilt-Trial Experience, and Premature Decision Making." *Cornell Law Review* 83:1476–1556.

Bowers, William J. and Benjamin D. Steiner. 1999. "Death by Default: An Empirical Demonstration of False and Forced Choices in Capital Sentencing." *Texas Law Review* 77:605–717.

Bowers, William J., Benjamin D. Steiner, and Marla Sandys. 2001. "Death Sentencing in Black and White: An Empirical Analysis of the Role of Jurors' Race and Jury Racial Composition." *University of Pennsylvania Journal of Constitutional* Law 3:171–274.

Bowers, William J., Margaret Vandiver, and Patricia H. Dugan. 1994. "A New Look at Public Opinion on Capital Punishment: What Citizens and Legislators Prefer." *American Journal of Criminal Law* 22:77–150.

Bright, Stephen B. 1994. "Counsel for the Poor: The Death Sentence Not for the Worst Crime but the Worst Lawyer." *Yale Law Journal* 103:1835–1883.

Chalmers, Mike, 2006. "Jurors Less Likely to Vote for Execution: Exonerations Based on DNA Evidence Turned Tide Since 1990s." *The News Journal*, January 12, 1A.

Dieter, Richard C. 1993. "Sentencing for Life: Americans Embrace Alternatives to the Death Penalty." (http://www.deathpenaltyinfo.org/article.php?scid=45&did=481).

Ehrhard, Susan. Forthcoming 2008. "Plea Bargaining and the Death Penalty: An Exploratory Study." *Justice System Journal* 29.

Eisenberg, Theodore, Stephen P. Garvey and Martin T. Wells. 2001. "Forecasting Life and Death: Juror Race, Religion, and Attitude Toward the Death Penalty." *Journal of Legal Studies* 30:277–311.

Eisenberg, Theodore and Martin T. Wells. 1993. "Deadly Confusion: Juror Instructions in Capital Cases." *Cornell Law Review* 79:1–42.

Fagan, Jeffery, Franklin E. Zimring, and Amanda Geller. 2006. "Capital Punishment and Capital Murder: A Market Share Test of Deterrence." *Texas Law Review* 84:1803–1867.

Gregg v. Georgia (1976). 428 U.S. 153.

Henderson, Stephen. 2007. "Defense Often Inadequate in 4 Death-Penalty States." *McClatchy Newspapers,* January 16. (http://www.mcclatchydc.com/201/story/15394.html).

Joint Legislative Audit and Review Commission. 2001. Draft: "Review of Virginia's System of Capital Punishment." (http://jlarc.state.va.us/Meetings/December01/capital.pdf).

Jones, Jeffrey M. 2003. "Support for the Death Penalty Remains High at 74%." *The Gallup Poll Tuesday Briefing,* May, 28.

Jones, Jeffrey M. 2005. "Americans' Views of Death Penalty More Positive This Year." *The Gallup Poll Tuesday Briefing,* May, 104.

Knight, Al. 2005. "Whither the Death Penalty?" *The Denver Post,* April 27, B07.

Lane, Charles. 2004. "Less Support for Death Sentence Cited for Decline in Executions. *The Washington Post,* December 15, A08.

Lane, J. Mark. 1993. "Is There Life Without Parole? A Capital Defendant's Right to a Meaningful Alternative Sentence." *Loyola of Los Angeles Law Review* 26:327–393.

Liebman, James S., Jeffrey Fagan, and Valerie West. 2000. "Capital Attrition: Error Rates in Capital Cases, 1973–1995." *Texas Law Review* 78:1839–1865.

Liptak, Adam. 2003. "Number of Inmates on Death Row Declines as Challenges to Justice System Rise." *The New York Times,* January 11, A11.

Liptak, Adam. 2004. "Fewer Death Sentences Being Imposed in U.S." *The New York Times,* September 15, A16.

Masters, Brooke A. 2001. "Executions Decrease for the 2nd Year; Va., Texas Show Sharp Drops Amid a National Trend." *The Washington Post,* September 6, A01.

McCleskey v. Kemp (1987). 481 U.S. 279.

McMenamin, Jennifer. 2006. "Balto. Co. Capital Sentences on Decline; Set of Factors Cited for Drop Mirroring Nationwide Trend." *The Baltimore Sun,* April 24, 1A.

Morgan v. Illinois (1992). 504 U.S. 719.

Nakell, Barry and Kenneth Hardy. 1987. *The Arbitrariness of the Death Penalty.* Temple University Press.

North Carolina Coalition for a Moratorium. [N.d.] "Poor Lawyering and the Death Penalty." (http://www.ncmoratorium.org/documents/issue_poorlawyer.pdf).

Pastore, Ann L. and Kathleen Maguire, eds. 2006. *Bureau of Justice Statistics, U.S. Department of Justice, Sourcebook of Criminal Justice Statistics.* (http://www.albany.edu/sourcebook/).

Paternoster, Raymond, Robert Brame, Sarah Bacon, Andrew Ditchfield, David Biere, Karen Beckman, Deanna Perez, Michael Strauch, Nadine Frederique, Kristin Gawkoski, Daniel Zeigler, and Katheryn Murphy. 2004. "Empirical Analysis of Maryland's Death Sentencing System with Respect to the Influence of Race and Legal Jurisdiction." (http://www.newsdesk.umd.edu/pdf/finalrep.pdf).

Pierce, Glenn L. and Michael L. Radelet. 2002. "Race, Region, and Death Sentencing in Illinois, 1988–1997." *Oregon Law Review* 81:39–69.

Rompilla v. Beard (2005). 545 U.S. 374.

Smith, Jeffrey R. 2004. "Death Sentences Hit 30-Year Low in U.S.; Activists See Shift in Juries' Attitudes." *The Washington Post,* November 15, A02.

Snell, Tracy. L. 2006. "Capital Punishment, 2005." *Bureau of Justice Statistics Bulletin.* (http://www.ojp.usdoj.gov/bjs/pub/pdf/cp05.pdf).

Songer, Michael and Isaac Unah. 2006. "The Effect of Race, Gender, and Location on Prosecutorial Decisions to Seek the Death Penalty in South Carolina." *South Carolina Law Review* 58:161–182.

Steiker, Carol S. 2002. "Capital Punishment and American Exceptionalism." *Oregon Law Review* 81:97–130.

Steiner, Benjamin D., William J. Bowers, and Austin Sarat. 1999. "Folk Knowledge as Legal Action: Death Penalty Judgments and the Tenet of Early Release in a Culture of Mistrust and Punitiveness." *Law & Society Review* 33:461–505.

Sundby, Scott E. 2006. "The Death Penalty's Future: Charting the Crosscurrents of Declining Death Sentences and the McVeigh Factor." *Texas Law Review* 84:1929–1972.

_____. 2005. *A Life and Death Decision: A Jury Weighs the Death Penalty.* New York, NY: Palgrave Macmillan.

_____. 1998. "The Capital Jury and Absolution: The Intersection of Trial Strategy, Remorse, and the Death Penalty." *Cornell Law Review* 83:1557–1598.

_____. 1997. "The Jury as Critic: An Empirical Look at How Capital Juries Perceive Expert and Lay Testimony." *Virginia Law Review* 83:1109–1188.

Unah, Isaac. 2003. "Electoral Proximity and Prosecutorial Decision to Seek the Death Penalty." Presented at the Annual Meeting of the American Political Science Association, Philadelphia, PA. August 31.

Wainwright v. Witt (1985). 469 U.S. 412.

Weisburd, David and Joseph Naus. 2005. "Report to Special Master David Baime: Applying the Race Monitoring System to Proportionality Review Data." (http://www.judiciary.state.nj.us/pressrel/2005_Weisburd_Naus_Report.pdf).

Wiggins v. Smith (2003). 539 U.S. 510.

Williams v. Taylor (2000). 529 U.S. 362.

CHAPTER 5

THE ABA DEATH PENALTY MORATORIUM IMPLEMENTATION PROJECT: SETTING THE STAGE FOR FURTHER RESEARCH

Deborah Fleischaker

For the past thirty years, the American Bar Association (ABA) has become increasingly concerned that there is a crisis in our country's death penalty system and that capital jurisdictions too often provide neither fairness nor accuracy. In response to this concern, on February 3, 1997, the ABA called for a nationwide moratorium on executions until serious flaws in the system are identified and eliminated. The ABA urges capital jurisdictions to (1) ensure that death penalty cases are administered fairly and impartially, in accordance with due process, and (2) minimize the risk that innocent persons may be executed.

To assist the majority of capital jurisdictions that have not yet conducted comprehensive examinations of their death penalty systems, the ABA Death Penalty Moratorium Implementation Project (the Project) decided in February 2003 to examine a number of state death penalty systems and preliminarily determine the extent to which they achieve fairness and provide due process. The Project thus far has released state assessments in Arizona, Alabama, Florida, Georgia, Indiana, Ohio, Pennsylvania and Tennessee. The assessments are not designed to replace the comprehensive state-funded studies necessary in capital jurisdictions, but instead are intended to highlight individual state systems' successes and inadequacies.

The assessments were designed to provide information about how state death penalty systems are intended to function and, to the extent the ABA could determine, how those systems are functioning in practice. Because capital punishment is the law in each of the assessment states and because the ABA has no position on the death penalty *per se*, the ABA focused exclusively on capital punishment laws and processes and did not consider whether states, as a matter of morality, philosophy, or penological theory, should have the death penalty.

Methodology

The first step in each of the states was recruiting a state-based assessment team that would be responsible for overseeing its state assessment. Each team was chaired by a law school professor and included or had access to current or former defense attorneys, current or former prosecutors, individuals active in the state bar association, current or former judges, state legislators, and anyone else whom the Project and/or team leaders felt should be included to complete the assessment in a timely, comprehensive manner. Team members were recruited without regard for their position on the death penalty or their position on a moratorium on executions and were asked only to approach the issue with an open mind. Once recruited, Assessment Team members provided guidance during the research process and served as reviewers as the report was being drafted. Each team leader hired law students to collect the data, review the case law, and conduct the necessary interviews.

At the same time that state teams were being recruited, the Project also drafted a data collection instrument, called an Assessment Guide. In the Assessment Guide, the Project broke each of the protocols and/or recommended policies into their most basic research components. All of the assessments use as a benchmark the protocols set forth in the ABA Section of Individual Rights and Responsibilities' 2001 publication, *Death Without Justice: A Guide for Examining the Administration of the Death Penalty in the United States* (the Protocols). While the Protocols were not intended to cover all aspects of the death penalty, they do encompass seven key aspects of death penalty administration: defense services, procedural restrictions and limitations on state post-conviction and federal habeas corpus proceedings, clemency proceedings, jury instructions, an independent judiciary, racial and ethnic minorities, and mental retardation and mental illness. Additionally, the Project added five new areas to the Assessment Guide to be reviewed as part of the assessments: preservation and testing of DNA evidence, identification and interrogation procedures, crime laboratories and medical examiners, prosecutors, and the direct appeal process.

The Assessment Guide was organized into chapters, one for each of the twelve substantive areas mentioned above, and a thirteenth for basic demographic information. Each of the chapters began with an introduction, which explained the relevant substantive issues and identified potential problems concerning the administration of the death penalty. Each chapter also contained a list of documents, including laws, rules, procedures, standards, guidelines, and leading case law, which the Project recommended that the state team gather, review, and explain, and a list of questions pertaining to these documents that, to the extent possible, should be answered by the team.

Given the detail of the Assessment Guide, the Project encouraged each local team to use it as a guide, and not as a checklist of required tasks. Thus, the state team was not compelled to collect every recommended document or answer every question contained in the Assessment Guide, as the Project believed that a thorough yet preliminary study of the death penalty system could be completed without collecting all of the recommended documents and/or answering all of the questions. The Assessment Guide attempted to reduce each issue into its most basic parts. For example, in determining whether the state preserves evidence in death penalty cases, including DNA evidence, the Assessment Guide posited the following:

a. Is your state required to preserve evidence in death penalty cases?
   i. If yes, what type of evidence is it required to preserve?
      - Is the state required to preserve DNA?
        o If yes, is the state required to preserve all DNA or only DNA that was not previously tested?
        o If yes, how long is the state required to preserve DNA? Is the state required to preserve the DNA after the defendant's trial where s/he was convicted?
      - What other types of evidence is your state required to preserve?
        o How long is the state required to preserve this evidence?
   ii. If no, does anyone possess the ability to request and/or the discretion to decide that certain evidence be preserved?
      - If yes, who has the right to request that evidence be preserved?
      - If yes, who has the discretion to decide whether certain evidence should be preserved? Are there any limitations to this discretion?
b. Where is the evidence preserved?
   i. Who possesses the discretion to determine where the evidence is preserved?
c. What information exists regarding what evidence actually is preserved?

Once the data had been collected, they were sent to the Project. The attorneys at the Project then used the research to draft chapters of the report. Each chapter was revised by the team leader and sent to the entire team for review. Once all of the chapters had been drafted, circulated, and revised, the team met in person to make final revisions and decide upon any additional recommendations that would be included in the final report, including whether the state team would recommend a moratorium on executions.

Over the course of conducting these assessments, the ABA learned an enormous amount about how state death penalty systems work, and often, how they do not work. At the same time, however, the ABA was unable to address a large number of issues that it had hoped to analyze because of a lack of data. This chapter will identify the key findings of the assessments, along with those areas where a lack of data limited the ABA's ability to analyze state death penalty systems, and additional areas where the ABA could assess compliance or noncompliance but other related questions remained.

Key Findings: The Death Penalty's Fatal Flaws

While the data necessary to conduct analysis were often not collected, maintained, or made available in a way that made analysis possible, general themes emerged in each of the research areas. Ultimately, serious problems were found in every state death penalty system, which call the fairness and accuracy of state death penalty systems into question. The key findings from the eight state assessments include:

Law Enforcement and Crime Lab Issues
- States generally fail to require the preservation of physical and/or biological evidence through the entire legal process and until after release from prison or execution, thereby increasing the possibility that crucial evidence that could prove innocence will be destroyed.
- States are not requiring law enforcement agencies to adopt procedures that comport with identified national best practices on identifications and interrogations.
- States do not require that crime laboratories and medical examiner offices be accredited.

Lawyering Issues
- States have not established, nor are they requiring prosecutors' offices to establish, policies on the exercise of prosecutorial discretion, or on evaluating cases that rely on eyewitness identification, confessions, or the testimony of jailhouse snitches, informants, and other witnesses who receive a benefit.

- Many states fail to require that prosecutors who handle capital cases receive any specialized training.
- Many states fail to provide a statewide indigent capital defense system, providing services instead on a county-by-county basis.
- Many states fail to provide for the appointment of two lawyers at all stages of a capital case, nor are they guaranteeing access to investigators and mitigation specialists.
- Many states require only minimal training and experience for attorneys handling death penalty cases.

Appellate Issues
- Some states are not required to conduct a proportionality review and, in those that are, the review tends to be cursory and include only cases where death was imposed, leaving out potentially important cases where death was sought but not imposed and where death could have been, but was not sought.
- Few, if any, states maintain the sort of capital case database that would include case information on actual and potential capital cases to make meaningful proportionality review easier to achieve.
- DNA testing statutes often are drafted too narrowly, with strict filing deadlines and onerous procedural hurdles, making it difficult for a wrongfully convicted person to successfully file for and obtain DNA testing.
- Many states make it difficult to obtain an evidentiary hearing and afford the post-conviction judge many opportunities to summarily deny a post-conviction petition.
- Some states make it difficult to raise claims of error, including wrongful conviction errors, in post-conviction proceedings.
- Most states fail to require any specific type or breadth of review in considering clemency petitions.

Jury Issues
- Jurors in many states appear to have difficulty understanding their roles and responsibilities as described by the judge in his/her jury instructions.
- Many states fail to provide, as a matter of course, written jury instructions.

Racial Disparity Issues
- Every state studied appears to have significant racial disparities in its capital system, particularly those associated with the race of the victim.
- Even in states with acknowledged racial disparities, little, if anything, has been done to rectify the problem.

- Generally, states are not keeping the data necessary to conduct the sort of analysis necessary to quantify any problem with bias and identify its causes, making the process of conducting analysis difficult, if not impossible.

Information Exists, and Conclusions Were Drawn, but Additional Questions Remain

While there were many areas in which the ABA was able to assess compliance or non-compliance, the analysis often raises as many questions as it answers. Most notably, while the ABA was able to identify many of the problems that exist in state death penalty systems, it was not able to determine why some of the problems existed (for example, racial disparity in capital sentencing), nor was it able to assess the effectiveness of the potential responses to the problems. These additional questions are substantive areas ripe for further research.

Proportionality

Comparative proportionality review—the process through which a sentence of death is compared with sentences imposed on similarly situated defendants to ensure that the sentence is not disproportionate—is the best method available to identify and quantify any arbitrariness in capital sentencing. Meaningful comparative proportionality review helps to (1) ensure that the death penalty is being administered in a rational, non-arbitrary manner, (2) provide a check on broad prosecutorial discretion, and (3) prevent discrimination from playing a role in the capital decision-making process.

In most capital cases, juries determine the sentence, yet they neither are equipped nor do they have the information necessary to evaluate the propriety of that sentence in light of sentences in similar cases. In the relatively small number of cases in which the trial judge determines the sentence, meaningful proportionality review still is important, as the judge may be unaware of statewide sentencing practices or be affected by public or political pressure. Regardless of who determines the sentence, dissimilar results are virtually ensured without the equalizing force of meaningful proportionality review.

Simply stating that a particular death sentence is proportional is not enough, however. Proportionality review should not only cite previous decisions, but should analyze their similarities and differences and the appropriateness of the death sentence. In addition, proportionality review should include cases in which a death sentence was imposed, cases in which the death penalty was sought but not imposed, and cases in which the death penalty could have been sought but was not.

Because of the role that meaningful comparative proportionality review can play in identifying and eliminating arbitrary and excessive death sentences, states that do not engage in the review, or that do so only superficially, substantially increase the risk that their capital punishment systems will function in an arbitrary and discriminatory manner. And while the U.S. Supreme Court does not require comparative proportionality review, proportionality—or the appearance of proportionality—still is required because the Eighth Amendment forbids arbitrary capital sentencing practices.

The results of the ABA assessments on the issue of proportionality are not encouraging. In state after state, comparative proportionality review is being conducted in a cursory and incomplete manner, if at all. For example, while the Indiana Supreme Court often conducts a thoughtful and searching review to ensure that similar, non-capital defendants who commit similar crimes are receiving similar sentences, it does not appear to do so in death penalty cases.

In Tennessee, while the State Supreme Court and the Court of Criminal Appeals are required to determine whether a death sentence "is excessive or disproportionate to the penalty imposed in similar cases, considering both the nature of the crime and the defendant," the Tennessee Supreme Court has limited the courts' duty to ensuring that "no aberrant death sentence is affirmed" (*State v. Godsey* 2001:781–84). Accordingly, a death sentence will be found disproportionate only "if the case, taken as a whole, is plainly lacking in circumstances consistent with those in similar cases in which the death penalty has been imposed" (*State v. Holton* 2002:27). So far, under this standard, the court has only found one death sentence to be disproportionate.

Most egregiously, Arizona no longer requires *any* sort of proportionality review. Prior to 1992, the Arizona Supreme Court would determine whether a death sentence was "excessive or disproportionate to the penalty imposed in similar cases, considering both the crime and the defendant" (*State v. Richmond* 1977:51). In 1992, however, the Arizona Supreme Court held that proportionality review was not mandated by statute or by the United States or Arizona Constitutions (*State v. Salazar* 1992:583–84). Since then, the Court has rejected any argument that the absence of proportionality review denies capital defendants equal protection and due process of law, or that it is tantamount to cruel and unusual punishment.

Yet while the evidence exists to clearly identify the absence of proportionality—and hence arbitrariness—as a problem, the research that would quantify the extent of the problem has not been done. There are two reasons for this. First, states generally are not collecting data on all death-eligible cases, including cases in which death could have been sought but was not. This makes any proportionality analysis that is conducted incomplete, at best. Second, even in states where some case data are collected, the states generally are not keeping the information in an organized manner. To conduct its limited analysis of proportionality, the ABA had to rely on incomplete trial judge reports and appellate decisions. Limiting analysis to the information contained in these two tools ensures that the review is only partially complete. Systemic-level, thorough review remains absent. The creation of a true case database that includes all death-eligible cases, along with research that looks at the murder cases in a particular jurisdiction to determine whether like crimes and like defendants are being punished similarly, is essential.

Defense Lawyering

Defense counsel competency is perhaps the most critical factor determining whether a capital offender/defendant will receive the death penalty. Although anecdotes about inadequate defense counsel have long been part of death penalty lore, and a comprehensive study by James Liebman and colleagues (Liebman, Fagan, and West 2000) shows definitively that poor representation has been a major cause of serious errors in capital cases as well as a major factor in the wrongful conviction and sentencing to death of innocent defendants, much research remains to be done.

While the assessments reaffirmed that the system of providing defense counsel to capital defendants and death row inmates is problematic, significant research still must be carried out to quantify the scope of the problem. For example, research into whether, to what extent, and why different state systems are broken, and how to fix systems that are broken, would be useful in forging new solutions to the long-identified problem surrounding indigent defense.

Additional research that delves more deeply into claims of ineffective assistance of counsel would be useful. We know that ineffective assistance is a problem, yet in most states, we do not have a sense of how often ineffective assistance of counsel claims are made, the factual basis for those claims, or the frequency with which those claims are succeeding. It also would be useful to know how frequently courts are finding that defense attorneys were deficient, but fail to grant relief due to the doctrine of harmless error.

For example, the Texas Defender Service (TDS) issued a report examining the quality of defense lawyers in state post-conviction proceedings (2002). The TDS reviewed 251 of the 263 state habeas petitions submitted between 1995 and

2001, quantifying the types of claims made and the quality of the petitions. The report concluded that many death row inmates are moved through the state post-conviction process with inadequate defense counsel and "an indifferent Court of Criminal Appeals" (2002: ix). This sort of research can have a significant impact on the death penalty policy debate, yet similar studies have not been conducted in other states.

Racial Disparity

Over the past twenty-five years, numerous studies evaluating decisions to seek and to impose the death penalty have found that race is all too often a major explanatory factor. Most of the studies have found that, holding other factors constant, the death penalty is sought and imposed significantly more often when the murder victim is white than when the victim is African-American.

The studies conducted as a part of four of the state death penalty assessments reached the same conclusions. In Georgia, the data demonstrated that among all homicides with known suspects, those suspected of killing whites are 4.56 times as likely to be sentenced to death as those who are suspected of killing blacks. In Indiana, the odds of a death sentence among homicides with a similar level of aggravation were 16 times higher for cases where whites were suspected of killing whites than for cases in which blacks were suspected of killing blacks. Ohio had similar race-of-victim disparities, with those who kill whites being 3.8 times more likely to receive a death sentence than those who kill blacks.

While the ABA was successful in conducting racial disparity studies in four states, it was not able to conduct them in all of the assessment states, in part because of the difficulty in obtaining the data. For example, while the ABA attempted to collect the data necessary to conduct a racial disparity study in Pennsylvania, we were unable to do so; even when we were able to collect data, we often received conflicting information about the same case. Even in the states where the ABA did collect the necessary data, the information was not as simple to collect as it should have been. For example, in Tennessee, while trial judge reports are required in all first-degree murder cases, and these reports would provide the data necessary to conduct a disparity study, three in five trial judge reports on first-degree murder convictions were missing, one in five reports on death sentences were missing, and "hundreds of cases included in the database have holes and are missing important details about the crime, defendant and victim" (Shiffman 2001).

More work remains to be done on the issue of racial disparity. The studies conducted as a part of the ABA assessments were rudimentary. More complex studies, which include significantly more data points, would be useful to identify the exact nature of the racial disparity and where in the legal process it surfaces. This data could then be used to develop strategies to eliminate or minimize the impact of race on capital sentencing.

Mental Illness

In the wake of the U.S. Supreme Court exempting mentally retarded and juvenile offenders from the death penalty (*Atkins v. Virginia* 2002; *Roper v. Simmons* 2005), the execution of mentally ill defendants has emerged as one of the next important subjects of death penalty discussion and advocacy. Groups like the American Bar Association (2006), the American Psychological Association (2006a; 2006b), and the American Psychiatric Association (2006a; 2006b; 2006c) have all have come out against the execution of people suffering from serious mental illness at the time of the crime or at the time of the scheduled execution.

As soon as the ABA passed its policy opposing the execution of people with serious mental illness, the Project began to include an analysis of mental illness issues in its state death penalty assessments. It confirmed what many already believed—that states generally are not providing the necessary protections to people with serious mental illness, including such protections as providing training to all actors in the criminal justice system to recognize mental illness in capital defendants and death row inmates, taking steps to ensure that the *Miranda* rights of mentally ill people are protected, giving jury instructions that clearly communicate that a mental disorder or disability is a mitigating factor rather than an aggravating factor, and allowing "next friends" to act on a death-row inmate's behalf in initiating or pursuing remedies. Yet despite the ABA's recognition that many states do not provide the necessary safeguards for defendants and inmates with serious mental illness, more data on the scope of the problem are needed. No one currently knows how many people on death row have serious mental illness. Furthermore, it is unclear how states are dealing with these issues on a case-by-case basis.

Given that policy proposals to exempt people with serious mental illness from the death penalty are already appearing, advocates must be equipped to answer basic questions about the scope of and remedies for the problem.

A Lack of Data: Is Anyone Minding the Store?

Central to assessing a state's death penalty system is the ability to collect data about that system. Yet, in state after state, the ABA could not reach conclusions about whether a state complied with many of its recommendations because no one collects and maintains much of the necessary data. Despite the fact that lives are in jeopardy and that the adequacy of state judicial systems are at stake, states routinely fail to keep comprehensive and searchable records of their death penalty systems and cases in one central location.

Because the ABA worked with a state-based assessment team in every assessment state, each of which used its own discretion in determining whether a state met or failed to meet ABA recommendations, it is not possible to conclude which state has the "best" death penalty system and which has the "worst." However, patterns emerged when teams in a majority of the states reached similar conclusions. These comparisons allow the ABA to identify problems that exist across states. Furthermore, this sort of pattern analysis reveals the areas in which the ABA could not assess state compliance because of insufficient data. In fact, of the 93 standard recommendations contained in every state assessment report, at least one-third could not be assessed in at least half of the states[1] due to the lack of data. Some types of data proved particularly difficult to collect, including:

Basic Statistics/Information

As part of each state death penalty assessment, the ABA intended to include a detailed section on demographics that would discuss crime data and details about the death row population. To accomplish this, the ABA requested state assessment teams to collect the following information:

- Number of and demographic information about capital homicides in each jurisdiction/county per year.
- Number of and demographic information about capital homicides with a known suspect, regardless of whether the individual has been charged or convicted in each jurisdiction/county per year.
- Number of and demographic information about capital homicides with a known victim in each jurisdiction/county per year.
- Number of and demographic information about arrests for capital homicides in each jurisdiction/county per year.

---

1. Because the mental illness recommendations were not adopted by the ABA until the Alabama, Arizona, and Georgia assessment reports already had been released, a majority of states is considered to be two out of three for the mental illness recommendations. For all other recommendations, at least three out of the six states had insufficient information to allow a conclusion to be reached about compliance or noncompliance.

- Number of and demographic information about individuals who were charged with capital homicides in each jurisdiction/county per year.
- Number of and demographic information about individuals against whom the prosecutor filed a notice of intent to seek the death penalty in each jurisdiction/county per year.
- Number of and demographic information about individuals against whom the prosecutor filed, but did not withdraw, a notice of intent to seek the death penalty against in each jurisdiction/county per year.
- Number of and demographic information about life sentences (including life without the possibility of parole) imposed by each jurisdiction/county per year;
- Number of and demographic information about death sentences imposed by each jurisdiction/county per year.
- Number of and demographic information about cases in which the judge overrode the jury's recommendation of life imprisonment (including life without the possibility of parole) or death by each jurisdiction/county per year.
- Number of and demographic information about death row inmates by jurisdiction/county per year.
- Number of and demographic information about individuals who: (a) had been convicted and sentenced to death, and subsequently had their conviction overturned and were acquitted at a re-trial, or against whom all charges were dropped; or (b) were given an absolute pardon by the governor based on new evidence of innocence; or (c) were released upon reaching a compromise with the prosecution by pleading to a lesser offense; or (d) were released when a parole board became convinced of their innocence; or (e) were acquitted at a retrial of the capital charge but convicted of lesser related charges, by jurisdiction/county per year.
- Number of and demographic information about individuals who died while on death row by jurisdiction/county per year.
- Number of and demographic information about individuals who were executed by jurisdiction/county per year.
- All cases in which identifiable doubt exists about the defendant's guilt.

While the teams were able to collect some of the most basic information, including the number of death sentences, number of executions, and number of exonerations, the majority of this information simply was not available. In particular, the data prior to sentencing, including the number of and demographic information about capital homicides, number of arrests, number of capital charges, and number of defendants against whom the death penalty was sought, almost universally were not found. These deficiencies in data result in the unfortunate conclusion that even the most basic information about the application of the death penalty is unavailable for review.

Prosecutors

Each prosecutor has responsibility for deciding whether to bring charges and, if so, what charges to bring against the accused. S/he must also decide whether to prosecute or dismiss charges or to take other appropriate actions in the interest of justice. Moreover, in cases in which capital punishment can be sought, prosecutors have enormous discretion in deciding whether or not to seek the death penalty. The character, quality, and efficiency of the whole death penalty system are shaped in great measure by the manner in which the prosecutor exercises his or her broad discretionary powers. And although the prosecutor operates within the adversary system, the prosecutor's obligation is to protect the innocent as well as to convict the guilty, and to guard the rights of the accused as well as to enforce the rights of the public.

While the great majority of prosecutors are ethical, law-abiding individuals who seek justice, the existence of prosecutorial misconduct and its impact on innocent lives and society at large cannot be ignored. Prosecutorial misconduct can encompass a variety of actions, including but not limited to: failing to disclose exculpatory evidence; abusing discretion in seeking the death penalty; allowing racial discrimination to affect the selection of jurors; covering-up and/or endorsing perjury by informants and jailhouse snitches; and making inappropriate comments during closing arguments.

Because of the broad discretion vested in prosecutors and their pivotal role in capital cases, the issues of prosecutorial discretion and prosecutorial misconduct are vitally important to understanding the death penalty. While the ABA worked to obtain prosecutorial participation in its state death penalty assessments and was successful in recruiting prosecutors to serve on several of its state death penalty assessment teams, it had a great deal of trouble securing prosecutorial participation, both as official team members and in providing information about their work. Ultimately, because of the lack of prosecutorial participation, a majority of the assessment reports were unable to assess compliance with a majority of recommendations relating to prosecutors, including the following:

- Each prosecutor's office should have written policies governing the exercise of prosecutorial discretion to ensure the fair, efficient, and effective enforcement of criminal law.

- Each prosecutor's office should establish procedures and policies for evaluating cases that rely on eyewitness identification, confessions, or the testimony of jailhouse snitches, informants, and other witnesses who receive a benefit.
- Prosecutors should ensure that law enforcement agencies, laboratories, and other experts under their direction or control are aware of and comply with their obligation to inform prosecutors about potentially exculpatory or mitigating evidence.

We cannot hope to fully understand how the death penalty is working without a clearer picture of the prosecutor's role. Unfortunately, the ABA was not successful in this endeavor and much work remains to be done. Some of the future work in this area could include research into: (1) why prosecutors tend to be unwilling to participate in research about capital punishment; (2) whether and in what circumstances prosecutors' offices and bar associations sanction prosecutors for misconduct; and (3) how often official claims of prosecutorial misconduct arise in capital cases, how often courts find that such misconduct actually occurred, and the judicial response offered when misconduct is found.

Clemency

Under a state's constitution and/or clemency statute, the governor or entity established to handle clemency matters is empowered to pardon an individual's criminal offense or commute an individual's death sentence. In death penalty cases, the clemency process traditionally was intended to function as a final safeguard to evaluate: (1) the fairness and judiciousness of the penalty in the context of the circumstances of the crime and the individual; and (2) whether the individual should be put to death. This process can only fulfill this critical function when the exercise of the clemency power is governed by fundamental principles of justice, fairness, and mercy, and not dominated by political considerations.

The clemency process should provide a safeguard for claims that have not been considered on the merits, including claims of innocence and claims of constitutional deficiencies. Clemency also can be a way to review important sentencing issues that were barred in state and federal courts. Because clemency is the final avenue of review available to a death-row inmate, the state's use of its clemency power is an important measure of the fairness of the state's justice system as a whole.

Clemency has been granted in a significantly lower proportion of death penalty cases recently than before 1972, when the U.S. Supreme Court temporarily barred the death penalty as unconstitutional (*Furman v. Georgia* 1972). Between 1976, when the Court authorized states to reinstate capital punishment, and April 2006, clemency was granted on humanitarian grounds only 229 times, in 19 of the 38 death penalty states and by the federal government (Death Penalty Information Center 2007). One hundred sixty-seven of these cases involved action taken in 2003 by the former governor of Illinois, George Ryan, out of concern that the justice system in Illinois could not ensure that an innocent person would not be executed.

Due to restrictions on the judicial review of meritorious claims, the need for a meaningful clemency power is more important than ever. As a result of these restrictions, clemency can be a state's only opportunity to prevent miscarriages of justice, even in cases involving actual innocence. The clemency decision-maker may be the only person or body that has the opportunity to evaluate all of the factors bearing on the appropriateness of the death sentence without regard to constraints that may limit a court or jury's decision-making. Yet as the capital punishment process currently functions, meaningful review frequently is not obtained and clemency too often has failed to be the critical final check against injustice in the criminal justice system.

While the clemency process is an important safeguard, it generally is shrouded in secrecy. Standards frequently are lacking and, owing in part to the secrecy of the process, it may be difficult to determine how clemency decisions are made. While this opaqueness may be purposeful, it increases the risk of arbitrariness in the capital system.

Because of the difficulty in obtaining information about the clemency process, a majority of the assessment reports were unable to assess compliance with a majority of the recommendations, including:

- The clemency decision-making process should not assume that the courts have reached the merits on all issues bearing on the death sentence in a given case; decisions should be based upon an independent consideration of facts and circumstances.
- The clemency decision-making process should take into account all factors that might lead the decision-maker to conclude that death is not the appropriate punishment.
- Clemency decision-makers should consider any pattern of racial or geographic disparity in carrying out the death penalty in the jurisdiction, including the exclusion of racial minorities from the jury panels that convicted and sentenced the death row inmate.
- Clemency decision-makers should consider the inmate's mental retardation, mental illness, or mental competency, if applicable, the inmate's

age at the time of the offense, and any evidence of lingering doubt about the inmate's guilt.
- Clemency decision-makers should consider an inmate's possible rehabilitation or performance of positive acts while on death row.
- To the maximum extent possible, clemency determinations should be insulated from political considerations or impacts.

A fuller picture of the clemency process would have several benefits. Given the significant decrease in granted clemency applications in recent years, information about what decision-makers consider in weighing a clemency application would allow future clemency applications to focus on matters considered relevant to the clemency authority's decision. In addition, further information about how clemency decisions are made would enable researchers to identify: (1) whether the clemency process appears to be producing arbitrary outcomes, and if it is, how that arbitrariness is being manifested; (2) whether political concerns are trumping concerns over fairness and justice and to begin to identify practical solutions if this turns out to be the case; and (3) where in the legal process concerns might arise that the process is failing to provide justice or due process so those areas can be examined and potentially changed.

Law Enforcement

Eyewitness misidentification and false confessions are two of the leading causes of wrongful convictions. Between 1989 and 2003, approximately 205 previously convicted "murderers" were exonerated nationwide (Gross, Jacoby, and Matheson 2005). In about 50% of these cases, there was at least one eyewitness misidentification, and 20% involved false confessions. Given that greater accuracy in law enforcement investigations would both exonerate the innocent and help inculpate the guilty, these sorts of reforms can and should be viewed as pro-law enforcement.

While information on law enforcement policies, including those on eyewitness identification and custodial interrogations, is sometimes available, it can be difficult and time consuming to obtain. Individual states have many—sometimes hundreds—of law enforcement agencies. If no statewide laws or rules exist governing the way these agencies conduct their work, and if no one entity serves as a clearinghouse for this sort of information, it becomes difficult to assess how these agencies are working on a statewide level. Because these laws and rules tend not to exist, and because many of the law enforcement agencies the state teams approached ignored the requests for information or refused the requests, the ABA was not able to collect the majority of the needed information on a statewide basis. Consequently, many of the assessment reports left compliance with a majority of the law enforcement recommendations unevaluated, including:

- Law enforcement agencies should adopt guidelines for conducting lineups and photospreads in a manner that maximizes their likely accuracy. Every set of guidelines should address at least the subjects, and should incorporate at least the social scientific teachings and best practices, set forth in the *ABA's Best Practices for Promoting the Accuracy of Eyewitness Identification Procedures* (2004).
- Law enforcement officers and prosecutors should receive periodic training on how to implement the guidelines for conducting lineups and photospreads, and training on non-suggestive techniques for interviewing witnesses.
- Law enforcement agencies and prosecutors' offices should periodically update the guidelines for conducting lineups and photospreads to incorporate advances in social scientific research and in the continuing lessons of practical experience.
- Ensure adequate funding to ensure proper development, implementation, and updating of policies and procedures relating to identifications and interrogations.

Effective law enforcement procedures are essential to protecting the innocent and convicting the guilty. Unfortunately, as matters currently stand, we do not have a good sense of how many law enforcement agencies utilize them.

Judicial Independence

The American criminal justice system relies on the independence of the judicial branch to ensure that judges decide cases to the best of their abilities without political or other bias and notwithstanding official and public pressure. However, judicial independence increasingly is threatened by judicial elections, appointments, and confirmation proceedings that are affected by nominees' or candidates' purported views on the death penalty or by judges' decisions in capital cases.

During judicial election campaigns, voters often expect candidates to assure them that they will be "tough on crime," that they will impose the death penalty whenever possible, and that, if they are or aspire to be appellate judges, they will uphold death sentences. In retention campaigns, judges are asked to defend decisions in capital cases and sometimes are defeated because of unpopular decisions, even when the decisions are reasonable, involve binding applications of the law, or reflect the prevailing interpretation of the Constitution. Prospective and actual nominees for judicial appointments often are subjected to scrutiny on these same bases. Generally, when such scrutiny occurs, the discourse is *not* about the constitutional doctrine in the case, but rather about the specifics of the crime.

Despite the importance of judicial independence, however, a majority of the assessment reports were unable to evaluate compliance with the vast majority of the ABA recommendations. The unevaluated recommendations include:

- A judge who has made any promise regarding his/her prospective decisions in capital cases that amounts to prejudgment should not preside over any capital case or review any death penalty decision in the jurisdiction.
- Bar associations and community leaders should speak out in defense of judges who are criticized for decisions in capital cases; bar associations should educate the public concerning the roles and responsibilities of judges and lawyers in capital cases; bar associations and community leaders should publicly oppose any questioning of candidates for judicial appointment or re-appointment concerning their decisions in capital cases; and purported views on the death penalty or on habeas corpus should not be litmus tests or important factors in the selection of judges.
- A judge who observes ineffective lawyering by defense counsel should inquire into counsel's performance and, where appropriate, take effective actions to ensure that the defendant receives a proper defense.
- A judge who determines that prosecutorial misconduct or other unfair activity has occurred during a capital case should take immediate action to address the situation and to ensure the capital proceeding is fair.
- Judges should do all within their power to ensure that defendants are provided with full discovery in capital cases.

A lack of judicial independence increases the possibility that judges will decide cases not on the basis of their best understanding of the law, but rather on the basis of how their decisions might affect their careers, and makes it less likely that judges will be vigilant against prosecutorial misconduct and incompetent representation by defense counsel. Given the stakes associated with ensuring judicial independence, the fact that we do not have the data necessary to assess the quality of judicial independence is troublesome. Consequently, further research would be beneficial and could include research into the use of pro-death penalty and "tough on crime" language in judicial elections and confirmation proceedings, combined with an analysis of future decisions by those judges in death penalty cases, the timing of those decisions as they relate to retention elections, and whether those findings of guilt or the imposition of death sentences are later overturned and, if so, for what reason.

Conclusion

Through its state death penalty assessments, the ABA has been able to document some of the overarching problems plaguing the administration of the death penalty. Yet in too many cases, the ABA was unable to conduct its analysis due to a lack of data. In still other cases, the ABA was able to conduct its analysis, but more research would strengthen its evaluations.

The need for continuing social science research remains as strong as ever. Whether the goal is fairness and accuracy in capital systems or evaluation of related policies, the research identified throughout this discussion is urgently needed. Change will occur only when state-specific data are supplied to advocates and politicians that fully demonstrate the scope and range of problems that exist. While the ABA state death penalty assessments have begun this process, much remains to be done.

References

American Bar Association. 2006. "Special Feature: Recommendation and Report on the Death Penalty and Persons with Mental Disabilities." *Mental & Physical Disability Law Reporter* 30:668–677.
_____. 2004. "Best Practices for Promoting the Accuracy of Eyewitness Identification Procedures." (http://www.abanet.org/leadership/2004/annual/111c.doc).
_____. 2001. "Death Without Justice: A Guide for Examining the Administration of the Death Penalty in the United States." (http://www.abanet.org/irr/finaljune28.pdf).
American Psychiatric Association. 2006a. "Death Sentences for Persons with Dementia or Traumatic Brain Injury." (http://www.psych.org/edu/other_res/lib_archives/archives/200508.pdf).
_____. 2006b. "Diminished Responsibility in Capital Sentencing. (http://www.psych.org/edu/other_res/lib_archives/archives/200406.pdf).
_____. 2006c. "Mentally Ill Prisoners on Death Row." (http://www.psych.org/edu/other_res/lib_archives/archives/200505.pdf).
American Psychological Association. 2006a. Excerpt from the Council of Representatives 2005 Meeting Minutes. Feb.18–20.

_____. 2006b. Excerpt from the Council of Representatives 2006 Meeting Minutes. Feb.17–19.

Atkins v. Virginia (2002). 536 U.S. 304.

Death Penalty Information Center. 2007. "Clemency." (http://www.deathpenaltyinfo.org/article.php?did=126&scid=13).

Furman v. Georgia (1972). 408 U.S. 238.

Gross, Samuel R., Kristen Jacoby, and Daniel Matheson. 2005. "Exonerations in the United States, 1989 through 2003." (http://www.law.umich.edu/NewsAndInfo/exonerations-in-us.pdf).

Liebman, James, Jeffrey Fagan, and Valerie West. 2000. "A Broken System: Error Rates in Capital Cases, 1973–1995." (http://www2.law.columbia.edu/instructionalservices/liebman/).

Roper v. Simmons (2005). 534 U.S. 551.

Shiffman, John. 2001."Missing Files Raise Doubts About Death Sentences." *Tennesseean*, July 22, A1.

State v. Godsey (2001). 60 S.W.3d 759 (Tenn.).

State v. Holton (2002). WL 1574995 (Tenn. Crim. App.).

State v. Richmond (1977). 560 P.2d 41 (Ariz.).

State v. Salazar (1992). 844 P.2d 566 (Ariz.).

Texas Defender Service. 2002. *Lethal Indifference*. Houston, TX: Texas Defender Service.

CHAPTER 6

THE NATIONAL DEATH PENALTY ARCHIVE (NDPA): "THE GREATEST BODY OF EVIDENCE EVER COLLECTED ABOUT THE DEATH PENALTY IN THE UNITED STATES"

Charles S. Lanier

> "The National Death Penalty Archive constitutes the greatest body of evidence ever collected about the death penalty in the United States. I think it will have an enormous impact on public understanding about the ultimate punishment."
>
> Scott Christianson

The National Death Penalty Archive (NDPA), which is one of the primary goals of the Capital Punishment Research Initiative (CPRI),[1] is an archive for historical documents and data on the death penalty (Lanier, Bowers, and Acker, this volume). The formation of this repository was acknowledged in 2005 when the National Death Penalty Archive (NDPA) was formally dedicated at a Presidential Event, hosted by late University at Albany President and constitutional scholar Kermit L. Hall, at the University at Albany Libraries (University at Al-

---

1. "The CPRI has three primary purposes: (1) to build and maintain a national archive for historical documents and data on the death penalty; (2) to plan and conduct basic and policy related research on capital punishment; and (3) to encourage scholarship, conduct graduate and undergraduate training, and disseminate scientifically grounded knowledge about the ultimate penal sanction" (School of Criminal Justice 2008a).

bany 2005). While the gathering of documents and papers on the death penalty had been underway for several years, this ceremonial launch announced publicly that "a national repository of archival material devoted solely to the death penalty" now existed at the M.E. Grenander Department of Special Collections and Archives. How did this important development occur, how has it evolved, what type of material does the Archive contain, and where is it headed in the years to come?

Background and Evolution

> "There will be some who will insist that such an archive as this belongs in New York [City], Boston or Philadelphia.... My reply is this—It was open to any scholar or librarian to undertake in New York, Boston or Philadelphia—only no scholar or team of scholars at any of the major universities in those cities undertook to do so."
>
> Hugo Adam Bedau

History

The National Death Penalty Archive is the product of a partnership between the University at Albany Libraries and the Capital Punishment Research Initiative at the School of Criminal Justice, University at Albany. The idea of establishing an Archive for materials related to the death penalty was born as part of the agenda of the CPRI in 1995. As New York State was preparing to enact new death penalty laws in September of that year, formation of the CPRI as a center for the study of capital punishment already was underway. One of the early aims of the CPRI was to obtain and preserve documents and data related to the incipient legislation. As events unfolded, the ambit of the Archive was expanded to include documents other than those New York State collections originally envisioned.

As the CPRI extended its reach and contacts in the latter part of the 1990s, people began to learn more about the work and efforts underway at Albany. One of those persons was Rick Halperin, from Southern Methodist University in Texas. In 1999, as researchers at the School of Criminal Justice formally established the CPRI, Professor Halperin contacted them to see if they were interested in his collection of news clippings and other articles dealing with capital punishment. Shortly afterward, an attorney who worked to preserve the life of Alvin Ford in Florida, inquired about whether his files on this important case (*Ford v. Wainwright* 1986), would be of interest. Today, both collections reside in the National Death Penalty Archive (see Appendix). These collections have been supplemented by many others in the intervening years. In fact, by the time of its formal Dedication in 2005 (University at Albany 2005), the NDPA already possessed over a million documents.

Journey to a Collection

In both instances noted above, the donors made an initial inquiry about whether their papers would be of interest to this embryonic enterprise tasked with saving and preserving papers germane to the history and administration of capital punishment. As time passed, other potential donors made contact through an intermediary. In still other instances, personnel from the CPRI have reached out to scholars, activists, and others about their papers. Serendipity also has accounted for several collections; these came about after chance encounters at conferences, and even as an outgrowth of interviews conducted as part of the CPRI's Oral History of the Death Penalty in America Project.

Once a donor and the CPRI agree that his or her papers will form a collection at the NDPA, both parties sign a Memorandum of Agreement (MOA) that transfers ownership of the collection to the University at Albany Libraries. While the MOA is fairly straightforward, some conditions can be requested by donors. For example, some "sensitive" papers or data can be restricted until a specific date in the future. Importantly, the collections are "gifted" to the NDPA, not purchased, and in return the Archive organizes, preserves, and makes available the contents of the various collections in perpetuity. Also noteworthy is that donors can (and do) add to their collections over time. For instance, if someone continues to do work in this area, subsequent efforts can be included in the NDPA. Sometimes additional material is located with the passage of time and then is forwarded to the NDPA.

Some collections are boxed up by the donors or their assigned representatives and then shipped to the NDPA for processing. Other collections are retrieved by CPRI personnel and transported by them back to the M.E. Grenander Department of Special Collections and Archives at the University at Albany Libraries. Some collections have even been brought in person to the NDPA by their donors (*e.g.*, Bill Babbitt; Abe Bonowitz; Bill Pelke). Some of these collections are comprised of only a few boxes (*e.g.*, November Belford, three boxes), while transporting others necessitated renting a truck (*e.g.*, M. Watt Espy, 131 boxes).

Collections vary in another important aspect as well—the degree to which they are organized. Many collections come to the NDPA in boxes of all sizes and shapes, with no organization. In many instances, papers, photographs, correspondence, and other items are haphazardly packed for transportation to the NDPA. Other donations come in neatly numbered storage boxes containing folders and/or with a computerized index of the contents. This level of organization is important for the next step in the journey—processing and creating a Finding Aid.[2]

Collections are processed by assigned library employees, while at other times trained volunteers donate their time and effort to facilitate making the contents of collections available. For instance, correspondence, papers and documents have to be culled for non-relevant material.[3] The contents of the boxes also have to be inspected to ensure they are free from infestation,[4] as well as other types of damage, like that resulting from exposure to water. All relevant materials then must be sorted, identified, boxes coded and labeled, and eventually recorded on the path to creating a Finding Aid. Some photographs need to be logged and in some cases digitized; some documents also need to be scanned for making online access a reality. In short, there are numerous and time-consuming steps in processing collections and developing useful Finding Aids. Thus the effort to build and maintain this collection of archival materials documenting the history of capital punishment, and to preserve and make available these resources for historical scholarship, is a time-consuming and costly undertaking, which by necessity requires considerable resources in personnel and money.

Contents of the NDPA

This growing collection of archival materials is housed in the M.E. Grenander Department of Special Collections and Archives, which is located in the University's state of the art Science Library. Open since 1999, the new archival repository for the University includes climate-controlled storage for more than 25,000 cubic feet of material. The NDPA itself contains papers, records and research data from the nation's leading scholars and researchers, as well as organizations like the National Coalition Against the Death Penalty.

---

2. "A finding aid is a description of an archival collection, usually containing a history of the person or organization that produced the collection and an inventory of its contents" (Duke University Libraries 2008).

3. On occasion, personal papers that have nothing to do with the death penalty, and were not intended to be sent to the NDPA, are found in the boxes. In such instances, the donors are notified and asked whether they want the items returned or destroyed.

4. One of the reasons the NDPA was initiated was to save and preserve historical and other documents from ruin. In some instances, these papers and other items are left in storage sheds, wet basements, and other areas where they are vulnerable to insects, rodents, as well as the elements.

The following examples provide some insight into the contents of some of the collections already acquired for the NDPA. Among the documents included in the papers of William J. Bowers is a series of exchanges by letter between Dr. Bowers and Isaac Ehrlich over the data he used in his much-debated study on deterrence. In David Von Drehle's collection are copies of papers from the Library of Congress containing the handwritten notes of Justice Harry Blackmun attesting to the actual communications between the justices on death penalty cases pending before the Court. Bill Babbitt's collection includes a poem written by his brother Manny at the time of his execution by the State of California, in which he hoped his death would satisfy and bring peace to his victim's family. Among the items brought to the NDPA in person by Norma Herrera[5] is the videotaped testimony about her brother Leonel's innocence which was sent to the United States Supreme Court (*Herrera v. Collins* 1993), an original execution warrant, and the Our Lady of Guadalupe medal that her brother wore the night he was executed by the State of Texas.

Beyond these compelling examples, the NDPA holds collections for serious study in a variety of disciplines. One future donor, author Scott Christianson, suggests that his papers contain research material for "two dissertations." Another complex and varied collection that should return years of research activity is the collection of data and documents contained in the papers of the Capital Jury Project. The life work of Hugo Adam Bedau also contains reams of information and files about the work of a renowned scholar who devoted a great portion of his life to studying capital punishment. Moreover, the M. Watt Espy collection contains abundant resources for books, scholarly papers, photographic displays, and a legion of ancillary writing (*e.g.*, newspaper, magazine articles, monographs).

The commanding information contained in The M. Watt Espy Executions in the United States Collection already has proven its worth in previous studies, and of course has the potential for future research. For instance, the "inventory" of "Executions Under State Authority" first presented in *Executions in America* (Bowers 1974) was later amended using Espy data. In fact, a decade later the author noted numerous corrections and additions to his original listing of executions (Bowers 1984), which originally was compiled without reference to the Espy data. Future research also might utilize Espy's historical data on slave executions to help understand the experience and differential treatment

---

5. On January 14, 2008, shortly after her visit to Albany to establish the Norma Herrera Collection at the NDPA (School of Criminal Justice 2008b), Norma Herrera—activist, author, and sister to Leonel—died unexpectedly. All of those who met Norma and spent time with her while she visited the University at Albany mourn her passing.

of African-Americans, at the same time it informs scholars about the practice of capital punishment in earlier periods of history.

These collections thus can be used by a wide array of people and organizations, for any number of purposes. Some documents will be of interest primarily to scholars and students; others to organizations, legislators, political commentators who influence public opinion, and pro- as well as anti-death penalty activists. Filmmakers and documentarians also will find some of the audio- and videotaped contents compelling, as will those writing for the media. The collections transcend academic disciplines as well. Papers already collected should be of interest to the fields of sociology, political science, history, psychology, government, public policy, and criminal justice, not to mention journalism and the visual arts. Outcomes can be as varied as writing a historical treatment of the execution of slaves, as personal as authoring a biography of a scholar, as clinical as compiling narratives on the social movement to abolish the death penalty, or as poignant as reporting on the lives of those personally affected by the practice of capital punishment.

Beyond its obvious value to the research community and interested others, it is important to recognize that the NDPA also serves to inspire others around the nation to identify and preserve related documents before it is too late. Not all collections have to come to the National Death Penalty Archive. At the same time, the existence of the NDPA can prevent some collections from being thrown away or destroyed because they are thought to be of little value. This repository is national in scope, and as such, can provide a home for such accumulations—both those already identified, and those waiting to be discovered.

The Future

"The National Death Penalty Archive is a landmark development in the history of capital punishment."

William J. Bowers

As Dr. Bowers' words suggest, establishing the National Death Penalty Archive has implications for the future. Indeed, plans are underway in several areas that will greatly increase the utility of this unique repository. One aspect of this planned trajectory now underway is to build a "virtual" archive of death penalty documents and collections currently scattered in libraries across the country. Second, the National Death Penalty Archive intends to continue collecting hard evidence, including quantitative data, which can be made available for future instruction as well as for research purposes. Finally, the search continues for outstanding collections across the nation that can and should be added to the NDPA. Taken together, this effort will yield a peerless resource that will enable researchers and scholars to conduct studies and respond equitably and judiciously to questions about the administration of the death penalty.

A Virtual Archive

Plans to establish a Virtual Archive to supplement the NDPA already are underway. A variety of papers, documents, and even some collections related to the death penalty already exist in public and private libraries scattered around the country. These records are maintained in other facilities and presumably covered under agreements that prevent them from being physically moved to the National Death Penalty Archive in Albany. For example, the death penalty writings of some scholars, public servants, attorneys, and even Supreme Court justices are housed with the larger collections of their papers and thus would not be physically located at the NDPA. Some entire collections, like the Sara R. Ehrmann papers at Northeastern University, already are gifted to other archives and thus are ineligible to be moved to the NDPA.

Notwithstanding their geographic location, these collections need to be identified, organized, and their contents made known to researchers and others. Thus the goal of the Virtual NDPA is to pull together these extant collections and related resources in a comprehensive index. This online resource would aid those conducting research, or looking for documents on capital punishment, by making available an online searchable database. This comprehensive aid will direct researchers, and others, to relevant documents archived in libraries around the United States. This supplementary resource will not only help facilitate research on the death penalty, but it also will reveal publicly the depth, duration, and scope of America's relationship with capital punishment.

The Virtual Archive can be built most efficaciously and thoroughly by seeking and accepting assistance not only from other archivists, but also from educators, researchers, students, and other volunteers including the family members of individuals connected to the materials. For example, "agents" of the Virtual Archive can be located in any jurisdiction around the country. From their particular vantage, they can identify existing collections, regardless of whether they are online, and share that information with the NDPA. Beyond serendipitously locating such collections, agents also can be enlisted in a systematic search of public and private libraries, and government archives; they even can post inquiries among archivists and librarians. Thus, in keeping with the leitmotif of the CPRI, the Virtual Archive will be constructed in the most comprehensive fashion through the assistance and dedication of individuals across the nation.

Quantitative Data

Data sets. A further outgrowth, or future goal of the NDPA, is the acquisition of data sets or collections that can be accessed and used by scholars and others investigating the capital sanction. One start in this area is the Capital Jury Project (CJP) data provided to the Archive by William J. Bowers, architect and Principal Investigator of the CJP.[6] Completed data collection instruments from approximately 1,200 interviews with capital jurors from Phase One of the CJP are housed in the NDPA and will be made accessible once resources become available.

Another extant data set is the collection of Executive Clemency Petitions in capital cases. Unlike judicial proceedings, claims raised in clemency petitions are free of procedural defaults that can mask error, unfairness, or irrationality in a given death sentence. Petitions thus can reveal what the sentencing authority may not have known because of attorney error, prosecutorial misconduct, newly discovered evidence, or other reasons. The approximately 150 petitions housed in the NDPA exist in their original hard copy format, but also in PDF files that are available online (http://library.albany.edu/speccoll/findaids/apap214.htm).

This collection already has been used by researchers, reporters, and capital attorneys, and is ideal for future research like that suggested by Austin Sarat: "... we know relatively little about this power to undo death, about the clemency process and how it operates, about the political and moral forces that are brought to bear in considering clemency petitions, and about the narrative strategies and rhetoric used by those seeking to persuade chief executives to spare their lives" (Sarat, this volume).

Trial transcripts from death penalty cases also are part of the future data collection plans at the NDPA. Approximately 15 trial transcripts in hard copy format already are present in Albany and have been used in previous research (Lanier 2004). Additionally, trial transcripts form part of the data source for the third phase of the Capital Jury Project, now underway at the CPRI in Albany; when completed, the transcripts (some of which are electronic) will be added to the transcript collection.[7] Importantly, the eventual collection of trial

---

6. For additional information on the CJP, as well as a list of the research published using this information, see "Capital Jury Project" (School of Criminal Justice 2008c).

transcripts will be instrumental for conducting the type of research on the downturn in death sentences advanced by Bowers and Sundby (this volume). These, as well as additional transcripts gathered during data collection will eventually reside in the NDPA, where they can be accessed for research and/or heuristic purposes. As time passes, additional trial transcripts, clemency petitions, and survey data from other researchers and scholars will be sought in an effort to gather, preserve, and make available information on the death penalty.

Data expansion. As noted elsewhere in this volume (Acker, Bowers, and Lanier; Fleischaker), one of the greatest impediments to conducting a wide range of study that is critical to assessing the administration of capital punishment is the dearth of reliable data. Information, on a variety of fronts, often is simply just not available. Court analysts responsible for allocating scarce judicial resources, defense counsel representing capital clients facing trial, lawmakers trying to decide on legislation, and even government-sanctioned bodies often are frustrated in their attempts to locate information integral to making informed and reliable decisions.[8]

The reasons for this privation vary, but include poor record keeping, a lack of foresight, difficulty in obtaining records from disparate agencies, finite resources, and a lack of uniformity in data sources. In some cases, moreover, keeping accurate records, like videotaped interrogations and/or confessions, might be inimical to law enforcement attempts to clear cases. What is eminently clear, though, is that accurate and reliable records are essential to research on the administration of the death penalty; because of data inadequacies, we do not know enough about how the system of capital justice is working.

In collaboration with others, the CPRI will seek to set forth a "data agenda"—*i.e.*, to identify the most essential and relevant information that should be collected and made available for research. This agenda should be jointly developed and priorities set by a variety of researchers, scholars, court

---

7. The CJP already has collected approximately 150 death penalty trial transcripts in electronic format.

8. "Throughout the nearly two years that the Commission has studied the capital punishment system in Illinois, Commission members had to contend with an astonishing lack of data about how the capital punishment system works. There is no organized state-wide effort to gather information about cases in which the death penalty is imposed. The efforts undertaken by the Commission to collect data revealed how important factual information about these cases is to a complete understanding about how the system has (or has not) been working" (Commission on Capital Punishment 2002: 189).

analysts, attorneys, and legislators. Once articulated, attempts should be made to secure the funding that is essential to fulfilling this goal. Moreover, notwithstanding the import of this goal, some individuals and agencies will be unwilling to voluntarily comply with the data needs of scholars and others. They may have an institutional bias, be ill-equipped to gather data, or suffer from shortages in resources and personnel. Accordingly, stakeholders should coalesce in an effort to convince lawmakers to provide force to their requests. This might include penalties for non-compliance with mandated data collection provisions. To the extent that such a data acquisition strategy can be implemented, the NDPA could then serve as an accessible repository for such data.

In keeping with research directions advocated in other chapters, among the kinds of information that might be sought are: costs of capital punishment at the local level (*e.g.*, the expense of court, prosecution and defense trial preparation, including especially background mitigation investigation of the defendant; see Gradess and Davies, this volume); costs of state and federal appeals (*e.g.*, in terms of additional time spent by appellate judges and staffing needs for capital appeals); and cost to the prison system of maintaining death row (*e.g.*, additional staffing, training, and construction and security costs).

For such cost estimates, of course, data are needed on the criminal justice processing of potentially capital cases from crime to final disposition. For instance, jurisdictional data on the number of potentially capital cases that end with a life or death outcome after trial and related information (*e.g.*, number of capital homicides, number of arrests, number of capital charges, number of defendants against whom the death penalty was sought) are largely unavailable. Data on the impact of sentences of LWOP on the prison system also would be important to have for future study. To the extent that any of these data are collected, they are neither available for research purposes in most states (Fleischaker, this volume), nor employed within states for management purposes (Pierce and Radelet 2008).

In the past, some elements of these data have been available from both governmental (*e.g.*, FBI Supplemental Homicide Reports provide data on potentially capital murders, victims and suspected offenders, and clearance rates in these cases) and non-governmental (*e.g.*, the NAACP Legal Defense Fund provides some race information on persons sentenced to death and executed for all death penalty jurisdictions) sources. Information about the various points in the processing of capital cases *may* be obtained from other sources (*e.g.*, the record of the trial proceeding preserved in the trial transcripts may be obtained in electronic form from court reporters; clemency petitions from parole boards; information on prisoners' disciplinary records and criminal histories, and sentencing information from state corrections departments), but it is not guaranteed to be available.

In addition to acquiring data like those mentioned directly above, a viable collection strategy also might seek to identify strategic court jurisdictions (*i.e.*, counties, cities, and states), where especially comprehensive and detailed information is obtainable, with an eye toward enlarging this group of rich data sites over time. The identification of such sites and the development of data within these locations has been the research strategy of David Baldus (see Baldus, Woodworth and Weiner, this volume), and was institutionalized at the state level in New Jersey. In sum, the CPRI is committed to developing a data acquisition strategy that will incorporate the acquisition of comparable data from sites on a widespread basis, as well as more comprehensive and richly detailed information for selected sites, and to make both kinds of data available through the NDPA.[9]

New Collections

Currently, there are several dozen collections in the National Death Penalty Archive, some of which are discussed in the Appendix to this chapter. This number includes a half-dozen collections that have been received at the CPRI, but not yet processed into the NDPA. Of course, the CPRI also maintains its focus on adding to existing collections, and at the same time attracting new collections of significance to the Archive. Several patrons already have supplemented their initial gift of papers with newly discovered documents or with additions based on their more recent work. These come to the Archive when past donors either ship new materials unannounced or otherwise notify personnel at the University about their predetermined contribution.

As noted above, collections come to the NDPA in a variety of ways, including at the behest of a potential donor, serendipity, and by request. Yet, new collections also can be sought predicated on their value to the field as a whole. It may be that as both funding and space become strained, the CPRI by necessity will be more limited in the collections it solicits. Nevertheless, as with the construction of the Virtual Archive mentioned above, the quest for adding executive clemency petitions, capital trial transcripts, even locating new collections and papers, remains by design, a collaborative enterprise.

---

9. The author thanks Bill Bowers for his insightful comments and suggestions on the foregoing discussion about the elements of a data acquisition strategy at the CPRI.

Conclusion

"This collection is vital to the future of the study of capital punishment. The death penalty is one of the most contentious issues in American jurisprudence and culture."

Kermit L. Hall

It is critically important—even "vital" in the words of the late constitutional scholar Kermit L. Hall—to collect, preserve, and make available historical and other materials related to the practice of capital punishment in the United States. That has been one of the foundational goals of the Capital Punishment Research Initiative—to establish an Archive for materials related to the death penalty. In fact, the various collections of historical and related materials already processed in the nascent National Death Penalty Archive provide an unrivaled resource for lawmakers, scholars, students, members of the public, and others interested in the history of capital punishment in America, and in the legal and political battles engendered by this sanction.

Collections in the NDPA already have been accessed and used by a variety of people. For instance, these papers have been reviewed by representatives of the media, on both a local level as well as by the Associated Press. Students also have made use of the NDPA, including a law student in Pennsylvania who sought access to the personal papers of Steve Hawkins, the former Executive Director of the National Coalition Against the Death Penalty. A noted scholar accessed the entire collection of Capital Punishment Clemency Petitions for research on executive clemency in death penalty cases. Likewise, a team of attorneys working on an executive clemency application in Virginia contacted the NDPA to seek previously filed petitions with similar claims. Others, including a documentary filmmaker, a law professor from Vermont, and numerous organizations have expressed an interest in perusing and using the papers housed in the National Death Penalty Archive.

Prior scholarship has demonstrated how and why history is important to contemporary research about the death penalty. Historical data have been integral to a number of scholarly accounts on capital punishment. Books such as *Legal Homicide: Death as Punishment in America, 1864–1982* (Bowers 1984); *Rites of Execution: Capital Punishment and the Transformation of American Culture, 1776–1865* (Masur 1989); *The Death Penalty: An Historical and Theological Survey* (Megivern 1997); *The Death Penalty: An American History* (Banner 2002); and *The Contradictions of American Capital Punishment* (Zimring 2003) all drew heavily on historical sources. The Supreme Court also regularly integrates the lessons of history in many of its decisions dealing with death (see, e.g., *Furman v. Georgia* 1972; *Gregg v. Georgia* 1976; *McCleskey v. Kemp* 1987). In short, documents and records testifying to this nation's past relationship with the death penalty have been, and should continue to be, collected, preserved, and used to inform the future.

As additional collections are gifted and processed into the NDPA, and as the Archive itself becomes more widely known, the value of this unique repository will be realized. Accordingly, the Capital Punishment Research Initiative, in conjunction with the NDPA, will continue to gather records that can be used by a variety of those interested in capital punishment, to inform the public about this preeminent repository and to disseminate historical and other information about the ultimate sanction—including public displays of relevant documents. This central athenaeum for the preservation of historic documents related to the death penalty, and the virtual and tangible additions planned above, will make it possible for litigators, criminal justice administrators, scholars, and the general public to better understand this complex and contentious issue which has had such a profound impact on American society and jurisprudence.

References

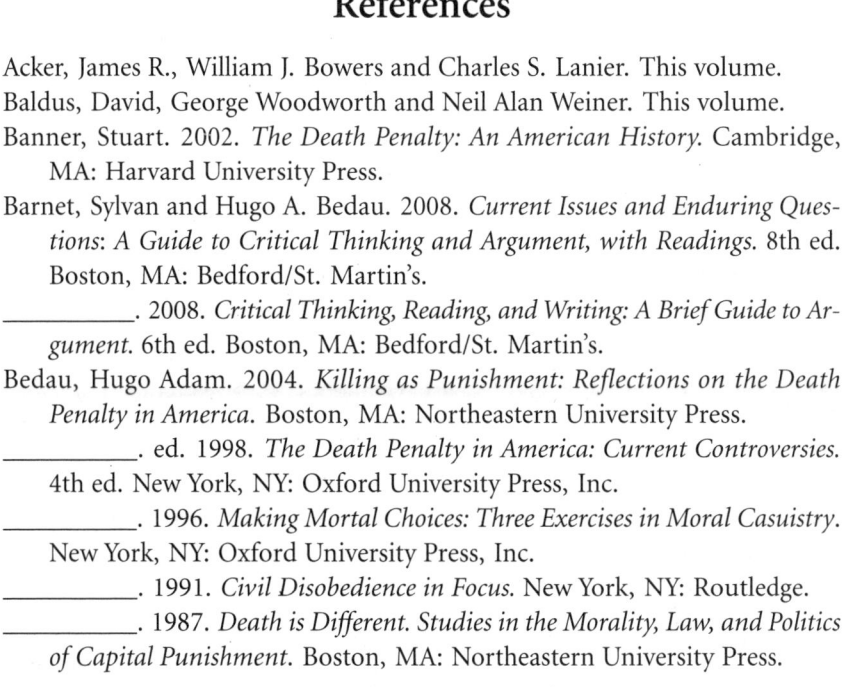

Acker, James R., William J. Bowers and Charles S. Lanier. This volume.
Baldus, David, George Woodworth and Neil Alan Weiner. This volume.
Banner, Stuart. 2002. *The Death Penalty: An American History*. Cambridge, MA: Harvard University Press.
Barnet, Sylvan and Hugo A. Bedau. 2008. *Current Issues and Enduring Questions: A Guide to Critical Thinking and Argument, with Readings*. 8th ed. Boston, MA: Bedford/St. Martin's.
_____. 2008. *Critical Thinking, Reading, and Writing: A Brief Guide to Argument*. 6th ed. Boston, MA: Bedford/St. Martin's.
Bedau, Hugo Adam. 2004. *Killing as Punishment: Reflections on the Death Penalty in America*. Boston, MA: Northeastern University Press.
_____. ed. 1998. *The Death Penalty in America: Current Controversies*. 4th ed. New York, NY: Oxford University Press, Inc.
_____. 1996. *Making Mortal Choices: Three Exercises in Moral Casuistry*. New York, NY: Oxford University Press, Inc.
_____. 1991. *Civil Disobedience in Focus*. New York, NY: Routledge.
_____. 1987. *Death is Different. Studies in the Morality, Law, and Politics of Capital Punishment*. Boston, MA: Northeastern University Press.

Bedau, Hugo Adam and Paul G. Cassell, eds. 2005. *Debating the Death Penalty: Should America Have Capital Punishment? The Experts on Both Sides Make Their Case.* New York, NY: Oxford University Press, Inc.

Bowers, William J. 1984. *Legal Homicide: Death as Punishment in America, 1864–1982.* Boston, MA: Northeastern University Press.

_____. 1974. *Executions in America.* Lexington, MA: D.C. Heath.

Bowers, William J. and Scott E. Sundby. This volume.

Bowers, William J., Thomas E. Brewer and Charles S. Lanier. This volume.

Christianson, Scott. 2000. *Condemned: Inside the Sing Sing Death House.* New York, NY: New York University Press.

Commission on Capital Punishment. 2002. "Chapter 14: General Recommendations." (http://www.idoc.state.il.us/ccp/ccp/reports/commission_report/chapter_14.pdf).

Duke University Libraries. 2008. "Finding Aids." (http://library.duke.edu/digitalcollections/rbmscl/inv/).

Fleischaker, Deborah. This volume.

Ford v. State (1979). 374 So.2d 496 (Fla.).

Ford v. Wainwright (1986). 477 U.S. 399.

Furman v. Georgia (1972). 408 U.S. 238.

Gradess, Jonathan E. and Andrew L. B. Davies. This volume.

Gregg v. Georgia (1976). 428 U.S. 153.

Herrera, Norma. 2007. *Last Words from Death Row: The Walls Unit.* Mequon, WI: Nightengale Press.

Herrera v. Collins (1993). 506 U.S. 390.

Lanier, Charles S. 2004. "The Role of Experts and Other Witnesses in Capital Penalty Hearings: The Views of Jurors Charged With Determining 'The Simple Sentence of Death.'" Doctoral Dissertation, University at Albany, State University of New York.

Lanier, Charles S., William J. Bowers and James R. Acker. This volume.

Masur, Louis P. 1989. *Rites of Execution: Capital Punishment and the Transformation of American Culture, 1776–1865.* New York, NY: Oxford University Press.

McCleskey v. Kemp (1987). 481 U.S. 279.

Megivern, James J. 1997. *The Death Penalty: An Historical and Theological Survey.* New York, NY: Paulist Press.

Mello, Michael A. 2002. *Deathwork: Representing the Condemned.* Minneapolis, MN: University of Minnesota Press.

_____. 2001. *The Wrong Man: A True Story of Innocence on Death Row.* Minneapolis, MN: University of Minnesota Press.

_____. 1999. *Dead Wrong.* Madison, WI: The University of Wisconsin Press.

_____. 1996. *Against the Death Penalty: The Relentless Dissents of Justices Brennan and Marshall*. Boston, MA: Northeastern University Press.

People v. McCoy (2004). 1 N.Y.3d 856, 808 N.E.2d 351, 776 N.Y.S.2d 216.

Pierce, Glenn L. and Michael L. Radelet. 2007. "Monitoring Death Sentencing Decisions: The Challenges and Barriers to Equity." *Human Rights Magazine* 34. (http://www.abanet.org/irr/hr/spring07/pieraspr07.html).

Radelet, Michael L., Hugo Adam Bedau and Constance E. Putnam. 1992. *In Spite of Innocence: Erroneous Convictions in Capital Cases*. Boston, MA: Northeastern University Press.

Sarat, Austin. This volume.

School of Criminal Justice, University at Albany. 2008a. "CPRI Mission Statement." (http://www.albany.edu/scj/CPRImission.htm).

School of Criminal Justice, University at Albany. 2008b. "Author of *Last Words from Death Row* Speaks at UAlbany." (http://www.albany.edu/scj/Herrera_Presentation_Oct07.htm).

School of Criminal Justice, University at Albany. 2008c. "Capital Jury Project." (http://www.albany.edu/scj/CJPhome.htm).

Special Report on Capital Punishment. 1965. New York, State Temporary Commission on Revision of the Penal Law and Criminal Code. Albany, NY.

University at Albany. 2005. "University at Albany Establishes National Death Penalty Archive," August 9 Office of Media Relations. (http://www.albany.edu/news/releases/2005/aug2005/death_penalty.shtml).

Von Drehle, David. 1995. *Among the Lowest of the Dead: The Culture of Death Row*. New York, NY: Times Books.

Zimring, Franklin E. 2003. *The Contradictions of American Capital Punishment*. New York, NY: Oxford University Press.

Appendix: Selected Holdings of the National Death Penalty Archive

BABBITT, BILL

The Bill Babbitt Collection consists of materials related to the execution of Manny Babbitt in California on May 4, 1999, and the subsequent activism of his brother Bill Babbitt, who is a Board Member of Murder Victims' Families for Human Rights. Manny, who received a Purple Heart for his service in Vietnam, was a paranoid schizophrenic who suffered from post-traumatic stress disorder. He was convicted for the murder of an elderly woman who had died of a heart attack after a break-in and beating, and sent to death row in 1982. The collection includes personal effects from Manny's cell after he was put to death, court documents, photos of his friends and their families, family photos, Manny's poems and other writings, books in his library, and cards and letters sent to him from around the world. Also included are newspaper clippings of the arrest, clemency campaign and execution of Manny Babbitt, VCR tapes of news coverage of the clemency campaign with David Kaczynski, VCR and CD tapes of documentaries featuring Bill Babbitt, and several books on the Babbitt story.

BEDAU, HUGO ADAM

Hugo Adam Bedau (PhD, Harvard, 1961) is a leading scholar, commentator, and active opponent of the death penalty. Bedau was a Professor of Philosophy at Tufts University from 1966–1999 and author, co-author, or editor of *Death is Different* (1987); *Civil Disobedience in Focus* (1991); *In Spite of Innocence* (1992); *The Death Penalty in America* (4th edition, 1998); *Killing as Punishment* (2004); *Debating the Death Penalty* (2005); *Current Issues and Enduring Questions* (8th edition, 2008); *Critical Thinking, Reading, and Writing* (6th edition, 2008); and contributor to many other volumes. His Romanell-Phi Beta Kappa lectures delivered at Tufts in the spring of 1995 were published by Oxford University Press, Inc. under the title, *Making Moral Choices* (1996). Bedau was recently the chairman of the board for the National Coalition Against the Death Penalty and a member of the board for the American Civil Liberties Union of Massachusetts.

BELFORD, NOVEMBER

November Belford, a long time activist, was married to Texas Death Row prisoner Bobby West in 1988; about a decade later he was executed. Belford launched a newspaper with West called *Endeavor*. Belford later started a second newspaper, *The Gathering*. The collection includes personal correspondence with a number of death row prisoners; newsletters published by death row prisoners; memorabilia; various publications from the National Execution Alert Network dating back to the 1980s; a copy of a signed petition requesting clemency from former Texas Governor Ann Richards for Warren E. Bridge; news articles on botched electrocutions; photographs; books, including some written by prisoners; and original copies of her two newspapers.

BONOWITZ, ABRAHAM J.

This collection includes photographic prints, negatives, digital images, clippings, and records from Bonowitz's time as Director of Citizens United Against the Death Penalty (CUADP). The organization works to end the death penalty in the United States through aggressive campaigns of public education and the promotion of grassroots activism. Bonowitz was also national coordinator for the Journey of Hope ... From Violence to Healing, Inc. as well as being active in other anti-death penalty events and actions including Floridians for Alternatives to the Death Penalty.

BOWERS, WILLIAM J. & THE CAPITAL JURY PROJECT

The Capital Jury Project was initiated in 1991 by a consortium of university-based researchers with support from the National Science Foundation. The Project is administered nationally by Dr. William J. Bowers, Senior Research Associate at the Capital Punishment Research Initiative (CPRI). The findings of the CJP are based on three- to four-hour, in-depth interviews with persons who have served as jurors in capital trials. Phase I of the Project has completed over 1,200 interviews with jurors in 353 capital trials in 14 states. These interviews chronicle the jurors' experiences and decision-making over the course of the trial, identify points at which various influences come into play, and reveal the ways in which jurors reach their final sentencing decision. The latest phase of the CJP research, which focuses on the decision-making of capital jurors at the penalty phase, is being continued at the CPRI in Albany (see Bowers, Brewer, and Lanier, this volume).

CAPITAL PUNISHMENT CLEMENCY PETITIONS

As part of his work with The Constitution Project, Dr. William J. Bowers has established The Clemency Petitions in Capital Cases Collection at the NDPA. The clemency process varies from state to state and typically involves the governor, a board of advisors, or both. Clemency refers to the lessening of the penalty of the crime without forgiving the crime itself, and in this context typically involves a request for the commutation of a capital sentence to a sentence of life imprisonment without possibility of parole. This collection includes approximately 150 clemency petitions in death penalty cases from almost two dozen jurisdictions. It is the initial installment in a collection that attempts to gather all death penalty clemency petitions filed in the United States during the modern era of capital punishment.

DEATH PENALTY IN NEW YORK TESTIMONY

The Death Penalty in New York Testimony Collection includes transcripts of testimony given to the New York State Assembly Standing Committee on Codes, Assembly Standing Committee on Judiciary, and Assembly Standing Committee on Corrections, on December 14, 2004, January 21 and 25, 2005, and February 8 and 11, 2005. The collection includes testimony from 137 witnesses, including officials from grass roots organizations, practicing lawyers, law professors, concerned citizens, religious leaders, former prisoners, and families of victims. The collection also includes the Public Hearing reports for each day of hearings, recorded verbatim; a copy of the 1965 Committee for the Revision of the Penal and Criminal Legal Code *Special Report on Capital Punishment*; and an amicus ("friend of the court") brief filed by Stewart F. Hancock in *People v. McCoy* (2004).

THE M. WATT ESPY EXECUTIONS IN THE UNITED STATES COLLECTION

M. Watt Espy, from Headland, Alabama, has documented more than 18,000 executions in this country beginning with executions that occurred in colonial Jamestown (http://www.dothaneagle.com/gulfcoasteast/dea/lifestyle.apx.-content-articles-DEA-2007-11-25-0001.html). His work is unique as a contribution to the history of capital punishment in this country. Among other significant historical facts about the death penalty, this collection documents the widespread practice of compensating slave owners for the execution of their slaves. This collection includes books, photographs, unpublished writings, letters, and other archival material gathered by Espy in the course of his research on executions in America.

FORD, ALVIN

Alvin Ford was convicted of first-degree murder in Broward County, Florida on December 17, 1974, and sentenced to death on January 6, 1975. He appealed his murder conviction and death sentence to the Supreme Court of Florida, which upheld both in *Ford v. State* (1979). After spending years on death row during which Ford became incompetent, his case eventually was heard by the United States Supreme Court. In *Ford v. Wainwright* (1986), the Court concluded that the 8th Amendment prohibits the State from inflicting the death penalty on a prisoner who is insane, and that Florida's procedures for determining competency for execution were constitutionally inadequate. This collection includes portions of the legal case file created by Ford's legal team during the period 1974–1990.

HALPERIN, RICK

Since 1972, Rick Halperin has been actively involved in the effort to abolish the death penalty in the United States. He works with many anti-death penalty organizations, capital defense attorneys, representatives of various communities of faith, newspaper editorial boards, victims' rights groups, members of the families of the condemned, and death row prisoners throughout the country. The collection consists of news clippings; newsletters; campaign materials; letters, flyers, and notices of rallies; research materials; organizational reports; and publications about the death penalty and death penalty issues.

HAWKINS, STEVEN

Steven Hawkins and his staff created these papers during his tenure as Executive Director of the National Coalition Against the Death Penalty, now called the National Coalition to Abolish the Death Penalty. The papers contain subject files that include extensive minutes of board meetings, speeches, travel arrangements, fundraising and reception notes, and pamphlets and other papers relating to his attendance at various board and committee meetings with related organizations, such as the Death Penalty Information Center and Amnesty International. The papers also contain copies of police reports, witness and investigator statements, and defendant testimony regarding the cases of certain high-profile death row inmates, such as Mumia Abu-Jamal, Delma Banks Jr., Kenneth Reams, and Keith Versie. These documents were retained by Hawkins and his staff in order to provide legal advocacy in attempts to obtain commutation, clemency, or exoneration for these death-sentenced prisoners.

HERRERA, NORMA

Norma Herrera is the sister of Leonel Herrera, whom the State of Texas executed following the U.S. Supreme Court's decision in *Herrera v. Collins* (1993). The Supreme Court reviewed Leonel Herrera's claim that newly discovered evidence demonstrated that he was innocent of the crime for which he was executed, but the justices rejected the claim and allowed the execution to go forward. Herrera has written a book about the case and her brother's life and death, entitled *Last Words from Death Row: The Walls Unit* (2007). In addition to donating materials to the NDPA, Herrera presented a lecture before the School of Criminal Justice, discussing capital punishment and issues of criminal justice, including the execution of her brother following the 1993 Supreme Court decision.

JOURNEY OF HOPE/BILL PELKE COLLECTION

Journey of Hope ... from Violence to Healing is an organization that is led by murder victims' family members. It conducts public education speaking tours and addresses alternatives to the death penalty. The collection includes public materials from the Journey of Hope co-founder, descriptions of events, t-shirts, and videos of marches.

MELLO, MICHAEL A.

Michael A. Mello is an internationally recognized authority on the death penalty and capital punishment issues. Examples of cases that he has been involved in or in which he has served as an informal advisor include those of Theodore Kaczynski, Joseph Robert "Crazy Joe" Spaziano, Theodore Bundy, and

Paul Hill. Professor Mello's courses taught at Vermont Law School have included Constitutional Law, Criminal Law, Criminal Procedure, Ethics, a Capital Punishment seminar, and a Search and Seizure seminar. The collection includes material related to Professor Mello's publications; research files; files related to both individual capital (*e.g.*, Spaziano) and potentially capital cases (*e.g.*, Kaczynski); and publications including *Death Work: Representing the Condemned* (2002); The Wrong Man: A True Story of Innocence on Death Row (2001); *Dead Wrong* (1999); *Against the Death Penalty: The Relentless Dissents of Justices Brennan and Marshall* (1996); and related material.

NATIONAL COALITION TO ABOLISH THE DEATH PENALTY

The National Coalition to Abolish the Death Penalty collection includes records that document the NCADP's mission and activities such as conference materials, publications, and death row and clemency case files. The NCADP was founded in 1976 in response to the Supreme Court's decision in *Gregg v. Georgia* (1976), which reinstated the use of the death penalty in the United States. As a Washington-based advocacy group, the NCADP lobbies against capital punishment through a variety of methods which include organizing protests and increasing public awareness. Through the efforts of its "Stop Killing Kids" Campaign, a movement that sought to bring an end to the death penalty for offenders whose crimes were committed while they were under the age of 18, the NCADP was successful in helping end the death penalty for juveniles in several states. In 2006 the NCADP successfully fought death penalty reinstatement efforts in Wisconsin.

NEW YORK STATE DEFENDERS ASSOCIATION (NYSDA)

The New York State Defenders Association (NYSDA) is a not-for-profit, membership organization which has provided support to New York's criminal defense bar since 1967. The NYSDA collection is composed of news articles about capital punishment and related issues.

ORAL HISTORY OF THE DEATH PENALTY IN AMERICA PROJECT (OHDPA)

The OHDPA is an ongoing research effort conducted under the auspices of the CPRI. Through interviews with a wide variety of activists, scholars, attorneys, and others whose lives have intersected the death penalty, the OHDPA is building an oral history of the post-*Furman* era of capital punishment in America. As such, these interviews create an important historical record and develop an invaluable resource for future research purposes. This collection entails audio- and videotaped interviews with numerous individuals, biographical information, and personal documents and/or papers associated with these interviews.

Among those people interviewed to date are Demaris Maguire, former Executive Director, New Yorkers Against the Death Penalty; Scott Christianson, historian and author of *Condemned: Inside the Sing Sing Death House* (2000); Jonathan E. Gradess, Executive Director, New York State Defenders Association; David Kaczynski, Executive Director, New Yorkers Against the Death Penalty; Abraham J. Bonowitz, Director and Co-Founder, Citizens United for Alternatives to the Death Penalty; Bill Pelke, Board Member, Murder Victims' Families for Reconciliation, Journey of Hope, and National Coalition Against the Death Penalty; Juan Melendez, former and exonerated death row prisoner; Steven W. Hawkins, former Executive Director of the National Coalition to Abolish the Death Penalty; Norman L. Greene, The Association of the Bar of the City of New York Committee on Capital Punishment 1997, 2002–present; Greg Wilhoit, former and exonerated death row prisoner; M. Watt Espy, historian extraordinaire and architect of the M. Watt Espy Executions in the United States Collection; Bill Babbitt, activist and brother of Manny Babbitt.

SOUTHERN COALITION ON JAILS AND PRISONS

Organized in 1974, the Southern Coalition on Jails and Prisons was formed to promote greater awareness of the problems of prisons and corrections, improve communication between the prison population and the outside world, and advocate for alternatives to the death penalty. The Coalition was active in Alabama, Arkansas, Florida, Georgia, Kentucky, Louisiana, Mississippi, North Carolina, South Carolina, Tennessee, and Virginia through the early 1990s. The records are primarily the files of Joe Ingle, co-founder of the Coalition.

VAN DEN HAAG, ERNEST

Ernest van den Haag (1914–2002) was a conservative commentator of social issues, especially crime, and one of America's foremost proponents of the death penalty. The publications in this collection include articles in published form, drafts, and related correspondence. Types of publications include transcripts from appearances on television shows in the 1970s and 1980s, files on the books which he authored, rough drafts for chapters, and hundreds of articles written for various journals, magazines, and newspapers from 1950–2000. The collection's publications cover a wide array of social science issues pertaining to the mid- to late-20th century from the perspective of an intellectual conservative. Topics include American culture, criminal justice, education, conservatism versus liberalism, and American politics. Van den Haag had a special political interest in U.S. foreign policy and commented on the Vietnam War, foreign wars, and issues relating to the Cold War.

VON DREHLE, DAVID

The papers in this collection were compiled during Von Drehle's writing of *Among the Lowest of the Dead: The Culture of Death Row* (1995), a history of Florida's experience with the death penalty between the *Furman* decision in 1972 and 1989. For 11 years, Von Drehle covered Florida's death row for the *Miami Herald*, and the collection comprises a comprehensive record of that period and Florida's experience with the death penalty. The collection includes virtually every relevant newspaper clipping from Florida newspapers during that period, notes from 100-plus interviews, government reports, law review articles and some ephemera, copies of letters from prisoners and diaries, and transcripts of testimony in major appeals and clemency hearings. Recent additions include Von Drehle's notes on Justice Harry Blackmun's papers from the Library of Congress (including copies of communications between the justices), which deal with his death penalty jurisprudence, and a transcript of television news coverage during the week leading up to the execution of John Spenkelink in Florida in 1979.

Section II

The Process Leading to a Capital Sentence

CHAPTER 7

Racial and Ethnic Disparities in Resolving Homicides[*]

Michael L. Radelet and Glenn L. Pierce

Introduction

Capital punishment is increasingly justified on the ground that it is needed to bring relief to the families of homicide victims. With only a minority of cases in which the death penalty is sought ending with a death sentence imposed, and fewer still ending with an execution (in which case the execution will come a decade or two after the trial), any benefits to the families of the victims are difficult to measure. In this chapter, we argue that instead of focusing scarce resources on executions, which (at best) can benefit only a few families of victims, increasing the proportion of homicide offenders who are arrested should attract much more attention from the criminal justice system. Furthermore, we present data that show that homicides with Black or Hispanic victims are less likely to result in the identification of a suspect than are homicides with White victims. In short, we show that in addition to those suspected of killing Whites being more likely to be sentenced to death *at trial*, similar racial disparities characterize the homicide suspects who are identified, long before the trial starts. This latter finding supports the contention that racial bias has a cumulative effect on who ends up on death row, with early disparities *hidden* to those who attempt to spot disparities only at the latter stages of the criminal justice process.

---

[*] The authors thank David Baldus and William J. Bowers for helpful comments on an earlier draft of this paper.

Justifications supporting the death penalty in the United States have changed dramatically in the past three decades. When Gary Gilmore began the modern history of executions by facing the firing squad in Utah in 1977, the top pro-death penalty argument was deterrence, a claim that suggested the death penalty was needed as a means of lowering the homicide rate. Other popular pro-death penalty arguments were based on cost-savings ("Why should my tax money be used to feed murderers?"), biblical verses ("Eye for eye; tooth for tooth"), and concerns for safety (without the death penalty, the murderers will kill again). With scant empirical support and effective challenges by foes of the death penalty, these justifications have declined in popularity since the time of Gilmore's death (Radelet and Borg 2000).

In their stead, retributive justifications have risen in popularity. In general, retributive justifications for executions are based on the proposition that the death penalty is the most painful of allowable criminal punishments. For various reasons, death penalty supporters contend that this anguish is both intended and good. To be sure, retributive justifications for executions have always been present, but the precise role of retribution in defending the death penalty has fluctuated through time (Banner 2002:116–23, 208–16). At one point, the prisoner's suffering was widely thought to increase the deterrent effects of capital punishment, thus intermingling retributive and deterrent justifications. To maximize the deterrent effects, executions were public events where citizens (even children) could come to witness the suffering and have their criminal tendencies restrained. Retribution also has been justified in religious terms. Throughout the nineteenth century, and even at the time when Gilmore was put to death, some of the leading voices in favor of the death penalty were from religious leaders who invoked the biblical principle *lex talionis*, "an eye for an eye and a tooth for a tooth."

In the 1970s and 1980s, as empirical studies undermined the deterrent rationale for the death penalty (Peterson and Bailey 2003) and most religious leaders began to join the opposition's ranks (Religious Organizing Against the Death Penalty 2007), attempts were made to justify the death penalty solely on retributive grounds. Under this view, the pain caused by executions is seen as a goal in itself, not as a means to another end (such as deterrence or carrying out God's will). No matter how much pain is imposed by the death penalty, it is defensible under the umbrella of "just deserts"—that is, the offender "deserves" it (Berns 1979).

The retributive justification, however, has always been problematic (Bedau 1978). Arguments based on just deserts invariably run into the problem of calculating how much of whatever sanction (whether it be reward or punishment) a given person (whether a Nobel Prize winner or a mass murderer) "deserves." In addition, it simply is not polite to argue that we need to execute prisoners because of pure unadulterated hatred. Those who call for retributivism also conflict with a centuries-old move away from the most painful methods of execution (such as burning at the stake or crucifixion), and the ongoing search for more humane methods of execution (such as lethal injection or, at other times, electrocution or asphyxiation).

In the past 15 years the retributive justification for the death penalty has taken on a relatively new slant: we need executions to help families of homicide victims. While the family of the victim has never been totally absent from discussions about the death penalty, during the 1970s and 1980s there was a wider recognition of the rights and needs of crime victims (and those of their families), and an increasing recognition of the need to involve victims and "co-victims" in criminal justice proceedings (Acker and Karp 2006). Here, supporters of the death penalty argue that we need retribution not as an end in itself, but instead because it helps facilitate the healing of families of homicide victims. This premise has made prosecutors see themselves as the champion of victims' rights, lawyers for the individual victim rather than for the state, striving to win death penalty cases as a way to honor the deceased. As Zimring puts it:

> The death penalty ... is regarded as a policy intended to serve the interests of the victims of crime and those who love them, as a personal rather than a political concern, an undertaking of government to serve the needs of individual citizens for justice and psychological healing. (2003:49)

The death penalty has been symbolically transformed into a "victim-service program" (Zimring 2003:62), and opposing it is depicted by its supporters as opposing families of homicide victims.

Countering this argument has been a difficult challenge for death penalty opponents. To be sure, the argument has been partially challenged by families of homicide victims who oppose the death penalty, such as Murder Victims' Families for Reconciliation, founded in 1976, or Murder Victims' Families for Human Rights, founded in 2004 (MVFR 2007; MVHR 2007). While these voices have presented formidable challenges to the idea that executions can help survivors, they are limited by the counterargument that families of homicide victims are diverse, and although some families reject the idea that executions can bring healing, other families just as forcefully applaud it.

On the other hand, while case studies of families of homicide victims are available (e.g., Acker and Karp 2006; Magee 1983), there has been no systematic research on how executions actually affect the homicide victims' survivors. Zimring argues that empirical studies of this impact are not needed because it is a justification based on faith (2003:63). If conducted, such research would involve complicated methodological challenges (Vandiver, this volume, 2006).

The execution may not occur until 15 years or more after the homicide, and by that time the survivors who are available and willing to voice their reactions are a biased sample of all homicide victim survivors. Within one homicide victim's family, reactions to an execution may vary widely. Any positive effects may also represent a self-fulfilling prophecy: after so many years of ups and downs and being told by prosecutors that they will feel better when the offender is dead, following an execution the survivors of the homicide victim may simply say what they feel they are expected to say. Another problem is confounding the effects of having the case finally resolved with the *method* of resolution.

Assisting Families of Homicide Victims

Supporters of the death penalty are correct when they argue that we need to do more about high rates of criminal violence (deterrence) and find better ways to prevent those convicted of murder from committing more criminal acts (incapacitation). They are also right in arguing that we need to do more to assist families of homicide victims.

One important issue regarding the types of assistance that can be given to families of homicide victims is whether resources should be invested proportionally across all cases, or invested disproportionately in a small number. This choice is also found in other social policy arenas; if we devote $10 million to fighting poverty in a given community, we could give large sums of money to a few people or small amounts of relief to larger numbers. Since only about one percent of those who commit criminal homicides are sentenced to death, and a smaller number actually executed, if we grant (for the sake of argument) that executions actually can help the families, then America's death penalty policy is analogous to transforming a few poor people into millionaires: a few of the needy get a widely disproportionate share of the resources. Only a few families of homicide victims derive whatever benefits may attach to executions.

Although criminal homicides in the United States disproportionately victimize African Americans, it is clear that the alleged beneficiaries of America's capital punishment practices are disproportionately White. In the 2000 census, approximately 13 percent of the American population identified themselves as African American (McKinnon 2007). In 2004, of the 13,926 homicides where the victim's race was known, 49.8 percent were White, 47.6 percent were Black, and 2.6 percent were "Other" races (U.S. Department of Justice 2007a:Table 2.3). Of the 1,099 executions between January 1, 1977 and December 31, 2007, some 79.8 percent (n=877) of the offenders were put to death for killing Whites, and just 13.7 percent were executed for killing Blacks (n=151) (Death Penalty Information Center 2007). Dozens of studies have found that, given similar homicides, disparities in the application of the death penalty in the end disproportionately make the supposed beneficiaries of America's death penalty practices the families of homicide victims who are White (Baldus and Woodworth 2003).

For nearly twenty years, one of the present authors has been working with families of homicide victims and trying to learn what social policies can be implemented that may assist them in responding to and living with the loss of their loved ones (Radelet and Stanley 2006). Because the alleged benefits of capital punishment are directed at only a small minority of families of homicide victims, our interactions with these families have focused on learning how to assist larger numbers than can be or are affected by the death penalty. Again and again, we have found that the single most important public policy that needs to be addressed is the falling proportion of cases that are resolved through identification and/or arrest of the suspected perpetrator. In 1961, the proportion of homicides cleared by arrests stood at 94 percent (Wellford and Cronin 1999:5). In 1976, at the dawn of the modern history of the death penalty, the clearance rate had dropped to 79 percent. By 1992 it had declined to 65 percent (U.S. Department of Justice 2007b). In 2005, 62.1 percent of murders in the United States were cleared by arrest or by exceptional means (U.S. Department of Justice 2007c). Wellford and Cronin (1999:7) suggest three general reasons for the declining proportion of homicide arrests: changes in the nature of homicide (a growing proportion of homicides between strangers or drug-related murders), changes in the nature of police resources, and changes in the degree of cooperation that police receive from witnesses or informants. Still unclear, however, is the answer to the question of what types of homicides are most likely to result in a perpetrator being identified by the police, and whether the resolution of the homicide varies with the race and ethnicity of the victim.

Research on Homicide Clearance Rates

Police detectives have a high degree of discretion regarding how various crimes are investigated, allowing them much leeway in using their judgment to give higher priority to some cases than to others. In a Canadian study, Corsianos (2003) interviewed 50 current and former police detectives from one police department. She focused on the "social construction" of high profile cases by police detectives and the differential treatment of crimes in their manner of investigation. She found that cases with victims with a higher socioeconomic status attracted more time and resources. Cases were also prioritized if the detective thought that the case would attract scrutiny by the media.

Wellford and Cronin (1999; 2000) studied factors that led to an arrest in 798 homicide cases that occurred in four large cities in 1994 and 1995. They found that certain police actions, such as the number of detectives assigned to the case and the prompt arrival by the police at the scene of the murder, were strong predictors of the probability that the case would be solved. They found no differences in the probability of clearing a case related to the victim's race or ethnicity (Wellford and Cronin 1999:21).

Puckett and Lundman (2003) studied homicide clearances in Columbus, Ohio, using data from 802 homicides that occurred between 1984 and 1992. They found that the social class of the victim and other extra-legal victim characteristics (*i.e.*, the race and gender of the victim) had no effect on homicide clearance rates. No separate results were presented for Hispanic victims (2003:180). The authors suggest that the absence of a relationship between victim characteristics and case resolution rates is explained because the high importance of homicide cases forces detectives to work earnestly to try to solve all cases, regardless of victim characteristics. Murders in Black neighborhoods had lower clearance rates than murders in White neighborhoods, an effect the authors attribute to a lower level of cooperation with police by witnesses to the homicides in the Black neighborhoods.

Litwin (2004) studied factors that affected homicide clearance rates for Chicago homicides from 1989 to 1991. Like Puckett and Lundman, Litwin found that, in general, few disparities were evident in the discretion used by police to investigate homicides. However, clearance rates were lower in cases with Latino victims and higher in neighborhoods with higher homeowner rates. In fact, the data showed that the odds of homicides with Latino victims being solved were 2.5 times less than the odds of White victims cases being solved, a finding that demonstrates the necessity of measuring both race and ethnicity in studies of homicide clearance rates. The author, like Puckett and Lundman, believes that these results may be a function of varying levels of cooperation with the police by potential witnesses, rather than by any "devaluing" of Latino-victim cases by the investigative agencies.

Working with Yili Xu, Litwin expanded this analysis to include Chicago homicides over three decades, from 1966 through 1995. They found that the race and ethnicity of the victim has had an increasing effect on homicide clearance rates over time, with cases with African American or Latino victims less likely to be cleared in more recent years covered in the study, especially in the period 1986–1995 (Litwin and Xu 2007).

Also using Chicago data, Alderden and Lavery (2007) found that the odds of resolving homicides with Hispanic victims, over the period 1991 to 2002, were 36 percent lower than for homicides with White victims. They found no differences in clearance rates between cases with White and Black victims (2007:123).

Regoeczi, Kennedy and Silverman (2000) studied clearance rates for homicides in both the United States and Canada. Their U.S. data were taken from the FBI's Supplemental Homicide Reports, 1976 through 1992, providing some 305,482 cases for analysis. Using odds ratios, the authors found that the strongest correlate of whether or not the U.S. homicides were solved is the presence of a concomitant felony, with the odds of clearing such cases 2.75 times lower than the odds of solving cases where no felony circumstances are found. Only small effects of the gender or race of the victim on clearance rates were found, with cases with non-White victims slightly more likely than other cases to be resolved (Regoeczi et al. 2000:148–149). No analysis was completed to determine whether the factors that help predict clearance rates were changing over the 27-year study period.

Because only one of the above studies used national data (Regoeczi et al. 2000) and the others focused only on large cities, much more needs to be learned about what types of homicides are most likely to remain unsolved. The study by Regoeczi et al. also ended in 1992; it is possible that the tiny race-of-victim effects they found have changed since then, as suggested by the findings of Litwin and Xu (2007). The variables that predict clearances in large cities may not be the same that predict clearances in smaller communities. We know that most death penalty studies have found that the race of the victim is a significant correlate of who is sentenced to death (for a review of recent studies, none of which measure any possible race/ethnicity effects prior to the charging decision, see Baldus and Woodworth 2003), but we do not know how soon after a homicide the race of the victim begins to shape which homicide defendants end up on death row. Because most studies on homicide clearance rates have been confined to large cities, and the effects of race and ethnicity are inconsistent, we designed a study using recent national data to see what patterns could be found in sorting out which homicide cases are most likely to be resolved by the investigating police department.

Methodology

To find out if homicides with White victims are more likely than homicides with Black or Hispanic victims to have a suspected perpetrator identified by the police, we analyzed data from the Supplemental Homicide Reports (SHR), which are annual data on homicides in American jurisdictions compiled by the Federal Bureau of Investigation. Our analysis focused on 164,000 homicides reported in the SHR over a ten-year period, 1993–2002.

"Homicides" are defined by FBI as murders and non-negligent manslaughters (Federal Bureau of Investigation 2006). Specifically, they are defined as:

> the willful killing of one human being by another. The general analyses excluded deaths caused by negligence, suicide, or accident; justifiable homicides; and attempts to murder. Justifiable homicides based on the reports of law enforcement agencies are analyzed separately (Bureau of Justice Statistics 2006).

For the purposes of the Supplemental Homicide Reports, the determination of whether an offense is a murder or non-negligent manslaughter is based solely on police investigation. As the Bureau of Justice Statistics notes, "The classification of this offense is based solely on police investigation as opposed to the determination of a court, medical examiner, coroner, jury, or other judicial body" (Federal Bureau of Investigation 2006).

Unfortunately, the SHR data are limited. They do not identify which homicides were cleared by an arrest or resulted in a conviction. However, they do give information on the suspected perpetrator, and in most cases where a suspect is known to the police, he or she will later be arrested. In this chapter, we define "resolved" or "cleared" homicides as those with an identified suspect, and "unresolved" homicides as those where the perpetrator is not known to the police. Hence, not all the cases we label as "resolved" actually result in an arrest. The resolved homicides have information about the suspect in the SHR data set, and since the suspect's gender is the easiest attribute for the police to identify, we coded any homicide where the suspect's gender is identified by the police in the SHR data as "resolved."

We measure victims' race and ethnicity in four categories. First we identify all Hispanics, regardless of race, based on the designation in the SHR data. Then we identify White non-Hispanics, Black non-Hispanics, and Other races non-Hispanic. In fact, most Hispanics are also White, but for our purposes we decided not to distinguish White and Black Hispanics in the analysis.

Findings

Our analysis proceeds as follows. We begin by examining whether the probability that a homicide will be resolved varies with the race and ethnicity of the victim. And we indeed find that homicide resolution rates do vary by the race and ethnicity of the victim. We then attempt to assess alternative explanations for the race and ethnicity finding by cross-tabulating homicide resolution rates by race and ethnicity while controlling for a set of factors known to be associated with arrest resolution rates, including the size of the city in which the homicide occurred, the circumstances surrounding the homicide, the victim-defendant relationship, and the number of homicide victims. In general, we find that the relationships between victims' race and ethnicity and resolution rates consistently hold even after controlling for each of these other potential determinants of homicide clearances. Following this assessment, we conduct a logistic regression analysis that examines the effects of victims' race and ethnicity on resolution rates while simultaneously controlling for each of the control variables previously examined. This analysis shows that the correlations between resolution rates and the victims' race and ethnicity hold even when controlling for these other factors.

Table 1 cross-classifies homicides by whether or not they have been resolved with the race and ethnicity of the victim. The analysis focuses on 164,578 cases for which data are available on the race and/or ethnicity of the victim. It can be seen in the last column of Table 1 that, as we measure it, 67.8 percent of all homicides are resolved (conversely, we do not know the gender of the suspect in 32.2 percent of the cases, and thus consider those cases "unresolved"). As expected, this proportion is a bit higher than the proportion of homicides cleared by arrest, as some homicides with an identified suspect will not result in arrest if the suspect is dead, "on the lam," or otherwise avoids arrest.

Table 1.
Homicide Resolution Rates by the Race and Ethnicity of the Victim

	White Non-Hispanic Victim	Black Non-Hispanic Victim	Hispanic Victim	Other Victim	TOTAL
Unresolved Homicides	.245	.370	.371	.291	.322
Resolved Homicides	.755	.630	.629	.709	.678
TOTAL	60,605	80,570	19,107	4,296	164,578

The second row of Table 1 shows that the probability of having an identified suspect significantly varies by the race and ethnicity of the homicide victim.[1] Whereas three-quarters of the homicides with White non-Hispanic victims are resolved (.755), only 63 percent of those with Black non-Hispanic victims

---

1. We do not report Chi-Square tests of statistical significance because such tests are a function of both sample size and the strength of the relationship. With more than 160,000 cases in our sample, it would be odd to find relationships that are not statistically significant. Instead, we focus attention on substantive differences between the groups of race/ethnicity.

and Hispanic victims (.629) result in the identification of a suspect by the police. Among the 4,296 cases where the victim's race is classified as "Other," 70.9 percent are resolved.

While not presented in a Table, our data further show that the probability that the homicide was resolved also varies by the size of the community in which the homicide occurred. Overall, the probability that a homicide is resolved is inversely related to the size of the community in which the crime occurred. In large cities (250,000+), only 60.5 percent of the homicides are resolved, but this figure increases to 67.7 percent in medium-sized cities (50,000–250,000), and 82 percent in smaller communities (<50,000). Clearly, research that studies homicide resolutions in large cities will miss a significant portion of the overall story.

We might hypothesize that the race and ethnic differences in the probabilities of resolving homicides would be largest in the larger cities. If, for example, felony or gang-related murders are more common in larger cities, and those killed in felony or gang-related homicides are more likely to be non-White or Hispanic, then the differences in resolution rates between non-Hispanic White victim homicides and other homicides will be particularly acute in the largest cities. In addition, to the degree that urban minorities are more likely than Whites to see the police as repressive, and hence to cooperate less than Whites in helping to solve homicides, then the racial differences in clearance rates would be especially high in urban centers. However, the data presented in Table 2 lead us to reject that hypothesis.

Table 2.
Homicide Resolution Rates by Size of City and Race/Ethnicity of Victim (N=164,578)

Community Size		White Non-Hisp. Victim	Black Non-Hisp. Victim	Hispanic Victim	Other Victim	TOTAL
250,000+	Unresolved	.363	.422	.344	.327	.395
	Resolved	.637	.578	.656	.673	.605
	TOTAL	19,527	46,666	9,423	1,925	77,541
50,000–250,000	Unresolved	.240	.355	.437	.294	.323
	Resolved	.760	.645	.563	.706	.677
	TOTAL	17,205	21,493	6,879	1,262	46,839
Smaller Than 50,000	Unresolved	.153	.201	.304	.226	.180
	Resolved	.847	.799	.696	.774	.820
	TOTAL	23,873	12,411	2,805	1,109	40,198

We see in the last column in Table 2 that in the largest cities (>250,000), 60.5 percent of the homicides are resolved. However, the differences in resolution rate by the race and ethnicity of the victim in large cities are relatively small, ranging from .656 among Hispanic victims, to .637 for White non-Hispanics, and .578 for non-Hispanic Blacks (the clearance rate for "Other" victims is .673, but given the ambiguity of "Other," we will not interpret that finding herein). Homicides with Hispanic victims actually have the highest rates of resolution. Among the three groups, the rate of resolution varies by 7.8 percent (.656 minus .578). These small differences in race/ethnicity-of-victim effects in large cities echo the results of studies reviewed above that were completed in Columbus, Ohio (Puckett and Lundman 2003), Chicago (Alderden and Lavery 2007; Litwin 2004; Litwin and Xu 2007), and the four large cities studied by Wellford and Cronin (2000; 1999).

Among medium-sized cities, the rate of homicide resolution ranges from .76 among homicides with non-Hispanic White victims, to .645 among non-Hispanic Black victims, to .563 among Hispanic victims. Among the three groups, the rate of resolution varies by 19.7 percent. Note that the overall results in Table 1 show that homicides with Hispanic victims are the least likely to be solved, and Table 2 shows that this relatively low closure rate is confined to medium-sized and small communities.

Finally, in the smallest communities (<50,000), the resolution rates are .847 for non-Hispanic White victims, .799 for non-Hispanic Blacks, and .696 for Hispanic victims. The total variation is 15.1 percent.

Overall, the data in Table 2 show that the largest race/ethnicity differences in the resolution rate for homicides are in medium-sized communities, followed by the smallest communities. In large urban centers, the race/ethnic differences are smaller. But overall, the racial/ethnic differences in the probabilities that homicides are resolved are not explained by the size of the cities in which the homicides occur.

Another hypothesis suggests that the reason why homicides with White victims are more likely to be resolved than those with Black or Hispanic victims involves differences in the circumstances surrounding the homicides that make murders with White victims easier to solve. Data not presented in a Table show that whether or not a homicide is resolved is related to the circumstances: almost 92 percent of homicides involving arguments are solved, but rates fall to 59.4 percent for gang-related homicides, 35.7 percent for homicides where the circumstances are unknown, and 27.8 percent for homicides accompanied by "suspected felonies."

However, the race differences persist even within categories of "circumstance." Table 3 shows that homicides with White victims are more likely to be resolved than homicides with Black or Hispanic victims regardless of circumstance. For every known circumstance (*i.e.*, Felony, Argument, or Gang-related), homicides with White victims are more likely to be resolved than homicides with Black or Hispanic victims.

Table 3.
Homicide Resolution Rates by Circumstance and Race/Ethnicity of Victim (N=164,578)

Circumstance		White Non-Hisp. Victim	Black Non-Hisp. Victim	Hispanic Victim	Other Victim	TOTAL
Felony	Unresolved	.239	.313	.315	.317	.280
	Resolved	.761	.687	.685	.683	.720
	TOTAL	9,261	8,423	2,014	838	20,536
Narcotic	Unresolved	.254	.347	.398	.295	.325
	Resolved	.746	.653	.602	.705	.675
	TOTAL	2,726	5,970	902	105	9,703
Argument	Unresolved	.051	.095	.125	.071	.081
	Resolved	.949	.905	.875	.929	.919
	TOTAL	19,549	24,347	6,390	1,426	51,712
Gang	Unresolved	.299	.399	.463	.413	.406
	Resolved	.701	.601	.537	.587	.594
	TOTAL	1,902	4,258	4,094	438	10,692
Other	Unresolved	.106	.208	.173	.133	.153
	Resolved	.894	.792	.827	.867	.847
	TOTAL	10,670	9,038	1,640	600	21,948
Suspected Felony	Unresolved	.620	.729	.866	.821	.722
	Resolved	.380	.271	.134	.179	.278
	TOTAL	353	391	209	28	981
Undetermined	Unresolved	.562	.673	.763	.662	.643
	Resolved	.438	.327	.237	.338	.357
	TOTAL	16,144	28,143	3,858	861	49,006

Another possible explanation for why homicides with White victims are the most likely to be resolved is that Whites may be more likely to be murdered by friends, family members, or acquaintances, and those types of murders are the easiest to solve. Data not presented in a Table reveal that when the relationship is known (Specific, General, or Stranger), the probability that the homicide will be resolved is quite high, with resolution rates ranging from 99.6 percent of those with a specific relationship between suspect and victim, to 93.6 percent when the assailant is a stranger, to 90.3 percent when there is only a general relationship. The rate falls to 35.8 percent when the relationship is undetermined. However, Table 4 shows that among murders committed between people with a general relationship and among murders committed between strangers, those with White victims are more likely than other homicides to be resolved. Only when the suspect and the victim have a known and specific relationship identified (*e.g.*, husband, wife, child, boyfriend, etc.) do the differences by race and ethnicity disappear, which is understandable because the clearance rate for this category is so high. The homicides involving a specific relation between the suspect and the victim are primarily intra-familial, which are the cases that are easiest to resolve, whereas homicides involving general or stranger relationships are more difficult to solve and invoke greater police discretion regarding what resources are devoted to solving the case.

Table 4.
Homicide Resolution Rates by Relation and Race/Ethnicity of Victim
(N=164,578)

Relationship		White Non-Hisp. Victim	Black Non-Hisp. Victim	Hispanic Victim	Other Victim	TOTAL
Specific Relation	Unresolved	.003	.003	.016	.004	.004
	Resolved	.997	.997	.984	.996	.996
	TOTAL	24,629	23,646	4,368	1,468	54,017
General Relation	Unresolved	.026	.096	.174	.091	.097
	Resolved	.974	.904	.826	.909	.903
	TOTAL	3,016	3,327	2,933	328	9,604
Stranger	Unresolved	.032	.051	.158	.085	.064
	Resolved	.968	.949	.842	.915	.936
	TOTAL	8,619	8,778	4,066	868	22,331
Undetermined	Unresolved	.594	.646	.759	.684	.642
	Resolved	.406	.354	.241	.316	.358
	TOTAL	24,341	44,819	7,740	1,672	78,572

Data not presented in a Table also reveal that the probability of resolving homicides increases with the number of victims. Virtually no differences exist in resolution rates among cases with one (67.5 percent) or two murder victims (67.2 percent), but with three victims the resolution rate increases to 76.7 percent, and it increases to 84 percent in cases with four or more victims. Table 5, however, shows that the differences in resolution by the race/ethnicity of the victim are not explained by differences in the number of victims in the

126   7 · RACIAL AND ETHNIC DISPARITIES IN RESOLVING HOMICIDES

cases. Regardless of the number of victims, homicides with White victims continue to be resolved at higher rates than those with Black, Hispanic, or victims of "Other" races.

Table 5.
Homicide Resolution Rates by Number of Victims and
Race/Ethnicity of Victim (N=164,284)

		White Non-Hispanic	Black Non-Hispanic	Hispanic	Other Non-Hispanic	TOTAL
One Victim Homicide	Unresolved	.251	.369	.368	.294	.325
	Resolved	.749	.631	.632	.706	.675
	TOTAL	54,210	75,378	17,363	3,711	150,662
Two Victim Homicide	Unresolved	.227	.407	.422	.321	.328
	Resolved	.773	.593	.578	.679	.672
	TOTAL	4,470	4,125	1,324	361	10,280
Three Victim Homicide	Unresolved	.140	.306	.391	.234	.233
	Resolved	.860	.694	.609	.766	.767
	TOTAL	1,075	719	304	124	2,222
Four + Victim Homicide	Unresolved	.104	.267	.259	.150	.160
	Resolved	.896	.733	.741	.850	.840
	TOTAL	850	348	116	100	1,414

In Tables 6 through 8B we examine the combined effects of the four control variables discussed above (city size, circumstance, victim-suspect relationship, and number of victims) and the race/ethnicity of the victim to assess the unique ability of each to predict the probabilities that homicides will be resolved. To do so, we use logistic regression analysis, which is a standard method for examining the combined effects of a series of independent variables on a dichotomous (resolved or not resolved) dependent variable (*see, e.g.*, Pierce and Radelet 2002:59). The independent variables are all entered into the analysis as dichotomous measures. To interpret the results, we use the exponentiated value of the beta (ß) coefficient, which is the logistic regression beta coefficient, Exp(ß), or the ß coefficient expressed as an odds ratio. Because of space limitations, we focus our discussion herein on the effects of race and ethnicity.

Table 6 shows that the beta coefficients for the three dichotomous race/ethnicity variables are negative, meaning that homicides with Black non-Hispanic, Hispanic, and "Other Race non-Hispanic" victims are less likely than those with White non-Hispanic victims to be resolved, controlling for the other independent variables. For cases with Black non-Hispanic victims, the exponentiated value of the beta coefficient is .878, which is the odds ratio for a homicide with a Black victim to be resolved. An odds ratio of 1.0 means that the likelihood of the resolution of the homicide changed by a factor of 1, or not at all, compared to cases with White victims. Therefore, the odds of a homicide being resolved in cases with Black victims are 12.2 percent lower (1.0 minus .878) than homicides with White victims. Similarly, the odds of homicides with Hispanic victims being solved are 60.7 percent lower than those in cases with White victims (1.0 minus .393), and the odds of resolving homicides with victims of "Other" races are 40 percent lower than cases with White victims. Of special note is the large difference in the odds of resolving cases with Hispanic victims compared to those with White victims.

Table 6.
Logistic Regression of Homicide Characteristics and the Race and Ethnicity of Victims with the Resolution Status of Homicides[1]

	B	Sig.	Exp(B)
City size[2] — 250,000 +	-.514	.000	.598
City size[2] — 50,000 to 250,000	-.583	.000	.558
Crime circ[3] — Felony	.898	.000	2.455
Crime circ[3] — Drug related	.956	.000	2.602
Crime circ[3] — Argument	2.148	.000	8.570
Crime circ[3] — Gangland	.247	.000	1.280
Crime circ[3] — Other circum.	1.430	.000	4.178
Crime circ[3] — Suspected Felony	-1.001	.000	.367
Relationship[4] — Specific Relation	5.516	.000	248.579
Relationship[4] — General Relation	3.049	.000	21.084
Relationship[4] — Stranger	3.242	.000	25.587
# of Homicide Victims[5] — one	-.589	.000	.555
# of Homicide Victims[5] — two	-.688	.000	.503
# of Homicide Victims[5] — three	-.299	.013	.741
Black non-Hispanic Victim[6]	-.131	.000	.878
Hispanic Victim[6]	-.935	.000	.393
Other Race non-Hispanic Victim[6]	-.510	.000	.600
Constant	-.109	.261	.896

1. Homicides Resolved = 1 and Unresolved Homicides = 0
2. Reference category for City size is City size under 50,000
3. Reference category for Crime Circumstance is Unknown
4. Reference category for Relationship is Unknown
5. Reference category for Number of Homicide Victims is four+
6. Reference category victim race and ethnicity is White non-Hispanic

Model Summary

-2 Log likelihood	Cox & Snell R Square	Nagelkerke R Square
106774.461	.456	.637

Table 7 shows how the race and ethnicity results are significantly modified when *only* the race of the victim is considered in the analysis (*i.e.*, White, Black and Other), and ethnicity (Hispanic or not) is *not* considered. Table 7 uses all the independent variables presented in Table 6 with the exception that ethnicity is not measured—we use only race—so all victims, including Hispanic, are classified only in terms of their race (*i.e.*, White, Black, or "Other"). In effect, this means that almost all the Hispanic victims are classified as "White," and to the extent that Hispanic victim homicides are resolved less often than White victim homicides, including them as one category with Whites will systematically underestimate any higher probability of resolution that cases with White non-Hispanics typically hold. The results in Table 7 show that two types of errors are introduced into the analysis when victims are identified only in terms of their race. First, the negative association with Hispanic victims and the resolution of homicide cases is *hidden* because almost all the Hispanic victim cases are in the same category as non-Hispanic Whites. Second, exclusion of ethnicity from the analysis also produces errors in the estimation of the association between victims' race and homicide resolution rates. If we look only at race, as in Table 7, cases with Black victims are actually more likely than cases with White victims to be resolved. However, when we look at both race and ethnicity, as in Table 6, we see that White non-Hispanic victim cases have the highest probability of being resolved. Note in Table 7 that the beta coefficient for Black victims is positive, meaning that cases with Black victims are more likely to be resolved than cases with White victims, not less likely as we saw in Table 6. This finding shows that previous researchers who did not measure and control for "Hispanic" status (Puckett and Lundman 2003), and who treat most Hispanic victims as White, shroud the Black-White differences in resolution probabilities. It is important to note that even in the present analysis we have probably underestimated the number of Hispanic homicide victims and overestimated the number of White non-Hispanic victims, because some police departments appear to be less likely to consistently record the ethnicity of homicide victims than to record the race of victims. Clearly, failure to obtain accurate measures of race and ethnicity may have resulted in the systematic underestimation of the effects of race on criminal justice outcomes.

Recall that the data presented in Table 2 show that in large cities, the probability of resolving a homicide with Hispanic victims is actually higher than the probability of resolving other homicide cases. Tables 8A and 8B zero in on different race/ethnicity effects by city size. Table 8A displays results for large cities (250,000-plus). Here, cases with Black victims are only slightly less likely than cases with White victims to be resolved (1.0 minus .938 = 6.2 percent), but when other factors are controlled for, cases with Hispanic victims and "Other"

Table 7.
Logistic Regression of Homicide Characteristics and the Race,
but Not Ethnicity, of Victims with the Resolution Status of Homicides[1]

	B	Sig.	Exp(B)
Control variables shown in Table 6 are included but not presented			
Black Victim[2]	.108	000	1.114
Other Race Victim[2]	-.236	000	.790
Constant	-.158	.105	.854

1. Homicides Resolved = 1 and Unresolved Homicides = 0
2. Reference category victims' race and ethnicity includes both non-Hispanic and Hispanic White victims

Model Summary

-2 Log likelihood	Cox & Snell R Square	Nagelkerke R Square
107881.580	.452	.632

races are 38 and 40 percent less likely (respectively) than cases with White victims to be resolved. In smaller cities and communities (under 250,000), differences in the arrest resolution rates between cases with White victims and those with victims from other race/ethnicity groups (*i.e.,* Black non-Hispanic, Hispanic and Other race victims) all grow larger.[2] Table 8B, with data only from communities with fewer than 250,000 residents, shows that the odds of resolving cases with Black victims are 16 percent lower than cases with White victims (1.0 minus .084), whereas the odds of resolution of cases with Hispanic victims are 76 percent lower than cases with White victims. The odds of resolving cases with victims of Other races are 39 percent lower than the odds of resolving cases with White victims (1.0 minus .606). Finding that differences in race/ethnicity arrest resolution are greater for smaller versus larger communities is important because we expect witness reluctance to support police investigations to be greatest in larger cities, where there are more developed youth gang organizations and perhaps greater opposition to snitching and/or cooperation with law enforcement. Thus, we find the greatest race/ethnic discrepancies in arrest resolution in smaller communities, not in the larger cities where we might expect potential witnesses to be more reluctant to assist the police in finding the killers.

---

2. The substantially lower probability of homicides being resolved for Hispanics in Table 8A compared with the results found in the bivariate crosstabular analysis presented in Table 2 arises from Hispanic ethnicity being associated with variables such as "Relationship— General" and "Relationship—Stranger," which when controlled affect the association between Hispanic ethnicity and resolution of homicides in cites with populations greater than 250,000.

Table 8A.
Logistic Regression of Homicide Characteristics and the Race and Ethnicity of Victims with the Resolution Status of Homicides[1] for Cities of 250,000 or More

	B	Sig.	Exp(B)
Control variables[2] shown in Table 6 are included but not presented			
Black non-Hispanic Victim[3]	-.064	009	.938
Hispanic Victim[3]	-.485	000	.616
Other Race non-Hispanic Victim[3]	-.509	000	.601
Constant	-.448	.002	.639

1. Homicides Resolved = 1 and Unresolved Homicides = 0
2. City size is not included as a control variable because City size has been used to specify the sample
3. Reference category for victim race and ethnicity is White non-Hispanic

Model Summary

-2 Log likelihood	Cox & Snell R Square	Nagelkerke R Square
58815.061	.442	.598

Table 8B.
Logistic Regression of Homicide Characteristics and the Race and Ethnicity of Victims with the Resolution Status of Homicides[1] for Cities of under 250,000

	B	Sig.	Exp(B)
Control variables shown in Table 6 are included but not presented			
Black non-Hispanic Victim[2]	-.174	010	.840
Hispanic Victim[2]	-1.445	000	.236
Other Race non-Hispanic Victim[2]	-.501	000	.606
Constant	-.275	.035	.760

1. Homicides Resolved = 1 and Unresolved Homicides = 0
3. Reference category for victim race and ethnicity is White non-Hispanic

Model Summary

-2 Log likelihood	Cox & Snell R Square	Nagelkerke R Square
47408.896	.449	.660

Conclusion

In this chapter we have attempted to zero in on the relationships between the race and ethnicity of the victim and the probability that the investigating police department will be able to identify a homicide suspect. The data suggest that there are widespread disparities in how homicides are treated by the criminal justice system, and these disparities correlate with characteristics of the homicide incident, the community, and the racial and ethnic characteristics of the victim. To the degree that defenders of the death penalty argue that executions help families of homicide victims, these data add to the evidence that not all victims are treated equally at various stages of the criminal justice system, and that those who arguably benefit from the death penalty are a lopsided sample of all families of homicide victims.

Clearly, additional research needs to be carried out to help close the gaps in what we know about how race influences who is sentenced to death. A comprehensive monitoring program needs to be instituted that can track all homicide cases from the time they first come to the attention of law enforcement officials through arrest, trial, and appeal. As we wrote in 2005:

> To accurately assess the full range of factors that may or may not affect criminal justice decisions, all links and actors in the decision-making process must be monitored. This necessitates collecting information from the very start of the process, including information on the character of police investigations and prosecutorial charging decisions. For example, if police devote more resources to the investigation of the homicides of wealthy white victims than to other cases, and/or prosecutors modify their charging decisions in such circumstances, even if all subsequent decisions are fair, then racial and class bias will still permeate the system and potentially affect the outcome. Improper decisions made earlier in the process later become invisible if they are not properly documented. As a result, some cases may be pursued more vigorously "based on the evidence" when, in fact, the evidentiary collection process and/or the charging process were themselves potentially biased to an unknown and undocumented degree (Pierce and Radelet 2005:37).

It would also be valuable to interview homicide detectives, their supervisors, and higher level police officials to get their impressions about why certain homicide cases appear much less likely to be resolved than others. Do language barriers restrict potential witnesses? Are relations between the police and the community so poor that potential witnesses are reluctant to assist with an investigation? Are there political or administrative pressures to pursue some cases? Are some cases given a lower administrative priority because of the neighborhood where the crime occurred, who the victim was, or just a general lack of public interest and/or media interest? Are the demands on the detectives' time so strong that promising leads cannot be pursued? Does the racial composition of the police department, the department's administration, and/or the detective unit correlate with differential attention to various homicides?

These findings underscore the point that understanding the effects of race on death penalty decisions requires researchers to examine what we elsewhere have called the "continuous chain" of decisions in homicide cases, "from the initial police investigation through appellate and clemency decisions, that result in (some) executions" (Pierce and Radelet 2002:41). To a degree, the evidence in homicide cases can be viewed as socially constructed. Evidence in some cases can be developed and aggrandized, and in other cases ignored or discounted (Radelet and Pierce 1985). If we study only one stage in the decision-making process that results in death sentences, biases that permeate earlier stages will not be spotted. Looking only at cases where jurors were asked to make death penalty decisions will miss any biases in prosecutorial behavior whereby some cases are deemed as warranting the death penalty, while others are not. Studying only how prosecutors deal with murder suspects would not reveal any biases that police departments may have if they devote more resources to homicides with White victims than homicides with Black victims. A thorough understanding of who is sent to death row and who is not requires looking at the continuous chain of decisions, with prior decisions affecting subsequent ones. Understanding this process requires researchers to begin with the day of the homicide and to develop measures of the quality of the investigation conducted by homicide detectives, and end with decisions on the eve of execution to see who is and is not awarded executive clemency (Wolfgang, Kelly, and Nolde 1962).

References

Acker, James R. and David R. Karp, eds. 2006. *Wounds That Do Not Bind: Victim-Based Perspectives on the Death Penalty*. Durham, NC: Carolina Academic Press.

Alderden, Megan A. and Timothy A. Lavery. 2007. "Predicting Homicide Clearances in Chicago: Investigating Disparities in Predictors Across Different Types of Homicide." *Homicide Studies* 11:115–132.

Baldus, David C. and George Woodworth. 2003. "Race Discrimination in the Administration of the Death Penalty: An Overview of the Empirical Evidence with Special Emphasis on the Post-1990 Research." *Criminal Law Bulletin* 39:194–226.

Banner, Stuart. 2002. *The Death Penalty: An American History*. Cambridge, MA: Harvard University Press.

Bedau, Hugo Adam. 1978. "Retribution and the Theory of Punishment." *The Journal of Philosophy* 75:601–620.

Berns, Walter. 1979. *For Capital Punishment: Crime and the Morality of the Death Penalty*. New York, NY: Basic Books.
Bureau of Justice Statistics. 2006. "Homicide Trends in the U.S.: Additional Information About the Data." (http://www.ojp.usdoj.gov/bjs/homicide/addinfo.htm).
Corsianos, Marilyn. 2003. "Discretion in Detectives' Decision Making and 'High Profile' Cases." *Police Practice and Research* 4:301–314.
Death Penalty Information Center. 2007. "Searchable Data Base of Executions." (http://www.deathpenaltyinfo.org/executions.php).
Federal Bureau of Investigation. 2006. "Uniform Crime Reports, Crime in the United States 2004 (Murder)." (http://www.fbi.gov/ucr/cius04/offenses_reported/violent_crime/murder.html).
Litwin, Kenneth J. 2004. "A Multilevel Multivariate Analysis of Factors Affecting Homicide Clearances." *Journal of Research in Crime and Delinquency* 41:327–351.
Litwin, Kenneth J. and Yili Xu. 2007. "The Dynamic Nature of Homicide Clearances: A Multilevel Model Comparison of Three Time Periods." *Homicide Studies* 11:94–114.
Magee, Doug. 1983. *What Murder Leaves Behind: The Victim's Family*. New York, NY: Dodd, Mead & Co.
McKinnon, Jesse. 2007. "The Black Population in the United States: March 2002." (http://www.census.gov/prod/2003pubs/p20-541.pdf#search=%22%22census%22%20proportion%20black%22).
Murder Victims' Families for Human RightsWebsite. 2007. (http://www.mvfhr.org/).
Murder Victims' Families for ReconciliationWebsite. 2007. (http://www.mvfr.org/).
Peterson, Ruth D. and William C. Bailey. 2003. "Is Capital Punishment an Effective Deterrent for Murder? An Examination of Social Science Research." Pp. 251–282 in *America's Experiment with Capital Punishment*. 2nd ed., edited by James R. Acker, Robert M. Bohm, and Charles S. Lanier. Durham, NC: Carolina Academic Press.
Pierce, Glenn L. and Michael L. Radelet. 2005. "The Impact of Legally Inappropriate Factors on Death Sentencing for California Homicides, 1990–1999." *Santa Clara Law Review* 46:1–47.
_____. 2002. "Race, Region, and Death Sentencing in Illinois, 1988–1997." *Oregon Law Review* 81:39–96.
Puckett, Janice L. and Richard J. Lundman. 2003. "Factors Affecting Homicide Clearances: Multivariate Analysis of a More Complete Conceptual Framework." *Journal of Research in Crime and Delinquency* 40:171–193.

Radelet, Michael L. and Marian J. Borg. 2000. "The Changing Nature of Death Penalty Debates." *Annual Review of Sociology* 2000:43–61.

Radelet, Michael L. and Glenn Pierce. 1985. "Race and Prosecutorial Discretion in Homicide Cases." *Law and Society Review* 19:587–621.

Radelet, Michael L. and Dawn Stanley. 2006. "Learning from Homicide Co-Victims: A University-Based Project." Pp. 397–409 in *Wounds That Do Not Bind: Victim-Based Perspectives on the Death Penalty*, edited by James R. Acker and David R. Karp. Durham, NC: Carolina Academic Press.

Regoeczi, Wendy C., Leslie W. Kennedy, and Robert A. Silverman. 2000. "Uncleared Homicides: A Canada/United States Comparison." *Homicide Studies* 4:135–161.

Religious Organizing Against the Death Penalty. 2007. "Statements of Opposition to Capital Punishment from Faith Groups." (http://www.deathpenaltyreligious.org/education.html).

U.S. Department of Justice. 2007a. "Crime in the U.S.: Murder." (http://www.fbi.gov/ucr/cius_04/offenses_reported/violent_crime/murder.html).

_____. 2007b. "Homicide Trends in the U.S.: Clearances." (http://www.ojp.usdoj.gov/bjs/homicide/cleared.htm).

_____. 2007c. "Clearances." (http://www.fbi.gov/ucr/05cius/offenses/clearances/index.html#figure).

Vandiver, Margaret. This Volume. "Capital Punishment and the Families of the Victims and Defendants."

_____. 2006. "The Death Penalty and the Families of Victims: An Overview of Research Issues." Pp. 235–252 in *Wounds That Do Not Bind: Victim-Based Perspectives on the Death Penalty*, edited by James R. Acker and David R. Karp, Durham, NC: Carolina Academic Press.

Wellford, Charles and James Cornin. 2000. "Clearing Up Homicide Clearance Rates." *National Institute of Justice Journal* June:3–7.

_____. 1999. "An Analysis of Variables Affecting the Clearance of Homicides: A Multistate Study." (http://www.jrsa.org/pubs/reports/Clearance_of_Homicide.html).

Wolfgang, Marvin E., Arlene Kelly, and Hans C. Nolde. 1962. "Comparison of the Executed and Commuted Among Admissions to Death Row." *Journal of Criminal Law, Criminology, and Police Science* 53:301–311.

Zimring, Franklin E. 2003. *The Contradictions of American Capital Punishment*. New York, NY: Oxford University Press.

CHAPTER 8

Perspectives, Approaches, and Future Directions in Death Penalty Proportionality Studies

David Baldus, George Woodworth and Neil Alan Weiner

Introduction

The subject of this chapter is empirical studies of proportionality and fairness in decision-making at one or more procedural stages in the processing of death-eligible cases in the criminal justice system. The principal focus of these studies is on systemic disparities in capital charging and sentencing outcomes based on the race or socioeconomic status (SES) of the defendant and victim and the geographic location of the prosecution. The purpose of this research is to assess the extent to which contemporary American death penalty systems deliver evenhanded justice at individual stages of the process and across multiple stages in the system.[1]

---

1. The Equal Protection Clause of the Fourteenth Amendment bars purposeful discrimination in the administration of the death penalty. However, *McCleskey v. Kemp* (1987) held evidence of systemic racial discrimination irrelevant under the Equal Protection Clause. The Court now requires direct smoking gun evidence of discrimination on the part of the prosecutor or jury in the defendant's case, which is impossible to develop. As a result, *McCleskey* has legitimated race discrimination, and for this reason no claims have been successfully presented in a federal court. New Jersey has the only state Supreme Court that has

To put the discussion in context, Figure 1 depicts 11 stages of the criminal justice system for processing death-eligible cases from arrest (Stage 1) to execution (Stage 11). The figure oversimplifies the actual process, particularly in stages 3 through 5, because plea bargaining, noted at stage 5, often precedes the charging and notice decisions at stages 3 and 4. Nevertheless, the figure reasonably depicts the flow of death eligible cases through the death penalty systems of most American death penalty jurisdictions.

Figure 1
Stages in Processing Death-Eligible Cases*

1. Investigation—victim focused
2. Arrest
3. Capital murder charge?
4. State's notice to the defendant of its intent to seek the death penalty?
5. Charge reduction/waiver of death penalty? Plea bargaining?
6. Capital murder conviction?
7. Penalty trial outcome—life or death?
8. Direct appeal
9. Post conviction proceeding—state court and federal court?
10. Clemency proceeding?
11. Execution

---

*For the purposes of this table we define a death-eligible case as one whose facts will support a capital murder conviction and a finding of the presence of one or more statutory aggravating factors regardless of how the case is charged and prosecuted.

As suggested above, there are two common approaches to analyses of case flows through the procedural stages depicted in Figure 1. First are analyses *within* a procedural stage that advances cases to the next procedural stage. Examples are separate analyses of stage 4 prosecutorial decisions to notify defendants of the state's intent to seek the death penalty, and stage 7 jury penalty trial decisions.[2] Second are analyses *across* multiple procedural stages that re-

---

rejected *McCleskey* as a matter of state constitutional law and recognizes the validity of claims of systemic discrimination when they are proven. However, the New Jersey court has established a very high burden of proof to make out such a claim. *Proportionality Review Project II* (2000). As of November 2007 it has recognized no race claims.

2. One advantage of the approach is that it can identify variations in the rates that cases advance from stage to stage. Typically, the rate of advancement of death-eligible cases to a capital guilt trial, Stages 3 through 5 in Figure 1, is low whereas the conviction rate is high at Stage 6 for cases that advance to capital murder trial.

8 · PERSPECTIVES, APPROACHES, AND FUTURE DIRECTIONS 137

flect the combined effects of decisions at multiple decision points in the process. One example is an analysis of the combined effects of prosecutorial decisions at stages 3 through 6 that advance cases to a capital guilt trial. The most common example in the literature is the analysis of death sentencing outcomes among all death-eligible cases which reflects the combined effects of decisions at stages 3 through 7. With both of these approaches, the most common objective is to document *systemic* effects of individual case characteristics, such as the race and socioeconomic status of the defendant and victim or the county and region in which the case was prosecuted.[3]

Before the 1960s, proportionality studies were infrequently conducted and principally of interest to sociologists. However, since the 1960s when the law began to focus on issues of evenhanded justice, numerous studies have been conducted by sociologists, lawyers, and psychologists. Because the focus of legal interest has been on the exercise of discretion by prosecutorial, judicial, and juror decision makers, independently or in combination, most of the studies have focused on the charging and sentencing outcomes depicted at decision points 3 though 7 in Figure 1.[4]

---

3. Systemic effects of the impact of a given variable in a system, such as the race of the victim, measure the average impact of that case characteristic across all cases in the analysis. However, in some legal contexts, for example in cases involving claims of selective prosecution based on the race of an individual defendant, the law may require proof of racial discrimination against an individual. This typically requires the application of both quantitative evidence of systemic discrimination and qualitative evidence of individual cases, which permits close case comparison of the outcomes of similarly situated cases with different defendant/victim racial combinations. A recent example is *Belmontes* v. *Brown* (2005:1125–29).

4. Baldus, Woodworth, and Pulaski (1990:228–65) summarizes the pre-1990 studies. Studies between 1990 and 2003 include those collected in Baldus and Woodworth (2003:215–26) and Thompson (1997—Arizona); Sorensen and Wallace (1995—Missouri); Bohm (1994—Georgia); and Williams and Holcomb (2001—Ohio). Empirical studies of capital charging and sentencing systems since 2003 include Paternoster *et al.* (2004—Maryland, which surveys the literature); Pierce and Radelet (2005—California); Pierce, Radelet, and Paternoster (2006—Georgia); Pierce, Radelet, and Paternoster (2007a—Indiana); Pierce, Radelet, and Paternoster (2007b—Tennessee); Pierce, Radelet, and Paternoster 2007c—Ohio); Songer and Unah (2006—South Carolina); Eberhardt *et al.* (2006—Philadelphia County); Hindson, Potter, and Radelet (2006—Colorado), McNally (2004—federal death penalty); Klein, Berk, and Hickman (2006—federal death penalty), and Blume, Eisenberg, and Wells (2004—multi state evidence). Post-2003 studies of the determinants of race discrimination in post-*Furman* capital charging and sentencing are reported in Baldus and Woodworth (2004); Bowers, Sandys, and Brewer (2004); Eisenberg and Johnson (2004); and Haney (2004).

In "The Basic Approaches" and "The Pros and Cons" in this chapter, we describe and evaluate the two most frequently used approaches that have been developed for the conduct of capital charging and sentencing studies. In chapter 9 of this book, we also present a primer on the key methodological issues presented by the conduct of such studies. In "Studies That Focus" in this chapter, we describe additional lines of research that have focused on how race may impinge at specific stages of the process. In that regard, we emphasize the importance of valid and complete data regardless of the procedural stage under analysis. In fact, the reason the nation remains in the dark about the fairness of the administration of the death penalty in most states is the nearly universal paucity of rich statewide data on each death-eligible offense prosecuted in the jurisdiction. Absent such data, even the most powerful analytical tools are rendered powerless. In "Potential Legal and Policy Implications," we consider the potential legal and policy implications of research findings in this field, and in "The Direction of Future Research," we consider the direction of future research.

The Basic Approaches to Capital Charging and Sentencing Decisions: Supplemental Homicide Reports and *McCleskey*-Style Analyses

The empirical literature on post-*Furman* capital charging and sentencing reflects two basic approaches. The first, the *Supplemental Homicide Report* (SHR) approach, uses an existing database maintained by the Federal Bureau of Investigation (FBI). The SHR was first used for a capital sentencing study in the early 1980s (Bowers and Pierce 1980) and successfully applied later in that decade (Gross and Mauro 1989; Radelet and Pierce 1985).[5] Since then, it has been used extensively (Pierce and Radelet 2002, 2005; Pierce, Radelet, and Paternoster 2006, 2007a, and 2007b; Radelet and Pierce 1991; Songer and Unah 2006; Sorensen and Wallace 1995; Thompson 1997; Williams and Holcomb 2001).

The SHR database contains the following information for each reported homicide "incident": (a) background information on the month, year, and county of the offense; and (b) the age, sex, race, and ethnicity of the victims

---

5. The SHR national database is maintained by the U.S. Department of Justice, Federal Bureau of Investigation on the basis of standardized reports submitted by local police departments to state agencies that are mandated to compile and forward the data to the FBI.

and offenders, when they are known.[6] This information provides a basis for estimating unadjusted race and geographic disparities.[7] The database also contains information on the following non-racial case characteristics that support the estimation of adjusted race and geographic disparities: contemporaneous offenses (*e.g.*, rape or robbery), the type of weapon used (knife, gun, etc.), the number of victims and offenders involved, and the prior relationship between the victim(s) and the offender (*e.g.*, acquaintance, stranger). This information provides a basis for estimating adjusted race and geographic disparities that control for offender culpability, a process that we discuss in chapter 9.

What the SHR database does not contain, however, is charging, conviction, and sentencing data for those who were prosecuted.[8] Nor does it include the suspect's name or the exact date of the offense.[9] Thus, especially in large counties, matching known death-charged and death-sentenced cases in the SHR database can be difficult, and it is precisely this information that is needed in order to examine the relationship between incident characteristics captured by the SHR and procedural outcomes like death sentencing. Filling the gap on the charging and sentencing outcomes of the SHR cases calls for additional research, which we discuss in chapter 9, that matches the known death sentenced and capitally charged defendants identified from sources outside the SHR database with counterpart offenders in the SHR database. With this information, it is possible to estimate statewide race and geography disparities with controls for the non-racial case characteristics in the SHR database.

A second approach to capital charging and sentencing studies is exemplified by the Georgia research presented in *McCleskey* v. *Kemp* (1987) (Baldus, Woodworth, and Pulaski 1990) ("*McCleskey*-style studies"). The distinguishing features of *McCleskey*-style studies as they have evolved over the past 25 years are: (a) a sample of cases from a specific jurisdiction that is limited to death-eligible murder cases; (b) comprehensive and detailed information on the presence of both statutory and non-statutory aggravating and mitigating non-racial case characteristics which, under the law of the jurisdiction, bear on the defendant's criminal culpability; (c) procedural detail on start-to-finish decision

---

6. FBI SHR (2004). Submission rates and the accuracy of the data submitted vary considerably by local agency (Maxfield 1989).

7. Unadjusted disparities do not account for and "control for" offense characteristics, such as the level of harm and mitigating factors in the case that might account for observed differences in the capital charging and sentencing rates.

8. Many SHR cases are never prosecuted because the suspect is never apprehended or died before prosecution and conviction.

9. The file includes only the year and the month of each offense.

making in each case that facilitates describing and then statistically modeling the flow of cases through the system; (d) the inclusion in the sample of all penalty trial cases, which embrace all death sentenced cases; (e) variables for the race and socioeconomic status of all defendants and victims; (f) to the extent possible, reliance on primary source materials such as case files and court records; and (g) mixed methods (qualitative—case study/narratives and quantitative—aggregate/structural) for documenting systemic race and geographic disparities.[10]

The Pros and Cons of the Two Basic Approaches

The first advantage of the SHR approach vis-a-vis the *McCleskey*-style approach is its lower complexity and cost. Its second advantage is that it embraces the beginning of the charging and sentencing process emphasizing the importance of capturing the earliest procedural points in the "continuing chain" of charging and sentencing decisions (Pierce and Radelet 2002:41). The SHR approach also avoids the potential risk of sample selection bias (Sorensen and Wallace 1995:563) and the potential risk that the "facts" bearing on the death eligibility and criminal culpability of the offender that evolve in the record of a case as it is processed through the system may be partially a "social" construct created (though not necessarily consciously so) by decision makers that justify initial charging decisions (Radelet and Pierce 1985). The latter risk may be greatest for cases with middling levels of culpability because these mid-range cases are relatively more ambiguous in terms of the presence and importance of aggravating and mitigating facts, which makes it easier for other, extra-legal factors to creep into prosecutorial, judicial, and juror decision making. The third advantage of the SHR approach is the readily available data maintained by the FBI on race and a number of other highly relevant variables

---

10. *McCleskey*-style studies build upon the methodology developed by Marvin Wolfgang and Marc Riedel in the 1960s in their study of race discrimination in the pre-*Furman* use of the death penalty in southern rape cases (Wolfgang and Riedel 1976). Because of the comparative simplicity of the law and procedure applicable in the southern states embraced in their study, their methodology was not tailored to the law and procedure of each state. Also, their study did not include all death-eligible cases and contained variables for fewer non-racial factors that bear on criminal culpability than have been included in the typical post-*Furman* studies.

that bear on death eligibility and criminal culpability.[11] Also, the database can be expanded to include legally meaningful variables that correspond to geographical boundaries such as counties. These variables might also include the racial composition of the county and the political affiliation of the prosecutor (Songer and Unah 2006). Fourth, although most applications of the SHR methodology focus only on the death-sentencing outcome, it also is possible to examine prosecutorial charging decisions when charging data are available (Songer and Unah 2006).

There are two principal limitations of the SHR methodology. The first is that the database includes many offenders who were never apprehended (up to 25–30% in many jurisdictions), which might bias findings if these offenders differ systematically from those who were apprehended. These cases are routinely identified by missing information on defendant sex and race and, therefore, are excluded from the database (Gross and Mauro 1989:35–39). Additionally, there are offenders whose sex and race is reported in the SHR database who avoid apprehension. This appears to be a small subset of cases.

The second weakness of the SHR methodology is the limited number of variables for non-racial case characteristics in the SHR database (Sorensen and Wallace 1995:64). For race studies, the most important omitted variable is the socioeconomic status of the defendant and victim. Missing data in the SHR database can be filled in and corrected with data from other sources, such as state maintained vital statistics records (Pierce and Radelet 2005). Despite these limitations, properly developed SHR-based studies can provide a very credible basis for estimating race and geographic disparities. Our confidence in the validity of the SHR studies is strengthened by the fact that when studies of both types have been conducted in the same jurisdiction, the race disparities estimated by the two approaches are comparable in both the direction of their effects and in their orders of magnitudes (*e.g.*, in Georgia, Gross and Mauro (1989:66), reported a 7.2 white victim odds multiplier (1976–1980) compared to Baldus *et al.* (1990:320), who reported a 4.3 white victim odds multiplier (1973–1980)).[12]

The principal advantage of the *McCleskey*-style approach is its greater potential to develop a more comprehensive, sharply focused, and well-measured

---

11. There are, however, missing data issues in the SHR database (Sorensen and Wallace 1995:63). For example, in the nationwide 2004 database, the race of the offender was unknown in 33% of the cases, while race was unknown for 1.3% of the victims (FBI SHR Codebook 2004).

12. The smaller race effect in the *McCleskey* research completed by Baldus *et al.* (1990) is, we think, the result of controlling for many more non-racial variables in the *McCleskey* regression models.

database, particularly with respect to the critical stage-specific decision making, the socioeconomic status of the defendant and victim, and other non-racial statutory and non-statutory case characteristics that bear on death eligibility and criminal culpability. However, the comprehensiveness of a study in this regard depends strictly on the quantity and quality of the primary data sources available to researchers. The likelihood of obtaining access to such data should be determined before a significant effort is made in planning such a study. For example, even if reliable race-of-defendant and race-of-victim data are available, a lack of data on basic control variables, which enable adjusted procedural-advancement rates to be calculated, such as statutory aggravating circumstances in the cases, should draw into question the utility of committing significant resources to the project.

Studies That Focus on How Race Impinges on Decision Making at Specific Stages in the Process

One little studied but important issue is the impact of the race of the defendant and victim on the development of evidence at successive stages of the pretrial process (Pierce and Radelet 2007; Radelet and Pierce 1985). For example, if a police department devotes more time and resources to the investigation of white victim cases, then white victim cases may appear to be more aggravated than similarly situated black victim cases that were only superficially investigated. As a consequence, prosecutors may base their charging decisions on evidence that distorts their perceptions of the culpability of the white and black victim cases. Similarly, if prosecutors consciously or unconsciously more thoroughly develop the evidence of statutory and non-statutory aggravation in white victim than in black victim cases, sentencing jurors will have a distorted picture of the culpability of the defendants that they sentence. Moreover, if investigators study the outcomes of white and black victim cases on the basis of evidence that overstates the culpability of the white victim cases, white victim disparities in the system may go undetected because the white victim cases will be read in the quantitative analysis as being more aggravated than they actually are.[13]

---

13. For example, if there are 100 white victim and 100 black victim cases with the same levels of criminal culpability and the capital charging rate is 80% for the white victim cases and 40% for the black victim cases, one would see a large adjusted white victim effect if the

Another line of profitable research concerns the process by which prosecutors inform their decisions about whether to seek death in a given case. For example, one study documented that from 1973 to 1990, prosecutors in a Georgia judicial circuit often met with the families of murder victims to discuss whether to seek a death sentence in the case (Bright 1995:454). However, these visits were limited to the families of white victims. As a result, while blacks were the victims in 65% of the murders in the circuit, only 15% of the capital cases involved black victims.

Another useful line of research concerns jury selection processes in capital cases. This is a story of how two important actors in the process—the prosecutor and defense counsel—select a vital decision maker—the capital jury (Baldus *et al.* 2001b). At one level, these studies assess the impact of United States Supreme Court decisions that prohibit the use of race as a basis for the exercise of peremptory strikes by prosecutors and defense counsel.[14] At another level, these studies focus on an important outcome in the process—the racial, gender, and age composition of the jury. Jury composition is important because juror characteristics, which reflect the jurors' experiences and preferences, are a key determinant of the outcomes of penalty trial sentencing decisions—measured both in terms of the probability of a death sentence and the level of race discrimination in the outcomes (Baldus *et al.* 2001b; Bowers, Steiner, and Sandys 2001). The flow of publications from the Capital Jury Project (CJP), which evaluate jury composition in rich detail, continues to expand this growing body of knowledge.

Potential Legal and Policy Implications of Findings

A motivation for both Marvin Wolfgang's research in the 1960s and the SHR-based research in the late 1970s and early 1980s was to support judicial claims alleging systemic racial discrimination in the administration of the death

---

criminal culpability of the cases was accurately coded. However if the coding of the white victim cases is biased upward, the white victim cases will be viewed in the quantitative analysis as being more culpable than the black victim cases. If in the system under review the criminal culpability of the defendants influences charging decisions, the biased culpability of the white victim cases would likely explain away or reduce and thereby bias the magnitude of the adjusted white victim disparity.

14. *Batson v. Kentucky* (1986) (prosecutors); *Georgia v. McCollum* (1992) (defense counsel).

penalty under the Eighth and Fourteenth Amendments. In each instance, the research was rejected by federal courts on methodological grounds, such as the omission from the database of all death-eligible cases in the defendant's county (*Maxwell v. Bishop* 1968:144, 147–49) and inadequate controls for non-racial factors bearing on defendant death eligibility and culpability (Baldus *et al.* 1990:309). Those decisions motivated the development of more extensive studies with hundreds of variables for non-racial case characteristics of the type that evolved in the 1980s and were used in *McCleskey v. Kemp* (1987) (Baldus *et al.*1990; Nakell and Hardy 1987). However, because *McCleskey* ruled that statewide statistically based claims of systemic race discrimination are not actionable under the Eighth and Fourteenth Amendments, a major judicial forum for the use of such evidence has been foreclosed for the foreseeable future.[15]

Potential consumers of the results of capital charging and sentencing studies now include state courts that recognize the relevance of statistically based claims of discrimination under state law, legislatures, and government-appointed advisory bodies that consider the issues relevant to the legality and legitimacy of their death penalty systems. Several such bodies have supported extensive studies. A good example is the long-term empirical research project sustained by the New Jersey Supreme Court since 1989.[16] In the early 1990s, the Racial and Ethnic Bias Study Commission of the Florida Supreme Court supported a study of the Florida system (Radelet and Pierce 1991). The Nebraska legislature funded a study of its system in 2002 (Baldus *et al.* 2002). The Governors of Maryland and Illinois recently funded studies of their respective

---

15. Professor Anthony Amsterdam believes that statewide studies like the *McCleskey* Georgia research may lay the foundation for successful federal and state claims in southern states with long histories of discrimination if they focus on black defendant/white victim cases prosecuted in jurisdictions with substantial racial disparities across the entire criminal justice system and "a legacy of racial bias embedded in the local institutions and ways of life that process and surround capital prosecutions." The goal of this litigation is to link the statewide and local evidence of race discrimination in a manner that will convince courts that race pervades the process and that the only appropriate relief is invalidation of the death penalty statute "leaving legislatures to enact new ones that restrict capital punishment to a narrower class of offenses and regulate the sentencing process more tightly..." (Amsterdam Forthcoming).

16. *Proportionality Review Project (II)* (2000:172) ("The court perseveres with the difficult methodological issues presented by the empirical research it supports because we know of no other means by which the relationship, if any, between race and the death penalty system in New Jersey may be reviewed. The importance of understanding whether racial discrimination infects our system of capital punishment requires that we make this effort.").

states' death-penalty systems (Paternoster *et al.* 2004; Pierce and Radelet 2002). The recently completed study of the federal death penalty system during the Clinton administration was funded by the National Institute of Justice at the urging of the Senate Judiciary Committee (Klein, Berk, and Hickman 2006). Public defenders and advisory commissions have also supported capital charging and sentencing studies with the hope of influencing state legislation (such as moratoria on executions and possible abolition) and judicial decision making (Baldus *et al.* 1998).

The Direction of Future Research

We have learned much over the past 25 years. We learned from the New Jersey Supreme Court the importance of institutionalizing within government the systematic collection of data on all homicides in a state, a task that no other entity could manage. In the absence of a reliable database, state courts have no capacity to evaluate claims of arbitrariness and discrimination in their capital sentencing systems. New Jersey has also taught us the importance of state supreme courts monitoring their own systems. That experience indicates that government-sponsored and especially court-sponsored research gives legitimacy not only to the research but also to the claims of death-sentenced offenders who rely on those research findings. Experience suggests that litigant claims are more likely to be treated seriously when the court is vested in the database, as is the New Jersey court.[17] To the extent that state courts are reluctant to undertake such research because of the financial cost, foundations with interests in these issues may be an important source of support.

The record of gubernatorial support for research in Illinois and Maryland provides helpful precedent for additional research, as has legislative support in Congress and Nebraska. Concerns about the cost of *McCleskey*-style studies suggest the utility of SHR-based pilot studies to determine the need for more extensive studies. The continuing ABA Moratorium Evaluation Project, which has focused thus far on SHR work (Pierce *et al.* 2006, 2007a, 2007b, and 2007c), may lead to *McCleskey*-style studies in states if there is sufficient concern about the current systems to marshal the resources and cooperation of courts and state agencies to undertake more detailed research.

---

17. The experience in New Jersey also indicates that conscientious judges are capable of handling the methodological issues that arise in the course of such research (*Proportionality Review Project* 1999).

In the conduct of capital charging and sentencing studies, we perceive a need for the introduction into the core statistical analytical models of variables that reflect the potential effect of the social context on how homicide cases are investigated and move forward through the criminal justices system (*e.g.*, the amount of publicity surrounding each case, the proximity of the prosecution to closely contested county prosecutor elections, and whether there were racial tensions in the community at the time of the prosecution). The research completed by Songer and Unah (2006:178–82) is a good step in this direction. There is also a need for introducing into analyses organizational variables that focus on how death-eligible cases are investigated and prosecuted (*e.g.*, the record of the prosecutor's office in seeking death sentences and the quality of the public defender's office and the local police department).

Empirical studies have traditionally focused on charging and death sentencing disparities in different areas of a state, such as broadly defined regions, although the moral and legal implications of those disparities are not well understood. Recent studies in Maryland and New Jersey highlight the importance of focusing on smaller organizational units within states, such as counties and individual prosecutors. We need to concentrate more on how the magnitude of the racial and SES disparities vary among different parts of the state ("interactions" in statistical parlance) and the most plausible explanations for those variations.

A related and useful research case-control design would focus on distinctions between otherwise comparable local jurisdictions *in different states* in which adjusted race effects are documented and those in which they are not. This strategy focuses attention on legal, institutional and social circumstances that account for the observed differences among the different jurisdictions. For example, a recent Georgia study revealed no race effects in prosecutorial charging decisions in Fulton and DeKalb county (the Atlanta urban area) (Paternoster 2007:15), whereas studies of Baltimore (Paternoster 2004a:19–24) and Chicago (Pierce and Radelet 2002) have found robust race of victim effects in the surrounding collar counties of these two urban centers. These findings suggest the importance of identifying the circumstances that explain the differential racial disparities documented in these systems.

Another direction with promise is an exploration of the interface between the findings of *McCleskey*-style studies within individual states and the findings of studies based on in depth juror interviews of the type developed by the Capital Jury Project. While the *McCleskey*-style research traces the effects of race at successive stages in the processing of capital cases, the CJP style research gives a "close-up" of how race figures in the critical final stage of the process. Joining the two styles of research in a state would considerably deepen courts' and policymakers' understanding of racial bias in death sentencing in their state and may shed light on how the law may reduce race effects in the system. In addition, the statistical finding from a *McCleskey*-style study may help inform and shape the content of the interview schedules used for the juror interviews in CJP studies. Similarly, the results of juror interviews may inform the construction of the data collection instruments used in *McCleskey*-style studies.

Finally, we clearly perceive a need for research to identify the mechanisms that produce the patterns of arbitrariness and discrimination that are not explained by legally relevant factors. We also need research that will build a model of the causes of these outcomes beyond the case-specific factors that are associated with arbitrariness and discrimination. More specifically, what is it about the broader proximate social context that produces or contributes in a systematic way to these disparities? Possible explanations include race-related conditions such as poverty and urbanization, lack of electoral competition, predominantly black populations, or, as in Maryland, the presence of neighboring counties with and without high proportions of blacks. In this tradition of research, we need to focus on the systemic social conditions that contribute to such arbitrariness and discrimination, apart from the characteristics of cases and defendants, as well as on the intermediary processes that link decision makers and the decisions they make to the broader contributing context. An examination of county-level SHR data, supplemented with available data on death row admissions by county could serve as a valuable step on this path.

References

Amsterdam, Anthony G. Forthcoming. "Opening Remarks to Symposium, Pursuing Racial Fairness in the Administration of Justice: Twenty Years After *McCleskey v. Kemp*." *Columbia Human Rights Law Review*.

Baldus, David and George Woodworth. 2004. "Race Discrimination and the Legitimacy of Capital Punishment: Reflections on the Interaction of Fact and Perception." *DePaul Law Review* 53:1411–96.

_____. 2003. "Race Discrimination in the Administration of the Death Penalty: An Overview of the Empirical Evidence with Special Emphasis on the Post-1990 Research." *Criminal Law Bulletin* 39:194–226.

_____. 2001a. *Race-of-Victim and Race-of-Defendant Disparities in the Administration of Maryland's Capital Charging and Sentencing System 1978–1999: Preliminary Findings* (unpublished manuscript on file with the authors).

_____. 2001b. "The Use of Peremptory Challenges in Capital Murder Trials: A Legal and Empirical Analysis." *University of Pennsylvania Journal of Constitutional Law* 3:3–169.

Baldus, David, George Woodworth and Catherine Grosso. 2002. "Arbitrariness and Discrimination in the Administration of the Death Penalty: A Legal and Empirical Analysis of the Nebraska Experience (1973–1999)." *Nebraska Law Review* 81:486–756.

Baldus, David, George Woodworth, and Charles Pulaski, Jr. 1990. *Equal Justice and the Death Penalty: A Legal and Empirical Analysis*. Boston, MA: Northeastern University Press.

Baldus, David, George Woodworth, David Zuckerman, Neil Alan Weiner, and Barbara Broffitt. 1998. "Racial Discrimination and the Death Penalty in the Post-*Furman* Era: An Empirical and Legal Overview, With Recent Findings from Philadelphia." *Cornell Law Review* 83:1638–1770.

Batson v. Kentucky (1986). 476 U.S. 79.

Belmontes v. *Brown* (2005). 414 F. 3d 1094 (9th Cir.).

Blume, John, Theodore Eisenberg, and Martin T. Wells. 2004. "Explaining Death Row's Population and Racial Composition." *Journal of Empirical Legal Studies* 1:165–207.

Bohm, Robert. 1994. "Capital Punishment in Two Judicial Circuits in Georgia." *Law and Human Behavior* 18:319–338.

Bowers, William and Glenn Pierce. 1980. "Arbitrariness and Discrimination Under Post-*Furman* Capital Statutes." *Crime and Delinquency* 26:563–632.

Bowers, William, Marla Sandys, and Thomas Brewer. 2004. "Crossing Racial Boundaries: A Closer Look at the Roots of Racial Bias in Capital Sentencing When the Defendant is Black and the Victim is White." *DePaul Law Review* 53:1497–1538.

Bowers, William, Benjamin Steiner, and Marla Sandys. 2001. "Death Sentencing in Black and White: An Empirical Analysis of the Role of Jurors' Race and Jury Racial Composition." *University of Pennsylvania Journal of Constitutional Law* 3:171–274.

Bright, Stephen. 1995. "Discrimination, Death and Denial: The Tolerance of Racial Discrimination in the Infliction of the Death Penalty." *Santa Clara Law Review* 35:433–483.

Eberhardt, Jennifer, Paul Davies, Valerie Purdie-Vaughns, and Sheri Lynn Johnson. 2006. "Looking Deathworthy: Perceived Stereotypicality of Black Defendants Predicts Capital-Sentencing Outcomes." *Psychological Science* 17:383–386.

Eisenberg, Theodore and Sheri Lynn Johnson. 2004. "Implicit Racial Attitudes of Death Penalty Lawyers." *DePaul Law Review* 53:1539–1556.

Georgia v. McCollum (1992). 505 U.S. 42.

Gross, Samuel, and Robert Mauro. 1989. *Death and Discrimination: Racial Disparities in Capital Sentencing.* Boston, MA: Northeastern University Press.

Haney, Craig. 2004. "Condemning the Other in Death Penalty Trials: Biographical Racism, Structural Mitigation, and the Empathic Divide." *DePaul Law Review* 53:1557–1589.

Hindson, Stephanie, Hillary Potter, and Michael Radelet. 2006. "Race, Gender, Region, and Death Sentencing in Colorado, 1980–1999." *University of Colorado Law Review* 77:549–594.

Klein, Stephen, Richard Berk, and Laura Hickman. 2006. "Race and the Decision to Seek the Death Penalty in Federal Cases." Rand Corporation Technical Report.

Maxfield, Michael. 1989. "Circumstances in Supplementary Homicide Reports: Variety and Validity." *Criminology* 27:671–695.

Maxwell v. Bishop (1968). 398 F.2d 138 (8th Cir.).

McCleskey v. Kemp (1987). 481 U.S. 279.

McNally, Kevin. 2004. "Race and the Federal Death Penalty: A Nonexistent Problem Gets Worse." *DePaul Law Review* 53:1615–46.

Nakell, Barry, and Kenneth Hardy. 1987. *The Arbitrariness of the Death Penalty.* Philadelphia, PA: Temple University Press.

Paternoster, Raymond. 2007. *The Death Penalty in Georgia 1995–2004.* (http:alt.coxnewsweb.com/ajc/deathpenalty/finalreport.doc).

Paternoster, Raymond. 2004a. *The Administration of the Death Penalty in Baltimore City, Maryland 1978–1999* (unpublished manuscript).

Paternoster, Raymond, Robert Brame, Sarah Bacon and Andrew Ditchfield. 2004. "Justice by Geography and Race: The Administration of the Death Penalty in Maryland, 1978–1999." *Margins: The University of Maryland Law Journal of Race, Religion, Gender, and Class* 4:1–99.

Pierce, Glenn and Michael Radelet. 2007. "Monitoring Death Sentencing Decisions: The Challenges and Barriers to Equity." *American Bar Association Human Rights Magazine* 34:2–4;24.

_____. 2005. "The Impact of Legally Inappropriate Factors on Death Sentencing for California Homicides, 1990–1999." *Santa Clara Law Review* 46:1–47.

_____. 2002. "Race, Region, and Death-Sentencing in Illinois." *Oregon Law Review* 81:39–96.

Pierce, Glenn, Michael Radelet, and Raymond Paternoster. 2007a. "Race and the Death Penalty in Indiana, 1981–2000" in "American Bar Association, Evaluating Fairness and Accuracy in State Death Penalty Systems: The Indiana

Death Penalty Assessment Report," Appendix at pp. 366–398 (A-GG). (http://www.abanet.org/moratorium/assessmentproject/indiana/report.pdf).

_____. 2007b. "Race and Death Sentencing in Tennessee, 1981–2000" in "American Bar Association, Evaluating Fairness and Accuracy in State Death Penalty Systems: The Tennessee Death Penalty Assessment Report," Appendix A at pp. 384–422. (http://www.abanet.org/moratorium/assessmentproject/tennessee/finalreport.pdf).

_____. 2007c. "Racial and Geographic Disparities in Death Sentencing in Ohio, 1981–2000" in "American Bar Association, Evaluating Fairness and Accuracy in State Death Penalty Systems: The Ohio Death Penalty Assessment Report," Appendix A. (http://www.abanet.org/moratorium/assessmentproject /ohio/finalreport.pdf).

_____. 2006. "Race and the Death Penalty in Georgia, 1989–1998" in "American Bar Association, Evaluating Fairness and Accuracy in State Death Penalty Systems: The Georgia Death Penalty Assessment Report," Appendix at pp. 324–350 (A-Y). (http://www.abanet.org/moratorium/assessmentproject/georgia/report.pdf).

Proportionality Review Project. 1999. 735 A.2d 528 (N.J.).

Proportionality Review Project (II). 2000. 757 A.2d 168 (N.J.).

Radelet, Michael and Glenn Pierce. 1991. "Choosing Those Who Will Die: Race and the Death Penalty in Florida." *Florida Law Review* 43:1–34.

_____. 1985. "Race and Prosecutorial Discretion in Homicide Cases." *Law and Society Review* 19:587–621.

Songer, Michael and Isaac Unah. 2006. "The Effect of Race, Gender, and Location on the Prosecutorial Decision to Seek the Death Penalty in South Carolina." *South Carolina Law Review* 58:161–209.

Sorensen, Jonathan and Donald Wallace. 1995. "Capital Punishment in Missouri: Examining the Issue of Racial Disparity." *Behavioral Sciences and the Law* 13:61–80.

Thompson, Ernie. 1997. "Discrimination and the Death Penalty in Arizona." *Criminal Justice Review* 22:65–76.

United States Department of Justice, Federal Bureau of Investigation, "Uniform Crime Reporting Program Data: Supplementary Homicide Reports, 2004 (Codebook)."

United States Department of Justice, Federal Bureau of Investigation. UNIFORM CRIME REPORTING PROGRAM DATA [UNITED STATES]: SUPPLEMENTARY HOMICIDE REPORTS, 2004 [Computer file]. Compiled by the U.S. Dept. of Justice, Federal Bureau of Investigation. ICPSR04465-v1. Ann Arbor, MI: Inter-university Consortium for Political and Social Research [producer and distributor], 2006-08-18. (http://www.icpsr.umich.edu/cocoon/ICPSR/STUDY/04465.xml).

Williams, Marian and Jefferson Holcomb. 2001. "Racial Disparity and Death Sentences in Ohio." *Journal of Criminal Justice* 29:207–218.

Wolfgang, Marvin and Marc Riedel. 1976. "Rape, Racial Discrimination and the Death Penalty in Georgia." Pp. 99–121 in *Capital Punishment in the United States*, edited by Hugo Bedau and Chester Pierce. New York, NY: AM Press.

CHAPTER 9

Empirical Studies of Race and Geographic Discrimination in the Administration of the Death Penalty: A Primer on the Key Methodological Issues

David Baldus, George Woodworth, David Zuckerman, Neil Alan Weiner and Catherine M. Gross

Introduction

This chapter focuses on the key methodological issues in the conduct of empirical studies of race and geographic discrimination in the administration of the death penalty in the United States. There is an extensive literature on the impact of race on prosecutorial charging and jury death sentencing decisions in capital cases since *Furman v. Georgia* (1972).[1] These studies assess the extent

---

1. Baldus, Woodworth, and Pulaski (1990:228–65) summarizes the pre-1990 studies. Studies between 1990 and 2003 include those collected in Baldus and Woodworth (2003:215–26) and Thompson (1997—Arizona); Sorensen and Wallace (1995—Missouri); Bohm (1994—Georgia); and Williams and Holcomb (2001—Ohio). Empirical studies of capital charging and sentencing systems since 2003 include Paternoster *et al.* (2004—Maryland); Pierce, Radelet, and Paternoster (2007—Tennessee); Pierce and Radelet (2005—California); (Pierce, Radelet, and Paternoster 2006—Georgia), Songer and Unah (2006—

to which a death sentencing system is characterized by systemic race discrimination that cannot be plausibly explained by the influence of legitimate non-racial case characteristics.[2] Investigators have also focused on the impact of geography on death sentencing outcomes (Paternoster *et al.* 2004; Songer and Unah 2006).[3] These studies assess the extent to which county and regional disparities in charging and sentencing outcomes are the product of variations in non-racial case characteristics that bear on offender criminal culpability or reflect different prosecutorial charging policies and practices among similarly situated cases; they also assess determinants of the identified disparities. This chapter provides guidance for investigators and funding agencies contemplating the conduct and support of such studies, and for consumers of the results of the studies (*e.g.*, students, scholars, interested public officials, and the general public). One theme of the chapter is that the resolution of methodological issues in this body of research should be guided first by *legally based considerations* of relevance and evidentiary requirements for inferences of systemic discrimination, and second, by generally accepted *statistical* practices.[4] Another theme is that when the appropriate methodological choice is not clearly dictated by legal or statistical considerations, prudence calls for the conduct of plausible alternative analyses, followed by an analysis of the convergence and stability of the substantive results. This convergence/stability approach has particular appeal when one of the methodological alternatives will materially reduce the sample size and, consequently, the power of the analysis.

The empirical literature on post-*Furman* capital charging and sentencing reflects two basic approaches, which we outline in chapter 8. The first, the *Supplemental Homicide Report* (SHR) approach, uses an existing database main-

---

South Carolina); Eberhardt *et al.* (2006 — Philadelphia County); Hindson, Potter, and Radelet (2006 — Colorado); McNally (2004 — federal death penalty); Klein, Berk, and Hickman (2006 — federal death penalty), and Blume, Eisenberg, and Wells (2004 — multi state evidence). Post-2003 studies of the determinants of race discrimination in post-*Furman* capital charging and sentencing are reported in Baldus and Woodworth (2004); Bowers, Sandys, and Brewer (2004); Eisenberg and Johnson (2004); and Haney (2004).

2. Purposeful race discrimination in this setting is prohibited by the Eighth and Fourteenth Amendments of the United States Constitution.

3. Although geographic discrimination currently does not implicate the Constitution, in the minds of many it has significant fairness implications.

4. This principle has been well stated in the context of the proportionality review of death sentences by New Jersey Special Master for Proportionality Review, David S. Baime: "When statistics enter the courtroom, the law must remain king. Legal principles must thus determine what statistical models are appropriate, what questions should be asked of the data and what inferences the statistical analyses ultimately yield. Having said this, our studies must be guided by reliable statistical methodology" (Baime 2005:8).

tained by the Federal Bureau of Investigation (FBI). This database contains the following information for each reported homicide "incident": (a) background information on the month, year, and county of the offense; and (b) the age, sex, race, and ethnicity of the victims and offenders, when they are known. The second basic approach to capital charging and sentencing studies is exemplified by the Georgia research presented in *McCleskey* v. *Kemp* (1987) (Baldus, Woodworth, and Pulaski 1990) ("*McCleskey*-style studies"). The distinguishing features of *McCleskey*-style studies as they have evolved over the past 25 years are: (a) a sample of cases from a specific jurisdiction that is limited to death-eligible murder cases; (b) comprehensive and detailed information on the presence of both statutory and non-statutory aggravating and mitigating non-racial case characteristics which, under the law of the jurisdiction, bear on the defendant's criminal culpability; (c) procedural detail on start-to-finish decision making in each case that facilitates describing and then statistically modeling the flow of cases through the system; (d) the inclusion in the sample of all penalty trial cases, which embrace all death sentenced cases; (e) variables for the race and socioeconomic status (SES) of all defendants and victims; (f) to the extent possible, reliance on primary source materials such as case files and court records; and (g) mixed methods (qualitative—case study/narratives and quantitative—aggregate/structural) for documenting systemic race and geographic disparities. Nearly all of the issues which we consider in this chapter apply both to studies based on the FBI's Supplemental Homicide Report (SHR) and to *McCleskey*-style longitudinal studies. We note in the margin the issues that are unique to the latter.[5]

The Research Team

The research team should include individuals with a variety of skills and expertise. Like all other parts of a project, these issues may be heavily influenced by the resources available to support the research. The first *sine qua non* is detailed knowledge of the substantive law and procedure as it is applied in the system to be studied. This expertise will inform the identification of the procedural stages in the decision-making process in the jurisdiction, the creation of measures of offender criminal culpability, and the creation of the data collection instrument and a quality assurance protocol when the data for the study go beyond the SHR database. A second requirement in *McCleskey*-style studies is

---

5. Two sections in this chapter address issues that are unique to *McCleskey*-style studies—sampling issues and screening cases for death eligibility.

expertise in research design, especially with respect to sampling methods. Sampling expertise is particularly important in *McCleskey*-style studies if the project contemplates the possibility of endogenously or exogenously stratified sampling methods.

A third essential requirement for *McCleskey*-style studies is access to the primary data sources required for the study, such as prison records, police reports, judicial opinions and appellate briefs. Ideally, data will be available on: (a) charging, conviction, and sentencing outcomes; (b) statutory aggravating and mitigating circumstances; (c) a wide array of non-statutory aggravating and mitigating circumstances; and (d) the race and socioeconomic status of the defendant and victim. Prudent planning will take into account how a lack of data in any of these categories may impair the validity and credibility of the final results. The fourth requirement is expertise in data entry, management, and statistical analysis. Fifth, projects require expertise in the interpretation of both the quantitative and qualitative (case review) results of the research. The final skill is the ability to present the findings in a manner that is accessible to judges, policy makers, lawyers, and informed lay readers, as well as to statisticians and social scientists.[6]

Research Design Issues

For *McCleskey*-style studies, the time frame and scope (*e.g.*, statewide or countywide) of the study are materially shaped by resources and the availability of data. Currency of the sample is a virtue for any study, as evidence of disparities from earlier times is often legally discounted as stale or irrelevant. Also, the inclusion of current death row inmates at risk of execution in the sample may be an important consideration because it underscores the stakes that are at play in death penalty research and the litigation informed by it.

Given the uncertainties concerning data availability and the likely substantive results of *McCleskey*-style studies, a pilot study is always worth considering. The principal *McCleskey* study was preceded by two statewide pilot studies—one limited to appellate court records and one limited to cases that resulted in murder trial convictions (Baldus *et al.* 1990:42–44). The design of the Pater-

---

6. Justice O'Hern of the New Jersey Supreme Court has noted the danger in the use of statistics to assess issues of proportionality, of permitting "technical debate to obscure substantive meaning. Our task is to ensure that technical problems with issues such as confidence intervals, model convergence, and more (or less) parsimonious models, be translated into an understandable legal format that we and the parties can apply" (*Proportionality Review Project* 1999:543–44).

noster-Brame study in Maryland was informed in part by the results of a statewide pilot study that was limited to cases in which the government had filed notice of its intent to seek death and contained no information on offender culpability beyond the statutory aggravators stated in the government's notice of that intention (Baldus and Woodworth 2001). Another useful pilot for a more detailed study, whether statewide or in selected counties, is an SHR study. These studies are helpful because they expose early in the analyses strengths and weaknesses of the data and can yield early signals of legally impermissible disparities.

A pilot study conducted in a small number of representative counties may provide useful guidance on the potential utility of a broader study. In this regard, it may also be useful to concentrate scarce resources on counties with substantial numbers of death sentences imposed. Here again a SHR pilot study may be very helpful.

The Unit of Analysis

The first issue is whether the unit of analysis should be homicide defendants or victims.[7] Since the focus of criminal prosecutions is individual defendants, there is consensus that each defendant/offender should define a separate case regardless of the number of victims. This also means that a single murder with co-perpetrators will produce a separate case for each defendant. It does not imply, however, that multiple defendants tried before the same jury are treated as statistically independent.

A more difficult issue concerns the treatment of prosecutions that follow a judicial guilt trial reversal or sentence vacation in a case that originally resulted in a death sentence.[8] Given the high reversal rates in some jurisdictions, a significant number of additional prosecutions could be added to the analysis. The issue is when and how to include subsequent prosecutions in specific analyses.

---

7. The SHR database contains "offender" and "victim" files. The former provides the foundation for an offender-focused file.

8. When a defendant is convicted in separate prosecutions of more than one murder committed at different times in *completely unrelated incidents*, the inclusion of both cases in the analysis does not per se raise independence issues. However, the presumption of independence may be drawn into question if the cases are prosecuted in the same jurisdiction, especially if by the same prosecutor, or the prosecutions occur close in time. When such circumstances raise serious concerns about the independence of the second charging decision, the second prosecution should be treated as a subsequent prosecution in the same case. The New Jersey Master for Proportionality Review appears to follow a per se rule of including only the first case, which is certainly safe (Proportionality Review Project (II) 2000:176).

The concern is whether the decisions that drive subsequent prosecutions are "independent," because decisions in the first prosecution may influence decisions in subsequent prosecutions even though the key underlying facts of the case remain the same. There is a substantial risk in this regard with respect to prosecutorial decision making because discretionary judgments made in the earlier case may simply be repeated in the later case(s). In such situations, current expert statistical practice is shifting to the use of hierarchical models that handle "multiple levels of randomness" (Carlin and Louis 2000). Software currently available for implementing such analyses in logistic regression requires high levels of statistical expertise, and requires Bayesian statistical inference, which has not yet been widely tested in social science research or litigation.[9] Investigators should seek the advice of a skilled statistician on these issues.

Because of the complexity of these issues, we recommend three technically simple alternatives with an evaluation of the consistency of the results produced in each analysis. The first alternative is to limit the analysis of prosecutorial decision making to the first prosecution. The second alternative, which also avoids the independence problem, is to limit the analysis to the most recent prosecution.[10] The third alternative includes all successive prosecutions in the analysis, with each case coded to reflect its status as an initial or subsequent prosecution.[11] These codes reduce but do not eliminate the risk of bias in estimated race disparities that may flow from the inclusion of subsequent prosecutions in an analysis. We recommend the same approach in the analysis of death sentencing outcomes among all death-eligible cases.[12]

---

9. While 12% of statistics journal articles and 2.6% of business, economic, and finance articles archived in JSTOR (a large archive of scholarly publications) over the last 10 years included the word "Bayesian," only 0.16% of peer reviewed law articles, 0.22% of sociology articles, and 0.28% of political science articles did so. A LEXIS search of federal district court cases over the same period of time found only 12 containing the word "Bayesian" but over 1000 containing the phrase "statistically significant," which is a non-Bayesian statistical concept. See Woodworth (2004) for an introduction to Bayesian analysis in biostatistics.

10. The New Jersey special master adopted the "first" and "last" prosecution alternatives (Baime 2005:9). Another alternative is to randomly select one case from each set of multiple prosecution cases and assess the extent to which the disparities estimated in that analysis are stable and comparable to those estimated with alternative populations of successive population cases.

11. This information can be carried in two subsequent prosecution variables, say D1 and D2. Single prosecution cases will be coded "0" for both variables. For the second prosecution, D1 is coded "1" and D2 is coded "0." For the third or more prosecution both D1 and D2 are coded "1."

12. The reason is that these outcomes also reflect the prosecutorial decisions that may not be independent.

Two important issues arise regarding death sentencing outcomes. First, multiple victim cases may result in multiple death sentences imposed for different victims in the same case. Courts view such cases as single death-sentenced cases (Proportionality Review Project (II) 2000). Moreover, serious concerns exist about the statistical independence of multiple death sentences imposed in a single case. In a given prosecution, therefore, each death-sentenced case should be limited to a single death sentence no matter how many are imposed. However, if a multiple victim case results in separate prosecutions for different victims, each prosecution should be treated as a separate case. Moreover, if a defendant is prosecuted and tried for homicides that occurred in different incidents at different times, each homicide should be treated as a different case.

Second, in studies with sufficient data to model penalty trial outcomes, an independence issue arises with respect to the inclusion of subsequent penalty trial sentencing decisions in the analysis. In contrast to prosecutorial decision making, subsequent penalty trial decisions are reasonably treated as independent of previous decisions unless there is evidence that a subsequent jury was told that the defendant had earlier been sentenced to death. However, if a subsequent prosecution advances to a bench trial, the judge would be aware of the earlier decision, suggesting that such a case should be treated like a subsequent prosecutorial charging decision and coded accordingly. A statistician should be consulted in such cases for advice on the current state of the art.

Defining the Universe

SHR-Based Studies

A SHR-based study requires the identification of two populations—a broad population of murder and non-negligent homicides reported to the FBI, and a smaller population of cases within that larger pool that were capitally charged and/or sentenced to death.[13] Each population must be assembled from separate datasets and then the second, narrower population has to be matched to the first. There appears to be a consensus on the exclusion from the broad population of offender/suspects who (a) were not apprehended[14] or (b) because of their age, were not death eligible under state law or the Constitution. In addition, some investigators have incorrectly deleted cases for which there is missing data on relevant case characteristics, such as race or aggravating

---

13. The SHR database includes other homicides, such as negligent homicides, but they are always excluded from the analysis.
14. The proxy for this circumstance is missing race and sex data for the offender.

circumstances. Unless there are massive amounts of missing information on important variables, missing information can be handled either by adding a dummy (1 or 0) variable to indicate a missing value for the substantive variable in question, or by some form of imputation using collateral information (Allison 2001; Little and Rubin 2002; Schafer and Graham 2002. *See, e.g.*, Baldus *et al.* 2001:136–61 (imputation of venire member and juror race, gender, and age in a study of peremptory strikes in capital cases)).

The second step in the process requires identifying within the broader SHR universe a smaller population of cases that have been capitally charged and/or death sentenced. This requires the identification and collection of information on the cases that actually sustained these outcomes so they can be matched to the unnamed cases in the SHR database on the basis of one or more variables in it. The question is how closely the facts of a known capitally charged or death-sentenced case must match a case in the broader SHR database to qualify for inclusion in the final substantive analysis. Current practice varies on this issue, with some studies matching only on the core variables of geography, race, and ethnicity of the defendant. This approach normally brings all but a handful of the known death-sentenced cases into the analysis (Pierce and Radelet 2005:13–14). However, it has been reported that when the investigators match on a substantial number of SHR variables, say up to nine, the number of cases known to have been capitally charged or death sentenced that are brought into the analysis can be reduced by 25% to 33% (Radelet and Pierce 1985:596–97; Songer and Unah 2006:186).[15] Resources permitting, we recommend the use of alternative matching approaches, from deep to shallow, with comparisons made of the resulting racial and geographic disparities to ascertain whether they are sensitive to the different matching rules.

McCleskey-*Style Studies*

A good first step in defining the "universe" of cases for a *McCleskey*-style study is to secure a master list of homicide convictions that have been obtained during the time period of the study. Ideally, the master list should contain all homicide convictions from first degree murder through voluntary manslaughter because many death-eligible cases terminate in guilty pleas to voluntary manslaughter.[16] This population of cases or a stratified sample thereof is then

---

15. In this situation, in the absence of other information, it is reasonable to assume that the capitally charged and/or death-sentenced cases that enter the analysis are a random sample of the entire group of offenders who were capitally charged or death sentenced.

16. Experience demonstrates that death-eligible cases are rarely pled to involuntary manslaughter or less.

screened to identify the death-eligible cases (Baldus *et al.* 2002; Paternoster *et al.* 2004).[17]

If resource limitations require a sample of homicide cases rather than the entire universe, it is important to avoid the temptation of limiting the study to first-degree murder cases. Experience indicates that a large proportion of cases that result in second-degree murder and voluntary manslaughter plea bargains are death-eligible (Sorensen and Wallace 1995:66). The preferred alternative is to include in the universe all homicides through voluntary manslaughter and draw a manageable sample of both kinds of cases stratified, for example, by crime of conviction and the number of convictions in the county.

Master lists with procedural details for each case and all of its stages are essential for the development of a stratified sampling plan because stratified sampling rates may vary for cases depending on the crime of conviction and the sentence imposed. Some state supreme courts maintain such records, as do most state prisons. Local courts also may have such lists and public defenders often maintain them. Because these lists frequently are not a matter of public record, a formal application for access may be required. Reported state appellate court opinions are another common source for the construction of such lists.

Sampling Issues

Sampling issues arise in *McCleskey*-style studies when the collection of data on the whole universe of death-eligible cases is unmanageable in light of available resources. When this issue materializes, a natural instinct is to randomly sample from the universe. However, this approach runs the risk of omitting from the final sample highly relevant cases with penalty trials resulting in life and death sentences. For example, if a study is used on behalf of a death-sentenced offender who had not been identified at the time the study was designed and conducted it may happen that the client's case is not included in the final sample. This is the *Maxwell v. Bishop* problem, in which all death-eligible cases

---

17. In a well-controlled study, the inclusion of cases that are not death-eligible does not threaten the validity of estimated race and geographic disparities because those estimates are based only on the information and outcomes of the death-eligible cases. Cases that lack death-eligibility are not comparable to the death-eligible cases in terms of the aggravating circumstances that define the similarly situated groups of cases that support the substantive analysis. As a result, they contribute nothing to the analysis. For this reason, a principle of economy calls for a limitation of the cases to those that are death-eligible.

from the defendant's county, including his own case, were omitted by chance from the sample because of random sampling (*Maxwell v. Bishop* 1968:144, 147–49).

The optimal strategy to handle this situation is a stratified random sampling design that includes all cases in the sample that advanced to a penalty trial, but is limited to samples of cases (possibly at different rates) among the death-eligible cases that: (a) were not capitally charged, or (b) were capitally charged but did not advance to a penalty trial. Stratification based on the size of each county may also be advisable, with 100% coverage of the very small counties, to avoid the risk of missing all or most of the cases from these counties and much lower proportionate coverage in the large, urbanized counties.

However, stratification comes at a cost. It requires access to data on the entire universe and procedural information on each case to determine whether a case qualifies for admission to the sample. Stratification also introduces technical complications into the analysis to compensate for "over sampling" parts of the universe. The analysis of stratified data requires the use of special procedures to estimate disparities and to compute the statistical significance of the estimated disparities.[18]

Another consideration is the acceptance in recent years of the argument that evidence of race effects in prosecutorial decisions is a matter of concern only when the analysis is limited to individual counties. Under this scenario, a sufficiently large sample of cases is needed in the most active death penalty counties to support reliable inferences of systemic discrimination at the county level.[19]

The Data Collection Instrument (DCI)/Codebook

The SHR data collection instrument/codebook is well designed. Although the non-racial variables are few in number, the large number of responses/foils for the key variables, such as the weapon, the defendant/victim relationship, contemporaneous offenses, and other circumstances provides many opportunities to create useful recoded variables that track both statutory aggravating factors in the jurisdiction's capital sentencing statute and important non-statutory aggravating and mitigating circumstances (Songer and Unah 2006).

---

18. Software such as SUDAAN (RTI International *undated*) is available but should be used under the guidance of a statistician or social scientist experienced in its use.

19. Here a SHR pilot study may be the optimal approach.

In the *McCleskey*-style studies, attention to detail in raw variable content and coding format is vital for the development of the recoded variables that are actually used in the statistical analysis.[20] The DCI in such studies additionally should include a detailed narrative summary of each case. These summaries are indispensable for validating the database throughout the process of analysis and for conducting qualitative analyses of the comparative culpability of death-eligible offenders. Many well developed DCIs are either in the public domain or available upon request from the investigators in earlier studies of Georgia (Baldus *et al.* 1990:Appendix E), Maryland (Paternoster *et al.* 2004), Philadelphia (Baldus *et al.* 1998), Nebraska (Baldus *et al.* 2002), and federal (Klein *et al.* 2006) death-penalty systems.

Data Collection, Coding, and Entry for Machine Analysis

The SHR database is available electronically. However, the additional data required for the capitally charged/death-sentenced database in an SHR study and for all of the variables in *McCleskey*-style studies are rarely available in electronic form. Moreover, when the data are available electronically, which they might be for a few procedural variables, they are often incomplete or inaccurate. This limitation often requires access to hard-copy records for the cases in order to correct the electronic database.

One commonly used source in SHR studies is trial court reports in cases that are charged capitally or result in death sentences. In some states, these reports are filed with the state supreme court, while in others, they are only available in the trial court. Additionally, sources used in *McCleskey*-style studies include the papers of the case in the trial court (available in county court houses throughout the state), appellate court case records (available in the state supreme court), probation reports (generally confidential documents requiring legislative or judicial authority to access), and files maintained by boards of pardons and paroles.

The race of the defendant may be included in prison data and police reports and we have successfully ascertained it from defendant and victim pho-

---

20. Very few of the variables in a typical DCI can be used without transformation through a "recoding" process into binary/dummy variables or counter variables such as the number of victims or the number of aggravating circumstances in the case. This also holds for the variables in the SHR database.

tographs contained in the papers of the case. Victim death certificates are also a good source of victim race and socioeconomic status (to the extent it can be deduced from the victim's occupation at the time of death).[21]

Statutory aggravating circumstances are often alleged in the prosecution's notice of its intent to seek death. However, even when they are included, independent verification is advisable, which requires access to data and detailed knowledge of the substantive law and procedure as applied in the jurisdiction under study. The inquiry should also strive to identify all aggravating and mitigating circumstances (both statutory and non-statutory) in each case. This can be a real challenge in cases that end in plea bargains.[22]

When access to hard copy files is available, it is prudent to copy the relevant portions of the case file to create a record that can later be used to validate or "clean" the data, to obtain information (later deemed relevant) that may not be contained in the data collection instrument, and to rebut challenges to the fidelity of the recorded data. When copying the relevant portions of the case files is not feasible and the coder can only access them for the time required to code them, a good substitute is the preparation of a detailed narrative summary that covers the procedural features of the case and the non-racial variables that bear on the offender's criminal culpability.

The data transcription or "coding" process, particularly in *McCleskey*-style studies, requires a good understanding of the decision making process, the substantive law defining death-eligibility, and the interpretation of individual statutory aggravating circumstances. For example, what facts support an inference that a case involved a "heinous, atrocious, and cruel" murder? A minimum of one year of law school or its equivalent is an essential coder qualification. In addition, preliminary training and close supervision are required along with the preparation and regular updating and documentation of a coding protocol on the coding issues that arise.

Coding has typically been executed in a hard copy data collection instrument. Currently in development are systems in which coders can access a web page for the project, access a blank, electronic DCI, and code the instrument electronically instead of in hard copy. This process avoids the additional data entry step that involves time, expense, and the introduction of data entry error

---

21. The SHR has good data here that can be used to fill in missing race of victim in *McCleskey*-style studies.

22. Another challenge in terms of modeling the exercise of prosecutorial discretion is to determine whether cases that advance to a guilt trial do so because no plea bargain was offered by the prosecution or the prosecution offered a plea bargain that was rejected by the defendant.

into the database. Electronic coding systems also enable validity checks to be conducted on the database as it develops, which allows the investigator to correct common coding errors early in the process.

Setting the Stage for Substantive Analysis

Screening Cases for Factual Death-Eligibility

In *McCleskey*-style studies, a crucial task is limiting the sample to cases that are factually death-eligible. This means that the facts of the cases could have supported a capital murder conviction and the finding of one or more statutory aggravating circumstances regardless of the actual outcome of the case. In cases that result in guilty pleas, the coder's assessment of factual death eligibility will be based on the facts of the case reported in the data sources. Cases that advance to a guilt trial, however, may present a complication. Because such cases involve a legally authoritative determination of facts, in either a bench or jury trial, we recommend the application of what has been called the controlling fact finding (CFF) rule. This rule provides that, in the absence of compelling evidence of jury nullification, where a judge or jury has made an authoritative finding of fact on a factual issue (concerning criminal liability or the presence or absence of aggravating circumstances), the coders must accept that finding and code accordingly.[23] It is essential, therefore, for the coders to have sufficient procedural information to determine whether the CFF rule applies to liability, and in cases that advance to a penalty trial, whether it applies to statutory aggravating circumstances.

Issues of jury nullification that would justify overriding a fact finder's decision rarely arise with respect to liability findings of less than capital murder, since those judgments generally turn on subtle mens rea issues that are hard to second guess. The situation is quite different, however, when the fact finder fails to find a statutory aggravating circumstance in the case when it is plainly present. This situation most commonly arises in armed robbery and multiple victim cases in which the fact finder, as an abbreviated method of voting for a life sentence, fails to find an aggravating circumstance that is clearly present in the case. Such determinations are based on deathworthiness judgments rather than findings of fact.

---

23. For example, if the defendant is charged with capital murder and the fact finder finds the defendant not guilty or guilty of only a lesser included noncapital crime, the case cannot be considered a "factually" death-eligible case in the absence of compelling evidence of jury nullification.

When a case is deemed to be not death-eligible as a result of the application of the CFF rule to an authoritative fact finding of liability for less than capital murder, it is properly excluded from any analysis of death sentencing outcomes. However, if on the basis of credible evidence, the prosecution viewed such a case as death-eligible, as evidenced by the advancement of the case to trial with the government seeking a death sentence, it would be appropriate to include the case in the sample of death-eligible cases that is used to model prosecutorial decision making.

Experience suggests that the death-eligibility (or not) of most cases is clear. However, for close cases, we recommend the solicitation of expert opinion from prosecutors and defense counsel (actual and/or retired) and retired judges (Paternoster *et al.* 2004).

Modeling the Stage-Wise Flow of Cases through the System

The first step in the process is to compute outcomes for death-eligible cases at successive charging and sentencing stages in the process, and overall among all death-eligible cases. The Paternoster-Brame Maryland study suggests the following for *McCleskey*-style studies:

1. Stage-wise models
   a. Prosecutorial decisions to serve notice of the state's intent to seek a death sentence in the case;
   b. Prosecutorial refusals to withdraw the notice of intent to seek a death sentence (thereby advancing the case to a guilt trial with the state seeking a death sentence); and
   c. Penalty trial life or death decisions.

2. Outcomes among all death-eligible cases that reflect the combined effects of multiple charging and/or sentencing decisions among all death-eligible cases:
   a. Death-eligible cases advanced to:
      (i) a capital guilt trial with the government seeking a death sentence;
      (ii) a penalty trial.[24]

---

24. The guilt trial outcomes are relevant but of less interest because they do not formally reflect a deathworthiness judgment. Moreover, defendants convicted of less than capital murder at trial are not properly considered death-eligible in the absence of overwhelming evidence of jury nullification.

b. Cases with death sentences imposed.[25]

Joint Legislative Audit (2002:17) provides another good example of the "funneling" of death-eligible cases through a system.

Typically, SHR-based studies have focused only on death sentencing outcomes. However, when data are available on prosecutorial decisions to seek death during the time period of the study, it is possible to model that decision as well (Songer and Unah 2006).

Unadjusted Race and Geographic Disparities

An important issue in this research concerns the distinction between the *practical* and *statistical* importance of race and geographic disparities. We believe that both are important because they address different aspects of the system. Measures of practical significance (effect size) focus on the magnitude of the harm to the protected group, while measures of statistical significance focus on the likelihood that documented disparities are the product of chance factors introduced through sampling or random shocks in the system that affect charging and sentencing outcomes.[26]

Another important distinction is between *unadjusted* and *adjusted* race and geographic disparities. Unadjusted disparities measure differential race- and geographic-based outcomes without regard to differences in the criminal culpability of the defendants. Adjusted disparities take into account and control for the impact of differences in the degree of criminal culpability of the defendants in the analysis as well as the county of prosecution.

Measures of Race and Ethnicity Disparities: The Basics

The Race and Ethnicity Measures

The first issue calls for the identification of the "protected" groups who may be adversely affected in a capital charging and sentencing system. Given the

---

25. Traditionally, the final outcome modeled has been the imposition of a death sentence. In jurisdictions with substantial numbers of executions, that outcome can also be usefully modeled (McAdams 2002:181).

26. Tests of statistical significance are also relevant if one views capital prosecutions within a given period (even if they include the universe of cases from a given period of time) as a sample of cases of the operation of the system over the long run.

uncertainty of the law and the literature, good practice calls for a justification of the race-based and ethnicity-based measures used in the analysis. For example, in most systems the concern is not about the risk of discrimination against "white" defendants but against "black" or "racial minority" defendants and "black defendants and racial minority defendants whose victims are white." The race variables should be coded in a manner that directly addresses those concerns.

In multiple victim cases, the most common approach is to classify the case as a white victim case if it has one or more white victims. The robustness of the results of this analysis can be tested to determine if the race of victim effect persists by deleting the cases with mixed race victims and comparing the substantive results with the results obtained when one or more white victim qualifies a case for a white victim classification.

Whichever racial categories are considered relevant in a jurisdiction, the analysis should focus on the impact of: (a) individual defendant and victim classifications, such as black or minority defendants and white or black victims; and (b) defendant/victim racial combinations, such as black/white, white/white, black/black, and white/black.[27] When "interaction terms" for defendant/victim racial combinations are included in a statistical analysis such as a logistic regression model, an important question concerns the identification of a "reference group" with whom the other racial subgroups are compared. For example, if theory, history, or unadjusted disparities in the data suggest the possibility of black defendant/white victim discrimination in the system, those cases are a good reference category because they will shed light on race of defendant effects (in contrast with the white defendant/white victim cases) and on the race of victim effects (in contrast with black defendant/black victim cases) (Paternoster *et al.* 2004:86).[28] Preliminary bivariate analyses may suggest other interaction terms, such as race by multiple victims or rural counties.

The use in a logistic regression model of separate main effect racial variables, such as "white victim" (WV) and "black defendant" (BD) calls for a

---

27. To facilitate comparisons with other studies, we recommend coding "1" for the group that the discrimination hypothesis posits will suffer a disparity in treatment. Thus, when used in dummy variables, white victim, minority/black defendant, and black defendant/white victim cases should be coded "1."

28. The reference category should have a reasonable sample size vis-a-vis the other comparison groups. This makes the white defendant/black victim a questionable reference category in most studies. In statistical parlance, one omits the "design variable" for the reference category. In this example, this means that the defendant/victim variable is omitted for the black defendant/white victim cases even though the black defendant/white victim cases are included in the analysis.

straightforward interpretation. The same holds for models limited to interaction terms, such as "WD/WV," "BD/BV," and "WD/BV," with "BD/WV" serving as the reference population.

However, models which mix main effect race variables and race-based interaction terms create risks of error in interpretation in the absence of a more complicated coding regime and interpretative strategy. Take, for example, a model with two main effect variables (BD and WV) and one race-based interaction term (BD x WV), with each variable coded as a 0/1 dummy variable (a "mixed measures of race" model). The results (odds ratios) produced in such analysis cannot be understood with the principles of interpretation that are applied to the results of models that are limited either to main effect race variables or multiple interaction terms with a reference population. In fact, the odds ratios in a mixed measures of race model like the above illustration are not interpretable. Moreover, because of the collinearity between the BD/WV variable and the main effect race variables, the standard errors of the coefficients for each race measure will be inflated upward ("variance inflation" in statistical parlance).

To avoid these problems, the interaction term in the model must be recoded in a manner that creates challenging issues of interpretation that call for consultation with someone who can deduce what the betas estimated in the resulting model actually represent.[29] In the example above, the proper recode for the interaction term is: BD x WV = (BD-0.5) * (WV-0.5), while the main effect variables for the BD and WV remain 0/1 dummies.[30] Now assume that

---

29. The "betas" estimated in a multiple regression analysis have two main features critical to explaining procedural outcomes: (1) their signs (valences) and (2) their magnitude. First, a beta's sign can be either positive or negative. A positive beta indicates that the variable to which it corresponds is related to a higher probability of a case moving ahead procedurally or resulting in a death sentence, as the case may be. Conversely, a negative beta is related to a reduced probability of a case's procedural advancement. Second, with regard to magnitude, a large beta implies a large influence on case advancement compared to a variable with a small beta. Of course, signs and magnitudes matter when other relevant issues are considered, such as statistical significance and substantive relevance. Betas estimated in a logistic regression analysis are difficult to interpret. For that reason we recommend principal reliance on odds multipliers/ratios computed from the betas and estimates of the impact of an independent variable on the estimated probabilities of the outcome of interest (Roncek 1991). See infra notes 36 and 37 and accompanying text.

30. The coding shown in the text ensures that the antilog of the interaction beta is the WV odds ratio in black victim cases divided by the WV odds ratio in non-black victim cases (or vice versa), the antilog of the BD beta is the geometric average of the BD odds ratio in WV cases and the BD odds ratio in non-WV cases, and the antilog of the WV beta is the geometric average of the WV odds ratio in BD cases and the WV odds ratio in non-BD cases.

with this new coding in place, the model produced the following odds ratios: BD (1.4), WV (1.5), and BD x WV (2.0). The BD odds ratio is the geometric mean/average of: (a) the BD odds ratio among the white victim cases; and (b) the BD odds ratio among the non-white victim cases, and the WV odds ratio has an analogous interpretation.

The antilog of the interaction logistic regression coefficient (BD x WV) has two interpretations: it is simultaneously (a) the ratio of the WV odds ratios among the black- and non-black defendant cases; and (b) the ratio of the BD odds ratios among the white- and non-white victim cases. Thus, if the interaction logistic regression coefficient is 0.00 (and its antilog is 1.00), then: (a) the white victim variable has the same odds ratio among the black- and non-black defendant cases; and (b) the black defendant variable has the same odds ratio among the white- and non-white victim cases.

Returning to the hypothetical with which we commenced this analysis, the (geometric) average BD odds ratio is 1.4; however the BD odds ratio is twice as large among the WV cases as it is among the non-WV cases. Similarly, the (geometric) average WV odds ratio is 1.5, but is twice as large in BD cases as in non-BD cases.

An additional issue arises with respect to the coding of Hispanic defendants and victims. Under current practice, defendant and victim "ethnicity" refers to Hispanic status for defendants and victims (DOJ FBI SHR Codebook 2004). The complexity in the process is that Hispanic defendants may also be characterized as black, white, or any other "race," which can result in problems with the interpretation of race effects and potential error if not captured. Hispanic status, is not a "racial" classification even though studies continue to characterize the "racial" categories as "black, white, Hispanic, Asian, and others." A significant problem in the SHR database is the large percentage of data for ethnicity that is coded as unknown or simply missing.

In spite of these complexities, a fairly standard way of classifying race and ethnicity is as follows: (a) White-non Hispanic; (b) Black-non Hispanic; (c) Hispanic; and (d) Other races-non Hispanic. This classification system conflates black and white Hispanics, which should be recognized, although the number of black Hispanics is small in most states.

Disparity Measures of Practical Significance
The Basic Approaches

There are two basic approaches to computing and presenting measures of practical significance. The first is to compare the "representation rates" of protected group cases, such as the percentage of white victim cases at successive stages in the decision making process. A good example of this approach is provided in the Paternoster-Brame Maryland study. Their study (Paternoster *et al.* 2004:Figure 3, p. 54) indicates that 44% of the death-eligible cases involved white victims, while 66% of the death-noticed cases involved white victims. This 22 percentage point (66%–44%) disparity in representation rates clearly indicates that white victim cases were more likely to be death noticed at the outset of the prosecution. The disparity can also be expressed as a ratio, *e.g.*, 1.5 (66%/44%).[31] The limitation of these measures, however, is that they do not quantify the *degree* to which the protected group cases, in this example, the white victim cases, were treated more punitively than the death-eligible case with non-white victims.

For this reason, the second approach—comparisons of "selection/outcome" rates—provides a more probative and relevant measure of the harm experienced by the protected group cases. The Paternoster-Brame example makes the point with respect to death notice rates among Maryland death-eligible cases. Among all death-eligible cases, 37% of the white victim cases were death noticed compared to 24% of the other cases.[32] This comparison provides the foundation for a series of disparity measures. The first is the arithmetic difference between the two selection rates, which in the Maryland study is a 13 percentage point (37%–24%) disparity in the rates that the two groups were death noticed. The selection rates also inform the "relative risk" measure that provides a commonly used basis for expressing the comparative risk of an adverse outcome faced by the two groups of cases. In the Maryland example, the relative risk is 1.5 (37%/24%), *i.e.*, the white victim cases were 1.5 times more likely to be death noticed.[33] A comparison of the two rates also tells us that the 37% death notice rate in the white victim cases was 54% (13/24) higher than the 24% rate in the other cases. Moreover, since this disparity is statistically significant beyond the .05 level, we have confidence that the data have correctly identified a positive disparity.[34]

---

31. Brock, Cohen, and Sorensen (2000:68) is a good example in a SHR-based study of applying a ratio measure, e.g., white victim cases were 34% of homicide arrestees and 69% of those were sentenced to death, a ratio of 2.04. Joint Legislative Audit and Review Commission (2002:14) is another good example (blacks constituted 86% of those sentenced to death before *Furman* and 52% of those sentenced to death after *Furman*).

32. In SHR-based studies, because of the large number of cases in the broader database, selection rates are sometimes presented as adverse outcomes per 100 or 1000 cases (Blume *et al.* 2004:197).

33. Pierce and Radelet 2005:23 (Table 6) is a good example in an SHR-based study.

34. The *p* (probability) value estimated for a disparity indicates the probability that such a disparity could occur by chance. A disparity with a *p* value of .05 or less is deemed to be "statistically significant."

Disparities based on selection rates can also be expressed in terms of odds,[35] which are not well understood in the legal community,[36] although they are the standard for risk comparisons in medicine. There is no generally accepted odds-based equivalent to the arithmetic difference between selection rates. There is, however, an odds-based measure of relative risk known as an "odds ratio" or "odds multiplier." In the Maryland example noted above, the odds of a death notice in the white victim cases were .59 (37%/63%), compared to the .32 (24% /76%) odds in the non-white victim cases. The ratio of these two odds is 1.8 (.59/.32). The adjusted "odds ratio," or "odds multiplier" as it is sometimes called, is a core measure of the impact of race and other variables in logistic regression analyses. For example, the core finding on which *McCleskey* relied was that after adjustment for legitimate non-racial case characteristics, the odds of a death sentence in white victim cases were on average 4.3 times higher than the comparable odds for the black victim cases.[37]

Increases in the Percentage of Statistically Accurate Outcome Predictions Associated with Protected Group Status— The CART (Classification and Regression Trees) Approach

A handful of investigators have applied a racial disparity measure to this field of research that focuses on the statistical impact of a protected status variable on the percentage of accurately predicted outcomes in a charging and sentencing system (Berk, Li, and Hickman 2005; Klein and Rolph 1991; Steinberg

---

35. Odds (O) and probabilities (P) have the following relationship: Odds = P/1-P and Probability = O/1+O.

36. In *McCleskey v. Kemp*, the court conflated odds and probabilities. The evidence in the case documented that the *odds* of a death sentence in white victim cases were "4.3 times higher" than they were in other cases, but the Court stated that defendants in white victim cases were "4.3 times as likely" to be sentenced to death (*McCleskey v. Kemp* 1987:287). Odds and probabilities have a direct computational relationship to one another. However, when the odds of a white victim case receiving a death sentence is "4.3 times higher" than that of other cases, that multiplier, technically called an odds multiplier, does not directly convert into a probability that is "4.3 times as likely." In other words, when the "4.3" odds that is associated with white victim cases receiving a death sentence is converted into a probability, the probability will *not* be 4.3 times as likely.

37. The estimated impact of an independent variable in a logistic regression can also be expressed in terms of its impact on the estimated probabilities. For example, white victim cases on average are 5 percentage points more likely to be capitally charged (Roncek 1991).

and Colla 1992).[38] Assume, for example, that the introduction of a variable for the race of the victim in a multivariate model increases the number of correctly predicted outcomes from 45% to 50%. This effect would be expressed as a 5-percentage point increase in the rate that the statistical model of this charging and sentencing system correctly "predicts" the actual outcome. We consider this a largely irrelevant measure of racial disparity because of its weak relationship to the harm experienced by the protected group of defendants. Specifically, the measure of impact in comparable situations, such as employment discrimination litigation and epidemiology (*e.g.*, the impact of cigarette smoking on cancer rates) is *effect size*—whether, for example, the exercise of discretion in employment contexts or cigarette smoking has the effect of increasing the rate at which members of a designated or protected group of people experience an unfavorable outcome (Woodworth forthcoming).

Measures of Geographic Disparities

Measures of geographic disparities are based on dummy variables that reflect the county or region of prosecution without regard to the racial or SES makeup of the community in which prosecutions occur (Brock et al. 2000; Paternoster *et al.* 2004; Songer and Unah 2006). For example, the Paternoster-Brame Maryland study documents well the vast disparity in capital charging and sentencing rates between Baltimore County and Baltimore City, and the less substantial variations in those rates among the other counties of the state. The inference of interest in the geographic analyses is the impact of prosecutorial charging practices after adjustment for the criminal culpability of the offenders. Because of the importance of county-wide charging practices, when they are considered to be legally relevant, the county of prosecution should be a control variable in the computation of adjusted race disparities.

---

38. A death sentence is "correctly" predicted if the death sentence prediction for the case was greater than 50% while a life sentence is correctly predicted if the death sentence prediction for the case was 50% or less. A death sentence is incorrectly predicted if the prediction is less than 50% and a life sentence is incorrectly predicted if the death sentence prediction for the case is greater than 50%.

"Adjusted" Race Disparities Computed with Controls for Legitimate Non-Racial Case Characteristics that Bear on Offender Criminal Culpability

Basic Approaches

Two approaches are used in this context that employ well-established, statistical methods that are widely used in employment discrimination cases, epidemiology, and demographics. They are the "model-based" approach, and the direct standardization or "culpability scale" approach. Each can be applied at successive decision making stages in the process and used to estimate adjusted disparities among all death-eligible cases (*e.g.*, those that advance to a guilt or penalty trial or result in a death sentence).[39]

Model-Based Methods

The model-based approach typically employs logistic regression models in which racial and other illegitimate factors are "adjusted" for legitimate and relevant non-racial variables that best explain the charging or sentencing outcomes for each defendant. The identification of the non-racial variables included in the model is informed by: (a) the legal status and importance of the non-racial variables; and (b) their power in explaining statistically the outcome of interest.[40] Although the number of candidate variables for inclusion in the models is normally larger in *McCleskey*-style studies, the process of screening variables for inclusion in the core model is the same (compare, for example, Baldus *et al.* 2002, and Songer and Unah 2006). In this regard, "screening" or model selection involves systematically selecting a subset of candidate explanatory variables on the basis of the impact of the candidate variables on the goodness of fit and coherence of the model involved. The practice is in-

---

39. To facilitate understanding of the impact of controls on estimated race and geographic disparities, we recommend reporting adjusted and unadjusted disparities with the same measures (Paternoster *et al.* 2004:92, Table 9G).

40. We recommend an initial model containing statutory aggravating and mitigating circumstances supplemented with additional non-racial variables that improve the fit of the model. Sample size will often influence the number of independent variables that a model can carry. Variables entering the model with unexpected/perverse signs should be carefully scrutinized to determine if they reflect a real effect in the system (in which event they should be retained) or noise (in which event they should be excluded from the model).

ferentially controversial (Raftery 1995a; 1995b) and should be viewed as a method of verifying whether racial and/or geographic disparities derived from models selected a priori on the basis of the law of the jurisdiction (for example, a model controlling for statutory aggravating and mitigating circumstances) are not accounted for by other variables.

Upon the development of an optimal model, racial variables are forced into the analysis to estimate their practical and statistical significance.[41] This process enables the investigators to determine the extent to which the magnitude and statistical significance of the unadjusted race and geographic disparities are diminished or enhanced by the introduction of controls for legitimate non-racial factors.

The logistic procedures provide two adjusted measures of interest, both of which are illustrated in the Paternoster-Brame Maryland study. The first is an adjusted "odds multiplier," which measures the protected group's harm in terms of the enhanced odds of being selected vis-a-vis the other cases. For example, their study indicates that on average defendants in white victim cases face odds of being death noticed that are 1.96 times higher than similarly situated defendants in other cases (Paternoster *et al.* 2004:35, 79, Table 8A).[42] The disparity can also be expressed in terms of enhanced probabilities, *e.g.*, in Maryland after adjustment for non-racial factors, the white victim cases on average face a 10-percentage point (25%–15%) greater risk of being death noticed than the other cases (Paternoster *et al.* 2004:37, 85, Table 8G). The Maryland study also illustrates the use of interaction terms based on the defendant/victim racial combinations. For example, after adjusting for non-racial factors, the odds of a white defendant/white victim case being death noticed are 55% (100%–45%) lower than the odds faced by similarly situated defendants in black defendant/white victim cases (Paternoster *et al.* 2004:38, Tables 86, 9A).[43] When expressed in terms of probabilities, the Maryland study documents that black

---

41. Because white victim effects in a system normally bias downward black/minority defendant effects, models should include main effect variables for the race of both the defendant and victim, or interaction terms based on the principal and most relevant defendant/victim racial combinations.

42. The .669 white victim logistic regression coefficient reported in Table 8A translates into an odds multiplier of 1.96. See *supra* note 36 and accompanying text for a discussion of odds ratios/multipliers generally.

43. In Table 9A, the black defendant/white victim cases are the reference category. Compared to those cases the -.786 regression coefficient for the white defendant/white victim cases translates into odds that the white defendant/white victim cases will be death noticed are only .45 of the odds faced by the black defendant/white victim cases. This results in the 55% (100%–45%) lower odds for the white defendant/white victim cases.

defendant/white victim cases have a 15-percentage point (34%–19%) higher probability of being death noticed than similarly situated white defendant/white victim cases (Paternoster *et al.* 2004:39, 92 Table 9G).[44]

Scale-Based Methods

The second, "scale-based," approach involves a two-step process. The first step is the development of scales that measure the comparative culpability of each offender in the analysis. The second step involves the application of a "nonparametric" statistical method known as the "direct standardization" of rates.[45] This procedure estimates the overall race disparity after correcting for differences in the distribution on the culpability scale of the two racially defined groups of offenders, such as black and non-black defendants. This process also enables investigators to determine the extent to which the magnitude and statistical significance of the unadjusted race and geographic disparities are diminished or enhanced by the introduction of controls for legitimate non-racial factors. Figure 1 presents such an analysis, which measures culpability with a scale relying on the number of aggravating circumstances in the cases (Baldus *et al.* 2002:570, Fig. 8, Part II). Column A documents an unadjusted 14-point race of defendant disparity in the rates that cases advance to a penalty trial, while Columns B through E document the disparities in four groups of increasingly aggravated cases. Footnote 1 indicates that after adjustment for the number of aggravating circumstances in the cases, the overall adjusted disparity is 15 percentage points, significant at the .06 level.[46]

An important virtue of the scale-based approach is its capacity to reveal in a straightforward fashion interactions (by not requiring the introduction of interaction terms into a regression model) between offender culpability levels and the magnitude and significance of the race effects. In many studies, the largest race effects have been concentrated among the mid-range of cases in terms of offender culpability, but that pattern does not hold in Figure 1.

---

44. To facilitate interpretation, we recommend reporting the results of basic regression diagnostics for the core logit models.

45. The most commonly used procedure for this purpose was developed by Mantel Haenszel. "Nonparametric" statistics address situations in which the "rank order" of a property of interest is known but the specific distribution is not. For example, various metals may be ranked in order of hardness without having any measure of hardness.

46. In some studies, the results for the impact of race at different levels of a culpability scale are reported without an overall adjusted disparity (Pierce, Radelet, and Paternoster 2006:V, Table 2).

Figure 1
Minority-Defendant Disparities in the Rates That Cases Advance to Penalty Trial Controlling for the Number of Aggravating Circumstances in the Cases: Nebraska, 1973–1999[1]

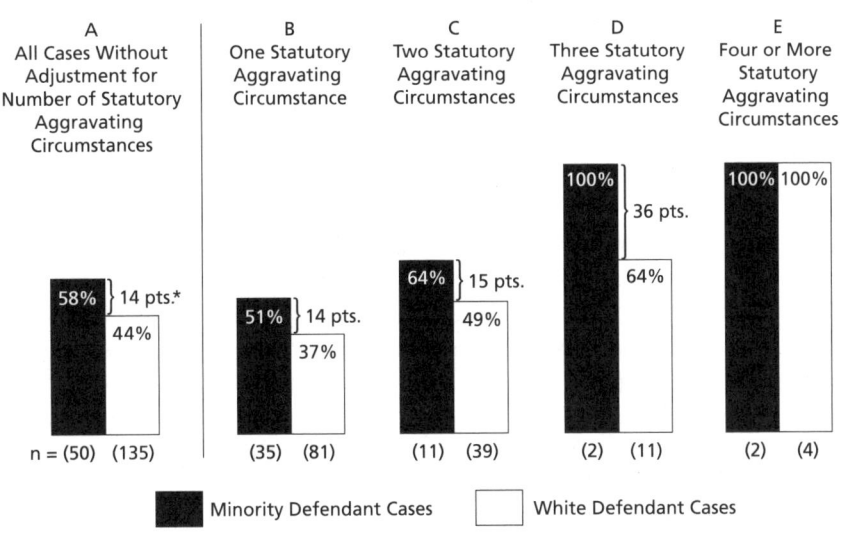

A	B	C	D	E
All Cases Without Adjustment for Number of Statutory Aggravating Circumstances	One Statutory Aggravating Circumstance	Two Statutory Aggravating Circumstances	Three Statutory Aggravating Circumstances	Four or More Statutory Aggravating Circumstances
58% / 44% (14 pts.*)	51% / 37% (14 pts.)	64% / 49% (15 pts.)	100% / 64% (36 pts.)	100% / 100%
n = (50) (135)	(35) (81)	(11) (39)	(2) (11)	(2) (4)

■ Minority Defendant Cases   ☐ White Defendant Cases

---

1. Source: Baldus *et al.* (2002: 570, Fig. 8, Part I). After adjustment for the number of statutory aggravating circumstances, the overall minority defendant disparity was 15- percentage points (.59 - .44), significant at the .06 level.
Level of Significance of Disparity: * = .10.

The culpability scales used for this purpose may also be used as additional independent variables in the model-based approach discussed above.[47]

A final issue concerns possible approaches to handling missing data, especially for the race of the defendant and victim variables. Two alternatives, noted above, are: (a) to delete such cases from the substantive analyses; and (b) to retain the cases in the analysis while adding a missing data variable. A further consistency check is to conduct "worst case" analyses in which missing data are given alternative race codes or are replaced by the mean/average for the variable on which the data are missing. For example, cases missing race of victim information may be coded "white" and "non-white" in different analyses to es-

---

47. We present below brief guidelines on the development of culpability scales.

timate the extent to which the missing race data have an impact on the documented race effects in the system.

Alternative Approaches

Propensity Analysis

A procedure known as "propensity analysis" seeks to identify non-racial control variables by identifying the non-racial variables that are highly correlated with the relevant racial characteristics of the cases, such as the race of the defendant or the victim. This procedure rests on the fact that a non-racial case characteristic can reduce the magnitude of a race effect, *e.g.*, based on the race of the victim, only if it is correlated with the racial variable of interest and the outcome variable. Thus, if a non-racial variable is correlated with the race variable it has the potential to explain away or reduce the impact of race on the outcome variable if it is also correlated with the outcome variable.

A propensity analysis employs a "propensity scale" that divides the cases into categories that are homogenous with respect to the proportion of each racial category of cases that is included in the substantive analysis. The race effects for the included racial categories are then estimated controlling for the propensity scale with the direct standardization method described above for scale-based methods (Rosenbaum and Rubin 1985; Rubin and Thomas 2000; Winship and Morgan 1999; Woodworth forthcoming).

We consider propensity analysis useful to supplement the two previously discussed basic procedures by providing a further test of whether the introduction of controls for non-racial variables will explain away or substantially minimize the race effects documented in the model- and scale-based approaches. The principal limitation of propensity analysis is that it lacks the foundation of a well-specified model of the most legally relevant case characteristics with a capacity to explain meaningfully and coherently the charging and sentencing outcomes of each case. For example, the procedure may produce models that contain no statutory aggravating circumstances. In addition, propensity analysis may be misapplied with adverse consequences (Woodworth, forthcoming).

Data Mining without Regard to Legal Relevance and Importance

Another approach to the identification of non-racial control variables is to screen the database for and include in the model any variable that is associated with the outcome variable at issue regardless of its plausibility and coherence under the law. This approach can produce models that have little relationship to the core aggravating and mitigating circumstances that inform charging and sentencing decision making. However, after the investigator has produced a core model based on the principal statutory aggravating and mitigating circumstances, the identification of additional plausible non-racial factors that add explanatory power to the core models is appropriate, and may stimulate thoughtful discussion, even if the procedures used might be characterized as "data mining."[48]

Guidelines for Creating Culpability-Based Scales

Scales Based on Counts of Aggravating Circumstances

Figure 1 above illustrates a straightforward scale based on the number of aggravating circumstances in a study tailored to Nebraska law and procedure (Baldus *et al.* 2002). Similar scales based on statutory and non-statutory factors have been used in a number of SHR studies (Brock *et al.* 2000; Gross and Mauro 1989; Pierce and Radelet 2005).

Scales Based on Qualitative Analyses of the Cases

While it may seem straightforward, the creation of qualitatively based culpability scales of the type created by Arnold Barnett with the *McCleskey* data require considerable insight into the decision making process. Barnett created three salient factors based on:

(a) The certainty the defendant was a deliberate killer ((0) Clearly no; (1) Neither 0 nor 2); (2) Clearly yes);
(b) A close or prior relationship between the defendant and the victim ((0) Yes; (1) No); and
(c) The vileness or heinousness of the crime ((0) Element of self-defense; (1) Neither 0 nor 2); (2) A vile killing (Baldus *et al.* 1990:51–52, 116–17)).

He identified these salient factors on the basis of the existing literature and his close reading of detailed narrative summaries of more than 500 life- and death-sentenced Georgia cases prosecuted between 1973 and 1978. He also developed a codebook to classify factually each case on these three dimensions. Finally, he combined the three salient factors into a 15-level culpability scale

---

48. However, the inclusion of variables with perverse signs, such as aggravating circumstances with negative/mitigating signs and mitigating circumstances with positive/aggravating signs requires careful scrutiny and justification.

with remarkable powers of discrimination for that dataset. The scale has had limited though successful replication.

Culpability Scales Based on Logistic Regression Models

Core logistic outcome models provide the foundation for the creation of defendant culpability scales (Baldus *et al.* 2002:536–37; Baldus *et al.* 1990:56). The first step in this process is to identify a well-specified model whose non-racial case characteristics represent a plausible measure of offender culpability. In this regard, a well-specified model is one to which the addition of further explanatory variables does not materially reduce the divergence between the data and the model. The second step is to add to the model race and SES variables for the defendant and victims. Step three estimates for each case a p-hat (a regression-based estimate of the likelihood of an adverse outcome) after purging the model of its race and SES effects. The purging of race and SES variables is crucial because the model should be free of any possible race or SES effects. The alternative of using p-hats based only on the non-racial variables runs a substantial risk of inadvertently incorporating into the scale the effects of race because of associations between race and SES and the non-racial variables (Blumstein *et al.* 1983:22–23). By including the race and SES variables in the model and basing the p-hats for the scale strictly on the non-racial variables after adjustment for the racial and socioeconomic variables, investigators will ensure that the scale is free of the effects of race and SES. Technical details are presented in the Appendix. Fourth, the distribution of p-hats is used to create a multi-level culpability scale.

Figure 2, which is based on Nebraska data, illustrates the process with respect to the rates that cases terminate in a negotiated plea/unilateral waiver of the death penalty (Baldus *et al.* 2002:571). Column A documents an unadjusted -18 percentage point minority defendant disparity, significant at the .05 level, while Columns B through H document the disparities among the cases at each level of the culpability scale. Footnote 1 reports the directly standardized rates and -16 point disparity significant at the .04 level computed after controlling for defendant culpability levels in a Mantel Haenszel procedure.[49]

This procedure has two virtues. First, it provides a straightforward measure of the adjusted disparities that does not require the interpretation of logistic based odds multipliers. Moreover, the validity of the estimated race disparities

---

49. When modeling this decision point it is important to determine, data permitting, the rates at which prosecutorial plea offers were made as well as were accepted among all death-eligible cases.

Figure 2
Statewide Minority Defendant Disparities in the Rates at Which Death-eligible Cases Terminated in a Negotiated Plea/Unilateral Waiver of the Death Penalty, Controlling for Defendant Culpability with a Regression Based Scale: Nebraska, 1973–1999[1]

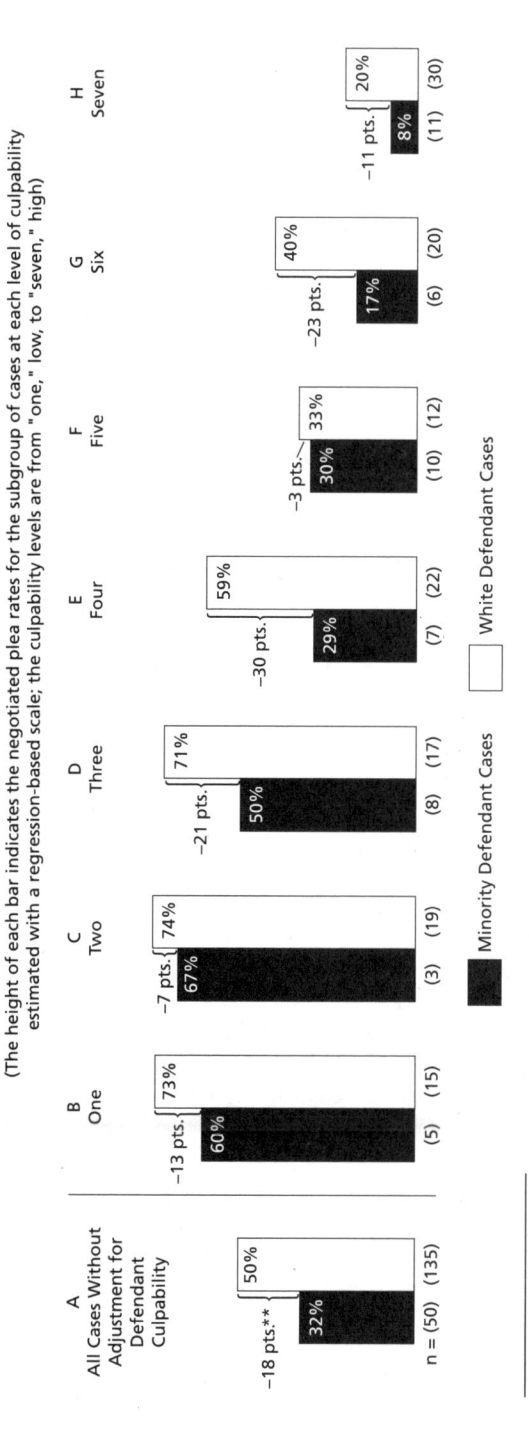

(The height of each bar indicates the negotiated plea rates for the subgroup of cases at each level of culpability estimated with a regression-based scale; the culpability levels are from "one," low, to "seven," high)

	A All Cases Without Adjustment for Defendant Culpability	B One	C Two	D Three	E Four	F Five	G Six	H Seven
White Defendant Cases	50%	73%	74%	71%	59%	33%	40%	20%
Minority Defendant Cases	32%	60%	67%	50%	29%	30%	17%	8%
Disparity	–18 pts.**	–13 pts.	–7 pts.	–21 pts.	–30 pts.	–3 pts.	–23 pts.	–11 pts.
n (Minority)	(50)	(5)	(3)	(8)	(7)	(10)	(6)	(11)
n (White)	(135)	(15)	(19)	(17)	(22)	(12)	(20)	(30)

1. Source: Baldus *et al.* (2002: 571, Fig. 9, Part I) The overall adjusted minority-defendant disparity is –16 percentage points (.34 - .50), significant at the .04 level. The outcome measure in the model underlying this scale is a negotiated guilty plea/unilateral waiver of the death penalty (*Id.* at 553, col. c). Thus, the least aggravated cases in Column B have the highest probability of obtaining such a waiver and the most aggravated cases in Column H have the lowest probability of obtaining one. In a scale based on a logistic model of death sentencing outcomes, the probability of a death sentence increases as the cases become more aggravated (*see e.g.*, Baldus *et al.* 1990:152)

Level of statistical significance: ** = .05

does not turn on the validity of the assumptions that underlie model-based methods such as logistic regression analysis. The only question is whether the cases are properly classified in terms of their criminal culpability. This question can be answered to some extent through an assessment of the charging and sentencing outcomes associated with each level of the scale (ideally the more culpable cases are treated more punitively at each ascending level of culpability). In addition, a qualitative analysis of the cases at each culpability level on the scale (accomplished through a comparative reading of their factual narrative summaries) will indicate whether the model-based categories correlate strongly with the rater's intuitive sense of the culpability of the cases in each category (see, *e.g.*, Baldus *et al.* 1990:602–09).

As noted above, a second virtue of a scale-based presentation is its capacity to identify interactions between criminal culpability and the magnitude of the race effects. For example, in Figure 2, the probability of a negotiated plea/unilateral waiver of the death penalty declines as the cases become more aggravated from Column B through Column H.

Presenting the Results

The Basics

To the extent that the purpose of the presentation is to inform the consideration of policy and legal issues, its hallmark should be accessibility for informed lay audiences with little understanding of statistics. We believe that the technical discussion should be relegated to footnotes and appendices, and that text should lead the reader "by the hand" through the tables and figures and assume a near zero level of sophistication in the interpretation of the findings. In that regard, clarity is achieved with an initial presentation of unadjusted disparities for all relevant race and geographic factors.[50] Tables with regression results should be presented with plain English descriptions of the variable names with rows and columns numbered or lettered for ease of reference. Crucial is a balanced recognition of the evidence that supports or undercuts the discrimination hypothesis.

Variations

Syntheses and overviews are often helpful. We present two below.

---

50. We recommend reporting the frequency distribution of all variables used in the analysis including an indication of the proportion of cases with missing values or the mean/proportion for each variable (Paternoster *et al.* 2004:57–59).

An Overview of Adjusted Stage-Wise Disparities

Figure 3 (on the next page) presents a stage-wise overview of adjusted black defendant/white victim disparities based on the Paternoster-Brame Maryland findings. Columns A through D present adjusted disparities (adjusted disparities in outcome rates and measures of relative risk) for the key decision points in the study, while Column E presents the comparable disparities for death sentencing rates among all death-eligible cases. Footnote 1 of the figure indicates that the underlying data come from a series of tables in the paper that document regression-based estimates of the enhanced impact of the black defendant/white victim circumstance on the enhanced probability that the defendant will be sentenced to death. For example, Column A indicates that there is a statistically significant 17-percentage point adjusted black defendant/white victim disparity in the death notice rates at the first stage of the process. The critical finding in Column E for death sentences imposed among all death-eligible cases is that the death sentencing rates for both racially defined groups are low, but the rate for the black defendant/white victim cases is a statistically significant 4.1 times higher rate than the rate for the other cases.

An Overview of Race and Culpability Interactions

Philadelphia research for the case of *Commonwealth* v. *Arrington* (2002) developed interesting evidence of interactions between offender culpability and race. The case involved evidence of systemic discrimination against black defendants in the weighing stage of 338 penalty trials conducted between 1978 and 2000. At this stage of the penalty trial, the jurors base their life or death decision on a weighing of the statutory and non-statutory aggravating and mitigating circumstances of the case. The unadjusted disparity was a statistically significant 12-percentage point (24%–12%) black defendant disparity in the imposition of death sentences in the weighing stage of the penalty trial. In the core logistic regression model, which controlled for statutory and non-statutory aggravating and mitigating factors, and the race and SES of both the defendants and victims, black defendants faced odds of receiving a death sentence that, on average, were 3.8 times higher than the odds faced by non-black defendants.

The second part of Arrington's case is presented in Figure 4, which plots the weighing stage sentencing outcomes for each case by its culpability level, along the horizontal X axis, and by its estimated probability of a death sentence, p-hat, along the vertical Y axis. There are four plots broken down by the defendant/victim racial combinations. The black defendant cases are in the two upper plots and the non-black defendants are in the two lower plots.

Figure 3
Adjusted Black Defendant/White Victim Disparities in Capital Charging and Sentencing Decisions: Maryland, July 1978–December 1999[1]

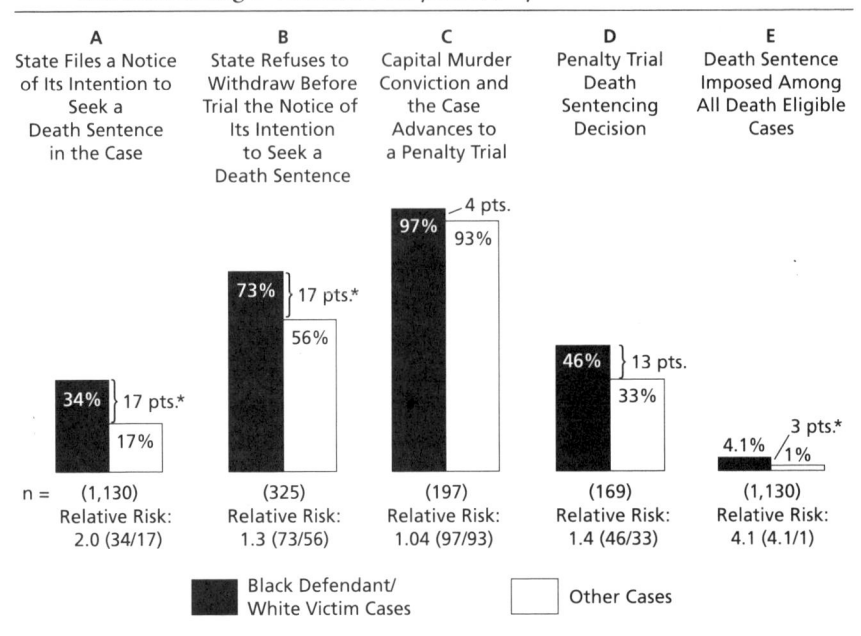

A	B	C	D	E
State Files a Notice of Its Intention to Seek a Death Sentence in the Case	State Refuses to Withdraw Before Trial the Notice of Its Intention to Seek a Death Sentence	Capital Murder Conviction and the Case Advances to a Penalty Trial	Penalty Trial Death Sentencing Decision	Death Sentence Imposed Among All Death Eligible Cases

A: 34% vs 17%, 17 pts.*
B: 73% vs 56%, 17 pts.*
C: 97% vs 93%, 4 pts.
D: 46% vs 33%, 13 pts.
E: 4.1% vs 1%, 3 pts.*

n = (1,130) | (325) | (197) | (169) | (1,130)
Relative Risk: 2.0 (34/17) | 1.3 (73/56) | 1.04 (97/93) | 1.4 (46/33) | 4.1 (4.1/1)

■ Black Defendant/White Victim Cases   □ Other Cases

---

1. Source: Paternoster *et al.*, 2004: Tbls. 9A, 9B, 9C, 9D, 9E, 9F, and 9G. The disparities reported in Columns A. B and E adjust for non-racial case characteristics and county of prosecution (Tbls. 9A, 9B, and 9F). The disparities reported in Columns C and D (Tbls. 9D and 9E) do not control for county of prosecution. The adjusted rates in Columns A-E are reported in Tbl. 9G. The adjusted rate for the "Other Cases" in each column is the average rate for the three other defendant victim racial combinations reported in Tbl. 9G.

Level of Statistical Significance: * = .05

At each point on the aggravation scale, the gap between the upper plots for the black defendant cases and the lower plots for the non-black victim cases indicates the magnitude of the black defendant disparity. For example, at point 3 on the aggravation scale, the estimated death sentencing rate for the black defendant cases is 80% while the estimated rate for the non-black victim cases is about 50%. As in *McCleskey*, the race effects are strongest in the mid-range of cases at levels 2–3 on the "Level of Aggravation" scale.

Figure 4
A Plot of Race-of-Defendant and Race-of-Victim Effects Estimated among Jury Weighing Decisions: Philadelphia, 1978–2000[1]

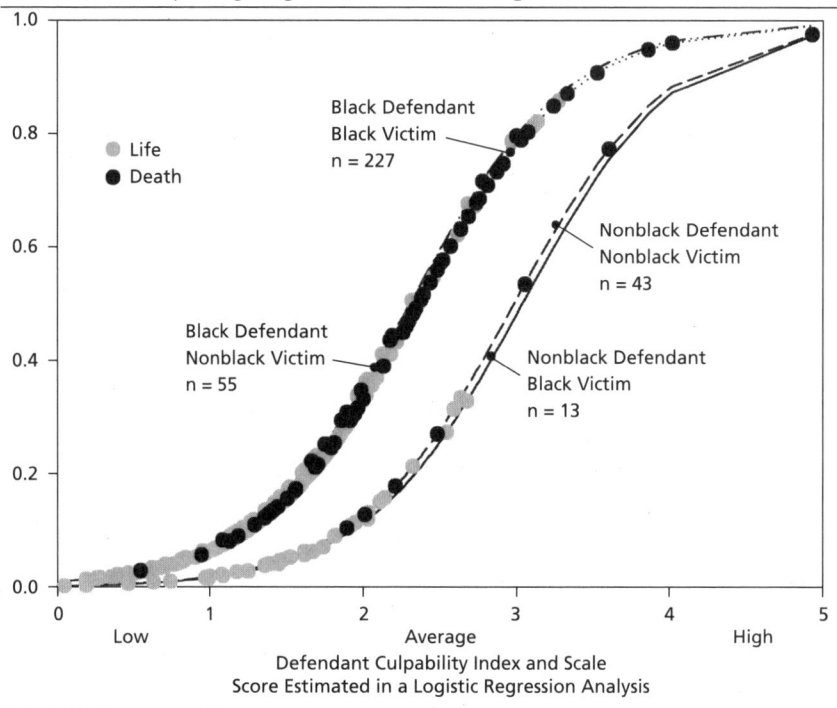

1. Source: Baldus and Woodworth (2003:211).

Conclusion

Empirical studies of capital charging and sentencing are similar to many empirical studies of legal systems. However, numerous features of charging and sentencing studies raise distinct methodological issues. This chapter presents a road map and guidelines on the best methodological approaches to these issues in SHR-based and *McCleskey*-style studies. Our first theme is that regardless of the strategy used and the particular legal questions of concern, at each step along the way, the assessment of the methodological issues by funders, investigators, evaluators, and consumers should be guided, *first, by legally based considerations* of relevance and evidentiary requirements for inferring racial and geographic discrimination and, *second, by generally accepted statistical practices*. Our second theme is that when the appropriate methodological choice is not clearly dictated by legal or statistical considerations, prudence calls for the conduct of plausible alternative analyses of the substantive results followed up with analysis of their consistency and stability.

Appendix

Creating a race-neutral defendant culpability control variable by purging racial influences

A. Overview

Let R denote a racial variable (such as the presence/absence of one or more white victims) and let X_1, X_2, $\cdots$, X_m represent the non-racial variables in the model. Initially we assume that none of the non-racial variables has an interaction with R. Let the estimated regression coefficients be α, the intercept, γ, the regression coefficient of the racial variable, R, and let β_2, $\cdots$, β_m be the regression coefficients of the non-racial variables.

The predicted probability, $\hat{p}$, is defined by the logit (Woodworth 2004, chapter 10): $logit = \ln(\hat{p}/1-\hat{p})) = \alpha + \gamma \cdot R + \beta_1 \cdot X_1 + \cdots + \beta_m \cdot X_m$. The logit is the Naperian logarithm of the odds on an unfavorable outcome, so that the predicted probability is non-linearly related to the explanatory variables and to the regression coefficients, $\hat{p} = \exp(logit)/(1 - \exp(logit))$. The purged logit is obtained by removing γ and R from the logit equation: $purged\ logit = \beta_1 \cdot X_1 + \cdots + \beta_m \cdot X_m$. The intercept can be retained or dropped as it does not alter the intervals between cases on the purged logit scale.

The purged logit is a single variable that involves only legitimate factors. It has the characteristic that if two cases have the same racial composition and the same value of the purged logit, then they have the same probability of an adverse outcome even though the two cases might have different values of the non-racial variables. In practice, the purged logit is "binned" into five to ten categories, within which cases of the same racial composition have nearly the same probability of an adverse outcome. Consequently, any method of estimating the race effect that controls for the purged logit, such as the Mantel-Haenszel procedure or direct standardization, will control for all non-racial variables in the model.

When one or more of the legitimate variables interacts with race the purging method is somewhat more complicated. Say, for example, the model contains an interaction between the racial variable and the first non-racial variable: $logit = \ln(\hat{p}/1-\hat{p})) = \alpha + \gamma \cdot R + \delta \cdot R \cdot X_1 + \cdots + \beta_m \cdot X_m$. In this case the purged logit is obtained by replacing the racial variable by its average value, $purged\ logit = (\delta \cdot \bar{R} + \beta_1) \cdot X_1 + \cdots + \beta_m \cdot X_m$. The effect is to replace the logistic regression coefficient of X_1, the variable involved in the racial interaction, by $\delta \cdot \bar{R} + \beta_1$, which is the effect of X_1 averaged over races.

The purged logit is a single variable that involves only legitimate factors. It has the characteristic that if two cases have the same racial composition, the same value of the purged logit, *and the same value of the interacting variable*, X_1, then they have the same probability of an adverse outcome. In practice, the purged logit is "binned" into five to ten categories, within which cases of the same racial composition *and the same value of the interacting variable*, X_1, have nearly the same probability of an adverse outcome. Consequently, any method of estimating the race effect that controls for the purged logit, and for *the interacting variable*, X_1, such as the Mantel-Haenszel procedure or direct standardization, will control for all non-racial variables.

The purpose of purging and binning is to make it possible to produce valid, corrected estimates of the racial disparity by easily understood categorical analyses.

B. Instructions for copying, changing, and running the SAS procedures

1. Copy the SAS source code to the local directory from which you wish to run the race purging procedure.
2. Make the following changes to your local copy of the source code:

    A. PATH and SAS DATA LIBRARY:
    ```
    /* specify your local path and library names */
    %LET PATH=path_to_project_directory;
    LIBNAME project_name "&PATH\sas_data_directory";
    ```

    B. *SAS data file to be analyzed:*
    ```
    /* STEP 2: Set up data to be analyzed */
    data temp;
        SET project_name.sas_data_file_name;
    ```

3. Execute Step 1 to load the MACRO procedure.
4. Execute Step 2 to set up your local SAS data file to be analyzed.
5. Execute Step 3 to Invoke the MACRO statement. Samples are shown below:

    The following describes all parameters that are passed to the MACRO:
    ```
    /* STEP 3: Invoke the Purge macro this way:
    %PURGE(name_of_new_index,
        name_of_dep_var,
        list_of_all_model_variables_and_interactions,
        list_of_race_variables,
        name_of_input_data_file,
    ```

name_of_output_data_file
name_of_reversed_variable);

The following shows an example of invoking the MACRO with actual data:
/* Example 1. BD effect depends on # vics */

%**PURGE**(d1_twovic,
    death1,
    num_agg mit2 twovic wv bd*VIC2 bd*VIC1,
wv bd,
temp,
temp2,
wv);

Note that the actual data replaces the described data in the same order. Therefore:
name_of_new_index is **d1_twovic**
name_of_dep_var is **death1**
list_of_all_model_variables_and_interactions: **num_agg mit2 twovic wv bd*VIC2 bd*VIC1**
list_of_race_variables is **wv and bd**
name_of_input_data_file is **temp**
name_of_output_data_file is **temp2**
name_of_reversed_variable is **wv**

additional examples:
/* Example 2 The same unpurged */

%**PURGE**(d1_unpurged,
    death1,
    num_agg mit2 twovic wv bd*VIC2 bd*VIC1,
    ,
    Temp2,
    Temp3);

/* Example 3 BD depends on WV   */
/* note that wv and wnv must be purged   */
%**PURGE**(d1_wvbd,
    death1,
    num_agg mit2 twovic BD*WV BD*NWV,
wv nwv bd,

```
          temp3,
          temp4);
```

6. Step 3 can be run as many times as you wish with different parameters.
7. If your variables have different names you may have to re-run Step 2.

C. The SAS macro required to implement the instructions in Part B of this Appendix[51]

The following SAS macro computes, among other things, the purged logit, here referred to as an *index*. In addition, it computes the unpurged logit and the unpurged logit with all racial variables reversed. Of course, the user will have to change the data set name, the path, the LIBNAME, and the variable names.

```
%MACRO purge(indexname,dep,vars,racevars,infile,outfile,reversed_vars);
    DATA &INFILE;
        LENGTH _LINK 4;
        RETAIN _OBS_ 0;
        SET &INFILE;
        _OBS_+1;
        _LINK=1;
    RUN;

    /* COMPUTE RAW BETAS */
    PROC GLMMOD NOPRINT DATA=&INFILE
        OUTDESIGN=_DESIGN;
        MODEL &DEP=&VARS;
    RUN;
    PROC TRANSPOSE DATA=_DESIGN
        OUT=_DESIGN(DROP=_NAME_
        RENAME=(_LABEL_=_NAME_));
    RUN;
    DATA _DESIGN;
        SET _DESIGN;
        IF _N_=1 THEN _NAME_="&DEP";
    RUN;
    PROC TRANSPOSE DATA=_DESIGN
        OUT=_DESIGN(DROP=_NAME_ _LABEL_);
```

---

51. Copy this part C to your SAS procedure library.

```
RUN;
DATA _DESIGN(DROP=&DEP intercept RENAME=(OUT-
COME=&DEP));
   LENGTH OUTCOME $1;
   SET _DESIGN;
   IF &DEP NOT IN (0,1) THEN OUTCOME="";
   ELSE OUTCOME=INPUT(PUT(&DEP,1.0),$1.);
RUN;

proc logistic noprint data=_design descending
OUTEST=_Ubetas(DROP=_LABEL_ _LINK_ _TYPE_ _STA-
TUS_ _NAME_ _LNLIKE_);
   model &dep(event="1") = _numeric_ ;
RUN;

/* CREATE PURGED DESIGN VARIABLES */
PROC MEANS DATA=&INFILE NOPRINT;
   BY _LINK;
   VAR &RACEVARS;
   OUTPUT OUT=_MEANS(DROP=_TYPE_ _FREQ_)
      MEAN=&RACEVARS;
RUN;
DATA _pDESIGN(DROP=&RACEVARS);
   SET &INFILE;
RUN;
DATA _pDESIGN;
   MERGE _MEANS _PDESIGN ;
   BY _LINK;
RUN;

PROC GLMMOD NOPRINT DATA=_PDESIGN
   OUTDESIGN=_PDESIGN;
   MODEL &DEP=&VARS;
RUN;
PROC TRANSPOSE DATA=_PDESIGN
   OUT=_PDESIGN(DROP=_NAME_
   RENAME=(_LABEL_=_NAME_));
RUN;
DATA _PDESIGN;
   SET _PDESIGN;
```

```sas
    IF _N_=1 THEN _NAME_="&DEP";
RUN;
PROC TRANSPOSE DATA=_PDESIGN
    OUT=_PDESIGN(DROP=_NAME_ _LABEL_ &DEP);
RUN;

    DATA &INFILE;
    LENGTH _LINK 4;
    RETAIN _OBS_ 0;
    SET &INFILE;
    _OBS_+1;
    _LINK=1;
RUN;

/* COMPUTE Reversed Design */
DATA _REVERSED;
    SET &INFILE;
    ARRAY RVARS &REVERSED_VARS;
    DO OVER RVARS;
        RVARS=1-RVARS;
    END;

PROC GLMMOD NOPRINT DATA=_REVERSED
    OUTDESIGN=_RDESIGN;
    MODEL &DEP=&VARS;
RUN;
    PROC TRANSPOSE DATA=_RDESIGN
    OUT=_RDESIGN(DROP=_NAME_
    RENAME=(_LABEL_=_NAME_));
RUN;
DATA _RDESIGN;
    SET _RDESIGN;
    IF _N_=1 THEN _NAME_="&DEP";
RUN;
PROC TRANSPOSE DATA=_RDESIGN
    OUT=_RDESIGN(DROP=_NAME_ _LABEL_);
RUN;
DATA _RDESIGN(DROP=&DEP intercept RENAME=(OUTCOME=&DEP));
    LENGTH OUTCOME $1;
```

```
    SET _RDESIGN;
    IF &DEP NOT IN (0,1) THEN OUTCOME="";
    ELSE OUTCOME=INPUT(PUT(&DEP,1.0),$1.);
RUN;

/* COMPUTE UnPurged PURGED AND REVERSED INDEX
AND P-HAT */

PROC IML;
    USE _PDESIGN;
        READ ALL VAR _all_ into PX;
    USE _RDESIGN;
        READ ALL VAR _all_ into RX;
    USE _DESIGN;
        READ ALL VAR _num_ into X;
    n=nrow(x);
    X=J(N,1,1)||X;
    RX=J(N,1,1)||RX;
    USE _UBETAS;
        READ ALL VAR _ALL_ into _ubeta;
    _ubeta=_ubeta';
    Ulogit=x*_ubeta;
    Uphat=1/(1+exp(-Ulogit));
    _purged=Ulogit||Uphat;
    Plogit=Px*_ubeta;
    Pphat=1/(1+exp(-Plogit));
    _purged=_purged||Plogit||Pphat;
    Rlogit=Rx*_ubeta;
    Rphat=1/(1+exp(-Rlogit));
    _purged=_purged||Rlogit||Rphat;

    create _purged from _purged
        [colname={U&indexname Up&indexname
        P&indexname Pp&indexname
        R&indexname Rp&indexname }];
    append from _purged;
    _pbeta=fuzz(ginv(X'*X)*X'*Plogit);
    create _pbetas from _pbeta [colname={"purged"}];
        append from _pbeta;
    quit;
```

```
RUN;
DATA &OUTFILE;
   MERGE &INFILE _PURGED;
RUN;

proc transpose data=_ubetas
   out=betas(rename=(col1=beta) drop=_label_);
run;
data betas;
   merge betas _pbetas;
run;

TITLE2 "Betas and purged betas for &INDEXNAME";
proc print noobs data=betas;
RUN;
TITLE2 "";
/* PROC DATASETS LIBRARY=WORK;
   DELETE _design _pdesign _means _pbeda _pbetas
   _purged _ubetas betas;
   QUIT;
   RUN; */
%MEND PURGE;
```

References

Allison, Paul D. 2001. *Missing Data.* Thousand Oaks, CA: Sage.

Baime, David S. 2005. Systemic Proportionality Review Project 2004–2005, Report to the New Jersey Supreme Court.

Baldus, David and George Woodworth. 2004. "Race Discrimination and the Legitimacy of Capital Punishment: Reflections on the Interaction of Fact and Perception." *DePaul Law Review* 53:1411–1496.

_____. 2003. "Race Discrimination in the Administration of the Death Penalty: An Overview of the Empirical Evidence with Special Emphasis on the Post-1990 Research." *Criminal Law Bulletin* 39:194–226.

_____. 2001. "Race-of-Victim and Race-of-Defendant Disparities in the Administration of Maryland's Capital Charging and Sentencing System 1978–1999: Preliminary Findings." Unpublished manuscript.

Baldus, David C., George G. Woodworth, and Catherine M. Grosso. 2002. "Arbitrariness and Discrimination in the Administration of the Death

Penalty: A Legal and Empirical Analysis of the Nebraska Experience (1973–1999)." *Nebraska Law Review* 81:486–756.

Baldus, David, George Woodworth, and Charles Pulaski, Jr. 1990. *Equal Justice and the Death Penalty: A Legal and Empirical Analysis*. Boston, MA: Northeastern University Press.

Baldus, David C., George Woodworth, David Zuckerman, Neil Alan Weiner and Barbara Broffitt. 2001. "The Use of Peremptory Challenges in Capital Murder Trials: A Legal and Empirical Analysis." *University of Pennsylvania Journal of Constitutional Law* 3:3–170.

_____. 1998. "Racial Discrimination and the Death Penalty in the Post-*Furman* Era: An Empirical and Legal Overview, With Recent Findings from Philadelphia." *Cornell Law Review* 83:1638–1770.

Berk, Richard, Azusa Li, and Laura Hickman. 2005. "Statistical Difficulties in Determining the Role of Race in Capital Cases: A Reanalysis of Data From the State of Maryland." *Journal of Quantitative Criminology* 21:365–390.

Blume, John, Theodore Eisenberg, and Martin T. Wells. 2004. "Explaining Death Row's Population and Racial Composition." *Journal of Empirical Legal Studies* 1:165–207.

Blumstein, Alfred, Jacqueline Cohen, Susan Martin, and Michael Tonry. 1983. National Research Council Panel on Sentencing Research. 1983. *Research on Sentencing: The Search for Reform*. Vol. I. Washington D.C. National Academy Press.

Bohm, Robert. 1994. "Capital Punishment in Two Judicial Circuits in Georgia." *Law and Human Behavior* 18:319–338.

Bowers, William, Marla Sandys, and Thomas Brewer. 2004. "Crossing Racial Boundaries: A Closer Look at the Roots of Racial Bias in Capital Sentencing When the Defendant is Black and the Victim is White." *DePaul Law Review* 53:1497–1538.

Brock, Deon, Nigel Cohen, and Jonathan Sorensen. 2000. "Arbitrariness in the Imposition of Death Sentences in Texas: An Analysis of Four Counties by Offense Seriousness, Race of Victim, and Race of Offender." *American Journal of Criminal Law* 28:43–71.

Carlin, Bradley P. and Thomas A. Louis. 2000. *Bayes and Empirical Bayes Methods for Data Analysis*. 2nd ed. Boca Raton, FL: Chapman & Hall.

Commonwealth v. Arrington (1998). CP-51-CR-0812071-1998 (1st Judicial District, Philadelphia County, Pennsylvania).

Department of Justice, Federal Bureau of Investigation, "Uniform Crime Reporting Program Data: Supplementary Homicide Reports. 2004 (Codebook)."

Eberhardt, Jennifer, Paul Davies, Valerie Purdie-Vaughns, and Sheri Lynn Johnson. 2006. "Looking Deathworthy: Perceived Stereotypicality of Black Defendants Predicts Capital-Sentencing Outcomes." *Psychological Science* 17:383–386.

Eisenberg, Theodore and Sheri Lynn Johnson. 2004. "Implicit Racial Attitudes of Death Penalty Lawyers." *DePaul Law Review* 53:1539–1556.

Furman v. Georgia (1972). 408 U.S. 238.

Gross, Samuel and Robert Mauro. 1989. *Death and Discrimination: Racial Disparities in Capital Sentencing.* Boston, MA: Northeastern University Press.

Haney, Craig. 2004. "Condemning the Other in Death Penalty Trials: Biographical Racism, Structural Mitigation, and the Empathic Divide." *DePaul Law Review* 53:1557–1589.

Hindson, Stephanie, Hillary Potter, and Michael Radelet. 2006. "Race, Gender, Region, and Death Sentencing in Colorado, 1980–1999." *University of Colorado Law Review* 77:549–594.

Joint Legislative Audit and Review Commission of the Virginia General Assembly. 2002. "Review of Virginia's System of Capital Punishment." (http://jlarc.state.va.us/reports/rpt274.pdf).

Klein, Stephen, Richard Berk, and Laura Hickman. 2006. "Race and the Decision to Seek the Death Penalty in Federal Cases." Rand Corporation Technical Report.

Klein, Stephen and John Rolph. 1991. "Relationship of Offender and Victim Race to Death Penalty Sentences in California." *Jurimetrics Journal* 32:33–48.

Little, Roderick and Donald Rubin. 2002. *Statistical Analysis with Missing Data.* 2nd ed. Hoboken, NJ: Wiley.

Maxwell v. Bishop (1968). 398 F.2d 138 (8th Cir.).

McAdams, John. 2002. "Race and the Death Penalty." Pp. 175–193 in *The Leviathan's Choice: Capital Punishment in the Twenty-First Century,* edited by Michael Martinez, William Richardson, and Brandon Hornsby. Lanham, MD: Rowan & Littlefield Publishers.

McCleskey v. Kemp (1987). 481 U.S. 279.

McNally, Kevin. 2004. "Race and the Federal Death Penalty: A Nonexistent Problem Gets Worse." *DePaul Law Review* 53:1615–1646.

Paternoster, Raymond, Robert Brame, Sarah Bacon, and Andrew Ditchfield. 2004. "Justice by Geography and Race: The administration of the death penalty in Maryland, 1978–1999." *Margins: The University of Maryland Law Journal of Race, Religion, Gender, and Class.* 4:1–99.

Pierce, Glenn and Michael Radelet. 2005. "The Impact of Legally Inappropriate Factors on Death Sentencing for California Homicides, 1990–1999." *Santa Clara Law Review* 46:1–47.

Pierce, Glenn, Michael Radelet & Raymond Paternoster. 2007. "Race and Death Sentencing in Tennessee, 1981–2000" in "American Bar Association, Evaluating Fairness and Accuracy in State Death Penalty Systems: The Tennessee Death Penalty Assessment Report," Appendix A at pp. 384–422. (http://www.abanet. org/moratorium/assessmentproject/tennessee/finalreport.pdf).

_____. 2006. "Race and the Death Penalty in Georgia, 1989–1998" in "American Bar Association, Evaluating Fairness and Accuracy in State Death Penalty Systems: The Georgia Death Penalty Assessment Report," Appendix at pp. 324–350 (A-Y). (http://www.abanet.org/moratorium/assessmentproject/georgia/report.pdf).

Proportionality Review Project. 1999. 735 A.2d 528 (N.J.).

Proportionality Review Project (II). 2000. 757 A.2d 168 (N.J.).

Radelet, Michael L. and Glenn L. Pierce. 1985. Race and Prosecutorial Discretion in Homicide Cases. *Law and Society Review* 19:587–621.

Raftery, Adrian E. 1995a. "Bayesian Model Selection in Social Research." *Sociological Methodology* 25:111–163.

_____. 1995b. "Rejoinder: Model Selection is Unavoidable in Social Research." *Sociological Methodology* 25:185–195.

Roncek, Dennis. 1991. "Using Logit Coefficients to Obtain the Effects of Independent Variables on Changes in Probabilities." *Social Forces* 70:509–518.

Rosenbaum, Paul R. and Donald B. Rubin. 1985. "Constructing a Control Group Using Multivariate Matched Sampling Methods that Incorporate the Propensity Score." *The American Statistician* 39:33–38.

RTI International [N.d.]. "SUDAAN: 30 Years in the Making." (http://www.rti.org/sudaan/page.cfm?nav=910).

Rubin, Donald B. and Neal Thomas. 2000. "Combining Propensity Score Matching With Additional Adjustments for Prognostic Covariates." *Journal of the American Statistical Association* 95:573–585.

Schafer, Joseph L. and John W. Graham. 2002. "Missing Data: Our View of the State of the Art." *Psychological Methods* 7:147–177.

Songer, Michael and Isaac Unah. 2006. "The Effect of Race, Gender, and Location on the Prosecutorial Decision to Seek the Death Penalty in South Carolina." *South Carolina Law Review* 58:161–209.

Sorensen, Jonathan and Donald Wallace. 1995. "Capital Punishment in Missouri: Examining the Issue of Racial Disparity." *Behavioral Sciences and the Law* 13:61–80.

Steinberg, Dan and Phillip Colla. 1992. *Cart: A Supplementary Module for SYSTAT.* Evanston, IL: SYSTAT Inc.

Thompson, Ernie. 1997. "Discrimination and the Death Penalty in Arizona." *Criminal Justice Review* 22:65–76.

Williams, Marian and Jefferson Holcomb. 2001. "Racial Disparity and Death Sentences in Ohio." *Journal of Criminal Justice* 29:207–218.

Winship, Christopher and Stephen L. Morgan. 1999. "The Estimation of Causal Effects from Observational Data." *Annual Review of Sociology* 25:659–706.

Woodworth, George. Forthcoming. "Statistical Issues in Recent Re-Analyses of Capital Charging and Sentencing Data."

_____. 2004. *Biostatistics: A Bayesian Introduction.* Hoboken, NJ: Wiley.

CHAPTER 10

THE CAPITAL JURY EXPERIMENT OF THE SUPREME COURT

William J. Bowers, Thomas W. Brewer and Charles S. Lanier[1]

The capital jury decides whether a convicted murderer should live or die, but it is not free to make this decision however it pleases. Indeed, the Supreme Court brought capital punishment to a halt 35 years ago in *Furman v. Georgia* (1972) because of the "arbitrary" and "capricious" way death sentences were being imposed. Seeking to remedy these ills, state legislatures enacted statutes that separated the capital trial into guilt and penalty phases and provided guidelines in terms of aggravating and mitigating factors for jurors to consider at the penalty stage of the trial. The Supreme Court accepted these "guided discretion" capital statutes in *Gregg v. Georgia* (1976) and companion cases,[2] saying that "on its face" such a bifurcated trial with explicit sentencing guidelines "is more likely to ensure elimination of the constitutional deficiencies identified in *Furman*" (p. 192).[3] Notably, saying "on its face" and "likely" implies that

---

1. The authors gratefully acknowledge Susan Ehrhard's assistance in the preparation of this chapter.
2. The Supreme Court approved three forms of guided discretion threshold, weighing, and directed statutes in *Gregg v. Georgia* (1976), *Proffitt v. Florida* (1976), and *Jurek v. Texas* (1976). *See* Acker and Lanier (1995:33, 52); Gillers (1980); and Note (1974:1699, 1712) for detailed discussions of these statutory distinctions.
3. Writing for the Court in *Gregg*, Justice Stewart explained how these statutory guidelines are presumed to remedy the *Furman* ills:
    Left unguided, juries imposed the death sentence in a way that could only be called freakish. The new Georgia sentencing procedures, by contrast, focus the jury's attention on the particularized nature of the crime and the particularized characteristics of the individual defendant.... In this way the jury's discretion is chan-

this was a legal experiment—a presumptive remedy subject to scrutiny and possible invalidation.

The Court's experiment with guided discretion represented a turnaround in its stand on sentencing guidelines. A year before *Furman*, in *McGautha v. California* (1971) the Court explicitly rejected the argument that the constitution requires that capital trials have separate guilt and penalty phases[4] and that jurors be guided by sentencing standards at the penalty stage of the trial. Indeed, the *McGautha* Court observed that, "[t]o identify before the fact those characteristics of criminal homicides and their perpetrators which call for the death penalty, and to express these characteristics in language which can be fairly understood and applied by the sentencing authority, appear to be tasks which are beyond present human ability" (p. 204). In effect, *McGautha* held that such standards were illusory and unworkable; *Furman* held that (in the absence of such guidelines) capital sentencing as then practiced was constitutionally unacceptable; and *Gregg* held, *McGautha* notwithstanding, that states had devised and implemented standards and guidelines that could be expected, at least on their face, to remedy the arbitrariness declared unconstitutional in *Furman*.

At the same time that the Supreme Court endorsed "guided discretion" in *Gregg*, it also held that "individualized" consideration of the crime and the defendant was indispensable in making the life or death punishment decision (*Woodson v. North Carolina* 1976). The requirement of individualized treatment figured in later rulings allowing the consideration of any mitigating factors, not just those enumerated in the statutes (*Lockett v. Ohio* 1978); requiring the sentencer to consider "any relevant mitigating evidence" (*Eddings v. Oklahoma* 1982); permitting the sentencing decision to be unguided once the jury finds a single statutory aggravating factor and considers mitigation (*Zant v. Stephens* 1983); and not requiring states to monitor the proportionality or evenhandedness of capital sentencing under their statutes (*Pulley v. Harris* 1984). These and related decisions had the effect of circumscribing sentencing guidelines, of "deregulating death," in the words of Robert Weisberg (1983), to the point, he contends, where capital juries function much as they had before *Furman* ruled standardless decision-making unconstitutional.

---

neled. No longer can a jury wantonly and freakishly impose the death sentence; it is always circumscribed by the legislative guidelines (*Gregg v. Georgia* 1976:206, 207, opinion of Stewart, J.).

4. "The Constitution does not prohibit the States from considering that the compassionate purposes of jury sentencing in capital cases are better served by having the issues of guilt and punishment resolved in a single trial than by focusing the jury's attention solely on punishment after guilt has been determined" (*McGautha v. California* 1971:221).

In light of further Supreme Court rulings, the capital sentencing decision is now supposed to be a "reasoned moral choice" (*Penry v. Lynaugh* 1989).[5] Unlike the guilt decision, which entails assessing whether the facts that establish every legal element of the crime charged have been proven beyond a reasonable doubt to all twelve jurors, the punishment decision is subject to a very different set of considerations and procedures, appropriate for a fundamentally moral judgment. Each juror is responsible for making the punishment decision on the strength of his or her own personal satisfaction with the evidence of mitigation and his or her own moral consciousness about the appropriateness of the punishment. Thus, in selecting the punishment, a juror is not required to agree with others on the presence or weight he or she assigns to various aspects of mitigation. Nor must he or she observe the standard of reasonable doubt in assessing the evidence of mitigation. The standards of proof beyond a reasonable doubt and of unanimous jury findings of fact generally required for the determination of guilt and of aggravation simply do not apply to the consideration of mitigation (*McKoy v. North Carolina* 1990; *Mills v. Maryland* 1988).

Making such a reasoned moral choice requires that jurors be able and willing to consider and give effect to mitigation in making their punishment decisions. Otherwise they are explicitly disqualified from serving as capital jurors (*Morgan v. Illinois* 1992). It presupposes that jurors correctly know the alternative punishments from which they choose. They should not have mistaken impressions of the punishment options that confront them with a "false choice" (*Simmons v. South Carolina* 1994 and *Shafer v. South Carolina* 2001).[6] It pre-

---

5. The requirement of individualized treatment was fundamental to the Court's emergent conception of the capital sentencing decision as a "reasoned moral choice" in *Penry v. Lynaugh* (1989). Accordingly, the decision must be an "individualized assessment" of the character and record of the particular offender and the circumstances of the particular offense, unencumbered by ignorance or emotion, and supported with information sufficient and relevant for reliable rational decision making. For sentencing:

[f]ull consideration of evidence that mitigates against the death penalty is essential if the jury is to give a "reasoned moral response to the defendant's background, character, and crime." In order to ensure "reliability in the determination that death is the appropriate punishment in a specific case," the jury must be able to consider and give effect to any mitigating evidence relevant to a defendant's background and character or the circumstances of the crime (*Penry v. Lynaugh* 1989:328, citations and internal quotation marks omitted).

6. The Court has so far made this a constitutional requirement only when the prosecution has alleged the future dangerousness of the defendant and the death penalty alternative is a sentence of life without the possibility of parole. For evidence that knowledge of the death penalty alternative influences jurors' decision making in cases not limited to these conditions, see Bowers and Steiner (1999:Table 6).

sumes that they take responsibility for the choice they make, for the punishment they impose. They should not see the law as the responsible agent, or believe that others who may review their verdict thereby relieve them of responsibility for the punishment they impose (*Caldwell v. Mississippi* 1985). And it presupposes that the punishment they impose not be biased by improper considerations. In choosing between life or death, jurors' sentencing decisions must not be influenced, consciously or unconsciously, by the race of the defendant, by the race of the victim, or by their own race (*Turner v. Murray* 1986).

Evidence of Jurors' Failure to Meet Constitutional Requirements

Following the Supreme Court's concern about the absence of research on "actual jurors in real cases" (*Lockhart v. McCree* 1986) and the need to know about the sentencing process and not just sentencing outcomes (*McCleskey v. Kemp* 1987), a consortium of university-based researchers in fourteen states undertook a nationwide study of how actual jurors made the life or death capital sentencing decision. Begun in 1990, this continuing program of research, known as the Capital Jury Project (CJP), conducted 3–4 hour in-depth personal interviews with 1,198 jurors from 353 capital trials in 14 states. The states were chosen to represent the principal variations in capital sentencing statutes.[7] Jurors were interviewed in Alabama, California, Florida, Georgia, Indiana, Kentucky, Louisiana, Missouri, North Carolina, Pennsylvania, South Carolina, Tennessee, Texas, and Virginia. Within each state, twenty to thirty capital trials were picked to represent both life and death sentencing outcomes, and from each trial, a target sample of four jurors was systematically selected for interviewing. The interviews trace the juror's trial experience with questions on jury selection, the guilt trial, jury deliberations on guilt, the penalty trial including the judge's sentencing instructions, and jury deliberations leading to the final life or death decision. Jurors were asked both structured questions with designated response options and open-ended questions that invite extended narrative responses. Some forty articles presenting and discussing the

---

7. The sample includes states with "threshold," "balancing," and "directed" statutory guidelines for sentencing discretion. It also includes states with "traditional" and "narrowing" definitions of capital murder and states in which the jury decisions are binding and those in which the judge currently can override the jury recommendations. For further details of the sampling procedure, see Bowers (1995).

findings of the CJP have appeared in scholarly and scientific journals; they are listed and some are posted in full on the CJP website at http://www.albany.edu/scj/CJPhome.htm. The website also cites court opinions, including those of the United States Supreme Court, that refer to CJP research.

The research of the Capital Jury Project has revealed that the decision-making of capital jurors is at odds with constitutional directives in at least seven respects (Bowers and Foglia 2003; Bowers, Steiner, and Antonio 2003). In particular, the data show:

1. *Premature punishment decision-making.* Despite the two-phase capital trial procedure designed to reserve the punishment decision for a second separate penalty stage of the trial in which the jury's sentencing discretion is to be guided by special circumstances usually identified as aggravating and mitigating factors, half of the jurors interviewed by CJP investigators (49.2%) said they felt they knew what the punishment should be during the guilt stage of the trial; three of ten (30.3%) said it should be death and two in ten (18.9%) said it should be life. Seven of ten (70.4%) who thought it should be death said they were "absolutely convinced" of that stand, and most adhered to that stand over the course of the trial (Bowers and Foglia 2003:Table 1).

2. *Pro-death predisposition of jurors.* Contrary to the requirement that individuals must be able and willing to give effect to aggravating and mitigating evidence in making the punishment decisions in order to qualify as capital jurors, more than half of the CJP jurors indicated that death was the only punishment they considered acceptable for a murder committed by someone previously convicted of murder (71.6%), a planned or premeditated murder (57.1%), or a murder in which more than one victim is killed (53.7%). Close to half could accept only death as punishment for the killing of a police officer or prison guard (48.9%), or for a murder committed by a drug dealer (46.2%). For a killing that occurs during another crime roughly a quarter of the jurors (24.2%) believed death was the only acceptable punishment. Eight out of ten jurors (81.8%) saw death as the only acceptable punishment for at least one of these kinds of killings (Bowers and Foglia 2003:Table 2).

3. *Failure to understand sentencing requirements.* Although what constitutes mitigation cannot be restricted by statute, the "beyond a reasonable doubt" standard of proof applies to aggravating but not to mitigating factors, and unanimity is not required for a juror to find evidence mitigating, many jurors failed to understand each of these requirements. A sizable minority (44.6%) failed to realize that they were allowed to consider mitigating factors not listed in the statute, half (49.2%) erroneously assumed that "beyond a reasonable doubt" was the standard of proof for mitigating evidence, three in ten (29.9%) did

not think they had to find aggravation beyond a reasonable doubt[8] and two-thirds (66.5%) of the jurors failed to realize that unanimity was not required for findings of mitigation. Fully ninety three out of one hundred jurors (93.4%) were mistaken about at least one of these sentencing requirements (Bowers and Foglia 2003:Table 3).

4. *Mistakenly believing the death penalty is required by law.* Contrary to the ruling that the law cannot direct jurors to impose the death penalty without considering mitigation, half of the jurors wrongly believed that the law made the death penalty mandatory under certain circumstances; a little more than four in ten (43.9%) thought death was required when the defendant's conduct was "heinous, vile or depraved," and a little fewer than four in ten (36.9%) thought death was required if they found that the defendant "would be dangerous in the future." Fully half (50.3%) thought the law required them to impose the death penalty under one or the other of these circumstances (Bowers and Foglia 2003:Table 4).

5. *Underestimating the death penalty alternative.* Despite the Court's admonition that jurors must base their decision on accurate information about the sentencing alternatives, most jurors thought that defendants not sentenced to death would usually be back on the streets well before they first become eligible for parole. In every state, the median estimate of the time usually served was less than the mandatory minimum for parole eligibility in that state, and the sooner jurors believed a defendant not given the death penalty would return to society, the more likely they were to impose the death penalty. Even in the four states that had life without the possibility of parole as the death penalty alternative at the time of the trials from which jurors were interviewed (Alabama, California, Missouri, and Pennsylvania), sizable majorities of the jurors thought that defendants would usually be released from prison if not given death (Bowers and Steiner 1999).

6. *Evasion of responsibility for the defendant's punishment.* At odds with the Supreme Court's insistence that capital jurors must see themselves as the ones most responsible for the defendant's punishment, only about one in twenty jurors (5.5%) saw the individual juror as most responsible, and less than one in ten (8.9%) saw the jury as a whole as most responsible for the defendant's punishment. Having found the defendant responsible for the crime at the guilt stage of the trial, half of the jurors said the defendant was the one most responsible for the punishment as well. Three of ten assigned primary responsibility to the

---

8. Jurors from three states where this issue had not been resolved were deleted from the estimate.

law (32.8%). When the assignment of responsibility was restricted to the judge and the jury, only 33.0% thought the jury was strictly responsible in the eleven states where the jury decision was binding on the trial judge. (In Alabama, Florida, and Indiana, the trial judge could impose death even if the jury voted for life (Bowers and Foglia 2003:Table 5; Bowers et al. 2006:Table 1).)

7. *Racial contamination of jury decision-making.* Notwithstanding the Court's expressed recognition of the need to purge the influence of conscious and unconscious racism from the decision-making of jurors, especially in black defendant, white victim cases, the CJP data demonstrate substantial disparities in the treatment of defendants both by race of individual juror and by the racial composition of the jury. Black and white jurors from the same black defendant, white victim cases differ substantially in lingering doubt about the defendant's guilt, impressions of the defendant's remorsefulness, and views of the defendant's future dangerousness. And, having five or more white male jurors increased death sentences by 41 percentage points (from 30.0% to 70.7%); having a black male on the jury reduced death sentences by 34 points (from 71.9% to 37.5%) (Bowers, Steiner, and Sandys 2001:193).

These departures from sentencing standards are not superficial or idiosyncratic, not slight or marginal. In fact, most of the specific mistakes and misunderstandings reviewed above are common to half or more of the jurors, and virtually none of the jurors are free of all such mistakes and misunderstandings. Nor can the presence or magnitude of these departures from constitutional standards be attributed to faulty memory on the part of the former jurors. A detailed examination of jurors' responses by how well the jurors say they remembered the trial, by their interviewer's assessment of their recall, and by the elapsed time from the trial to the interview, gives no indication that jurors' responses at odds with the law are owing to faulty memory or hindsight bias (Bowers and Foglia forthcoming).[9] What is more, these understandings and practices contrary to constitutional requirements are common to all states; they are not faults that the statutes or procedures of some states have overcome.[10] The fact that these flaws in jury decision-making are so common among

---

9. The "best estimates" based on the responses of jurors who report remembering "very well," for whom interviewers reported no memory problems, and who were interviewed soonest after the trial, were typically no more than a few percentage points from the sample wide estimates.

10. Some of these faults are exacerbated in states where the jury's sentencing decision is not binding but merely a recommendation to the trial judge (Bowers et al. 2006), but they are common in substantial measure to all states, regardless of the form their statutes

jurors and pervasive across states suggests that the guidelines they violate may be fundamentally incompatible with making the capital sentencing decision.

Plainly, many jurors do not know the rules for considering aggravating and mitigating factors; they do not realize that the law never requires the death penalty, even for heinous crimes or for defendants who would be dangerous in the future; they do not wait for the penalty stage of the trial to take a stand on the punishment, to be absolutely convinced of that stand, and to stick to it thereafter; they vastly underestimate the death penalty alternative; they do not see themselves as the ones most responsible for the punishment, and so on. Hence, the reality that comes into view when we interview actual jurors about their decision-making is that a great many are oblivious to legal requirements for making their decisions. This is not because many jurors do not take their task seriously; to the contrary, the CJP investigators found that nearly all jurors were extremely well-intentioned and conscientious. Can these departures from sentencing requirements be remedied by reforms in jury selection or jury instructions, or does the daunting character of the life or death decision render such decision rules irrelevant or distracting to most people when they are confronted with the reality of such an overwhelming decision?

The Capital Jury Project Research Agenda

The continuing work of the Capital Jury Project is now taking as its focus jurors' receptivity to mitigation, which is at the core of capital sentencing as a reasoned moral judgment. This research draws upon trial transcripts for documentation of the mitigation to which jurors were exposed. It brings the social context of the punishment decision process under scrutiny by mapping the flow of interpersonal influences and pressures that come to bear. And it brings the confounding effects of race into the picture, race of juror, race of defendant and victim, and even race of the jury itself. This research will also update the earlier findings reviewed above with interviews conducted during the present downturn in death sentences since the mid 1990s (Bowers and Sundby, this volume). This section sketches the details of this new phase of CJP research and the section that follows considers directions other future studies of the capital jury might take.

---

take (Bowers and Foglia 2003; Bowers et al. 2003). For example, the percent taking a premature stand on punishment at the guilt stage of the trial departs from the sample wide figure by as much as ten percentage points for only one state and by five to nine points for only another three (Bowers and Foglia 2003:Table 1).

Assessing Receptivity to Mitigation

The CJP data reveal that many presumptively mitigating considerations are not strongly or consistently viewed as mitigation by jurors (Bowers et al. 1998:Table 12). In many instances jurors' responses indicate uncertainty or ambiguity about the mitigating role of the factor. And even for factors found to be among the most consistently mitigating,[11] investigators have nevertheless found that the importance or weight of these factors in mitigation is "tempered" (Eisenberg, Garvey, and Wells 1998), "dampened" or "undermined" (Sundby 1998) by other factors that appear to serve as impediments to the consideration of mitigation. A pervasive example is the mistaken perception that convicted capital offenders not sentenced to death would usually be back in society well before they even become eligible for parole (Bowers and Steiner 1999), or in the case of mentally retarded offenders, the belief that they would be dangerous in the future (Sandys, Trahan, and Pruss forthcoming).

Initial steps have been taken to assess jurors' receptivity to mitigation. Brewer (2003) contrasted jurors' responses to questions in the CJP interview instrument on what was presented to the jury in mitigation with their responses to questions about what they regarded as mitigating. For specific mitigating factors, he matched the juror's reports of whether such evidence and arguments were presented to the jury against that juror's judgment of how important that mitigating factor was in his or her sentencing decisions. He developed an index that scored the importance to the juror of the various mitigating factors presented to the jury according to that juror's report and found considerable differences in receptivity to mitigation associated with the manner in which defense attorneys treat the defendant (Brewer 2005), and by race of juror in black defendant white victim cases (Brewer 2004). Yet Brewer's index of receptivity to mitigation relies upon jurors' accounts for what defense attorneys presented and argued in mitigation, and by virtue of interviewing several, usually four, jurors from each trial, we know that jurors from the same trial sometimes disagree on what mitigation was presented to the jury.

A further step was taken by Lanier (2004) who examined trial transcripts from 14 cases tried capital and interviews with 49 people who had served as jurors at these trials. One focus of the research was to see from the trial transcripts

---

11. Factors found to be among the most mitigating in jurors' reports of their decision-making include the defendant's remorse (Eisenberg, Garvey, and Wells 1998; Sundby 1998), the defendant's lack of future dangerousness (Blume, Garvey, and Johnson, 2001; Haney, Sontag and Costanzo 1994), and residual doubt about the defendant's guilt (Bowers et al. 1998; Geimer and Amsterdam 1988).

what mitigating evidence and arguments were actually presented to the jury and how the jurors responded to the evidence and arguments documented in the transcripts. Lanier found that jurors' reports of what was presented in mitigation, and even of who presented it, was not always faithful to what the transcript revealed. He found discrepancies between the transcripts and the reports of one or more jurors in most of the 14 cases. Jurors incorrectly recounted the substance of the evidence presented and the number or identity of witnesses who appeared for the defense. And, when the questioning moved to the main points of those who testified, jurors were often not able to give a coherent retelling of the testimony. In effect, trial transcripts provide empirical grounding for the assessment of receptivity to mitigation.

These studies underscore the importance of what we believe is an indispensable next step for understanding the role of mitigating evidence in capital sentencing. The critical contribution trial transcripts make to investigating receptivity to mitigation among capital jurors is the information they provide on the arguments advanced by the defense as mitigation; the testimony and other evidence presented to the jury; and the "orchestration" of that evidence in terms of the kinds of witnesses who appeared, and the substance, consistency, coherence and integration of the testimony they provided. They are the ideal source of information for determining the orchestration of mitigation as conceived by Sundby (1997) who was concerned chiefly with the reinforcement of expert witness testimony with the testimony of lay witnesses and family members. From a practical research standpoint, trial transcripts are increasingly available in electronic formats that make them far more accessible, searchable, and sharable for research purposes.

Trial transcripts also make it possible to objectively establish a number of other empirically grounded facts of critical importance in refining and enhancing our understanding of the decision-making process. Specifically, the portion of the transcript that pertains to jury selection contains the precise questions jurors were asked and the answers they gave that might correlate with whether they saw death as the appropriate or only acceptable punishment for the offense in question. The portion of the transcript on guilt trial evidence provides details about the character of the killing, the testimony of prosecution witnesses, and the possibility of "front loading" mitigation by the defense. And the penalty stage portion of the transcript contains exactly what jurors were told in the judge's sentencing instructions, the opening and closing arguments advanced by both defense and prosecuting attorneys, and, of course, a complete rendition of the testimony of both aggravation and mitigation witnesses.

The research strategy will further capitalize on trial transcripts in the interviewing of jurors. In preparation for the interview, the interviewer will read and prepare a summary of the testimony and arguments advanced at the penalty stage of the trial. The interview instrument contains a series of questions about those who testified and the nature of their testimony. After the juror has responded to these questions, the interviewer will then probe for additional reactions to the witnesses and their testimony, informed by his/her review of the penalty phase of the transcript. This will permit the interviewer to probe for additional information with questions about any witnesses the juror may have overlooked and any testimony that s/he might have forgotten. The fact that jurors may not remember or may mistakenly recall will be valuable data for analysis in its own right. In essence, this mitigation grounded interviewing strategy will seek to learn the juror's reaction to evidence and arguments known to have been presented at the penalty trial, both those readily recalled and those initially forgotten, in order to see how the full complement of mitigation evidence was understood, ignored, or otherwise interpreted by the juror.

Social Pressures on Individual Decision-Making

Jurors' accounts of how they reached their punishment decisions often reveal an intense social persuasion process. In such cases, the punishment decision appears to be less the exercise of an individual's reasoned moral judgment than the product of a social interaction process characterized by the successive hardening of punishment stands often buttressed with rhetorical claims more vigorously and emphatically advanced as punishment deliberations proceed. Such arguments often go beyond standards supposed to guide the capital sentencing decision, arguments that seek to deny, discredit and invalidate not merely the evidence but also the legitimacy of mitigating considerations in sentencing and discredit those who hold them (for examples from jurors' narrative accounts, see Bentele and Bowers 2001; Bowers and Steiner 1999; Bowers et al. 2001). This kind of an interpersonal persuasion process is a reality apt to compromise underlying legal assumptions about how the decision should be made, especially the place and effect to be accorded mitigation.

The CJP has previously examined the way individual jurors arrived at their punishment stands with open-ended questions about their decision-making. While this has revealed aspects of the social dynamics involved in the decision process, it has done so incidentally and indirectly, not with systematic data on how the punishment decision is affected by an interactive social influence process. For this research on receptivity to mitigation, the CJP has adopted a more direct and systematic way of learning how advocacy and interpersonal pressures among jurors figure in the decision-making process and influence the final decisions of the individual jury members. For this purpose, we employ an interpersonal influence mapping procedure that enables us to trace the influence of other members of the jury on the initial punishment stands jurors take and on the changes or hardening of those stands over the course of the trial. With such information from a sample of jurors in a given trial, it should be possible to identify jurors who were able to influence others by enlisting partisans, by breaking opposition among holdouts and by engineering consensus, and thus permit us to trace the development of the sentencing verdict and ultimately to map the interpersonal dynamics of the decision process.

For the mapping of interpersonal influences, the CJP interviewers provide jurors with a copy of the jury list and ask them to identify jurors from the list according to the role they played and the influence they exerted on the respondent during guilt and penalty deliberations. Jurors are asked which jurors were most outspoken, most opinionated, most influential; which jurors advanced particular arguments; which jurors formed coalitions; and which jurors had the most influence on them and in what ways. With each additional interview in a given case, further details about the events and actors in the influence process will emerge. Interviewers will be able to focus questioning and probing in later interviews on critical points in the decision-making process that were revealed in earlier interviews. Such probing will be contingent upon issues raised in reading the trial transcript, upon the leads developed in interviews completed with other jurors, and upon the developing pattern of responses of the juror being interviewed.

There will naturally be discrepancies in jurors' perceptions of the decision-making process and hence in the accounts they give of the stands and actions of various others. The strength of this social influence and network mapping strategy is that it will enable us to trace the decision process from the vantage point of jurors with different perspectives and experiences, to compare the perspectives of particular jurors with the perceptions other jurors have of them, and to assess the centrality/marginality of the various jurors in the social group. The more jurors we can interview in a given case, the more reliably we will be able to map the networks of influence and trace the formation of pro-death and pro-life coalitions of jurors. A target sample of six juror interviews per case will be sought for a coherent picture of the influence process.

The Confounding Role of Race

Receptivity to mitigation as an individual disposition and as a product of interpersonal pressures has been found to differ by race of juror, as well by racial composition of the jury itself. Thus, an investigation of race linked perspectives in capital sentencing that examined three consistently mitigating factors found that whites on the same juries as blacks were much less likely to see the defendant as remorseful, to believe the defendant will not be dangerous in the future, and to feel lingering doubt about the defendant's guilt in black defendant/white victim cases (Bowers et al. 2001). Blacks in these cases more often see the defendant as remorseful and therefore deserving of mercy, and even more apt to wonder whether the defendant was the actual killer or at least whether the killing was a capital murder. These differences between black and white jurors are not simply the product of selective perceptions of defense evidence and arguments, but of a differential appreciation or receptivity to that evidence and those arguments by race of juror (Brewer 2004). In other words, however much black and white jurors may have differed in what they thought they heard, Brewer's research established that they also differed in their willingness to give effect to what they heard. Nor was the lower receptivity of white jurors to mitigation in these cases prompted by heightened receptivity to aggravation on their part; in fact, black and white jurors did not differ appreciably in receptivity to aggravation in these cases (Bowers, Sandys, and Brewer 2004). Hence, the very low level of receptivity to mitigation among white jurors in these cases suggests that, contrary to the law, many white jurors are simply failing to give effect to mitigation in black defendant/white victim cases.

Furthermore, in black defendant/white victim cases, black jurors believed more often than whites that the jury rushed to judgment, was intolerant of disagreement, and was dominated by a few outspoken jurors. Moreover, these differences between black and white jurors were greater between the males of the two races and in cases with white male dominated juries. Black jurors report that many of their white fellow jurors came to the trial with their minds made up about punishment and that they either ignored evidence of mitigation or treated it as trivial. For instance, in a case where a black juror said the defendant "seemed sorry and pled for his life," a white juror saw "the coldness of the man" (Bowers et al. 2001:249, 250).

According to the statistical data, black jurors more often feel that the jury was in a rush to reach a verdict and intolerant of disagreement; they feel more emphatically so in cases with five or more white male jurors. Further, these white-male-dominated juries appear to exacerbate the fissures between black and white jurors in lingering doubt, remorse, and dangerousness. And, as the trial proceeds, black and white jurors grow farther apart in their thinking about what the punishment should be. Jurors' narrative accounts of punishment deliberations reveal tactics of ostracism, deception, and intimidation in black defendant/white victim cases; they reflect tension, hostility, mistrust, and misunderstanding between black and white jurors. These decision-making dynamics appear to be driven by a determination to impose a particular verdict, not by a commitment to making a reasoned moral judgment on the part of individual jurors.

To further assess the confounding effect of race on receptivity to mitigation entails representing cases that vary in the number of black jury members, and cases that vary in the racial character of the crime (*i.e.*, white defendant and white victim killings, black defendant and white victim killings, and black defendant and black victim killings). Since blacks are usually in the minority on such juries, they must be given interviewing priority to ensure the representation of both black and white jurors who have served as members of the same juries, so that we can extend and refine our earlier comparisons of their thinking of black and white jurors about the same crime, the same defendant and the same victim.

Looking Ahead

Beyond these extensions of research on the capital jury now underway by CJP investigators, other research could be expected to contribute significantly to what we should know about the role of the jury in capital trials. Some directions that such research might take are sketched out below.

1. *The effect of punishment considerations on guilt decision-making.* The CJP findings that most jurors reported that during guilt deliberations the jury talked about the likely or appropriate punishment and that half of the jurors said they knew what the punishment should be at the guilt stage of the trial, strongly suggests that punishment considerations could have influenced their deliberations and decisions about guilt. This CJP evidence has prompted trial and appellate judges to call for separate juries at the guilt and penalty stages of the trial (*State of New Mexico v. Good* 2007; *United States v. Green* 2004). Matching a sample of cases tried capitally with those tried non-capitally might be one way to learn whether the prospect of making the life or death punishment decision affects jurors' decisions about guilt. The capital and non capital cases must be selected to be comparable in aspects of aggravation and mitigation, defendant and victim racial combination and similar attributes. The matched samples could be drawn within a state or between states with and without the death penalty. Within a state, the matching could be difficult because the cases tried capital are presumptively more aggravated, though disparate charging practices of prosecutors in different jurisdictions within a state might facilitate such matching. Matched samples of such cases from neighboring death penalty and abolitionist states would be the presumptively most serious murder cases in the

respective jurisdictions, and the findings could be more readily generalized to the difference between having and not having capital punishment.[12]

2. *The effects of the guilt trial experience on punishment decision-making.* Jurors' narrative accounts of their decision-making in cases where they voted for a death sentence reveal that the aggravated character of the crime was dispositive for many jurors. The jurors find the flood of horrifying details overwhelming; they become convinced that the aggravation requires death. By the time of the penalty stage many jurors simply see the mitigation as "no excuse" (Bentele and Bowers 2001). The death qualification process as an element of "structural aggravation" (Haney 1997; 1984), tends further to foster a pro-death disposition among jurors. The pro death influence of the guilt stage experience is also suggested by the fact that among death cases remanded for re-sentencing, juries exposed only to a penalty stage presentation of evidence and argument were much more likely to impose life than to renew the death sentence (Liebman, Fagan, and West 2000). A more focused assessment of the possibly biasing effect of the guilt trial on the punishment decision might compare jurors who served only on sentencing juries with those who served at both guilt and sentencing stages of capital trials. The cases would need to be comparable or matched in terms of crimes and defendant characteristics and in other aspects of aggravation and mitigation. This might best be accomplished by interviewing jurors who served on re-sentencing juries lacking guilt trial exposure and those who served on the original trial juries in the very same cases remanded for re-sentencing, and hence cases matched in aggravation and mitigation (though not necessarily in the presentation of these factors to the respective juries).

3. *The effects of interpersonal dynamics and the decision-making of capital jurors.* Much might be learned about the decision-making process in capital cases, and especially about the interpersonal dynamics involved, by reconvening capital juries (after perhaps a "decompression" delay of three to six months). The jurors in a given case, preferably most of the twelve, might be brought together to revisit their deliberations, to reiterate some of their own thinking, and to replay some of their interactions with others as they occurred during the original jury room exchanges. These group sessions might be expected to remind jurors of events, encounters, and exchanges they may have forgotten or selectively recounted in individual interviews, and they may re-ignite conflicts or

---

12. Notably, observed differences between the two samples could be owing to death qualification of the jurors in one but not the other sample as well as to the anticipation of making the punishment decision. The effects of these two factors might be distinguished through interviewing but it is their joint effect that is of interest.

disputes that erupted between jurors during the deliberations. Having jurors reenact portions of the decision-making process could yield insights about the nature and dynamics of such decision-making beyond what interviews with individual jurors would reveal. If these were cases where interviews with individual jurors had already been conducted, such interviews could serve as background that would point to issues and directions that those conducting the meeting should pursue. Researchers could raise questions about salient exchanges and key turning points in the deliberations and how they occurred. They could ask the various jurors what they said and felt at these critical points in the deliberations. This meeting should give jurors a chance to exchange views and voice disagreements with one another about the experience and personal meaning of serving as a capital juror on the case. From the vantage point of this retrospective, jurors could also be asked what they would do differently if they had it to do over again. Such sessions should be video taped for further analyses.[13]

4. *The effects of felt responsibility on decision-making.* Much might also be learned about the decision-making process in capital cases by selecting a shadow jury of persons that match those chosen as jurors for a capital trial, exposing them to the evidence, arguments and jury instructions at the guilt and penalty stages of that trial and asking them to reach a sentencing verdict at the same time the actual jurors are doing so. The shadow jurors' guilt and punishment deliberations could be directly observed and they could be interviewed about their decision-making at selected points during the trial and after their deliberations. Directly observing their deliberations could yield further insights about the nature and dynamics of such decision-making. While the use of shadow jurors who attend the trial and are exposed to the evidence might be challenged because they are not the ones who bear responsibility for the defendant's punishment, as has the use of mock jurors (*Lockhart v. McCree* 1986), this

---

13. Of course, having a video transcription of the actual deliberations would have definite advantages over a reconvening of the jury to prompt recall and to focus faithfully on what transpired. Efforts to arrange to record jury deliberations have met with considerable opposition in the past and in the capital context this might be expected to be especially difficult to navigate. The work of Kalven and Zeisel (1966) prompted lawmakers to block the direct observation of real juries for research purposes. Following the disclosure in 1955 of the audio taping of jury deliberations in connection with their research, the U.S. Attorney General publicly censured "eavesdropping" on jury deliberations. Congress and more than 30 states responded by enacting statutes prohibiting jury taping (Kalven and Zeisel 1966). Such barriers have occasionally been relaxed for media interests (e.g., the airing of video taped deliberations of a Wisconsin criminal jury on the PBS "Frontline" program, April 11, 1986 and of four Arizona juries on a two-hour NBC Special aired on April 16, 1997).

might in its own right make research with shadow jurors quite illuminating. In particular, working with a shadow jury and the actual jury on the same case might reveal problems in the decision-making of actual jurors associated with the weight of responsibility for the defendant's life or death punishment. Researchers could bring together members of both the real and the shadow juries and raise questions in the presence of both about salient exchanges and turning points in the deliberations and decisions of each group. This might reveal subtle but important differences in making a reasoned moral choice between jurors who actually have responsibility for the life or death punishment and those alleviated of that responsibility.

5. *The psychological/emotional effect of capital jury service.* Some research suggests that jurors who serve in capital trials may suffer intense and prolonged trauma owing to their role in deciding on the fate of another human being (Bienen 1993; Lanier 2004).[14] This impact has been identified alternatively as "vicarious traumatization," "secondary traumatization," "compassion fatigue," or Post Traumatic Stress Disorder (PTSD). Capital jurors should therefore be questioned about their death penalty experiences in an effort to detect, understand and assess the magnitude of any psychological problems stemming from their jury service. The limited focus to date suggests that making the capital sentencing decision generates "secondary victims," and these citizens should be identified, clinically assessed, and offered care for any problems stemming from their capital jury experience. Lanier (2004) further noted that almost a quarter of the respondents in his study claimed they would either "try to get out of it," or "refuse to do so" when asked if they would serve on a capital jury in the future (p. 613). This expressed unwillingness to accept future jury service in a capital case may be a subtle indication that those jurors who become averse to sitting on another death-penalty case were not able to remain fair and impartial during the term of their present jury service. Future research thus also should examine the potential biasing effects of emotionally troubling jury duty in a death penalty case on the individual juror's decision-making in that case.

---

14. Hoffmann (1995) also remarks on the discomfort of capital jurors: "Almost all of the jurors mentioned how they initially felt uncomfortable, sometimes even overwhelmed, by the role that they were being asked to play during the sentencing portion of the capital trial. And, after the trial was over, many jurors suffered lingering traumatic effects from their experience" (pp. 1155–1156). Jurors' attempts to "shift responsibility" for the death sentence from themselves to others, as detected during interviews of capital jurors (Hoffmann 1995), also might be understood as their attempt to deal with the emotions involved in their decision to take a life.

6. *The assessment of prospective reforms.* Courts or legislatures may adopt reforms intended to rid their capital statutes of the flaws demonstrated in the CJP research. These might include altering jury selection to improve the identification and barring of jurors with pro-death predispositions, or modifying jury instructions to achieve better understanding among jurors of their duties and responsibilities in making the punishment decision. Assessing such reforms should employ a scientifically developed and pre-tested interview instrument. The evaluation must cover a long enough post-reform period to obtain data on a sufficient sample of trials and jurors for reliable estimates of jurors' post-reform understandings and behavior. Similar data should be collected from a comparable sample of jurors who sat on cases prior to the reform that could serve as a baseline and facilitate the analysis of any changes that occurred. Care should be taken to detect any "announcement" effect that might be owing to publicity and special precautions taken at the introduction of the reform but not persisting thereafter. Further, such an evaluation should be authorized, funded, and carried out in conjunction with the court or legislative committee that initiated the changes so that the results will be heeded by the policy makers responsible for the reforms.

Studies conducted under experimental conditions with prospective or "mock jurors" might help to identify impediments to the selection and instruction of jurors who would perform their duties in accord with constitutional standards. Concerning jury selection, such studies have identified psychological predispositions that bias the decision-making of prospective jurors (O'Neil, Patry, and Penrod 2004) and shown that death qualification questioning tends to convey the assumption that the punishment should be death (Haney 1984). Concerning jury instructions, such research shows that current instructions do not adequately convey the concepts and processes essential to guiding penalty phase judgments nor does jury deliberation correct for jurors' errors in comprehension (Wiener *et al.* 2004), and that the rewording of instructions can modestly improve juror comprehension (Diamond and Levi 1996). Further studies of these kinds might suggest reforms that could alleviate some of the most egregious departures from constitutional standards.

While well executed reforms might improve jurors' comprehension of the guidelines they must follow in considering aggravating and mitigating circumstances, or improve jury selection and in so doing even bring down premature punishment decision-making, the question is not merely whether improvements can be made but whether such improvements would be substantial and comprehensive enough to render the demonstrated flaws constitutionally negligible. Furthermore, the seven constitutional flaws reviewed above are by no means a complete inventory. The CJP research now underway may well uncover evidence of additional departures from constitutional requirements, especially perhaps in the realms of receptivity to mitigation, social pressures on individual decision-making, and the confounding role of race.

Where Do We Stand?

The presently prevailing legal assumption is that the law can remedy the *Furman* ills of arbitrariness and discrimination. This is the stand the Court took in *Gregg*, though not without acknowledging that the remedy appeared "on its face" [only] "more likely" (than its absence) to banish the arbitrariness. While the problem was seen as faulty decision-making on the part of capital jurors, and the solution would be new laws that guide jurors' exercise of sentencing discretion, it is now evident that the guidelines are not working, that jurors are not following this guidance.

The natural inclination of those trained and accomplished in the law is to look for the solution to this problem in legal reforms — i.e., to think that the guidelines are not quite right yet, or that they are not being conveyed clearly or forcefully enough in the belief that the solution is to revise and refine the laws and to provide better instructions on how to implement them. Maybe a more formal screening and schooling of prospective jurors would help. Just as judges, prosecutors and defense attorneys can benefit from special preparation for their roles in capital cases, perhaps jurors also need special training for the proper performance of their role. The schooling might involve indoctrination in the decision-making guidelines and role playing to perfect their implementation in a simulated trial, a kind of professionalization of the jurors. Beyond this, the selection of jurors might require screening that would entail psychological testing to detect unconscious predispositions and biases, and to ensure that the prospective jurors had the right intellectual and emotional make up for the task. But, obviously, such a "Brave New World" transformation, nay professionalization of the capital jury, is hardly acceptable or workable within the constitutional bounds of our judicial system.

Another possibility is that the burden of deciding whether someone should live or die is a responsibility that many or most persons serving as jurors are simply not able or willing to accept or to carry out in accord with the legally prescribed directives. Perhaps the mix of fear and vengeance that capital crimes inspire make it impossible for many jurors to make a reasoned moral judgment that gives effect to mitigation. Perhaps the awful details of the crime and the evident emotional loss of victims' family members prompt jurors to begin to think about punishment, indeed become absolutely convinced of what the punishment should be, well before the penalty stage of the trial. Perhaps the death penalty advocacy of other jurors before the penalty stage of the trial, or even during penalty deliberations, overwhelms jurors' capacity for "individualized treatment," undermines jurors' reliance on sentencing guidelines, and forfeits their potential for a "reasoned moral judgment." And surely, the culturally ingrained element of race is not readily swept away by legal admonitions to overcome racial bias.

Can the manifest failures of capital sentencing to comport with constitutional standards eventually be fixed? Perhaps legal reforms can alleviate the departures from constitutional standards, at least to some extent. Or maybe Justice Harlan's pronouncement in *McGautha* (1971) that the task is "beyond present human ability" will be confirmed. Further research of the kinds outlined above should bring us closer to the answer. But, critically, the unrivaled evidence presently available on jurors' decision-making demonstrates that capital statutes and their implementation are now falling woefully short of constitutional standards. So far, America's experiment with the death penalty in the post *Furman* era has failed. The death sentences and executions imposed since *Furman* are sacrifices to legal fiction.

References

Acker, James R. and Charles S. Lanier. 1995. "Statutory Measures for More Effective Appellate Review of Capital Cases." *Criminal Law Bulletin* 31:211–258.

Bentele, Ursula and William J. Bowers. 2001. "How Jurors Decide on Death: Guilt is Overwhelming; Aggravation Requires Death; and Mitigation is No Excuse." *Brooklyn Law Review* 66:1011–1080.

Bienen, Leigh B. 1993. "Helping Jurors Out: Post-Verdict Debriefing for Jurors in Emotionally Disturbing Trials. *Indiana Law Journal* 68:1333–1355.

Blume, John H., Stephen P. Garvey, and Sheri L. Johnson. 2001. "Future Dangerousness in Capital Cases: Always 'At Issue.'" *Cornell Law Review* 86:397–410.

Bowers William J. and Wanda D. Foglia. Forthcoming. "Does Faulty Memory Distort the Evidence of Law's Failure to Purge Arbitrariness from Capital Sentencing?"

Bowers, William J. and Wanda D. Foglia. 2003. "Still Singularly Agonizing: Law's Failure to Purge Arbitrariness from Capital Sentencing." *Criminal Law Bulletin* 39:51–86.

Bowers, William J., Wanda D. Foglia, Jean E. Giles, and Michael E. Antonio. 2006 "The Decision Maker Matters: An Empirical Examination of the Way the Role of the Judge and the Jury Influence Death Penalty Decision-Making. *Washington and Lee Law Review* 63:931–1010.

Bowers, William J., Marla Sandys, and Thomas W. Brewer. 2004. "Crossing Racial Boundaries: A Closer Look at the Roots of Racial Bias in Capital Sentencing When the Defendant is Black and the Victim is White." *DePaul Law Review* 53:1497–1538.

Bowers, William J., Marla Sandys, and Benjamin D. Steiner. 1998. "Foreclosed Impartiality in Capital Sentencing: Jurors' Predispositions, Guilt-Trial Experience, and Premature Decision Making." *Cornell Law Review* 83:1476–1556.

Bowers, William J. and Benjamin D. Steiner. 1999. "Death by Default: An Empirical Demonstration of False and Forced Choices in Capital Sentencing." *Texas Law Review* 77:608–717.

Bowers, William J., Benjamin D. Steiner, and Michael E. Antonio. 2003. "The Capital Sentencing Decision: Guided Discretion, Reasoned Moral Judgment, or Legal Fiction." Pp. 413–467 in *America's Experiment with Capital Punishment: Reflections on the Past, Present, and Future of the Ultimate Penal Sanction*. 2nd ed., edited by James R. Acker, Robert M. Bohm, and Charles S. Lanier. Durham, NC: Carolina Academic Press.

Bowers, William J., Benjamin D. Steiner, and Marla Sandys. 2001. "Death Sentencing in Black and White: An Empirical Analysis of the Role of Jurors' Race and Jury Racial Composition." *University of Pennsylvania Journal of Constitutional Law* 3:171–274.

Bowers, William J. and Scott E. Sundby. This Volume. "Why the Downturn in Death Sentences?"

Brewer, Thomas. 2005. "The Attorney-Client Relationship in Capital Cases and Its Impact on Juror Receptivity to Mitigation Evidence." *Justice Quarterly* 22:340–363.

_____. 2004. "Race and Jurors' Receptivity to Mitigation in Capital Cases: The Effect of Jurors', Defendants', and Victims' Race in Combination." *Law and Human Behavior* 28:529–545.

_____. 2003. "Don't Kill My Friend: The Attorney-Client Relationship in Capital Cases and its Effect on Jury Receptivity to Mitigation Evidence." Doctoral Dissertation, University at Albany, State University of New York. *Dissertation Abstracts International* 64:631–764.

Caldwell v. Mississippi (1985). 472 U.S. 320.

Diamond, Shari Seidman, and Judith N. Levi. 1996. "Improving Decisions on Death by Revising and Testing Jury Instructions." *Judicature* 79:224–232.

Eddings v. Oklahoma (1982). 455 U.S. 104.

Eisenberg, Theodore, Stephen P. Garvey, and Martin T. Wells. 1998. "But Was He Sorry? The Role of Remorse in Capital Sentencing." *Cornell Law Review* 83:1599–637.

Furman v. Georgia (1972). 408 U.S. 238.

Geimer, William and Jonathan Amsterdam. 1988. "Why Jurors Vote Life or Death: Operative Factors in Ten Florida Death Penalty Cases." *American Journal of Criminal Law* 15:1–54.

Gillers, Stephen. 1980. "Deciding Who Dies." *University of Pennsylvania Law Review* 129:1–124.

Gregg v. Georgia (1976). 428 U.S. 153.

Haney, Craig. 1997. "Violence and the Capital Jury: Mechanisms of Moral Disengagement and the Impulse to Condemn to Death." *Stanford Law Review* 49:1447–1486.

_____. 1984. "On the Selection of Capital Juries: The Biasing Effects of the Death Qualification Process." *Law and Human Behavior* 8:121–132.

Haney, Craig, Lester Sontag, and Sally Costanzo. 1994. "Deciding to Take a Life: Capital Juries, Sentencing Instructions, and the Jurisprudence of Death." *Journal of Social Issues* 50:149–176.

Hoffmann, Joseph L. 1995. "Where's the Buck?—Juror Misperception of Sentencing Responsibility in Death Penalty Cases." *Indiana Law Journal* 70:1137–1160.

Jurek v. Texas (1976). 428 U.S. 262.

Kalven, Harry and Hans Zeisel. 1966. *The American Jury.* Boston, MA: Little, Brown.

Lanier, Charles S. 2004. "The Role of Experts and Other Witnesses in Capital Penalty Hearings: The Views of Jurors Charged With Determining the 'Simple Sentence of Death.'" Doctoral Dissertation, University at Albany, State University of New York.

Liebman, James S., Jeffrey Fagan, and Valerie West. 2000. "Capital Attrition: Error Rates in Capital Cases, 1973–1995." *Texas Law Review* 78:1839–1865.

Lockett v. Ohio (1978). 438 U.S. 586.

Lockhart v. McCree (1986). 476 U.S. 162.

McCleskey v. Kemp (1987). 481 U.S. 279.

McGautha v. California (1971). 402 U.S. 183.

McKoy v. North Carolina (1990). 494 U.S. 433.

Mills v. Maryland (1988). 486 U.S. 367.

Morgan v. Illinois (1992). 504 U.S. 719.

Note. 1974. "Discretion and the Constitutionality of the New Death Penalty Statutes." *Harvard Law Review* 87:1690–1719.

O'Neil, Kevin M., Marc W. Patry, and Steven D. Penrod, (2004). "Beyond Death Qualification: Exploring the Effects of Attitudes Toward the Death Penalty on Capital Sentencing Verdicts" *Psychology, Public Policy, and Law* 10:443–470.
Penry v. Lynaugh (1989). 492 U.S. 302.
Proffitt v. Florida (1976). 428 U.S. 242.
Pulley v. Harris (1984). 465 U.S. 37.
Sandys, Marla, Adam Trahan, and Heather Pruss. Forthcoming. "Taking Account of 'the Diminished Capacity of the Retarded:' Are Capital Jurors Up to the Task." *DePaul Law Review*.
Shafer v. South Carolina (2001). 532 U.S. 36.
Simmons v. South Carolina (1994). 512 U.S. 154.
State of New Mexico v. Good (2007) No. D-0101-CR-200400522 N.M. Dist. Ct., 1st Dist.
Sundby, Scott E. 1998. "The Capital Jury and Absolution: The Intersection of Trial Strategy, Remorse, and the Death Penalty." *Cornell Law Review* 83:1557–1598.
_____. 1997. "The Jury as Critic: An Empirical Look at How Capital Juries Perceive Expert and Lay Testimony." *Virginia Law Review* 83:1109–1188.
Turner v. Murray (1986). 476 U.S. 28.
United States v. Green (2004). 348 F. Supp. 2d 1; 2004 U.S. Dist.
Weisberg, Robert. 1983. "Deregulating Death." *The Supreme Court Review* 1983:305–395.
Wiener, Richard L., Melanie Rogers, Ryan Winter, Linda Hurt, Amy Hackney, Karen Kadela, Hope Seib, Shannon Rauch, Laura Warren, and Ben Morasco. 2004. "Guided Jury Discretion in Capital Murder Cases: The Role of Declarative and Procedural Knowledge" *Psychology, Public Policy, and Law* 10:516–576.
Woodson v. North Carolina (1976). 428 U.S. 280.
Zant v. Stephens (1983). 462 U.S. 862.

Section III
The Process Beyond the Sentencing Decision

CHAPTER 11

The Future of Innocence

Richard C. Dieter

Introduction

The issue of innocence has had a profound impact on the death penalty debate in the United States in recent years. Since 1973, one hundred and twenty-four people have been exonerated and freed from death row (Death Penalty Information Center (DPIC) 2007a). About half of these exonerations took place in the past ten years. Many other people not on death row have been freed from prison through newly discovered DNA evidence, also in the past decade (Innocence Project 2007).

Although support for the death penalty is subject to a complex array of influences, it should be possible to quantify some of the effect of the innocence issue on the use of capital punishment. Moreover, it would be very worthwhile to identify the problem areas in the criminal justice system that have led to death penalty exonerations so that changes can be implemented to prevent these mistakes. Finally, analyzing the trends of the past ten years may provide insight into the future of capital punishment, especially in light of the changes spurred by the issue of innocence.

The Impact of Innocence

The dramatic decline in the use of the death penalty since 2000 has been a surprising development. Given the steady rise in executions in the 1990s, the constant flow of new cases into the system, and the political climate that elected a strong pro-death penalty candidate as President in 2000, it would have been natural to expect a broad increase in the use of capital punishment. Moreover, the tragic events of September 11, 2001, might have completely solidified this country's commitment to a broad and expanding death penalty.[1]

But that did not happen. Instead, we have seen death sentences decline by nearly 60 percent since the start of 1999. Executions are down 45 percent. The size of death row has declined each year after 25 years of constant increases (Bureau of Justice Statistics 2006; DPIC 2006). Even public opinion, which still favors the death penalty, has dropped noticeably from its high point of 80% support in 1994 to 65% in 2006 (Gallup 2006).

Many factors besides innocence, such as the wider use of life-without-parole sentencing, may have contributed to the decline in death sentences (Bowers and Sundby, this volume). But the innocence issue has captured the attention of Supreme Court justices, religious and political leaders, and even former supporters of the death penalty (DPIC 2007b). Moreover, the innocence issue has firmly established itself in the popular culture through books by authors such as John Grisham (2006) and Scott Turow (2003), movies by directors such as Clint Eastwood (1999), and in the ubiquitous "CSI" television programs. Since no one supports the taking of innocent life,[2] and since the risk of wrongful executions cannot be entirely eliminated, the punishment itself is on the defensive, not just its use against innocent defendants.

Areas of Research

The issue of innocence presents the field of criminal justice with numerous opportunities for research. Generally, it would be helpful to measure the impact that innocence has had on the declining use of the death penalty. Cre-

---

1. Indeed, following the terror attack in Oklahoma City in 1995, there was a marked increase in the use of the death penalty and in the passage of legislation such as the "Anti-terrorism and Effective Death Penalty Act of 1996" to speed up executions. On the other hand, there is evidence that the attacks of September 11 might have tempered the country's punitive response to crime. A survey by the Pew Research Center shortly after September 11 found that 78% of the public believed that the influence of religion in American life was growing. A similar survey taken six months before the attack showed that only 37% believed that religion was becoming more prominent (Pew Research Center 2007).

2. Polls do indicate that Americans support the death penalty even while believing that innocent people have been executed (Dieter 2007d). But that does not mean that they support the taking of innocent life. Rather, it may only represent the belief that some mistakes are tolerable to achieve a higher goal: "Society has a right to protect itself from capital offenses even if this means taking a finite chance of executing an innocent person" (Pojman 2004:68).

ative research has been conducted by Professor Frank Baumgartner and colleagues (Baumgartner, De Boef, and Boydstun forthcoming), who have correlated the number of media stories about the death penalty (stories frequently focused on the possible innocence of a defendant) with the number of death sentences imposed on a national basis. Their research revealed that as the number of media stories increased, the number of death sentences declined.

Opinion research could be conducted into how the public perceive the issue of innocence and what effect it is having on their views of the death penalty. Research similar to that already conducted by the Capital Jury Project (Bowers, Sandys, and Steiner 1998) into whether jurors in capital cases are becoming more hesitant to impose death sentences because of the lingering doubts they may have about the defendant, or about the justice system generally, could also be instructive.

The Death Penalty Information Center recently conducted a national opinion poll to measure the impact of the innocence issue on the public's death penalty views (Dieter 2007). According to the poll conducted in 2007, nearly 40% of the public believe that they would be disqualified from serving on a jury in a death penalty case because of their moral beliefs. Over two-thirds (68%) of African-Americans in this survey believe they would be excluded as capital jurors; 48% of women reached the same conclusion, and 47% of Catholics. While these latter numbers are based on sub-samples with a larger margin of error than the whole poll, they point to a problem of unrepresentative capital juries that do not reflect the country's diversity.

By a wide margin, the American public believe that the most significant development in the death penalty in recent years has been the advent of DNA testing and the proof that many who were sentenced to death were innocent. Only 39% of the public expressed either complete or "quite a bit" of confidence that the justice system sentences only the guilty to death. A strong majority (75%) of those polled believe that we need a higher standard of proof for guilt in death penalty cases.

Most Americans have been affected by the news of the many exonerations in death penalty cases. Only 37% said that such news had no effect on their position on the death penalty. Sixty percent said that these wrongful convictions had either lessened their support for the death penalty or strengthened their already existing opposition.

From a research perspective, it would be helpful to know to what extent the decline in death sentences has been due to fewer jury verdicts, and to what extent it is due to fewer capital prosecutions. Are these two causes related: *i.e.*, are prosecutors electing to settle more cases with a lesser sentence because they know it is harder to obtain a death sentence from a jury? Are the growing expense of capital prosecutions and heightened risk of penalty-phase deliberations ending with a life sentence steering more cases out of death penalty consideration?

The issue of innocence is an important ground for empirical research because its impact is not only felt when the innocent go free, but in every case to which reforms are applied. Awareness of this problem is not only significant when it leads people to denounce the execution of the innocent, but also when it draws them into a discussion of the inherent risks in the punishment itself.

When an inmate like Anthony Porter is exonerated and freed from death row in Illinois in 1999 primarily through the investigative work of journalism students (Belluck 1999), the question arises: "How did that happen?" The answers vary with each case, but consistent themes run through these miscarriages of justice: faulty eyewitness identifications, ineffective counsel, withheld evidence, and false confessions. As a result, innocence cases have sparked a series of reforms that affect every death penalty prosecution and many non-death penalty cases as well. For example, some states have adopted standards for capital representation, lifted unreasonable caps on compensation, and allowed the admission of new evidence arising after conviction (DPIC 2007c). Moreover, many jurors are demanding a higher degree of proof of guilt before they are willing to impose a death sentence (Dieter 2005).

Counting the Cases of Innocence

The issue of innocence, of course, has been the subject of much research in the past. Surprisingly, one of the areas that still stirs controversy is the question of *who is innocent*. The resolution of this issue is clearly important for future research.

In 1993, DPIC became directly involved in quantifying the issue of innocence through the collection of cases in which people were exonerated and freed from death row. DPIC's "Innocence List" originated in a request from Representative Don Edwards of California in 1993. Rep. Edwards was then the Chairman of the House Subcommittee on Civil and Constitutional Rights, and he asked DPIC to assess the risk that innocent people might be sentenced to death or executed under current laws. DPIC prepared a draft report that resulted in the publication of a Staff Report of the Subcommittee later that year (Subcommittee on Civil and Constitutional Rights 1993). As part of that report analyzing the risks of sentencing innocent people to death, DPIC included a list of individuals who had been on death row and who subsequently had their convictions overturned. In almost all of the 48 cases listed, the end result was either a retrial in which the defendant was acquitted, or the dismissal of all charges by the prosecution.

In preparing this list, DPIC relied on the research of others, particularly the contributions of Michael Radelet, Hugo Bedau, and Constance Putnam (1992). However, DPIC sought to apply a more restrictive and objective definition of innocence. It chose not to rely on the collective judgment of researchers that a defendant was probably innocent, despite the value of such opinions. Rather, it elected to employ only the decisions rendered by the justice system, as it applied its traditional procedures and criteria for determining guilt or innocence, and to restrict DPIC's role primarily to recording the history of those judgments.

In the years since that initial report, DPIC has continued to maintain this innocence list, which now consists of 124 cases. The criteria for inclusion on the list are clearly stated in its reports on this issue (Dieter 2004, 1997 and 1993) and on its website. DPIC's list consists only of:

Cases involving former death row inmates who have since 1973:

- Been acquitted of all charges related to the crime that placed them on death row; or
- Had all charges related to the crime that placed them on death row dismissed by the prosecution; or
- Been granted a complete pardon based on evidence of innocence.

Others have compiled innocence lists that differ from DPIC's. However, a far different approach to how innocence cases should be counted has recently arisen as a response to the widespread attention this issue has been receiving.

This approach, voiced in op-eds, amicus briefs and other venues, attempts to diminish the importance of the innocence issue by drastically reducing the number of cases (Ponnuru 2002). The thrust of this approach can be summarized fairly simply: defendants are not "innocent" just because they have been acquitted at a trial or have no charges pending against them. The basis for denying these individuals the status of innocence is the opinions of prosecutors, investigating officers, and sometimes judges, expressing the view that a defendant is still *likely* guilty, despite his or her legal exoneration.

Typically, this approach does not clearly define how a person, once convicted of a crime, can ever be deemed innocent. This highly restrictive use of innocence is premised on the notion that even when defendants who have been charged with a crime have been acquitted of all charges at trial, they still have more to prove to be considered "innocent." A person must additionally pass a subjective test of "actual innocence" set by prosecutors or other advocates. If these self-appointed judges determine that the person is *probably* guilty—despite an official determination that their guilt does not meet the time-honored standard of "beyond a reasonable doubt"—then that person is not innocent and should not be included on DPIC's, or anyone else's, innocence list.

This is a very different notion of innocence than traditionally used in our justice system. DPIC specifically avoided such subjective second-guessing and vague judgments that would surely have left it open to claims of bias.[3] Such an extra requirement of a person's status of innocence is also contrary to our country's long-standing traditions and constitutional principles. The bedrock principle that a person is innocent until proven guilty beyond a reasonable doubt is the individual's protection in society against the unchecked power of the state to diminish a person's status through mere suspicion.

A particularly noteworthy example of this extra requirement for innocence occurred in Justice Scalia's concurrence in *Kansas v. Marsh* (2006). Justice Scalia took strong exception to the dissent's contention that, because of all the mistakes made in capital cases, we should be erring on the side of caution even when it comes to death sentencing. Justice Souter, writing for the four dissenters in *Marsh*, had stated that:

> [A] new body of fact must be accounted for in deciding what, in practical terms, the Eighth Amendment guarantees should tolerate, for the period starting in 1989 has seen repeated exonerations of convicts under death sentences, in numbers never imagined before the development of DNA tests (*Kansas v. Marsh* 2006:2544).

For Justice Scalia, the claim of "repeated exonerations ... in numbers never imagined before" was grossly exaggerated. He specifically criticized DPIC and others for overstating the innocence issue. In particular, he attempted to discredit the innocence list by discussing the case of one of the people on the list, Delbert Tibbs.

Justice Scalia's opinion would give the distinct impression that Tibbs escaped death unjustly on the barest of technicalities. What he failed to mention is that mistaken eyewitness identifications (and Tibbs' conviction was based largely on a single eyewitness) are one of the primary reasons for wrongful convictions. He leaves out that Tibbs was black and that the witness was white, that she was a drug-user at the time of the crime, and that he was tried by an

---

3. In a subsequent letter, Chairman Edwards thanked DPIC on behalf of his Subcommittee for this objectivity: "This document and the Center's other reports serve as the basic reference materials for objective, relevant data on the death penalty" (Letter from Don Edwards, Subcommittee on Civil and Constitutional Rights, Oct. 22, 1993 (on file with DPIC)).

all-white jury for rape and murder in Florida. Tibbs' conviction was thrown out by the Florida Supreme Court because the *state's case lacked sufficient credibility* (*Tibbs v. State* 1976). Given the reluctance of any appellate court to make such a judgment overturning a jury's verdict, this is far more than a technicality. Furthermore, Justice Scalia does not mention that the prosecutor from the original trial later called the case "tainted from the beginning," and vowed to be a witness for the defense if the case was tried again (Radelet *et al.* 1992:59).

For Justice Scalia, Tibbs was merely "a lucky man," not an innocent one. He maintains that cases in which the state drops all charges should not be counted as innocence cases. Besides the fact that this approach strips away a person's fragile right on the basis of unproven suspicion, it also tends to obscure the overriding importance of these cases.

However one may label the people who have been freed, their cases should raise concerns across the country. In each of the 124 innocence cases, the justice system unanimously convicted an individual and expressed such certainty in its decision that it then sentenced the person to death. This same justice system then reviewed the cases and concluded that each person could not even be convicted of the slightest offense, and each one was set free. That reflects a disturbing record and should be ample cause for the Court's attention. Even if one were to refuse to grant these individuals the status of innocence, their cases represent the tremendous risks and unreliability involved in death sentencing.

Future Research Related to Innocence

In addition to the areas of possible research mentioned above—measuring the impact of the innocence issue on juries, prosecutors, and public opinion, and the need for properly defining the concept of innocence—a number of other research areas related to this issue present themselves. One such topic is the potential use of innocence commissions.

Innocence Commissions

The frequency of mistakes in capital cases has led some jurisdictions to consider extra-judicial bodies to explore two areas of concern. One area is to examine cases that have already been overturned to discern how the system failed and what changes need to be made to prevent a reoccurrence. This was the principal task given to the Illinois Death Penalty Commission in the wake of Governor George Ryan's imposition of a moratorium on executions in that state in 2000 (Associated Press 2003). The Illinois Commission consisted of a broad spectrum of prominent state individuals concerned about the justice system. It deliberated for over two years and produced an impressive array of recommendations. Only a small portion of the recommendations has been adopted by the state legislature, but the moratorium on executions remains in place. Although it was not delegated with the question of whether the death penalty should be continued in any form, the Commission noted that its majority view was that it would be better to simply abolish the death penalty (Illinois 2007). If the death penalty was to be continued, it offered 85 changes to current law and practice to make the system fairer and more reliable.

By way of contrast, a government commission in Florida also considered that state's cases of innocence. Its conclusions were far different than those drawn by the commission in Illinois. Florida has had more people exonerated and freed from death row than any other state. Its commission reviewed the cases of 23 people who had been freed from death row (21 of whom were on DPIC's innocence list) (Florida Commission on Capital Cases 2002). Citing mostly comments from prosecutors and police, the commission concluded that *none* of the 23 defendants was innocent, and that the guilt of only four could be doubted. One member of the commission went even further in comments to the press, concluding that no one on *death row* was innocent, even though the Commission never looked at those cases (Associated Press 2002).

The radical differences between these two commissions had to do with the perception of the gravity of the problem of innocence, the selection of who would serve on the commission, and on the definition of innocence. The mere establishment of a review process is not always sufficient to get to the heart of the problem.

A second kind of commission could be established to explore the possible innocence of people presently in prison or on death row. Although courts and the appellate process already exist to distinguish the guilty from the innocent, procedural barriers to bringing claims of innocence have often prevented the truth from coming out. Almost all states have specific time restrictions on presenting new evidence after trial. In other cases, defense attorneys have failed to investigate and present claims that their clients urged them to explore. And, of course, in death penalty cases, the execution of the defendant makes it almost impossible for the judicial system to reverse a prior conviction.

The model for a body to review claims of innocence from those in prison and on death row is the Criminal Cases Review Commission established in the United Kingdom in 1997 (Criminal Cases Review Commission 2007). The Commission reviews both convictions and sentences. Cases that merit further consideration are sent to a court of appeals. The Commission has received almost 9,000 applications since its inception.

This model was recently adopted by the state of North Carolina in the wake of a number of high profile exonerations there. The Innocence Inquiry Commission was promoted by the former Chief Justice of the North Carolina Supreme Court, I. Beverly Lake. It is the first of its kind in the United States (Woolverton 2006).

The commission consists of eight members, including a prosecutor and a sheriff. The commission has subpoena power to pursue evidence. If an appeal to the commission is found to have sufficient merit, it is sent to a three-judge panel, which would have to agree unanimously in order to overturn a conviction. If an inmate pleaded guilty, he or she must wait two years before applying for relief from the commission. As presently constituted, the commission will only hear claims filed through 2010.

This commission is certainly not without its critics. It is possible that, given its mix of members and cumbersome procedures, it will have only a minimal impact on freeing the innocent. The existence of the commission does not take away any rights that defendants have of pursuing their appeals in the traditional fashion. However, once someone files a petition with the commission, he or she can be required to testify. Moreover, the commission can use evidence that would not otherwise be admissible in court, such as evidence obtained without a warrant or without *Miranda* rights being given, in its deliberations.

Given the unique structure and power of this body, research into its use would be very helpful:

- Do such commissions lessen the importance of the courts, or the responsibility of the jury in the criminal justice system?
- If there are flaws in the regular courts, does the establishment of such a commission relieve the burden of remedying those flaws?
- What rights does a defendant have if denied relief by the commission?
- What power does the public have to affect the composition and decisions of the commission?
- Should such a commission consider the case of someone who was executed, but where new evidence of their innocence has emerged?

Innocent and Executed

In Texas, the need for an independent commission to examine claims that an innocent person has been executed recently became clear in a case from San Antonio. Following an investigation by attorneys associated with the NAACP Legal Defense and Educational Fund, the *Houston Chronicle* conducted its own inquiry and concluded that Ruben Cantu, who was executed in 1993, was likely innocent of the murder for which he was condemned to death (Olsen 2005).

The former District Attorney of Bexar County, Samuel Milsap, who approved of Cantu's original capital prosecution, now believes that Cantu was "probably innocent," and he has taken full responsibility for the error (Pew Forum 2006). However, the actual investigation of the innocence claim is being handled by the present District Attorney, Susan Reed, who as a judge, signed Cantu's death warrant (Houston Chronicle 2006). Witnesses who have come forward concerning the original crime have been mocked by prosecutors in the D.A.'s office, and some have been threatened with charges of perjury (Olsen 2006). This conflict of interest and possible prejudgment have prompted calls for an independent investigation, but to no avail.

In July 2007, the D.A.'s office issued its report on the Cantu case, concluding that there was no credible evidence pointing to his innocence. Their investigation included interviews with 80 people involved in the case, and claimed to have uncovered even more evidence pointing to Cantu's guilt. Critics pointed to flaws in the investigation and called for an independent investigation (Robbins and Olsen 2007).

A similar scenario played out regarding the possible innocence of Larry Griffin, who was executed in Missouri in 1995. An investigation by the NAACP Legal Defense and Educational Fund had revealed considerable evidence casting doubt on Griffin's guilt in the murder for which he was sentenced to death. The prosecutor's report, issued on July 12, 2007, however, concluded that Griffin was guilty and challenged some of the Legal Defense Fund's assertions (Patrick and Ratcliffe 2007). Such cases illustrate the precarious nature of innocence claims where an objective standard is not available—different conclusions will be drawn by different observers (Kirchmeier 2006).

In these and similar cases (see, *e.g.*, Cameron Willingham executed in Texas in 2004 and Carlos DeLuna executed in Texas in 1989 (DPIC 2007d)), an independent state or national innocence commission could conduct an inquiry that would engender greater public confidence. Researchers could play a pivotal role in identifying potential cases of innocence meriting fuller investigations by a commission. The potential impact of such cases is illustrated by the posthumous royal pardon of Timothy John Evans in England in 1966 (Bedau and Radelet 1987). Evans had been executed in 1950 and his pardon coincided with suspension of executions and eventual abolition of the death penalty in that country.

In its recent report on the death penalty in Florida, a panel convened by the American Bar Association's Death Penalty Moratorium Implementation Project recommended the establishment of two innocence-related commissions, one of each type mentioned above. The first commission would pursue the causes of the wrongful convictions in capital cases that have already occurred and recommend changes to prevent future mistakes. The second commission would review claims of innocence from those on death row (American Bar Association 2006). Similarly, legislation to establish a commission like the one in North Carolina has already passed one house of the Pennsylvania legislature, and been proposed in New York (Christianson 2007).

Legislation

Another area to be explored in the realm of legislative activity concerns two recent efforts to reinstate the death penalty in non-death penalty states. In Massachusetts, then-Governor Mitt Romney proposed a "gold-standard" death penalty law: defendants would only be eligible for a death sentence if the jury believed they were guilty beyond any doubt and the conviction was obtained through the use of scientific evidence. The bill followed the recommendation of a committee appointed by the governor to study this issue. The bill was soundly defeated by the legislature (Helman 2005).

- Would such a law have been practical?
- If a jury can consider even *un*reasonable doubts, is there any limit to what they might imagine in considering the credibility of the state's evidence?
- Even if it would have been unwise for Massachusetts to base reinstatement of the death penalty on the promise of a "fool-proof" statute, would a variation on such a system be an improvement in states that do have the death penalty currently?
- Should states with the death penalty formally allow juries to consider lingering doubts about the guilt of the defendant whom they have already convicted when considering to sentence him to death?

In the 2006 elections, voters in Wisconsin were asked whether the death penalty should be reinstated with a law that would require that a capital conviction be supported by DNA evidence.

- Is that a reliable criterion for eliminating the risks of our present system?
- What are the chances that DNA evidence can be faulty?
- Would such a criterion interfere in selecting the "worst of the worst" from among those who have committed murder by choosing only those who happen to leave DNA evidence?

Voters approved the referendum by a majority of 56%, though they also strengthened the hand of the legislators who opposed the death penalty, so no re-instatement is likely. Interestingly, the legislator who proposed the referendum conceded that the DNA requirement for conviction was only a starting point for the legislation and was not likely to be included in a final law (Capital Times 2006).

Other Questions

In looking forward to using the issue of innocence to explore broader problems in the criminal justice system, two general areas could also be the basis for further research:

1. Many states, prompted by errors that have been revealed in recent years, have empanelled study commissions to review their death penalty systems. Some, like the commission in Illinois, recommended extensive changes to the death penalty, if it was to be kept at all. In New Jersey (Associated Press 2007) and New York (New York State Assembly 2005), hearings conducted over many days with testimony from state and national experts resulted in reports that found compelling reasons to end the death penalty. In other states, such as Georgia, Alabama, Florida, Tennessee and Arizona, the American Bar Association sponsored reviews and produced reports calling for broad changes in the respective state systems (American Bar Association 2006; Fleischaker, this volume). Still other legislative investigations in states like Nebraska and Indiana found only narrow areas requiring reform (DPIC 2007c).

From this extensive body of knowledge about the practice of the death penalty in states across the country:

- Are there common problem areas identified in these investigations?
- What are the consensus recommendations for change from these reviews?
- How many states have adopted recommended changes as a result of these reviews?
- Are errors in capital cases decreasing because of these changes?
- What are the political and practical obstacles to further reform?
- How much would such reforms add to the costs of the death penalty?
- Would such expenses be justified?

2. As discussed above, there has been a recent sharp decline in the use of the death penalty. This, too, raises a series of questions and research possibilities:

- Is the decline in death sentences and executions likely to continue, to level off, or to reverse direction?
- Is the decline in death sentences due to fewer judgments of death, fewer prosecutions, a drop in the murder rate, or other causes?

- What has been the role of life-without-parole sentences in the decreased use of the death penalty?
- When did the various states adopt life without parole and what happened to their death sentencing rate after adoption?
- Have there been previous drops in the use of the death penalty in the United States, and if so, why did the use rise again?
- What has been the international experience when the death penalty has been used less? Has declining use been a precursor to abolition, or is the use of the death penalty cyclical?
- The expansion of the federal death penalty has run counter to the death penalty trends in the states. The number of people on the federal death row has more than doubled since 2000 and federal capital trials are being conducted in many states that do not have their own death penalty (Schmitt 2004). What are the implications of the broader use of the federal death penalty?

Conclusion

The issue of innocence has received a high level of attention since the late 1990s and the early 2000s. It continues to have a profound effect on the death penalty in the U.S. today. Efforts to empirically measure the importance of innocence, through public opinion research, systematic interviews with jurors, through a quantification of the legislative and policy changes that have occurred, and by exploring the notion of innocence commissions and other initiatives, could give the country a better idea of where the death penalty is headed, and could help the public discern whether continuing this punishment makes good public policy sense.

References

American Bar Association. 2006. "Evaluating Fairness and Accuracy in State Death Penalty Systems." See Florida Death Penalty Assessment Report. (http://www.abavideonews.org/ABA340/index.php).

Associated Press. 2007. New Jersey Death Penalty Study Commission's report. Jan. 2.

_____. 2003. "Illinois Reforms System for Death Penalty." *Washington Post*, Nov. 20, A11.

_____. 2002. "State Senator Says Review of Cases Finds No Innocence." June 20.

Baumgartner, Frank, Suzanna De Boef, and Amber E. Boydstun. Forthcoming 2008. *The Decline of the Death Penalty and the Discovery of Innocence.* New York, NY: Cambridge University Press.

Bedau, Hugo and Michael Radelet. 1987. "Miscarriages of Justice in Potentially Capital Cases." *Stanford Law Review* 40:21–179.

Belluck, Pam. 1999. "Convict Freed After 16 Years on Death Row." *New York Times*, Feb. 6, A7.

Bowers, William, Marla Sandys, and Benjamin D. Steiner. 1998. "Foreclosed Impartiality in Capital Sentencing: Jurors' Predispositions, Guilt-Trial Experience, and Premature Decision Making." *Cornell Law Review* 83:1476–1566.

Bowers, William J. and Scott E. Sundby. This Volume. "Why the Downturn in Death Sentences?"

Bureau of Justice Statistics. 2006. "Capital Punishment 2005." (http://www.ojp.gov/bjs/pub/pdf/cp05.pdf).

Capital Times, The (Wisconsin). 2006. Nov. 8.

Christianson, Scott. 2007. "Perspective: Appoint Commission to Study Wrongful Convictions." *New York Law Journal*, May 15.

Criminal Cases Review Commission. 2007. (http://www.ccrc.gov.uk/).

Death Penalty Information Center. 2007a. "Innocence: List of Those Freed From Death Row." (http://www.deathpenaltyinfo.org/article.php?scid=6&did=110).

_____. 2007b. "New Voices." (http://www.deathpenaltyinfo.org/article.php?did=482&scid=16).

_____. 2007c. "Recent Legislative Activity." (http://www.deathpenaltyinfo.org/article.php?did=236&scid=40).

_____. 2007d. "Executed But Possibly Innocent." (http://www.deathpenaltyinfo.org/article.php?&did=2238).

_____. 2006. "The Death Penalty in 2006: Year End Report." (http://www.deathpenaltyinfo.org/2006YearEnd.pdf).

Dieter, Richard C. 2007. "A Crisis of Confidence: Americans' Doubts About the Death Penalty." Death Penalty Information Center Report. (http://www.deathpenaltyinfo.org/CoC.pdf).

_____. 2005. "Blind Justice: Juries Deciding Life and Death With Only Half the Truth." Death Penalty Information Center Report. (http://www.deathpenaltyinfo.org/BlindJusticeReport.pdf).

_____. 2004. Innocence reports on Death Penalty Information Center Website. (http://www.deathpenaltyinfo.org/article.php?did=404&scid=45).

_____. 1997. Innocence reports on Death Penalty Information Center Website. (http://www.deathpenaltyinfo.org/article.php?did=404&scid=45).

_____. 1993. Innocence reports on Death Penalty Information Center Website. (http://www.deathpenaltyinfo.org/article.php?did=404&scid=45).
Eastwood, Clint. 1999. Director of the movie "True Crime."
Fleischaker, Deborah. This Volume. "The ABA Death Penalty Moratorium Implementation Project: Setting the Stage for Further Research."
Florida Commission on Capital Cases. 2002. Report: June 20.
Gallup News Service. 2006. Press release, June 1.
Grisham, John. 2006. *The Innocent Man: Murder and Injustice in a Small Town*. New York, NY: Doubleday.
Helman, Scott. 2005. "Death Penalty Bill Fails in House: Romney Initiative Roundly Defeated." *Boston Globe*, November 16, B1.
Houston Chronicle. 2006. Editorial, "Mistrust: Court's Decision to Leave a Wrongful Execution Inquiry With a Tainted DA Clouds Texas Justice." Sept. 5, B6.
Illinois 2007. "Capital Punishment: Commission on Capital Punishment Report, April 2002." (http://www.idoc.state.il.us/ccp/ccp/reports/index.html).
Innocence Project, The. 2007. (http://www.innocenceproject.org/).
Kansas v. Marsh (2006). 126 U.S. 2516.
Kirchmeier, Jeffrey. 2006. "Dead Innocent: The Death Penalty Abolitionist Search for a Wrongful Execution." *Tulsa Law Review* 42:403–435.
McAdams, John. 2002. "Race and the Death Penalty." Pp. 175–193 in *The Leviathan's Choice: Capital Punishment in the Twenty-First Century*, edited by Michael Martinez, William Richardson, and Brandon Hornsby. Lanham, MD: Rowan & Littlefield Publishers.
New York State Assembly. 2005. Press Release, "Assembly Releases Death Penalty Report." April 4.
Olsen, Lise. 2006. "Candid Phone Calls Cast Doubt on Cantu Review." *Houston Chronicle*, July 22, A1.
_____. 2005. "Did Texas Execute an Innocent Man?" *Houston Chronicle*, Nov. 20, A1.
Patrick, Robert and Heather Ratcliffe. 2007. "Circuit Attorney Says Executed Man Was Guilty." *St. Louis Post-Dispatch*, July 12.
Pew Forum on Religion and Public Life. 2006. Event Transcript, July 21. (http://pewforum.org/events/index.php?EventID=122).
Pew Research Center. 2007. "Post September 11 Attitudes." (http://people-press.org/reports/display.php3?ReportID=144).
Pojman, Louis. 2004. "Why the Death Penalty is Morally Permissible." Pp. 51–75 in *Debating the Death Penalty: Should America Have Capital Punishment?: The Experts on Both Sides Make Their Best Case*, edited by Hugo Bedau and Paul Cassell. New York, NY: Oxford University Press.

Ponnuru, Ramesh. 2002. "Bad List: A Suspect Roll of Death Row 'Innocents.'" *National Review* 54:27–28.

Radelet, Michael, Hugo Bedau, and Constance Putnam. 1992. *In Spite of Innocence: Erroneous Convictions in Capital Cases.* Boston, MA: Northeastern University Press.

Robbins, Maro and Lise Olsen. 2007. "Cantu Case Report Hasn't Shut Door on Debate; Critics Say First State Review of Possible Wrongful Execution Wasn't a Fair Evaluation." *San Antonio Express-News,* July 8, B4.

Schmitt, Richard. 2004. "Ashcroft is Undeterred in Push for Capital Cases." *Los Angeles Times,* Sept. 29.

Subcommittee on Civil and Constitutional Rights.1993. Staff Report, U.S. House of Representatives, Committee on the Judiciary, "Innocence and the Death Penalty: Assessing the Danger of Mistaken Executions." 103 Cong., 1st Sess.

Tibbs v. State (1976). 337 So. 2d 788 (Fl.).

Turow, Scott. 2003. *Ultimate Punishment: A Lawyer's Reflections on Dealing with the Death Penalty.* New York, NY: Farrar, Straus, and Giroux.

Woolverton, Paul. 2006. "Innocence Panel Advances." *Fayetteville Observer,* July 13.

CHAPTER 12

Mental Retardation and the Death Penalty Five Years after *Atkins*

John H. Blume, Sheri Lynn Johnson and Christopher Seeds

Cooperation between social science and the law is essential to a growing understanding of how the death penalty operates. This chapter considers an issue that has consumed a great deal of litigation effort nationwide in the recent past and which we anticipate will do so in the foreseeable future: mental retardation and the death penalty.[1]

Introduction

Almost five years ago in *Atkins v. Virginia* (2002), the United States Supreme Court held that the Eighth Amendment prohibits the execution of persons with mental retardation. *Atkins* reversed the Supreme Court's earlier ruling that mental retardation, while a mitigating factor that jurors may consider as

---

1. In this chapter, we use the term "mental retardation" as it is used in *Atkins* and as it is commonly understood by attorneys and courts to refer to the class of individuals exempt from the death penalty. Efforts are underway, however, to replace the term "mental retardation" with the term "intellectual and developmental disabilities" (*see Mental Retardation is No More—New Name Is Intellectual and Developmental Disabilities: Name Change Reflects Society's Efforts to Appropriately Address People with Cognitive Disabilities*, at www.aamr.org/About_AAIDD/MR_name_change.htm). The former American Association on Mental Retardation, now the American Association on Intellectual and Developmental Disabilities, prefers the term intellectual and developmental disabilities because it is "less stigmatizing" than "mental retardation." The journal formerly titled Mental Retardation has likewise been renamed Intellectual and Developmental Disabilities.

a reason to find the death penalty inappropriate in a given case, was not an absolute bar to the execution of an offender (*Penry v. Lynaugh* 1989). In the dozen years between *Penry*, in which the Court approved of the execution of persons with mental retardation, and *Atkins*, in which the Court condemned it, the state legislative landscape dramatically shifted away from the practice. During that period, sixteen more states determined that persons with mental retardation were categorically ineligible for the death penalty; and in the states that continued to permit execution of persons with mental retardation, it was increasingly uncommon for juries to sentence mentally retarded defendants to death (*Atkins v. Virginia* 2002:314–16). This shift away from executing persons with mental retardation formed the basis for the Court's conclusion that "the evolving standards of decency that mark the progress of a maturing society" preclude the execution of persons with mental retardation (*Atkins v. Virginia* 2002:316, 321).

Because states' definitions of mental retardation varied, however, as did the procedures the states used to determine whether a person suffered from mental retardation, the legislative and jury-sentencing trends did not supply a comprehensive answer to either definitional or procedural questions. The *Atkins* opinion implies a resolution of the definitional question (*Atkins v. Virginia* 2002:317). The Court did not explicitly define the "range" supported by national consensus, but pointed to two clinical definitions—those of the American Association on Mental Retardation (AAMR) and the American Psychiatric Association (APA), suggesting that state measures for ascertaining mental retardation in capital cases would be "appropriate" so long as they "generally conformed" to these clinical definitions (*Atkins v. Virginia* 2002:nn. 3, 22). The Court left entirely to the states the selection of procedures for assessing who "fall[s] within the range of mentally retarded offenders about whom there is a national consensus" (*Atkins v. Virginia* 2002:317).[2]

Unfortunately, five years of litigation has served to illuminate the difficulties inherent in judicial application of any clinical definitions, and those years have also revealed the reluctance of many states to embrace aspects of the clinical definitions that seemed unambiguous at the time of *Atkins*. Moreover, assigning responsibility to the states to select procedures with which to implement

---

2. In leaving "to the State[s] the task of developing appropriate ways to enforce the constitutional restriction upon its execution of sentences," the Court anticipated "serious disagreement ... in determining which offenders are in fact retarded" (*Atkins v. Virginia* 2002:317). "Not all people who claim to be mentally retarded," the Court cautioned, "will be so impaired as to fall within the range of mentally retarded offenders about whom there is a national consensus" (*Atkins v. Virginia* 2002:317).

the Court's ruling has exacerbated the diversity with which the categorical exemption is applied. This chapter surveys the range of issues that have arisen with respect to criteria for deciding who is categorically ineligible for the death penalty by reason of their cognitive limitations, and the interaction of procedural variations with the substance of the exclusion, with an eye to identifying areas for productive future research.

Issues Arising from State Applications of the Clinical Definitions

In an early footnote, *Atkins* recites two definitions of mental retardation, the AAMR's definition and the American Psychiatric Association's (APA) definition, which is published in the Diagnostic and Statistical Manual, Version IV (DSM-IV). The Court notes that the definitions are "similar" (*Atkins v. Virginia* 2002:n. 3). Subsequent references in the opinion imply that the constitutional boundary incorporates the common ground between these definitions (*Atkins v. Virginia* 2002:n. 22). Both definitions have three requirements. They word the first criterion the same way, "significantly subaverage intellectual functioning," as measured by IQ tests. The second criterion relates to the manifestation of the intellectual deficits in the individual's life: the AAMR requires "related limitations in two or more of the following adaptive skills areas: communication, self-care, home living, social skills, community use, self-direction, health and safety, functional academics, leisure, and work"; the APA utilizes the same categories, and similarly requires "significant limitations in adaptive functioning in at least two of [those] areas." Finally, both definitions require "manifestation" (AAMR) or "onset" (APA) before the age of 18.

The first two prongs of the definitions, IQ and adaptive functioning or behavior deficits, have engendered substantial litigation, often resulting in state court rulings that are at odds with the consensus of mental retardation professionals. The third prong, onset before age 18, has been less contended thus far, though behind initial quiet on that front lurks the potential for additional controversy.

Subaverage Intellectual Functioning

Intelligence is "a general mental ability" that "includes reasoning, planning, solving problems, thinking abstractly, comprehending complex ideas, learning quickly, and learning from experience" (AAMR 2002:51). Subaverage intellectual functioning is measured by intelligence tests.³ The most widely accepted tests for intellectual functioning are the Stanford Binet, the Wechsler Adult Intelligence Scale (WAIS), and the Wechsler Intelligence Scale for Children (WISC) (AAMR 2002:59–62).⁴ On these tests, the mean IQ score is 100, and in order to satisfy the first prong of the definitions for mental retardation, a person must score "two standard deviations below the mean, considering the standard error of measurement for the specific assessment instruments used and the instruments' strengths and limitations" (AAMR 2002:13). The tests are normed so that a standard deviation is fifteen points. Thus, a person with an IQ of 70 or below meets the first prong of the definition of mental retardation (AAMR 2002:60–62, 63–66 (discussing intelligence tests)).

Of course, the preceding statement assumes perfect measurement, and measurement of intelligence is far from flawless. If a person is tested on more than one occasion, it is quite likely that the scores on the two occasions will be different. Thus, to interpret scores, understanding of the Standard Error of Measurement (SEM) is necessary (AAMR 2002:67–71 (charting SEM for common intelligence scales)). SEM "estimate[s] the amount of error usually attached to an examinee's obtained score" (Sattler 1992:28). SEM is critical and "must be part of any decision concerning a diagnosis of mental retardation" (AAMR 2002:57). The standard error of measurement for IQ tests is approximately five points, which means that an expert would be reasonably confident that a person's true IQ was no more than five points above or five points below the score the subject received. Thus, a measured score of 75 might reflect a true score as low as 70, or on the other hand a true score as high as 80. A person may have a measured IQ as high as 75, in other words, and still satisfy the first prong of subaverage intellectual functioning.⁵

Many courts across the country have correctly held that SEM is an important consideration when deciding whether a person is mentally retarded (*see,*

---

3. The AAMR notes that secondary conditions, such as general physical and mental health, "can affect the assessment of intelligence" (AAMR 2002:46). Language and cultural differences may also impair the effectiveness of these intelligence tests on a given individual (AAMR 2002).

4. Achievement tests, grades, or group-administered IQ tests can be relevant to adaptive functioning—in particular, to the adaptive skill area of functional academics—but they are not appropriate measures of IQ. Grades are even less appropriate, as they may reflect performance within a particular lower track, or a teacher's estimate of the amount of effort a child is putting forth. Group IQ tests, with their high potential for "cooperative" work products, and inadequate norming, are not reliable measures of anything.

5. The DSM-IV provides the example that a Wechsler IQ score of 70 could obtain from a reported testing range of 65 to 75. "In effect," the AAMR points out, "[the practice effect] expands the operative definition to 75" (AAMR 2002:59).

e.g., In re Hearn 2004; *Rogers v. State* 1998:1178 (holding measuring intellectual functioning through standardized IQ tests includes assessing "a margin of error of five points in either direction"); *State v. Dunn* 2002:867 (recognizing that "[r]egardless of the test administered, each test is burdened with a range of plus/minus number of IQ points known as the standard error measurement (SEM)"); *State v. Williams* 2002:853 n. 26 (holding that "the assessment of intellectual functioning through the primary reliance on IQ tests must be tempered with attention to possible errors in measurement.... The concept of standard error of measurement (SEM) is an aid."); *Walker v. True* 2005; *Walton v. Johnson* 2005). However, seven states (Alabama, Delaware, Florida, Indiana, Maryland, North Carolina, and Tennessee) apply 70 as a strict IQ cut-off score, holding in effect that a person who scores above 70 is not mentally retarded within the meaning of *Atkins*.[6] Such strict cutoffs are inconsistent with the clinical definition of mental retardation.[7]

Moreover, strict cut-offs ignore two other factors that artificially inflate IQ scores.[8] The first recognized inflationary factor is the practice effect. Repetition of the same IQ test may increase a test-taker's score, depending on the interval between tests, the age of the test-taker, and the number of retests (WAIS III Manual:57). For example, retesting after 2–12 weeks has been found to result, on average, in a 2.5–8.3-point increase in performance IQ (WAIS III Manual:57). Practice effects are particularly important in capital litigation because both parties may wish to administer an IQ test within a fairly short period prior to trial. One of the scores may be much inflated by a practice effect (Bonnie and Gustafson 2007:839–840).

An additional, and often misunderstood aspect of IQ testing is referred to as "the Flynn effect" (Flynn 2006). The Flynn effect is an accepted scientific phenomenon that yields an inflated IQ score when an older test is administered. It is based on the fact that scores on standardized measurements of intelligence have been rising steadily during the last century. Therefore, in order to maintain the true relationship between an IQ score and the number of persons in the pop-

---

6. *See Ex parte Perkins* (2002); Del. Code Ann. 4209 ("'Significantly subaverage intellectual functioning' means an intelligence quotient of 70 or below...."); *Cherry v. State* (2007) (interpreting Fla. Stat. Ann. 921.137 and Fla. R. Crim. Proc. 3.203); *State v. McManus* (2007); Ann. Code Md. 2-202; N. Carolina Gen. Stat. Ann. 15A-2005; *Howell v. State* (2005) (applying Tenn. Code Ann. 39-13-203).

7. Mossman (2003) states that "Using such precise cut-offs mistakenly suggests that a one-point difference in two persons' scores reflects a significant difference in their cognitive capacity" (p. 269).

8. In some instances, those factors render invalid not only a cut-off score of 70, but even a higher cut-off score of 75, which Mississippi has adopted. *See Chase v. State* (2004).

ulation above and below that score, adjustments must be made to compensate for the obsolescence of the tests (Flynn 2006). "[W]hen an examinee's performance is referenced to outdated norms rather than to current ones, the IQ score may be inflated" (Kaufman and Lichtenberger 1999). The size of the Flynn effect depends upon the country in which the test is administered and how many years prior to its administration the test was normed; the effect varies from two to four points per decade (in the United States the annual national performance increase is approximately 0.3 points), and can be accurately and easily calculated by an expert for any given administration of an outdated test.

Thus, assuming a subject has taken an older test re-administered in a short period of time, and taking account of the standard error of measurement, one can imagine a defendant with a tested IQ of 85 who actually has subaverage intellectual functioning.[9] This is not to say that such occurrences will be common, only to point out that a strict cut-off score, beyond being inconsistent with the consensus among experts, creates unnecessary dangers of underinclusion. In a slight twist on the cut-off score, Ohio and South Dakota have established a presumption that an IQ score greater than 70 means the defendant is not mentally retarded.[10] Such presumptions may be acceptable if the law permits testimony concerning recognized phenomena such as the SEM, the Flynn effect, and the practice effect.

Adaptive Functioning Deficits

The second requirement for a diagnosis of mental retardation looks at the expression of intellectual deficits in the life of an individual. The text of the *Atkins* opinion refers to "significant limitations in adaptive skills such as communication, self-care, and self-direction," and quotes approvingly the two dominant definitions (*Atkins v. Virginia* 2002:n. 3), the first of which was adopted by the AAMR in 1992, and the second by the American Psychiatric Association in the DSM-IV. At the time of *Atkins*, both required significant deficits in at least two of ten listed areas.[11]

---

9. For example, a five-point SEM may decrease the score to 80, practice effect may decrease the actual score another five points to 75, and the Flynn effect—caused by taking a test that was normed seventeen years prior (17 x 0.3 = 5.1)—could then place the actual IQ score under 70.

10. *See State v. Lott* (2002:1012); S.D. Codified Laws 23A-27A-26.

11. The AAMR revised its formulation of adaptive functioning deficits in 2002. Instead of requiring limitations in at least two of the ten itemized "adaptive skills areas," the new definition more concisely refers to "significant limitations ... in adaptive behavior as expressed in conceptual, social, and practical adaptive skills," requiring a showing of limitations in

The AAMR defines adaptive behavior as "the collection of conceptual, social, and practical skills that have been learned by people in order to function in their everyday lives" (AAMR 2002:73). Deficits in adaptive behavior reduce the personal culpability of a defendant charged with a crime because they contribute to "[a] diminished capacit[y] to understand and process information, to communicate, to abstract from mistakes and learn from experience, to engage in logical reasoning, to control impulses, and to understand the reactions of others" (*Atkins v. Virginia* 2002:318). The DSM uses the similar term "adaptive functioning," which refers to "how effectively individuals cope with common life demands and how well they meet the standards of personal independence expected of someone in their particular age group, sociocultural background, and community setting" (DSM-IV-TR: 42).

Principles underlying the clinical definitions are critical to interpreting adaptive behavior or adaptive functioning limitations. Mental retardation experts agree that an individual's limitations often coexist with strengths. A person with mild mental retardation, for example, may be able to master reading, writing, or math up to the level of a sixth grader of average intelligence — and thus may be able to read a newspaper, write a story or a short essay, or do long division. Some people with mental retardation have a high degree of independence in daily living, and are even totally self-supporting (AAMR 2002:83).[12]

Most capital defendants that fail to establish mental retardation under *Atkins* lose on this second prong, perhaps in part because the evidence on the adaptive functioning prong is less cut and dried than on the first prong and requires greater scrutiny by the factfinder. Sometimes a finding of death eligibility based on a lack of significant adaptive functioning deficits is appropriate, but many *Atkins* claims are denied for reasons that clearly do not accord with expert understanding of adaptive functioning. All of the following reasons have been cited as disproving mental retardation:

---

one of the broader categories (AAMR 2002:1). In practice, the change is more often semantic than outcome-determinative because, as the AAMR Manual notes, each of the ten skill areas of the 1992 definition is "conceptually linked" to at least one of the broader categories of the 2002 definition (AAMR 1992; AAMR 2002:81).

12. The AAMR manual explains: "Within an individual, limitations often coexist with strengths. This means that people with mental retardation are complex human beings who likely have certain gifts as well as limitations. Like all people, they often do some things better than other things. Individuals may have capabilities and strengths that are independent of their mental retardation. These may include strengths in social or physical capabilities, strengths in some adaptive skill areas, or strengths in one aspect of an adaptive skill in which they otherwise show an overall limitation" (AAMR 2002:8).

The defendant could "read, write, and perform rudimentary math";
The defendant had "adapted to the criminal life";
The defendant was married three times (!);
The defendant maintained construction jobs;
The defendant could drive;
The defendant gave a detailed confession;
The defendant gave the police an alias;
The defendant was in the army;
The defendant could use a phone;
The defendant was never in special education classes;
The defendant cooked for his mother;
The defendant could operate a microwave;
The defendant could make a sandwich;
The defendant read children's books and the Bible;
The defendant had magazine subscriptions;
The defendant's employer testified he was a good worker who took directions well;
The defendant took notes during trial;
The defendant gave a coherent statement at sentencing.

None of these facts taken alone, however, demonstrate that a defendant is not mentally retarded. To conclude otherwise implies one of two fundamental errors: the factfinder has an image of persons with mental retardation as drooling idiots, or else the factfinder fails to comprehend that among this population (as among persons with higher intelligence) strengths coexist with weaknesses and the question is not whether the defendant is competent in some areas, but whether in addition to suffering from subaverage intellectual functioning he demonstrates significant adaptive functioning *deficits*—in *some* areas. Moreover, it is important to remember that many persons with mental retardation attempt to conceal their disability, so some behaviors—such as ordering magazines or appearing to take notes—may not in fact reflect competencies at all, but an understandable pretense at normality (Ellis and Luckasson 1988:429–431).

There are other concerns with the measurement of adaptive skill limitations. An individual's limitations must be considered "within the context of the community environment typical of the individual's age peers and culture" (AAMR 2002). Similarly, a "[v]alid assessment considers cultural and linguistic diversity" (AAMR 2002:8–9, 13). Consistent with these principles, assessments must, in addition to focusing on limitations not strengths and recognizing that strengths and limitations coexist, take into account the context of community and cultural environment. Context may also affect the choice of measurement instrument (*see* Bonnie and Gustafson 2007:848–849; *Van Tran v. State* 2006: finding two standardized adaptive behavior measures, Vineland and Independent Living Scales, inapplicable to a defendant who grew up in Vietnam and had spent much of his adult life in prison).

Onset before the Age of 18

Because both *Atkins*-approved clinical definitions of mental retardation require onset before the age of 18, one might expect uniformity on this prong. But several states (Indiana, Maryland, and Utah) depart from the AAMR and APA definitions, and require onset before the age of 22.[13] This deviation of course is permissible because it broadens rather than narrows the class of constitutionally ineligible defendants. Normally this prong is not contested, though occasionally cases arise where the state contends that drug use or brain injury occurring after the age of majority caused the defendant's subaverage intellectual functioning or adaptive skills deficits. If that is established, the defendant can be eligible for the death penalty, or more precisely, not *Atkins*-ineligible.

It is inconsistent with the *Atkins*-approved definitions, however, to insist on an IQ score demonstrating significantly subaverage intellectual functioning obtained prior to the age of 18. Generally, whether an individual was IQ tested before the age of 18 depends on the school district's policy and resources (Bonnie and Gustafson 2007:855, noting that requiring onset before 18 "would be unconstitutional because it would amount to discrimination against people whose need for special education was overlooked and who did not have access to adequate clinical or social services as a child"). Particularly with older defendants or defendants from underdeveloped countries, IQ tests may not have been administered, even when signs of mental retardation were present. Thus, *Atkins* requires professionals to evaluate scanty childhood evidence along with more recent and detailed information to determine age of onset. It is worth noting that outside the capital trial context, experts will not have had much experience with this issue, and that finding experts who are confident in drawing conclusions about age of onset absent such childhood testing is often difficult.

One might ask why age of onset matters at all. To our knowledge, no court has asked this question. Given the rationale of *Atkins*, it is difficult to see why age of onset should matter. It is true that age of onset is part of the AAMR and APA definitions, but this appears to be for the purpose of ascertaining the appropriate services to be supplied, and/or determining etiology,

---

13. Ann. Ind. Code 35-36-9-2; Md. Ann. Code, 2-202; Utah Code Ann. 77-15a-102.

neither of which is relevant in the capital prosecution context. If a person has significantly subaverage intellectual functioning and displays significant adaptive functioning deficits *at the time of the crime*, then it would seem that his moral culpability for the crime is lessened to a degree that the death penalty would be cruel and unusual punishment, whether or not he suffered from the condition causing those deficits as a child, or only came to suffer them as an adult. In sum, although it serves a useful etiological function and diagnostic function in the psychological community in which it was developed, the onset requirement seems to make little sense in the death penalty context.[14]

Additional Requirements Employed by States

Despite *Atkins'* holding that all persons with mental retardation are exempt from imposition of the death penalty, and its strong implication that mental retardation should be measured by the three-prong tests to which the opinion refers (*Atkins v. Virginia* 2002:nn. 3, 22), several states have not been content with these prongs and have added further requirements. Delaware and Kentucky have, quite inexplicably, held that the defendant must be "seriously mentally retarded."[15] While those states' intentions are unclear, *Atkins'* is not: mild mental retardation (as reflected in an IQ of 55 to 70) suffices for categorical ineligibility. In Kansas, in order to exempt the defendant from capital punishment, mental retardation must substantially impair the defendant's ability to appreciate the criminality of his conduct or to conform his conduct to the requirements of law.[16] This ruling confounds the definition of insanity with the definition of mental retardation, and again, is contrary to *Atkins*.[17]

To take another example, Texas requires by case law its own novel measurements of whether an individual has adaptive skills deficits. The Texas Court

---

14. *See* James Ellis, Mental Retardation and the Death Penalty: A Guide to State Legislative Issues, at http://www.deathpenaltyinfo.org/MREllisLeg.pdf, at 9–10. *See* American Bar Association Task Force on Mental Disability and the Death Penalty (2006).

15. Del. Code Ann. 4209(3)(b), (3)(d)(1); Ky. Rev. Stat. Ann. 532.140, 532.135, 532–130.

16. Kan. Stat. Ann. 21-4634(f).

17. *Cf.* Bonnie and Gustafson, 2007:819 ("[A] statute using a definition based on diminished capacity to appreciate the wrongfulness of specific conduct or to conform that conduct to the law would run afoul of the rationale for the Atkins decision because it would allow a defendant to receive the death penalty as long as he possessed whichever capacities were required by the statute, even if he is mentally retarded according to the prevailing professional criteria.").

of Criminal Appeals holds that courts should evaluate adaptive functioning by considering the following factors (*Ex parte Briseno* 2004):

> Did those who knew the person best during the developmental stage—his family, friends, teachers, employers, authorities—think he was mentally retarded at that time, and, if so, act in accordance with that determination?
>
> Has the person formulated plans and carried them through or is his conduct impulsive?
>
> Does his conduct show leadership or does it show that he is led around by others?
>
> Is his conduct in response to external stimuli rational and appropriate, regardless of whether it is socially acceptable?
>
> Does he respond coherently, rationally, and on point to oral or written questions or do his responses wander from subject to subject?
>
> Can the person hide facts or lie effectively in his own or others' interests?
>
> Putting aside any heinousness or gruesomeness surrounding the capital offense, did the commission of that offense require forethought, planning, and complex execution of purpose?[18]

Without question the *Briseno* factors do not address the full scope of the AAMR and APA skill areas. Further, certain factors plainly focus on strengths rather than deficits. At best, these factors could only be acceptable as a complement to the AAMR and APA definitions. But the Texas Court of Criminal Appeals on more than one occasion has applied these factors to determine adaptive functioning without any reference to the AAMR or APA (*see generally Chester v. Texas* 2007).

Issues Arising from State Procedures for Determining Mental Retardation

There has been little exploration thus far of the interaction between states' chosen procedures for determining mental retardation and the likelihood of finding a defendant mentally retarded. Yet, there are many procedural issues of

---

18. *Ex parte Briseno* (2004:8–9).

importance to the legal and social science communities that need exploration. Significant procedural issues that states approach in different ways include: Who decides the issue? What is the burden of proof and which party bears it? And when should the determination of mental retardation occur relative to the capital sentencing proceeding?

With regard to whether judge or jury should be the fact finder, twenty states (Alabama, Arizona, Colorado, Delaware, Florida, Idaho, Illinois, Indiana, Kansas, Kentucky, Mississippi, Nebraska, Nevada, New Mexico, Ohio, Pennsylvania, South Carolina, South Dakota, Texas, Utah, and Washington) have determined that the judge decides the issue. In five states (Connecticut, Georgia, Louisiana, Maryland, and Oklahoma) the jury decides, although in two of those states (Connecticut and Georgia) a defendant may waive the jury and in one (Louisiana) the parties may agree to judicial determination. In California, the defendant may elect whether a judge or jury decides the issue of mental retardation. And in seven states (Arkansas, Missouri, New York, North Carolina, South Carolina, Tennessee, and Virginia) the defendant gets two bites at the apple, with either two independent determinations, or judicial review of a jury's determination that the defendant is not mentally retarded.

Another aspect of difference among states is the burden of proof, both its allocation and its magnitude. Twenty-one states (Arkansas, California, Idaho, Illinois, Louisiana, Maryland, Mississippi, Missouri, Nebraska, Nevada, New Mexico, New York, Ohio, Oklahoma, Pennsylvania, South Dakota, Tennessee, Texas, Utah, Virginia, and Washington) assign the burden to the defendant by a preponderance of the evidence. Five states (Arizona, Colorado, Delaware, Florida, and Indiana) assign the burden to the defendant by clear and convincing evidence. North Carolina assigns the burden to the defendant, but by a preponderance of the evidence standard when considered in front of a jury and by a clear and convincing evidence standard when the issue is decided by a judge before trial. Georgia assigns the burden to the defendant beyond a reasonable doubt.

Another significant issue is when during the capital proceedings the issue of mental retardation should be determined. Does it matter whether the issue is resolved before or after the guilt-innocence phase, or after or during the sentencing phase? If the mental retardation hearing occurs after jurors have been exposed to the facts of the crime during the guilt-innocence trial, to what extent might the heinousness of the crime play into the factfinders' mental retardation determination? Infusing culpability based on the heinousness of the offense into the mental retardation determination arguably conflicts with the rationale of *Atkins* that the impairments associated with mental retardation ("diminished capacities to understand and process information, to communicate, to abstract from mistakes and learn from experience, to engage in logical reasoning, to control impulses, and to understand the reactions of others" (*Atkins v. Virginia* 2002:318)) diminish the defendants' moral culpability (*Atkins v. Virginia* 2002:320–21; Tobolowsky 2003:113). A jury's knowledge, or lack thereof, of the fact that the defendant will not be eligible for the death penalty upon a finding of mental retardation may also impact determinations.

In section IV, below, we suggest some issues of interaction between procedure, outcome, and receptiveness that might be fruitfully explored through collaboration between lawyers and social scientists in the next wave of research on *Atkins*.

Additional Significant Issues

Race

Race intersects with virtually every significant criminal law or procedural issue in some way. In the context of mental retardation and the death penalty, however, there are reasons to expect multiple intersections. Given the strength and pervasiveness of stereotypes about race and IQ, it would be surprising if factfinders could make race-neutral evaluations of evidence of mental retardation. In some cases, factfinders may be more ready to believe that a defendant is mentally retarded because he is black (or Latino) and less willing to do so when the defendant is white (or Asian). On the other hand, some factfinders may dismiss evidence of limitations in adaptive functioning (*e.g.,* poor employment history, failure to finish school) as simply consistent with their stereotypes of the group to which the defendant belongs rather than giving it the significance it deserves as probative of mental retardation. The extent to which factfinders rely on stereotype plays to a general problem of perception: are decision makers more likely to find a defendant not mentally retarded based on appearance (including attractiveness, dress, affect or demeanor)? (*See* Eberhardt *et al.* 2006). We know from empirical studies that the race of jurors and the race of the defendant affect the extent to which jurors perceive the defendant to be dangerous and the extent to which they fear the defendant (Bowers, Brewer and Sandys 2004; Bowers, Sandys and Steiner 2001; Garvey 2000; Thompson 2001). *Atkins* sought to eliminate the possibility of jurors treating mental retardation as a fear-driven aggravating circumstance rather than as a mitigating circumstance. But irrational fear could enter the equation nevertheless through racial bias (Slobogin 2004).

Race may further impact a lawyer's investigation of mental retardation. First, a lawyer's investigation may be impeded by his own stereotypes about intelligence and race. Second, the client may be more hesitant to cooperate with a mental retardation defense, viewing it as the product of the lawyer's racial stereotypes—whether it is or not. And third, the lawyer will have to cope with resistance from witnesses, some based upon reluctance to acknowledge cognitive limitations for a person of color, and some based on stereotypes that such limitations are consequences of race rather than mental retardation.

Finally, culture plays a significant role in accurately identifying and diagnosing adaptive skills deficits. In this context, as in any other, investigation into the cultural subtleties of an individual's adaptive functioning must be done carefully and competently (Cross *et al.* 1989).[19]

Experts

Atkins litigation cries out for expert testimony. But what kind of expert is appropriate? In preparing mental retardation claims, attorneys rely principally upon academics and independent practicing psychologists, both of which are especially skilled in interpreting tests results. A somewhat different kind of "expert" is a professional (variously trained) who has worked with the state department of disability in assessing whether individuals have mental retardation. But are such persons neutral experts? Of course, a person with a disability may be biased, and of course many professionals from social service departments are solely focused on the welfare of the clientele they serve. Nonetheless, factfinders will have to face the question of whether those who are paid by the state to determine whether someone should receive services or payments may not often perceive their job as rooting out malingerers, or saving the state money. Regardless of whether accusations of less than neutral evaluations are founded or unfounded, one can expect a battle between the more academically oriented

---

19. *See* Cross *et al.*(1989) (defining cultural competency as a "set of congruent behaviors, attitudes, and policies that come together in a system or agency or among professionals and enable the system, agency, or professionals to work effectively in cross-cultural situations. 'Culture' refers to integrated patterns of human behavior that include the language, thoughts, communications, actions, customs, beliefs, values, and institutions of racial, ethnic, religious, or social groups. 'Competence' implies having the capacity to function effectively as an individual and an organization within the context of the cultural beliefs, behaviors, and need presented.").

expert and such social services professionals, a battle that the factfinders will need to resolve (Note 2003:2584–2585). Concerning how they will do so, and what they will find persuasive, we know very little (*see* Sundby 1997).

Areas for Future Research

The previous discussion surveys current issues with respect to the interpretation and implementation of *Atkins*. The following are some areas that we view as productive avenues for future social science and empirical research:

- Based on cases that have gone to hearing or determination, by jurisdiction, who is found to be mentally retarded? What is the demographic background (by class, race, ethnicity) of these defendants?
- For those defendants not found mentally retarded, again by jurisdiction, on which prong (IQ, adaptive limitations, age of onset) do they lose? To what extent is each prong a determinative factor in denials?
- What is the demographic background of the defendants that lose on each prong? For example, research might consider the extent to which defendants lose on the second prong because there are no standardized measurements appropriately normed for their background or the extent to which courts refuse to give greater credence to a measurement based on a defendant's background.
- How many defendants lose on additional requirements (such as those imposed by states such as Kansas or Texas)? And, implicating Eighth Amendment concerns with arbitrariness, how many of those would have met the AAMR and APA definitions? What is the demographic background of these defendants?
- Efforts should be made to assess the impact of knowledge of the crime on determinations of mental retardation: for example, by giving the same facts to two sets of decision makers—one set who know the facts of the crime and one set who do not. How does race intersect with this determination? Similarly, efforts should be made to assess the impact of knowledge of the defendant's ineligibility for the death penalty if a determination of mental retardation is made.
- We should study the neutrality of experts who testify with regard to mental retardation. For example, facts could be provided from cases that have gone to hearing to neutral experts who are not retained by a party to the litigation, and assessment made of how their findings compare to those of the testifying experts in the actual case(s).

- The degree of deference that factfinders will give to different types of experts should be examined. In addition, the reasons that courts give for imposing limitations on the types of professionals who may assess mental retardation in a capital case should be analyzed.
- Determinations of mental retardation across states should be studied to gauge the impact of procedures and procedural differences—for example, examining the different rates of findings of mental retardation in states that have a single agency making the determination in every case and states that have a variety of decision makers. The agencies and organizations that do the evaluations should be examined and, where applicable, the competency and neutrality of those agencies' evaluations should be assessed.
- In addition, with regard to procedure, correlations might be expected between both the burden of proof and the likelihood of a finding of mental retardation, and between the identity of the factfinder and the finding, but to date no studies have explored those correlations in actual cases or in laboratory studies. We might also question whether variations in the burden of proof and in the selection of the factfinder reflect receptiveness or resistance to *Atkins*—a question that could be studied by considering whether states' pre-*Atkins* position and practice on the execution of persons with mental retardation bears any connection to the procedures they have adopted to implement *Atkins*.

Conclusion

Atkins was viewed as a victory by many, including death penalty abolitionists, death penalty lawyers, and experts whose understanding of mental retardation paved the way for the Supreme Court's understanding. But if the *Atkins* decision was enormously encouraging on its own terms, its potential has not been fully realized. Further research and cooperative effort on the issues touched on herein are necessary to clarify the meaning of *Atkins*. Nor is *Atkins* the last frontier of categorical exclusion from the death penalty. Severe mental illness has many characteristics that overlap with the characteristics of mental retardation that the Supreme Court found supported categorical exclusion in *Atkins* (Mossman 2003:279–287). On this basis, many have already called for a death penalty exemption for defendants who suffer from severe mental illness (Allen 2005; Izutsu 2005; Slobogin 2005; Tabak 2005, 2006). Complicated issues await on how to define the scope of mental illness that would qualify for an exemption.

References

Allen, Aletheia V.P. 2005. "State v. Flores: In The Wake Of *Atkins v. Virginia*, New Mexico Tackles Capital Punishment For Defendants With Mental Disabilities." *New Mexico Law Review* 35:557–586.

American Association on Intellectual and Developmental Disabilities. 2007. "Mental Retardation Is No More—New Name Is Intellectual and Developmental Disabilities: Name Change Reflects Society's Efforts to Appropriately Address People with Cognitive Disabilities." (http://www.aamr.org/About_AAIDD/MR_name_change.htm).

American Association on Mental Retardation. 2002. *Mental Retardation: Definition, Classification, and Systems of Support.* 10th ed. Washington D.C.: American Association on Intellectual and Developmental Disabilities.

_____. 1992. *Mental Retardation: Definition, Classification, and Systems of Support.* 9th ed. Washington D.C.: American Association on Intellectual and Developmental Disabilities.

American Bar Association Task Force on Mental Disability and the Death Penalty. 2006. "Recommendation and Report on the Death Penalty and Persons with Mental Disabilities." *Mental & Physical Disability Law Reporter* 30:668–677.

American Psychiatric Association. 2000. *Diagnostic and Statistical Manual of Mental Disorders.* 4th ed (DSM-IV-TR). Arlington, VA: American Psychiatric Publishing, Inc.

Atkins v. Virginia (2002). 536 U.S. 304.

Bonnie, Richard J. and Katherine Gustafson. 2007. Allen Chair Symposium: The Role of the Death Penalty in America: Reflections, Perceptions, and Reform Articles. "The Challenge of Implementing *Atkins v. Virginia*: How Legislatures and Courts Can Promote Accurate Assessments and Adjudications of Mental Retardation In Death Penalty Cases." *University of Richmond Law Review* 41:811–860.

Bowers, William J., Thomas W. Brewer and Marla Sandys. 2004. "Crossing Racial Boundaries: A Closer Look at the Roots of Racial Bias in Capital Sentencing When the Defendant Is Black and the Victim Is White." *DePaul Law Review* 53:1497–1537.

Bowers, William J., Marla Sandys and Benjamin D. Steiner. 2001. "Death Sentencing in Black and White: An Empirical Analysis of the Role of Juror's Race and Jury Racial Composition." *University of Pennsylvania Journal of Constitutional Law* 3:171–274.

Chase v. State (2004). 873 So.2d 1013 (Miss.).

Cherry v. State (2007). 959 So.2d 702 (Fla.).

Chester v. Texas (2007). 2007 WL 602607 (Tex. Crim. App.).

Cross, Terry L., Barbara J. Bazron, Karl W. Dennis and Mareasa Isaacs. 1989. *Towards a Culturally Competent System of Care, Volume I.* Washington, D.C.: Georgetown University Child Development Center, CASSP Technical Assistance Center.

Eberhardt, Jennifer L., Paul G. Davies, Sheri L. Johnson and Valerie J. Purdice-Vaughns. 2006. "Looking Deathworthy: Perceived Stereotypicality of Black Defendant Predicts Capital-Sentencing Outcomes." *Psychological Science* 5:383–386.

Ellis, James W. and Ruth A. Luckasson. 1988. "Mentally Retarded Defendants." *George Washington Law Review* 53:414–493.

Ellis, James W. (N.d.). Death Penalty Information Center. "*Mental Retardation and the Death Penalty: A Guide to State Legislative Issues.*" (http://www.deathpenaltyinfo.org/MREllisLeg.pdf).

Ex parte Briseno (2004). 135 S.W.3d 1 (Tex. Crim. App.).

Ex parte Perkins (2002). 851 So.2d 453 (Ala.).

Flynn, James R. 2006. "Tethering the Elephant: Capital Cases, IQ, and the Flynn Effect." *Psychology, Public Policy & Law* 12:170–178.

Garvey, Stephen P. 2000. "The Emotional Economy of Capital Sentencing." *New York University Law Review* 75:26–73.

Howell v. State (2005). 151 S.W.3d 450 (Tenn.).

In re Hearn (2004). 376 F.3d 447 (5th Cir.).

Izutsu, Laurie T. 2005. "Applying *Atkins v. Virginia* to Capital Defendants with Severe Mental Illness." *Brooklyn Law Review* 70:995–1043.

Kaufman, Alan S. and Elizabeth O. Lichtenberger. 1999. *Essentials of WAIS-III Assessment.* Indianapolis, IN: Wiley Publishing.

Mossman, Douglas. 2003. "*Atkins v. Virginia*: A Psychiatric Can of Worms." *New Mexico Law Review* 33:255–291.

Note. 2003. "Implementing Atkins." *Harvard Law Review* 116:2565–2587.

Penry v. Lynaugh (1989). 492 U.S. 302.

Rogers v. State (1998). 698 N.E.2d 1172 (Ind.).

Sattler, Jerome M. 1992. *Assessment of Children.* 3rd ed. La Mesa, CA: Jerome M. Sattler, Publisher, Inc.

Slobogin, Christopher. 2005. "Mental Disorder As An Exemption From The Death Penalty: The Aba-Irr Task Force Recommendations." *Catholic University Law Review* 54:1133–1152.

Slobogin, Christopher. 2004. Symposium: Disability Law, Equality, and Difference: American Disability Law and the Civil Rights Model. "Is Atkins The Antithesis Or Apotheosis Of Anti-Discrimination Principles?: Sorting Out The Groupwide Effects Of Exempting People With Mental Retardation From The Death Penalty." *Alabama Law Review* 55:1101–1107.

State v. Dunn (2002). 831 So.2d 862 (La.).
State v. Lott (2002). 779 N.E.2d 1011 (Ohio).
State v. McManus (2007). 868 N.E.2d 778 (Ind.).
State v. Williams (2002). 831 So.2d 835 (La.).
Sundby, Scott E. 1997. "The Jury As Critic: An Empirical Look at How Capital Juries Perceive Expert and Lay Testimony." *Virginia Law Review* 83:1109–1188.
Tabak, Ronald J. 2006. "Executing People With Mental Disabilities: How We Can Mitigate An Aggravating Situation." *St. Louis University Public Law Review* 25:283–306.
_____. 2005. "Overview Of Task Force Proposal On Mental Disability And The Death Penalty." *Catholic University Law Review* 54:1123–1131.
Thompson, Kim-Taylor. 2001. "Empty Votes in Juror Deliberations." *Harvard Law Review* 113:1261–1320.
Tobolowsky, Peggy M. 2003. "Atkins Aftermath: Identifying Mentally Retarded Offenders and Excluding Them From Execution." *30 Journal of Legislation* 33:77–141.
Van Tran v. State (2006). 2006 WL 3327828 (Tenn. Crim. App.).
Walker v. True (2005). 399 F.3d 315 (4th Cir.).
Walton v. Johnson (2005). 407 F.3d 285 (4th Cir.).
Wechsler, David. 1997. *Wechsler Adult Intelligence Scale. Technical Manual.* 3rd ed. San Antonio, TX: The Psychological Corporation.

CHAPTER 13

THE EFFECTS OF AEDPA ON JUSTICE

David R. Dow[1] and Eric M. Freedman

Introduction

We know that through the course of American history federal habeas corpus has been a critical mechanism for preventing injustice in capital cases. We also know that through the 1980s and 1990s Supreme Court doctrine erected a series of legal barriers to the availability of habeas corpus that caused many scholars to question whether the goal of achieving justice was being threatened. And we know from a major empirical study covering the years 1973–1995 what success rate death row inmates achieved in federal habeas corpus actions during that period.

The Anti-terrorism and Effective Death Penalty Act of 1996 (AEDPA) "dramatically altered the landscape for federal habeas corpus petitions" (*Rhines v. Weber* 2005) by making legal alterations that were designed, as President Clinton said in signing the legislation, "to streamline Federal appeals for convicted criminals sentenced to the death penalty," while preserving "independent review of Federal legal claims and the bedrock constitutional principle of an independent judiciary" (Hertz and Liebman 2005b:2124). We have now learned, from a study covering the years 2000–2006 and here reported in full for the first time,[2] that, insofar as the published cases reveal, the success rate for capital inmates on federal habeas has fallen dramatically—to levels about a fifth of what they previously were.

---

1. I thank the University of Houston Law Foundation for support and Jennifer Hannigan and Matt Kita for superb research assistance. My special thanks to Melissa Azadeh both for superb research assistance and for additional contributions that warrant calling her a co-author.
2. A very preliminary set of results has been published previously (Dow 2006:xxii).

These results raise pressing questions of public policy for empirical research. The mere fact that the relief rate in capital federal habeas corpus litigation has plummeted since the enactment of AEDPA does not itself establish causation, much less answer the normative question of whether that rate is an appropriate one in light of the error rate in the underlying cases. But given the many causes for concern about the functioning of the contemporary system of capital punishment, there is an urgent need to do the empirical research that will create a complete database for study. Until then, proposals to impose yet further restrictions on the availability of habeas corpus are—as all knowledgeable organizations have already told Congress—simply premature. Once the study has been completed and Congress is in a position to legislate on the basis of facts rather than anecdote, it may well find that the path towards achieving speed and justice together lies in some hitherto-neglected directions.

Getting to 1995

As one of us has previously described in some detail (Freedman 2003a:554–560), there is a close historical connection between federal habeas corpus and the imposition of capital punishment by the states. Summarizing briefly, as Figure 1 illustrates, a state criminal defendant has the right after conviction in a state trial court to pursue a direct appeal to one or more state appellate courts (typically in capital cases directly to the state's supreme court), and then to seek discretionary review in the United States Supreme Court by a petition for a *writ of certiorari*. Thereafter, most states provide for some form of state post-conviction review to allow for the examination of issues that could not have been addressed during the appeal. Where such procedures exist, defendants must utilize them before seeking the federal habeas corpus remedy.

Figure 1. Typical State and Federal Trial and Post-Conviction Procedure

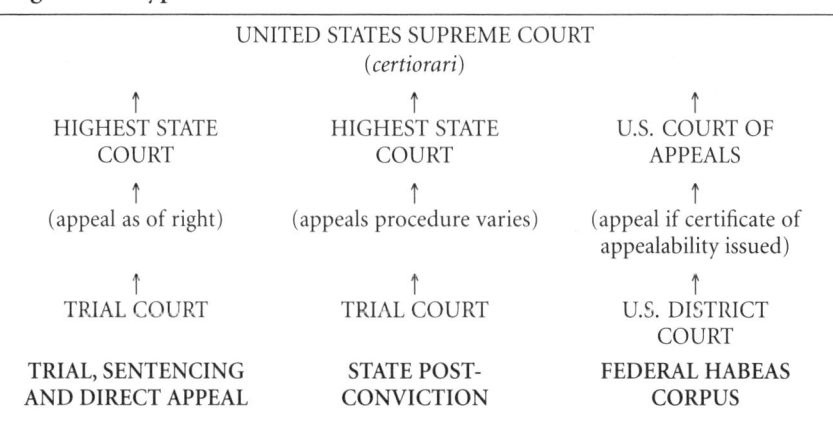

UNITED STATES SUPREME COURT (*certiorari*)		
↑	↑	↑
HIGHEST STATE COURT	HIGHEST STATE COURT	U.S. COURT OF APPEALS
↑	↑	↑
(appeal as of right)	(appeals procedure varies)	(appeal if certificate of appealability issued)
↑	↑	↑
TRIAL COURT	TRIAL COURT	U.S. DISTRICT COURT
TRIAL, SENTENCING AND DIRECT APPEAL	**STATE POST-CONVICTION**	**FEDERAL HABEAS CORPUS**

This is not a system designed for efficiency. It is instead intended as a constraint on government power. As famously expressed by James Madison in *The Federalist* (No. 51), "In the compound republic of America, the power surrendered by the people is first divided between two distinct governments, and then the portion allocated to each subdivided among distinct and separate departments. Hence a double security arises to the rights of the people. The different governments will control each other, at the same time that each will be controlled by itself" (Madison 1788:323).

In the years prior to the Civil War, however, "the rights of the people" came under unremitting stress from the philosophical and political challenges generated by the peculiar institution of slavery:

> During the period that slavery existed in a colony or state, African-Americans were usually judged and summarily punished in special courts by all-white judges or juries for alleged crimes committed against whites. Violent acts by whites against blacks were rarely defined as criminal and then only as property crimes committed against the slave's white owner. Not only did the legal structure of slavery fail to protect blacks against the violent acts of whites, but it denied African-Americans the right to seek legal redress, or to testify as a witness against whites (Colbert 1990:13).

The 13th, 14th, and 15th Amendments, passed in the aftermath of the Civil War, were designed to end this two-tier system within the states. But the framers of those Amendments had little faith in the willingness of the state courts to discharge the responsibility of guaranteeing the rights of equal protection and due process of law to all citizens. It was in this context that Congress passed the federal habeas corpus act of 1867 (Amsterdam 1965), whose basic structure survives to this day. In the face of "the state courts' expected systematic resistance," the "Congress sought to assure prisoners of one full opportunity to enforce their newly given national rights in a national court" (Hertz and Liebman 2005a:52). Although its enthusiasm for the implementation of this purpose wavered during the Reconstruction period (Freedman 2003a:558–560), the Supreme Court in 1923 reaffirmed the critical importance of independent federal judicial review of claims that state criminal proceedings had violated the Constitution (*Moore v. Dempsey* 1923:90–92).

During the twentieth century and into the twenty-first, the death penalty in America has been the subject of extensive empirical study. Its principal features from the viewpoint of achieving justice are quite clear (Freedman 2005:667–672) and have been fully documented in a comprehensive anthology (Acker, Bohm, and Lanier 2003). In brief:

[C]apital defendants systematically receive less due process than others. Their cases are more likely than those of defendants not facing execution to have been infected by distortions arising from racism, the incompetence of defense counsel, their own mental limitations, public passion, political pressures, or jury prejudice or confusion (Baldus and Woodworth 2003; Bowers, Fleury-Steiner, and Antonio 2003; Bright 2003; Mello and Perkins 2003; Sandys and McClelland 2003). Of course, the result is a dangerous increase in the risk that the system will make a fatal error (Freedman 1990–1991; Gross 1996; Radelet and Bedau 2003) (Freedman 2003a:560).

This risk is compounded by the fact that capital cases are tried under unique rules that systematically increase the chances of conviction. Although death penalty trials are bifurcated into guilt and penalty phases, they are heard before a single jury. States are entitled to exclude from the penalty phase jury those with a fixed conviction in opposition to capital punishment. But such individuals also are denied participation in the trial's guilt phase, where they generally would be more likely to acquit defendants of capital murder than would their death-qualified counterparts. Repeated studies have shown that capital cases are tried before jurors who are more apt to convict than jurors sitting on non-capital cases (Freedman 2005:667–668; Liptak 2007).

For all of these structural reasons, in the decades following *Moore* robust federal habeas corpus review in capital cases was repeatedly recognized as being of especial importance for preventing miscarriages of justice (Association of the Bar 1996:177–181; Hertz and Liebman 2005a:§2.6). Nevertheless, following its ruling in *Gregg v. Georgia* (1976) that procedures could be designed to meet the constitutional mandate "that the penalty of death not be imposed in an arbitrary or capricious manner" (p. 195), the Supreme Court throughout the 1980s and 1990s systematically built up "a legalistic maze of restrictions on the availability of the habeas corpus remedy" (Freedman 2003a:567).

Among the most entangling vines in this dense thicket were doctrines of harmless error (*Brecht v. Abramson* 1993), whose incoherence had the practical effect of encouraging federal judges to ignore serious claims of constitutional violations (Amsterdam 2004; Dow and Rytting 2000); the universally condemned ruling in *Teague v. Lane* (1989), which arbitrarily constricted the universe of favorable legal rules available to federal habeas corpus petitioners (Freedman 2003a:566–567); and a series of cases involving the doctrines of procedural default, abuse of the writ, and exhaustion of remedies (Freedman 2006a:1097–1098). To take just one of many examples, in *Coleman v. Thompson* (1991) the Court ruled that a capital prisoner whose lawyer had filed his state habeas corpus appeals papers three days late had thereby forfeited federal habeas corpus review. This decision was premised on the explicit view that the outcome represented the appropriate "allocation of costs" between the interests of the State in avoiding a federal review of its conviction that might lead to an expensive retrial and those of the prisoner in not being executed pursuant to a possibly unconstitutional judgment (p. 754).

We have reliable empirical knowledge of how death row inmates fared in attempting to traverse this legal landscape, because a landmark study by Professor James S. Liebman and his colleagues examined every capital case in the United States in the period between 1973 and 1995, including more than 4,500 habeas petitions (Liebman, Fagan, and West 2000). The study found that petitioners in capital cases that reached federal habeas review succeeded approximately 40% of the time in overturning either the verdict or the sentence (Liebman et al. 2000). Specifically, for each 100 death verdicts returned, approximately 47 were overturned during state appeals; of the remaining 53, approximately 21 were invalidated on federal habeas corpus review—a total error rate of 68% (pp. 5–6). Even then—noting the systemic sources of error inherent in the design of death penalty systems and the legal difficulties in correcting them on federal habeas review—the authors expressed "grave doubt" about whether all errors were indeed being caught (a doubt reinforced by the observation that in 82% of the cases in which a death sentence was overturned the defendant subsequently received a sentence less than death, including 7% of cases in which he was found to be innocent of the capital offense) (pp. i–ii).

AEDPA and After

The last year covered by the Liebman study was 1995. In 1996, Congress enacted AEDPA. The statute, which was complex and convoluted—"in a world of silk purses and pigs' ears, the Act is not a silk purse of the art of statutory drafting" (*Lindh v. Murphy* 1997: 336)—made a plethora of highly technical changes to the rules governing federal habeas corpus proceedings. These changes included the creation of a statute of limitations and the imposition of constraints on federal review of legal and factual issues that had been, or might have been, litigated during the antecedent state proceedings (Hertz and Liebman 2005a:114–117).[3]

---

3. With the exception of certain provisions contained in Chapter 154 of the statute, these changes apply to capital and non-capital cases alike. Although, in keeping with the concerns of this volume, our discussion is limited to capital cases, it is worth noting that as a matter of design of the criminal justice system the effects of AEDPA on non-capital cases—

Arguably, AEDPA was principally motivated by an impetus to speed the federal habeas review of state death penalty cases, "while making no fundamental alteration in the existing role of the federal courts inquiring into state capital convictions" (Freedman 2003a:568). The Supreme Court certainly has frequently read the statute that way (Hertz and Liebman 2005a:120–132), which is consistent with the view that the Court had already shaped the field to its liking prior to 1996 (Freedman 2003a:569). This premise also is consistent with a recent study by Professor Blume finding that AEDPA made no difference to petitioners' success rate at the Supreme Court level (Blume 2006). But Professor Blume went on to caution:

> However, AEDPA does seem to have made it more difficult, especially in recent years, for petitioners to succeed in the federal courts of appeals. Given the number of exonerations in recent years, the scope of the writ—if it is to retain its historical function as a safeguard of freedom in our criminal justice system—should be expanded, not contracted, before the "bite" of judicial and congressional habeas reform exceeds the "hype" and effectively insulates even the most egregious state court decisions from federal collateral attack (p. 297).

Our statistical data show Professor Blume's warning to have been entirely correct. If the statute was intended to speed up federal habeas corpus proceedings in the lower federal courts without making relief any more difficult to obtain than it already was, the legislation has most certainly failed. Whatever may have been the effect on speed of disposition (which we have not studied) the success rate of capital federal habeas corpus petitioners in the lower federal courts has fallen sharply—so sharply as to raise a serious doubt whether those courts are in fact conducting the independent review of state law that Article III of the Constitution mandates (Liebman and Ryan 1998). Quite apart from legal considerations, our results warrant an urgent look at a grave policy question: has the statute in practice imperiled the bedrock role of capital habeas proceedings as "a safeguard against injustice" (American Bar Association 2003:931)?

We have examined the published results on appeal of all federal habeas corpus applications filed by all death row inmates between 2000 and 2006, inclu-

---

which greatly outnumber capital ones and which in an era of sharply rising rates and lengths of incarceration are consuming enormous resources (Amsterdam 2007:53; Liptak 2005)—are also in urgent need of study. An initial effort in this direction has been announced by Vanderbilt Law School (http://law.vanderbilt.edu/article-search/article-detail/index.aspx?nid=55).

sive.[4] The data can be summarized simply: whereas prior to AEDPA death row inmates prevailed somewhere between half and two-thirds of the time, they now prevail, nationwide, approximately 12 percent of the time. Further, the success rate, in most jurisdictions, appears to be declining.[5]

Although the entire data are reported in the Appendix, several aspects of our findings are worth highlighting here. First, although the overall rate of relief nationwide is around 12 percent, the figure varies significantly from circuit to circuit. Thus, for example, the rate of relief in the Fourth Circuit is less than two percent; in the Fifth and Eleventh Circuits it is less than four percent. In contrast, the Ninth Circuit shows a relief rate of 35 percent, while the Seventh and Tenth Circuits have relief rates of around 23 percent.

Second, relief rates do not appear to be adumbrated by grants of certificates of appealability in any of the circuits. Thus, in the Fourth and Fifth Circuits, where relief rates are lowest, the rates for COA grants are also low (at 45 and 43 percent, respectively). However, in the Eleventh Circuit, which also has an extremely low rate of relief, the courts grant a COA more than 84 percent of the time. In contrast, while the Ninth Circuit has the highest rate of relief, its rate of granting COA is in the middle of the pack, at 68 percent. The Seventh Circuit, which has a relatively high relief rate, has the lowest COA grant rate, only 37 percent. The highest COA grant rate of 91 percent is in the Eighth Circuit, which has a relief rate of only 17 percent.

Third, although relief rates have been declining over the last three years of the period we have studied, there is not a clearly defined trend line that stretches across all circuits over the entire seven-year period that we have examined. For example, the overall relief rate in 2000 was around six percent, but it shot up to around 27 percent in 2003, and was at 19 percent in 2005 (having declined to seven percent in 2004). These variations may reflect no more than random fluctuations and relatively small sample sizes, but they merit further study.

---

4. The Supreme Court ruled in *Lindh* that habeas petitions filed before the effective date of AEDPA would not be governed by the statute. We therefore began our analysis with calendar year 2000 in a rough effort to exclude most of the habeas petitions that would continue to be adjudicated under pre-AEDPA law.

5. Our data also capture the distinction between cases where an inmate obtained a certificate of appealability (COA) and those where he did not. Under AEDPA, before a U.S. Court of Appeals may adjudicate the merits of a claim on which a death row inmate has been denied relief, the inmate must make a "substantial showing of denial of a constitutional right" and obtain from either the District or Circuit Court a COA to that effect (28 U.S.C. §2253(c)(2)). The statute has been interpreted to mean that the issue the inmate seeks to have adjudicated is "debatable" among reasonable jurists (*Slack v. McDaniel* 2000:484; *Miller-El v. Cockrell* 2003).

The Road Ahead

We can think of three possible explanations for the contemporary state of affairs described by the data we have collected. One is that death penalty trials are fairer today and involve dramatically fewer constitutional violations than was the case a decade ago. There is no evidence in support of this hypothesis and a good deal against it (American Bar Association 2003:928–930; Death Penalty Information Center 2007; Lindell 2006).

A second possible explanation is that the trials are just as unfair today as they once were but death row inmates are obtaining relief in state courts and therefore do not need to resort to federal court as frequently. Although more detailed statistical studies would be welcome, this hypothesis, too, may appropriately be described as distinctly implausible. Liebman et al. (2000), for example, found low reversal rates in the state courts in Texas and Virginia, and a later study, that included an analysis of some post-AEDPA cases, found that the Texas and Virginia reversal rates remained low (Lofquist 2002:1513–1520).

The third possibility is that trials are just as unfair today as they ever were, and that state courts continue to deny relief to death row inmates, but that AEDPA now precludes the federal courts from issuing relief that they would have issued prior to AEDPA's enactment. Although this explanation seems to be the most likely one—and, indeed, we predict that it will prove to be correct—empirical validation of it will require careful analysis since, as indicated above, the legal environment for death row inmates was darkening in any event in the years before AEDPA took effect.

Such a study could be designed in several ways. One would be to focus on individual judges of the Courts of Appeals. Suppose that a particular judge voted to grant relief in capital habeas corpus cases at a 40% rate in the period 1981–1986, at a 30% rate in 1986–1991, at a 25% rate in 1991–1996, and at a 5% rate in both 1996–2001 and 2001–2006. And suppose further that this pattern—a sharp drop in votes to grant relief by the same judge following the enactment of AEDPA—turned out to be typical. Such findings would certainly be strongly suggestive that AEDPA, rather than the doctrinal changes made by the Supreme Court before the enactment of the statute, caused the drop.

Another highly important need is the compilation of a comprehensive and detailed database recording the grounds on which habeas relief is being granted or denied. Only with this information in hand will policymakers be able to sensibly assess and address the underlying public policy issues. As matters currently stand, when proposals for legislative reform of the capital habeas corpus process are made to Congress they are tested by a process consisting of no more than a duel of anecdotes. Given the stakes, this practice should be unacceptable to any serious person—which is precisely why such mainstream groups as the American Bar Association, the United States Judicial Conference, and the Conference of Chief Justices have all told Congress that it should provide for an independent empirical study of the current workings of the system before legislating (McMillion 2006).

We agree, and would only add our hope that the contents of legislative proposals be guided by the empirical findings. If, for instance, AEDPA, rather than any improvement in the fairness of state court proceedings, has caused the decline in grants of relief, then one might plausibly seek to improve the quality of defense representation in capital cases in those courts at trial, on direct appeal, and in state post-conviction proceedings (American Bar Association 2003:924–935; Freedman 2003b:1100–1103; Freedman 2006b:190–191).

Regardless of their views on the death penalty, legislators, social scientists, lawyers, and ordinary citizens might well benefit from pausing to reflect that each execution takes place in the name of all of us.

AEDPA Stats — Totals 2000–2006

Judicial Circuit	Relief Denied — Affirm Denial	Relief Denied — Reverse Grant	Relief Granted — Conviction Vacated	Relief Granted — Sentence Vacated	Unresolved — Remanded Denial	Unresolved — Remanded Grant	TOTAL	UNFILTERED HITS
1st	0	0	0	0	0	0	0	9
2d	0	0	0	0	0	0	0	22
3d	5	3	1	2	3	2	16	58
4th	49	5	1	0	5	0	60	75
5th	175	7	4	4	8	4	202	282
6th	35	9	3	5	14	2	68	139
7th	15	1	3	2	0	0	21	53
8th	17	3	2	3	3	1	29	44
9th	8	0	1	6	5	0	20	136
10th	45	1	5	10	3	0	64	113
11th	42	2	1	1	4	2	52	103
DC	0	0	0	0	0	0	0	3
TOTAL	391	31	21	33	45	11	532	1037
	422		54		56			
% TOTAL	73.50%	5.83%	3.95%	6.20%	8.46%	2.07%	100.00%	
	79.32%		10.15%		10.53%			

Grant of a COA are treated as "Unresolved"
Denial of a COA are treated as "Relief Denied"
Grant of a COA where the denial was Affirmed are treated as "Affirmed Denial"
Grant of a SOE are treated as "Remanded Grant"
Denial of SOE are treated as "Relief Denied"

AEDPA Stats — Year-By-Year

2000

Judicial Circuit	Relief Denied — Affirm Denial	Relief Denied — Reverse Grant	Relief Granted — Conviction Vacated	Relief Granted — Sentence Vacated	Unresolved — Remanded Denial	Unresolved — Remanded Grant	TOTAL
1st	0	0	0	0	0	0	0
2d	0	0	0	0	0	0	0
3d	2	0	0	0	0	0	2
4th	13	1	0	0	0	0	14
5th	21	0	0	1	1	1	24
6th	4	1	0	0	0	0	5
7th	0	0	0	0	1	0	1
8th	1	0	0	1	0	0	2
9th	2	0	0	0	0	0	2
10th	8	0	0	2	1	0	11
11th	1	0	0	0	1	0	2
DC	0	0	0	0	0	0	0
TOTAL	52	2	0	4	4	1	63
% TOTAL	82.54%	3.17%	0.00%	6.35%	6.35%	1.59%	100.00%
	85.71%			6.35%	7.94%		

AEDPA Stats — Year-By-Year

2001

Judicial Circuit	Relief Denied		Relief Granted			Unresolved		TOTAL
	Affirm Denial	Reverse Grant	Conviction Vacated	Sentence Vacated	Remanded Denial	Remanded Grant	
1st	0	0	0	0	0	0	0
2d	0	0	0	0	0	0	0
3d	0	0	0	1	0	0	1
4th	2	1	0	0	0	0	3
5th	17	1	1	0	1	1	21
6th	4	0	0	0	3	0	8
7th	2	0	0	0	0	0	2
8th	1	0	1	0	0	1	3
9th	1	0	0	0	0	1	2
10th	8	0	1	4	0	0	13
11th	2	0	0	1	0	1	4
DC	0	0	0	0	0	0	0
TOTAL	37	3	3	6	4	4	57
	40			9		8	
% TOTAL	64.91%	5.26%	5.26%	10.53%	7.02%	7.02%	100%
	70.18%			15.79%		14.04%	

AEDPA Stats — Year-By-Year

2002

Judicial Circuit	Relief Denied — Affirm Denial	Relief Denied — Reverse Grant	Relief Granted — Conviction Vacated	Relief Granted — Sentence Vacated	Unresolved — Remanded Denial	Unresolved — Remanded Grant	TOTAL
1st	0	0	0	0	0	0	0
2d	0	0	0	0	0	0	0
3d	1	0	0	0	1	0	2
4th	4	2	0	0	1	0	7
5th	35	1	0	0	1	0	37
6th	5	1	0	0	2	0	8
7th	4	0	0	1	1	0	6
8th	4	1	0	1	0	0	6
9th	0	0	1	3	0	0	4
10th	15	0	2	0	1	0	18
11th	9	1	0	0	1	0	11
DC	0	0	0	0	0	0	0
TOTAL	77	6	3	5	8	0	99
	83		8		8		
% TOTAL	77.78%	6.06%	3.03%	5.05%	8.08%	0.00%	100.00%
	83.84%		8.08%		8.08%		

AEDPA Stats — Year-By-Year

2003

Judicial Circuit	Relief Denied — Affirm Denial	Relief Denied — Reverse Grant	Relief Granted — Conviction Vacated	Relief Granted — Sentence Vacated	Unresolved — Remanded Denial	Unresolved — Remanded Grant	TOTAL
1st	0	0	0	0	0	0	0
2d	0	0	0	0	0	0	0
3d	1	0	0	0	0	0	1
4th	11	0	1	0	0	0	12
5th	25	0	0	1	0	1	27
6th	4	0	0	2	1	1	8
7th	0	0	1	0	0	0	1
8th	2	0	1	0	1	0	4
9th	0	0	0	2	0	0	2
10th	5	1	1	3	0	0	10
11th	5	0	1	9	1	0	16
DC	0	0	0	0	0	0	0
TOTAL	53	1	5	17	3	2	81
	54		22		5		
% TOTAL	65.43%	1.23%	61.17%	20.99%	3.70%	2.47%	100.00%
	66.7%		27.16%		6.17%		

AEDPA Stats — Year-By-Year

2004

Judicial Circuit	Relief Denied		Relief Granted			Unresolved		TOTAL
	Affirm Denial	Reverse Grant	Conviction Vacated	Sentence Vacated	Remanded Denial	Remanded Grant	
1st	0	0	0	0	0	0	0
2d	0	0	0	0	0	0	0
3d	0	2	0	0	1	0	3
4th	4	1	0	0	1	0	6
5th	21	1	1	0	1	1	25
6th	3	1	0	1	1	1	7
7th	6	0	0	0	0	0	6
8th	4	1	0	0	0	0	5
9th	3	0	0	1	2	0	6
10th	1	0	1	1	1	0	4
11th	3	0	0	0	1	0	4
DC	0	0	0	0	0	0	0
TOTAL	45	6	2	3	8	2	66
% TOTAL	68.18%	9.09%	3.03%	4.55%	12.12%	3.03%	100.00%
	77.27%		7.58%			15.15%		

AEDPA Stats — Year-By-Year

2005

Judicial Circuit	Relief Denied - Affirm Denial	Relief Denied - Reverse Grant	Relief Granted - Conviction Vacated	Relief Granted - Sentence Vacated	Unresolved - Remanded Denial	Unresolved - Remanded Grant	TOTAL
1st	0	0	0	0	0	0	0
2d	0	0	0	0	0	0	0
3d	0	0	1	1	0	2	4
4th	8	0	0	0	1	0	9
5th	24	1	2	1	1	0	29
6th	7	3	1	1	3	1	16
7th	6	0	6	3	0	0	15
8th	1	1	0	0	0	0	2
9th	0	0	0	0	1	0	1
10th	4	0	0	0	0	0	4
11th	7	1	0	1	0	0	9
DC	0	0	0	0	0	0	0
TOTAL	57	6	10	7	6	3	89
	63		17		9		
% TOTAL	64.04%	6.74%	11.24%	7.87%	6.74%	3.37%	100.00%
	70.79%		19.10%		10.11%		

13 · THE EFFECTS OF AEDPA ON JUSTICE

AEDPA Stats — Year-By-Year

2006

Judicial Circuit	Relief Denied		Relief Granted			Unresolved		TOTAL
	Affirm Denial	Reverse Grant	Conviction Vacated	Sentence Vacated	Remanded Denial	Remanded Denial	Remanded Grant	
1st	0	0	0	0	0	0	0	0
2d	0	0	0	0	0	0	0	0
3d	1	1	0	0	1	0	0	3
4th	7	0	0	0	1	0	0	8
5th	34	2	1	3	1	0	1	42
6th	8	3	1	2	3	0	0	17
7th	1	0	0	0	0	0	0	1
8th	4	0	0	1	1	0	0	6
9th	2	0	0	0	1	0	0	3
10th	4	0	0	0	0	0	0	4
11th	15	0	0	0	0	0	0	15
DC	0	0	0	0	0	0	0	0
TOTAL	76	6	2	6	8	8	1	99
	82		8		6	9		
% TOTAL	76.77%	6.06%	2.02%	6.06%	8.08%	8.08%	1.01%	100.00%
	82.83%		8.08%			9.09%		

AEDPA Stats — Subsection 1 — COA Granted by District Court

2000

Judicial Circuit	Relief Denied		Relief Granted			Unresolved		TOTAL
	Affirm Denial	Reverse Grant	Conviction Vacated	Sentence Vacated	Remanded Denial	Remanded Grant	
1st	0	0	0	0	0	0	0
2d	0	0	0	0	0	0	0
3d	1	0	0	0	0	0	1
4th	0	0	0	0	0	0	0
5th	9	0	0	0	1	0	10
6th	3	0	0	0	1	0	4
7th	0	0	0	0	0	0	0
8th	0	0	0	0	0	0	0
9th	0	0	0	0	0	0	0
10th	6	0	0	2	0	0	8
11th	0	0	0	0	1	0	1
DC	0	0	0	0	0	0	0
TOTAL	19	0	0	2	3	0	24
% TOTAL	79.17%	0.00%	0.00%	8.33%	12.50%	0.00%	100.00%
	79.17%		8.33%		12.50%		

AEDPA Stats — Subsection 1 — COA Granted by District Court

2001

Judicial Circuit	Relief Denied - Affirm Denial	Relief Denied - Reverse Grant	Relief Granted - Conviction Vacated	Relief Granted - Sentence Vacated	Unresolved - Remanded Denial	Unresolved - Remanded Grant	TOTAL
1st	0	0	0	0	0	0	0
2d	0	0	0	0	0	0	0
3d	0	0	0	0	0	0	0
4th	0	0	0	0	0	0	0
5th	8	0	0	0	0	0	8
6th	1	0	0	0	2	0	3
7th	1	0	0	0	0	0	1
8th	1	0	0	0	0	0	1
9th	0	0	0	0	0	0	0
10th	3	0	1	2	0	0	6
11th	1	0	0	0	0	0	1
DC	0	0	0	0	0	0	0
TOTAL	15	0	1	2	2	0	20
% TOTAL	75.00%	0.00%	5.00%	10.00%	10.00%	0.00%	100.00%
	75.00%		15.00%		10.00%		

13 · THE EFFECTS OF AEDPA ON JUSTICE

AEDPA Stats — Subsection 1 — COA Granted by District Court

2002

Judicial Circuit	Relief Denied — Affirm Denial	Relief Denied — Reverse Grant	Relief Granted — Conviction Vacated	Relief Granted — Sentence Vacated	Unresolved — Remanded Denial	Unresolved — Remanded Grant	TOTAL
1st	0	0	0	0	0	0	0
2d	0	0	0	0	0	0	0
3d	1	0	0	0	1	0	2
4th	0	0	0	0	0	0	0
5th	3	0	0	0	1	0	4
6th	1	0	0	0	0	0	1
7th	0	0	0	0	0	0	0
8th	3	1	0	1	0	0	5
9th	0	0	0	0	0	0	0
10th	6	0	0	0	0	0	6
11th	7	1	0	0	0	1	9
DC	0	0	0	0	0	0	0
TOTAL	21	2	0	1	2	1	27
% TOTAL	77.78%	7.41%	0.00%	3.70%	7.41%	3.70%	100.00%
	85.19%		3.70%		11.11%		

AEDPA Stats — Subsection 1 — COA Granted by District Court

2003

Judicial Circuit	Relief Denied			Relief Granted			Unresolved		
	Affirm Denial	Reverse Grant	Conviction Vacated	Sentence Vacated	Remanded Denial	Remanded Grant	TOTAL
1st	0	0	0	0	0	0	0
2d	0	0	0	0	0	0	0
3d	0	0	0	0	0	0	0
4th	0	0	0	0	0	0	0
5th	5	0	0	1	0	0	6
6th	2	0	0	1	1	1	5
7th	0	0	0	0	0	0	0
8th	1	0	0	0	0	0	1
9th	0	0	0	1	0	0	1
10th	1	0	0	2	0	0	3
11th	2	0	1	0	1	0	4
DC	0	0	0	0	0	0	0
TOTAL	11	0	1	5	2	1	20
% TOTAL	55.00%	0.00%	5.00%	25.00%	10.00%	5.00%	100.00%
	55.00%		30.00%		15.00%		

AEDPA Stats — Subsection 1—COA Granted by District Court

2004

Judicial Circuit	Relief Denied		Relief Granted			Unresolved		TOTAL
	Affirm Denial	Reverse Grant	Conviction Vacated	Sentence Vacated	Remanded Denial	Remanded Grant	
1st	0	0	0	0	0	0	0
2d	0	0	0	0	0	0	0
3d	0	1	0	0	0	0	1
4th	0	0	0	0	0	0	0
5th	5	1	0	0	1	0	7
6th	2	0	0	0	0	0	2
7th	1	1	0	0	0	0	1
8th	2	0	0	0	0	0	3
9th	1	0	0	0	1	0	2
10th	1	0	1	0	1	0	3
11th	1	0	0	0	0	0	1
DC	0	0	0	0	0	0	0
TOTAL	13	3	1	0	3	0	20
% TOTAL	65.00%	15.00%	5.00%	0.00%	15.00%	0.00%	100.00%
	80.00%		5.00%		15.00%		

13 · THE EFFECTS OF AEDPA ON JUSTICE

AEDPA Stats — Subsection 1—COA Granted by District Court

2005

Judicial Circuit	Relief Denied		Relief Granted			Unresolved		TOTAL
	Affirm Denial	Reverse Grant	Conviction Vacated	Sentence Vacated	Remanded Denial	Remanded Grant	
1st	0	0	0	0	0	0	0
2d	0	0	0	0	0	0	0
3d	1	0	0	0	0	0	1
4th	5	0	0	0	0	0	5
5th	4	0	0	0	0	0	4
6th	6	1	0	0	2	0	9
7th	1	0	0	0	0	0	1
8th	0	1	0	0	0	0	1
9th	0	0	0	0	1	0	1
10th	4	0	0	0	0	0	4
11th	3	1	0	0	0	0	4
DC	0	0	0	0	0	0	0
TOTAL	24	3	0	0	3	0	30
	27		0			3		
% TOTAL	80.00%	10.00%	0.00%	0.00%	10.00%	0.00%	100.00%
	90.00%		0.00%			10.00%		

AEDPA Stats — Subsection 1—COA Granted by District Court

2006

Judicial Circuit	Relief Denied		Relief Granted			Unresolved		TOTAL
	Affirm Denial	Reverse Grant	Conviction Vacated	Sentence Vacated	Remanded Denial	Remanded Grant		
1st	0	0	0	0	0	0		0
2d	0	0	0	0	0	0		0
3d	1	1	0	0	1	0		3
4th	2	0	0	0	0	0		2
5th	8	0	0	0	1	0		9
6th	5	2	1	1	2	0		11
7th	0	0	0	0	0	0		0
8th	3	0	0	1	0	0		4
9th	2	0	0	0	1	0		3
10th	4	0	0	0	0	0		4
11th	6	0	0	0	0	0		6
DC	0	0	0	0	0	0		0
TOTAL	31	3	1	2	5	0		42
	34		3		5			
% TOTAL	73.81%	7.14%	2.38%	4.76%	11.90%	0.00%		100.00%
	80.95%		7.14%		11.90%			

AEDPA Stats — Subsection 2—COA Denied by District Court

2000

	Relief Denied		Relief Granted			Unresolved		TOTAL
	Affirm Denial	Reverse Grant	Conviction Vacated	Sentence Vacated	Remanded Denial	Remanded Grant	
1st	0	0	0	0	0	0	0
2d	0	0	0	0	0	0	0
3d	1	0	0	0	0	0	1
4th	0	0	0	0	0	0	0
5th	0	0	0	0	0	0	0
6th	1	0	0	0	1	0	2
7th	0	0	0	0	0	0	0
8th	0	0	0	0	0	0	0
9th	0	0	0	0	0	0	0
10th	1	0	0	0	0	0	1
11th	1	0	0	0	0	0	1
DC	0	0	0	0	0	0	0
TOTAL	4	0	0	0	1	0	5
% TOTAL	80.00%	0.00%	0.00%	0.00%	20.00%	0.00%	100.00%
	80.00%		0.00%			20.00%		

AEDPA Stats — Subsection 2—COA Denied by District Court

2001

	Relief Denied		Relief Granted			Unresolved		TOTAL
	Affirm Denial	Reverse Grant	Conviction Vacated	Sentence Vacated	Remanded Denial	Remanded Grant	
1st	0	0	0	0	0	0	0
2d	0	0	0	0	0	0	0
3d	0	0	0	0	0	0	0
4th	1	0	0	0	1	0	2
5th	1	0	0	0	1	0	2
6th	1	0	0	0	1	0	2
7th	1	0	0	0	0	0	1
8th	0	0	0	0	0	0	0
9th	0	0	0	0	1	0	1
10th	1	0	0	0	0	0	1
11th	1	0	0	0	0	0	1
DC	0	0	0	0	0	0	0
TOTAL	6	0	0	0	4	0	10
% TOTAL	60.00%	0.00%	0.00%	0.00%	40.00%	0.00%	100.00%
	60.00%		0.00%			40.00%		

AEDPA Stats — Subsection 2 — COA Denied by District Court

2002

	Relief Denied		Relief Granted			Unresolved		TOTAL
	Affirm Denial	Reverse Grant	Conviction Vacated	Sentence Vacated		Remanded Denial	Remanded Grant	
1st	0	0	0	0		0	0	0
2d	0	0	0	0		0	0	0
3d	0	0	0	0		0	0	0
4th	0	0	0	0		0	0	0
5th	0	0	0	0		0	0	0
6th	1	0	0	0		1	0	2
7th	0	0	0	0		1	0	1
8th	1	0	0	0		0	0	1
9th	0	0	0	0		0	0	0
10th	2	0	0	0		0	0	2
11th	1	0	0	0		0	0	1
DC	0	0	0	0		0	0	0
TOTAL	5	0	0	0		2	0	7
% TOTAL	71.43%	0.00%	0.00%	0.00%		28.57%	0.00%	100.00%
	71.43%		0.00%			28.57%		

AEDPA Stats — Subsection 2 — COA Denied by District Court

2003

	Relief Denied		Relief Granted			Unresolved		TOTAL
	Affirm Denial	Reverse Grant	Conviction Vacated	Sentence Vacated		Remanded Denial	Remanded Grant	
1st	0	0	0	0		0	0	0
2d	0	0	0	0		0	0	0
3d	1	0	0	0		0	0	1
4th	2	0	0	0		1	0	3
5th	2	1	0	0		1	0	4
6th	1	0	0	0		0	0	2
7th	0	0	0	0		0	0	0
8th	1	0	0	0		0	0	1
9th	0	0	0	0		0	0	0
10th	0	0	0	0		0	0	0
11th	0	0	0	0		0	0	0
DC	0	0	0	0		0	0	0
TOTAL	7	1	0	1		2	0	11
% TOTAL	63.64%	9.09%	0.00%	9.09%		18.18%	0.00%	100.00%
	72.73%		9.09%			18.18%		

AEDPA Stats — Subsection 2—COA Denied by District Court

2004

	Relief Denied		Relief Granted			Unresolved		TOTAL
	Affirm Denial	Reverse Grant	Conviction Vacated	Sentence Vacated		Remanded Denial	Remanded Grant	
1st	0	0	0	0		0	0	0
2d	0	0	0	0		0	0	0
3d	0	0	0	0		1	0	1
4th	2	0	0	0		4	0	6
5th	2	1	1	0		6	0	10
6th	0	0	0	1		0	1	2
7th	0	0	0	0		0	0	0
8th	2	0	0	0		0	0	2
9th	1	0	0	1		0	0	2
10th	1	0	0	0		1	0	2
11th	0	0	0	0		0	0	0
DC	0	0	0	0		0	0	0
TOTAL	8	1	1	2		12	1	25
	32.00%	4.00%	4.00%	8.00%		48.00%	4.00%	
% TOTAL	36.00%		12.00%			52.00%		100.00%

AEDPA Stats — Subsection 2 — COA Denied by District Court

2005

	Relief Denied		Relief Granted			Unresolved		TOTAL
	Affirm Denial	Reverse Grant	Conviction Vacated	Sentence Vacated		Remanded Denial	Remanded Grant	
1st	0	0	0	0		0	0	0
2d	0	0	0	0		0	0	0
3d	0	0	0	0		0	0	0
4th	3	0	0	0		1	0	4
5th	2	0	0	1		3	0	6
6th	0	0	0	0		0	0	0
7th	1	0	0	0		0	0	1
8th	1	0	0	0		0	0	1
9th	0	0	0	0		0	0	0
10th	0	0	0	0		0	0	0
11th	4	1	0	0		0	0	5
DC	0	0	0	0		0	0	0
TOTAL	11	1	0	1		4	0	17
	64.71%	5.88%	0.00%	5.88%		23.53%	0.00%	100.00%
% TOTAL	70.59%		5.88%			23.53%		

AEDPA Stats — Subsection 2—COA Denied by District Court

2006

	Relief Denied		Relief Granted			Unresolved		TOTAL
	Affirm Denial	Reverse Grant	Conviction Vacated	Sentence Vacated		Remanded Denial	Remanded Grant	
1st	0	0	0	0		0	0	0
2d	0	0	0	0		0	0	0
3d	0	0	0	0		0	0	0
4th	5	0	0	0		1	0	6
5th	7	0	0	0		1	0	8
6th	2	1	0	1		1	0	5
7th	1	0	0	0		0	0	1
8th	1	0	0	0		1	0	2
9th	0	0	0	0		0	0	0
10th	0	0	0	0		0	0	0
11th	7	0	0	0		0	0	7
DC	0	0	0	0		0	0	0
TOTAL	23	1	0	1		4	0	29
	24					4		
% TOTAL	79.31%	3.45%	0.00%	3.45%		13.79%	0.00%	100.00%
	82.76%		3.45%			13.79%		

Summary of All Federal Capital Habeas Dispositions, 2000–2006

Rate of Total Relief Granted—2000 to 2006

Circuit	Total Cases (filtered)	Granted (Raw #)	Granted (%—rounded to 3rd decimal point)
1st	0	n/a	n/a
2d	0	n/a	n/a
3d	16	3	18.75
4th	60	1	1.667
5th	202	8	3.960
6th	68	8	11.765
7th	21	5	23.81
8th	29	5	17.241
9th	20	7	35.00
10th	64	15	23.438
11th	52	2	3.846
Average	48.364	4.909	12.68

Rate of COA's granted (by Either District Court or Court of Appeals)—2000 to 2006

Circuit	Relief Denied by DC	COA granted by Either (Raw)	Rate of COA granted by either (%)
1st	0	n/a	—
2d	0	n/a	—
3d	13	11	84.616
4th	59	27	45.763
5th	198	86	43.434
6th	60	49	81.667
7th	16	6	37.5
8th	24	22	91.667
9th	16	11	68.75
10th	57	38	66.667
11th	51	43	84.314
Average	44.9091	26.636	54.944

Rate of Relief Granted Upon Grant of COA
(by Either Court) — 2000 to 2006

Circuit	# of COA's Granted	Relief Granted As result of COA	Rate (%)
1st	n/a	n/a	n/a
2d	n/a	n/a	n/a
3d	11	0	0
4th	27	0	0
5th	86	4	4.651
6th	49	6	12.245
7th	6	0	0
8th	22	1	4.546
9th	11	3	27.27
10th	38	8	21.053
11th	43	1	2.326
Average	26.636	2.091	6.554

References

Acker, James R., Robert M. Bohm, and Charles S. Lanier, eds. (2003) *America's Experiment With Capital Punishment: Reflections on the Past, Present and Future of the Ultimate Penal Sanction*. 2nd edition. Durham, NC: Carolina Academic Press.

American Bar Association. 2003. "Guidelines for the Appointment and Performance of Defense Counsel in Death Penalty Cases" (rev. ed.) with Commentary. Reprinted in *Hofstra Law Review* 31:913–1090.

Amsterdam, Anthony G. 2007. "Lady Justice's Blindfold Has Been Shredded." *The Champion* 51–53 (May).

_____. 2004. "Remarks." *Hofstra Law Review* 33:403–416.

_____. 1965. "Criminal Prosecutions Affecting Federally Guaranteed Civil Rights: Federal Removal and Habeas Corpus Jurisdiction to Abort State Court Trial." *University of Pennsylvania Law Review* 113:793–912.

Association of the Bar of the City of New York. 1996. "The Crisis in Capital Representation." *Record of the Association of the Bar of the City of New York* 51:169–206.

Baldus, David C. and George Woodworth. 2003. "Race Discrimination and the Death Penalty: An Empirical and Legal Overview." Pp. 501–551 in *America's Experiment With Capital Punishment: Reflections on the Past, Present and Future of the Ultimate Penal Sanction*, edited by James R. Acker,

Robert M. Bohm, and Charles S. Lanier. 2nd edition. Durham, NC: Carolina Academic Press.
Blume, John H. 2006. "AEDPA: The 'Hype' and the 'Bite'" *Cornell Law Review* 91:259–298.
Bowers, William J., Benjamin D. Fleury-Steiner and Michael E. Antonio. 2003. "The Capital Sentencing Decision: Guided Discretion, Reasoned Moral Judgment or Legal Fiction?" Pp. 413–467 in *America's Experiment With Capital Punishment: Reflections on the Past, Present and Future of the Ultimate Penal Sanction*, edited by James R. Acker, Robert M. Bohm, and Charles S. Lanier. 2nd ed. Durham, NC: Carolina Academic Press.
Brecht v. Abramson (1993) 507 U.S. 619.
Bright, Stephen B. 2003. "The Politics of Capital Punishment: The Sacrifice of Fairness for Executions." Pp. 127–146 in *America's Experiment With Capital Punishment: Reflections on the Past, Present and Future of the Ultimate Penal Sanction*, edited by James R. Acker, Robert M. Bohm, and Charles S. Lanier. 2nd edition. Durham, NC: Carolina Academic Press.
Colbert, Douglas L. 1990. "Challenging the Challenge: The Thirteenth Amendment as a Prohibition Against the Racial Use of Peremptory Challenges." *Cornell Law Review* 76:1–128.
Coleman v. Thompson (1991). 501 U.S. 722.
Death Penalty Information Center (2007). "*Innocence and the Death Penalty.*" (http://www.deathpenaltyinfo.org/article.php?did=412&scid=6).
Dow, David R. and James Rytting. 2000. "Can Constitutional Error be Harmless?" *Utah Law Review* 2000:483–536.
Dow, David R. 2006. *Executed on a Technicality: Lethal Injustice on America's Death Row.* New York, NY: Beacon Press.
Freedman, Eric M. 2006a."*Girratano* is a Scarecrow: The Right to Counsel in State Capital Post-Conviction Proceedings." *Cornell Law Review* 91:1079–1103.
_____. 2006b. "Fewer Risks, More Benefits: What Governments Gain by Acknowledging the Right to Competent Counsel on State Post-Conviction Review in Capital Cases." *Ohio State Journal of Criminal Law* 4:183–193.
_____. 2005. "Mend It or End It? The Revised ABA Capital Defense Representation Guidelines as an Opportunity to Reconsider the Death Penalty." *Ohio State Journal of Criminal Law* 2:663–675.
_____. 2003a. "Federal Habeas Corpus in Capital Cases." Pp. 553–571 in *America's Experiment With Capital Punishment: Reflections on the Past, Present and Future of the Ultimate Penal Sanction*, edited by James R. Acker, Robert M. Bohm, and Charles S. Lanier. 2nd ed. Durham, NC: Carolina Academic Press.

———. 2003b. "Add Resources and Apply Them Systemically: Governments' Responsibilities Under the Revised ABA Capital Defense Representation Guidelines." *Hofstra Law Review* 31:1097–1115.

———. 1990–1991. "Innocence, Federalism, and the Capital Jury: Two Legislative Proposals for Evaluating Post-Trial Evidence of Innocence in Death Penalty Cases." *New York University Review of Law and Social Change* 18:315–324.

Gregg v. Georgia (1976). 428 U.S. 123.

Gross, Samuel R. 1996. "The Risks of Death: Why Erroneous Convictions are Common in Capital Cases." *Buffalo Law Review* 44:469–500.

Hertz, Randy and James S. Liebman 2005a. *Federal Habeas Corpus Practice and Procedure*. Vol. 1. 5th ed. Charlottesville, NC: The Michie Company.

———. 2005b. *Federal Habeas Corpus Practice and Procedure*. Vol. 2. Fifth edition. Charlottesville, NC: The Michie Company.

Liebman, James S. and William F. Ryan 1998. "'Some Effectual Power': The Quantity and Quality of Decisionmaking Required of Article III Courts." *Columbia Law Review* 98:696–791.

Liebman, James S., Jeffrey Fagan, and Valerie West. 2000. *A Broken System: Error Rates in Capital Cases.* New York, NY: Columbia University.

Lindell, Chuck. 2006. "Sloppy Lawyers Failing Clients on Death Row." *Austin American-Statesman,* Oct 29.

Lindh v. Murphy (1997). 521 U.S. 320.

Liptak, Adam. 2007. "Court Ruling Expected to Spur Convictions in Capital Cases." *N.Y. Times,* Jun 9.

———. 2005. "Serving Life, With No Chance of Redemption." *N.Y. Times,* Oct 5.

Lofquist, William S. 2002. "Putting Them There, Keeping Them There, and Killing Them: An Analysis of State-Level Variations In Death Penalty Intensity." *Iowa Law Review* 87:1505–1557.

Madison, James. [1788] 1999. "The Federalist, No. 51." Pp. 320–325 in *The Federalist Papers,* edited by Charles R. Rossiter. New York, NY: Mentor Publishing.

McMillion, Rhonda. 2006. "Not So Fast." ABA Journal 92:65–65.

Mello, Michael and Paul J. Perkins 2003. "Closing the Circle: The Illusion of Lawyers for People Litigating for Their Lives at the *Fin de Siècle*." Pp. 347–84 in *America's Experiment With Capital Punishment: Reflections on the Past, Present and Future of the Ultimate Penal Sanction,* edited by James R. Acker, Robert M. Bohm, and Charles S. Lanier. 2nd ed. Durham, NC: Carolina Academic Press.

Miller-El v. Cockrell (2003). 537 U.S. 322.

Moore v. Dempsey (1923). 261 U.S. 86.

Radelet, Michael L. and Hugo A. Bedau. 2003. "The Execution of the Innocent." Pp. 325–344 in *America's Experiment With Capital Punishment: Reflections on the Past, Present and Future of the Ultimate Penal Sanction,* edited by James R. Acker, Robert M. Bohm, and Charles S. Lanier. 2nd ed. Durham, NC: Carolina Academic Press.

Rhines v. Weber (2005). 544 U.S. 269.

Sandys, Marla and Scott McClelland. (2003). "Stacking the Deck for Guilt and Death: The Failure of Death Qualification to Ensure Impartiality." Pp. 385–411 in *America's Experiment With Capital Punishment: Reflections on the Past, Present and Future of the Ultimate Penal Sanction,* edited by James R. Acker, Robert M. Bohm, and Charles S. Lanier. 2nd ed. Durham, NC: Carolina Academic Press.

Slack v. McDaniel (2000). 529 U.S. 473.

Teague v. Lane (1989). 489 U.S. 288.

CHAPTER 14

Toward a New Perspective on Clemency in the Killing State

Austin Sarat

"*Legal interpretation demands that we remember the future.*"
Drucilla Cornell,
"From the Lighthouse: The Promise of Redemption and the
Possibility of Legal Interpretation" (1990)

Introduction

Clemency in capital cases is today an endangered species and, yet one of the most important parts of the death penalty system in the United States. The importance of clemency arises, in part, from the fact that courts, including the Supreme Court, have grown impatient with the complex legal process which the Court itself constructed to ensure fairness in the administration of law's ultimate penalty (Anti-Terrorism and effective Death Penalty Act 1996; Greenberg 1982; Zimring 1992). They have gradually cut back on the availability of federal habeas corpus relief in death penalty cases (see *Wainwright v. Sykes* 1977). Decisions dealing with procedural default (*Wainwright v. Sykes* 1977), exhaustion (*Rose v. Lundy* 1982), and abuse of the writ through the filing of successive habeas petitions (*McCleskey v. Zant* 1991), have made it increasingly difficult for federal courts to reach the merits of a defendant's habeas claims.

A defendant who receives a death sentence now often finds it impossible to obtain federal habeas review of the merits of whatever decisions or rulings might have been made by the judge during his capital trial (Goldstein 1990–91;

Liebman 1990–91; see Dow and Freedman, this volume). Due to the imposition of procedural bars and default rules, and the resulting limits on judicial review of convictions and sentences in death cases, gubernatorial clemency has become, in essence, the court of last resort, providing what Chief Justice Rehnquist in *Herrera v. Collins* (1993) called a "fail safe" mechanism in the death penalty system.

Despite its importance, research on clemency has not occupied a large and important place in death penalty scholarship. While much has been said and written about the power to kill within the confines of modern law (Sarat 2001), that sustained focus on the right to impose death sometimes eclipses its essential corollary—the sovereign right to spare life (for exceptions see Davis 1987 and Hay 1975). Executive clemency in capital cases is distinctive in that it is the only power that can *undo death*—the only power that can prevent death once it has been prescribed and, through appellate review, approved as a legally appropriate punishment. Yet we know relatively little about this power to undo death, about the clemency process and how it operates, about the political and moral forces that are brought to bear in considering clemency petitions, and about the narrative strategies and rhetoric used by those seeking to persuade chief executives to spare their lives. Moreover, most of the existing scholarship on capital clemency focuses on the dynamics of decision making by those who have the power to grant clemency or takes the form of normative argument about the appropriateness of the clemency power (see, *e.g.*, Breslin and Howley 2002; Dinsmore 2002; Garvey 2004; Heise 2003; Kobil 2002; Love 2000–01; Moore 1989; Radelet and Zsemblik 1992–93; Rapaport 2001). As a result, our understanding of the nature and importance of clemency in the killing state is somewhat impoverished.

In what follows I offer a framework for future research on the clemency process. This framework takes a bottom-up rather than top-down view of that process and helps explain the significance of clemency petitions even when the chances that any narrative strategy or rhetoric will produce a favorable result are so remote.

Playing Long Odds in the Lottery for Life

With the exception of a rare dramatic gesture, like Governor Ryan's mass commutation in Illinois, the long-held constitutional right of chief executives to spare life seems to have "died its own death, the victim of a political lethal injection and a public that overwhelmingly supports the death penalty" (Salladay 1998). During the 1990s, from one to eight death row inmates had their sentences commuted every year—compared to approximately 20 to 90 executions.[1] This represents a radical shift from several decades ago, when governors granted clemency in 20 to 25 percent of the death penalty cases they reviewed (Banner, 2002).[2] In Florida, for example, one of the states most firmly in the "death belt," between 1924 and 1966, there were 59 commutations and 196 executions in capital cases. However, between 1983 and 2000, the clemency requests of all 161 Florida prisoners on death row were denied (Sarat 2005:Appendix B).

The rarity of capital clemency is not just a southern, death-belt phenomenon. Thus, "since at least 1965, no Washington Governor has intervened to overturn a death sentence, and in only one instance was an execution postponed by a Governor's action" (Washington State Office of the Attorney General 2000). From 1964 to 2003, the year of Governor Ryan's action, clemency was granted in only one Illinois capital case. And, in Pennsylvania, another state with a large death row population, the last death penalty commutation took place in the early 1960s (Sarat 2005:Appendix B).

Rejecting appeals from the Pope, Mother Teresa, televangelist Pat Robertson, former prosecutors and even judges and jurors in death cases, governors reserve their clemency power for "unusual" cases in which someone clearly has been erroneously convicted (Acker and Lanier 2000). Thus, at the outset of his administration, Texas Governor George Bush embraced a standard for clemency that all but ensured that few if any death sentences would be seriously examined. Writing about Bush's views, Alan Berlow (2003) noted:

> "In every case," [Bush] wrote in *A Charge to Keep*, "I would ask: Is there any doubt about this individual's guilt or innocence? And, have the courts had ample opportunity to review all the legal issues in this case?" This is an extraordinarily narrow notion of clemency review: it seems to leave little, if any, room to consider mental illness or incompetence, childhood physical or sexual abuse, remorse, rehabilitation, racial discrimination in jury selection, the competence of the legal defense, or disparities in sentences between co-defendants or among defendants convicted of similar crimes. Neither compassion nor "mercy," which

---

1. Looking at 1998, for example, reveals that 68 people were executed. Only one death row inmate was granted clemency, a Texas man who "confessed" to 600 murders but was found to be in Florida during the one killing for which he received a death sentence.

2. As Banner (2002:291–92) notes, "For centuries governors commuted death sentences in significant numbers. That pattern continued for the first two-thirds of the twentieth century. Florida commuted nearly a quarter of its death sentences between 1924 and 1966; North Carolina commuted more than a third between 1909 and 1954. Those figures dropped close to zero under new sentencing schemes."

the Supreme Court as far back as 1855 saw as central to the very idea of clemency, is acknowledged as being of any account.... During Bush's six years as governor 150 men and two women were executed in Texas—a record unmatched by any other governor in modern American history.... Bush allowed the execution to proceed in all cases but one.

Similarly, then-Governor Bill Clinton explained his reluctance to grant clemency by saying, "The appeals process, although lengthy, provides many opportunities for the courts to review sentences and that's where these decisions should be made" (cited in "Clemency Becoming Rare as Executions Increase" 1987:2).

The Bush and Clinton views are today the norm.[3] Governors are reluctant to substitute their judgment for those of state legislators and courts, and, in death cases, to use clemency as an expression of mercy (see Breslin and Howley 2002:239; Dinsmore 2002; Kobil 2002:567, 572).[4] What this means is that filing clemency petitions is a bit like buying a lottery ticket in a contest for a multimillion dollar payoff. Filing them, death row inmates participate in this lottery for life, hoping against long odds that they will draw the winning number.

Some speculate that capital clemency has fallen into disfavor because of increased public support for the death penalty. Thus, Richard Dieter, executive director of the Death Penalty Information Center, observes, capital punishment is "the answer to the public's fear of crime, so [clemency] just goes against the grain" (quoted in Salladay 1998).[5] Even as crime rates fell during the 1990s, fear of crime persisted and, in this climate, mercy fell into disfavor, compassion went out of style.[6]

---

3. These views have a long history, reaching back at least to the early 19th century. However, "the actual record of gubernatorial pardons ... [in that period] shows that in practice the pardon process was not so cut and dried" (Brown 2003:191).

4. Love (2000–01:125–26) notes a similar reluctance at the federal level. Beginning with the Reagan Administration, she says, "the number of pardons each year began to drop off." Rita Radostitz (quoted in Salladay 1998), co-director of the Capital Punishment Clinic at the University of Texas and an attorney for Henry Lee Lucas, who was granted clemency in Texas, says about clemency: "I think that clearly a miscarriage of justice should be raised, but in other cases, mercy could also come into play.... That's what clemency has historically been about—mercy."

5. As Fiskesjo (2003: 46) puts it, "In light of 'domestic' opinion, it is very often not the decision to pardon but the decision not to pardon that best furthers the political standing of the power-holder...."

6. As Cobb (1989:394) argues, "Political considerations have figured prominently in the unwillingness of many governors to be merciful. The popularity of the death penalty suggests to these officials that the safest course of action is to avoid the exercise of their clemency powers."

Others suggest that capital clemency has been a victim of the rejection of rehabilitation as the guiding philosophy of criminal sentencing and the increasing politicization of issues of crime and punishment since the 1960s. In this climate governors seek, in Jonathan Simon's (2006) evocative phrase, to "govern through crime," to turn crime fighting, tough-on-crime policy into a strategy for building coalitions and strengthening the state (see also Kennedy 2000:829, 832).[7] Many have used the death penalty in their campaigns, promising more and quicker executions (Simon 2006). Simon's work suggests that the political power of governors depends:

> in large part on their power to mobilize the state around crime fears. In numerous states and on many occasions the death penalty has been the venue for the assertion of a governor's power by campaigning for, or signing into law, a new death penalty statute ... or signing a death warrant authorizing the execution of a particular prisoner. Clemency provides another occasion when, in effect, the Governor can assert

---

This is not to say that capital clemency has completely disappeared. It has not. For example, in 2002, "Hours before Charlie Alston was scheduled to be executed in North Carolina, Governor Mike Easley commuted Alston's sentence to life without parole. Although Easley did not give a specific reason for the reprieve, he stated, 'After long and careful consideration of all the facts and circumstances of this case in its entirety, I conclude that the appropriate sentence for the defendant is life in prison without parole.' Alston's commutation marks the 2nd time Easley has granted clemency, and the 5th time a North Carolina governor has done so since 1976. During that same time, 47 death row inmates nationally have had their sentences commuted for humanitarian reasons" (Death Penalty Information Center 2006).

In Oklahoma, Governor Brad Henry recently granted a request for clemency in the case of Osvaldo Torres, a Mexican foreign national on the state's death row, in part because of a recent International Court of Justice decision ordering the United States to review the cases of 51 Mexican foreign nationals because they were denied their right to seek consular assistance following their arrest. Henry's "decision to commute Torres' sentence to life in prison without parole marks the first time that the Governor has granted clemency to an individual on death row. In his statement, Henry said the International Court of Justice ruling is binding on U.S. courts, and that the U.S. State Department had contacted his office to urge that he give careful consideration to the fact that the U.S. signed the 1963 Vienna Convention on Consular Relations, which ensures access to consular assistance for foreign nationals who are arrested. 'The treaty is also important to protecting the rights of American citizens abroad,' Henry noted" (Death Penalty Information Center 2006).

7. Kennedy (2000:832) argues that, "The breadth and depth of the political consensus behind ... increases in the severity of criminal sentences may be without parallel in contemporary political history."

his or her support for the death penalty (and empathy with ordinary citizens) by rejecting clemency (Simon 2006:chapter 5).

These are valuable and important speculations, yet they tell us little about the meaning and significance of seeking clemency in the current legal and political climate. In the next section I sketch a framework for reorienting research on clemency in the contemporary killing state.

Creating an Archive of Injustice

As Drucilla Cornell (1990:1084) reminds us in the epigraph to this chapter: "Legal interpretation demands that we remember the future." In that phrase, Cornell suggests that legal processes fix their gaze temporally, not just on the possibilities (or impossibilities) of the present, but on a future promise of Justice. She reminds us that there are, in fact, two audiences for every legal act, the audience of the present (to which one might appeal to spare the life of the condemned), and the audience of the future (which stands as a figure of law's redeeming promise of Justice). In this sense, processes like clemency, as Robert Cover (1983:9) writes, provide "a bridge" to "'alternity.'" In this sense, clemency petitions also record a history of the present, and, in that history, preserve the present's pained voice.

Taking Cornell's and Cover's perspective, one might say that clemency petitions, which have so little chance of immediate success, nonetheless participate in the logic of what Cover (1983:34) called "redemptive constitutionalism." Those who file them refuse to recognize the violence of the present moment as the defining totality of law and are the carriers of a vision of a future in which Justice prevails over that violence. For these people, as Cover (1983:34) argues, "Redemption takes place within an eschatalogical schema that postulates: (1) the unredeemed character of reality as we know it, (2) the fundamentally different reality that should take its place, and (3) the replacement of one with the other."

Cover (1983:39) uses the example of an abolitionist struggle of another era, namely anti-slavery activism in the mid-nineteenth century, to suggest that the work of "redemptive constitutionalism" reveals "a creative pulse that proliferates principle and precept, commentary and justification, even in the face of a state legal order less likely to hold slavery unconstitutional than to declare the imminent kingship of Jesus Christ on Earth." In this view, those who file clemency petitions speak in a prophetic voice even as they supply the argumentative and interpretive resources to bridge the gap between the violence of the present and the beckoning possibility of Justice (see Lobel 1995:1337).

But there is perhaps a second way of understanding the meaning of clemency petitions in the contemporary killing state. In this second understanding Cover's image is reversed, and redemption gives way to Judgment. As redemption gives way to Judgment, the future is called on to remember the injustices of the present (see Le Goff 1992). Given this imperative to remember, those who ask for clemency serve as witnesses testifying against those injustices. Their petitions provide:

> the testimonial *bridge* which, mediating between narrative and history, guarantees their correspondence and adherence to each other. This bridging between narrative and history is possible since the narrator is both an *informed* and an *honest* witness.... All the witness has to do is to *efface himself*, and let the *literality of events* voice its own *self-evidence*. "His business is only to say: *this is what happened,* when he knows that it actually did happen" (Felman and Laub 1992:101).

Like lawyers in the mitigation stage of a capital trial or those pursuing habeas relief (Sarat 1998), those filing clemency petitions can take advantage of one of the legitimating promises of law, namely its commitment to giving everyone a hearing. They can use the clemency process to create a record which serves as the materialization of memory (Nora 1989:7). They can use those processes to speak to the future and turn them into museums of unnecessary, unjust, undeserved pain and death.[8] They can write and record history by creating narratives of present injustices. By recording such history and constructing such narratives they call on an imagined future to choose Justice over the jurispathic tendencies of the moment (Cover 1983). Constructing such narratives, those seeking clemency ensure that, even when no one (including the governors to whom they are addressed) seems willing to listen, the voices of the "oppressed" will not be silenced.

The movement from giving testimony to writing history is a movement from the immediacy of the eyewitness report to the mediation produced through narrativization (Felman and Laub 1992). In this movement clemency petitions may, as Robert Gordon (1996:36) indicates, frame the stories they seek to record in what he calls "legalist" style. This narrative treats the injustices of the present as wrongs "done by specific perpetrators to specific victims" (Gordon 1996:36). It stays within the frame of liberal-legalism and describes present injustice in terms of the remedies that governors, should they be willing, could easily supply.

---

8. As Minow (1987:1860) suggests, legal rights matter not just because they provide dignity to law's victims, or because they help to mobilize them to undertake political action, but because they provide an opportunity to tell a story that might not otherwise get to be told.

Alternatively the petitions may speak about "bad structures rather than bad agents.... This historical enterprise takes the form of a search for explanations rather than a search for villainous agents and attribution of blame" (Gordon 1996:36–37). In this narrative style, they expand the scope of inquiry by linking the particular stories of the condemned inmate with broader patterns of injustice and institutional practice.

The ability to use the clemency process to speak to the future and memorialize the present, to both give testimony and write history, has been ignored by those who have tried to document the possibilities and problems of the present moment. For them, its value resides exclusively in its most immediate effects. But, as Cornell reminds us, legal processes, like clemency, are as much about the future as the present, and as much about the possibilities of memory as the current prospects of success. Thus, when the condemned and their advocates file their petitions, they:

> posit the very ideal ... [they] purportedly find "there" (in those processes) ... as [they] posit the ideal or the ethical [they] promise to remain true to it. [Their] promise of fidelity to the ethical or to the ideal is precisely what breathes life into the dead letter of the law and provides a barrier against the violence of the word.... To heed the call to responsibility within law is to remind ... [ourselves] of the disjuncture between law and the ideal and to affirm our responsibility to make the promise to the ideal, to aspire to counter the violence of our world in the name of universal justice (Cornell 1988:1628).

The clemency process provides one method of "remembering the future" and of insuring that the future remembers. It is both a kind of testimony and a way of recording a history of injustice. Those seeking clemency put state killing in a narrative context which juxtaposes it to the Good, and preserve "the versions of legal meaning created by groups outside the mainstream of American law" (Lobel 1995:1337). They turn clemency boards and governors' offices into memorials to present injustice. Perhaps by paying attention to this function of the clemency process, we can gain a new perspective on its value in the contemporary killing state.

Conclusion

Future research should examine the clemency process not just as the moment when chief executives decide whether to spare the life of someone condemned to death, but as a moment when the history of the present is recorded.

Understood in this way clemency petitions may be understood to speak to two audiences, the pardon boards and governors who are their literal addressees, but also to the future, calling the future to attend to the injustices of the present moment, cumulating, despite their often narrow legalist frames, in a broad indictment of the inequities and injustices of America in the late twentieth century.

Despite the overwhelming futility of their appeals to spare a particular life, clemency petitions are documents that refuse despair. They embody the hope that narratives of present inequities and injustices will someday move the United States away from the daily reality of state killing and toward their particular vision of the Good.[9] In those narratives, the condemned and their advocates give content both to the possibility of Justice as well as to its deferred presence in law. Taken together, those narratives are powerful reminders of law's intimate association with violence even as they call on law to stay its bloody hand. They confront the possibility that law may be little more than a killing machine, yet they hold out hope that it is, and will be, something more (Alfieri 1996:352). They call on us to join in using the present moment in America's history of state killing to speak to the future and devise ways to ensure that the future remembers and redeems this moment.

References

Acker, James R. and Charles Lanier. 2000. "May God—Or the Governor—Have Mercy: Executive Clemency and Executions in Modern Death-Penalty Systems." *Criminal Law Bulletin* 36:200–237.

Alfieri, Anthony. 1996. "Mitigation, Mercy, and Delay: The Moral Politics of Death Penalty Abolitionists." *Harvard Civil Rights-Civil Liberties Law Review* 31:325–352.

Anti-Terrorism and Effective Death Penalty Act. 1996. (http://www.fas.org/irp/crs/96-499.htm).

Banner, Stuart. 2002. *The Death Penalty: An American History.* Cambridge, MA: Harvard University Press.

Berlow, Alan. 2003. "The Texas Clemency Memos." *The Atlantic Monthly,* July/August. (http://www.theatlantic.com/issues/2003/07/berlow.htm).

---

9. As Lobel (1995:1333) notes, "Law ... arises from the clash between the state seeking to enforce its rules and ... activist communities seeking to create, extend, or preserve an alternative vision of justice"(*see also* Alfieri 1986:352).

Breslin, Beau and John J.P. Howley. 2002. "Defending the Politics of Clemency." *Oregon Law Review* 81:231–254.

Brown, Richard. 2003. *The Hanging of Ephraim Walker: A Story of Rape, Incest, and Justice in Early America.* Cambridge, MA: Harvard University Press.

"Clemency Becoming Rare as Executions Increase." 1987. *Corrections Digest,* July 8:2.

Cobb, Paul. 1989. "Reviving Mercy in the Structure of Capital Punishment." *Yale Law Journal* 99:389–409.

Cornell, Drucilla. 1990. "From the Lighthouse: The Promise of Redemption and the Possibility of Legal Interpretation." *Cardozo Law Review* 11:1687–1714.

_____. 1988. "Post-Structuralism, the Ethical Relation, and the Law." *Cardozo Law Review* 9:1587–1628.

Cover, Robert. 1983. "The Supreme Court, 1982 Term-Foreword: Nomos and Narrative." *Harvard Law Review* 97:4–68.

Davis, Natalie Zemon. 1987. *Fiction in the Archives: Pardon Tales and Their Tellers in Sixteenth Century France.* Stanford, CA: Stanford University Press.

Death Penalty Information Center. 2006. "Clemency News and Developments." (http://www.deathpenaltyinfo.org/article.php?scid=13&did=850).

Dinsmore, Alyson. 2002. "Clemency in Capital Cases: The Need to Ensure Meaningful Review." *UCLA Law Review* 49:1825–1858.

Dow, David R. and Eric M. Freedman. This Volume. "The Effects of AEDPA on Justice."

Felman, Shoshana and Dori Laub. 1992. *Testimony: Crises of Witnessing in Literature, Psychoanalysis, and History.* New York, NY: Routledge.

Fiskesjo, Magnus. 2003. *The Thanksgiving Turkey Pardon, The Death of Teddy's Bear, and the Sovereign Exception of Guantanamo.* Chicago, IL: Prickly Paradigm Press.

Garvey, Stephen. 2004. "Is It Wrong to Commute Death Row? Retribution, Atonement, and Mercy." *North Carolina Law Review* 82:1319–1343.

Goldstein, Steven. 1990–1991. "Chipping Away at the Great Writ: Will Death Sentenced Federal Habeas Corpus Petitioners Be Able to Seek and Utilize Changes in the Law?" *New York Review of Law & Social Change* 18:357–414.

Gordon, Robert. 1996. "Undoing Historical Injustice." Pp. 35–75 in *Justice and Injustice in Law and Legal Theory*, edited by Austin Sarat and Thomas Kearns. Ann Arbor, MI: University of Michigan Press.

Greenberg, Jack. 1982. "Capital Punishment as a System." *Yale Law Journal* 91:908–936.

Hay, Douglas. 1975. "Property, Authority, and the Criminal Law." Pp. 17–63 in *Albion's Fatal Tree: Crime and Society in Eighteenth-Century England,*

edited by Douglas Hay, Peter Linebaugh, John G. Rule, E.P. Thompson, and Cal Winslow, New York, NY: Pantheon Books.
Heise, Michael. 2003. "Mercy by the Numbers: An Empirical Analysis of Clemency and Its Structure." *Virginia Law Review* 89:239–310.
Herrera v. Collins (1993). 506 U.S. 390.
Kennedy, Joseph E. 2000. "Monstrous Offenders and the Search for Solidarity Through Modern Punishment." *Hastings Law Journal* 51:829–980.
Kobil, Daniel. 2002. "Chance and the Constitution in Capital Clemency Cases." *Capital University Law Review* 28:567–577.
Le Goff, Jacques. 1992. *History and Memory*. Translated by Steven Randall and Elizabeth Clamon. New York, NY: Columbia University Press.
Liebman, James. 1990–1991. "More Than 'Slightly Retro': The Rehnquist Court's Rout of Habeas Corpus Jurisdiction in *Teague v. Lane*." *New York University Review of Law & Social Change* 18:357–414.
Lobel, Jules. 1995. "Losers, Fools & Prophets: Justice as Struggle." *Cornell Law Review* 80:1331–1421.
Love, Margaret Colgate. 2000–2001. "Fear of Forgiving: Rule and Discretion in the Theory and Practice of Pardoning." *Federal Sentencing Reporter* 13:125–133.
McCleskey v. Zant (1991). 499 U.S. 467.
Minow, Martha. 1987. "Interpreting Rights: An Essay for Robert Cover." *Yale Law Journal* 96:1860–1915.
Moore, Kathleen Dean. 1989. *Pardons: Justice, Mercy, and the Public Interest*. New York, NY: Oxford University Press.
Nora, Pierre. 1989. "Between Memory and History: *Les Lieux de Memoire*." *Representations* 26:7–24.
Radelet, Michael and Barbara Zsembik. 1992–93. "Executive Clemency in Post-*Furman* Capital Cases." *University of Richmond Law Review* 27:289–314.
Rapaport, Elizabeth. 2001. "Staying Alive: Executive Clemency, Equal Protection, and the Politics of Gender in Women's Capital Cases." *Buffalo Criminal Law Review* 4:967–1007.
Rose v. Lundy (1982). 455 U.S. 509.
Salladay, Robert. 1998. "Clemency: Slim Chance These Days." *San Francisco Examiner*, Nov. 29, A. (http://www.sfgate.com/cgi-bin/article.cgi%3Ff=/examiner/archive/1998/11/29/NEWS8622.dtl&type=printable).
Sarat, Austin. 2005. *Mercy on Trial: What It Means to Stop an Execution*. Princeton, NJ: Princeton University Press.
_____. 2001. *When the State Kills: Capital Punishment and the American Condition*. Princeton, NJ: Princeton University Press.
_____. 1998. "Between (the Presence of) Violence and (the Possibility of) Justice: Lawyering against Capital Punishment." Pp. 317–346 in *Cause*

Lawyering: Political Commitments and Professional Responsibilities, edited by Austin Sarat and Stuart Scheingold. New York, NY: Oxford University Press.

Simon, Jonathan. 2006. *Governing Through Crime: The War on Crime and the Transformation of American Governance, 1960–2000.* New York, NY: Oxford University Press.

Wainwright v. Sykes (1977). 433 U.S. 72.

Washington State Office of the Attorney General. 2000. *Reprieves, Pardons and Commutations in Death Penalty Cases.* (http://www.atg.wa.gov/deathpenalty/pardons.shtml).

Zimring, Franklin. 1992. "Inheriting the Wind: The Supreme Court and Capital Punishment in the 1990s." *Florida State University Law Review* 20:7–19.

SECTION IV
THE UTILITY AND EFFICACY OF THE CAPITAL SANCTION

CHAPTER 15

Death and Deterrence Redux: Science, Law and Causal Reasoning on Capital Punishment[+]

Jeffrey Fagan* and Valerie West**

"Things are seldom what they seem ... Skim-milk masquerades as cream ..."

Gilbert and Sullivan

The Current Controversy

Long before the U.S. Supreme Court restored capital punishment in 1976, proponents of the death penalty claimed that executions save lives by deter-

---

[+] An earlier version of this chapter was published in the *Ohio State Journal of Criminal Law* 4:255–320 (2006). Permission to print this chapter has been granted by the *Ohio State Journal of Criminal Law*.
* Professor of Law and Public Health, Columbia University. Outstanding research assistance was provided by Arie Rubinstein, Ethan Jacobs, Michel Werschtenschlag, David Finkelstein and Jason Stramaglia. Amanda Beth Geller provided excellent assistance in the empirical analyses. I am indebted to the Criminal Justice Research Center at The Ohio State University for their invitation to deliver the Walter C. Reckless Lecture in April 2005, which was the basis for this essay. Brandon Garrett, Michael Maltz, Christopher Maxwell, Justin Wolfers, Avery Katz and Franklin Zimring provided helpful comments and advice on earlier versions of the article.
** Assistant Professor and Doctoral Faculty at John Jay College/CUNY.

ring would-be murderers from lethal violence. The more recent ascension of deterrence as a rationale for capital punishment in the 1970s coincided with a series of landmark Supreme Court cases that first abolished and then reinstated the death penalty, and with the publication of a series of articles that claimed a scientific basis for the assertion that potential murderers can be deterred from homicide by the threat of execution. The originator of these claims was Professor Isaac Ehrlich (1975a; 1975b; 1977) who, inspired by the theoretical work of economist Gary Becker (1968; 1978), developed a theoretical model that explained crime as a process of rational choice between illegal and legal behavior; the choices were shaped by how law enforcement reacted to illegal activities. Such rationality, Ehrlich (1977) argued, would influence would-be offenders to avoid punishment and forego violent crime.

Ehrlich published a highly influential article in 1975 that tested this model with the use of econometric methods, in the case of murder and capital punishment. Although a technical piece, its influence went far beyond the economics profession. Ehrlich's work was cited in *Gregg v. Georgia* (1976), the central U.S. Supreme Court decision restoring capital punishment. No matter how carefully Ehrlich qualified his conclusions, his article had the popular and political appeal of a headline, a sound bite and a bumper sticker all rolled into one: "One execution saves eight innocent lives" (p. 398). Ehrlich's work was cited favorably in *Gregg* (1976), and it was later cited in an amicus brief filed by the U.S. Solicitor General in *Fowler v. North Carolina* (1976). Even though Ehrlich's findings were disputed in academic journals such as the *Yale Law Journal* (Baldus and Cole 1975; Bowers and Pierce 1975; Ehrlich 1975b), the proponents of deterrence had gained the upper hand in how this research was interpreted and how its findings were applied.

Ehrlich's work became the focal point for research on deterrence and the death penalty, launching an era of contentious arguments in the press and in professional journals (Chressanthis 1989; Cover and Thistle 1988; Grogger 1990; Layson 1985; Leamer 1983; McAleer and Veall 1989; McManus 1985). Over the next two decades, economists and other social scientists attempted to replicate Ehrlich's results using different data, alternative statistical methods, and other twists that tried to address glaring errors in Ehrlich's techniques and data (Layson 1986; 1985). The accumulated scientific evidence from these later studies weighed heavily against the claim that executions deter murders (Bowers and Pierce 1975; McGahey 1980; Passell and Taylor 1977). Ehrlich's findings were challenged by many scholars as to the sample period and/or the variables he chose, and the murder supply equation and the functional form of the equations he estimated (Mocan and Gittings 2003:454). Also, Ehrlich's methodology, the aggregation of data from all states within the U.S., led to his conclusion that "a decrease in the execution risk in one State combined with an increase in the murder rate in another State would, all other things being equal, suggest a deterrent effect that quite obviously would not exist" (Albert 1999:356). Within three years of the publication of Ehrlich's study, an expert panel appointed by the National Academy of Sciences issued strong criticisms of his work (Klein, Forst, and Filatov 1978). Despite the weight of technical economic and other social science evidence condemning Ehrlich's work, each new study that followed supporting the deterrence conclusion found uncritical acceptance among proponents of the death penalty, while the critiques failed to gain popular or political traction.

History is now repeating itself. In the past five years, a new wave of a dozen or more studies have appeared, reporting deterrent effects of capital punishment that go well beyond Ehrlich's findings. The new deterrence studies analyze data that spans the entire period since the resumption of executions in the U.S. following the 1972 decision in *Furman v. Georgia*. The new studies go farther, though, claiming that exonerations cause murders to increase. Several claim that pardons, commutations, and exonerations cause murders to increase (Mocan and Gittings 2003:453). Some say that even murders of passion, among the most irrational of lethal acts, can be deterred (Shepherd 2004).

At least one study, by Professor Zhiqiang Liu (2004), claims that executions not only deter murders, but they also increase the deterrent effects of other punishments. Following this logic, the new deterrence research has been applied to justify punitive criminal justice policies in several areas: mandatory minimum sentences and "three strikes" laws, zero tolerance policies for school children and drug offenders, and mandatory transfer of adolescent offenders from the juvenile court to the criminal court. Thus, the deterrent effects of capital punishment are apparently indefinite and offer execution as a cure-all for everyday crime (Liu 2004).

Many of these studies have already appeared in leading academic journals, while others are working their way through the review process. These studies have been reported favorably and uncritically by leading newspapers (*e.g., Washington Post, Boston Globe, Wall Street Journal*), and they have been broadcast widely by pro-death penalty advocacy groups to state legislators (Jacoby 2003:H11; Morin 2002a:B5; 2002b:B5). Many were cited in major newspapers prior to undergoing some major changes after peer evaluation. Newspapers of record, such as the *Washington Post*, quoted in their headlines findings that were later proven to be wrong (Lardner 2003). Pro-death penalty advocacy groups including Justice for All, The Criminal Justice Legal Foundation, and American Voice, are widely disseminating the results of the new studies as scientific evidence of the deterrent effects of capital punishment. State groups in

California and North Carolina also are citing this evidence to oppose local moratorium efforts. As in the *Gregg* era, these studies have been cited without challenge in amicus briefs in recent capital cases including *Schirro v. Summerlin* (2004). In April 2004, Professor Joanna Shepherd, co-author of some of these studies, summarized the new deterrence evidence in testimony before the federal House Judiciary Committee, claiming that there is sound scientific evidence that each execution deters between three and eighteen murders.

Accordingly, the reach of the new deterrence research seems quite long, and its potential impact on criminal justice politics and policies extends beyond the death penalty. This new deterrence research also benefits advocates of capital punishment by competing with death penalty opponents who cite high rates of errors in capital cases and wrongful convictions as arguments for state moratoria or abolition (Marshall 2004; Warden 2005). If these claims are true, the new evidence would not only fundamentally change the roiling discourse on capital punishment, it could influence both the politics and substance of criminal law and policy.

What are we to make of these claims? We want to answer this question in two ways. First, we will look at the evidence itself. What claims are made in the various studies, and what might we conclude about executions and deterrence scanning across the new body of evidence? What is the structure of the data and what do the data tell us, even before we look at the modeling process itself? What cautions should we place on the interpretation and application of this information?

Second, we ask how well these claims stand up to scientific scrutiny. Have these analyses asked too much of the data? What happens when the data are subject to alternatives in measurement and analysis? Do the studies pay sufficient attention to the conceptual details of deterrence, murder itself, and alternate explanations for the complex relationships that influence changes in murder rates over time? Here, we consider some serious omissions in the construction of this paradigm, both conceptually and in the details of some modeling decisions.

Replication is one of the cornerstones of the scientific process. In an earlier version of this chapter one of us did as much and found that the claims of the new deterrence literature are unfounded (Fagan 2006). As we discuss below, the structure of the data and modeling deficiencies combine to undermine the conclusions of the new deterrence literature.

Finally, we will consider the tensions at the intersection of science and law that these episodes raise. Here, we examine the recurring phenomenon of what we might conveniently call a "rush to judgment" when science—whether behavioral or natural—dangles the promise of simple answers to very complex yet urgent questions (Epstein and King 2002; Rein and Winship 1999).

The remainder of this essay shows that the new deterrence studies are fraught with numerous technical and conceptual errors: inappropriate methods of statistical analysis, failures to consider several relevant factors that drive murder rates such as drug epidemics, missing data on key variables in key states, the tyranny of a few outlier states and years, weak to non-existent tests of concurrent effects of incarceration, statistical confounding of murder rates with death sentences, failure to consider the general performance of the criminal justice system, artifactual results from truncated time frames, and the absence of any direct test of the components of contemporary theoretical constructions of deterrence. Social scientists have failed to replicate several of these studies, and in some cases have produced contradictory or unstable results with the same data, suggesting that the original findings are unreliable and perhaps inaccurate. The central mistake in this enterprise is one of causal reasoning: the attempt to draw causal inferences from a flawed and limited set of observational data, and the failure to address important competing influences on murder. Murder is a complex and multiply-determined phenomenon, with cyclical patterns for over forty years of distinct periods of increase and decline that are not unlike epidemics of contagious diseases. There is no reliable, scientifically sound evidence that pits execution against a robust set of competing explanations to identify whether it can exert a deterrent effect that is uniquely and sufficiently powerful to overwhelm these consistent and recurring epidemic patterns. Nor can it be shown that capital punishment has a greater deterrent effect than any other sanction currently available. These flaws and omissions in a body of scientific evidence render it unreliable as a basis for law or policy that generate life-and-death decisions. To accept it uncritically invites errors that have the most severe human costs.

The New Deterrence Literature

Over a dozen new studies appeared since the mid-1990s, mainly in economics journals, with most claiming new evidence that executions have strong and powerful deterrent effects on homicide. The studies have quickly found their way into the courts. Similar to the immediate citations of Ehrlich's work in *Gregg* (1976) and other cases, the new deterrence studies were cited in *Schirro v. Summerlin* (2004) in an amicus brief and in a *certiorari* petition to the United States Court of Appeals for the Ninth Circuit (Criminal Justice Legal Foundation 2004:23–4). The studies gained attention in Congress (Rubin 2006; Shepherd 2003), in the popular press (Jacoby 2003; Koretetz 2003; Morin 2002a; 2002b; Nicholson 2002; Rubin 2002; Seper 2001), among death penalty advocates (Criminal Justice Legal Foundation 2004), and now, among legal scholars

(Becker 2005; Posner 2005; Steiker 2005; Sunstein and Vermeule 2005). Professors Sunstein and Vermeule (2005) find the new deterrence evidence "powerful" (p. 745) and "impressive" (p. 713), and they couple it with "many decades of reliable data about [capital punishment's] deterrent effects"(p. 751) as the "foundation" of their argument that since "capital punishment powerfully deters killings"(p. 735), there is a moral imperative to aggressively prosecute capital crimes.

The studies use several designs that conceptualize capital punishment as a "treatment" that would deter homicides. The designs include classical panel studies that co-vary homicide rates and deterrence measures that incorporate executions, quasi-experiments testing the effects of moratoria, natural experiments comparing homicide rates in death penalty and non-death penalty states, nested (hierarchical) designs of counties within states that provide more fine-grained analyses of local homicide rates, and instrumental variables designs that attempt to disentangle spurious effects due to factors other than deterrence. The estimation techniques vary from standard Ordinary Least Squares models to complex equilibrium models with simultaneous equations, to negative binomial estimators of homicides. Several have used a relatively new dataset on death sentences and executions to operationalize and measure deterrence. The data are produced by the U.S. Department of Justice (Bonczer and Snell 2002; U.S. Department of Justice 2004), and are updated and revised annually. They include all death sentences and their dispositions following the resumption of capital punishment after *Furman* (1972). The conclusions these studies derive are wedded to the methods and sources that are used to compile these data. The studies have appeared both in peer-reviewed journals, primarily in economics, and law reviews; a few have been published online as working papers.

The studies are listed in Appendix A. Their claims are strong, far stronger than results produced in most social policy experiments on education, welfare, or crime control. A detailed analysis of the methods and results of these studies is not the purpose here; instead, what follows is a representative sampling of the results and claims made by these authors.

- Mocan and Gittings (2003): "[A]n additional execution generates a reduction in homicide by five, an additional commutation increases homicides by four to five, and an additional removal brings about one additional murder"(p. 469).
- Dezhbakhsh, Rubin, and Shepherd (2003): "Our results suggest that capital punishment has a strong deterrent effect; each execution results, on average, in eighteen fewer murders—with a margin of error of plus or minus ten"(p. 344).

- Shepherd (2004): "[E]ach execution results in, on average, three fewer murders.... [C]apital punishment deters murders previously believed to be undeterrable: crimes of passion and murders by intimates.... [L]onger waits on death row before execution lessen the deterrence.... [O]ne less murder is committed for every 2.75-year reduction in death row waits. Thus, recent legislation to shorten the wait should strengthen capital punishment's deterrent effect" (p. 283).
- Dezhbakhsh and Shepherd (2006): "Results suggest that capital punishment has a deterrent effect, and that executions have a distinct effect which compounds the deterrent effect of merely (re)instating the death penalty" (p. 512).
- Cloninger and Marchesini (2001): As a result of the unofficial moratorium on executions during most of 1996 and early 1997, the citizens of Texas experienced a net 90 additional innocent lives lost to homicide (p. 575).
- Liu (2004): From the econometric standpoint, this suggests that the structure of the murder supply function depends on the status of the death penalty, which is in itself endogenous. Liu goes on to claim that executions deter crimes other than murder, suggesting collateral benefits of capital punishment for public safety more broadly (p. 238).
- Shepherd (2005): The impact of executions differs substantially among the states. Executions deter murders in six states, executions have no effect on murders in eight states, and executions increase murders in thirteen states. Additional empirical analyses indicate that there is a threshold effect that explains the differing impacts of capital punishment. On average, the states with deterrence execute many more people than do the states where executions increase crime or have no effect to achieve deterrence, states must execute several people (p. 205).

Readers can easily see the appeal of these findings. Just as the Ehrlich (1975a) findings were quickly embraced in popular and political culture, these new studies make strong claims that have the same appeal. It is not surprising that they have been quickly embraced and disseminated as a counterweight against the cultural and political narratives of innocence (Dieter 2004; Gross *et al.* 2005; Scheck, Neufeld, and Dwyer 2000) and errors (Liebman *et al.* 2000).

Social Science Reasoning

These strong claims of powerful deterrent effects are not without contradictions and serious limitations. When the elements of the scientific enterprise are decomposed and evaluated, we can identify a series of recurring challenges in the conceptualization, model specification, measurement, and causal reasoning in these studies. The totality and cumulative weight of these challenges yields to strong reasonable doubts about the reliability of these claims. There are errors both of commission and omission in this oeuvre of research, as we discuss below. Then, some simple empirical exercises reveal problems in the sensitivity of the results to alternate measurement and model specification assumptions, producing different results whose instability and fragility undermine the strong claims of death penalty proponents.

The Structure of the Data

To some degree, the findings of a negative correlation between executions and murder seem to be structured into the data in a way that weakens generalizations or predictions. Indeed, executions in most states in most years since *Gregg* are very rare. According to the Death Penalty Information Center (2008a; 2008b), there have been 1099 executions since 1976; more than one in three (405) have been in Texas. A simple average of executions per state per year would be deceptive, since state laws were enacted in different years, but even a simple estimate—based on thirty-eight death penalty states, each with a valid law in effect for an average of twenty years since *Gregg* (1976)—suggests that on average, there is fewer than one execution per year per state. In states other than Texas, the median state-year average is far lower.

The distribution is highly skewed, and the mean is dominated by a few extreme values. Most states in most years execute no one. In Mocan and Gittings' analysis (2003:458), for example, eighty-six percent of the state years equal zero. As a result, the median is also zero. There are but eleven cases with values greater than five. Accordingly, the low number of events in most states suggests that there is hardly enough of what Mocan and Gittings (p. 460) refer to as a "signal" to reach a disparate and heterogeneous population of would-be murderers (Berk 2005; Cheung 2002; Zorn 1998).

Both the problem of low base rates and the hegemony of Texas in the new deterrence studies have been illustrated by Professor Richard Berk (2005:304), who re-analyzed data from Mocan and Gittings to show some simple trends and empirical facts in the data. Berk constructed a simple deterrence measure, lagging executions one year behind homicides, to show several underlying trends in these data. First, a deterrent effect—that is, a negative slope in the murder rate relative to the execution rate—occurs when the number of executions within a state over a single year is five or more. Figure 1, from Professor Berk's analysis, illustrates this point. But even at this extreme tail of the distribution, the confidence intervals are so large as to render a claim of prediction meaningless.

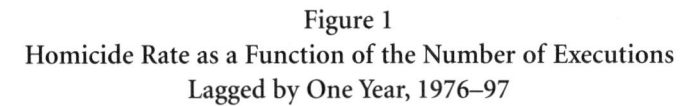

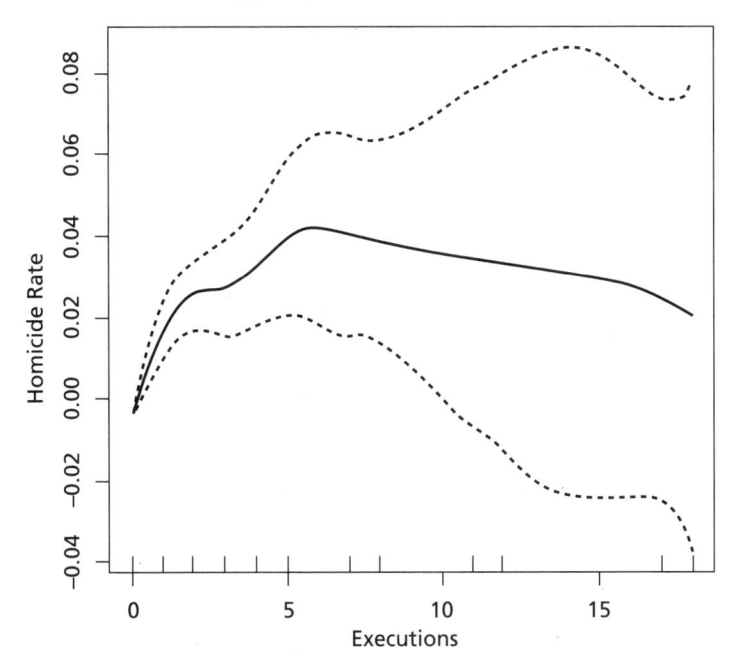

Figure 1
Homicide Rate as a Function of the Number of Executions Lagged by One Year, 1976–97

Source: Berk (2005). Note: Solid line is smoothed fitted values. The dotted lines contain the approximate 95 percent confidence interval. The relationship between the homicide rate and the lagged number of executions is generally positive for up to five executions and uncertain thereafter.

Second, Professor Berk (2005:319) shows that after controlling both for the initial and average murder rate per state over the full twenty-one year study interval and state population size over time, the trends become unstable and unpredictable. Third and most important, he shows that once Texas is removed from the analysis, all deterrent effects disappear (pp. 321–324).

The deterrent effect, according to Professor Berk (2005:318), reflects extreme cases, not the mass of the data. The leverage of these cases is transformed into influence when extreme values of a predictor—executions—are likely to be paired with extreme values of a response variable—homicides. By "influence" one means that the potential impact of leverage in a model's fit becomes a reality, reinforcing the illusion of a statistical relationship, which—in this case—

actually is simply a product of one small set of observations. When he eliminates Texas, where these extremes are concentrated, Professor Berk shows that the relationship between execution and homicide disappears (p. 322).

Some analysts have tried to overcome these difficulties by disaggregating murders to the county level (Shepherd 2005:223), but the extreme cases still unduly influence the execution-homicide trends. No matter how deterrence is measured, the analyses remain captives of the structure of the data, and that structure ordains a particular result. If there is an effect of executions on homicides, it is the result of eleven extreme values, and from the influence of Texas. Generalizations from the eleven observations with values greater than five to the remaining 99% would be unstable and inappropriate.

Theory and Specifications

The current set of deterrence tests typically takes the form of a regression model predicting murder rates. The predictors include measures of deterrence in the form of executions per death sentence; a lag function expresses assumptions about the delay from sentence to execution, and from execution to the deterrent effect on murder. At least one study includes "announcement effects" of executions by including newspaper reports of executions (Shepherd 2005:253). Controls are sometimes introduced to account for different assumptions about the production of the "supply" of offenders eligible for execution: murder arrests, population size and demography. Rarely are there measures that capture the punitiveness of the criminal justice system or its incapacitative effects. Some try to estimate the risks of detection by indexing the number of police. Few estimate the aggressiveness of law enforcement by looking at the general behavior of legal institutions toward crime generally. Socioeconomic contexts associated with homicide may be introduced via measures of the age distribution of the population, poverty and unemployment rates, and the extent of urbanization of the population. These structural factors have been identified as homicide risks over time and across different units of analysis including states, cities, and neighborhoods (Krivo and Peterson 2000; Land, McCall, and Cohen 1990; Sampson and Lauritsen 1994). Most of the new deterrence studies measure both murder and structural risk at the state level, but others are based on a county-within-state analysis (Shepherd 2005:223).

The approach in the new deterrence studies involves estimation of regressions with different combinations of variables, with sensitivity or robustness estimated from variation in the size of the regression coefficient for execution or the statutory presence of the death penalty in different configurations of predictors. Covariates associated with the production of homicides are included, but often excluded to form a sensitivity test for the specifications. These strategies often omit a range of important factors that have stable and recurring effects on murder rates, leading to specification errors that tend to inflate the significance of the deterrence factors that are included. As we shall see below, some are more important than others, but the cumulative effect of these omissions or conceptual strategies is a distortion and inflation of execution effects.

Deterrence, Incapacitation and Life without Parole

Perhaps the most important theoretical misspecification in the new deterrence studies is the omission of the incapacitative effects of imprisonment generally, and Life Without Parole (LWOP) sentences in particular. Of the thirty-six states that currently have valid death penalty statutes, thirty-five also have LWOP statutes. Only New Mexico does not. Of the fourteen states without the death penalty, thirteen have life without parole. Only Alaska does not (Death Penalty Information Center 2008c; Lane 1993; Wright 1990:546). Even if LWOP were available as a sentencing option in cases other than capital trials, incarceration of persons with lengthy histories of violent crimes for non-capital offenses would likely exert some prophylactic effect on murder, given the prevalence of felony murders such as robbery-homicides (Fagan, Zimring, and Geller 2006). Accordingly, the omission of LWOP from research on legal interventions to reduce homicide is a potentially biasing omission.

But how much of an effect might LWOP have on homicide rates? Systematic data on the extent to which juries return LWOP sentences in capital cases is difficult to obtain; when available, it often is only for periods beginning in 1990 or later. Information is available on when each state passed its LWOP statute or modified it to make it a sentencing alternative in capital cases (Death Penalty Information Center 2008c) so the effects at least of the availability of LWOP as a sentencing option could be modeled and estimated. None of the new deterrence studies do so.

Yet data from a small number of states shows ample evidence that LWOP is used far more often than are death sentences in capital cases and cannot be ignored in estimating reasons for the decline in homicide rates (Death Penalty Information Center 2008c). For example, data from the Pennsylvania Department of Corrections (1999) shows that there were 139 LWOP sentences in Pennsylvania in 1999, compared to 15 death sentences. In 2000, there were 121 life sentences compared to 12 death sentences (Pennsylvania Department of Corrections 2000). In California, there were 3,163 inmates serving life without parole on February 29, 2004, compared to 635 on death row, and zero executions (California Department of Corrections 2004; Zimring, Hawkins, and

Kamin 2001). In South Carolina, 485 defendants have received LWOP sentences since 1996, compared to 27 executions (South Carolina Department of Corrections 2005). One final illustration comes from Georgia. Georgia has sentenced 369 persons to death since passing its LWOP statute in 1993, while death sentences have declined from about ten per year to four during this time (Associated Press 2003). Georgia has executed 21 persons since passing its LWOP statute (Georgia Department of Corrections 2004). Overall, data from the National Judicial Reporting Program in 2002 show that LWOP sentences were more than three times more frequent in murder cases than were death sentences, and nearly 10 times more common than executions (U.S. Department of Justice 2002).

Obviously, LWOP has incapacitative effects, as does execution, and the two are exceedingly difficult to disentangle empirically. The 1978 National Research Council Panel on Research on Deterrence and Incapacitation noted the complex relationship between the two and the difficulty of separating the effects of each (Klein *et al.*1978:336). Using a longer time series, Professors Katz, Levitt and Shustarovich (2003) compare deterrence (executions per 1,000 prisoners) with incapacitation and conclude that the death rate among prisoners, which they view as a proxy for prison conditions, has a significant deterrent effect on violent crime rates, but they find no robust evidence of a deterrent effect of capital punishment (p. 327). And in one study that does compete incarceration and deterrence, Mocan and Gittings (2003:464) report larger regression coefficients for incarceration (-.0354) than executions (-.0063). Mocan and Gittings call no attention to this very interesting finding that competes well with execution as an explanation for the decline in murders. Few other studies in the new deterrence literature report incarceration effects, and when they do, the effects either compete with or overwhelm execution effects.

To claim that executions deter homicides when there may be equally strong simultaneous effects from incarceration—whether incapacitative or deterrent—introduces an omitted variable bias that potentially inflates the effects of execution. Indeed, with the exceptions noted above, most of the new deterrence studies simply ignore incarceration or understate its effects (*see e.g.* Shepherd 2005). Incarceration effects argue against the *marginal* deterrent effects of execution threats. Felony murder offenders should be deterred both by the threat of prison and the threat of execution. But when both are included in multivariate models, there seems to be no greater marginal threat from execution than from a generalized effect from incarceration. Indeed, one sensitivity test that was not conducted by Mocan and Gittings (2003) is a model that includes incarceration but not execution.

Parsing the deterrent effects of incarceration from its incapacitative effects is a task for another chapter. But for this essay, it is important to note that high incarceration rates across most states are exerting a significant downward pressure on homicide rates (Blumstein and Beck 1999). Moreover, these rates are highest for violent crimes (Durose and Langan 2005; Harrison and Beck 2005). This is important for two reasons. First, most capital-eligible homicides are felony murders: homicides committed in the course of other crimes, specifically robbery and rape (Fagan *et al.* 2006). No offense category has grown faster in the run-up of incarceration than violent crimes (Durose and Langan 2005). Removing a segment of serious offenders through incarceration has contributed to a reduction in the base rate of robbery and assault, and lowered the probability of such crimes escalating to homicides. While Shepherd controls for the robbery rate in one of the new deterrence studies, she does not control for robbery incarcerations or any other incarceration category (Shepherd 2005). Second, the high rate of incarceration and the increasingly lengthy sentences imposed for violent offenses may leave little margin for additional deterrent effects from the threat of execution. Certainly, a robust test of deterrence, as well as a fully specified conceptual theory, would address the separate if not conditional effects of incarceration on murder rates. Unfortunately, the current crop of deterrence studies overlooks this question.

Co-Morbid Epidemics

Homicide was not the only epidemic social problem in the U.S. in the years following *Furman* (1972). *Furman* was decided just as a five year epidemic of heroin use had begun to wane in the U.S. in the early 1970s (Musto 1995; 1987). An era when homicide rates also rose sharply across American cities (Blumstein and Rosenfeld 1998; Rosenfeld 2000; Zimring and Hawkins 1997) linked temporally and spatially to an epidemic of heroin use (Agar and Reisenger 2002; Egan and Robinson 1979; Hunt and Chambers 1976; Inciardi 1979). Over the next two decades, homicide rates rose and fell concurrently with other drug epidemics. Homicide rates spiked again from 1979 to 1981, concurrent with the emergence of street drug markets in major cities where powdered cocaine was openly sold (*see e.g.,* Johnson *et al.*1990; Williams 1989; Zimmer 1990; 1987). Record homicide rates in American cities in the early 1990s coincided with the crack epidemic that lasted nearly a decade after 1986 (*see e.g.,* Baumer 1994; Baumer *et al.* 1998; Grogger and Willis 2000).

The temporal and spatial dependence of murder and drugs is an epidemiological fact that deserves serious attention as a competing influence on the murder rate. One might see drug epidemics and murder as simply co-morbid problems that share common etiologies or that combine to weaken the resources needed to resist such social problems. Or, one might see them as causally related, in which case the rise and fall of one epidemic would predict concurrent or closely spaced changes in the other (*see e.g.,* Chaiken and Chaiken 1990; MacCoun and Reuter 2003). The latter view dominated criminological research through the 1990s. Through mechanisms that connect drug sales and gun violence, the crack epidemic exerted a strong push on murder rates and spread across American cities in a pattern similar to a contagious disease (*see e.g.,* Blumstein 1995; Cork 1999; Fagan 1990).

The decline in homicides through the late 1990s and into the early part of this decade has been linked to the decline in the crack epidemics, specifically changes in street markets where drugs had been openly sold amidst much violence a decade earlier (*see e.g.,* Curtis 1998). Drug sales declined in volume and moved indoors as demand shrunk and also as police focused on drug sales. Competition between sellers waned, reducing the incidence of disputes implicated in many murders during the height of the epidemic (National Institute of Justice 1998).

None of the new deterrence studies consider the epidemics of drug use and related violence. Perhaps the declines in drug markets were due to police efforts to deter drug selling through intensive drug enforcement and high volumes of drug arrests. But these direct or indirect effects of policing were also not given close attention. As in policing, the inattention to the effect of drug epidemics on crime is an omission that challenges, if not impeaches, the conclusions of the new deterrence studies of a singular effect of execution on homicide.

Are All Homicides Deterrable?

Most of the new deterrence studies regard homicide as a homogeneous criminal behavior. With one exception, these studies make no distinctions between homicides committed in varying contexts or with different motivations. The assumption is that all are equally deterrable. This logic is challenged in at least two different ways. First, several decades of empirical research on homicide that cut across the social sciences suggests that homicides are variably rational; some, such as crimes of jealousy or unplanned and highly contingent events, are simply poor candidates for deterrence. Second, the law makes these distinctions explicit in felony murder rules, and carves out a particular set of homicides—such as homicides committed in the course of other crimes—as eligible for capital punishment. The most accurate test of the underlying rationale for deterrence would be the sensitivity of these homicides to the threat of execution.

Only one among the new studies, by Professor Joanna Shepherd (2004), offers estimates of the deterrent effects of execution on specific categories of homicide. Shepherd's study finds that "domestic" or intimate partner homicides are more deterrable than others. Shepherd reports that executions deter all types of murder, including "crimes of passion" that so often are considered to be irrational and spontaneous acts that are beyond the rational reach of execution threats.

The high rate of murder-suicides in domestic homicides is one clue to the irrationality if not mental illness of this subset of murderers, limiting the prospects for deterrence (*see e.g.*, Bennett, Goodman, and Dutton 2000; Campbell, Sharps, and Class 2001; Weisz, Tolman, and Saunders 2000). The gradient of uncontrolled rage that precedes many domestic homicides also suggests the inelasticity of motivation and arousal among men who kill or nearly kill their intimate partners (Polk 1994; *see also* Browne, Williams, and Dutton 1999; Fagan and Browne 1994). The steady decline over nearly 30 years in "domestic" or intimate partner homicides (*see e.g.*, Dugan, Nagin, and Rosenfeld 1999) suggests a secular trend that is insensitive to fluctuations in the number of executions since capital punishment was reinstated following *Gregg*.

The literature on homicide events shows that many homicide offenders are simply unresponsive to punishment threats (Katz 1988; *see also* Pallone and Hennessy 1996). Professor Jack Katz (1988) offers an analysis of homicide events and offenders that portrays some as "stone cold killers" while others simply take pleasure from killing, even as they remain indifferent to punishment threats or even death by retaliation in the moment of the homicide. Using a social interactionist framework, several sociologists conclude that most homicide events are largely unplanned products of complicated social interactions—disputes that escalate from minor conflicts into threatening conflicts where the fear of injury or death motivates lethally violent responses to even minor provocations (Felson and Steadman 1983; Luckenbill 1977; Oliver 1994). Deanna Wilkinson and Jeffery Fagan (2001) suggest that the presence of firearms short-circuits the decision stages where the perceived cost of not killing a possibly armed opponent is one's own death from the opponent's firearm. There is no planning in these events; the emotional arousal in the moment trumps all restraint and compromises the type of reasoning and calculation necessary for deterrence (Pallone and Hennessy 1996).

Measurement and Specification Errors

Three types of measurement error undermine the claims of the new deterrence studies: large amounts of missing data on key indices of murder, overinclusion of persons who are eligible for capital punishment in the estimates of deterrence, and arbitrary and artifactual temporal truncation in the panel designs. Each source of error independently leads to inflated estimates of deterrence.

Missing Data

To measure both homicides and homicide arrests, most of the new deterrence studies rely on data published by the Federal Bureau of Investigation through its Uniform Crime Reporting (UCR) program. However, the UCR data have large amounts of missing data from critical states. For example, data on homicide and robbery arrests in Florida are missing for many local police departments in 1988 and 1989 and again in 1997 through 2002. A more recent analysis by Professors Michael Maltz and Harald Weiss (2006) of monthly data on crimes reported to the police shows that many years have only partial data: reports in fewer than the full twelve months of the calendar year. For example, Florida reported homicides to the UCR system for no months in 1988, five months in 1989, and no more than two months in 1997 through 1999. Yet Florida is one of the nation's most active death penalty states, with fifty-seven executions from *Gregg* through 2003, so the importance of its omission and the potential bias in estimating the deterrent effects of execution due to incomplete data are obvious. In general, non-reporting by police agencies is a recurring problem in the UCR program. For example, from 1992 to 1994, 3,516 of the 18,413 (19%) agencies participating in the UCR system made no reports at all to the UCR program (Maltz 1999:Table 1). According to Professor Michael Maltz (1999), the non-reporting agencies included the primary police agencies in three counties and cities with populations greater than 100,000, and also the primary agencies in 200 cities with populations greater than 10,000. By 1995, the proportion of the U.S. population covered by agencies reporting crimes to the UCR system declined from nearly 100% in 1980 to less than 90% (Maltz 1999:Figure 3). By 1997, the proportion of the U.S. population covered by agencies reporting UCR arrest records had declined from 95% in 1977 to 73% (Maltz 1999:Figure 10).

The new deterrence studies are generally silent on the patterns of missing data and offer no adjustments that might compensate the biases from excluding key states and years. When not silent, the adjustments for missing data are often puzzling, but more worrisome is their potential for introducing bias. In one study, Professor Shepherd (2004) takes heart in the fact that over 90% of the homicides are reported by the FBI, ignoring the weighting and distribution of the missing homicide statistics. Instead, she simply dropped those data points "so that the missing data do not bias my results" (Shepherd 2004:304). Quite the contrary, simply leaving out these state-months raises doubts about the accuracy and absence of bias in her results. The 10% of the population that is not included in the UCR's crime reports is not normally distributed, nor is the 27% that is not included in the arrest statistics. The bias from ignoring the processes generating such large amounts of missing data is potentially quite large.

Even within states, the omission of these key agencies and years in places like Florida introduces a selection bias that is likely to distort both the regression coefficients and the standard errors. Professors Jon Sorensen and Rocky Pilgrim (2006) showed an undercounting of 137 homicides in a two-year span from 1996 to 1997 by Cloninger and Marchesini (2001) in their analysis of the impacts on homicide of the short moratorium on executions in Texas in the mid-1990s. Similarly, Mocan and Gittings (2003) use a substitute of .99 to replace cases divided by zero (in computing executions per lagged death sentence), a decision that increases the size of the deterrence coefficient by approximating a value of one rather than a value of zero. When this coding decision is corrected, the deterrence variable is no longer statistically significant.

The new deterrence studies also fail to address the missing data problems or investigate alternate data sources that might fill in important gaps in annual homicide rates. One such dataset is available from the mortality and morbidity files of the National Center for Health Statistics (NCHS 2007).[1] Information on all deaths classified as homicides by local coroners or medical examiners are compiled by NCHS and reported annually. The data are available for counties as well as states, and have been used in research on capital punishment to develop a metric of the use of the death penalty relative to local homicide rates (Blume and Eisenberg 1999; Liebman et al. 2002). The extent of the missing data bias is evident when we substitute a complete record of homicides in regression models estimating the deterrent effects of capital punishment. For example, when the complete NCHS homicide victimization dataset is substituted for the incomplete FBI homicide data in the Mocan and Gittings (2003) dataset, regression model results change dramatically and the magnitude of a putative deterrent effect is significantly reduced.

Early Cutoffs in Panel Designs

A third concern is the artifactual truncation of observations that excludes data points where execution and homicide show no relationship. What would happen if there were five to eight more years added to these panels, years when

---

1. State homicide and victimization data, including by race, are from the Vital Statistics of the United States or other data compilations generated by the Centers for Disease Control and Prevention National Center for Health Statistics (2007). Data for 1973–1992 are from Vital Statistics of the United States, Mortality Detail Files, 1968–1992. Data for 1993–1998 are from Centers for Disease Control and Prevention National Center for Health Statistics. Data after 1998 are from Centers for Disease Control Wonder (2007). Through 1992, the relevant data sources list homicide victims by state of death. After 1993, the relevant data source lists homicide victims by state of residence. Data for 2001 exclude all victims from the events of September 11th.

homicide rates were stable while executions were sharply declining? That is the case in the new deterrence studies, and the result is that the current estimates suffer from period effects that produce artifactual and elevated estimates of deterrence.

Many of the studies include data from 1977 through 1996 (Shepherd 2005), 1997 (Mocan and Gittings 2003; Yunker 2001; Zimmerman 2004), or 1999 (Shepherd 2004). Only one panel study extended the observational window through 2000 (Zimmerman 2004). But the pattern of executions and homicides in the five years following these studies suggests that murder was insensitive to the levels of execution in this interval: executions declined nationwide from ninety-eight in 1999 to fifty-nine in 2004, but the murder rate remained nearly stable, varying between 5.5 and 5.6 per 100,000 population. Perhaps there were changes in the predictors of homicide in that period that helped stabilize the murder rate, such as shifts in demography, incarceration patterns, drug epidemics, or other factors such as the robbery rate that influence the crimes that typically lead to capital-eligible felony murders. But there is no reason to believe that homicide rates had become insensitive to the pace of change in these externalities. Nor did these factors decline at a rate greater than the 40% decline in executions. If homicides were sensitive to executions, we would expect an uptick in the homicide rate as executions declined. But this distinctive footprint of deterrence is not evident in the patterns of murder through 2004, which remained nearly flat across the nation since 1999.

The flat pattern of homicides and executions since 1999 is likely to influence both the regression coefficient for any of the measures of execution-based deterrence, as well as the standard errors of the estimates. Whatever the form of the model before 2000, it is now different. Throughout the late 1990s, as executions increased while homicides declined, there was nearly a linear relationship between execution and murder. But the addition of five more years with a different pattern of executions and homicides, where the relationship is no longer tightly defined, makes the earlier model at a minimum less accurate because the overall fit of the trend line is no longer comfortable. In other words, the shape of the curve is now different, and so too should be the functional form of the equation that predicts it.

Computation and Model Specification Errors

Other computational and model specification errors have been noted in two articles by Professors John Donohue and Justin Wolfers (2006a; 2006b), including conceptual and measurement errors in the selection of instrumental variables by Dezhbakhsh *et al.* (2003). Instrumental variables should be correlated with the predictor—in this case, executions—but not with the dependent variable, murders. This technique allows analysts to conduct quasi-experiments that simulate the conditions of true experiments. Dezhbakhsh and colleagues (2003) use instruments that are in all likelihood correlated with executions: prison admissions, Republican voters, and police payrolls. It is hard to imagine that the same social and political dynamics, including higher crime rates, that contribute to higher prison admissions do not also contribute to harsher criminal justice policies including the aggressive application of the death penalty. Indeed, Professor Liebman and his colleagues (2002) show that these measures—political dynamics, punitive criminal justice policies, high murder rates, and aggressive use of the death penalty—are correlated with errors in death sentences.

When Donohue and Wolfers (2006b) make minor adjustments to avoid the confounding of the instruments with the other design elements, the estimates of deterrence become very unstable and range so widely (from 429 lives saved per execution to 86 lives lost) as to become meaningless. They also show that when computational errors by Mocan and Gittings (2003) are corrected, their estimates are no longer statistically significant. Overall, these types of computational errors lead to biased estimates. The biases affect both the size of the regression coefficients and the standard errors. Both biases suggest that the published estimates are unacceptably sensitive to even minor modifications in measurement and estimation techniques. This is the opposite of robustness, and shows the risks of a utilitarian approach to vetting claims of deterrence.

Estimation Techniques

The new deterrence studies share a common econometric language and preference for analytic strategies. All the studies use panel data examining murder rates over time within states or counties over a number of years. The general analytic form is a regression equation where the murder rate in each state and year in the time series (or panel) is the dependent variable, and the predictors are a linear combination of factors including the presence of a death penalty law in a given state, the predictability of execution given a death sentence in some previous era, state effects that account for differences between the states, and year effects that account for national time trends that affect the states. Most studies estimate models with states as the unit of analysis, while others include models where county murder rates are predicted from a combination of state- and county-level predictors (*see e.g.*, Dezhbakhsh *et al.* 2003).

As discussed earlier, most designs include statistical controls or covariates that represent factors within states or counties that may affect the homicide rate, including demographic and socio-economic conditions, law enforcement indicia, and political forces that may encourage use of the death penalty (*see* Donohue and Wolfers 2006a). But these factors also influence the presence and use of the death penalty, introducing an analytic confound that can bias results and give misleading and inflated estimates of deterrence. To avoid this, and to approximate an experiment where experiments are not possible, some studies use instrumental variables designs, where variables are included that might affect the use of the death penalty but not necessarily murder (*see e.g.,* Dezhbakhsh *et al.* 2003). These studies assume that this durable functional form can produce accurate results; however, we saw earlier that measurement and model specification errors can produce misleading, if not inaccurate, results.

Put that aside for the moment, and consider the analytic strategy on its own terms. Two connected assumptions in this strategy may undermine the stability and accuracy of the claims of the new deterrence studies. First, the state-fixed effects strategy assumes that any variance that is not accounted for by the covariates remains stable over time. In other words, state- or county-level factors that might produce initial differences are assumed to be invariant. This is probably incorrect, especially for longer time periods: the assumption that the states or counties are invariant with respect to stability in these exogenous factors places a huge burden on the covariates to do all the work in accounting for meaningful change within the states over time. The assumption of stability is only as good as the selection of the covariates. Earlier, we discussed limitations and errors in these predictors and covariates that are likely to produce biased and inaccurate estimates. If this is true, then analytic strategies that rely on the assumptions of stability (or the absence of cross-sectional heteroskedacity) in the predictors are quite risky and probably wrong.

Second, using fixed effects for years treats each year as a separate experimental period that is independent from the previous year's outcomes. The year-fixed effects may account for national trends over time, but it ignores the effects of time within states. In effect, this approach to understanding time in panel data ignores the fact that murder rates within states vary *through* time, and that murder rates within states or counties are serially correlated over time. This is the problem of autoregression, or serial correlation. Autoregression is the tendency of trends in longitudinal or time series data to be heavily influenced by the trends in preceding years. In other words, the best predictor of what the murder rate will be next year is what it was last year. Statistically and conceptually, it is unlikely that effects of extremely rare events, such as executions, can impact trends that are so heavily influenced by their own history (Berk 2005). The problem is compounded when there are patterns of missing observations in time series models when the data evidence autoregressive structures (Young and Pettit 2006). The problem is compounded again when there is serial correlation in the treatment variable, as is the case when estimating the effects of the presence of a death penalty statute, which nearly always is constantly present from year to year once a valid statute passes and goes into effect (Wooldridge 2002).

Many of the studies underplay the question of when and where executions take place and the differences in death penalty and non-death penalty states. Several of the studies include non-death penalty states as comparisons, but fail to address statistically the differences between the two groups of states. Simple contrasts between death penalty and non-death penalty states, even with covariates that characterize some of the differences, make strong identifying assumptions that in the absence of a treatment, the average murder rates for states in each group would have followed parallel paths over time. But if the murder rates are higher in death penalty states, then the antecedents of homicides are probably unbalanced in the two groups, and the estimates of treatment effects are biased. Simply controlling for state differences via state fixed effects, or inserting a variable for whether a valid death penalty statute was in effect in any year, raises a series of connected endogeneity problems that require an integration of econometrics with methods more familiar in the analysis of data in natural experiments.

Most of the new deterrence studies use standard errors computed from simple Ordinary Least Squares (OLS) regressions, but without correcting for autoregression, the standard errors in the estimates of the effects of execution are well understated (*see e.g.*, Bertrand, Duflo, and Mullainathan 2004). In at least two studies in the new deterrence literature, when the standard errors are corrected for autoregression, the standard errors increase, and the execution variable is no longer statistically significant (*see* Donohue and Wolfers 2006a). Such instability in the coefficients under different measurement and analytic conditions should be a serious warning sign to those who would uncritically embrace the new deterrence evidence.

Deterrence

Death sentences are rare, as are executions. One reason is that capital punishment is limited by a jurisprudence that recognizes that "death is different" and should, therefore, be reserved for only the most heinous murders (Abramson 2004; Bedau 1987). This jurisprudence leads to a necessary scarcity: most states have narrowly tailored capital punishment laws to constrain the number and types of homicides that are eligible for the death penalty. This scarcity undermines the logic of deterrence: is it reasonable to expect that rare execution events will have salience across large heterogeneous pools of potential offenders?

This problem is not just a matter of social science, but also of law. The Supreme Court concluded in *Furman* that when only a tiny fraction of persons who commit murder are sentenced to death, capital punishment is unconstitutionally irrational because it serves no identifiable penal function. Assuming rationality, for the moment, rare executions are unlikely to influence decision processes by motivating would-be killers to adjust to these punishment threats. A death penalty that is almost never used serves no deterrent function, because no would-be murderer can reasonably expect to be executed. In his concurrence in *Furman*, Justice White recognized that:

> [A] major goal of the criminal law—to deter others by punishing the convicted criminal—would not be substantially served where the penalty is so seldom invoked that it ceases to be the credible threat essential to influence the conduct of others.... [C]ommon sense and experience tell us that seldom-enforced laws become ineffective measures for controlling human conduct and that the death penalty, unless imposed with sufficient frequency, will make little contribution to deterring those crimes for which it may be exacted (p. 312).

The heart of the matter, then, is whether the criminal law can deter murder and if so, under what conditions. The contours of the modern deterrence argument in capital punishment were constructed by Professor Gary Becker (1968) in theoretical work that preceded and informed Ehrlich's empirical application to the death penalty (1975a, 1975b). Becker's framework was a decision heuristic informed by rational choice and information processing: "All human behavior can be viewed as involving participants who (1) maximize their utility (2) form a stable set of preferences and (3) accumulate an optimal amount of information and other inputs in a variety of markets" (Becker 1978:14; Becker 1968). In the decades following Ehrlich's publication, these theoretical propositions formed the core of discourse, theory and research on deterrence. Accordingly, the new deterrence studies are minor extensions of Becker's and Ehrlich's original theoretical formulations that rely on price theory.

Until recently, the crossfire between deterrence advocates and opponents focused not on the moving parts of deterrence theory, but on three methodological concerns: the econometrics to estimate deterrence, data and measurement concerns, and model specification problems such as those discussed earlier (*see e.g.,* Passell and Taylor 1977). Despite advances in theorizing deterrence in the context of public enforcement of law, including the addition of constructs such as tastes for risk or imperfect knowledge, empirical research on capital punishment has not been updated to test these propositions. In fact, there still have been *no* direct tests of deterrence among groups whose responses could be reasonably generalized to violent offenders. No studies have shown that murderers are aware of executions in their own state, much less in faraway states, and that they rationally decide to forego homicide and use less lethal forms of violence.

No one doubts that the criminal law, as well as other types of legal sanctions, have deterrent effects, but the evidence suggests that such effects may be confined to risk groups atypical of homicide offenders (Nagin 1998; *see e.g.,* Casey and Scholz 1991; Kinsey, Grasmick, and Smith 1991; Pogarsky and Piquero 2003). Deterrence research in the last half century is equivocal on the robustness of deterrent effects, and quite modest when extending deterrence rationales to groups of high-rate or serious offenders (Nagin 1998; Nagin and Pogarsky 2001). Professor Daniel Nagin's (1998) detailed review shows that deterrent effects in the criminal law are conditioned on the social position of the person and the type of crime. The evidence cannot be reliably extended to murderers, since the more persuasive deterrence experiments have been done using experimental paradigms with lower risk groups (*see e.g.,* Nagin and Paternoster 1994). Obviously, in experimental paradigms, it is unrealistic to simulate the contexts where lethal aggression tends to occur. But one could doubt that extreme violence might be deterred: Nagin reports no evidence of valid tests for deterrence of injury aggression.

With these limitations in mind, what conditions are necessary to reliably extend deterrence theory to the case of murder and capital punishment? Professors Paul Robinson and John Darley (2004) identify three conceptual and practical prerequisites to deterrence that are necessary to establish a plausible link between punishment contingencies and behavioral outcomes: rationality, knowledge, and choice. They characterize each as a conceptual hurdle that deterrence theory must overcome to attain empirical validity and conceptual legitimacy.

Rationality

The rationality test asks whether offenders, assuming they possess knowledge of the risks of detection and punishment, will apply their understanding to the decision to engage in homicide at the moment when they are making the choice. Studies that directly examine the reactions of individuals to punishment threats consistently show the limits of rationality, especially in the case of aggression or violence. For example, violence often is embedded in the contexts of the moment, where choices among alternatives are skewed by the demands of the situation. For murder, these contingencies include revenge, retaliation, fear of lethal attack, and nonnegotiable demands of peers or network cohorts (*see e.g.,* Ross and Nisbett 1991). Consequently, many situations that could end in lethal violence are highly volatile, where decisions are made under conditions of arousal, whether anger or fear (*see e.g.*, Fagan and Wilkinson 1998a; Pallone and Hennessy 1996). Rationality may be further impaired by cognitive, organic and neuropsychological factors that may occlude punishment risk from rational calculations (*see e.g.*, Gatzke-Kopp *et al.* 2001; Lewis *et al.* 2004; Raine *et al.* 1998).

The underlying assumptions of rationality depend on clarity and objectivity among offenders in cognition, risk analysis, cost measuring, future orientation and premeditation (Elster 1990). Such attributes are unknown in research on murder and murderers, except perhaps among the very small percentage of murder-for-hire and premeditated killings (Katz 1988). Rather, murderers are more likely to discount punishment risks, and inflate the present value of whatever gains the crime may offer (*see e.g.*, Pallone and Hennessy 1996). This amounts to economics minus the rationality assumptions (Jolls, Sunstein, and Thaler 1998).

The limitations in unreconstructed rationality led Professors Russell Korobkin and Thomas Ulen (2000) to recommend replacing the rationality assumption with a multi-disciplinary understanding of human behavior, drawing from such fields as cognitive psychology, sociology, and decision sciences. Along the same lines, Professor Robert Cooter (2005) says that economic theories of deterrence need a theory of endogenous preferences that will integrate cognitive psychology to incorporate motives and values into the deterrence calculus. These theories are unified in prospect theory, an alternate decision framework that describes how people actually make decisions (Guthrie 2003). Like rational choice theory, prospect theory assumes that decision makers will seek to maximize their outcomes, but in unpredictable ways. The theory assumes that people will make risk-averse decisions when deciding among options that seem to be gains, but will make risk-seeking decisions when faced with losses (Guthrie 2003). Offenders will value losses more than gains of a similar magnitude, and they will overvalue certainty (Kahneman and Tversky 1979). In other words, most people, including criminal offenders, are more likely to take risks to avoid losses than to accumulate gains.

This challenge to rationality and the movement toward disciplinary integration exposes the fault lines in assumptions of rationality among criminal offenders. As a group, offenders often are risk-seekers and prone to thrill seeking (Nagin and Paternoster 1994), and their impulsivity tends to be significantly higher than non-offenders (Cooter 2005). They value social rewards and status from crime over the social rewards of conventional roles and behaviors (Fagan and Wilkinson 1998a; Wilkinson and Fagan 1996), and they often are impaired from extensive careers of drug and alcohol abuse (Chaiken and

Chaiken 1990). Future consequences are either ignored or postponed, giving way to an orientation to consider only present contingencies (Nagin and Paternoster 1994). In one of the few studies with samples of criminal offenders, Professor Charles Dean and his research collaborators report that the stability of present orientation over a long developmental period explains long criminal careers (Dean, Brame, and Piquero 1996). These irrational orientations tend to co-exist in a cascade of organic and cognitive impairments to further weaken cognition and decision making.

In this framework, when faced with uncertainty, decision makers are likely to systematically depart from the rational actor model (Tversky and Kahneman 1986). Rationality is a familiar comfort zone for the law (*see e.g.*, Posner 1973). But rationality as a descriptive term for cognition has given way in social science to the concept of "bounded rationality." Professor Herbert Simon (1982) uses "bounded rationality" to describe the process of making decisions using decision making heuristics, limited time, and incomplete information. A rational choice would be one which maximizes utility, but Simon points out that in many cases the decision maker will aim to make only a satisfactory choice (Simon calls this "satisficing") (Simon 1957).

These shortcomings in rationality remind us that even when facts are known, they may be neither recalled in a particular event nor mobilized accurately as part of a decision heuristic. The facts themselves may or may not be relevant to the situation, and even if recalled, they may be interpreted incorrectly given the context. If a criminal offender is prone to discounting costs that create cognitive dissonance with the perceived benefits or their preferences, the facts that communicate those costs will be distorted if not ignored (*see e.g.*, Anderson 2002). Legal costs may be communicated as a distal influence via a set of rules, or more proximally via an updating based on how one perceives the risks. Yet both are unsatisfactory conditions in thinking about murderers and murders.

Knowledge

The second hurdle is knowledge: does the offender know and understand the implications of the law (Robinson and Darley 2004)? Does the offender know which actions are criminalized and at what schedule, or which actions will excuse one's crime or otherwise mitigate one's culpability?

There is little attention to this question in the new deterrence literature. For example, Professor Joanna Shepherd (2004) elaborates on the early deterrence theoretical framework, maintaining that executions deter all types of murder by allowing all would-be murderers to update their expectations of punishment risk, compensating for the uncertainty about whether the murder they are about to commit would be charged and prosecuted capitally. Such uncertainty, she claims, has less to do with the motivations of murderers than with their capacity to internalize exogenous factors such as prosecutorial discretion, quality of defense counsel, and juror preferences. There are no assumptions in her study nor in the other similar studies about where or how potential murderers acquire the information to do so.

Instead, the new deterrence studies seem to assume, incredibly, that murderers have perfect knowledge about the probability and magnitude of sanctions, and that their decisions about risk are neither discounted nor variable. One study, for example, includes measures of newspaper stories and other media reports of executions (Shepherd 2005). It is a causal story that assumes much about the reading habits and television viewing preferences of would-be murderers. Quite the opposite is probably true given literacy levels among most prison inmates. The new studies fail to show that murderers are aware of executions in their own state, much less in far-away states, and that they rationally decide to forego homicide and use less lethal forms of violence.

The rules—whether one faces execution for one type of murder versus another, or whether one faces execution at all given the circumstances producing a death—are too abstract and removed from the moment to be salient, even assuming that there is a small number of murderers or would-be murderers who have such knowledge. There is no evidence that information markets among would-be murderers are dense, efficient, or fueled by accurate information (*see e.g.*, Sunstein 2005). First, there is no evidence to suggest that there are networks among persons who commit murder. They may be embedded in social networks where violence is common—for example, in street gangs or drug selling networks—but homicide is far from a primary motivator of social cohesion in these groups (Papachristos 2006). Cass Sunstein (2005) also claims that in such markets, competition among group members may lead to gaming where some may withhold information or not disclose what they know. This has the unfortunate effect of propagating errors and corroding group cohesion.

While experience—whether direct or vicarious—may substitute for knowledge, these experiences may not be transferable to the specific situations that may lead to murder. Robinson and Darley (2004) suggest that offenders are unlikely to do the calculations necessary to decide correctly which rules apply in which situations. Indirect or vicarious knowledge is prone to error as well, as it is fueled by gossip and misinformation about the rules of law and the probabilities of detection and punishment.

Choice and Preferences

Assuming knowledge and rationality, will an offender make a behavioral choice consistent with deterrence? Robinson and Darley (2004) refer to this as the *Perceived Net Cost Hurdle*.

Decisions themselves—as a matter of human development and not just antisocial behavior—suggest that even in a "rational" estimation of costs and benefits, decision makers are more likely to use intuitive heuristics, shortcuts which may or may not result in wise decision making (Thaler 1991). Professors Amos Tversky and Daniel Kahneman (1974) note that although heuristics sometimes work well, they can also lead to irrational decisions or decisions that may not maximize utility but instead maximize short-term preferences that are framed by situational contingencies and present circumstances. "In general, these heuristics are quite useful, but sometimes they lead to severe and systematic errors" (Tversky and Kahneman 1974:1124). The moving parts in biased decision making heuristics include two dimensions: fallacies and skewed adjustments (Korobkin and Ulen 2000). Additionally, decisions are skewed by emotions. Preferences for utility, cognition and heuristics under conditions of arousal are all vulnerable to distortion under conditions of arousal or fear.

Emotion

One's emotional state plays a role in decision making, and can influence a person to act in ways that are not maximally optimal (or rational) (Dailey 2000). Obviously, anger and other forms of arousal can skew judgment in several ways, changing rationality and also reshaping the estimation of costs and benefits. Professor Anne Dailey (2000) argues that lawyers should focus more on the source of an individual's needs, feelings, and motives, which may be unconscious, irrational, or both. One example of how emotions can lead to irrational decision making is illustrated by the finding that, in general, people are willing to pay more for an emotionally meaningful item than for an equally valuable but emotionally neutral item. Professor Russell Korobkin (2003) calls this the *endowment* effect.

Weighing Net Costs

Assume that knowledge is internalized and a would-be murderer will put this information to work accurately and rationally. Theorists from Becker (1968) to Polinsky and Shavell (2007) have posited a calculus of decision making where actors weigh costs and benefits prior to action (or inaction). The decision making is complex, of course, with different actors assigning different utilities and preferences to the components of cost and return. For example, postponing reward is an expression of preference, as is discounting past (sunk) costs or postponing present costs. Deterrence will take place, to put it simply, when punishment is a cost worth avoiding—that is, when the costs of punishment outweigh the perceived rewards of the act. Put another way, is the offender likely to choose compliance as the more beneficial option?

Beginning with Bentham (1789), deterrence theorists have disaggregated costs into three dimensions: probability, severity, and delay. While there is no debate on severity,[2] there is strong evidence that death is delayed punishment owing to due process and the numerous errors in capital sentences (Liebman, Fagan, and West 2000). Probability also is low: no more than one homicide in four is capital-eligible (Fagan *et al.* 2006), few of these are selected for prosecution (*see e.g.*, Paternoster *et al.* 2004), and the percentage of death row cases that proceed to execution for states other than Texas remains very low (Death Penalty Information Center 2008d) As mentioned earlier, scarcity undermines the deterrent threat of death, and the marginal deterrence from this weak threat compared to the certainty and harshness of incarceration undermines this utilitarian argument for capital punishment.

The benefit side of the equation is more complex. Professors Fagan and Freeman analyzed a series of empirical studies on the tradeoffs between legal work and illegal income-producing criminal activity for young men in inner cities (Fagan and Freeman 1999). When faced with sharply escalating incarceration risks throughout the late 1980s and 1990s, robbers and drug dealers consistently valued the economic returns of illegal work over either the foregone opportunities for legal income or the punishment costs that jail would exact. Similar tradeoffs were reported by burglars (Wright and Decker 1994) and robbers (Wright and Decker 1997) in ethnographic studies of their crime decision making. Other studies have shown that drug offenders will heavily value the combined reward of relief from withdrawal symptoms and the pleasure of addiction (Kaplan 1983).

Scholars of homicide have long known that homicide is the result of complex social interactions that increase the present value of benefits and push costs to the background (*see e.g.*, Katz 1988; O'Kane 2005; Polk 1994; Wolfgang 1958). Recent studies on violence *in situ* confirm the salience of reward, and introduce an element of risk that attaches when extreme violence is *not* used. In interviews with 125 young males ages sixteen to twenty-four who were involved in over 300 incidents of gun violence in New York City from 1995–1997, Professors Jeffrey Fagan and Deanna Wilkinson collaborated to understand

---

2. Although there may be some debate on the severity of life imprisonment without the possibility of parole compared to execution, and the marginal deterrence of capital punishment relative to such life sentences is unknown.

decision making within violent events where guns were used, and other events where guns were almost used but avoided at some point during a confrontation (Fagan and Wilkinson 1998a). In these settings, lethal violence has both instrumental and intrinsic rewards that trumped the distal risks of detection and punishment. In fact, there was greater fear of retaliation from victims' families or friends than from what was perceived as the remote possibility of police involvement. Extreme violence was an expected and valued behavior and, for some, thought to be necessary to ensure their survival (Wilkinson 2003). Chance encounters with others in these neighborhoods were seen as potentially threatening or lethal—unknown others were widely thought to harbor hostile intentions and capacity to inflict harm. Extreme violence and toughness was the currency of respect, and respect had both strategic value and offered strong social reward. Violence was a public performance, designed to maintain a social identity that deters attack and reinforces a self-presentation of "toughness." Other acts of violence also were pathways to social status. For example, robbery not only generated material goods or cash and was helpful in sexual conquests, but it also established one's status in a social hierarchy where respect was a finite commodity (*see also* Anderson 1999; 1990). Of course, the danger that a robbery could escalate into a homicide was always present. Violence also functions as social control in these contexts, redressing grievances or peremptorily ending them before they ever begin.

In a similar study, Andrew Papachristos (2007) interviewed gang members in the Austin and North Lawndale neighborhoods of Chicago. Most had been involved either as witnesses or accomplices in murders committed in gang disputes. The risk of a death sentence was simply not a reality among gang members. This is not to say that rationality is not part of their decisions about crime and violence: gang members often think rationally about crimes, especially drug dealing, but usually as a matter of business details such as packaging, marketing and selling drugs to maximize their returns. Their knowledge of law clearly passed the knowledge hurdle (Papachristos 2007).

But the perceptions of risk and benefit were different for interpersonal violence, including murder. Compared with drug selling, gang members do not necessarily act "rationally" or weigh the prospects of execution in the course of violence. Although most of these gang members had been in and out of jail quite often, very few know anyone on "death row" or who has been executed. Rather, the greatest risk in murder was retaliation by members of rival gangs, not retribution by the state. A much broader and more pressing "threat of violence" looms over the gang world. Even more so than in "street culture" more generally, the consequences of victimization are the chief concern and are to be avoided at all costs. *Self-protection* and *mutual protection* are often key determinants in carrying weapons and engaging in violence. Violence was often reactionary and retaliatory, serving as a deterrent against future victimization, a form of self-protection, or a mechanism of social control. State sanctions, and especially the death penalty, rarely entered into the means-ends calculus of gang members on the street. Quite the opposite was true: gang members see prison sentences as "worth it" in order to maintain face and self-respect to deter the possibility of victimization. Often, receiving a prison sentence for maintaining personal honor can, in fact, *increase* one's personal reputation (Papachristos 2007).

There are numerous other examples of perceived benefits eclipsing risk in homicide: murders by violent spouses aimed at dominating and controlling intimate partners, retaliation and reprisal, or even robbery-homicides (Katz 1988). In fact, punishment costs may be discounted even more in the modal category of capital-eligible crimes: felony murders—homicides committed in the course of other crimes, especially robbery. Robbery is not a crime that is committed casually, nor are robbers a random sample of the criminal population: most have prior arrest records and many have completed spells in prison (*see e.g.*, Wright and Decker 1997). In felony murders, especially robbery-homicides which are more than half the capital-eligible murders (Fagan *et al.* 2006), struggles for weapons or fear of identification may escalate the crime to a homicide. There is a weak prospect that a risk heuristic of punishment will enter into the volatile and unpredictable street dynamics of robbery interactions to reduce the risk of lethality (Fagan *et al.* 2006), especially when a gun is present. Accordingly, the presence of a gun in a robbery further increases not just the risk of lethality but the decision by the robber to use it (Fagan and Wilkinson 1998b; Wilkinson and Fagan 1996; Zimring and Zuehl 1986). In other words, there is a strong risk of cognitive errors in situations of intense arousal, errors that are likely to overwhelm the evaluations of the benefits of crime and the risks and costs of punishments (*see e.g.*, Kahneman and Tversky 1984).

Cumulative and Conditional Corrosion

In the Robinson-Darley framework, "[s]etting any one of the variables to zero means that there is no deterrent effect whatever" (2004:196). Of course, none of these values reach zero in reality, except perhaps in the case of the mentally ill (*see e.g.*, Link, Steuve, and Phelan 1998). Nevertheless, the parts of this framework are neither exchangeable nor separate. Rather, they interact conditionally and multiplicatively to produce a robust deterrent effect, and weakness in any one domain will drag down the salience of the others. So, for example, prison may be worth avoiding if there is a positive benefit from compliance. If detached from conventional social worlds via joblessness or addiction, the exposure of violent offenders to the actuarial risks of detection declines, and their perception of detection risks—not inaccurately, from their perspective—declines with it (*see* Robinson and Darley 2004). The scarcity of execution, however salient executions may be, is unlikely to disturb their risk assessment. How deterrence works in this social system and skewed information markets is uncharted territory. Having said that, there is a large body of social science evidence that in the case of murder, each of the three hurdles in this framework becomes far higher than in the case of less complex or serious crimes, and their reciprocal and multiple effects are likely to militate against deterrence. That is, the cumulative effect of these hurdles for deterring murder is considerable, and their height casts doubt on the streamlined version of deterrence argued in the new deterrence studies.

Conclusion: A Cautionary Tale

The new deterrence studies claim that each execution prevents anywhere from three to thirty-two murders. This is hardly a new claim: about 30 years ago, similar claims about the death penalty were made just before executions resumed following the post-*Furman* moratorium. One thousand executions later, the claim has been revived by a small group of researchers touting advances in econometric techniques and new data sources that resolve technical problems in the earlier work. Endorsing these claims, Sunstein and Vermeule (2005) suggest that this evidence "morally" requires executions, a conclusion echoed by Becker (2005) and Posner (2005). These arguments too are neither new nor correct.

The new deterrence literature fails to provide a stable foundation of scientific evidence on which to base law or policy. Nor can this evidence be used to calibrate the normative implications of new "facts" about lives saved or lost. As in the debate over Ehrlich's (1975a; 1975b) findings, simple but necessary changes in the functional form of regression equations, combined with measurement strategies that provide more complete and accurate data, produce different results that differ from the current crop of studies, results that are far more equivocal. Even more significant modifications to these studies, such as using research designs that more closely approximate quasi-experiments that account for murder trends in states with no executions, also produce different and equivocal results (Donohue and Wolfers 2006a). Conceptual errors and omissions in specifying the multiple influences on murder rates seriously bias the estimates of deterrence.

The wide range of results, and the sensitivity of findings to even the most minor tweaks, introduces *model uncertainty*. Each study in the new deterrence literature, both those that confirm and those that challenge the deterrence claims, uses a particular model of crime that embodies a choice of data, time period, control variables, and statistical specifications. Variation in these choices is part of a vigorous scientific vetting of a theoretical proposition. While model uncertainty is endemic to this process, the uncertainty here is so wide and so profound as to raise strong cautions on reaching any conclusion about deterrence, much less policy. At the end of the day, econometric "pyrotechnics" (Donohue and Wolfers 2006a) may dazzle, but they are diversions that fail to advance the debate on capital punishment.

Sunstein and Vermeule (2005) embrace these findings, and then use the evidence to animate their calls for a more vigorous use of the death penalty. Sunstein and Vermeule are willing to tolerate error in the estimates of deterrence, arguing that doubts about their robustness should not stand in the way of increasing the use of execution if executions can avoid harm. The problem for them is that the fragility of the new deterrence evidence, a function of the fundamental empirical and theoretical errors in this body of work, raises concerns greater than simply just "doubt": the conclusions in this body of work are wrong, there is no reliable evidence of deterrence. The only scientifically and ethically acceptable conclusion from the complete body of existing social science literature on deterrence and the death penalty is that it is impossible to tell whether deterrent effects are strong or weak, or whether they exist at all (Donohue and Wolfers 2006b).

Social science sets a high bar for causal inference, demanding caution until such claims can be replicated under a variety of experimental conditions. Several such replication efforts, facilitated by generous sharing of data and statistical programs, suggest that these claims of deterrence are volatile and inconsistent, sensitive to alternate ways to measure murder rates and decisions on how to account for anomalies such as missing information and years with no homicides. Depending on commonplace methodological adjustments, regression models can just as easily show that executions increase murder or reduce murder (Donohue and Wolfers 2006a). In fact, this work fails the tests of rigorous replication and robustness analysis that are the hallmarks of good science. And the analyses here and elsewhere suggest that the prospect for replications that will produce a range of estimates that can confirm the core finding of deterrence are not forthcoming.

As a matter of social science, it is important to ask how this debate, in reality the second round in the debate over deterrence and the death penalty, arrived at this point. Like the cold fusion scandal in the 1980s, when bold scientific claims were greeted with widespread enthusiasm by the public that fueled a sharp mobilization of academic and political institutions, there was a quick and passionate embrace of the new deterrence claims by a small community of legal scholars and death penalty advocates. As the new evidence leeched into the mainstream media and eventually into political discourse and appellate arguments, the evidence was reified as scientifically rigorous. And as with the cold fusion episode, these claims seem to be unable to withstand scientific vetting.

There are several distinctions between cold fusion and the current deterrence debate. Cold fusion was the work of two scientists. The new deterrence is the work of several researchers, nearly all economists, using core elements of identical data sets on executions, death sentences, and murders, and submitting their papers to peer reviewed journals in economics and non-peer reviewed law reviews. One can only speculate about what happens between submission of an empirical article to a good journal and an editorial decision. But Walter McManus (1985) showed that it is not unreasonable to assume that a reviewer's priors influence her posteriors. When McManus introduced the priors of researchers into a representative regression model of murders and executions, he showed that "significant conflicts remain over the estimated deterrent effect of an additional execution, even after the researchers have confronted the same data. The conflicting interpretations of the data evidence are serious" (McManus 1985:423). Model uncertainty would be large in a condition such as this (Leamer 1983). The priors of the researchers, in other words, overwhelm the data, and the data simply are not strong enough to lead researchers to a consensus or convergent conclusion. It is not hard to see, given McManus' demonstration, how like-minded researchers would reach similar conclusions.

But understanding the priors of researchers cannot explain how reviewers and journal editors would overlook the same flaws that are apparent to many others who have critiqued this body of work. One assumes that reviewers and editors have a wider distribution of priors, but whether the priors of reviewers and editors enter into peer review decisions is unknowable for the moment. We suspect a different dynamic: a set of papers about murder were reviewed as part of an interior conversation among economists who have little or no familiarity with the dynamics of murder, murderers, and criminal legal institutions. Other opinions seem to be unwelcome. Editors and reviewers alike seem impervious to the kind of intellectual humility that would sustain a result at dissonance with the dominant paradigm of price theory. When discussing the study of deterrence as carried out by economists, Coase (1978:210) notes in *Economics and Contiguous Disciplines* that:

> Punishment, for example, can be regarded as the price of crime. An economist will not debate whether increased punishment will reduce crime; he will merely try to answer the question, by how much? The economist's analysis may fail to touch some of the problems found in the other social systems....

Indeed, potentially the most disturbing concerns in this interlude reside not just in the willingness (or preference) of good journals to publish stylized econometrics over substantive social science theory. Rather, these decisions also are rooted in the striking absence of either critical commentary or substantive contributions by scholars from other disciplines since the initial publication of these articles over the past decade. In fact, these other disciplines are marginalized or dismissed. Nor do editors or reviewers challenge this self-referential group with concerted attempts to test more rigorously for the immediate impact of a change in threatened punishment with more detailed crime data and a better causal theory. Unfortunately for anyone interested in the deterrent impact of harsher sentences, several of the built-in safeguards for self-correction within the social sciences have clearly failed in this instance. Whether the explanation resides in orthodox beliefs, lack of critical skepticism, or whatever else may be responsible, the failure to maintain scientific and intellectual rigor is particularly disturbing. Indeed, any study which is not adequately challenged by one's scholarly peers can only hinder rather than help the credibility of scholarly contributions to either side of the deterrence debate.

As a regulatory matter, embracing the new deterrence findings ignores risks of error that would have serious consequences. As a normative matter, the implications are dangerous. Research at Columbia Law School on reversals in capital sentences from 1973–1995 showed that the number of serious errors leading to reversal in capital sentences increased sharply with higher rates of death sentences per murder (Liebman et al. 2002). More than two death sentences in three during this time were reversed, and at resentencing, approximately five percent were exonerated (Liebman, Fagan, and West 2000). Even the harshest critics of the Columbia studies acknowledge that the lower bound on error rates is four in ten (Hoffman 2001). Making more people eligible for execution increases the risks of horrific errors of wrongful conviction that are far more likely in states that execute "many people." The clamor to make policy if not law under these conditions of uncertainty is expensive and dangerous.

In this episode, a group of scholars combine some sophisticated strategies to compare the use of the death penalty with a sample of state murder rates. They introduce a set of theoretically tangential controls, and reach a conclusion of deterrence that fails to replicate when more complete data is applied, when unsustainable coding decisions are corrected, and when the functional form is modified to account for the rigid structure of the data. The appeal of this simple story of deterrence is obvious. Sadly, though, "it is easier to muddy the waters than it is to calm them" (Dauber 2005), especially in the midst of recent erosion in popular support for the death penalty that followed the moratorium on executions in Illinois (see Warden 2005), the exoneration of the

100th person from death row (*see* Gross *et al*. 2005), and the revelations of widespread reversals and errors in capital sentences (*see* Liebman *et al.* 2000; 2002). Complexity and uncertainty, though, are what the data say. Until this research survives the rigors of replication and thorough testing of alternative hypotheses, this research provides no basis for decisions to take many more lives.

This cohort of studies and researchers, like Ehrlich before them, has created unjustified confidence in the minds of legislators, death penalty advocates, and a small group of legal scholars about the capacity of death sentences and executions to deter murder. They raise their concerns to a high moral ground, and brush off evidentiary doubts as unreasonable cautions that place potential beneficiaries at risk of severe harm. Although rebukes like this and others may put the brakes on the rush to once again embrace deterrence as the cure for murder, interludes such as this one also remind us to invoke the tough, neutral social science standards and commonsense causal reasoning before taking a path that can do far more harm than good.

References

Abramson, Jeffrey. 2004. "Death-is-Different Jurisprudence and the Role of the Capital Jury." *Ohio State Journal of Criminal Law* 2:117–164.

Agar, Michael and Heather Schacht Reisenger. 2002. "A Heroin Epidemic at the Intersection of Histories: The 1960s Epidemic Among African Americans in Baltimore." *Medical Anthropology* 21:115–156.

Albert, Craig J. 1999. "Challenging Deterrence: New Insights on Capital Punishment Derived from Panel Data." *University of Pittsburg Law Review* 60:321–371.

Anderson, David. 2002. "The Deterrence Hypothesis and Picking Pockets at the Pickpocket's Hanging." *American Law and Economics Review* 4:295–313.

Anderson, Elijah. 1999. *Code of the Street: Decency, Violence, and the Moral Life of the Inner City*. New York, NY: W.W. Norton & Company.

_____. 1990. Streetwise: *Race, Class, and Change in an Urban Community*. Chicago, IL: The University of Chicago Press.

Associated Press. 2003. "Georgia: Number of Death Penalty Cases Decline." Dec. 28. (http://www.democracyinaction.org/dia/organizations/ncadp/news.jsp?key=374&t=).

Baldus, David and James W.L. Cole. 1975. "A Comparison of the Work of Thorsten Sellin and Isaac Ehrlich on the Deterrent Effect of Capital Punishment." *Yale Law Journal* 85:170–186.

Baumer, Eric. 1994. "Poverty, Crack, and Crime: A Cross-City Analysis." *Journal of Research in Crime and Delinquency* 31:311–327.

Baumer, Eric, Janet L. Lauritsen, Richard Rosenfeld, and Richard Wright. 1998. "The Influence of Crack Cocaine on Robbery, Burglary and Homicide Rates: A Cross-city Longitudinal Analysis." *Journal of Research in Crime and Delinquency* 35:316–340.

Becker, Gary. 2005. "More on the Economics of Capital Punishment." (http://www.becker-posner-blog.com/archives/2005/12/more_on_the_eco.html).

_____. 1978. *The Economic Approach to Human Behavior*. Chicago, IL: University of Chicago Press.

_____. 1968. "Crime and Punishment: An Economic Approach." *Journal of Political Economy* 76:169–217.

Bedau, Hugo Adam. 1987. *Death is Different: Studies in the Morality, Law, and Politics of Capital Punishment*. Boston, MA: Northeastern University Press.

Bennett, Lauren, Lisa Goodman, and Mary Ann Dutton. 2000. "Risk Assessment Among Batterers Arrested for Domestic Assault: The Salience of Psychological Abuse." *Violence Against Women* 6:1190–1203.

Bentham, Jeremy. [1789] 1948. *An Introduction to the Principles of Morals and Legislation*. New York, NY: Hafner Publishing Company.

Berk, Richard. 2005. "New Claims About Executions and General Deterrence: Déjà Vu All Over Again?" *Journal of Empirical Legal Studies* 2:303–330.

Bertrand, Marianne, Esther Duflo, and Sendhil Mullainathan. 2004. "How Much Should We Trust Differences-in-Differences Estimates?" *The Quarterly Journal of Economics* 119:249–275.

Blume, John and Theodore Eisenberg. 1999. "Judicial Politics, Death Penalty Appeals, and Case Selection: An Empirical Study." *Southern California Law Review* 72:465–504.

Blumstein, Alfred. 1995. "Youth Violence, Guns, and the Illicit-Drug Industry." *Journal of Criminal Law and Criminology* 86:10–36.

Blumstein, Alfred, and Allen J. Beck. 1999. "Population Growth in U.S. Prisons, 1980–1996." *Crime and Justice* 26:17–61.

Blumstein, Alfred and Richard Rosenfeld. 1998. "Explaining Recent Trends in U.S. Homicide Rates." *Journal of Criminal Law and Criminology* 88:1175–1216.

Bonczar, Thomas P. and Tracy L Snell. 2002. "Capital Punishment." (www.ojp.usdoj.gov/bjs/pub/pdf/cp02.pdf).

Bowers, William J. and Glenn L. Pierce. 1975. "The Illusion of Deterrence in Isaac Ehrlich's Research on Capital Punishment." *Yale Law Journal* 85:187–208.

Browne, Angela, Kirk R. Williams, and Donald G. Dutton. 1999. "Homicide Between Intimate Partners: A 20-Year Review." Pp. 149–164 in *Homicide: A Sourcebook of Social Research*, edited by M. Dwayne Smith and Margaret A. Zahn. Thousand Oaks, CA: Sage Publications.

California Department of Corrections. 2004. "Facts and Figures Third Quarter. 2004." (http://www.corr.ca.gov/DivisionsBoards/AOAP/FactFigures Archive/FactsFiguresArchive.html).

Campbell, Jacquelyn C., Phyllis Sharps, and Nancy Glass. 2001. "Risk Assessment for Intimate Partner Homicide." Pp. 136–157 in *Clinical Assessment of Dangerousness*, edited by Georges-Franck Pinard & Linda Pagani. Cambridge: Cambridge University Press.

Casey, Jeff T. and John T. Scholz. 1991. "Beyond Deterrence: Behavioral Decision Theory and Tax Compliance." *Law & Society Review* 25:821–844.

Centers for Disease Control. 2007. Wonder, the Centers for Disease Control Data Extraction Engine. (http://wonder.cdc.gov).

Centers for Disease Control and Prevention National Center for Health Statistics 2007. (http://www.cdc.gov/nchs/).

_____. 1993–1998. "Compressed Mortality File, 1989–1998 CD-ROM Series 20, No 2C." (http://www.cdc.gov/nchs/).

Chaiken, Jan M. and Marcia R. Chaiken. 1990. "Drugs and Predatory Crime." *Crime and Justice* 13:203–239.

Cheung, Yin Bin. 2002. "Zero-Inflated Models for Regression Analysis of Count Data: A Study of Growth and Development." *Statistics in Medicine* 21:1461–1469.

Chressanthis, George A. 1989. "Capital Punishment and the Deterrent Effect Revisited: Recent Time-Series Econometric Evidence." *Journal of Behavioral Economics* 18:81–97.

Cloninger, Dale O. and Roberto Marchesini. 2001. "Execution and Deterrence: A Quasi-Controlled Group Experiment." *Applied Economics* 33:569–576.

Coase, Ronald H. 1978. "Economics and Contiguous Disciplines." *The Journal of Legal Studies* 7:201–211.

Cooter, Robert. 2005. "Treating Yourself Instrumentally: Internalization, Rationality and the Law." Pp. 95–110 in *The Law And Economics Of Irrational Behavior*, edited by Franco Parisi and Vernon L. Smith. Palo Alto, CA: Stanford University Press.

Cork, Daniel. 1999. "Examining Space-Time Interaction in City-Level Homicide Data: Crack Markets and the Diffusion of Guns Among Youth." *Journal of Quantitative Criminology* 15:379–406.

Cover, James P. and Paul D. Thistle. 1988. "Time Series, Homicide, and the Deterrent Effect of Capital Punishment." *Southern Economic Journal* 54:615–622.

Criminal Justice Legal Foundation. 2004. Brief of Amici Curiae in *Schirro v. Summerlin*, 542 U.S. 348 (No. 03-526). (http://www.cjlf.org/briefs/Summerlin.pdf).

Curtis, Richard. 1998. "The Improbable Transformation of Inner-City Neighborhoods: Crime, Violence, Drugs and Youth in the 1990s." *Journal of Criminal Law and Criminology* 88:1233–1276.

Dailey, Anne C. 2000. "The Hidden Economy of the Unconscious." *Chicago-Kent Law Review* 74:1599–1623.

Dauber, Michele Landis. 2005. "The Big Muddy." *Stanford Law Review* 57:1899–1914.

Dean, Charles, Robert Brame, and Alex Piquero. 1996. "Criminal Propensities, Discrete Groups of Offenders, and Persistence in Crime." *Criminology* 34:547–574.

Death Penalty Information Center. 2008a. "Executions by Year." (http://www.deathpenaltyinfo.org/article.php?scid=8&did=146).

─────────. 2008b. "Number of Executions by State and Region Since 1976." (http://www.deathpenaltyinfo.org/article.php?scid=8&did=186).

─────────. 2008c. "Life Without Parole." (http://www.deathpenaltyinfo.org/article.php?did=555&scid=59).

─────────. 2008d. "Death Sentencing Rate by State." (http://www.deathpenaltyinfo.org/article.php?scid=67&did=915).

Dezhbakhsh, Hashem, Paul H. Rubin, and Joanna M. Shepherd. 2003. "Does Capital Punishment Have a Deterrent Effect? New Evidence from Post-moratorium Panel Data." *American Law Economic Review* 5:344–376.

Dezhbakhsh, Hashem and Joanna M. Shepherd. 2006. "The Deterrent Effect of Capital Punishment: Evidence from a 'Judicial Experiment.'" *Economic Inquiry* 44:512–535.

Dieter, Richard C. 2004. "Death Penalty Information Center, Innocence and the Crisis in the American Death Penalty." (http://www.deathpenaltyinfo.org/article.php?scid=45&did=1149#ExSum).

Donohue, John and Justin Wolfers. 2006a. "Uses and Abuses of Empirical Evidence in the Death Penalty Debate." *Stanford Law Review* 58:791–846.

─────────. 2006b. "The Death Penalty: No Evidence for Deterrence." *The Economist's Voice* 3:5, Article 3 (April). (http://www.bepress.com/ev/vol3/iss5/art3).

Dugan, Laura, Daniel S. Nagin, and Richard Rosenfeld. 1999. "Explaining the Decline in Intimate Partner Homicide: The Effects of Changing Domesticity, Women's Status, and Domestic Violence Resources." *Homicide Studies* 3:187–214.

Durose, Mark R. and Patrick A. Langan. 2005. "Felony Sentences in State Courts, 2002." Bureau Justice Statistics Bulletin. (http://www.ojp.usdoj.gov/bjs/pub/pdf/fssc02.pdf).

Egan, Donald J. and David O. Robinson. 1979. "Models of a Heroin Epidemic." *American Journal of Psychiatry* 36:1162–1167.

Ehrlich, Isaac. 1977. "Capital Punishment and Deterrence: Some Further Thoughts and Additional Evidence." *Journal of Political Economy* 85:741–788.

———. 1975a. "The Deterrent Effect of Capital Punishment: A Question of Life and Death." *American Economic Review* 65:397–417.

———. 1975b. "Deterrence: Evidence and Inference." *Yale Law Journal* 85:209–227.

Elster, Jon. 1990. "When Rationality Fails." Pp. 19–50 in *The Limits of Rationality*, edited by Karen S. Cook and Margaret Levi. Chicago, IL: University of Chicago Press.

Epstein, Lee and Gary King. 2002. "The Rules of Inference." *University of Chicago Law Review* 69:1–133.

Fagan, Jeffrey. 2006. "Walter Reckless Memorial Lecture Death and Deterrence Redux: Science, Law and Causal Reasoning on Capital Punishment." *Ohio State Journal of Criminal Law* 4:255–320.

———. 1990. "*Intoxication and Aggression*". Pp. 241–320 in *Crime and Justice, Volume 13: Drugs and Crime: A Review of Research*, edited by Michael Tonry and James Q. Wilson. Chicago, IL: University of Chicago Press.

Fagan, Jeffrey and Angela Browne. 1994. "Violence Toward Spouses and Intimates: Physical Aggression between Men and Women in Intimate Relationships." Pp. 115–292 in *Understanding and Preventing Violence, Volume 3: Social Influences,* edited by Albert J. Reiss, Jr. and Jeffrey A. Roth. Washington DC: National Academy Press.

Fagan, Jeffrey and Richard B. Freeman. 1999. "Crime and Work." *Crime and Justice* 25:225–290.

Fagan, Jeffrey A. and Deanna L. Wilkinson. 1998a. "Guns, Youth Violence and Social Identity in Inner Cities." Pp. 105–188 in *Crime and Justice, Volume 24: Annual Review of Research*, edited by Michael Tonry and Mark H. Moore. Chicago, IL: University of Chicago Press.

———. 1998b. "Social Contexts and Functions of Adolescent Violence." Pp. 55–93 in *Violence in American Schools: A New Perspective*, edited by Delbert S. Elliott, Beatrix A. Hamburg, and Kirk R. Williams. Cambridge: Cambridge University Press.

Fagan, Jeffrey, Franklin Zimring, and Amanda B. Geller. 2006. "Capital Punishment and Capital Murder: Market Share and the Deterrent Effects of the Death Penalty." *Texas Law Review* 84:1803–1868.

Felson, Richard B. and Henry J. Steadman. 1983. "Situational Factors in Disputes Leading to Criminal Violence." *Criminology* 21:59–60.

Fowler v. North Carolina (1976). 428 U.S. 904.
Furman v. Georgia (1972). 408 U.S. 238.
Gatzke-Kopp, Lisa M., Adrian Raine, Monte Buchsbaum, and Lori LaCasse. 2001. "Temporal Lobe Deficits in Murderers: EEG Findings Undetected by PET." *Journal of Neuropsychiatry and Clinical Neurosciences* 13:486–491.
Georgia Department of Corrections. 2004. "Inmate Statistical Profile." (http://www.dcor.state.ga.us/pdf/lwop04-10.pdf).
Gregg v. Georgia (1976). 428 U.S. 153.
Grogger, Jeffrey. 1990. "The Deterrent Effect of Capital Punishment: An Analysis of Daily Homicide Counts." *Journal of the American Statistical Association* 85:295–303.
Grogger, Jeffrey and Michael Willis. 2000. "The Emergence of Crack Cocaine and the Rise in Urban Crime Rates." *The Review of Economics and Statistics* 82:519–529.
Gross, Samuel R., Kristen Jacoby, Daniel J. Matheson, Nicholas Montgomerry, and Sujata Patil. 2005. "Exonerations in the United States, 1989 Through 2003." *The Journal of Criminal Law and Criminology* 95:523–560.
Guthrie, Chris. 2003. "Prospect Theory, Risk Preference, and the Law." *Northwestern University Law Review* 97:1115–1163.
Harrison, Paige M. and Allen J. Beck. 2005. "Prisoners in 2004." Bureau of Justice Statistics Bulletin. (http://www.ojp.usdoj.gov/bjs/pub/pdf/p04.pdf).
Hoffmann, Joseph L. 2001. "Violence and the Truth." *Indiana Law Journal* 76:939–949.
Hunt, Leon G. and Carl D. Chambers. 1976. *The Heroin Epidemics: A Study of Heroin Use in the United States, 1965–75.* New York, NY: Spectrum Publications.
Inciardi, James A. 1979. "Heroin Use and Street Crime." *Crime and Delinquency* 25:335–346.
Jacoby, Jeff. 2003. "Execution Saves Innocents." *Boston Globe* Sept. 28, H11.
Johnson, Bruce D., Terry Williams, Kojo A. Dei, and Harry Sanabria. 1990. "Drug Abuse in the Inner City: Impact on Hard Drug Users and the Community." *Drugs and Crime: A Review of the Research* 13:9–67.
Jolls, Christine, Cass R. Sunstein, and Richard Thaler. 1998. "A Behavioral Approach to Law and Economics." *Stanford Law Review* 50:1471–1550.
Kahneman, Daniel and Amos Tversky. 1984. "*Choice, Values, and Frames.*" *American Psychologist* 39:341–350.
⸺⸺⸺. 1979. "Prospect Theory: An Analysis of Decisions Under Risk." *Econometrica* 47:263–269.
Kaplan, John. 1983. *The Hardest Drug: Heroin and Public Policy.* Chicago, IL: The University of Chicago Press.

Katz, Jack. 1988. *Seductions of Crime: Moral and Sensual Attractions in Doing Evil.* New York, NY: Basic Books.

Katz, Lawrence, Steven D. Levitt, and Ellen Shustorovich. 2003. "Prison Conditions, Capital Punishment, and Deterrence." *American Law and Economics Review* 5:318–343.

Kinsey, Karyl A., Harold G. Grasmick, and Kent W. Smith. 1991. "Framing Justice: Taxpayer Evaluations of Personal Tax Burdens." *Law & Society Review* 25:845–874.

Klein, Lawrence R., Brian E. Forst, and Victor Filatov. 1978. "The Deterrent Effect of Capital Punishment: An Assessment of the Estimates." Pp. 336–360 in *Deterrence and Incapacitation: Estimating the Effects of Criminal Sanctions on Crime*, edited by Alfred Blumstein, Jaqueline Cohn, and Daniel Nagin. Washington DC: National Academy of Science.

Koretetz, Gene. 2003. "Equality? Not on Death Row." *Business Week*, June 30, 28.

Korobkin, Russell. 2003. "The Endowment Effect and Legal Analysis." *Northwestern University Law Review* 97:1227–1291.

Korobkin, Russell and Thomas S. Ulen. 2000. "Law and Behavioral Science: Removing the Rationality Assumption from Law and Economics." *California Law Review* 88:1051–1144.

Krivo, Lauren J. and Ruth D. Peterson. 2000. "The Structural Context of Homicide: Accounting for Racial Differences in Process." *American Sociological Review* 65:547–559.

Land, Kenneth C., Patricia L. McCall, and Lawrence Cohen. 1990. "Structural Covariates of Homicides Rates: Are There Any Invariances Across Time and Social Space?" *American Journal of Sociology* 95:922–963.

Lane, J. Mark. 1993. "'Is There Life Without Parole?' A Capital Defendant's Right to a Meaningful Alternative Sentence." *Loyola of Los Angeles Law Review* 26:327–393.

Lardner, George. 2003. "The Role of the Press in the Clemency Process." *Capital University Law Review* 31:179–184.

Layson, Stephen A. 1986. "United States Time-Series Homicide Regressions with Adaptive Expectations." *New York Academy of Medicine Bulletin* 62:589–600.

_____. 1985 "Homicide and Deterrence: A Reexamination of the United States Time-Series Evidence." *Southern Economics Journal* 52:68–89.

Leamer, Edward E. 1983. "Let's Take the Con Out of Econometrics." *The American Economic Review* 73:31–43.

Lewis, Dorothy Otnow, Catherine A. Yeager, Pamela Blake, Barbara Bard, and Maren Strenziok. 2004. "Ethics Questions Raised by the Neuropsychiatric, Neuropsychological, Educational, Developmental, and Family Characteristics of 18 Juveniles Awaiting Execution in Texas." *Journal of the American Academy of Psychiatry and the Law* 32: 408–429.

Liebman, James S., Jeffrey Fagan, Andrew Gelman, Valerie West, Garth Davies, Alexander Kiss. 2002. "A Broken System, Part II: Why There Is So Much Error in Capital Cases, and What Can Be Done About It." (http://www2.law.columbia.edu/brokensystem2/).

Liebman, James S., Jeffrey Fagan, and Valerie West. 2000. "A Broken System, Part I: Error Rates in Capital Cases, 1973–1995." (http://www2.law.columbia.edu/instructionalservices/liebman/).

Liebman, James S, Jeffrey Fagan, Valerie West, and Jonathan Lloyd. 2000. "Capital Attrition: Error Rates in Capital Cases, 1973–1995." *Texas Law Review*, 78:1839–1865.

Link, Bruce G., Ann Stueve, and Jo Phelan. 1998. "Psychotic Symptoms and Violent Behaviors: Probing the Components of 'Threat/Control-Override' Symptoms." *Social Psychiatry and Psychiatric Epidemiology* 33:S55–S60.

Liu, Zhiqiang. 2004. "Capital Punishment and the Deterrence Hypothesis: Some New Insights and Empirical Evidence." *Eastern Economic Journal* 30:237–258.

Luckenbill, David F. 1977. "Criminal Homicide as a Situated Transaction." *Social Problems* 25:176–186.

MacCoun Robert J. and Peter Reuter. 2003. *Drug War Heresies: Learning From Other Vices, Times, and Places.* New York, NY: Cambridge University Press.

Maltz, Michael D. 1999. "Bridging Gaps in Police Crime Data." (http://www.ojp.usdoj.gov/bjs/pub/pdf/bgpcd.pdf).

Maltz, Michael D. and Harald E. Weiss. 2006. "Creating a UCR Utility." Final Report to the National Institute of Justice. (http://www.ncjrs.gov/pdffiles1/nij/grants/215341.pdf).

Marshall, Lawrence C. 2004. "The Innocence Revolution and the Death Penalty." *Ohio State Journal of Criminal Law* 1:573–584.

McAleer, Michael and Michael R. Veall. 1989. "How Fragile Are Fragile Inferences? A Re-Evaluation of the Deterrent Effect of Capital Punishment." *Review of Economics and Statistics* 71:99–106.

McGahey, Richard M. 1980. "Dr. Ehrlich's Magic Bullet: Economic Theory, Econometrics and the Death Penalty." *Crime and Delinquency* 26:485–502.

McManus, Walter S. 1985. "Estimates of the Deterrent Effect of Capital Punishment: The Importance of the Researcher's Prior Beliefs." *Journal of Political Economy* 93:417–425.

Mocan, H. Naci and R. Kaj Gittings. 2003. "Getting Off Death Row: Commuted Sentences and the Deterrent Effect of Capital Punishment." *Journal of Law & Economics* 46:453–478.

Morin, Richard. 2002a. "Murderous Pardons?" *Washington Post*, Dec.15, B5.

_____. 2002b. "Lame Ducks and the Death Penalty?" *Washington Post*, Jan. 20, B5.

Musto, David F. 1995. "Perception and Regulation of Drug Use: The Rise and Fall of the Tide." *Annals of Internal Medicine* 123:468–469.

_____. 1987. *The American Disease: Origins of Narcotic Control*. 3rd ed. New York, NY: Oxford University Press.

Nagin, Daniel. 1998. "Criminal Deterrence Research at the Outset of the Twenty-First Century." *Crime and Justice* 23:1–43.

Nagin, Daniel and Raymond Paternoster. 1994. "Personal Capital and Social Control: The Deterrence Implications of Individual Differences in Criminal Offending." *Criminology* 32:581–606.

Nagin, Daniel S. and Greg Pogarsky. 2001. "Integrating Celerity, Impulsivity, and Extralegal Sanction Threats into a Model of General Deterrence: Theory and Evidence." *Criminology* 39:865–889.

National Center for Health Statistics. 2007. (http://www.cdc.gov/nchs/howto/w2w/w2welcom.htm).

National Institute of Justice. 1998. "Annual Report on Cocaine Use Among Arrestees." NCJ 175657. (http://www.ncjrs.gov/pdffiles1/175657.txt).

Nicholson, Kieran. 2002. "Study: Race, Gender of Governors Affect Death-Row Decisions." *Denver Post*, Dec.19, A17.

O'Kane, James M. 2005. *Wicked Deeds: Murder in America*. New Brunswick, NJ: Transaction Publishers.

Oliver, William. 1994. *The Violent Social World of Black Men*. New York, NY: Lexington Books.

Pallone, Nathaniel J. and James J. Hennessy. 1996. *Tinder-Box Criminal Aggression: Neuropsychology, Demography, Phenomenology*. New Brunswick, NJ: Transaction Publishers.

Papachristos, Andrew V. 2007. "Murder by Structure: Dominance Relations and the Social Structure of Gang Homicide in Chicago" (http://ssrn.com/abstract=855304).

Passell, Peter and John B. Taylor. 1977. "The Deterrent Effect of Capital Punishment: Another View." *American Economic Review* 67:445–451.

Paternoster, Raymond, Robert Brame, Sarah Bacon, and Andrew Ditchfield. 2004. "Justice by Geography and Race: The Administration of the Death Penalty in Maryland, 1978–1999." *Margins: Maryland's Law Journal on Race, Religion, Gender and Class* 4:1–97.

Pennsylvania Department of Corrections. 2000. "Annual Statistical Report 19." (http://www.cor.state.pa.us/stats/lib/stats/Annual%20Report%202000.pdf).

_____. 1999. "Annual Statistical Report 18." (http://www.cor.state.pa.us/stats/lib/stats/ASR1999.pdf).

Pogarsky, Greg and Alex R. Piquero. 2003. "Can Punishment Encourage Offending? Investigating the 'Resetting' Effect." *Journal of Research in Crime and Delinquency* 40:95–120.

Polinsky, A. Mitchell and Steven Shavell. 2007. *"The Theory of Public Enforcement of Law."* Pp. 403–454 in *Handbook of Law and Economics, Volume 1*, edited by A. Mitchell Polinsky and Steven Shavell. Amsterdam: Elsevier Science Publishing.

Polk, Kenneth. 1994. *When Men Kill: Scenarios of Masculine Violence.* Cambridge: Cambridge University Press.

Posner, Richard. 2005. "The Economics of Capital Punishment." (http://www.becker-posner-blog.com/archives/2005/12/the_economics_o.html).

_____. 1975. "The Economic Approach to Law." *Texas Law Review* 53:757–782.

Raine, Adrian, J. Reid Meloy, Susan Bihrle, Jackie Stoddard, Lori Lacasse, and Monte S. Buchsbaum. 1998. "Reduced Prefrontal and Increased Subcortical Brain Functioning Assessed Using Positron Emission Tomography in Predatory and Affective Murderers." *Behavioral Sciences & the Law* 16:319–332.

Rein, Martin and Christopher Winship. 1999. "The Dangers of 'Strong' Causal Reasoning in Social Policy." *Society* 36:38–46.

Robinson, Paul H. and John M. Darley. 2004. "Does Criminal Law Deter? A Behavioral Science Investigation." *Oxford Journal of Legal Studies* 24:173–205.

Rosenfeld, Richard. 2000. "Patterns in Adult Homicide: 1980–1995." Pp. 130–163, in *The Crime Drop in America*, edited by Alfred Blumstein and Joel Wallman. New York, NY: Cambridge University Press.

Ross, Lee and Richard E. Nisbett. 1991. *The Person and the Situation: Perspectives of Social Psychology.* Philadelphia, PA: Temple University Press.

Ruben, Paul. 2006. Statement before *An Examination of the Death Penalty in the United States: Hearing Before the Subcommittee on the Constitution, Civil Rights and Property Rights of the Senate Committee on the Judiciary*, 109th Cong. (http://judiciary.senate.gov/testimony.cfm? id=1745& wit_id=4991).

Rubin, Paul H. 2002. "Study: Death Penalty Deters Scores of Killings." *Atlanta Journal Constitution*, Mar.14, 22A.

Sampson, Robert J. and Janet Lauritsen. 1994. "Violent Victimization and Offending: Individual-, Situational-, and Community-Level Risk Factors." Pp. 1–114 in *Understanding and Preventing Violence: Social Influences*, edited by Albert J. Reiss and Jeffrey A. Roth. Washington, DC: The National Academies Press.

Scheck, Barry, Peter Neufeld, and Jim Dwyer. 2000. *Actual Innocence: Five Days to Execution, and Other Dispatches From the Wrongly Convicted*. New York, NY: Doubleday.

Schirro v. Summerlin (2004). 542 U.S. 348.

Seper, Jerry. 2001. "Garza Executed for Drug Killings: Murderer Makes Deathbed Apology." *Washington Times*, June 20, A3.

Shepherd, Joanna M. 2005. "Deterrence Versus Brutalization: Capital Punishment's Differing Impacts Among States." *Michigan Law Review* 104:203–256.

——————. 2004. Statement Before the Subcommittee on Crime, Terrorism, and Homeland Security of the House Committee on the Judiciary, 108th Cong. 23–28 Hearing on H.R. 2934, the Terrorist Penalties Enhancement Act of 2003.

——————. 2004. "Murders of Passion, Execution Delays, and the Deterrence of Capital Punishment." *Journal of Legal Studies* 33:283–321.

Simon, Herbert A. 1982. "Theories of Bounded Rationality." Pp. 408–423 in *Models of Bounded Rationality, Vol. 2: Behavioral Economics and Business Organization*, edited by Herbert A. Simon. Cambridge, MA: MIT Press.

——————. 1957. "Rational Choice and the Structure of the Environment." Pp. 261–273 in *Models of Man: Social and Rational*, edited by Herbert A. Simon. New York, NY: John Wiley & Sons.

Sorensen, Jonathan and Rocky LeAnn Pilgrim. 2006. *Lethal Injection: Capital Punishment in Texas During the Modern Era*. Austin, TX: University of Texas Press.

South Carolina Department of Corrections. 2005. "Inmate Populations Statistics and Trends, Sentence Length Distribution FY-01-05." (http://www.amazon.com/PublicInformation/StatisticalReports/InmatePopulationsStatsTrend/AsOfTrendSentenceLengthDistributionFY01-05.pdf).

Steiker, Carol S. 2005. "No, Capital Punishment Is Not Morally Required: Deterrence, Deontology, and the Death Penalty." *Stanford Law Review* 58:751–790.

Sunstein, Cass R. 2005. "Group Judgments: Deliberations, Statistical Means, and Information Markets." *New York University Law Review* 80:962–1049.

Sunstein, Cass R. and Adrian Vermeule. 2005. "Is Capital Punishment Morally Required? Acts, Omissions, and Life-Life Tradeoffs." *Stanford Law Review* 8:703–750.

Thaler, Richard H. 1991. *Quasi Rational Economics*. New York, NY: Russell Sage Foundation.

Tversky, Amos and Daniel Kahneman. 1986. "Rational Choice and the Framing of Decisions." *The Journal of Business* 59: S251–S278.

_____. 1974. "Judgment Under Uncertainty: Heuristics and Biases." *Science* 185:1124–1131.

United States Department of Justice, Bureau of Justice Statistics. 2004. "Capital Punishment in the United States, 1973–2002." (http://webapp.icpsr.umich.edu/cocoon/ICPSR-DAS/03958.xml).

_____. 2002. "Bureau of Justice Statistics National Judicial Reporting Program 2002." Inter-University Consortium for Political Science and Social Research. (www.icpsr.com).

Vital Statistics of the United States, Mortality Detail Files, 1968–1992. Inter-University Consortium for Political Science and Social Research, Study No.7632, 6798. (http://www.icpsr.umich.edu/).

Warden, Robert. 2005. "Illinois Death Penalty Reform: How it Happened, What it Promises." *Journal of Criminal Law and Criminology* 95:381–426.

Weisz, Arlene N., Richard M. Tolman, and Daniel G. Saunders. 2000. "Assessing the Risk of Severe Domestic Violence: The Importance of Survivors' Predictions." *Journal of Interpersonal Violence* 15:75–90.

Wilkinson, Deanna L. 2003. *Guns, Violence, and Identity Among African American and Latino Youth*. New York, NY: LFB Scholarly Publishing.

Wilkinson, Deanna L. and Jeffrey Fagan. 2001. "A Theory of Violent Events." Pp. 169–196 in *The Process and Structure of Crime: Criminal Events and Crime Analysis*, edited by Robert F. Meier and Leslie Kennedy. New Brunswick, NJ: Transaction Publishers.

_____. 1996. "The Role of Firearms in Violence 'Scripts': The Dynamics of Gun Events Among Adolescent Males." *Law and Contemporary Problems* 59:55–89.

Williams, Terry. 1989. *The Cocaine Kids: The Inside Story of a Teenage Drug Ring*. New York, NY: Addison Wesley Publishing Company.

Wolfgang, Marvin E. 1958. *Patterns in Criminal Homicide*. Philadelphia, PA: University of Pennsylvania Press.

Wooldridge, Jeffrey M. 2002. *Econometric Analysis of Cross Section and Panel Data*. Cambridge, MA: MIT Press.

Wright, Julian H. Jr. 1990. "Life-Without-Parole: An Alternative to Death or Not Much of a Life at All?" *Vanderbilt Law Review* 43:529–568.

Wright, Richard T. and Scott H. Decker. 1997. *Armed Robbers in Action: Stickups and Street Culture*. Boston, MA: Northeastern University Press.

_____. 1994. *Burglars on the Job: Streetlife and Residential Break-Ins*. Boston, MA: Northeastern University Press.

Young, K. D. S. and L.I. Pettit. 2006. "The Effect of Observations on Bayesian Choice of an Autoregressive Model." *Journal of Time Series Analysis* 27:41–50.

Yunker, James A. 2001. "A New Statistical Analysis of Capital Punishment Incorporating U.S. Postmoratorium Data." *Social Science Quarterly* 82:297–311.

Zimmer, Lynn. 1990. "Proactive Policing Against Street-Level Drug Trafficking." *American Journal of Police* 9:43–74.

———. 1987. "Operation Pressure Point: The Disruption of Street-Level Drug Trade on New York's Lower East Side." Occasional Papers from the Center for Research in Crime and Justice, New York University School of Law, NY.

Zimmerman, Paul R. 2004. "State Executions, Deterrence, and the Incidence of Murder." *Journal of Applied Economics* 7:163–193.

Zimring, Franklin and Gordon Hawkins. 1997. *Crime is Not the Problem: Lethal Violence in America.* New York, NY: Oxford University Press.

Zimring, Franklin, Gordon Hawkins, and Sam Kamin. 2001. *Punishment and Democracy: Three Strikes and You're Out in California.* Oxford: Oxford University Press.

Zimring, Franklin and James Zuehl. 1986. "Victim Injury and Death in Urban Robbery: A Chicago Study." *The Journal of Legal Studies* 15:1–40.

Zorn, Christopher J. W. 1998. "An Analytic and Empirical Examination of Zero-Inflated and Hurdle Poisson Specifications." *Sociological Methods and Research* 26:368–400.

Appendix A

Partial List of Studies Published after 1990 on Deterrent Effects of the Death Penalty

Brumm, Harold J. and Dale O. Cloninger. 1996. "Perceived Risk of Punishment and the Commission of Homicides: A Covariance Structure Analysis." *Journal of Economic Behavior and Organization* 31:1–11.

Cloninger, Dale O. 1992. "Capital Punishment and Deterrence: A Portfolio Approach." *Applied Economics* 24:635–645.

Cloninger, Dale O. and Roberto Marchesini. 2005. "Executions, Moratoriums, Commutations, and Deterrence: The Case of Illinois." Unpublished. (http://econwpa.wustl.edu:8089/eps/le/papers/0507/0507002.pdf).

———. 2001. "Execution and Deterrence: A Quasi-Controlled Group Experiment." *Applied Economics* 35:569–576.

Dezhbakhsh, Hashem, Paul Rubin, and Joanna M. Shepherd. 2003. "Does Capital Punishment Have a Deterrent Effect? New Evidence from Postmoratorium Panel Data." *American Law and Economics Review* 5:344–376.

Dezhbakhsh, Hashem and Joanna M. Shepherd. 2006. "The Deterrent Effect of Capital Punishment: Evidence from a "Judicial Experiment." *Economic Inquiry* 44:512–535.

Katz, Lawrence, Steven D. Levitt, and Ellen Shustorovich. 2003. "Prison Conditions, Capital Punishment, and Deterrence." *American Law and Economics Review* 5:318–343.

Liu, Zhiqiang. 2004. "Capital Punishment and the Deterrence Hypothesis: Some New Insights and Empirical Evidence." *Eastern Economic Journal* 30:237–258.

Mocan, H. Naci and R. Kaj Gittings. 2003. "Getting Off Death Row: Commuted Sentences and the Deterrent Effect of Capital Punishment." *Journal of Law and Economics* 46:453–478.

Shepherd, Joanna M. 2005. "Deterrence versus Brutalization: Capital Punishment's Differing Impacts Among States." *Michigan Law Review* 104:203–256.

_____. 2004. "Murders of Passion, Execution Delays, and the Deterrence of Capital Punishment." *Journal of Legal Studies* 33:283–321.

Sorensen, Jon, Robert Wrinkle, Victoria Brewer, and James Marquart. 1999. "Capital Punishment and Deterrence: Examining the Effect of Executions on Murder in Texas." *Crime and Delinquency* 45:481–493.

Yunker, James A. 2002. "A New Statistical Analysis of Capital Punishment Incorporating U.S. Postmoratorium Data." *Social Science Quarterly* 82:297–311.

Zimmerman, Paul R. 2006. "Estimates of the Deterrent Effect of Alternative Execution Methods in the United States: 1978–2000." *American Journal of Economics and Sociology* 65:909–941.

_____. 2004. "State Executions, Deterrence, and the Incidence of Murder." *Journal of Applied Economics* 7:163–193.

CHAPTER 16

Researching Future Dangerousness

Jon Sorensen

Introduction

Nearing the close of session in 1973, the Texas Legislature reached an odd compromise between the House-sponsored "mandatory" and Senate-sponsored "guided discretion" versions of what was to become the state's new death penalty statute. The resulting "special issues" framework narrowed the circumstances in which a murderer could be deemed eligible for the death penalty. Following a capital murder conviction, jurors were required to address a series of special issues at the sentencing phase of the trial. "Whether there was a probability that the defendant would commit criminal acts of violence that would constitute a continuing threat to society," quickly became the issue that most often determined the fate of a defendant. Requiring a prediction of "future dangerousness" would also become the defining characteristics of, and most hotly debated provision within, the modern Texas death penalty statute (*Barefoot v. Estelle* 1983; *Estelle v. Smith* 1981; *Jurek v. Texas* 1976).

Since that time, other states and the federal government have either explicitly included future dangerousness as an aggravating factor in their capital murder statutes or allowed it as a non-statutory aggravating factor. Similarly, an assertion of a defendant's lack of future dangerousness is relevant as a mitigating circumstance in every jurisdiction with a capital punishment statute (*Lockett v. Ohio* 1978; *Skipper v. South Carolina* 1986). With future dangerousness ubiquitous in capital murder trials, the importance of empirical research in this context is apparent. The availability of objective information concerning the level of threat posed by capital murderers is crucial to juries with whom the responsibility for making individualized determinations of future dangerousness rests. Empirical studies of future dangerousness can also be useful to legislators in their consideration of policy options related to capital punishment. An accurate gauge of the level of violent risk posed by capital murderers is also relevant to correctional administrators who are responsible for making housing, security, classification, and programming decisions.

Under present laws, so few convicted capital murderers ever return to society that the question of whether they are "dangerous" translates, for all practical purposes, into how likely they are to be violent in prison. Reliable scientific assessments of dangerousness, consistent with jurisprudence, currently focus exclusively on future behavior in the prison system when estimating "the probability that the defendant would commit criminal acts of violence that would constitute a continuing threat to society."

The purpose of this chapter is to sketch an agenda for research on future dangerousness and the death penalty. First, the progression of published research in this area is briefly charted. Second, relevant methodological issues are identified and examples provided. Finally, strategies are formulated for the next generation of future dangerousness research.

Prior Studies

Commuted Capital Offenders

Prior to the explicit statutory nexus between future dangerousness and the death penalty, and during an era when capital offenders were more likely to return to society after a term of imprisonment, early research focused on the behavior of offenders released from death row. In the first study of this kind, Giardini and Farrow (1952) gathered data on 197 commuted capital offenders paroled from prisons in 22 states over follow-up periods ranging from one to 38 years. They found that 6% of the paroled offenders committed some type of new offense. Studies of former death-sentenced inmates in New Jersey, Oregon, and New York noted a similarly sparse pattern of re-offending among commuted capital offenders (Bedau 1964, 1965; Stanton 1969). Researchers following up on the behavior of 558 inmates purged from the death rows of 29 states (Illinois excluded) and the District of Columbia in the wake of *Furman v. Georgia* (1972) found that just over one percent killed again while in prison or on parole during 1973–1988 (Marquart and Sorensen 1989). Collectively, the early commutation studies suggested that capital murderers, upon release from death row, did not present a substantial threat of further criminal violence.

While these early commutation studies provided information concerning the relative necessity of using the death penalty to incapacitate capital murderers, the studies have been criticized on a number of grounds. First, the studies were criticized as not being generalizable to the modern era because they included inmates sentenced to death for murder under a broad range of circumstances, and even some who were sentenced to death for armed robbery and rape where no murder resulted. They consequently were not limited to the same types of murderers sentenced under post-*Furman* statutes, wherein death sentences have been restricted to a narrower range of eligible offenses occurring under specific circumstances, such as murders stemming from robberies or the murder of police officers. Responding to this criticism, researchers completed studies on inmates sentenced under post-*Furman* statutes and subsequently released from their death sentences. Those studies also documented low rates of subsequent violent prison misconduct (Marquart, Ekland-Olson, and Sorensen 1989; Reidy, Cunningham, and Sorensen 2001).

Another feature of the early studies makes generalizations to the modern era questionable; one of the major incentives for good prison behavior from the earlier era—parole eligibility—is almost completely lacking now. In most jurisdictions at the time of *Furman*, capital murderers under "life" sentences could expect to serve about 10 to 15 years prior to obtaining discretionary release. One could argue that the existence of parole as an incentive during the earlier era may have held in check the number of violent acts committed by former death row inmates hoping to gain early release from their "life" sentences. Parole provisions for capital murderers formerly available in many states, an impetus for "future dangerousness" aggravators in post-*Furman* capital sentencing schemes, have been considerably restricted since that time. All but two states (Alaska, which does not have the death penalty, and New Mexico, which does) now have life-without-parole (LWOP) as a sentencing option. While the major focus of early studies was recidivism upon release from prison, LWOP makes time spent in the community irrelevant to modern risk calculations. Hence, the question of a capital defendant's future dangerousness has shifted entirely to the level of threat he/she presents to other prisoners and staff members while incarcerated.

Aside from the downward bias in prison violence that may have resulted from capital murderers' hope of favorable consideration in parole hearings, a counteractive influence may inflate estimates of violence potential that attempt to extrapolate from data collected from earlier time periods. Advances in prison management, particularly classification systems that place progressively greater constraints on behavior (*e.g.*, supermax confinement), along with behavioral incentives and broader social changes, have resulted in safer prisons during recent years. For example, the rate of prison homicide declined from 54 per 100,000 inmates in 1980 to four per 100,000 in 2002 (Mumola 2005).

Another issue that arises in the commutation studies is differential attrition from death row. Aside from mass commutations, such as the one resulting from *Furman*, individual commutations have historically denoted something salvageable about the person spared execution. One might reasonably expect a lower level of violent behavior among these inmates than their counterparts whose death sentences were executed. To a lesser degree, the same sort of bias could result in a study of cases reversed by judicial decisions during the modern era (Marquart *et al.* 1989), some of which are based, for instance, on a jury's failure to consider or properly weigh mitigating evidence.

Beyond such potential differences between those released from, and those remaining on death row, two obvious confounds exist in any contemporary study of the behavior of released death row inmates. Age and time served are the strongest inverse correlates of violent misbehavior in prison. Inmates released from death row have spent some period of time incarcerated, albeit on death row, prior to entering the general prison population, and thereby have had time to adjust to the prison environment. Similarly, they have aged while incarcerated. As part of the natural maturation process, fewer acts of violence in the general prison population are to be expected than if the commuted inmates had been sentenced directly to a term of life imprisonment.

Related to the age and time-served confounds is the inability in these studies to include the entire observation period. Inmates are seldom followed through the entirety of their terms in general studies of prison behavior. As such, the inmates' likelihood of continuing, or beginning, to commit violent acts is difficult to estimate beyond the observed period. More insidious, however, is the practice of beginning the observation period at some stage during an ongoing process. Commutation studies that dealt only with parole behavior could not count dangerous acts committed during incarceration (*e.g.*, Sorensen, Marquart, and Bodapati 1990). Even when prison behavior was considered, the observation period in commutation studies was, with one exception (Reidy *et al.* 2001), limited to inmates' time spent in the general prison population, exclusive of time spent on death row. Violent acts committed outside the observation period thus were not counted, which could have resulted in a miscalculation of the prevalence or frequency of violence among the samples. One way to overcome this problem is to examine the behavior of death-sentenced inmates upon their initial entrance to death row.

Inmates under a Sentence of Death

Two studies have examined the behavior of inmates on Texas' death row. In the first, researchers studying the behavior of 421 death-sentenced inmates between 1974 and 1988 found that just over 10% had assaulted prison staff or inmates (Marquart, Ekland-Olson, and Sorensen 1994). In the second, John Edens and colleagues (2005) followed-up on the subsequent prison behavior of 155 Texas death-sentenced murderers; in each case an expert witness had testified that the defendant represented a "continuing threat to society." Employing a more restrictive definition of dangerous behavior, they found that just over 5% were involved in serious assaultive behavior during an average stay of 10 years on death row (Edens *et al.*).

Because these studies considered the behavior of death-sentenced inmates from the beginning of their sentences, they were not beset with some of the problems inherent in commutation studies. Their main methodological weakness results from the restricted environment of death row settings in most jurisdictions. When death-sentenced inmates serve time under conditions of super-maximum security confinement (single-celled; recreated individually; cuffed, searched and escorted outside of cells), their opportunity to commit violent acts is severely curtailed. Extrapolations based on inmates' death row behavior therefore would likely underestimate their violence potential in the general prison population.

The super-maximum security conditions under which most death-sentenced inmates serve time, however, have not been universal. Historical examples exist where inmates under a sentence of death were removed from the strict confines of death row without incident (Murton and Hyams 1969). Prior to 1999, death row confinement in Texas included two separate classifications, one of which allowed death-sentenced inmates to work in a self-contained garment factory on death row. Although sparsely supervised in a factory with dangerous weapons readily at their disposal (*e.g.*, scissors capable of cutting cloth), and allowed to congregate outside their cells for recreation and buffet-style food service, these inmates were involved in few incidents of violence (Sorensen and Marquart 1989).

Currently, Missouri is the only state that has a "mainstreamed" death-sentenced population. Death-sentenced inmates are intermixed in Potosi Correctional Center side-by-side with other maximum security inmates sharing the same conditions of confinement and levels of restriction on movement (Lombardi, Sluder, and Wallace 1997). A recent study, which posed the question, *Is Death Row Obsolete?*, found that Missouri death-sentenced inmates were no more likely to commit acts of violent misconduct than other inhabitants of Potosi (Cunningham, Reidy, and Sorensen 2005).

A criticism of these studies, as well as those described in the previous section, concerns the possibility that the death penalty itself influenced current or former death row inmates' behavior. The behavior of inmates under a sentence of death could be influenced by their hope of winning a life sentence on re-trial. Aware that good behavior on death row would bolster the case that they no longer present a danger to others, death-sentenced inmates have an unusually strong incentive to behave. Beyond this incentive, the death penalty itself could represent a "treatment effect." Current and former death row inhabitants have had the unique experience of living under a sentence of death, which alone could account for changes in their behavior. By studying the behavior of those sentenced directly to a term of life imprisonment, researchers are able to gauge the potential for future violent acts in prison among murderers who are spared a death sentence from the start.

Murderers Sentenced to Terms of Imprisonment

Various studies have examined prison behavior in an effort to determine the extent of dangerous acts committed by murderers spared a death sentence. Those employing the broadest samples compare the behavior of inmates convicted of homicide versus those convicted of other offenses. Researchers recently compared the disciplinary records of murderers to other inmates housed in the Florida Department of Corrections (FDOC) (Sorensen and Cunningham forthcoming). They found that murderers did not represent a disproportionate threat of violence to other inmates and staff. While murderers constituted 18.6% of the stock population of 51,527 inmates serving sentences the entire 2003 calendar year, they accounted for 17.7% of assaults, 19.4% of assaults resulting in any injury, and 15.8% of assaults resulting in serious injury. The rate of violence among murderers was almost identical to that of the remainder of the stock population, with assaultive behavior occurring at a rate of three per 100 inmates, assaults with any injuries at five per 1,000, and assaults resulting in serious injuries at two per 1,000.

The advantage of this type of study is the large sample size, which allows for greater stability in estimating base rates, identifying correlates, partitioning variance among predictors, and performing actuarial analyses. Further, the inclusion of inmates convicted of any degree of homicide ensures that all offenders for whom the death penalty was even a remote possibility were included. Therein lies one of the major weaknesses; the sample may be too inclusive. The crimes committed by incarcerated homicide offenders often did not meet the legal requirements of capital crimes. As such, these inmates may not represent the most appropriate group from which to extrapolate the likely behavior of death-sentenced offenders if they had been given an alternate sentence.

The Florida study supports the view that at least some homicide offenders are inappropriate for inclusion in an estimation sample. The rate of violent behavior was not consistent across all degrees of homicide conviction. While those convicted of first- and second-degree murder had similar rates of violent rule infractions, those convicted of lesser homicides (*e.g.*, manslaughter) had lower rates of violent rule infractions. Both studies of the behavior of incarcerated Texas homicide offenders, one examining violent acts occurring during the 1990s (Sorensen and Pilgrim 2000) and another examining violent acts during 2001–2003 (Sorensen and Cunningham 2007), found that inmates convicted of lesser homicides committed violent acts at lower levels than those convicted of murder. The studies split, however, on the issue of whether capital murderers had higher levels of violent misconduct than those convicted of simple murder. The earlier study found that the rates were similar and the latter study found that capital murderers were more violent. While the earlier study did not show capital murderers to be more dangerous across-the-board than non-capital murderers, the researchers did find some characteristics of capital murder (multiple victims, contemporaneous robbery/burglary) to be related to higher rates of violent rule infractions. The latter study did not control for these characteristics when it examined the relationship between degree of murder and violent prison infractions.

Overall, these studies suggest that base rates should be extrapolated from a more limited sample of inmates convicted of murder or capital (first-degree) murder, while the search for correlates, partitioning of variance among predictors, and performance of actuarial analyses may appropriately be completed on a broader sample of homicide offenders. What has not been discerned from these studies is how an inmate serving a life sentence without the possibility of parole is likely to behave in prison. One may intuitively expect that inmates sentenced to LWOP, who thus lack the prospect of freedom as an incentive to comply with rules, would be more recalcitrant and violent in prison than incarcerated murderers generally.

Several studies of LWOP inmates' institutional behavior do not support this assumption. One study found that the rate of assaultive rule infractions among 323 first-degree murderers sentenced to LWOP in Missouri, six per 100 annually, was identical to that of inmates serving life-with-parole during 1977–1992 (Sorensen and Wrinkle 1996). The study of mainstreamed death-sentenced prisoners described above found the rate of assaultive behavior among 1,054 first-degree murderers sentenced to LWOP to be far lower than other inhabitants of Potosi Correctional Center during 1991–2001 (Cunningham *et al.* 2005). Another study found the rate of violent rule infractions among 1,897 LWOP inmates in Florida during 1998–2003 to be similar to that of other long-term, high-security inmates (Cunningham and Sorensen 2006).

Even samples restricted to LWOP inmates might be considered overly inclusive when attempting to assess threats that would be posed to the prison community if inmates currently sentenced to death were instead imprisoned for life. After all, in a death penalty jurisdiction, a defendant's potential for future dangerousness is a consideration, even if implicit, in every capital murder case. One might expect that prosecutors are more likely to seek the death penalty, and jurors more likely to impose it, when the defendant presents a threat of future dangerousness. If death sentences accurately identify those most likely to commit acts of violence in the future, then the worst prospects have been preemptively culled from the LWOP pool. As such, even the behavior of LWOP inmates might not be an accurate gauge of how death-sentenced inmates may behave had they not been subjected to the rigors of death row confinement and executed.

There is one group of LWOP inmates, however, for whom this criticism is less applicable, those whose propensity for future dangerousness was asserted by prosecutors, but who received a sentence of LWOP rather than the death penalty. A recent study of capital murderers sentenced to LWOP in the federal system between 1991 and 2005 examined the prison conduct of inmates based on whether future dangerousness was alleged by the government when a notice to seek the death penalty was filed (Cunningham, Reidy, and Sorensen forthcoming). The U.S. Department of Justice alleged future dangerousness (*i.e.*, there is a probability the defendant would commit criminal acts of violence that would constitute a continuing threat to society) as a non-statutory aggravating circumstance in 104 out of 145 cases. The likelihood of various levels of violent outcomes in prison, from any violations to assaults resulting in injuries, was examined for offenders in all cases. When other relevant variables (*e.g.*, age, felony-related murder) were held constant, an allegation of future dangerousness was not a significant predictor of violent outcome in any of the models. Allegations of future dangerousness by prosecutors appear to have little relationship to the prison behavior of capital murderers.

The findings from the studies that focus on murderers not sentenced to death, like the findings concerning the behavior of offenders under sentence of death and offenders whose death sentences were commuted, suggest that defendants sentenced to death do not pose a disproportionate threat of criminal violence to other inmates and staff. That is, the modern prison system appears to be capable of restricting capital murderers' "dangerousness" to a level on par with other inmates housed under similar conditions.

Methodological Issues

Operational Definitions of Future Dangerousness and Their Effect on Base Rates

In defining future dangerousness, some researchers have included any type of inmate disciplinary infraction that has the potential to result in a violent outcome, such as possession of a weapon, rioting, escape (actual or attempted), and threatening to inflict harm. Such a broad definition can inflate the perceived dangerousness of incarcerated murderers. An expansive definition of "serious prison violence," in part, led DeLisi and Munoz (2003) to erroneously conclude that death-sentenced inmates were more dangerous than other inmates serving lesser sentences in the Arizona Department of Corrections. DeLisi and Munoz (2003) referred to their outcome measure as the "sum of eight criminal offenses roughly commensurate with the Part I Index Offenses in the *Uniform Crime Reports* [including] murder, rape, rioting, hostage taking, aggravated assault, escape, arson, and weapons possession" (p. 294). They failed to mention, however, their inclusion of mutually consensual fights and threats, although these offenses made up nearly half of their samples' total "serious prison violence." An independent review of the disciplinary histories of 127 Arizona inmates on death row in 2003 revealed that the "weapons/contraband" offenses (coded "A09" pursuant to Arizona Department of Corrections regulations) represented fully two-thirds of that subgroup's disciplinary violations categorized as "serious prison violence" by DeLisi and Munoz (Cunningham, Sorensen, and Reidy 2004).

The choice of operational definition has obvious consequences for studying inmate misconduct; the level of potential threat posed by capital murderers in prison will depend to a large extent on this definition. The study examining the behavior of federal inmates sentenced to LWOP for capital murder serves as an example (Cunningham *et al.* forthcoming). When an expansive definition of future dangerousness similar to that employed by DeLisi and Munoz was used, the annual rate of "potentially violent misconduct" was 147 per 1,000 inmates. However, this definition included many offenses for which, although the potential for violence was present, the likelihood of a violent outcome was much less certain, such as weapon violations and threats. Weapons may be held for defensive or deterrent purposes rather than to perpetrate an assault on another inmate. Inmates threatening bodily harm are typically "blowing off steam" rather than announcing intentions of an imminent violent attack. When these offenses and "fights" involving mutually consenting combatants were excluded from consideration, the rate of assaultive misconduct decreased to 56 per 1,000 inmates annually. While assaultive disciplinary infractions typically involve overt acts of violence, the seriousness of the assaults and the resulting harm varies from no injury to serious injury or even death. When the Federal Bureau of Prisons classification of serious (100 level) assaults was utilized, the rate of assaultive behavior decreased to 17 per 1,000 inmates annually. When restricted to assaults resulting in "moderate injuries" (warranting hospital treatment), the rate decreased to 1.1 per 1,000 inmates annually. When only those offenses resulting in "major injuries" (life threatening injuries or death) were considered, the rate dropped to zero. Changing operational definitions of future dangerousness in the federal LWOP study resulted in base rates that varied dramatically from the least to most restrictive definitions.

Further disaggregation of "officially" labeled serious assaultive behavior is warranted. A recent study of violent rule misconduct committed by a cohort of non-death sentenced capital murderers in Texas found a high rate of assault committed against officers, 84 per 1,000 inmates annually during February 2001 through May 2004 (Cunningham and Sorensen forthcoming). However, other indicators in the database revealed that these assaults were not as serious as one may suspect. For instance, one indicator revealed that only seven of the 27 assaults involved weapons, while another, "CH," revealed that most of the assaults with weapons actually involved the "chunking" of some substance rather than an assault with a shank. In fact, none of the assaults on staff resulted in serious injuries. Of the nine assaults listed as resulting in serious injuries, all were committed against an inmate, and only one involved the use of a weapon. Further, most of the inmate-on-inmate violations carried an additional "FT" descriptor, which indicated that the inmates involved in these incidents were mutual combatants caught "fighting." Without consulting actual incident and hearing reports, it is difficult to ascertain the actual culpability of a particular offender and the extent of injury resulting from the violation.

Choice of Comparison or Control Groups

Considering whether the rate of assault among convicted capital murderers is high or low may depend on the comparison group selected, such as the entire population of inmates, inmates housed under similar conditions of maximum security, incarcerated murderers, or some other subset. A comparison to the entire population of inmates may seem unreasonable because many are housed under less severe conditions of confinement and are under less scrutiny; hence, they have more opportunities to commit violent acts. On the other hand, inmates serving time in lower custody levels are typically there because they have committed less serious crimes or have proven themselves trustworthy throughout their incarceration. As such, these prisoners may be expected to be involved in less violence. The latter assumption is generally supported by the empirical evidence. Still, one may ask whether it is fair to compare the behavior of a capital murderer who is given an alternative to the death sentence to average, run-of-the-mill inmates. Perhaps the more appropriate comparison group would be other long-term inmates or murderers housed under similar conditions of confinement. This comparison raises problems of its own, mainly related to the differential attrition of better-behaved inmates into lower custody levels, and eventual release to society, along with the co-occurring selective migration of "bad actors" to higher security levels.

A recent study by DeLisi and Munoz (2003) illustrates how selection of a comparison group and related nonequivalent conditions of confinement can bias the results of an analysis. Their study searched for correlates of future dangerousness among a sample of 1,005 Arizona inmates sentenced to determinate, life, or death sentences. The authors concluded that death-sentenced inmates posed a greater danger in the prison system than inmates serving other sentences. One of the major problems with the comparison under scrutiny, however, was that unequal conditions of confinement had not been considered. Death-sentenced inmates in Arizona serve their sentences under a much different custodial regimen than most of the remaining comparison sample of general population inmates.

To determine whether death-sentenced inmates were truly more dangerous than other inmates would require utilizing a suitable group of inmates serving time under similarly restrictive conditions of confinement for comparison, a feat achieved in the study of mainstreamed death-sentenced inmates at Missouri's Potosi Correctional Center (Cunningham *et al.* 2005). The Potosi study, however, did suffer from the methodological weakness of including a nonequivalent comparison group due to the selective migration of bad actors to higher security levels. The comparison to LWOP inmates, who had rates of violent misconduct similar to the death-sentenced inmates, was reasonable because all LWOP inmates had to remain in Potosi throughout their entire term of incarceration. The comparison to other inmates who had worked their way up to Potosi or failed to work their way down to a lower custody level resulted in a somewhat biased comparison, with that group of term-sentenced inmates having a yearly rate of assaultive violent misconduct five times higher than those sentenced to death or LWOP.

In analyzing the behavior of murderers in the Florida Department of Corrections (FDOC) during 2003, potential problems with utilizing the remainder of the prison stock population as a comparison group were cataloged (Sorensen and Cunningham forthcoming). First, the possibility of differential attrition between murderers and the comparison group was at issue because of the comparison group's greater potential for early release based on good behavior. At any given point in time, the stock population from which the comparison group was drawn consisted of legions of newly admitted, youthful, short-term prisoners who were more prone to rule violations, as well as those who had failed to behave well enough to attain release. Murderers in the stock population, however, were less subject to this process of attrition, and as a result tended to be older, more settled, and predictably better behaved in the prison population. To control for differential attrition, a second analysis limited the comparison to a cohort of murderers versus other inmates entering the FDOC during the previous year, 2002. This comparison still did not account for the possibility that differences in behavior between murderers and the remainder of the entering cohort could be due to their serving time under different conditions of confinement. To eliminate initial custody classification as a potential confound, a third analysis limited the comparison to murderers and other inmates in the entering cohort who were initially classified to the highest security level. Although the use of any comparison group has shortcomings, showing that murderers were no more likely to commit violent acts in prison regardless of the comparison group strengthened the study's conclusion.

Utilizing Agency Records

Studies of future dangerousness have been based exclusively on data gathered from correctional agencies. As with all "official data," prison records may reflect errors, omissions, and other complications. Unlike a self-report or victimization survey, official records are prone to reflect differences in enforcement and reporting practices. While this is particularly true regarding one of the more expansive operational definitions of future dangerousness, even the most serious forms of prison violence may be misrepresented in the records.

In the Florida studies described above, for instance, gradations of assault were discerned from an injury indicator. A weakness not overcome regarding the database, however, was that the injury indicator was not specific about who caused the harm. While most of the time an inmate charged with an assault presumably would have caused the resulting harm, an injury code would be indicated in the inmate's electronic file even if the one charged with the assault had sustained the injury at the hands of another inmate or guard.

When studying the behavior of individual inmates, a related problem arises. One assaultive incident involving several inmates may be counted as several separate assaults, once again inflating the levels of violence recorded among a sample. Of course, reverting to the original incident or disciplinary hearing reports could clear up these problems (Cunningham *et al.* forthcoming), although those reports are often unavailable or difficult to obtain.

When utilizing a database or performing a manual search of inmate files, it is nearly impossible to detect certain omissions. For example, instances of violence that do not directly affect prison staff or inmates as victims may not be included as disciplinary misconduct. Capital murderers, particularly those under a sentence of death, often spend a significant amount of time in local jails awaiting appeal outcomes, re-trials, or re-sentencing hearings. Often less closely guarded in local jails, they have a greater opportunity to commit violent acts. At the same time, jail misconduct records do not always migrate to prison records. When they do, assaultive behavior occurring in local jails may translate into prison files as new crimes rather than disciplinary offenses.

Even within the prison system, some violent acts prosecuted as crimes may not be coded as disciplinary violations. In rare occurrences, capital murderers have been charged with crimes ranging from escape to ordering a "hit" by cell phone on an informant in the free world. Due to the structure of agency databases, where inmate-specific, conviction-related, and disciplinary misconduct information are typically held in separate electronic files, some instances of violence may be overlooked. Although it may be possible to match these files by identifying numbers, the hierarchical structure of the databases and different levels of data aggregation can lead to errors when the files are combined. Following these records longitudinally is an especially daunting task. Attempting to account for changes in housing assignments and security levels and their effect on an inmate's violent misconduct, for instance, would require time as well as considerable extraction and programming skills.

In their study of Arizona inmates, DeLisi and Munoz (2003) counted acts of misconduct committed by inmates during *prior* incarcerations as occurring during the *current* period of incarceration, the relevant observation period. This practice led to numerous errors in the analysis, including the misspecifications of time-at-risk and misinterpretation of the influence of predictors measured during the inmates' current incarceration—most importantly the relationship between the sentence being served (*i.e.*, a death sentence) and violent outcomes.

Individualizing Predictions Based on Specific Inmate Characteristics

Additional concerns arise in attempting to individualize a prediction of future dangerousness based on specific inmate characteristics. In death penalty trials across the United States, experts are called on to make assessments concerning the threat of future dangerousness, or lack thereof, posed by capital murder defendants. Few of them, however, anchor their estimates in base rates or rely on proven predictors; rather, they typically make predictions based on their own experience as clinicians (Cunningham and Reidy 1999). Consistent with general research on clinical predictions, Edens *et al.* (2005) found positive predictions of future violent behavior made by clinicians in death penalty cases to be wrong most of the time. Because many murderers have psychological profiles indicative of severe pathologies, such as antisocial personality disorder, psychometric instruments are not very useful for making predictions about violent outcomes in prison.

Nonetheless, as death penalty trials continue to involve the propensity for future dangerousness as an aggravator, or the lack thereof as a mitigator, expert testimony will continue to be utilized in this context. The empirical issues that arise concern how accurately, and on what basis, such an assessment can be made. While the best predictor of future behavior is an anamnestic one based on an individual's previous behavior, such predictions are context-specific. Bad acts generally do not necessarily translate into unruly behavior in prison, so free-world behavior must be used cautiously in making predictions about behavior in a controlled environment where access to alcohol, weapons, and vulnerable victims is restricted. A defendant's behavior during a previous incarceration or in jail awaiting trial is much more useful in making an anamnestic prediction, but often inmates have only a short track record in prison or jail from which to extrapolate their potential for future dangerousness. Inmates who are undergoing re-sentencing, and who have often spent a decade or more under various custodial regimes, are an exception, although their behavior during that period arguably could be influenced by their hopes of obtaining a new trial and a different outcome.

The actuarial method can also be used to estimate an inmate's likelihood of future dangerousness. In an actuarial prediction, a defendant is compared to other inmates who are already serving time and have a behavioral track record in prison. The matched group's characteristics and record of violent misconduct are used to estimate the level of violent threat posed by a particular capital murder defendant. The accuracy of such predictions depends on several factors. First, the smaller the base rate of violence (more restrictive definition), the more difficult it typically is to make a reliable prediction of violence. Second, the accuracy of an assessment depends on identifying reliable predictor variables associated with a violent outcome. Finally, a scale constructed from the predictors will vary in its ability to discriminate among cases based on the likelihood of a violent outcome.

A study of a cohort of Texas capital murderers provides an example (Cunningham and Sorensen forthcoming). A simple additive scale was used that assigned inmates one point for each of the following risk factors: prior prison incarceration, contemporaneous robbery or burglary, under the age of 35, and an additional point if under the age of 21. Although the sample size was small (N=136), the span of time at risk short (six to 40 months), and the predictor variables few, the predictive ability of the scale was among the most powerful noted in this type of research. Cases were sorted into three risk levels: high (3–4), average (2), and low (0–1). Nearly 60% of those in the highest risk category committed "potentially violent" rule infractions, but only 25% committed assaultive violations, and only 12% committed assaults resulting in serious injuries. Inmates in the lowest risk category committed potentially violent acts 10% of the time, and none of them engaged in assaultive acts during their incarceration.

While a scale such as the one described above sorts capital defendants into risk categories reasonably well, making predictions based on such an actuarial analysis nevertheless suffers from limitations. First, the probability of a capital defendant being involved in dangerous acts depends to a large degree on the operational definition of such acts. Second, estimating the probability of dangerous acts over a lifetime of incarceration is difficult because the observed period of time at risk is typically only a few years. Third, making a prediction of future dangerousness will always result in a large number of false positives because the base rate of serious forms of prison violence is quite low.

Given these limitations, the use of actuarial data is best restricted to depicting group base rates and relative probabilities using various operational definitions. Relying on the Texas data described above, for instance, one could say that a low-risk capital murder defendant is about one-third as likely to be involved in potentially violent acts as the average capital murder defendant (10.3% vs. 29.1% prevalence during the observation period).

Toward the Next Generation of Future Dangerousness Research

While empirical findings on future dangerousness appear to be consistent, most of these studies have been completed in Texas, Missouri, and Florida. Unique opportunities exist in other jurisdictions to advance the literature about future dangerousness. The mass commutation of Illinois death-sentenced inmates by Governor Ryan and the nationwide reversal of death sentences due to *Atkins v.* Virginia (2002) and *Roper v. Simmons* (2005) provide excellent opportunities to study the behavior of former death row inmates. The Illinois commutations include an entire population of death-sentenced inmates and thus, unlike reversals, an unbiased cross-section of modern-era former death row inmates. The reversals resulting from *Atkins* and *Roper* provide an opportunity to observe the behavior of high-risk (mentally retarded and youthful) subsets of former death row inmates across jurisdictions. It would be interesting to see how correctional officials in various states have assimilated these inmates into general prison populations, and whether differences in housing and security precautions affect their levels of institutional misbehavior.

Less dramatic natural experiments occur in every death penalty jurisdiction, providing an opportunity to examine issues related to future dangerousness. For instance, Texas recently replaced its former "life" sentence for capital murderers with LWOP. How prosecutors, defense attorneys, jurors, and defendants have responded to this policy change has not yet been fully analyzed. Such studies need not be limited to quantitative analyses measuring behavioral outcomes. Qualitative research is useful to examine the process by which prosecutors, clinicians, and jurors make decisions about a defendant's potential for future dangerousness (Blume, Garvey, and Johnson 2001).

Although many studies have measured the rate and correlates of prison violence, little is known about the context in which prison violence occurs. Where available, incident-level prison violence data could provide a more detailed picture of prison violence, including its precursors, actual level of resulting harm, and the characteristics and patterns of behavior among chronic offenders and victims. Such a detailed description or typology of the most extreme form of prison violence—murder—could be especially informative because little is known about the circumstances surrounding such events (Merillat, 2006; Porporino, Doherty, and Sawatsky 1987; Ralph and Marquart 1991).

The study of broader penological issues, including modern classification, safety procedures, and the conditions of confinement under which long-term inmates or troublesome inmates are housed is valuable for determining the effectiveness of practices designed to control potentially violent or disruptive behavior. In a recent study undertaken to inventory current knowledge about supermax prisons, Mears and Watson (2006) devote most attention to outlining a research agenda because so little is known about these institutions (*see also* Briggs, Sundt, and Castellano 2003). In-depth studies of these institutions along the lines suggested by Mears and Watson (2006) could dispel the "powder keg" myth that surrounds the housing of prisoners with "nothing to lose."

Finally, researchers should focus more attention on LWOP. In light of the number of inmates under sentence of LWOP—33,633 at the end of 2003 (Mauer, King, and Young 2004)—and since LWOP is the primary alternative to the death penalty, it is surprising how little research has been completed on this sentence. A host of factors related to the operation of LWOP are important areas for empirical research. Cross-jurisdictional and longitudinal research could provide insights into whether the availability of the death penalty, as opposed to LWOP, influences individual case outcomes (Kuziemko 2006), including convicted murderers' propensity to engage in prison violence. Through intensive case studies of the machinations of LWOP in non-death penalty jurisdictions, researchers may also gain insight into what occurs when capital punishment is unavailable.

A major limitation of existing research examining the behavior of LWOP inmates is that all studies were completed in death-penalty jurisdictions. It is unknown whether these findings would apply in jurisdictions that have abolished capital punishment. Studies restricted to death-penalty jurisdictions cannot rule out the possibility that the availability of the capital sanction may be effectively restraining LWOP inmates' violent tendencies, thus resulting in lower rates of violence than would be evidenced if that sanction were not available. Studies utilizing the full spectrum of research designs should be employed in an effort to estimate how LWOP inmates may behave when capital punishment is not an available sanction.

References

Atkins v. Virginia (2002). 536 U.S. 304.
Barefoot v. Estelle (1983). 463 U.S. 880.
Bedau, Hugo A. 1965. "Capital Punishment in Oregon, 1903–1964." *Oregon Law Review* 45:1–39.
_____. 1964. "Death Sentences in New Jersey, 1907–1960." *Rutgers Law Review* 19:1–55.
Blume, John H., Stephen P. Garvey and Sheri L. Johnson. 2001. "Future Dangerousness in Capital Cases: Always 'At Issue.'" *Cornell University Law Review* 86:397–410.
Briggs, Chad S., Jody L. Sundt, and Thomas C. Castellano. 2003. "The Effect of Supermaximum Security Prisons on Aggregate Levels of Institutional Violence." *Criminology* 41:1341–1376.
Cunningham, Mark D. and Thomas J. Reidy. 1999. "Don't Confuse Me with the Facts: Common Errors in Violence Risk Assessment at Capital Sentencing." *Criminal Justice and Behavior* 26:20–43.
Cunningham, Mark D., Thomas J. Reidy, and Jon R. Sorensen. Forthcoming. "Assertions of 'Future Dangerousness' at Federal Capital Sentencing: Rates and Correlates of Subsequent Prison Misconduct." *Law and Human Behavior*.

_____. 2005. "Is Death Row Obsolete? A Decade of Mainstreaming Death-Sentenced Inmates in Missouri." *Behavioral Sciences and the Law* 23:307–320.

Cunningham, Mark D. and Jon R. Sorensen. Forthcoming. "Capital Offenders in Texas Prisons: Rates, Correlates, and an Actuarial Analysis of Violent Misconduct." *Law and Human Behavior*.

_____. 2006. "Nothing to Lose? A Comparative Examination of Prison Misconduct Rates Among Life-Without-Parole and Other Long-Term High-Security Inmates." *Criminal Justice and Behavior* 33:683–705.

Cunningham, Mark D., Jon R. Sorensen, and Thomas J. Reidy. 2004. "Revisiting Future Dangerousness Revisited: Response to DeLisi and Munoz." *Criminal Justice Policy Review* 15:365–376.

DeLisi, Matt and Ed A. Munoz. 2003. "Future Dangerousness Revisited." *Criminal Justice Policy Review* 14:287–305.

Edens, John F., Jacqueline K. Buffington-Vollum, Andrea Keileen, Phillip Roskamp, and Christine Anthony. 2005. "Predictions of Future Dangerousness in Capital Murder Trials: Is It Time to 'Disinvent the Wheel?'" *Law and Human Behavior* 29:55–86.

Estelle v. Smith (1981). 451 U.S. 454.

Furman v. Georgia (1972). 408 U.S. 238.

Giardini, Giovanni I. and R.G. Farrow. 1952. "The Paroling of Capital Offenders." *The Annals* 284:85–94.

Jurek v. Texas (1976). 428 U.S. 153.

Kuziemko, Ilyana. 2006. "Does the Threat of the Death Penalty Affect Plea Bargaining in Murder Cases? Evidence from New York's Reinstatement of Capital Punishment." *American Law and Economics Review* 18:116–142.

Lockett v. Ohio (1978). 438 U.S. 604.

Lombardi, George, Richard D. Sluder, and Donald Wallace. 1997. "Mainstreaming Death-Sentenced Inmates: The Missouri Experience and Its Legal Significance." *Federal Probation* 61:3–11.

Marquart, James W., Sheldon Ekland-Olson, and Jonathan R. Sorensen. 1994. *The Rope, The Chair, and the Needle: Capital Punishment in Texas, 1923–1990*. Austin, TX: University of Texas Press.

_____. 1989. "Gazing into the Crystal Ball: Can Jurors Accurately Predict Dangerousness in Capital Cases?" *Law & Society Review* 23:449–468.

Marquart, James W. and Jonathan R. Sorensen. 1989. "A National Study of the Furman-Commuted Inmates: Assessing Threat to Society from Capital Offenders." *Loyola of Los Angeles Law Review* 23:5–28.

Mauer, Mark, Ryan S. King, and Malcolm C. Young. 2004. *The Meaning of "Life": Long Prison Sentences in Context*. Washington DC: The Sentencing Project.

Mears, Daniel P. and Jamie Watson. 2006. "Towards a Fair and Balanced Assessment of Supermax Prisons." *Justice Quarterly* 23:232–270.

Merillat, A.P. 2006. "The Question of Future Dangerousness of Capital Defendants." *Texas Bar Journal* 69: 738–741.

Mumola, Christopher J. 2005. *Suicide and Homicide in State Prisons and Local Jails.* Washington DC: Bureau of Justice Statistics.

Murton, Tom and Joe Hyams. 1969. *Accomplices to the Crime: The Arkansas Prison Scandal.* New York, NY: Grove Press.

Porporino, Frank J., Phyllis D. Doherty, and Terrence Sawatsky. 1987. "Characteristics of Homicide Victims and Victimizations in Prison: A Canadian Perspective." *International Journal of Offender Therapy and Comparative Criminology* 31:125–136.

Ralph, Paige H. and James W. Marquart. 1991. "Gang Violence in Texas Prisons." *Prison Journal* 71:38–49.

Reidy, Thomas J., Mark D. Cunningham, and Jon R. Sorensen. 2001. "From Death to Life: Prison Behavior of Former Death Row Inmates." *Criminal Justice and Behavior* 28:62–82.

Roper v. Simmons (2005). 543 U.S. 551.

Skipper v. South Carolina (1986). 476 U.S. 1.

Sorensen, Jon R. and Mark D. Cunningham. Forthcoming. "Conviction Offense and Prison Violence: A Comparative Study of Murderers and Other Offenders." *Crime and Delinquency.*

_____. 2007. "Operationalizing Risk: The Influence of Measurement Choice on the Prevalence and Correlates of Prison Violence Among Incarcerated Murderers." *Journal of Criminal Justice* 35:546–555.

Sorensen, Jonathan R. and James W. Marquart. 1989. "Working the Dead." Pp. 169–177 in *Facing the Death Penalty,* edited by Michael L. Radelet. Philadelphia, PA: Temple University Press.

Sorensen, Jonathan R., James W. Marquart, and Madhava Bodapati. 1990. "Two Decades After People v. Anderson." *Loyola of Los Angeles Law Review* 24:45–55.

Sorensen, Jonathan R. and Rocky L. Pilgrim. 2000. "An Actuarial Risk Assessment of Violence Posed by Capital Murder Defendants." *Journal of Criminal Law and Criminology* 90:1251–1270.

Sorensen, Jon R. and Robert D. Wrinkle. 1996. "No Hope for Parole: Disciplinary Infractions Among Death-Sentenced and Life-Without-Parole Inmates." *Criminal Justice and Behavior* 23:542–552.

Stanton, John M. 1969. "Murderers on Parole." *Crime & Delinquency* 15:149–155.

CHAPTER 17

CAPITAL PUNISHMENT AND THE FAMILIES OF VICTIMS AND DEFENDANTS

Margaret Vandiver[1]

Introduction

This chapter addresses the need for research on two closely related questions: the effect of the death penalty on the families of homicide victims and on the families of homicide offenders. We probably know less about this area than about any other important aspect of capital punishment. The emotional and political salience of the topic and the lack of research combine to encourage strong opinions and beliefs that may or may not be accurate, but are deeply held and frequently expressed.

The modern death penalty in America has failed to deliver its desired effects (*e.g.*, deterrence, incapacitation) and its administration has been wracked with problems (*e.g.*, racial disparities, arbitrary sentencing, wrongful convictions), all at great cost of money and resources (for an overview of these issues, see Acker, Bohm, and Lanier 2003). Thus, the question of the effect of capital punishment on families assumes particular importance. If the death penalty consistently provides victims' families with solace unobtainable through other punishments, then it offers a benefit that can be weighed against its failings in other areas. Any such benefit would have to be weighed as well against the cost of the death penalty to the families of offenders.

---

1. The author thanks the editors of this volume for their helpful comments and suggestions on this chapter.

Research on the effects of capital punishment on families of victims and offenders presents a number of challenges, some of which may never be fully met. Nonetheless, thoughtful, well-designed, and systematic research has recently significantly increased what we know about families of condemned prisoners and can be expected to do the same for families of victims.

This chapter presents a brief update and assessment of the research that has been done on families affected by capital punishment and then considers several factors that make research in this area particularly challenging: the rarity of death sentences and executions under current laws, the diffuse as well as direct influence of capital punishment, and the role of time and the process of adjustment after traumatic loss. I outline potential directions for future research, briefly noting the formidable challenges of carrying out well designed, methodologically sound, ethical research in this area. The chapter ends with a brief consideration of potential policy implications of research on families affected by the capital sanction.

A Brief Assessment of Existing Research

Families of Capital Defendants

Research on members of capital defendants' families is somewhat more developed than that on victims' family members (see Vandiver 2003, for a summary of the findings of relevant studies). In the 1980s, social scientists began exploring the experiences of families who had relatives on death row. The extremely low number of executions at this time prevented these studies from including relatives of inmates who had been executed. The best of these early studies, by John Smykla, concluded that every one of the 40 family members he interviewed experienced "prolonged suffering" and "distorted grief reactions," along with "an unbelievable mixture of other physical, emotional, and social problems" (Smykla 1987:338, 343).

Recent studies have made significant advances in the quality of research design and methods; additionally, these studies have been able to include respondents whose relatives have been executed as well as those with family members on death row. Rachel King's (2005) detailed study of eight families provides in-depth perspective with long quotations from interviews with relatives. Susan Sharp (2005) based her book *Hidden Victims* on interviews with 53 family members of capital defendants and 15 non-related but closely associated people. Sharp's research improved and extended earlier studies in several ways. She used a brief standard interview instrument for consistency, but encouraged her respondents to answer the questions in whatever depth they chose. Sharp interviewed people whose experiences covered the whole range of case processing, from those whose relatives had merely been threatened with capital charges to those whose relatives had been executed. She concluded that the death penalty is "incredibly traumatic" for families of defendants (Sharp 2005:177).

Elizabeth Beck and her colleagues studied a sample of 14 people identified as primary supporters of their condemned relatives (Beck, Blackwell, Leonard, and Mears 2003). The researchers assessed whether respondents who agreed to undergo the testing were experiencing symptoms consistent with post traumatic stress disorder (PTSD) and/or depression as measured by the Beck Depression Scale. The great majority had symptoms consistent with PTSD and had depression. Although the sample was small and nonrepresentative, the use of standard measurements for the dependent variables is an important methodological enhancement (Beck *et al.* 2003:405–06).

Elizabeth Beck, Sarah Britto, and Arlene Andrews (2007) based their book *In the Shadow of Death* on semi-structured interviews with a family member of each of 24 capital offenders. They supplemented this information with topical interviews on subjects of particular interest and with interviews with children and adults who as children had had parents or brothers as capital defendants. In addition, the authors held two focus groups and drew upon 14 psychosocial histories compiled by one of the authors. Beck *et al.* paid explicit attention to issues of reliability and validity, aiming both to "capture the lived experiences of family members" and to achieve an "objective understanding" (Beck *et al.* 2007:239).

An important contribution of the Beck *et al.* book is its consideration of the effect of the death penalty on children. The authors interviewed eight people whose parents were or had been capital defendants; four had been executed; three were on death row; one was awaiting a capital trial. Four of the respondents were underage at the time of the interview. In addition, the authors spoke with two people whose brothers were on death row when they were children; one of the condemned was still on death row and the other had been executed at the time of the interview. The authors concluded that "these children are the death penalty's dirty little secret" and that capital punishment "produces numerous long-term negative consequences on their lives" (Beck *et al.* 2007:112;113). Citing research documenting the negative effects of parental incarceration on children, they noted that the children of the condemned face those risks along with others unique to the death penalty.

Samples drawn from various jurisdictions, examination of reactions of people involved in varying stages of the criminal justice process, use of standardized interview instruments and psychological scales, and explicit attention to issues of reliability and validity all represent important advances. The conclusions of the Sharp (2005) and Beck *et al.* (2007) studies are consistent with the conclusions drawn by the authors of the earlier, simpler studies. In light of the increasingly sophisticated methods used and the overall agreement of studies done over a period of 25 years, it seems safe to say that we now know enough to conclude that the death penalty exacts a terrible price from the families of the condemned.

This is not to say that all methodological challenges have been surmounted or that all research issues have adequately been addressed. It is unlikely that research on this topic will ever be able to successfully use random sampling. Families interviewed probably differ from families who have not been contacted or who have refused to participate, thus limiting the degree to which findings can be generalized. For instance, families that have broken off contact with their condemned relative may have different reactions from those that remain in touch. (In very rare instances, family members of condemned prisoners have expressed support for the execution of their relatives. See Magee 1980:53 and Mohr 2005 for examples.) Longitudinal research designs would be useful in establishing time order and trying to sort out causes and effects. Additionally, studies that interviewed people many years after the condemnation and execution of a relative would provide information about the duration of effects. Studies using comparison groups of families of prisoners serving long sentences for violent crimes and families of condemned prisoners could clarify which reactions or intensity of reactions are unique to those facing a relative's death sentence.

Families of Homicide Victims

The simple answer to the question of what research remains to be done on the effects of capital punishment on family members of homicide victims is "almost everything." Although an extensive body of research exists on the impact of murder on surviving relatives, little work has systematically addressed the impact of the criminal justice system, and even less the impact of capital punishment on these families. In part, this may reflect the fact that until recently the effect of capital punishment on victims' families was not a central concern even of supporters of capital punishment. Frank Zimring documents that the rise of victim-focused justification for capital punishment and the "symbolic transformation of execution into a victim-service program" occurred only very recently (2003:62).

Several authors have written essays discussing the effects of capital punishment on homicide victims' families; these are useful in that they explicate the issues and point toward potential research questions, but they are not reports of original research on victims' families (Acker 2006a; Acker 2006b; Acker and Mastrocinque 2006; Armour and Umbreit 2006; Vandiver 2003; Zimring 2003). Other scholars have studied newspaper accounts of the immediate reaction of victims' families to the offender's execution (Gross and Matheson 2003; Vollum 2005) and have used interviews to study the effects of witnessing the offender's execution (Madeira Forthcoming).

Jaime Lynn Burns (2006) interviewed 23 family members of homicide victims about their experiences with and opinions of the criminal justice system and the death penalty. All the respondents interviewed supported capital punishment and in all of their cases the offender had been sentenced to death. Burns organized her summary of the interviews thematically and included extensive quotations from the respondents. She did not break down the percentage of her respondents who gave particular answers or reported certain experiences; rather, she noted that most, many, or the majority responded in certain ways. Burns found a high level of disillusionment and frustration with the criminal justice system, concerns that the needs of victims were not adequately addressed, resentment over the length of appeals in capital cases, and skepticism that the execution of the offender had or would provide real closure.

A popular misconception is that all, or nearly all, victims' families support capital punishment. In fact, the range of opinion among the relatives of homicide victims is as wide as among the general population, although it is probably distributed differently. In addition, individuals' feelings and opinions about the proper punishment may change over time. Far from presenting a monolithic outlook, victims' families cover a broad and shifting spectrum of opinion.

Within this broad range of opinion, researchers should focus special attention on those families who oppose the death penalty for the killer of their relative, including whether their opposition is to the death penalty in all cases or whether factors such as wishing to avoid prolonged involvement in appeals leads them to reject the sentence for practical reasons. Robert Renny Cushing and Susannah Sheffer (2002) have documented the isolation, lack of services, and sometimes abuse endured by families who face the capital prosecution of their relatives' killers over their own opposition (see also King 2003).

How families of homicide victims experience the criminal justice system probably depends on their punishment preferences as well as on the actual punishment received. Families who see the offender convicted and given the sentence they prefer—whether that sentence is death or not—are likely to have a more positive impression of the criminal justice system. Those who do not receive the desired sentence are likely to feel the criminal justice system did not serve their needs, although this may vary by whether prosecutors were responsive to their wishes (*i.e.*, a family that wanted a death sentence might feel less negatively about a jury's imposition of life than about a prosecutor's refusal to seek death).

Research on how the death penalty affects the families of homicide victims faces the same methodological challenges mentioned above in reference to the families of defendants. In addition, if we are to achieve a full understanding of the issue, it is essential that murder victims' relatives who support capital punishment, those who oppose it, and those whose opinions are shifting all be included in samples. It is also necessary to ensure that samples of homicide victims' families are representative of the class and racial distribution of homicide victimization and do not overrepresent white and wealthier families.

The Context of Research on Families and Capital Punishment

In what follows, I attempt to place the research topic within the context of the current administration of the death penalty in America. Hypothetical questions about how the death penalty might affect victims' and offenders' families under other systems of capital punishment are beyond the scope of this chapter; its focus is on the realities of the modern death penalty in the United States, with its characteristic rarity and slowness. I note as well that the effects of capital punishment are not confined to those cases in which it is imposed, but have wider scope.

The Frequency of Homicide and the Rarity of Capital Punishment

Research on the effects of capital punishment must be placed in the context of the frequency of homicide and the rarity of death sentences and executions. To say that the United States has a high rate of homicide is to repeat something so well known that it has almost lost its power to surprise. Looking closely at the numbers, however, reveals the shocking toll of murder in America. Since January 1977, when executions under modern statutes began, through the end of 2005, over 575,000 people have been the victims of murder and non-negligent manslaughter in the United States (Pastore and Maguire 2005: Table 3.106.2005). (This number is probably an undercount; some homicides may be wrongly classified as accidents or suicides; some victims may be classified as missing; and some data are missing. In addition, the count does not include deaths due to the terrorist attacks of September 11, 2001.)

This appalling number of victims is roughly ten times the number of American deaths in the Vietnam hostilities. It closely approaches the number of American battle deaths in all wars from the Revolutionary War through the present (Fischer, Klarman, and Oboroceanu 2007: Tables 1 and 15). Despite the steep fall in homicide starting in the mid-1990s, the number of people losing their lives to murder remains very large. In 1999, the year with the lowest number of homicides since executions resumed, 15,522 victims were killed (Federal Bureau of Investigation 2005).

Slightly under two-thirds of homicides are cleared by the police through arrest or exceptional means (Federal Bureau of Investigation 2005). Families whose relatives are killed by unknown parties face extraordinarily painful and problematic situations (Radelet and Stanley 2006), but a discussion of punishment is irrelevant when no offender has been identified. In another set of homicides, sometimes the most egregious, the offender kills himself or is killed at the scene of the crime. Thus, in something over a third of homicides, the offender is either unidentified or dead.

Among the cases in which an offender is identified, the death penalty is an exceptionally rare punishment. The Death Penalty Information Center (2007a) documents 6,940 death sentences imposed between January 1977 and the end of 2005. Over the same years, 1,004 people were executed (Death Penalty Information Center 2007b). Thus researchers seek to determine the effect of a punishment given as a sentence in approximately 1.2% of homicides and carried out in 0.17%. Not only is the death penalty rare, it is becoming rarer. Executions have fallen from a yearly high of 98 in 1999, to 53 in 2006. Perhaps more significantly for the future, the number of death sentences has plummeted. In 1995, 315 death sentences were imposed; in 2005, there were only 128. The average number of death sentences between 1995 and 1999 was 296; between 2000 and 2004, the average was 170 (Death Penalty Information Center 2007a; 2007b).

These numbers are significant for research on the effects of capital punishment. The death sentence is an exceedingly rare punishment; execution is even rarer. Whatever the impact of the death penalty on families of victims and offenders, not many people are directly affected. If executions have some benefit for victims' families, those benefits are available to fewer than one percent of the bereaved families. And it is important to note that the cases receiving death sentences are neither a random subset of all homicide cases nor do they consistently represent the very worst homicide cases, but rather reflect the pervasive influence of non-legal variables, especially the geographic location of the homicide and the race of the victims (Baldus and Woodworth 2003; Poveda 2006).

Time

The death penalty is not a single event that occurs in a brief period of time. Its influence extends from the first possibility of a capital prosecution all the way through the prisoner's execution or reduction of sentence. The present system of capital punishment in America is excruciatingly slow and the time spent on death row by many offenders has reached astonishing lengths. In Florida, for instance, at least ten prisoners have death sentences dating to 1976 or earlier; they have been on death row over thirty years (Florida Department of Corrections 2007). It is not unusual for a condemned inmate to live out half his life on death row before his death sentence is executed or reduced.

Time is therefore an essential element in this research. Families of victims and of offenders face years if not decades of involvement with the criminal justice system. For victims' families, these are years during which they will undergo the slow process of attempting to come to terms with their bereavement. For the offenders' families, the long period on death row is a time of anticipatory grieving as they attempt both to prevent and to prepare for the possibility of an execution.

For both sets of families, research needs to extend a number of years past the execution. Newspaper interviews with victims' families immediately after execution often quote people as feeling relief and hope for the future. Researchers should attempt to learn how long these feelings remain. The agony of the defendants' families in the aftermath of the execution is obvious, but we do not know much about the course their grieving takes or the long term effects of their loss, especially on children.

Time may also have an effect on the punishment preferences of homicide victims' families. Cross-sectional research designs that take a snapshot of the feelings of families at one time risk reaching misleading conclusions, especially if the research occurs soon after the crime or around the time of the execution. Longitudinal designs may be able to track changes over time as the families move through the stages of grieving and through various levels of the criminal justice system.

The Diffuse Effects of Capital Punishment

The rarity of death sentences and the prolonged length of time between sentence and execution do not necessarily indicate failures in the administration of the punishment. U.S. Supreme Court jurisprudence emphasizes that "death is different": capital punishment should be imposed only for the very worst crimes committed by the worst offenders and death sentences should be carried out only in accordance with high standards of due process (although in fact, proportionality of sentencing and procedural due process have not been achieved by modern death penalty laws). Whether the Court's logic is compelling for bereaved families is another question. Learning that the law and the people charged with carrying out the law do not consider the death of a family member to be among the worst of murders, as occurs in the overwhelming number of cases, is unlikely to be comforting. Statutory aggravating and mitigating factors and the extensive case law on their application are probably not of great interest to families hoping that the legal system can provide them with something to ease their pain. From the perspective of the offender's family, the threat of the death penalty casts a long shadow. The fear of a capital prosecution, even where that is unlikely, adds to the stress and unhappiness of the family as they await the outcome of their relative's case.

Thus capital punishment, although vanishingly rare in practice, has an influence far beyond what its low numbers would indicate, providing false expectations for victims' families and unnecessary dread for families of defendants. Researchers who want to try to study the full scope of the death penalty's influence must look beyond cases that are charged as capital offenses. The experiences of victims' families who believed that a death sentence should have been sought and carried out in their cases, and offenders' families who feared that outcome in their cases, are important to consider in assessing the broad impact of a system that provides capital punishment as one sentencing option for homicide.

Potential Directions for Future Research

In what follows, I attempt to sketch some directions that research on these issues could take and related methodological considerations (see also Vandiver 2006). I focus on research about victims' families, since so little has been done; many of the same considerations, however, apply to research on offenders' families. While it is tempting to try to design a comprehensive study, the obstacles to such an undertaking are considerable. Given the preliminary state of research on the topic and the substantial challenges the research presents, however, studies based on small samples of persons with homogeneous views are a helpful step in building knowledge.

Research in related areas can provide theoretical frameworks and guidance on research design. The experiences of homicide victims' families fall within the broad theoretical and research literature on the effects of criminal victimization. Families of condemned prisoners form a subset of other prisoners' families, a group that has received the attention of researchers in recent years.

The emerging literature on victims of human rights violations by governments may also provide relevant perspectives on the families of the condemned. Both families of homicide victims and families of executed offenders experience violent bereavement and research on both can be grounded in the growing literature on grieving and traumatic loss. Both have extended engagement with the criminal justice system; their experiences can be seen as a sort of second victimization in which the system itself adds to the distress of the event that put them in contact with the system. Scholars thus can draw upon substantial prior work in related areas as they design research to answer questions specific to the effect of capital punishment on families.

Stating the research question and operationalizing its variables are not as simple as may appear at first glance. If we want to know how the death penalty affects the families of offenders and victims, we will have to begin by deciding whether we are studying the effect of executions, or of executions and death sentences, or of even the potential for a death sentence to be imposed. It is necessary to define what relationships fall under the term "family." Are all types of homicide under consideration, or should the study include only cases in which the death penalty could have been sought under the law of the jurisdiction?

In order to test the effects of the different punishments, it will be necessary to compare the experiences of people based on the outcome of their relatives' cases. Subjects could be selected within one jurisdiction and compared based upon the outcome of their relative's case. Or homicide victims' families within an abolitionist jurisdiction could be compared with victims' families in a death penalty jurisdiction, with the latter group divided on the basis of case outcome. This would allow three-way comparisons among families for whom the death sentence was never an option, those in whose case the death sentence could have been but was not imposed, and those in whose case the offender was sentenced to death. A potential complication is that Americans in abolitionist states are well aware that the death penalty is an option in other states; this may blur comparisons based on the sharp distinction between abolitionist and non-abolitionist jurisdictions. To compensate for this, the design could be extended to include a comparison group in another country where capital punishment had been abolished decades ago; this of course raises issues of comparability of samples as well as a number of practical difficulties. A further refinement would compare the experiences of victims' families in jurisdictions where executions are infrequent with those where executions are more common. However the categories of respondents are defined, identifying and sampling individual respondents, then locating, contacting, and gaining consent from them will be neither simple nor quick.

Gathering data presents further challenges. Interviews are an obvious method for trying to learn about the families' experiences, opinions, and reactions. Interviews could cover everything from the facts of the case to the respondents' descriptions of their emotional state. If conducted at different times over a long period, especially after significant developments in the case, interviews could provide some longitudinal data about experience and emotions. While such interviews would provide rich descriptive materials, the resulting data would be unlikely to provide a basis for standardized coding and cross-group comparisons. Supplementing open-ended interviewing with the administration of standardized assessment inventories such as the Texas Revised Inventory of Grief and the Inventory of Complicated Grief could be helpful in gaining measurements that could provide a basis for comparisons. These inventories should be used with care and with special attention to issues of validity (Tomita and Kitamura 2002).

A different, or perhaps supplementary, way to gather data would be to use other sources of information on respondents' well-being. It might be possible to compare respondents on a number of indicators of well-being such as divorce, employment, substance abuse, suicide, stress-related illnesses, etc. Gathering such information would of course require respondents' permission, might be perceived by respondents as unduly intrusive, and would present many practical difficulties.

Whatever methods are used, researchers who wish to study the impact of executions on the families of offenders and victims must give careful consideration to the ethics of their work (see Beck and Britto 2006). In essence, we are asking strangers to confide in us the most terrible experience of their lives and their emotional responses to those experiences. We are asking them for honesty, even when the feelings they express may be socially undesirable. We expect them to revisit times in their lives when they have been overwhelmed by grief and we want them to express to us the intensity of what they felt (and may well still feel at the time of the study). We are asking them to summarize the storms of sorrow and pain they have endured in a way that will allow us to attempt to describe, if not to measure, in impartial scientific language, their internal emotional state. These are not small things to request. Some families may find the close attention and careful nonjudgmental listening of the interviewer to be comforting; others may not. But in either case, we are researchers, not therapists, and we must not confuse those roles.

The people who carry out the interviews and analyze the results will not emerge unscathed. The level of horror experienced by both sets of families exceeds anything people experience outside of war or armed conflict. Those who study them with the attention and sympathy they deserve will pay a personal price.

Policy Implications

Enough is known about the effects of the death penalty on the families of defendants to conclude that their suffering must be a consideration in any evaluation of the costs and benefits of capital punishment (Sheffer and Cushing 2006). Continuing the use of the death penalty inevitably means intentionally inflicting the traumatic loss of violent bereavement on innocent family members of the convicted person. This loss could be entirely avoided simply by ending the death penalty.

The research is not as extensive nor are its implications as clear for victims' families. As discussed above, we do not yet have sufficient evidence to reach conclusions about how the death penalty affects these families. If future studies conclude that capital punishment offers some unique benefit to the victims' families, the policy implications remain debatable. First, it becomes necessary to weigh the cost exacted on the defendant's family against the benefit provided to his victim's family, a destructive prospect in any event, and nonsensical when the victim and offender come from the same family and/or when the victim's family does not want the death sentence.

If the victim's family does want the offender executed, and the benefits of execution to them are determined to outweigh the cost to the offender's family, we then face both the legal and the practical issues raised by the rarity of executions. If executions offer some long term benefits to victims' families, can it be justifiable to reserve these benefits for fewer than one percent of homicide cases? Will doing so add to the pain of the 99% of homicide victims' families who do not receive those benefits? If it is determined that use of the death penalty should be expanded to a greater number of cases, how can this be undertaken when the few current capital cases are already straining judicial funding and resources? And how will this expansion fit with Supreme Court rulings that—at least in theory, if not in practice—reserve the capital sanction for the very worst offenses and offenders?

Finally there remains the question of what to do when the victim's family opposes the death penalty. Such opposition, whether based on broad moral grounds or on considerations particular to the family's situation, is not nearly as rare as is often assumed. Overriding the wishes of these families by sentencing the defendant to death is likely to be destructive to their well-being; honoring their wishes for a lesser sentence introduces yet another level of caprice to a system already riddled with the influence of extralegal factors.

In the end, the impact of the death penalty on victims' families may not be the most important question to ask. The focus on such a tiny subgroup of victims' families may be a disservice to homicide victims' survivors as a whole. A better question for researchers and for policy makers might be what can be done to assist the largest number of homicide victims' family members. Much—perhaps most—of what could be done, including interventions to lower the homicide rate, may lie outside the criminal justice system. But there are actions that the criminal justice system can take, and sometimes does take, that have the potential to broadly assist victims' families.

First, the most obvious and the most difficult: solving the crime is the fundamental task of the criminal justice system after a homicide. The national clearance rate for homicides has fallen from 91% in 1965 to 62.1 in 2005 (Federal Bureau of Investigation 1965; 2005). Michael Radelet's innovative and important work in Colorado demonstrates the overwhelming importance of this issue to survivors and the shocking lack of coordinated effort and even information on the part of law enforcement agencies (Radelet and Stanley 2006; see also Radelet and Pierce, this volume). This is a particularly timely area of interest, as recent developments with DNA technology open new potential for solving cases in which biological evidence exists, even ones that are decades old (Lagos 2007). Researchers, law enforcement personnel, and victims' families and advocates may be able to work together productively on this issue to the substantial benefit of victims' families.

A second area where research indicates that relatively simple changes can have a beneficial effect for homicide victims' survivors is death notification. The manner in which news of the death is delivered to the family can leave lasting wounds, complicating the trauma and the emotional aftermath of the death. Protocols and training in death notification are available, but unfortunately those who deliver the news of death often have not been trained in how to do so (Reed and Blackwell 2006:256–59; Stewart, Lord, and Mercer 2000).

Finally, it is important that victims' families have someone who can assist them in obtaining information and explanations of what is happening in their relative's case and who can ensure that they receive respectful treatment. Much progress has been made in this area in the last several decades (Karmen 2001:316–17); more remains to be done. There is preliminary evidence that involvement with the legal system under some conditions may have "positive effects on the mental health and well-being of crime victims," but much more study is necessary in order to "identify those policies and practices associated with the best outcome for victims, as well as those which may be detrimental" (Herman 2003:165). It is essential that the availability of support and information to the families be entirely independent of the families' punishment preference. Peter Loge (2006) suggests that victims' families would be better served if victim advocates were removed from prosecutors' offices and if neutral parties provided the families with overviews of the system and information specific to their cases.

Conclusion

The effect of capital punishment on families of offenders remains underresearched; almost no work has been done on the death penalty's effect on families of victims. Despite the methodological, practical, ethical, and emotional challenges of doing research in this area, both the intrinsic interest of the issues and their importance for policy make the effort worthwhile. Only when we know the effect of capital punishment on the families whose lives have been so tragically affected by homicide can we fully evaluate the ultimate penalty.

References

Acker, James R. 2006a. "The Myth of Closure and Capital Punishment." Pp. 167–176 in *Demystifying Crime and Criminal Justice*, edited by Robert M. Bohm and Jeffery T. Walker. Los Angeles, CA: Roxbury Publishing Co.

_____. 2006b. "Hearing the Victim's Voice Amidst the Cry for Capital Punishment." Pp. 246–260 in The *Handbook of Restorative Justice: A Global Perspective*, edited by Dennis Sullivan and Larry L. Tifft. London & New York: Routledge.

Acker, James R., Robert M. Bohm, and Charles S. Lanier (eds.). 2003. *America's Experiment with Capital Punishment: Reflections on the Past, Present and Future of the Ultimate Penal Sanction*, 2nd ed. Durham, NC: Carolina Academic Press.

Acker, James R. and Jeanna Marie Mastrocinque. 2006. "Causing Death and Sustaining Life: The Law, Capital Punishment, and Criminal Homicide Victims' Survivors." Pp. 141–160 in *Wounds That Do Not Bind: Victim-Based Perspectives on the Death Penalty*, edited by James R. Acker and David R. Karp. Durham, NC: Carolina Academic Press.

Armour, Marilyn Peterson and Mark S. Umbreit. 2006. "Exploring 'Closure' and the Ultimate Penal Sanction for Survivors of Homicide Victims." *Federal Sentencing Reporter* 19:105–112.

Baldus, David C. and George Woodworth. 2003. "Race Discrimination and the Death Penalty: An Empirical and Legal Overview." Pp. 501–551 in *America's Experiment with Capital Punishment: Reflections on the Past, Present and Future of the Ultimate Penal Sanction*, 2nd ed., edited by James R. Acker, Robert M. Bohm, and Charles S. Lanier. Durham, NC: Carolina Academic Press.

Beck, Elizabeth, Brenda Sims Blackwell, Pamela Blume Leonard, and Michael Mears. 2003. "Seeking Sanctuary: Interviews with Family Members of Capital Defendants." *Cornell Law Review* 88:382–418.

Beck, Elizabeth and Sarah Britto. 2006. "Using Feminist Methods and Restorative Justice to Interview Capital Offenders' Family Members." *Affilia: Journal of Women and Social Work* 21:59–70.

Beck, Elizabeth, Sarah Britto, and Arlene Andrews. 2007. *In the Shadow of Death: Restorative Justice and Death Row Families.* Oxford: Oxford University Press.

Burns, Jaime Lynn. 2006. "Families of Homicide Victims Speak: An Examination of Perceptions of the Criminal Justice System and Capital Punishment." Unpublished dissertation, Oklahoma State University.

Cushing, Robert Renny and Susannah Sheffer. 2002. "Dignity Denied: The Experience of Murder Victims' Family Members Who Oppose the Death Penalty." Cambridge, MA: Murder Victims' Families for Reconciliation. (http://www.mvfr.org/dignitydenied).

Death Penalty Information Center. 2007a. "Death Sentences by Year: 1977–2005." (http://www.deathpenaltyinfo.org/article.php?scid=9&did=873).

_____. 2007b. "Executions by Year." (http://www.deathpenaltyinfo.org/article.php?scid=8&did=146).

Federal Bureau of Investigation. 1965. *Uniform Crime Reports for the United States, 1965.* Washington, DC: U.S. Department of Justice, Federal Bureau of Investigation.

_____. 2005. *Crime in the United States, 2005.* Washington, DC: U.S. Department of Justice, Federal Bureau of Investigation. (http://www.fbi.gov/ucr/05cius/offenses/clearances/index.html#figure).

Fischer, Hannah, Kim Klarman, and Mari-Jana "M-J" Oboroceanu. 2007. "American War and Military Operations Casualties: Lists and Statistics." Washington, DC: Congressional Research Service. (http://www.fas.org/sgp/crs/natsec/RL32492.pdf).

Florida Department of Corrections. 2007. "Death Row Roster." (http://www.dc.state.fl.us/activeinmates/deathrowroster.asp).

Gross, Samuel R. and Daniel J. Matheson. 2003. "What They Say at the End: Capital Victims' Families and the Press." *Cornell Law Review* 88:486–516.

Herman, Judith Lewis. 2003. "The Mental Health of Crime Victims: The Impact of Legal Intervention." *Journal of Traumatic Stress* 16:159–166.

Karmen, Andrew. 2001. *Crime Victims: An Introduction to Victimology.* Belmont, CA: Wadsworth/Thompson Learning.

King, Rachel. 2005. *Capital Consequences: Families of the Condemned Tell Their Stories.* New Brunswick, NJ: Rutgers University Press.

_____. 2003. *Don't Kill in Our Names: Families of Murder Victims Speak Out Against the Death Penalty.* New Brunswick, NJ: Rutgers University Press.

Lagos, Marisa. 2007. "San Jose Cops Wake Up Dormant Case Files." *San Francisco Chronicle,* August 19, A1.

Loge, Peter. 2006. "The Process of Healing and the Trial as Product: Incompatibility, Courts, and Murder Victim Family Members." Pp. 411–430 in *Wounds That Do Not Bind: Victim-Based Perspectives on the Death Penalty*, edited by James R. Acker and David R. Karp. Durham, NC: Carolina Academic Press.

Madeira, Jody Lyneé. Forthcoming. "Blood Relations: Collective Memory, Cultural Trauma, and the Prosecution and Execution of Timothy McVeigh." *Studies in Law, Politics & Society*: 42. (http://ssrn.com/abstract=1007041).

Magee, Doug. 1980. *Slow Coming Dark: Interviews on Death Row*. New York, NY: The Pilgrim Press.

Mohr, Holbrook. 2005. "Family Says Hitman 'Causing Trouble' with Dying Words." *Gadsden (Alabama) Times*, December 18. (http://www.Gadsden-Times.com).

Pastore, Ann L. and Kathleen Maguire (eds.). 2005. *Sourcebook of Criminal Justice Statistics*. (http://www.albany.edu/sourcebook/pdf/t31062005.pdf).

Poveda, Tony G. 2006. "Geographic Location, Death Sentences and Executions in Post-*Furman* Virginia." *Punishment & Society* 8:423–442.

Radelet, Michael L. and Glenn Pierce. This volume. "Racial and Ethnic Disparities in Resolving Homicides."

Radelet, Michael L. and Dawn Stanley. 2006. "Learning from Homicide Co-Victims: A University-Based Project." Pp. 397–409 in *Wounds That Do Not Bind: Victim-Based Perspectives on the Death Penalty*, edited by James R. Acker and David R. Karp. Durham, NC: Carolina Academic Press.

Reed, Mark D. and Brenda Sims Blackwell. 2006. "Secondary Victimization among Families of Homicide Victims: The Impact of the Justice Process on Co-Victims' Psychological Adjustment and Service Utilization." Pp. 253–274 in *Wounds That Do Not Bind: Victim-Based Perspectives on the Death Penalty*, edited by James R. Acker and David R. Karp. Durham, NC: Carolina Academic Press.

Sharp, Susan F. 2005. *Hidden Victims: The Effects of the Death Penalty on Families of the Accused*. New Brunswick, NJ: Rutgers University Press.

Sheffer, Susannah and Renny Cushing. 2006. "Creating More Victims: How Executions Hurt the Families Left Behind." Cambridge, MA: Murder Victims' Families for Human Rights. (http://www.murdervictimsfamilies.org).

Smykla, John Ortiz. 1987. "The Human Impact of Capital Punishment: Interviews with Families of Persons on Death Row." *Journal of Criminal Justice* 15:331–347.

Stewart, Alan E., Janice Harris Lord, and Dorothy L. Mercer. 2000. "A Survey of Professionals' Training and Experiences in Delivering Death Notifications." *Death Studies* 24:611–631.

Tomita, Takuro and Toshinori Kitamura. 2002. "Clinical and Research Measures of Grief: A Reconsideration." *Comprehensive Psychiatry* 43:95–102.

Vandiver, Margaret. 2006. "The Death Penalty and the Families of Victims: An Overview of Research Issues." Pp. 235–252 in *Wounds That Do Not Bind: Victim-Based Perspectives on the Death Penalty*, edited by James R. Acker and David R. Karp. Durham, NC: Carolina Academic Press.

_____. 2003. "The Impact of Capital Punishment on the Families of Homicide Victims and Condemned Prisoners." Pp. 477–505 in *America's Experiment with Capital Punishment: Reflections on the Past, Present and Future of the Ultimate Penal Sanction*, 2nd ed., edited by James R. Acker, Robert M. Bohm, and Charles S. Lanier. Durham, NC: Carolina Academic Press.

Vollum, Scott. 2005. "Giving Voice to the Dead: An Exploratory Analysis of Executed Offenders' Last Statements and Statements of Their Co-victims." Unpublished Dissertation, Sam Houston State University.

Zimring, Franklin E. 2003. *The Contradictions of American Capital Punishment*. Oxford and New York: Oxford University Press.

CHAPTER 18

THE COST OF THE DEATH PENALTY IN AMERICA: DIRECTIONS FOR FUTURE RESEARCH[1]

Jonathan E. Gradess and Andrew L. B. Davies

In 2007, the case of Brian Nichols, accused of murdering four people including a judge, brought the public defender system of the state of Georgia to a standstill (Goodman 2007). The reason was a familiar one: this high-profile case had entirely drained that system's resources. Reluctantly, the judge ordered that the trial be suspended until later in the year. Cases such as this one, where vast costs associated with trying and then carrying out death sentences cripple the criminal justice system, are by no means uncommon (Dieter 1994). The Nichols case simply highlights an endemic problem which this chapter investigates in depth: the ruinous cost of the administration of the death penalty.

The intuitive assumption that, by foreshortening a convict's life, the state can save money has been under sustained attack for more than half a century (*e.g.*, Caldwell 1952). In that time, writings on the subject have developed from opinion pieces by academics and corrections professionals to systematic analyses and comparisons of the cost of life and death sentences. These latter studies support the suspicions of those working in the system. The belief that capital punishment saves the state money is a myth (Cochran, Sanders and Chamlin 2006). This chapter reviews the history of these developments, dividing them into three periods before considering possibilities for future research. The im-

---

1. The authors are grateful for the helpful comments of Mardi Crawford, Alexandra Avvocato, Kiley Oram, Bill Bowers and Elizabeth Brown in the preparation of this chapter.

portance of information on the cost of the death penalty for public opinion and policy is also discussed.

Policy makers are now obliged to confront the reality that the introduction or continuation of the death penalty will result in additional costs. Death penalty cases involve costly pre-trial investigations by both prosecution and defense, the appointment of higher numbers of attorneys, numerous unique pretrial motions, a complex voir dire process, frequent sequestering of juries, considerably longer trials which include an additional penalty phase, the employment of additional and non-traditional expert witnesses, a mandated appeals process, frequent venue changes and (often) extensive collateral proceedings (Bohm 2003; Costanzo and White 1994; Garey 1985; Tabak and Lane 1989; Wilson, Doss and Phillips 2004). States must also maintain a death row facility to house the condemned. The large number of overturned death sentences further reduces the system's cost-efficiency (Snell 2006).[2] The implications that policy makers now confront are both that the death penalty is inordinately expensive, and that it drains resources from other much needed services within criminal justice and beyond (Costanzo 2001).

A virtual consensus which crosses ideological lines has emerged on the matter of cost (Radelet and Borg 2000). County administrators across the nation have raised taxes, squabbled over borders, withheld paychecks to their employees, cut ambulance and fire services, and even gone to jail over the need to meet the costs of capital trials (Brooks and Erickson 1996; Costanzo 2001; Dieter 1994). A California district attorney complained in 1988 that the cost of capital trials in Sierra County robbed the residents of funds which could be better spent on law enforcement personnel (Dieter 1994). In one extraordinary case, the Nevada trial of Gerald Gallego was partly funded by public donations following the revelation that the cost would cripple the sparsely populated county in which the crimes had taken place (Roll 1984; Taylor 2002). The cost of the trial made the decision to prosecute an unpopular one, despite the horrific nature of Gallego's crimes. The district attorney was of the opinion that the donations saved his job (Gilliam 2006).[3]

Some members of the public, however, believe that the death penalty is cost-effective. 11% of death penalty supporters in a recent Gallup poll indi-

---

2. The latest Bureau of Justice Statistics figures show that of the 4,408 individuals removed from death row between 1973 and 2005, 61% were removed by sentence commutation (Snell 2006: Appendix Table 4).

3. Over $25,000 was raised toward the trial of Gerald Gallego for the murder of two Sacramento, California teenagers after *Sacramento Bee* columnist Stan Gilliam suggested readers send donations to Pershing County, Nevada to help fund the trial. Gallego was sentenced to death, but died of cancer in prison in 2002 (Taylor 2002).

cated their support was due in part to the fact that they believed it would save taxpayers money (Gallup 2003).[4] Historical data show this proportion has remained relatively stable over time (Ellsworth and Gross 1994; Gallup 2003). In addition to reviewing evidence on the cost of the death penalty itself, therefore, this chapter also examines the impact of information about cost upon death penalty opinions.

The Early Bewilderment Period

"When all is said and done, there can be no doubt that it costs more to execute a man than to keep him in prison for life." Thurgood Marshall, dissenting in *Furman v. Georgia* (1972).

During what we call the "early bewilderment period," little was known about the cost of the death penalty that was not the result of impressionistic observations. In 1972, when Justice Marshall expressed his opinion on the matter in *Furman*, the evidence available to him was scant. Practitioners had been expressing the opinion that the death penalty was inordinately costly to the correctional system for some time, but their warnings had yet to be tested by empirical research (*e.g.*, Eshelman and Riley 1962; McGee 1964). Indeed, for all his expressed confidence, Marshall's statement that the death penalty cost more than life imprisonment was based on very little evidence.

Marshall cited four sources for his opinion (*Furman v. Georgia* 1972:358 n. 140).[5] The sources themselves were in virtual unison: life sentences were almost certainly more economical than the death penalty. For one reason, life sentenced prisoners played an important role in the economy of any prison. They could be set to work in a variety of domestic functions (McGee 1964; Sellin 1961). The death penalty removed any possibility that they might be economically productive themselves or make restitution to the survivors of the victims they had murdered (Caldwell 1952). Aside from their economic contribution, the considerable additional burdens upon the correctional system of housing, guarding and then executing condemned prisoners were also emphasized (Caldwell 1952; Sellin 1961). Some even noted the disturbing but logical conclusion of the economy argument: would it not save the state even more money

---

4. The response was the third most popular answer after "it fits the crime" (37%) and "they deserve it" (13%). The argument that it will deter future crimes was also mentioned by 11% of respondents (Gallup 2003).

5. The sources were: Caldwell (1952); Eshelman and Riley (1962); McGee (1964); and Sellin (1961).

simply to execute all prisoners, whether capitally charged or not (Caldwell 1952; Hartung 1951)?

These authors represent a fair cross-section of writing on the cost of the death penalty during the early bewilderment phase. Two were practitioners working in corrections (a correctional administrator and a prison chaplain) who believed that the high costs of keeping an inmate on death row and then executing him or her were self-evident (Eshelman and Riley 1962; McGee 1964). The other two were academics discussing the utility of capital punishment (Caldwell 1952; Sellin 1961). All four were explicit in their writings about their personal abolitionist beliefs. All four also expressed the belief that, in the 1950s and 1960s, capital punishment was simply no longer relevant to modern, civilized America.

Only one of the authors Marshall cited could point to empirical data to support his arguments.[6] Evidence in favor of or against the positions espoused by death penalty proponents and opponents was arcane, and the debate rhetorical rather than empirical. The result was that the positions espoused by these ardent abolitionists continued to appear counterintuitive and suspect. As late as 1983, Ernest van den Haag, one of the foremost proponents of the death penalty of his generation, argued that the death penalty was no more costly than life imprisonment. He dismissed the greater cost of funding the many appeals associated with capital sentences. Any accused person, he argued, would be expected to appeal a conviction equally vigorously regardless of his or her sentence (van den Haag and Conrad 1983).[7]

But van den Haag, like Marshall, had no firm evidence with which to back up his claim. The time for empirical work had come.

The Study Period (1982–1993)

In 1982, the New York State Defenders Association published *Capital Losses: The Price of the Death Penalty in New York State*, the first state-level report of

---

6. Caldwell (1952) cited a crude study by Hartung (1951) — the earliest study known to the present authors to address the issue of cost empirically. Hartung found the death penalty to be costlier than life imprisonment, though this conclusion was based on an estimated life expectancy for life-sentenced prisoners of only eight years and two months.

7. See also Culver (1985:574). Van den Haag's argument has little merit, especially when one considers that no right to counsel attaches to discretionary review in the United States Supreme Court, state supreme courts or on habeas corpus. In non-capital cases, therefore, prisoners often languish without representation. Prisoners facing execution, by contrast, more often attract the attention of lawyers willing to take cases *pro bono* and are thus more likely to fully exhaust their post-conviction legal options.

its kind which attempted to quantify the cost to the state of a death penalty case. The study was an attempt to anticipate the impact of a death penalty bill which promised funding for high quality defense representation in capital cases. Breaking the capital litigation process down into eleven stages, costs were estimated for defense, prosecution, court, and other costs accruing to counties and states at each stage. The study focused on only the first three of these "stages," namely trial in state court, direct appeal, and first certiorari petition review in the United States Supreme Court. The report concluded that in a typical case "the costs of the first three stages of capital litigation will total no less than $1,828,100. By the time the first 40 New York death cases have been tried to verdict, over $59 million will have been expended" (New York State Defenders Association 1982:26). These figures were compared to the cost of maintaining a life-sentenced inmate for 40 years, calculated at $602,000 (New York State Defenders Association 1982:23).

Since 1982, a wide variety of surveys, analyses and evaluations have been carried out by government, media, and academic organizations. These evaluations have generally quantified the cost of the death penalty in one of three ways: the amount spent per capital trial, the amount per death sentence, or the amount per execution (Costanzo and White 1994; Tabak and Lane 1989). Each of these calculations yields different results. The decision to seek death in a case creates additional costs from the moment it is made: averaging these costs across all capital trials gives the cost per trial.[8] Not all trials end in death sentences, however. The cost per death sentence imposed is therefore higher than the cost per capital trial. In addition, not all death sentences result in executions, with the result that the cost per execution is higher still.[9] Some reports quantify the difference in still other ways, calculating the costs of administering the death penalty across an entire state or over several years (*e.g.*, Indiana Legislature 1989; Kansas Legislative Research Department 1987).

---

8. When conducting comparisons of the costs of death and non-death cases, the possibility that cases may be selected for death-notices non-randomly should be borne in mind. Cases selected for death are often characterized by greater aggravation and stronger evidence. In addition, decisions regarding death notices may vary by locality and time period due in part to cost considerations (Paternoster, Brame and Bacon 2003). Researchers must therefore be careful to compare like with like when making comparisons between death and non-death cases, in order to ensure that inherent differences between the cases themselves do not interfere with cost calculations.

9. Bureau of Justice Statistics figures show that of those removed from death row between 1973 and 2005 (n=4408), almost 23% were removed by execution. Among the entire population of those sentenced to death in the same period (n=7662), only 13% were executed (Snell 2006:Appendix Table 4).

Soon after the publication of *Capital Losses*, state governments began taking a renewed interest in the question of the cost of the death penalty. In 1983, the General Assembly, Public Defender, and Chief Judge of the Court of Appeals in the state of Maryland were asked by the House Appropriations Committee to provide information on the fiscal impact of processing death penalty cases in the state. They found that among cases where death was sought, those resulting in sanctions of death cost at least $24,082 more than those resulting in non-death sentences, not including appeals (Maryland House Appropriations Committee 1985). In 1987, the Kansas Legislative Research Department concluded that the cost of the re-imposition of the death penalty in Kansas would be $11,419,932 per year, excluding post-conviction review following direct appeals (Kansas Legislative Research Department 1987). In Indiana, a 1989 legislative study estimated the state could save $5 million a year by replacing the death penalty with life without parole (Indiana Legislature 1989). The same year, the New York Department of Correctional Services estimated that each capital trial in that state would cost $1 million (Moran and Ellis 1989). In 1991, the Iowa Legislative Fiscal Bureau calculated the cost of executing the first defendant under new death penalty legislation at approximately $2.1 million (Iowa Legislative Fiscal Bureau 1991).

In 1985, Margot Garey, an academic, published a widely cited study in which it was estimated that capital murder trials cost $201,510 more on average than non-capital trials in California (Garey 1985). A study by the *Sacramento Bee* in 1988 added weight to her finding, concluding that the death penalty cost California an additional $90 million a year, $78 million of which was in trial costs alone (Maganini 1988). Other media organizations also produced informative investigations into the issue. In Florida, a 1988 *Miami Herald* study concluded that every execution cost Florida $3.1 million, while the cost of life imprisonment under then-extant actuarial tables was only $515,964 (Von Drehle 1988). In 1992, the *Dallas Morning News* estimated that a single death penalty case cost an average of $2.3 million in that state, about three times the cost of imprisoning someone in a single maximum security cell for 40 years (Hoppe 1992).

Despite the seeming consensus of these studies, these early attempts were dogged by a variety of limitations. Often they focused on a specific area within capital litigation, such as the trial, and so did not fully reflect the cost of maintaining a system of capital punishment. Data limitations were often considerable, rarely permitting direct comparisons between life and death sentences (General Accounting Office 1989). The result was a call for further study with more sophisticated methodologies, designed to compare the costs of the two approaches. The ideal experimental design (where murder cases are randomly assigned either to a "capital" or "non-capital" condition and tried accordingly) was clearly impossible to implement. Researchers were instead obliged to develop increasingly sophisticated quasi-experimental approaches and adopt careful accounting methodologies to produce more valid results (Van Duizend et al. 1986). The call for more sophisticated methodological approaches would be heeded by a group of scholars from North Carolina, heralding the beginning of a new era for research and dissemination of information on the topic.

The Political Dissemination Period: 1993–2007

The Costs of Processing Murder Cases in North Carolina was the finest, most ambitious, and most credible study of the cost of the death penalty to date (Cook, Slawson and Gries 1993). Comparing the cost of a capital case to a non-capital one where the defendant served twenty years, the researchers estimated the additional cost to the state per trial to be in excess of $163,000. For every death sentence imposed, the cost to the state was more than $216,000 above what it would have paid had the same cases been prosecuted non-capitally. The additional cost to the state of each execution carried out was over $2.16 million.[10]

The North Carolina study was unique in its rigor and credibility. The authors carefully parsed out the costs of life and death sentences into a common set of elements. The additional costs of the death penalty were then quantified as the difference in the sums of the costs of each element, multiplied by the number of such elements in each case type. In this way, the costs of the resources expended on a sample of murder cases, including attorney time and court time at trial and appellate stages, and the maintenance of detention facilities, were all estimated. The only area in which the researchers found savings was the costs of imprisonment—which, given the condemned inmate's foreshortened life-span, was hardly surprising.

The North Carolina study brought a new credibility to the empirical argument for the costliness of capital prosecution. Its impact was heightened further by the near-simultaneous publication of *Millions Misspent: What Politicians Don't Say about the High Costs of the Death Penalty* (Dieter 1994). In this exhaustive review, Dieter concluded that a wealth of evidence, both scientific

---

10. The twenty year figure was chosen because it was the earliest date at which a defendant could be paroled under contemporaneous North Carolina law. The authors did not attempt to make the same comparison for "natural life" sentences (Cook, Slawson and Gries 1993:71).

and anecdotal, provided overwhelming support for the idea that the death penalty was a more costly option for states than life without parole.

After the North Carolina study, few could disagree that the argument that the death penalty cost more than life imprisonment had been settled definitively. In the face of increasingly credible and voluminous evidence, the issue of cost fully entered the debate on the death penalty, changing the nature of discussions on the issue (Radelet and Borg 2000). The costliness of the death penalty featured in discussions among policy-makers and in the media (*e.g.*, Moran and Ellis 1986, 1989; Morgenthau 1995), and also began to be used in court cases in support of ineffective assistance of counsel claims (Gradess 1992, 1995).

Evidence continued to mount. In 1998, the Judicial Conference adopted the conclusions of a study of the federal death penalty which found that defense costs were four times higher in federal death cases compared to non-death ones (Spencer, Cauthron and Edmunds 1998). In 2000, the *Palm Beach Post* found that Florida's death penalty cost the state an additional $51 million (Dáte 2000). A study carried out at Dartmouth University in 2001 estimated that the total burden the death penalty would place on county budgets across the country over 20 years would be $5.5 billion (Baicker 2004). A 2002 study by the Indiana Criminal Law Study Commission concluded that retention of the death penalty in that state would cost 38% more than its abolition (Janeway 2002).[11]

In anticipation of the reintroduction of the death penalty in Kansas, a legislative study commission found that the additional costs of a capital trial over a similar non-death trial would be $546,332. The additional costs per death sentence imposed would be $1,299,103. The additional costs per execution would be over $4.26 million (Carter 1995; Kansas Legislative Research Department 1994). A 2003 study in the same state found that each capital case cost the state $1.2 million, 70% more than the average non-capital case. The cost of a capital trial alone, at $508,000, was over fifteen times as much as in non-death penalty cases. The appellate process in capital cases was estimated to cost over twenty-one times as much per case (Audit of the Department of Corrections, State of Kansas 2003). A 2004 Tennessee study concluded on the basis of limited data that the cost of the death penalty in that state was higher than that for life sentences (Wilson *et al.* 2004). A study by the New Jersey Policy Perspective concluded that the death penalty had cost that state over $250 million since 1982, amounting to $4.2 million per death sentence, or $28 million after reversals (Forsberg 2005; Gradess 2006).

---

11. The Commission assumed that only 20% of cases would be overturned, a figure which research has shown to be a rather low estimate (Liebman, Fagan and West 2000; Snell 2006).

With this plethora of evidence about the costliness of the death penalty, ancillary questions of the effects of this new knowledge on public opinion and policy-making became salient. Justice Marshall had argued in his *Furman* opinion that the moral standards of members of the public were an important indicator for the manner in which the Eighth Amendment should be interpreted (*Furman v. Georgia* 1972). The famous "Marshall hypothesis" also was first stated in *Furman*. Marshall opined that a public which is generally more informed about the death penalty will tend toward its opposition. (*Furman v. Georgia* 1972).

Policy-makers and pollsters alike wondered whether opinion on the death penalty would be influenced by new knowledge about cost. Evidence to show that information on cost is material to opinions on the death penalty quickly accumulated. In 1989, an opinion poll in New York State showed that when respondents were told that the death penalty cost more than life imprisonment, support for it dropped by sixteen percentage points (Amnesty International USA 1989). A 1988 survey of Oklahoma residents revealed that 49% of respondents thought the cost of the death penalty was an important consideration in their opinion about the death penalty. Those who believed the death penalty cost more than life imprisonment were 17 percentage points less likely to support it (Grasmick and Bursik 1988). A 1984 Massachusetts poll showed that those who believed executions were more costly than life sentences were less likely to favor the death penalty by seven percentage points (Massachusetts Citizens Against the Restoration of the Death Penalty 1984). In 1993, the first nation-wide poll to address the issue was conducted by a bipartisan coalition of polling firms. It reported that 46% of Americans expressed doubts about the death penalty when presented with information on cost (Dieter 1993).

Corroboration of the importance of cost information for death penalty opinions also comes from scholarly work on the Marshall hypothesis. Work in this area has investigated the impact of a wide variety of information and other experiences on support for the death penalty, including information on the utilitarian and humanitarian consequences of capital punishment (Sarat and Vidmar 1976; Vidmar and Dittenhoffer 1981); information on innocence and deterrence (Lambert and Clark 2001); taking a class on the death penalty (Bohm, Clark and Aveni 1990; Bohm and Vogel 2004; Cochran and Chamlin 2005); and being required to answer questions on the subject (Murray 2003). Regarding cost, Cochran *et al.* (2006) found that individuals susceptible to capital punishment "myths" (including the belief that it was cost-effective) reduced their levels of support for the death penalty more than others when such myths were debunked. Bohm and Vogel (2004) also noted that the pattern of changes in opinions on the death penalty over a ten-year period for their subjects appeared similar to the pattern in their reported beliefs about its costliness.[12]

Areas for Future Research

We next discuss three issues which future research should address to improve our knowledge about the cost of the death penalty. First, more needs to be known about the indirect costs of the death penalty, particularly the high cost of maintaining a capital punishment system infrastructure. Second, future work needs to explore the argument advanced by capital punishment proponents that the death penalty reduces costs by persuading defendants to plead guilty. Finally, and most importantly, the concrete diversion of criminal justice and human service budgetary resources caused by the excessive cost of the death penalty should be measured and analyzed at the state and local levels.

Fortunately, for several of these inquiries a natural laboratory exists: New York.

Capital punishment was reintroduced in New York in 1995, after a period of nearly twenty years in which the death penalty was not used or useable.[13] From September 1, 1995 to June 24, 2004, during which time more than 10,000 murders were committed, New York had a viable, operating death penalty. During these nine years, district attorneys considered bringing 877 death-eligible cases, filed death notices in 58 cases, and brought in jury death verdicts

---

12. No rigorous analysis was presented to test the statistical significance of this superficial similarity, however. Elsewhere, Bohm and Vogel (1991) found no significant impact on opinions following a class discussion about costs. The authors argued instead that their subjects tended towards abolitionism as a result of the cumulative effect of discussions across a variety of topics.

13. After an extensive history of executions making New York a national leader in capital punishment, the Bartlett Commission in 1965 called for abolition (State of New York Temporary Commission on Revision of the Penal Law and Criminal Code 1965). The resulting compromise that entered New York's 1967 Penal Law provided a limited death penalty, struck down on constraint of *Furman v. Georgia* (1972) in *People v. Fitzpatrick* (1973). The next year the Legislature passed a death penalty statute providing mandatory capital punishment for those who kill police officers or correctional officers, and for lifers who kill while in prison. *People v. Davis* (1977) effectively eliminated the first two categories, although the death penalty ruling technically applied only to correctional officers. For the next 17 years vetoes by two governors, punctuated only briefly in 1984 by the ruling that struck the lifer exception, *People v. Smith* (1984), effectively made New York death penalty free.

in seven. On June 24, 2004, the State's death penalty statute was enjoined[14] and no murder case subsequently was charged capitally. Thus, the period before, during, and after New York's recent capital experiment represents a natural laboratory for assessing the propositions that should be addressed in future cost research.

Indirect Costs and the Cost of Infrastructure

Although a great deal of work has been done to estimate costs associated with court proceedings and imprisonment, few attempts have been made to quantify indirect costs.[15] Past focus on "cost per trial" or "cost per execution" has tended to obscure the fact that the death penalty costs states money even when no trials or executions are being carried out. Even where states execute no one, as in New York between 1995 and 2004, the cost of the death penalty can be vast (Lentol, Weinstein and Aubry 2005) because maintaining a capital punishment infrastructure incurs additional costs unrelated to the conduct of executions. Costs are high when no trials are being conducted, when no cases are going forward capitally, and when no one is being executed. Those costs need to be cataloged and measured in systematic analyses.[16]

With the onset of capital punishment, New York's court system added special death clerks for each of the judges on its high court. Special training units

---

14. In *People v. LaValle* (2004) the New York Court of Appeals vacated the defendant's death sentence, held that the statutory deadlock instruction prescribed in the 1995 statute was unconstitutional under the New York State Constitution, and concluded that the statute could "only be cured by a new deadlock instruction from the Legislature." The court further held that first-degree murder prosecutions could only go forward as non-capital cases unless and until such a legislative change took place.

15. Discussions of the true cost of the death penalty often make the point that capital punishment has psychological and social costs for individuals and communities alike, but much work remains to be done exploring these issues. Financial costs incurred by uncompensated trial participants (such as witnesses and the families of defendants) have, for example, been noted, but not calculated. Juror impact has begun to be studied, with significant fruitful pathways opened for further exploration (Dieter 2005; National Center for State Courts 1998). The costs of correction officer and executioner stress have been noted as well (Lifton and Mitchell 2000). All of these areas suggest valuable directions for future research; they are also emblematic of the kind of indirect costs that need to uncovered and studied.

16. New York provides the attractiveness of a natural "before, during, and after" laboratory, but similar analyses can be performed through independent rigorous analyses in all death penalty states by a comparison of capital vs. non capital infrastructure costs. This approach, taken within case studies, is similarly available for examining the cost of infrastructure.

and programs were developed for prosecutors, defense, and judiciary. Five revenue streams were created to help prosecutors and an independent Backup Center for District Attorneys was established. The costs of prosecution have been estimated at $150 million, overshadowing the defense costs (Gradess 2005). Yet at its height the Capital Defender Office had more than 70 staffers and an annual budget of more than $15 million. After a recent case reaffirming New York's judicial declaration of the death penalty statute's constitutional flaws,[17] the State Department of Correctional Services reported that it had been housing the last resident of death row with operational costs amounting to $300,000 per year (Stashenko 2007). None of the work regarding the costs of the recent New York death penalty experiment has represented anything more than informed projections. Concrete work to scientifically determine capital punishment's genuine cost to law enforcement, courts, prosecution, defense, judiciary, and corrections is sure to reveal current figures to be deeply discounted conservative estimates. Future research can fruitfully examine more about the costs of infrastructure and its relationship to the high cost of maintaining a death penalty system in New York and elsewhere.

Cost Savings through Coercion

Future work should address empirically the argument that the death penalty might marginally reduce costs by persuading defendants to plead guilty, saving the state the cost of a trial in some cases. It is certainly true that the pleading of capital cases reduces their costliness (Maryland House Appropriations Committee 1985). Yet, putting aside constitutional objections to a penal scheme that scares people into disposing of their cases by threatening to poison them if they are found guilty after trial, there are many reasons to doubt the argument that the death penalty gives prosecutors an additional weapon with which to negotiate with defendants. In some states, indeed, bargaining by prosecutors in capital cases is illegal (Brooks and Erickson 1996). During New York's experiment with capital punishment, non-capital murder cases were often disposed of by plea with attendant trial and appeal waivers at an unexpectedly high rate.[18]

---

17. *People v. Taylor* (2007).
18. New York data for the period 1994–2003 reveal that 47 percent of non-capital second-degree murder cases were disposed of by plea without the coercion urged by death penalty apologists to justify the high costs of the death penalty. And significantly, non-capital murder cases do not receive the resources of capital murder cases. Police and prosecutorial work in non-capital cases is often routine, motion practice is frequently limited, and

Meanwhile, Nakell (1978) asserted that death penalty cases go to trial more than ten times more often than other felony cases. Prosecutors are often hawkish about the death penalty during election campaigns, increasing the probability that they will press for it when in office and use it where available (Dieter 1996). Thus, the marginal savings that might be envisioned would surely also have to examine whether this political factor offsets such savings in cases that otherwise should, but for their politics, have been disposed of by a guilty plea. These two opposing hypotheses about the effect of the death penalty on prosecutorial discretion have never been rigorously tested. More importantly, they have not been examined against the rich backdrop of emergent evidence on wrongful convictions (Dieter 2004), which helps to reveal patterns of coercion that should give pause for thought about even asserting the legitimacy of using plea bargaining as a cost control mechanism.

This area of research is important because the argument concerning cost savings through coercion is morally unattractive and the idea appears to rest on a flawed premise. The cost-savings argument appears akin to holding a 40% discount sale in a retail store, after marking up the price 200%. It is only through the increased cost generated by the death penalty that the unconscionable suggested savings can be realized. The proponents of this argument thus first concede the increased cost of capital punishment and then suggest an "offset" from the waiver of trials and appeals. Research controlling for other variables will, we think, reveal this.

Diversion of Criminal Justice and Human Service Budgetary Resources

Governors and State Legislatures across the country have come in the last 30 years to recognize—often during their worst fiscal crises—that they have been wasting enormous amounts of taxpayer money for exceedingly little or no return by "banking" on capital punishment. They have learned the hard way that they cannot have a death penalty with all its unnecessary attendant costs *and* all the other things citizens need. This phenomenon, separate and distinct

---

investigation constrained. The amount paid to assigned counsel in such cases—beginning with the statutory cap of $4,400—is still often a pittance. Public defenders are provided with no extra resources for those cases; neither are there five special state revenue streams available for prosecutors in non-capital cases. Automatic appeals to the Court of Appeals are not required in a non-capital case, post-conviction practice is rare, and grants of *certiorari* even rarer.

from the political rhetoric which has long accompanied the passage of substantive death provisions, has emerged in the context of budget analyses.

The "guns vs. butter" and "guns vs. guns" choices have been stark. Expanding taxpayer funds to support the death penalty by definition means that less money can be spent on what is needed for spina bifida research, AIDS services, homeless housing subsidies, etc. (guns vs. butter). If large amounts of government money are expended on the death penalty, less is available for bullet proof vests, partners accompanying one another in police cars, hazardous waste investigations, etc. (guns vs. guns). In sum, Government has come to see that there are not two spigots from which appropriations can flow forth, one for capital punishment and one for other services. Choices must be made. This understanding, now prevalent at the state level in many places, must be examined at the local level in death penalty states.

Future research must explore the local analog of these phenomena by examining the exact and exacting policy choices being made in localities across the country.[19] Researchers should assess the diversion of resources at the local level.

In 2001, Senator Elaine Richardson of Arizona acknowledged that certain counties in her state could not afford death penalty prosecutions. "If you live in Pima or Maricopa County you're going to get one form of treatment," she is reported to have said, "while anywhere else you're going to get a different form of treatment." In the same year, several smaller Georgia counties reported that they could not afford the cost of pursuing capital prosecutions without compromising road building programs or their ability to pay the salaries of personnel in their fire and sheriff's departments (Death Penalty Information Center 2007).

These seemingly isolated responses from knowledgeable public officials must be collected and used in conjunction with local analyses of the actual reasons why death penalty prosecutions are not pursued. Large state and small state phenomena should be compared and analyzed; the reasons for resistance to capital prosecutions may differ but the high cost motivation should remain constant. In California, there may be local concerns with property taxes. In New York in 2005, the death penalty was opposed at the local level in Syracuse because of the need for more child care (Leeds 2005). More than seventeen years ago the much smaller state of Missouri saw Schuyler and Texas counties threatened with bankruptcy over the cost of the death penalty (Gradess 1995).

Researchers must not only catalog the kinds of events represented by the Gallego monetary collection referred to earlier in this chapter, or the example

---

19. Baicker (2004) already provides evidence of the substantial costs of death penalty prosecutions to local governments.

of counties disputing where a body fell to avoid local prosecution costs (Sherrill 2001), but should also pose other critical related questions and study them. What does the high cost of capital punishment actually make people do? How specifically does it affect policy? When capital punishment is imposed, what actual public benefits are traded off? What factors are used to support the decision not to go forward when cost is the motivator? How is the justification presented when cost is the known motivator for behavior? Does cost drive down death sentencing at the local level? If so, does knowledge about it drive it down further? If cost drops support by 16% in public opinion surveys, does broader knowledge in a population have real world implications for advocacy, sentencing strategy, or juror education? What happens in jurisdictions when prosecutors attempt to try all death-eligible cases? What happens to the reversal rate? What down-line effects arise from this expenditure in other areas of law enforcement, including at the local level? How do we assess the value in increased resources of abolition to the law enforcement community? And perhaps more importantly, how do we assess the ways the general public benefits from not going forward with the capital sanction?

A long hard look at the single spigot phenomenon for government funding at the local level will reveal much about the high cost of capital punishment. It will also provide another window into its arbitrary and capricious application.

Conclusions: The One Spigot Period— 2007 and Beyond

Data compiled for more than 25 years in virtually all of the states studied consistently show that the death penalty costs more than life in prison. Officials take cost issues into account in the death states and the issue emerges in reinstatement debates almost as a given. The "high cost" of the death penalty is almost an adjective describing the sanction. The media concedes the issue, advocates use it, and proponents and pro-death politicians, rather than debating it, have to absorb it by urging facilely against it.

The bold declaration often made by proponents of capital punishment is that "justice has no price," and of course that is true. But the administration of a justice system inevitably does. Such a system involves real choices between different punishment options, each of which incurs different costs, benefits, and dangers.

In March 2007, Montana Assistant Attorney General John Connor called for the repeal of the death penalty in his state on the grounds that he did not believe it deterred crime, and that it was costly:

> It seems to me to be the ultimate incongruity to say we respect life so much that we're going to dedicate all our money, all our resources, our legal expertise and our entire system to try and take your life.... Frankly, I just don't think I can do it any more. (Associated Press 2007)

Connor, like Justice Blackmun before him, came to the realization that he could no longer tinker with the machinery of death (*Callins v. Collins* 1994).

Thanks to the research outlined above, the cost-benefit analysis of the death penalty can now be rendered in real, practical terms. The result of over fifty years of debate and research on the cost of the death penalty is that policy-makers now realize that the death penalty is not a free choice. Rather, it is one with a calculable financial impact. Unlike fifty years ago, state officials in New Jersey are now aware that the $11 million they spent on the death penalty in 2005 (when they executed no one) could have paid for 160 new police officers to be deployed on the streets of the state.[20] Alternatively, they could have spent the money on grief counseling for more than 850 victims of violent crime (Gradess 2006). Dollars spent on the death penalty do not just represent expenditures and investments: they represent choices made and opportunities lost. Not only must states choose what to give up to pay for the death penalty, they must also face the fact that not all their subdivisions can apply the death penalty equally; some will always resist capital punishment because it is too costly to use, producing further evidence of its arbitrariness.

In the years since Hartung's early writing on the cost of the death penalty (Hartung 1951), the importance, credibility, and sheer weight of evidence on the cost of the death penalty have all only grown. Were Justice Marshall writing his *Furman* opinion today, he would have been able to draw upon a wealth of information produced by academics, media organizations, government research departments, and criminal justice professionals from across the ideological spectrum to fortify his opinion that the death penalty is more costly than life imprisonment.

The task for researchers going forward is to build on these studies and data to draw the final significant conclusions about the cost of the penalty of death, so that even the most principled proponents of capital punishment must ask themselves exactly how much they are willing to pay for so little.

---

20. The cost to New Jersey of a new state police officer's salary in 2005 was $68,737.11 according to the New Jersey State Police Payroll Unit (communication 9/12/06 on file with authors).

References

Amnesty International USA. 1989. "New York Public Opinion Poll—The Death Penalty: An Executive Summary." Amnesty International USA. On file with authors.

Associated Press. 2007. "Assistant AG Asks House to End Death Penalty." Reprinted at *Billings Gazette*. (http://www.billingsgazette.net/articles/2007/03/10/news/state/37-death.txt).

Audit of the Department of Corrections, State of Kansas. 2003. "Performance Audit Report: Costs Incurred for Death Penalty Cases: A K-GOAL Audit of the Department of Corrections." State of Kansas, December 2003. (http://www.kslegislature.org/postaudit/audits_perform/04pa03a.pdf).

Baicker, Katherine. 2004. "The Budgetary Repercussions of Capital Convictions." *Advances in Economic Analysis & Policy* 4:1311–1337.

Bohm, Robert. 2003. "The Economic Costs of Capital Punishment: Past, Present, and Future." Pp. 573–594 in *America's Experiment with Capital Punishment: Reflections on the Past, Present and Future of the Ultimate Penal Sanction*. 2nd ed., edited by James R. Acker, Robert M. Bohm, and Charles S. Lanier. Durham, NC: Carolina Academic Press.

Bohm, Robert M., Louise J. Clark and Adrian F. Aveni. 1990. "The Influence of Knowledge of Reasons for Death Penalty Opinions: An Experimental Test." *Justice Quarterly* 7:175–186.

Bohm, Robert M. and Brenda L. Vogel. 2004. "More Than Ten Years After: The Long-Term Stability of Informed Death Penalty Opinions." *Journal of Criminal Justice* 32:307–327.

Bohm, Robert M. and Ronald E. Vogel. 1991. "Educational Experiences and Death Penalty Opinions: Stimuli That Produce Changes." *Journal of Criminal Justice Education* 2:69–80.

Brooks, Justin and Jeanne H. Erickson. 1996. "The Dire Wolf Collects His Due While the Boys Sit by the Fire: Why Michigan Cannot Afford to Buy into the Death Penalty." *Thomas M. Cooley Law Review* 13:877–905.

Caldwell, Robert G. 1952. "Why is the Death Penalty Retained?" *Annals of the American Academy of Political and Social Science* 284:45–53.

Callins v. Collins (1994). 510 U.S. 1141.

Carter, Martha. 1995. "Cost of the Death Penalty: An Introduction to the Issue." Report # 95-2. Lincoln, NE: Legislative Research Division, Nebraska Legislature.

Cochran, John K. and Mitchell B. Chamlin. 2005. "Can Information Change Public Opinion? Another Test of the Marshall Hypothesis." *Journal of Criminal Justice* 33:573–584.

Cochran, John K., Beth Sanders and Mitchell B. Chamblin. 2006. "Profiles in Change: An Alternative Look at the Marshall Hypothesis." *Journal of Criminal Justice Education* 17:205–226.

Cook, Philip J., Donna B. Slawson and Lori A. Gries. 1993. "The Costs of Processing Murder Cases in North Carolina." Durham, NC: Terry Sandford Institute of Public Policy, Duke University. (http://www.thejusticeproject.org/press/reports/pdfs/21740.pdf).

Costanzo, Mark. 2001. *Just Revenge: Costs and Consequences of the Death Penalty.* 3rd ed. New York, NY: St. Martin's Press.

Costanzo, Mark and Lawrence T. White. 1994. "An Overview of the Death Penalty and Capital Trials: History, Current Status, Legal Procedures and Cost." *Journal of Social Issues* 50:1–18.

Culver, John H. 1985. "The States and Capital Punishment: Executions From 1977–1984." *Justice Quarterly* 2:567–578.

Dáte, Shirish V. 2000. "The High Price of Killing Killers." *Palm Beach Post,* Jan. 4, A1.

Death Penalty Information Center. 2007. "Costs News and Developments: 2001–1998." (http://www.deathpenaltyinfo.org/article.php?did=2061).

Dieter, Richard C. 2005. "Blind Justice: Juries Deciding Life and Death with Only Half the Truth." Washington DC: Death Penalty Information Center. (http://www.deathpenaltyinfo.org/BlindJusticeReport.pdf).

_____. 2004. "Innocence and the Crisis in the American Death Penalty." Washington DC: Death Penalty Information Center. (http://www.deathpenaltyinfo.org/article.php?scid=45&did=1150).

_____. 1996. "Killing for Votes: the Dangers of Politicizing the Death Penalty Process." Washington DC: Death Penalty Information Center. (http://www.deathpenaltyinfo.org/article.php?scid=45&did=260).

_____. 1994. "Millions Misspent: What Politicians Don't Say About the High Costs of the Death Penalty." 2nd ed. Washington DC: Death Penalty Information Center. (http://www.deathpenaltyinfo.org/article.php?scid=45&did=385).

_____. 1993. "Sentencing for Life: Americans Embrace Alternatives to the Death Penalty." Washington DC: Death Penalty Information Center. (http://www.deathpenaltyinfo.org/article.php?scid=45&did=481).

Ellsworth, Phoebe C. and Samuel R. Gross. 1994. "Hardening of the Attitudes: Americans' Views on the Death Penalty." *Journal of Social Issues* 50:19–52.

Eshelman, Byron E. and Frank Riley. 1962. *Death Row Chaplain.* Englewood Cliffs, NJ: Prentice-Hall.

Forsberg, Mary E. 2005. *Money for Nothing? The Financial Cost of New Jersey's Death Penalty.* Trenton, NJ: New Jersey Policy Perspective.

Furman v. Georgia (1972). 408 U.S. 238.

Gallup. 2003. "Death Penalty" [responses to question 'Why do you favor the death penalty for persons convicted of murder?'], for May 19–21, 2003. (http://www.galluppoll.com/content/?ci=1606&pg=1).

Garey, Margot. 1985. "The Cost of Taking a Life: Collars and Sense of the Death Penalty." *U.C. Davis Law Review* 18:1221–1273.

General Accounting Office. 1989. "Limited Data Available on Costs of Death Sentences: Report to the Chairman, Subcommittee on Civil and Constitutional Rights, Committee on the Judiciary, House of Representatives." Washington, DC: United States General Accounting Office.

Gilliam, Stan. 2006. Personal communication via email. Available from authors.

Goodman, Brenda. 2007. "Georgia Murder Case's Cost Saps Public Defense System." *New York Times,* March 22, A16.

Gradess, Jonathan. 2006. "New Jersey and the Cost of the Death Penalty" (written testimony before the New Jersey Death Penalty Study Commission), given September 13, 2006, Trenton, NJ. On file with authors.

_____. 2005. "The Death Penalty in New York State" (written testimony before the New York State Assembly Standing Committees on Codes, Judiciary and Correction), given January 25, 2005, Albany, NY. On file with authors.

_____. 1995. *Affidavit of Jonathan E. Gradess re: Cost of the Death Penalty in Willie Simmons v. State of Missouri.* On file with authors.

_____. 1992. *Affidavit re: Cost of Death Penalty in Tennessee v. Henry Hodges.* On file with authors.

Grasmick, Harold G. and Robert J. Bursik. 1988. "Attitudes of Oklahomans Toward the Death Penalty." Norman, OK: Center for the Study of Crime and Delinquency: Study 8802, Department of Sociology, University of Oklahoma.

Hartung, Frank E. 1951. *On Capital Punishment.* Wayne University. Unpublished manuscript.

Hoppe, Christy. 1992. "Executions Cost Texas Millions." *Dallas Morning News,* March 8, A1.

Indiana Legislature. 1989. *A Fiscal Impact Statement re: Senate Bill 531.* Indianapolis: Indiana Legislature.

Iowa Legislative Fiscal Bureau. 1991. *Senate File 384: Fiscal Note for Amendment H-3546.*

Janeway, Kathryn. 2002. "The Application of Indiana's Capital Sentencing Law: Findings of the Indiana Criminal Law Study Commission." (http://www.in.gov/cji/special-initiatives/law_book.pdf).

Kansas Legislative Research Department. 1994. "Memorandum: Cost Considerations of Implementing the Death Penalty." Topeka, KS: Kansas Legislative Research Department. Feb. 15.

_____. 1987. "Memorandum from Kansas Legislative Research Department Regarding Costs of Implementing the Death Penalty—House Bill 2062 as Amended by the House Committee of the Whole." Topeka, KS: Kansas Legislative Research Department. Feb. 11.

Lambert, Eric and Alan Clarke. 2001. "The Impact of Information on an Individual's Support of the Death Penalty: A Partial Test of the Marshall Hypothesis among College Students." *Criminal Justice Policy Review* 12:215–234.

Leeds, Stephanie F. 2005. "Focus on the Living." *Syracuse Post-Standard*, April 17.

Lentol, Joseph, Helene Weinstein and Jeffrion Aubry. 2005. *The Death Penalty in New York*. Albany, NY: New York State Assembly.

Liebman, James S., Jeffrey Fagan and Valerie West. 2000. "A Broken System: Error Rates in Capital Cases, 1973–1995." (http://www2.law.columbia.edu/instructionalservices/liebman/index.html).

Lifton, Robert J. and Greg Mitchell. 2000. *Who Owns Death: Capital Punishment, the American Conscience and the End of Executions*. New York, NY: HarperCollins.

Maganini, Stephen. 1988. "Closing Death Row Would Save State $90 Million a Year." *Sacramento Bee*, March 28, A1.

Maryland House Appropriations Committee. 1985. "Committee to Study the Death Penalty in Maryland, Final Report: The Cost and Hours Associated with Processing a Sample of First Degree Murder Cases for which the Death Penalty was Sought in Maryland Between July 1979 and March 1984." Maryland House Appropriations Committee.

Massachusetts Citizens Against the Restoration of the Death Penalty. 1984. "Death Penalty Opinion Poll Study." Unpublished manuscript. On file with authors.

McGee, Richard A. 1964. "Capital Punishment as Seen by a Correctional Administrator." *Federal Probation* 2:11–16.

Moran, Richard and Joseph Ellis. 1989. "Death Penalty: Luxury Item." *Newsday*, June 14, 60.

_____. 1986. "Price of Executions Is Just Too High." *Wall Street Journal*, Oct. 15, 34.

Morgenthau, Robert M. 1995. "What Prosecutors Won't Tell You." *New York Times*, Feb. 7, A25.

Murray, Greg. 2003. "Raising Considerations: Public Opinion and the Fair Application of the Death Penalty." *Social Science Quarterly* 84:753–770.

Nakell, Barry. 1978. "The Cost of the Death Penalty." *Criminal Law Bulletin* 14:69–80.

National Center for State Courts. 1998. "Through the Eyes of the Juror: A Manual for Addressing Juror Stress," NCSC Publication # R-209. National Center for State Courts.

New York State Defenders Association. 1982. "Capital Losses: The Price of the Death Penalty in New York State." Albany, NY: New York State Defenders Association.

Paternoster, Raymond, Robert Brame, and Sarah Bacon. 2003. "An Empirical Analysis of Maryland's Death-Sentencing System with Respect to the Influence of Race and Legal Jurisdiction: Final Report." Baltimore, MD: University of Maryland.

People v. Davis (1977). 371 N.E.2d 456 (N.Y.).

People v. Fitzpatrick (1973). 300 N.E.2d 139 (N.Y.).

People v. LaValle (2004). 817 N.E.2d 341 (N.Y.).

People v. Smith (1984). 468 N.E.2d 879 (N.Y.).

People v. Taylor (2007). 878 N.E.2d 969 (N.Y.).

Radelet, Michael L. and Marian J. Borg. 2000. "The Changing Nature of Death Penalty Debates." *Annual Review of Sociology* 26:43–61.

Roll, John. 1984. *"Citizens Donate Money to Pay for Trial of Accused Killer."* Associated Press feed, Mar 24.

Sarat, Austin and Neil Vidmar. 1976. "Public Opinion, The Death Penalty and the Eighth Amendment: Testing the Marshall Hypothesis." *Wisconsin Law Review* 1:171–206.

Sellin, Thorsten. 1961. "Capital Punishment." *Federal Probation* 25:3–11.

Sherrill, Robert. 2001. "Death Trip: The American Way of Execution." *The Nation*, Jan. 8.

Snell, Tracy L. 2006. "Capital Punishment, 2005." *Bureau of Justice Statistics Bulletin.* (http://www.ojp.usdoj.gov/bjs/pub/pdf/cp05.pdf).

Spencer, James R., Robin J. Cauthron, and Nancy G. Edmunds. 1998. "Federal Death Penalty Cases: Recommendations Concerning the Cost and Quality of Defense Representation." Report to the Judicial Conference of the United States, Sept. 15.

Stashenko, Joel. 2007. "Capital Defender Readies to Shut Doors." *New York Law Journal*, Oct. 29.

State of New York Temporary Commission on Revision of the Penal Law and Criminal Code. 1965. "Fourth Interim Report." Legislative Document # 25: Feb. 1.

Tabak, Ronald J. and J. Mark Lane. 1989. "The Execution of Injustice: A Cost and Lack-of-Benefit Analysis of the Death Penalty." *Loyola of Los Angeles Law Review* 23:59–146.

Taylor, Michael. 2002. "'Sex-Slave' Killer Dies of Cancer in Nevada Prison Hospital." *San Francisco Chronicle*, July 22, A15.

Van den Haag, Ernest and John P. Conrad. 1983. *The Death Penalty: A Debate*. New York, NY: Plenum.

Van Duizend, Richard, Mary E. Elsner, Don E. Hardenbergh and Howard Wainer. 1986. "Does the Death Penalty Impose Additional Costs on the Justice System? A Research Design." National Center for State Courts.

Vidmar, Neil and Tony Dittenhoffer. 1981. "Informed Public Opinion and Death Penalty Attitudes." *Canadian Journal of Criminology* 23:43–56.

Von Drehle, Dave. 1988. "The Death Penalty, A Failure of Execution." *The Miami Herald*, July 10–13.

Wilson, Emily, Brian Doss and Sonya Phillips. 2004. "Tennessee's Death Penalty: Costs and Consequences." Tennessee: Comptroller of the Treasury, Office of Research, Authorization Number 307321.

SECTION V

EXAMINING THE PUNISHMENT OF DEATH

CHAPTER 19

"Symbolic" and "Instrumental" Aspects of Capital Punishment[*]

David Garland

Introduction

In the last thirty years, studies of the symbolic aspects of action and institutions have become well established in social science and in socio-legal studies. The analysis of symbolic connotation, oblique meaning and indirect communication has become central to one field after another, as the "cultural turn" has re-oriented sociology (Friedland and Mohr 2004); historical work has focused on matters of culture and meaning (Hunt 1989); and expressive theories of law have prompted legal scholars to examine law's declarative, communicative aspects as well as its performative ones (Anderson and Pildes 2000). This general re-orientation has made the study of symbols and symbolic action much more common but also somewhat less precise. The subtlety and care brought to these problems by early analysts such as Joseph Gusfield (1963, 1986), Kit Carson (1974), and Murray Edelman (1964), or their common literary inspiration, Kenneth Burke (1968, 1969), is not always in evidence, nor is the precision with which they defined their concepts and applied them to their material. Thirty years on, we have followed their lead but not always fully absorbed the lessons they have to teach us.

---

[*] A different version of this paper appeared in A. Brannigan and G. Pavlich (eds.) *Governance and Regulation in Social Life: Essays in Honour of W.G.Carson* (Routledge-Cavendish 2007).

This chapter will discuss a field of research in which symbolism in general and the symbolic/instrumental distinction in particular are frequently invoked by socio-legal scholarship—the study of capital punishment. It will use Gusfield's and Carson's analyses as a point of departure in an attempt to identify the problems to be explained, to clarify the conceptual issues involved, and to refine the kind of analysis that ought to be brought to bear. It will also carry forward their insistence on historical and theoretical specificity by suggesting that we must forge new conceptual tools if we are to properly understand the various ways in which "the symbolic" and "the instrumental" (as well as other forms of action and communication) feature in the institution of capital punishment.

An inquiry of this kind seems timely. In recent years, it has become commonplace to discount the "instrumental" efficacy of capital punishment and to consider America's capital punishment laws and litigation as largely "symbolic" in motive and character. Commentators point to the death penalty's limited impact as an instrument of crime control (Garland 1990); to the limited protections of legal rules that are designed to provide the "reassuring symbolism of legal doctrine" rather than to confer any more robust rights to the defendant (Weisberg 1983:307); to the restricted role of instrumental (as opposed to symbolic) considerations in shaping public attitudes (Tyler and Weber 1982); and to the marked contrast between public enthusiasm for *enacting* death penalty statutes and institutional reluctance to *enforce* them (Weisberg 1996). These observations frequently prompt the conclusion that the system is oriented to symbolic rather than to instrumental ends—that capital punishment is all symbol and no substance (*cf.*, Zimring 2005).

Thus, Zimring and Hawkins (1986) assert that "the appeal of the death penalty derives not from its function as a particularly effective or appropriate penal method, but rather from its symbolic significance" (p. 19). They point out that, for all the public discussion that surrounds it, the death penalty is imposed on very few offenders (in 2004 the number was 130, out of approximately 15,000 homicide arrests), and of these sentences, fewer than half are actually executed (in 2004, the number was 59), typically after a decade and more of appeals, habeas corpus reviews and stays of execution. This pattern of administration implies a discrepancy between the public's idea of capital punishment and the actual practices through which that punishment is (or is not) carried out. To many analysts this suggests that the death penalty ought to be considered as a symbolic gesture rather than an operative system of penal justice or crime control—or, as they typically say, as "symbolic" and not "instrumental."

Research on public attitudes similarly suggests that individuals support or oppose capital punishment on the basis of "symbolic attitudes" rather than as an "instrumental response" to the problem of crime (Tyler and Weber 1982). And Ellsworth and Gross (1994) point out that individual attitudes on this issue are rooted in "symbolic" associations with specific styles of life and identity rather than in instrumental calculations about what will best reduce crime or secure justice: "[D]eath penalty attitudes came to have a powerful symbolic significance, [with] support for the death penalty representing an ideological self-definition of the person as unyielding in the war on crime, unwilling to coddle criminals, firm and courageous" (p. 19). The finding that attitudes regarding capital punishment reflect the individual's basic values rather than his or her assessment of the practical efficacy of death as a specific penal sanction suggests that symbolic appeals and associations play a major role in shaping public opinion. For many members of the public, the death penalty is a resonant symbol that they invoke to express a sentiment, rather than a practical policy option that they have decided is more effective than the alternatives. Public opinion polls probably reflect and reinforce this tendency.

A related point concerns the politics of law-making in this area. Despite the considerable political energy that goes into creating capital punishment legislation, death penalty laws are often enacted to great fanfare only to lie on the books for years without being enforced or executed. Commentators point out that some state statutes are so narrowly drafted—New York's 1995 statute is an example—that they are unlikely to result in any offenders ever being executed (Kahan 1999; Weisberg 1996; Zimring 2005). The inference drawn from this, once again, is that capital punishment ought to be viewed as a political symbol rather than a policy instrument: "The death penalty fails as a political tool but it is a highly effective means for politicians to manipulate political debates and public perceptions" (Pierce and Radelet 1990–1991:726).

Commentators also suggest that the emotional energy and political salience associated with capital punishment are explicable only by reference to its symbolic qualities, since the existence of the penalty directly affects very few people in material respects or in terms of their everyday lives. As one author puts it, "[n]o person's livelihood ... is at stake when executions are present or absent in state government—except of course the condemned.... Does not this inflated emphasis on a little used sanction show that the ultimate stakes are symbolic?" (Zimring 1999:140). Again, the inference being drawn is that the energy unleashed by this issue has to be understood in non-instrumental terms, as symbolic rather than material politics. "For many people, policies such as those regarding abortion and pornography regulation, gambling, the death penalty, and sex education symbolize the basic moral values affirmed by the state" (Mooney and Lee 2000:224). Like flag-burning or school prayer or gay marriages, it is a "social values" issue rather than a "pocketbook" one. And where social values are at stake, the evocation of symbolic associations often matters more than instituting of operative practices. All of this tends to support an understanding of capital punishment framed in symbolic rather than instrumental terms.

Yet this conventional characterization of capital punishment as a "symbolic," non-instrumental sanction may be less accurate and less helpful than it at first appears. In their eagerness to criticize an institution that is deeply controversial, commentators may be too quick to reduce a complex network of actors and system of practices to a singular "symbolic" dimension; too ready to ignore the instrumental uses to which capital punishment laws can be put, whether or not anyone is actually executed; too one-dimensional and unempirical in their discussion of symbolic communication; and too casual in their use of the term "symbolic" to effectively address what is at stake in this description.

I will argue that the original meaning of the symbolic/instrumental distinction is changed when translated into the capital punishment field, and that its conceptual precision is lost as a consequence. Once this original precision is abandoned, the idea of "the symbolic" becomes increasingly slippery and vague, as does its relation to "the instrumental." I argue that the current usage of this dichotomy is problematic, and that analysts should either use it in its original sense or else abandon these generic terms altogether and substitute some more precise descriptive terms.

This chapter is thus, in part, a critique of the transformation and misuse of what was originally an effective and precise conceptual distinction. Beyond this, my argument will be that the dichotomy developed by Gusfield and Carson remains valuable for the study of capital punishment, as do several related conceptual points that emerge from their work. But I will also suggest that the communicative and cultural dimensions of the death penalty raise explanatory issues that cannot be understood by reference to the symbol/instrument distinction nor by the status group and interest group politics to which this distinction originally referred. I will briefly identify some of the other dimensions of social meaning, social action, and social consequence that operate in this domain, and suggest some terms and concepts that might allow us to address them. My conclusion is that the analytical framework developed by Gusfield and Carson, properly understood, remains relevant to the study of capital punishment but does not exhaust the problems of symbolic action and social meaning that arise in that field. Scholars of capital punishment have conceptual as well as empirical work that still needs to be done.

The Meaning and Purpose of the Symbolic/Instrumental Distinction

The symbolic/instrumental distinction has become a standard reference point in socio-legal literature—so much so that it is often evoked without any explication, as if it were a natural way to classify action and phenomena in the world. But like all conceptual tools, this distinction was created to do some quite specific theoretical work. Reading the various ways in which this distinction is now deployed in the capital punishment literature, it seems to me that the particular explanatory use for which this dichotomy was originally designed may no longer be the one to which it is now typically put. Instead of being used to get at the specific explanatory issues with which Gusfield and Carson were concerned, these terms are now employed in a much looser sense and in a broader set of contexts. The result is that the meaning of the distinction tends to slip and the explanatory claims implied by its use become less clear. Before using these terms to analyze capital punishment we ought to recall why these concepts were originally developed and what theoretical work they were intended to do. By recalling the original meaning and use of these terms we may be able to sharpen our use of them in this domain, avoid misapplications and confusions, and relearn some of the lessons that Gusfield and Carson have to teach.

In *Symbolic Crusade: Status Politics and the American Temperance Movement*, first published in 1963,[1] Joseph Gusfield generated the idea of symbolic crusades and symbolic politics to explain actions that could not easily be explained by "interest politics"—which was at the time the dominant framework for understanding politically oriented collective action by social groups. The limited capacity of "interests"—understood as *material* interests, which is to say the pursuit of *economic* or *political* advantage—to explain the conduct of groups and individuals who pursued temperance reform prompted Gusfield to look for other kinds of motivational accounts.[2] In particular, it led him to focus upon *status* concerns and the ways in which group prestige is gained or lost in the course of legislative conflicts. To the extent that these conflicts come to be about the status, rather than about the legislation, the participants focus upon signs of respect and disrespect and shape their words and deeds in ways calculated to enhance their social standing. And since status is a matter of pub-

---

1. References here are to the 1984 reprint edition.
2. Similar concerns prompted Murray Edelman (1964) to look for non-economic ways to explain voting behavior, election campaigns, and the other rituals of political life.

lic regard rather than material resources, status struggles revolve around the symbols, signs and gestures that confirm the group's perceived place in the social hierarchy.

To understand this kind of action, the sociologist needs to chart struggles over symbolic goods as well as struggles over material ones. As Gusfield (1984) remarks, "We have always understood the desire to defend fortune. We should also understand the desire to defend respect. It is less clear because it is symbolic in nature but it is not less significant" (p. 11). In this competition for social status and esteem, the government's legislative acts take on an especially weighty character. "Since governmental actions symbolize the position of groups in the status structure, seemingly ceremonial or ritual acts of government are often of great importance to many social groups. Issues which seem foolish or impractical items are often important for what they symbolize about the style or culture which is being recognized or derogated. Being acts of deference or degradation, the individual finds in government action that his own perceptions of his status in the society are confirmed or rejected" (Gusfield 1984:11).

Gusfield's investigation of status politics allowed some otherwise inexplicable actions to be made intelligible.[3] In particular, it allowed him to explain why it was that such fierce energy was put into the pursuit of temperance legislation when it was widely believed that such legislation, even if passed, would not be enforceable and could not achieve its ostensible goal of compelling abstinence among alcohol users. In the course of his study, he effectively re-interprets the meaning of the American temperance movement and the constitutional prohibition on alcohol that it secured. What had previously been understood as a futile and misdirected effort to ban drinking was now viewed as a successful and well-aimed campaign to enhance the status of groups who led the temperance movement. The real goal was, in that sense, "symbolic" rather than "instrumental." Its aim was not to have the government end drinking but rather to have the government affirm the superior social status of rural Protestant Americans by contrastively degrading the values and lifestyles of urban immigrant groups whose drinking was now deemed a national problem.

In his 1974 article, Kit Carson takes up Gusfield's distinction and uses it as a heuristic for understanding the struggles over factory safety legislation in England in the 1830s—the proposed laws to regulate factory conditions, the

---

3. Tom Frank (2004) makes a similar move when he explains the voting behavior of poor electoral districts such as Kansas, which seem to be inexplicable if the explanatory framework foregrounds economic interests. But, in sharp contrast to Gusfield, Frank seems to believe that the pursuit of status recognition through symbolic politics is an irrational enterprise.

length of the working day, and health and safety at work. Legislation of this kind has obvious economic consequences, and can be expected to impinge in different ways on different interest groups (factory owners, firms, and employers, which vary in terms of size, sector, employment practices, etc.). Patterns of support and group mobilization might therefore be expected to follow the logic of economic interest. However, Carson shows that economic considerations are a poor guide to legislative politics here because other, non-economic issues were also at stake. He demonstrates that the enactment of factory safety laws was also understood by proponents and opponents as a means to a moral end—the fostering of humane conditions in the workplace—and as a marker of the social ascendancy and decline of different groups, as the new industrial economy began to acquire the marks of respectability and official recognition. As a result, status considerations and symbolic understandings shaped action as much as economic motivations did. Based on these insights, Carson's study is able to offer a powerful explanation of the calculations and strategic choices that lay behind the shifting positions and public statements of the key actors in this legislative campaign and the debates that surrounded it.

Capital Punishment and Status Politics

Central to Gusfield's and Carson's inquiries is a question about the motivations that prompted specific actions, attitudes and statements. How did particular social groups come to support or oppose specific legal provisions or proposed law reforms? Why did key players adopt a particular position or develop a particular attitude and why did these sometimes change over time? Why did particular actors do what they did and say what they said? It scarcely needs to be pointed out that these questions are of central importance in the study of capital punishment, particularly in the United States, where the policy-making process is closely attuned to public opinion and political leaders often claim to be following the preferences of the people they serve. As one might expect, there is a large body of work that investigates the motivational underpinning of these public attitudes: some of it examining the differential attitudes of specific demographic groups (Ellsworth and Gross 1994); some of it studying social movements and the groups who compose them (Haines 1996); and some of it exploring the emotional and cognitive roots of individual attitudes (Ellsworth and Gross 1994; Kahan 1999; Tyler and Weber 1982).

In Gusfield's work in particular, there is a concern with laws that are best understood as forms of symbolic action—which is to say, as governmental acts the primary impact of which is to shape ideas and attitude rather than directly regulate conduct. And while the laws that he mentions in this category—laws regulating gambling, birth control, prostitution and drinking—do not explicitly include capital punishment, it is clear that many of today's death penalty statutes can be thought of in this way.[4]

As noted above, the analytical frame that Gusfield and Carson use to explain the motivation of groups who pursue legislation that is (at least for them) primarily "symbolic" rather than "instrumental" is that of "status politics." Groups of actors form opinions about laws and take action with respect to them because they understand that these governmental decrees hold implications for the distribution of social prestige. They are motivated by the belief that their social standing will be positively or negatively affected by the fact that such legislation is contemplated and passed, whether or not it is ever effectively enforced. Their action is undertaken to advance these status interests.

Status politics of this kind are surely an aspect of the struggles over capital punishment—particularly in states where enactment is not backed up by enforcement—though the exact balance of status and economic interests (or symbolic and instrumental goals) will vary somewhat, depending upon which actors one is observing. Politicians who engage in death penalty politics in order to win votes and get elected might be said to be pursuing "instrumental" rather than "symbolic" interests, though they are using a symbolic means to do so. Prosecutors who bring a capital indictment to pressure defendants to enter a plea bargain—or else to win the approval of constituents and enhance their prospects of re-election—are likewise acting in a classically "instrumental" manner.[5] But for many other actors, including most members of the public, their attitude towards capital punishment may have no very clear instrumental aspect. For most members of the public, being for or against the death penalty brings nothing in the way of professional advancement or material gain. It is a matter of values rather than interests, if one might put it that way. For these individuals and groups, support for, or opposition to, the death penalty is a symbol expressing values and commitments rather than an instrumental means for pursuing material reward.

For these actors, their attitude towards the issue may be an expression of a commitment to "specific styles of life or identity" (Ellsworth and Gross 1994)

---

4. Gusfield was writing in the late 1950s and early 1960s, at which time capital punishment in America more frequently resulted in executions than was subsequently the case. The shift to a "symbolic" interpretation of the death penalty only began in the late 1970s and early 1980s, when laws were on the books and sentences were passed but very few condemned men were actually put to death.

5. Note that the threat of capital punishment must seem real enough to the defendant if it is to be effective as a means of forcing a guilty plea.

or, more broadly, to a set of (religious, political, moral or philosophical) values that somehow bear upon the question. As Kahan (1999) suggests, the politics of capital punishment pit "authoritarianism [against] egalitarianism, righteousness [against] tolerance, southernness and westernness [against] easternness, compassion for victims of crime [against] compassion for victims of social deprivation" (p. 488). These conflicting values map onto conflicts of class, region, race, religion and gender, albeit in a rather complex way. But whatever the exact linkages, the result is that the debate over capital punishment is always also a debate over social values and their competing claims to authority.

This may be true even when the idiom in which these struggles are pursued is a utilitarian one focused on questions of crime control and deterrence. In an argument that echoes Gusfield's, Kahan (1999) suggests that attitudes towards the death penalty are a form of status signaling, and that conflicts over capital punishment are best understood not as debates about penal policy but as displaced conflicts between status collectivities over what he calls "the expressive capital of the criminal law" (p. 416). Status concerns of this kind are no doubt part of the reason why so much public and political energy is expended on a penal measure that directly affects so few people.

But if status politics are a driving force here—in a way that economic interests evidently are not—we ought to bear in mind that their operation is complex: in the enactment of capital punishment laws there is always more than one kind of status at stake. To begin with, the primary status attribution does not directly implicate a social group at all, but instead refers to those individuals—nowadays persons convicted of aggravated murder—who are made subject to the penalty of death. Gusfield (1986) tells us that "[t]he language of status issues ... is the language of moral condemnation," and the chief target of the law's moral reproach and status degradation in capital punishment is the murderer himself (p. 184). By responding to the defendant's crime (and to the account of his life and character typically offered by the defense by way of mitigation) with the death penalty rather than life imprisonment, the jury makes a judgment about his social worth and his value as a human being. Of all the symbolic messages that such laws convey, the most obvious and explicit one is that capital murderers are human beings who do not deserve to live. As James Fitzjames Stephen (1864) put it: "When a man is hung, there is an end to our relations with him. His execution is a way of saying, 'You are not fit for this world, take your chance elsewhere'" (p. 763, quoted in *Furman v. Georgia* 1972:292).

We might pause here to note that this "symbolic," "communicative," or "expressive" aspect of capital punishment—the implied statement that aggravated murder is reprehensible in the extreme and that the defendant stands condemned of the worst of all crimes—is not an accidental afterthought, or an oblique symbolic aside. Nor is it separate from the punishment's instrumental aim. It is an intrinsic element of the punishment, a central part of the penalty's instrumentality and intended effect. The punishment of death is being used as a symbolic communication as well as an instrument of retribution, deterrence and incapacitation. It is an instrumental symbol as well as a symbolic instrument.

After the symbolic depiction and status degradation of the murderer, the next most explicit status attribution concerns the murder victim and the social or occupational group from which he or she is drawn. One of the distinctive features of today's capital punishment statutes is that they identify aggravating factors that elevate an ordinary homicide to a capital murder for which the penalty can be death. Aggravating factors take a variety of forms, including traditional ones such as felony murder, mass murder, murder in prison, or murder while lying in wait. But, as Simon and Spaulding (1999) have observed, many modern statutes also identify special classes of victims whose murder constitutes a capital offense—for instance police or prison officers, federal agents, pregnant women, young children, seniors, or individuals who were killed because of their race, religion, national origin or sexual orientation. By singling out these occupational and social groups for special protection, the state accords them a measure of social esteem that is denied to other victims—an obvious example of such non-favored victims being young black urban males who are, in fact, at greatest risk of being murdered.

Simon and Spaulding note that prosecutors and jurors have always tended to make covert judgments about the social worth of victims when they exercise their discretion over capital charges and verdicts. But now judgments of the victim's social worth are being made in advance, drawing law-makers directly and explicitly into the "politics of identity" and the "endless battle for prestige and power within the state" (Simon and Spaulding 1999:82). The political process that shapes these aggravating factors—campaigning for recognition by identity groups (gays and lesbians, the disabled, ethnic minorities) and by occupational groups (police and prison officers, federal agents, etc.) is precisely the symbolic pursuit of status that Gusfield describes. The Supreme Court's decision in *Payne v. Tennessee* (1991) that permitted the relatives of the deceased to make victim impact statements in the penalty phase of a capital murder trial might be understood in the same way—as a mark of esteem for victims and an institutionalized recognition of their worth. In effect, crime victims have operated as a mobilized status collectivity and have enhanced their social standing and visibility by means of legislation and legal decisions. Victim impact statements may or may not secure their declared instrumental aims of producing "closure" and enhancing "justice." But the very fact that the law now permits such statements to be made is, in itself, a symbol of the official esteem in which victims' survivors are now held.

In addition to these more or less direct attributions of status worth, the enactment and enforcement of capital punishment statutes send other messages, some of which may have significant implications—whether "symbolic" or "instrumental"—for particular social groups or status collectivities. When the New York State legislature enacted a death penalty law in 1995 the lawmakers' action had many meanings. Its most proximate meaning was a legal one: henceforth certain murderers in New York would be liable for the death penalty, assuming a capital charge is brought, appropriate procedures are followed and a jury chooses to impose a capital sentence. This, one might say, was the denotative meaning of their legislative act—a meaning clearly entailed by the passage of a death penalty law. But, as with any social practice, this action had other layers of significance and other social meanings.

Another core meaning was a political one. The passage of such a law was a defeat for Democratic Assembly representatives and Senators (many of whom were opposed to the death penalty) and a victory for Republicans (most of whom were for it). In one sense, there was nothing especially "symbolic" about this. The 1994 elections had produced a new Republican state governor who had promised to reintroduce the death penalty. The successful enactment of the 1995 statute was thus the predictable outcome of this new balance of political forces. To say that it "symbolized" a victory for the Republicans is to misuse the term—it would be clearer and more precise to say that it *was* a victory (or was the *product* of a victory) in the immediate, literal sense of this being an intrinsic aspect of the law-making event understood politically.

However, in the perceptions of many legislators and commentators (and, one assumes, in the perception of some members of the public), this legislative development had larger significance and further layers of meaning. The new law on capital punishment was not simply a Republican policy preference on a par with lowered property taxes or trimmed-back welfare spending. Rather, it was generally understood as a historic achievement given the fact that capital punishment bills had been introduced every session for 18 years, only to be vetoed by Democrats Mario Cuomo and Hugh Carey, the two previous governors. These prior defeats and recurring efforts heightened the significance of the law and intensified its political meaning. Its passage was therefore a major event, marking the passage of a long-established regime and the beginning of a new political era. In that sense, one might properly say that the bill's passage was a symbol of a political watershed, a metaphor of political change.

(That recently elected Governor George Pataki had distinguished himself from Governor Cuomo primarily on this issue helped sustain this metaphorical meaning.) This bill's passage—a very visible event, marked by an all-night sitting of the Assembly and extensive publicity—signaled the Republican party's newfound capacity for effective political action, succeeding where previous administrations had failed. Passing the bill did not give the Republicans more power. It did not increase their majority. It may even have lost them some public support. But the Republicans' success in overcoming long-standing opposition and enacting a highly visible bill produced a status gain for the party and its supporters. It was, in Gusfield's terms, a properly symbolic victory.

The passing of this statute also had repercussions for the distribution of social and political status more generally. In New York politics its passage was viewed as an important defeat for liberal elites for whom opposition to capital punishment was a signature position. It was understood as a victory for populist, law-and-order conservatives whose support for the measure was similarly intense and identificatory. In this sense too, the passage of the law could be seen to signal and affirm a shift in the prevailing political culture and status hierarchies. The enactment of this particular law thus had meanings that were exogenous to the statute itself: the capacity of the pro-death penalty lobby to pass the law signaled the decline of the political ascendancy of liberal opinion and an important accommodation of the state to "tough on crime" sentiment. Moreover, for certain sections of the public, and particularly for anti-death penalty activists, the enactment of the law represented not just a new statute on the books but a sign of New York State's changing identity. In this respect, capital punishment could be seen as emblematic of the state's changing political culture and status hierarchies and its new location on a mental map of liberal and conservative polities.

At the same time, Governor Pataki's success in passing a death penalty law in liberal New York enhanced his status as an effective political figure who might have the conservative credentials to run for national office. By the same token, Mario Cuomo's defeat in the election signaled to many commentators the near-impossibility of winning political office on an anti-capital punishment ticket, and thus crystallized the electoral significance of the issue. Henceforth, a pro-death penalty stance came to be the recognized symbol of "tough on crime" politics, a litmus test for politicians and federal judges alike, and an essential element of any viable election platform, even for Democrats.

One could go on. Clearly, the meanings attributed to the enactment of a capital punishment statute are multiple—indeed they are as numerous and varied as the actors who care to interpret the event and comment upon its significance. Faced with this multiplicity, sociologists typically search for those meanings that command most agreement, or that feature most prominently in political debate. They seek to identify culturally or politically dominant meanings, as well as the central oppositional ones, paying less attention to variants that command little support or media prominence. But notice that in talking here about "social meanings" instead of "symbols and status" we are beginning to move away from Gusfield's original conception. A social meaning is not quite the same as a symbolic meaning—unless we use the term "symbol" in its linguistic sense, thus rendering all words and signs as "symbolic."[6] More to the point, both Gusfield and Carson use the term "symbolic" in a quite restrictive sense, to mean the value attributions associated with a particular practice insofar as these bear upon the social status of a particular group or collectivity.

Does the passage of a capital punishment law mark a redistribution of group status beyond the mundane sense in which a legislative victory makes the bill's immediate proponents appear victorious? Do death penalty laws allocate group status as well as individual punishment? Given that capital punishment attitudes do not map directly onto group membership, this is a difficult question. There is no single group—white, black; protestant, Catholic; male, female; urban, rural; secular, religious; rich, poor—that is fully identified, pro or con, with the death penalty. The issue is certainly one that "liberal elites" oppose and "conservative populists" support, but people from all demographics show up on either side of the issue. (Most demographic groups exhibit a majority preference for the death penalty, but the size of that majority varies considerably.) Consequently, when a state legislature passes a capital punishment law it clearly embraces the preferences and perhaps enhances the status of those who support the law (conservatives, law and order advocates, pro-death penalty activists) and rejects the preferences and perhaps diminishes the status of those who oppose the law (liberals, defendants' rights advocates, anti-death penalty activists), but this does not send a clear status message about any particular group beyond the immediate protagonists.

At least not directly. The symbol-of-status effect is certainly not as clear-cut as it was in earlier historical periods. In 18th century Europe, for example, execution methods often varied according to the status of the offender (hanging for commoners, beheading for nobles, etc.). Similarly, in 19th century America, southern state legislatures passed statutes that made blacks but not

---

6. Since words stand for things, or more precisely, signifier refers to a signified, there is always a process of symbolization involved in using language. But we typically talk of "symbolic" meaning only when the word or sign or image also carries a non-literal reference or association—when it functions as a metaphor to connote an additional level of meaning.

whites liable to capital punishment for particular offences—either explicitly, before the 1860s, or implicitly thereafter, as with capital rape laws which were only enforced against African-American defendants. The passage and enforcement of such laws deliberately demeaned the status of African-Americans in a way that was well understood by all concerned. Today, things are not so straightforward. Constitutional law invalidates discriminatory statutes, capital rape laws are unconstitutional, and while there is much evidence to suggest racial bias in enforcement, the authorities contest that there is no such bias and no intent to discriminate.

The possibility that the 1995 Act could be read as a symbolic attack on the standing of the black community in New York is one that we ought to consider. Given the racialized history of capital punishment and the continuing evidence of its racially biased deployment in many states, it is no surprise that some commentators and Assembly representatives viewed the passage of this law as a status slight to African-Americans in the state. Some members of the Assembly took pains to deny this narrative, arguing that poor black communities were precisely the ones that would be most protected by the deterrent effects of capital punishment, and pointing to the safeguards against racial injustice that were included in the statute.[7] But such attempts to refute the imputation of racism could not succeed in allaying the suspicions of those for whom capital punishment is an enduring symbol of racial oppression and injustice.

Whatever its declared or intended meaning, the historical and political context ensured that the law would be interpreted by some as a sign of covert racism. The symbolic politics of race—focused, as Gusfield and Carson suggest, on perceived allocations of status and disrepute, honor and dishonor—are complex and, as in much American politics, unavoidably present. Proponents of the bill vigorously denied any such intention or inference, saying that they wanted to protect African-American communities from violent crime, but some of the bill's opponents insisted on this interpretation anyway, protesting that the act was a racist attack on the black community. What this suggests is that the symbolic meaning of a law and its implications for group status are themselves subject to controversy and varying interpretations. If the case studies of Gusfield and Carson make it appear that both sides of an issue agreed on what was at stake and fought to prevail, the politics of capital punishment suggest a more complex situation in which groups disagree about what is being fought over. The symbolic meaning of an act and its consequences for group status are not just the basis of conflicts—they are also the subject of conflict.

---

7. See transcript of Assembly floor debates.

Finally, we might note the observations of Robert Weisberg (1996), who offers an interpretation of the political and cultural meanings of the New York statute. One of his more interesting claims is that "the New York law essentially means nothing" (Weisberg 1996:284). Based on a prediction (subsequently proven to be accurate) that the act would never result in any offenders being put to death, Weisberg describes its passage as an empty political gesture that was never intended to have operative effect. (He describes politicians' statements of support for capital punishment as a vacuous religious oath, solemnly taken for purely political purposes.) Weisberg's point is nicely overstated for rhetorical effect. He knows full well that even empty gestures can be filled with meaning and practical social consequence. Such actions are not empty, or magical, or merely waste. They are *rhetorical*, which is to say, with Kenneth Burke (1969), an inducement to action or attitude. As Gusfield puts it, "[i]t is useful to think of symbolic acts as forms of rhetoric, functioning to organize the perceptions, attitudes, and feelings of observers. Symbolic acts 'invite consideration rather than overt action.' They are persuasive devices that alter the observer's view of the objects" (p.170). The symbolic politics of capital punishment operate in complex ways, and the grouping and value associations thus created link up with other fault lines in the American culture and polity.[8] The shaping of attitudes, the molding of associations, the clustering of issues, and the forging of value commitments is how the culture wars are fought, and the death penalty has been one of the recurring issues around which these conflicts have raged.

Shifts in the Meaning of the Symbolic/Instrumental Distinction

So far I have been discussing the status politics of capital punishment legislation using the analytical framework developed by Gusfield and Carson. But when death penalty commentators talk about the "symbolic" as opposed to "instrumental" aspects of capital punishment, they are generally not using

---

8. At one point, Gusfield notes that political symbolism can be distinguished into two separate forms: "*gestures of cohesion* and *gestures of differentiation*" (p. 171), but the enactment and enforcement of capital punishment laws continually creates new forms of cohesion and new forms of differentiation, depending upon the context and how it is represented and perceived. The capital conviction of Scott Peterson creates solidarities and divisions that are quite different from those that formed in the wake of cases of O.J. Simpson or Timothy McVeigh.

these terms in their original sense, nor are they talking about status politics. In the death penalty literature, for the most part, the symbolic/instrumental distinction has come to refer not to the contrast between status-oriented action and economically oriented action but instead to a rather different contrast between politically oriented or emotionally laden gestures (which are said to be "symbolic") on the one hand, and crime-control oriented policies (which are taken to be "instrumental") on the other.

These terms are typically used not to distinguish different forms of action, each of which has its own logic and rationality, as in the Gusfield-Carson usage, but rather as a critical device for debunking policies that pretend to be one thing (real crime control) while actually being something else (mere political symbolism or emotional acting out). This shift in usage, which as far as I am aware has never been properly discussed, subtly changes the meaning and implication of these concepts. An analytical distinction that originally differentiated between two forms of political action, each of them fully rational and goal-oriented, is thereby transformed into (1) a critical distinction that regards capital punishment as an irrational-because-symbolic form of action that can be contrasted to other forms of action (*e.g.,* imprisonment) that are rational-because-instrumental; or else (2) a distinction between two forms of institutional functioning: symbolic functioning—where various kinds of messages are sent—and instrumental functioning—where various kinds of control are imposed.

When critics characterize capital punishment as "symbolic" as opposed to "instrumental," they are often seeking to characterize capital punishment as an irrational policy that has no instrumental rationale and therefore no criminological justification. In other words, they are using the term "symbolic" to mean "merely symbolic" or else as a synonym for "irrational," "ineffective," or "unrelated to crime control." Thus, Kosinski and Gallagher (1995) describe capital punishment as an "expensive and distracting side-show" in the battle against crime (p. A21). Bowers (quoted in Lifton and Mitchell 2000) calls it "a hollow symbol" (p. 248–249). Greenberg (1981–1982) says "the system ... looks irrational ... and serves no purpose" (p. 927). Ellsworth and Gross (1994) suggest that "for most Americans capital punishment is an abstract social symbol rather than a seriously examined political issue" (p. 384). Pierce and Radelet (1990–1991) claim that "the death penalty is an inconsequential social policy" an "illusory solution ... to the crime problem" (p. 720). And Johnson (1998) says: "Capital punishment has ... become a commodity dispensed without any redeeming social or communal purpose" (p. 9).

But there are a number of problems with this approach. First of all, it tends to underplay the extent to which the current capital punishment system does, in fact, produce crime control effects. It is hard to gainsay the fact that the death penalty, if carried out, is the most effective means of incapacitating known murderers and preventing them from re-offending. Other means of permanent incapacitation are, in theory, available, but even a sentence of life without parole leaves some jurors worrying about future escapes, assaults upon prison staff, or changes in parole laws that might allow a killer back on the street. Justifiably or not, capital punishment is regarded by some people as an effective preventative instrument. The same is true of the supposed deterrent effects of the death penalty. Capital punishment opponents may insist that there is no good evidence that a death penalty deters more than life without parole, but the most balanced reading of the research suggests that the evidence is simply inconclusive, allowing commentators such as James Q. Wilson (1983) or Ernest van den Haag (1986) to argue that we ought to give the benefit of the doubt to potential future victims rather than condemned murderers. Elected officials in death penalty states often claim that capital punishment saves lives by deterring violent crime, and this possibility shapes public perceptions. Whatever critics of the system claim, "instrumental" crime control considerations still play a part in creating support for capital punishment.

In addition to these crime-control uses, we ought also to note that the death penalty can function effectively as a practical instrument of penal power. I have already mentioned the use prosecutors make of the threat of capital punishment to secure plea deals. The threat of capital punishment is also used by prosecutors to extract information from defendants, as in the case of the Green River killer in Washington State, where the defendant provided the names of his victims, and the recent Colorado case where the defendant revealed the whereabouts of bombs that he had made, each time in return for an agreement to drop capital charges. Prosecutors are among the most vocal interest groups supporting capital punishment, and the reason for their support is plain to see.

Second, this analysis fails to see the crucial role of "symbols" in pursuing the instrumental aims of criminal justice insofar as these aims are *penal* rather than crime-control-oriented. It dismisses the "symbolic" as non-instrumental, when in fact condemnation is a major end of criminal justice and symbolic communication a major means for achieving this end. The problem is that the sharp distinction that Gusfield and Carson draw between the symbolic and the instrumental does not survive its transformation of meaning and reference. The distinction between symbolic and instrumental is an intelligible one when the contrast is between status interests and material interests. It is less intelligible when applied to penal measures, which typically combine moral condemnation with some measure of control or restriction. When a death penalty law is passed, or a capital sentence imposed, a specific penal goal—that of public denunciation—is thereby achieved. Indeed, it is being achieved in the most emphatic way possible, since modern sensibilities and legal restraints make the death penalty today's "ultimate punishment."

Is this "instrumental" or "symbolic"? Perhaps we should ask ourselves instead, does the question make sense? When a defendant is sentenced to death a penal meaning is being communicated—he is being condemned in the most extreme fashion available. If condemnation is one of the court's aims in passing sentence then the death penalty is clearly an instrumentally effective means to secure this end. Under this analysis—phrased in penal rather than crime-control terms—capital punishment is clearly an instrumental measure. To pass a death penalty statute or impose a capital sentence is to wield an instrument of symbolic action, whether or not anyone is actually executed. Penal measures of this kind tend to confound the symbolic/instrumental distinction rather than exemplify it.

To talk about capital punishment—or about any penal sanction—as symbolic and therefore non-instrumental narrows the ways in which we think about penal sanctions, their social purposes, and their legitimacy. The discussion proceeds as if the only legitimate aim of penal measures is the utilitarian, instrumental aim of crime control and that any other motivation or purpose is a "side-show," "a distraction," "irrational," serving "no purpose." But it is not at all clear why social purposes other than crime control—*e.g.*, purposes such as expressing public sentiment, affirming social values, marking political distinction, promoting social solidarity, or merely denouncing specific crimes— may not also be legitimate and rational. Critics who wish to contest the legitimacy and rationality of imposing the death penalty in order to serve these extraneous purposes would do well to engage these issues, rather than define them out of existence.

Moreover, there is no need to take an "all-or-nothing" approach to these matters. Gusfield and especially Carson make it clear that we need not suppose that an action is motivated *either* by instrumental reasoning *or* by symbolic concerns. Their understanding of "symbolic" politics is nuanced and does not imply an absence of practical effects. As Gusfield puts it (1984): "Law contains a great deal which has little direct effect upon behavior.... [W]hile we do not maintain that [Temperance legislation] has no effect on behavior, we do find its instrumental effects are slight compared to the response which it entails as a symbol, irrespective of its utility as a means to a tangible end" (p. 169).

We might pause again here to note that a revealing ambiguity creeps into Gusfield's formulation here when he uses the terms "tangible" and "direct." It ought to be clear that symbolic acts have direct effects on attitude and perception and therefore, one might expect, indirect effects on action. The term "tangible" means material and would exclude ideational effects—but to say that something is not tangible does not mean it cannot be real, effective and powerful in its social effects. The intangible idea can produce very tangible effects (think of Max Weber's claim that the intangible idea of salvation drove the worldly callings of Calvinists and brought modern capitalism into being). Elsewhere, Murray Edelman echoes Gusfield's claim: "The most intensive dissemination of symbols commonly attends the enactment of legislation which is most meaningless in its effects upon resource allocation" (quoted in Gusfield 1986:182). Of course Edelman is forgetting that symbols are "resources" too.

There is no need to set the instrumental (or crime-control) dimension at zero in order to proceed to the symbolic or other dimensions. This is the mistake of reductionist, either/or thinking. (It was this kind of reductionist insistence that all action could be, and should be, analyzed in terms of economic interest—and the difficulties of interpretation that resulted—that first prompted Gusfield and Edelman to argue for the symbolic dimension.) Instead of assuming that an action can be categorized as instrumental or symbolic, crime-control or penal, we ought to think in terms of a *balance* of multiple aims or dimensions, and differentiate actions accordingly.[9]

Another problem of this framework's use in relation to the death penalty is that its specific application is often vague. Analysts often talk about "capital punishment" being symbolic rather than instrumental—by which they presumably mean the institution as a whole—but this is imprecise and overstated. The institution of capital punishment does not exist separately from its practices, and these practices are, in turn, undertaken by specific actors in specific situations. Consequently, it is always useful to identify which actors and which actions we are discussing and what kinds of action they are engaged in. There are many kinds of actors who pursue many forms of action in respect of capital punishment, make many kinds of representations, and express many kinds of attitude. Politicians, legislators, prosecutors, defense counsel, jurors, judges, governors, victims, defendants, members of the public, journalists, academics, activists, etc.: each of these groups exhibits different motivations, acts in different situations, and pursues different aims and interests. Each of them engages with capital punishment in a different way and for different purposes. And while their actions might be analyzed as symbolic or instrumental, the precise meaning of these terms, and the balance between them, will be different in each case.

These different usages of capital punishment may well require different kinds of analysis. The prosecutor uses the death penalty differently than the politi-

---

9. Note that the contemporary American death penalty exhibits a balance that is more penal and less crime control. The Chinese death penalty, with an estimated 10,000 or more executions per year, suggests a different balance.

cian. The victim's family relates to it differently than a respondent in a public opinion survey. The United States Supreme Court comes at the issue differently than the Texas Court of Criminal Appeals. In deciding to vote for a death penalty, different jurors may seek to achieve rather different ends—incapacitation, vengeance, closure for the victim's relatives, justice for the victim, a vindication of the law, or just a faithful implementation of the judge's instructions. The post-revolutionary regime in Romania may seek to make a statement by abolishing capital punishment that is different from one made by a stable liberal democracy like France. Turkey's abolition (undertaken as a step towards joining the European Union) may mean something else again. Capital punishment is used differently by Texas courts than by the Connecticut ones, differently by the Chinese or Singapore governments than those of Japan or Hong Kong.

The contrastive terms "symbolic" and "instrumental" do not begin to capture this variation and specificity. So why do analysts so frequently use such terms? My guess is that this situation is produced by the dominance of critical thought over analytical precision in the death penalty literature. Many commentators imply that anything other than an instrumental, crime control use of capital punishment is illegitimate. When they say the usage is "symbolic" (and not instrumental) they mean this claim to carry a critical connotation, to imply a frivolous or an illicit or an ideological usage—an implied meaning that is very far from that described in the work of Gusfield, Carson, Edelman, or Burke.

It seems to me that there are two problems with this practice. First, there is a conceptual problem. Used in this way, the concept of "symbolic" is a falsely generic category, since it means something different in each context. The result is conceptual confusion in which usages slip and slide. Sometimes "symbolic" is used to describe what Carson more precisely terms "a political reciprocal for other issues"—a trope in which capital punishment is used as a metaphor or a sign of something else, such as states' rights, traditional values, a tough stance on crime, etc. (p. 128). Sometimes it is used to name the expression of emotion—the venting of public fear and rage, the anger of the victim's survivor, sympathy for the victim, etc. Sometimes it is used to describe an action that is merely gestural, as when a measure is knowingly enacted without any likelihood of actual enforcement (Zimring 2005), or when a defendant's "right of allocution" comes after the court has determined the verdict and sentence.[10]

---

10. Discussing the continuation of the common law ritual of allocution, which allowed a defendant to address the court, in modern capital procedure Justice Harlan notes that the ritual had become "largely symbolic" (*McGautha v. California* 1971:202—its purpose now being to "avoid the possibility that a person might be tried, convicted and sentenced to

Rather than use the same word to refer to these rather different concepts, it might be more illuminating to use more specific and varied terms to describe the different kinds of conduct being discussed. We need to ask: "Symbolic of what?" "What is being symbolized?" Carson and Gusfield had an answer to this question—they made it clear that they were analyzing symbols of status, marks of esteem and disesteem. But analysts who have abandoned the original framework need to provide content for that empty category.[11]

The second problem is an evaluative one. It is perfectly cogent to argue that capital punishment is only legitimate if it is used as an instrumental means to control crime, and to regard all other uses of the death penalty as illegitimate. But we should see that this is only an argument and by no means a self-evidently valid one. Too many commentators assume that if they succeed in throwing doubt on the death penalty's crime-control effectiveness, then they have undermined its only valid rationale, leaving nothing more substantial than "symbolism" standing in the way of its abolition. But we need to see that criminal penalties in general and capital punishment in particular can be justified on grounds other than crime-control efficacy. One can argue that capital punishment is a valid means to express society's outrage in the face of an aggravated, unmitigated murder; that it is a necessary means to denounce the worst of crimes; that it is a means of honoring the victim and providing satisfaction to his or her survivors; that it is a valuable morale-boosting measure in the war against crime; that it reflects the democratic will of the majority of the people; or that it is a matter that the states are constitutionally permitted to decide for themselves. Each of these arguments has a certain cogency and force, and although each of them can be challenged they will not be rebutted simply by lumping them together as "merely symbolic" as opposed to properly instrumental. To suppose that this argument is an effective refutation is to fall victim to the materialist fallacy that ideas and symbols are somehow less real and less consequential than more solid, tangible forms of action.

To discredit these arguments, one has to recognize them for what they are and engage with them on their own terms. In other words, analytical precision will serve the cause of understanding *and* the cause of critique. Better, then, to engage in detailed description and analysis, specifying the motivations,

---

death in complete silence." (Originally, the defendant's allocution had a more "instrumental" impact, being an opportunity to avert the court's verdict by claiming benefit of clergy, benefit of belly, etc.)

11. For example, the concern to "hear the voice of the defendant," symbolizes a minimal concern for individualized justice and for the ritual recognition of the person being sentenced.

meanings and effects associated with particular uses of capital punishment, than to bundle these together as "symbolic" measures that fail to meet a spurious "instrumental" requirement. Each use of capital punishment should be analyzed in terms of motivation, meaning, purpose and effect. Following Weber, we can analyze such acts in terms of the different rationalities that they entail, breaking them down into three categories: (1) *value-rational forms of action* (declaring a set of social values, upholding specific cultural commitments, affirming a particular way of life)—a category that roughly corresponds to the "symbolic" as it is conventionally used; (2) *purpose-rational forms of action* (using capital punishment as an instrumental means to a specified end, such as deterring, or incapacitating, or pleasing voters, or satisfying victims)—which corresponds to "instrumental"; and also a third category, (3) *affective forms of action* (expressing passions, conveying sentiments, acting out emotional conflicts)—a category that is either absent from discussion or else conflated with value-rational conduct as one more kind of "symbolic" action.[12]

We might also note that while value-rational action is the most straightforward form of symbolic politics—if the symbols of a group's lifestyle or social values are reflected in public policy, the group thereby enjoys a kind of status reinforcement—affective action works in a rather similar way. Where sections of the public feel outraged by a heinous crime, angered by a wave of violence, or anxious about their physical security, they put pressure on their political representatives to "do something," to act upon these emotions in a way that gives them expression and resolution—*e.g.*, by enacting a capital law, bringing a capital indictment, or carrying out an execution. Where such action is taken, the public may feel satisfaction, just as they may feel frustration where such expression is denied to them.[13] (For the political representatives involved, on the other hand, such action may be chiefly instrumental, since giving the people what they want may bring rewards at the ballot box.) That capital punishment has come to be the favored means for expressing the public's outrage about crime—the very symbol of "doing something" serious—is, no doubt, another reason, beyond status politics, why so much emotional energy is expended on this measure.

We might note, in passing, that this observation contains the answer to Tom Franks' famous question, "What's the Matter with Kansas?", which asks why

---

12. Interestingly, Gusfield (1963) presents a three-type classification, distinguishing class politics (action aimed at redistributing economic resources); status politics (action aimed at redistributing prestige); and expressive politics (action, prompted by frustration or aggression, that has no immediate redistributive aim). This third category is not discussed in Carson (1974) and has tended to drop out of sight.

13. *Cf.*, Gusfield's third category of political action—"expressive politics."

so many working class voters are led to support Republican candidates by "social value" considerations despite the fact that Republican economic policies work to their material detriment. The answer is that there is nothing the matter. The voters in question are simply pursuing value-rational and affective ends, possibly at the cost of economic benefits. When voters in Kansas vote for pro-death penalty candidates (and against liberal anti-death penalty candidates) on the basis of "social values" or because they want to express their anger and resentment, they are not behaving irrationally. If there is a President in the White House who shares their values, and can be trusted to uphold capital punishment, this provides gratification of sorts—perhaps a more immediate and tangible form of gratification than that which might be derived from national economic policies that may or may not produce local benefits. Analysts of capital punishment—especially those who are critical of the system—need to realize that attitudes and actions of this kind are not irrational, as writers such as Frank would suggest. On the contrary, they involve a purposeful pursuit of status rewards and emotional gratifications.[14]

Conclusion: New Directions for Research

My argument has been that the critical literature on American capital punishment uses the symbolic/instrumental dichotomy in a manner that lacks the analytical precision and interpretive value that these terms initially possessed. I have shown that a return to the original usage of these concepts would lend a greater clarity of analysis, at least where status politics are involved, though I have also suggested that the original dichotomy might usefully be expanded into a more comprehensive typology by adding the category of affective action—a category that seems especially relevant to death penalty politics. I have also suggested that the precision of analysis—and also of critique—would be enhanced if accounts of capital-punishment-oriented action were to take more care to specify the motivations, meanings, and effects involved, rather than lump them together into an undifferentiated category of "the symbolic."

I draw two conclusions from this discussion, one conceptual, the other methodological, both of which have consequences for future research.

The underlying conceptual problem that affects the symbolic/instrumental distinction and its various synonyms (saying/doing; symbol/substance; ideal/material; speech/action; rhetoric/practice, ideology/reality, intangible/tangible;

---

14. Liberal critics of capital punishment have never understood the pleasures of punishing. They ought to read more Nietzsche and less Bentham.

etc.) is that the first of these terms is always marked as somehow less impactful, less important, less real. This is true, despite the protestations of analysts like Gusfield and Carson, for whom the symbolic is a realm of *action* as well as meaning (and who, following Kenneth Burke, regard rhetoric as the active shaping of attitude and hence of action). There is no way to avoid this perceived differential of ontological weight: it is a fact of our culture, and no amount of breast-beating on the part of analysts will change this. At the level of ordinary language—which exerts a constant gravitational pull on our theoretical analyses—when we talk of something having symbolic but not instrumental significance, we are already discounting its overall significance. Already, by using the term "symbolic," we are moving the phenomenon towards the world of empty gestures and hollow promises.

There is no avoiding this, but two conceptual strategies might reduce this problem somewhat. One is to insist that all actions involve both symbolic and instrumental aspects and accustom ourselves to talking about a symbolic/instrumental balance. The idea of a "both/and" balance rather than an "either/or" choice is helpful, but it does not fully resolve the problem: for one thing it limits the dimensions to two, when in fact there is often a third. For another, it passes over the fact that symbolic and instrumental mean different things in different contexts (the pursuit of status as opposed to economic advantage in one context, the pursuit of operational crime control instead of expressive punishment in another). Better, then, to say precisely what one means, identifying the motivational ends in question as being status-oriented, economic, religious, political, crime-control, penal, expressive, affective, or value-oriented. By replacing the symbolic/instrumental distinctions with more specific analytic descriptions we lose little and may gain some precision.

The other conclusion is methodological. Any move towards descriptive specificity requires that we study the "forest of symbols" empirically, as they emerge in historical situations, shaped by the intentions of the actors who communicate them, the interpretations of the audiences that perceive them, and the cultural conventions and frameworks of reference and meaning within which all communication takes place. Without this empirical grounding, analyses tend to become impressionistic inferences that analysts bring to the material rather than accounts of the meanings that were actually conveyed and understood.

But how ought one to research these questions? What kind of empirical studies can advance our knowledge of the meanings and motives that capital punishment symbols imply?

The research approach that comes most readily to mind is historical analysis—a form of study that has already been well established with respect to symbolic action and death penalty politics. When Gusfield and Carson, both sociologists, undertook to study symbolic action they chose to focus on specific historical episodes—the Temperance Movement in early 20th century America, the Factory Act struggles of early 19th England—and produced analyses that were empirically grounded and conceptually productive. Gusfield and Carson both develop interpretations that are anchored in the archive, in the records of things historical actors said and did, and the sociological accounts they produce are intended to contextualize these actions and explicate their meaning. We have many historical studies of capital punishment that do the same. Douglas Hay (1975) famously uncovered the symbolic functions of the 18th century English capital punishment system with its elaborate ceremonies, its strategic mixture of terror and mercy, and its extensive system of pardons, which shored up the private power of ruling class individuals. Randall McGowen (1987) has offered us exquisitely detailed analyses of the changing cultural frameworks in which the death penalty was successively enacted as English society moved from the early modern period into the secular modernity of the 19th century—the metaphor of "the body" taking on new meanings in the process. Philip Smith (2003) has done something similar with regard to execution technologies, the symbolic resonances they evoked and the struggles that went on to define their meaning.

This historical approach has all the advantages of hindsight (a capacity for detachment, an overview of surrounding and subsequent events, access to the work of other historians of the period, memoirs and biographies of the key actors, etc.) but it also limits possibilities for inquiry, restricting analysis to the study of surviving documents and obliging the researcher to rely on inferences from recorded statements and actions. Whereas researchers working on the present can generate data designed to answer their research questions, the historian must make do with what the historical record happens to provide. Historical studies may be analytically powerful and suggestive, but their bearing upon the present is often uncertain. They offer insights and conceptual tools, but they do not necessarily address the specific symbolic meanings that operate today. For that reason, contemporary empirical work is desirable.

What kind of contemporary research might deepen our understanding of the symbolic and cultural aspects of capital punishment? One possibility is to study the people most directly and deliberately engaged in symbolic struggles over the death penalty: the pro- and anti-capital punishment activists. People who routinely engage in practical forms of action often understand what they do rather better than those who theorize about them from the outside. Death penalty activists know all too well about the symbolic meanings of capital punishment, and in their political practice they seek to challenge unwelcome associations and establish preferred connotations that are more compatible with their cause. They struggle to frame the issue of capital punishment in specific ways, linking it with specific ways of thinking, seeking to fix its public meaning and symbolic associations.

In capital punishment politics, each side aims to shape the dominant narrative within which the death penalty is discussed. Traditionally, anti-death penalty activists have associated capital punishment with a savage, barbaric past, insisting that abolition is a sign of social progress and "civilization." In the legal battles of the 1960s and 1970s, this rhetoric was translated into the constitutional term of art, "evolving standards of decency." But the same rhetoric, the same symbolism of progress, decency, and civility, was also appropriated by the other side, who insist that a civilized society is one that secures citizen from violence, values innocent life, and humanely eliminates the threat of dangerous, asocial individuals who jeopardize the peaceful order of a civilized society.

In the United States, from the 1960s on, the preferred framing of the issue for death penalty critics linked the practice to racism, to lynching, and to America's history of racial oppression and violence. For these activists, the aim was to establish death penalty abolition as a civil rights cause, to associate it with oppression, injustice and the ill-treatment of powerless people from despised minorities and the poorest classes. The cases that were chosen to spearhead litigation campaigns were carefully selected to symbolize these issues (*e.g.*, capital rape cases from the South, involving black defendants and white victims), and the legal issues were framed so as to emphasize due process violations, rather than substantive claims of immorality.

More recently, abolitionists have sought to establish a different symbolic framing, forging an association between capital punishment and the wrongful conviction of innocent individuals. This "innocence" frame has been emblematically established by newspaper photographs of a large group of individuals on a stage in Chicago, all of them released from death row; by the figure of "the Exonerated"—as depicted in a star-cast, off-Broadway play and subsequent film; and by the idea of "a broken system," which refers to a widely circulated research report about the error-prone character of a system that "overproduces death" (Liebman 2000). The aim here is to associate the system with miscarriages of justice, an unacceptably high likelihood of mistakes, false convictions, and inappropriate sentences, and to do so in vividly concrete ways, telling the stories of innocent individuals who came close to death, using compelling human narratives to ram home a general critique.

Supporters of the death penalty fight back by trying to discredit the evidence upon which these powerful symbols and images are based. They challenge the ideas of "innocence" and "exonerated" as being inexact, suggesting that many of those whose sentences were overturned were nevertheless guilty of murder, though not deserving of a capital sentence. These counter-narratives aim to undermine the innocence frame by questioning the veracity and representative nature of its emblematic stories. Where instances of "exoneration" symbolize a broken system for the abolitionists, for death penalty supporters, they are to be understood as proof that the system's safeguards work or else examples of guilty individuals wrongly freed on procedural technicalities. For both sides, the concern is less with the individual case than with the symbolic meanings that can be around it.

Supporters of the system legitimate it as "closure" for family members, thereby displacing negative images of capital punishment as violent or barbaric and substituting connotations of healing for vulnerable, traumatized innocents. The modern lethal injection protocol, with its clinical trappings and medical atmospherics, likewise projects a symbolism of "caring" to counter the idea of an execution as state killing. Opponents challenge these associations, talking instead of "secondary victimization" suffered by the victim's family members, as drawn-out proceedings repeatedly revive traumatic memories, or else bringing evidence to suggest that the lethal injection is actually painful and inhumane, and is administered in ways that violate fundamental norms of medical treatment.

Finally, when proponents of capital punishment insist that any politician who takes public crime concerns seriously will support the death penalty, abolitionists seek to upset the idea that being tough on crime means being for the death penalty. They do so by claiming that the death penalty is an expensive distraction from real crime control, and pushing to redeploy the funds currently used on capital cases to increase support to murder victims, or to put in place better crime prevention policies.

What all of this amounts to is, quite simply, symbolic struggle. And today it is more important than ever, since anti-death penalty activists are increasingly bringing their case to the media, rather than the court, seeking to forge symbolic associations in the minds of the public and political actors, rather than concentrating on constitutional claims, as they did for much of the last thirty years. Researchers interested in the symbolic aspects of capital punishment might begin by researching what the activists do, what they say, and how they do or say it. They can study available texts and recorded statements, they can reconstruct the emergence of strategies and the thinking that lay behind them — often aided by memoirs of those who took part, such as Meltsner (1973), or Greenberg (1981–1982) — and they may be able to interview key actors to inquire about the meanings and motivations that directed their actions.

The primary symbolism at stake in these conscious struggles concerns what might be termed penal symbols or symbols of justice—the death penalty's most immediate criminal justice connotations—rather than its broader, more oblique associations, such as the link between capital punishment and states' rights, or the backlash against civil rights, or conservative values. Can these broader associations be studied? Perhaps. Here we might focus on political statements—reading between the lines for code words, oblique references, race cards, etc., when legislators act. What do they say in their press releases? What is the rhetoric of political exchange or legislative debate? What metaphors and analogies recur? What associations are forged, what connotations suggested? We can also read the media headlines, op eds, and editorials, as well as letters to the editors and comments to online blogs, to get some sense of how these issues are taken up and interpreted by public commentators, including, sometimes, members of the public.

One could also envision research focused on the specific symbolic functions that capital punishment supposedly serves. If the death penalty is perceived to be important as a symbolic token of esteem for victims and their survivors, as an emphatic denunciation of evil, or as a means of reassuring the community that danger has been eliminated, authority upheld, and moral order restored, abolitionists would be interested to know whether these same functions can be effectively fulfilled by alternative punishments, such as a life term of imprisonment, or life without parole. One could envision comparative work that studied parallel cases—for example, on how aggravated murders are handled, how their punishment is discussed, and how the issues are represented—in jurisdictions with and without the death penalty. It might also be possible to investigate the symbolic resonances of punishment in abolitionist nations where the death penalty is not a viable option. Do prison sentences there carry the weight of meaning and the symbolic resonance that capital punishment carries in American culture? Do people come to regard "life imprisonment" as a weighty, ultimate punishment, morally appropriate to the worst crimes? This would require careful, ethnographic research, reading texts, interviewing actors and spectators. Comparative work of this kind is not easy to carry out, but it is by no means impossible. If the death penalty's symbolic ends can be effectively served by other means, this is useful information for the institution's critics.

Comparative work might also reveal the mutability of metaphors and symbolic associations. If the relatives of murder victims in abolitionist Britain regard a life sentence of imprisonment as the ultimate punishment and have come to see proper retribution as entailing "a life for a life" (rather than a death for a death), this suggests that ideas of justice and moral order are conventions that can be altered rather than fixed points in the scheme of things. It might also be possible to undertake historical studies of transition periods—for example the forty years between Britain's repeal of capital punishment in the 1960s and the present—to trace how these associations and expectations gradually changed. Over the long-term, normative conventions regarding punishments, their severity and their symbolism, have undergone important changes. The death penalty that we now consider "the ultimate penalty" is actually a very restrained, relatively mild punishment compared to the aggravated death penalties involving torture, dismemberment, and the display of body parts that were a feature of the early modern period. Critics of these changes complained that the new, more lenient penalties could never function as effectively, but over time new expectations emerged and new conventions became established. The conventional understandings of today's death penalty, its immediate meanings and symbolic connotations, are historical and social constructs. Studying the historical processes of their construction may well provide useful knowledge for those who struggle to deconstruct them.

References

Anderson, Elizabeth S. and Richard H. Pildes. 2000. "Expressive Theories of Law: General Restatement." *University of Pennsylvania Law Review* 148:1503–2000.

Burke, Kenneth. 1969. *The Language of Symbolic Action*. Berkeley, CA: University of California Press.

_____. 1968. *A Rhetoric of Motives*. Berkeley, CA: University of California Press.

Carson, W.G. 1974. "Symbolic and Instrumental Dimensions of Early Factory Legislation: A Case Study in the Social Origins of Criminal Law." In *Crime, Criminology and Public Policy: Essays in Honour of Sir Leon Radzinowitz*, edited by Roger Hood. London: Heinemann.

Edelman, Murray. 1964. *The Symbolic Uses of Politics*. Urbana, IL: Illinois University Press.

Ellsworth, Phoebe C. and Samuel R. Gross 1994. "Hardening of Attitudes: Americans' Views on the Death Penalty." *Journal of Social Issues* 50:19–45.

Frank, Tom. 2004. *What's the Matter with Kansas? How Conservatives Won the Heart of America*. New York, NY: Metropolitan Books.

Friedland, Roger and John Mohr (eds). 2004. *Matters of Culture: Cultural Sociology in Practice*. Cambridge: Cambridge University Press.

Furman v. Georgia (1972). 408 U.S. 238.

Garland, David. 1990. *Punishment and Modern Society: A Study in Social Theory.* Chicago, IL: University of Chicago Press.

Greenberg, Jack. 1981–1982. "Capital Punishment as a System." *Yale Law Journal* 91:908–936.

Gusfield, Joseph, R. [1963] 1986. *Symbolic Crusade: Status Politics and the American Temperance.* Urbana, IL: University of Illinois Press.

Haines, Herbert. 1996. *Against Capital Punishment: The Anti-Death Penalty Movement in America, 1972–1994.* New York, NY: Oxford University Press.

Hay, Douglas. 1975. "Property, Authority and the Criminal Law." Pp. 17–63 in *Albion's Fatal Tree,* edited by Douglas Hay, Peter Linebaugh, John G. Rule, E.P. Thompson and Cal Winslow. New York, NY: Pantheon Books.

Hunt, Linda (ed.). 1989. *The New Cultural History.* Berkeley, CA: University of California Press.

Johnson, Robert. 1998. *Death Work: A Study of the Modern Execution Process.* Belmont, CA: Wadsworth.

Kahan, Dan. 1999. "Redrawing the Criminal-Civil Boundary." *Buffalo Criminal Law Review* 2:679–723.

Kosinski, Alex and Sean Gallagher. 1995. "For an Honest Death Penalty." *New York Times*, March 8, A21.

Liebman, James S. 2000. "The Overproduction of Death." *Columbia Law Review* 100:2030–2156.

Lifton, Robert J. and Greg Mitchell. 2002. *Who Owns Death? Capital Punishment, the American Conscience and the End of Executions.* New York, NY: Perennial.

McGautha v. California (1971). 402 U.S. 183.

McGowen, Randall. 1987. "The Body and Punishment in Eighteenth Century England" *Journal of Modern History* 59:651–679.

Meltsner, Michael. 1973. *Cruel and Unusual: The Supreme Court and Capital Punishment.* New York, NY: Random House.

Mooney, Christopher and Mei-Hsien Lee. 2000. "The Influence of Values on Consensus and Contentious Morality Policy: U.S. Death Penalty Reform, 1956–82" *Journal of Politics* 65:223–239.

Payne v. Tennessee (1991). 501 U.S. 808.

Pierce, Glenn L. and Michael L. Radelet. 1990–1991. "The Role and Consequences of the Death Penalty in American Politics." *New York University of Review of Law and Social Change* 15:711–728.

Simon, Jonathan and Christina Spaulding. 1999. "Tokens of Our Esteem: Aggravating Factors in the Era of Deregulated Death Penalties." Pp. 81–1147 in *The Killing State Capital Punishment in Law Politics, and Culture,* edited by Austin Sarat. Oxford: Oxford University Press.

Smith, Phillip. 2003. "Narrating the Guillotine: Punishment Technology as Myth and Symbol." *Theory, Culture and Society* 20:27–51.
Stephen, James F. 1864. "Capital Punishments." *Fraser's Magazine* 69:753–772.
Tyler, Tom R. and Renee Weber. 1982. "Support for the Death Penalty: Instrumental Response to Crime or Symbolic Attitude." *Law and Society Review* 17:21–45.
van den Haag, Ernest. 1986. "The Ultimate Punishment: A Defense." *Harvard Law Review* 88:1662–1669.
Weisberg, Robert. 1996. "The New York Statue as a Cultural Document: Seeking the Morally Optimal Death Penalty." *Buffalo Law Review* 44:282–302.
_____. 1983. "Deregulating Death." *Supreme Court Review* 1983:305–395.
Wilson, James Q. 1983. *Thinking About Crime*. New York, NY: Vintage Books.
Zimring, Franklin E. 2005. "Symbol and Substance in the Massachusetts Commission Report." *Indiana Law Review* 80:115–131.
_____. 1999. "The Executioner's Dissonant Song: On Capital Punishment and American Legal Values." Pp. 137–147 in *The Killing State*, edited by Austin Sarat. New York, NY: Oxford University Press.
Zimring, Franklin E. and Gordon Hawkins. 1986. *Capital Punishment and the American Agenda*. Cambridge: Cambridge University Press.

CHAPTER 20

Alternative Sanctions for Aggravated Murder: Form and Function

James R. Acker

Introduction

Murderers should be punished.

Much like the proposition that innocent people should not be executed, no one—neither supporters nor opponents of the death penalty—disputes this simple premise. Although disagreements arise about the appropriate form and severity of the sanctions for murder, and about which penal objectives should be prioritized (retribution, social protection, etc.), we are safe in presuming that people generally share an abhorrence of the unlawful taking of human life and agree that punishment should follow. The division of opinion about the death penalty, as reflected among the public and in laws in this country and worldwide, involves issues that lie more at the margins than the core of the punishment question. Death-penalty abolitionists and retentionists would appear to have more in common than is typically recognized. Research that focuses on whether, why, and how well alternative sanctions promote the essential functions of punishment, and at what potential cost, will be useful in locating this common ground and assessing the most appropriate legal response to murder.

To address these issues, it will be helpful to roam beyond the relatively narrow focus of capital punishment. We must first attempt to identify the most important social objectives fulfilled by punishing murder. Then we must gain a fuller understanding of public perceptions about the effectiveness of alternative punishments—including death and life imprisonment—in promoting those functions and, conversely, the extent to which the benefits associated with the different punishments should be discounted because they risk adverse unintended consequences. Finally, we must explore how the perceived benefits and costs of alternative punishments are best reconciled, with a willingness to consider nontraditional penal measures. Public opinion research that sheds light on the valued functions of punishment for murder, and citizens' and policymakers' perceptions about the respective benefits and drawbacks of alternative forms of punishment, promises to be useful to help inform future sentencing policies.

Why Punish Murder?

Before deciding *how* to punish murderers, it is important to clarify *why* they should be punished. The reasons may be obvious and many can be ventured, but it is difficult to envision a productive discussion about either the type or magnitude of a punishment response unless there is agreement about objectives. Murder is a violent crime, commonly considered to be the most serious of all offenses. Traditional justifications for punishing murderers include: (1) the primarily noninstrumental functions of denunciation and retribution—of expressing collective moral outrage about the offense and giving the offender his or her just deserts for committing it; (2) the utilitarian functions associated with social protection—including incapacitating potentially dangerous offenders and discouraging other prospective offenders by example; and (3) a somewhat related restorative function through which the harm inflicted on the individual murder victim is acknowledged and society signifies concern and interest by responding to the loss suffered by the victim's immediate survivors and the larger community.

Denunciation

The expressive function of punishment in denouncing criminal conduct is nowhere more evident than in the context of the death penalty. Capital punishment has long been imbued with public ceremony and ritual designed to reinforce government authority and respect for law. Thus, in a bygone era, British judges solemnly donned black caps atop their wigs before pronouncing a sentence of death, elaborate gallows processionals and pious speeches preceded public hangings, and bodies were prominently displayed following executions (Foucault 1979:10–14; Gatrell 1994:56–89; Harding 2000:231 n. 199; Hay 1975:17–63). As Lord Justice Denning remarked before the Royal Commission on Capital Punishment, "Punishment is the way in which society expresses its denunciation of wrong doing: and, in order to maintain respect for the law, it is essential that the punishment inflicted for grave crimes should adequately reflect the revulsion felt by the great majority of citizens for them. It is a mistake to consider the objects of punishment as being deterrent or reformative or preventative and nothing else" (quoted in Bilz and Darley 2004:1218 n. 7). Nineteenth century English judge and legal historian Sir James Fitzjames Stephen pithily captured the unique message of social condemnation embodied by capital punishment when he wrote, "When a man is hung, there is an end of our relations with him. His execution is a way of saying, 'You are not fit for this world, take your chance elsewhere'" (quoted in *Furman v. Georgia* 1972:290).

It bears noting that contemporary executions, which are deliberately hidden from public view and involve the largely "medicalized" process of lethal injection, may have robbed capital punishment of a good measure of its dramatic denunciative function (Bessler 1997; Sarat 2001:60–84). Still, in light of the tremendous divergence between the incidence of lethal criminal violence and society's use of the death penalty, it is hard to quarrel with the notion that the primary function of capital punishment in contemporary America is symbolic (Acker 2006; Garland, this volume). Roughly 16,000 to 24,000 intentional criminal homicides have been committed annually in this country since 1977, when executions resumed in the post-*Furman* era, yet never during this period have as many as 100 murderers a year been executed (Pastore and Maguire 2005: Table 6.79.2005). Moreover, a dramatic reduction has recently been evidenced in both the number of new death sentences imposed (approximately 114 in 2006, compared to 283 in 1999) and executions carried out (53 in 2006 vs. 98 in 1999) (Bowers and Sundby, this volume; Death Penalty Information Center 2006). Yet to question the practical efficacy of capital punishment in responding to criminal violence is not to dismiss it as insignificant. The death penalty is likely more important for what it represents than what it accomplishes tangibly. Among its plausible symbolic attributes is promoting interests linked to social cohesiveness, such as fortifying individuals' beliefs that they live in a world where good triumphs over evil, and that offers both security and justice (Beschle 1997; Blecker 2003).

Retribution is commonly recognized as a legitimate objective of criminal punishment generally (von Hirsch 1976:45–55) as well as for the death penalty (Ellsworth and Gross 1994:27–29; *Gregg v. Georgia* 1976:183–184). The principle of just deserts presumes a blameworthy offender and demands at least rough proportionality between the seriousness of the offense, including the offender's culpability and the harm caused, and the punishment inflicted. This precept finds constitutional stature in the death-penalty context and restricts the capital sanction from being used for utilitarian purposes, such as deterrence or incapacitation, unless it is first justified on retributive grounds (*Coker v. Georgia* 1977; cf., *Atkins v. Virginia* 2002; *Roper v. Simmons* 2005). Eighth Amendment prohibitions against mandatory capital punishment (*Sumner v. Shuman* 1987; *Woodson v. North Carolina* 1976) and using death to punish unaggravated murder (*Godfrey v. Georgia* 1980; *Zant v. Stephens* 1983) further signify that a capital sentencing decision requires a unique and individualized assignment of blame. A death sentence is both figuratively and literally a judgment of condemnation. Unlike any other sanction known to the law, capital punishment expresses society's moral outrage against the offender and his or her conduct (Berns 1979).

Social Protection

Murderers have demonstrated a capacity for violence and a disregard for human life, giving rise to the possibility that they might do so again. Their imprisonment protects society at large against the risk of repeat offending, while their execution additionally safeguards prison staff, inmates, and visitors against future violence. Punishing murder by lengthy incarceration or death also serves as a warning to others. Prospective killers should know about the harsh sanctions that accompany murder and presumably will be discouraged from committing homicide to avoid suffering them. Incapacitation and general deterrence are widely acknowledged as justifications for criminal punishment generally and each rationale figures prominently in the death penalty context.

Statutes may require (most notably, in Texas) or allow (in many other states) juries to make predictions about offenders' future dangerousness as a part of their death penalty deliberations (Acker and Lanier 1994:118–121). Indeed, jurors typically weigh concerns about future violence heavily in their capital sentencing decisions whether or not the law authorizes them to do so (Blume, Garvey, and Johnson 2001; Bowers 1995). Available evidence suggests that capital murderers in general are not unusually prone to engage in repeat acts of criminal violence compared to other offenders, and reflects that neither mental health experts nor jurors are very good at predicting specific murderers' violent propensities (Sorensen, this volume). Still, most people understandably are not inclined to ignore even a small to moderate risk that a convicted murderer will kill again, thus making incapacitation one consideration in fixing punishment.

Legislative debates have long been shaped by views regarding the death penalty's efficacy as a general deterrent to murder (Abernethy 1996; Galliher and Galliher 2001–2002). This issue remains the subject of lively academic discussion despite numerous studies' inability to uncover evidence that capital punishment uniquely influences murder rates (Berk 2005; Dezhbakhsh and Shepherd 2006; Fagan 2006; Shepherd 2005). Some policymakers prefer to err on the side of protecting innocent life and thus favor allowing convicted murderers to be executed even though evidence is sparse that capital punishment discourages would-be murderers from killing better than the alternative sanction of life imprisonment (*cf.*, van den Haag 2003:241). On the other hand, some research suggests that the death penalty has a "brutalizing" effect that actually may inspire unlawful killings (Bailey 1998; Bowers and Pierce 1980; Cochran and Chamlin 2000). Concerns for social protection promise to remain important in choosing a punishment for murder in the face of doubts about alternative sanctions' comparative effectiveness in promoting general deterrence.

Restoration: Victim-Centered Concerns

Individuals who suffered harm at others' hands before the emergence of the criminal law had no choice but to rely on self-help for redress. Homicide inspired the affected families and clans to retaliate in kind, leading to protracted and debilitating blood feuds. As populations grew and societies became increasingly complex, blameworthy conduct that caused harm to individuals became defined as crimes against the body politic. Centralized governments appropriated the peace-keeping function by punishing wrongdoers, an advance that not only displaced individual victims from exacting revenge but also denied them direct compensation from the lawbreakers who had harmed them. Individual crime victims became so ancillary to the justice system in this country that many believed that their interests were considered inferior to those of the offenders responsible for harming them. The late 20th century spawned concerted action and laws designed to correct this perceived imbalance. The "victim's rights" movement thus helped focus attention on the criminal justice system's obligations toward individual crime victims (Acker and Mastrocinque 2006).

One aspect of this movement embraced enhancing the law's responsiveness to the interests of murder victims and their surviving family members. Just four years after ruling that victim impact evidence was inadmissible in capital trials because it threatened to inject arbitrariness into sentencing deliberations, the Supreme Court reversed course, ruling that such testimony was relevant to allow jurors to gain a richer appreciation of the victim's personal qualities and the extent of the loss suffered by his or her survivors (*Booth v. Maryland* 1987; Logan 2006; *Payne v. Tennessee* 1991). Close in time to this legal development, the notion that executions were important to help provide "closure" to murder victims' survivors began to figure prominently in policy discussions about the death penalty (Acker 2006; Zimring 2003:58–63). Choices about the preferred punishment for murder thus became importantly linked to a restorative function involving the concerns and interests of victims' survivors (Kay 2005; Umbreit *et al.* 2003).

Death is Different, and So Are Its Costs

Owing to its unique severity and irrevocability, there is agreement that "death is qualitatively different from a sentence of imprisonment, however long.... Because of that qualitative difference, there is a corresponding difference in the need for reliability in the determination that death is the appropriate punishment in a specific case" (*Woodson v. North Carolina* 1976:305). This staple of Eighth Amendment jurisprudence also has important policy implications. Just as the benefits (denunciation, social protection, restoration) accompanying different legal sanctions for murder must be given weight, so must their potential costs. The consequences of error and procedural unfairness, which are of concern in all murder prosecutions, are magnified when life is in the balance.

It is fair to conclude that research results have been less equivocal regarding the occurrence of substantive mistakes and procedural irregularities in capital cases than whether death offers unique benefits as a punishment for murder. Errors and administrative problems in death penalty cases, including wrongful convictions, racial disparities, jurors' misunderstanding or disregard of judicial instructions, inadequate legal representation, and others—many of which are discussed in this volume—have been amply documented. Murder prosecutions, and the systems sustaining them, also appear to entail significantly greater financial costs when death sentences are pursued than when life imprisonment is the sought-after punishment (Gradess and Davies, this volume). We should not be surprised to learn that capital trials are not foolproof, cheap, or prone to the same kinds of problems that occur in other criminal cases. "One cannot have a system of criminal punishment without accepting the possibility that someone will be punished mistakenly" (*Kansas v. Marsh* 2006:2539, Scalia, J., concurring). However, we would be remiss if we failed to consider the heightened consequences of mistakes and unfairness in capital cases when making policy decisions about the preferred punishment for murder.

Maximizing Benefits and Minimizing Costs

In deciding whether murder should be punished by death or an alternative sanction, such as life imprisonment without parole or another, we might hazard that the preferred sentence will be revealed by the most advantageous calculus of benefits and costs, a process that first requires that the underlying strengths and weaknesses of the respective options be identified and weighted. Research will be needed to reveal the specific positive and negative attributes of different punishments relevant to this benefit-cost formula and to measure their significance. The analysis might begin, for example, by attempting to confirm that denunciation, social protection, and restoration are essential ingredients of punishment for aggravated murder, and determining whether important additional purposes exist. Then, the effectiveness of different punishments in promoting those objectives would have to be measured, as discounted by their drawbacks—*e.g.*, the consequence of exposing innocent persons to punishment, imposing the punishment arbitrarily or disproportionately based on the race of the offender or victim, relative expense, and so forth. We should be willing to consider punishments not traditionally or presently used for murder in the process of attempting to maximize the benefit-cost ratio.

For example, torture might emerge as the most dramatic form of denunciation for aggravated murder and as the punishment most likely to operate as a general deterrent, but it presumably would entail unacceptably high costs because it is considered degrading, could be abused, and is almost certainly unconstitutional and thus unenforceable. The death penalty might be perceived as superior to life imprisonment in serving expressive and social protection functions, although its relative severity and irrevocability suggest that the corresponding costs associated with substantive and procedural injustices would be compounded significantly. Life imprisonment without the possibility of parole (LWOP) presumably entails relatively diminished perceived costs because errors are correctable and not amplified by the magnitude of a capital sentence, but imprisonment also might be perceived as producing fewer benefits than the death penalty.

The search for a punishment with the optimal balance of benefits and costs should embrace novel alternatives. Those who have reservations about capital punishment for murder "must accept the challenge of providing alternative ways of allowing the community to effectively express its unity in opposing violent crime" (Beschle 1997:538). If the death penalty is undesirable, owing to doubts or disagreement about its benefits or in light of its considerable potential costs, a more desirable solution must be found. A replacement for the death penalty "will be effective only if it can satisfy the community's need to denounce the criminal, and treat him harshly, while stopping short of killing him.... [T]o the extent that the abolitionist movement is seen as simply a part of an overall movement to be less punitive, more understanding and sympathetic to, violent criminals, it is likely to meet fierce resistance" (Beschle 2001:787).

Virtually all states that retain the death penalty also make use of LWOP (Bowers and Sundby, this volume). The coexistence of these sanctions suggests that most legislative bodies do not perceive imprisonment to suffice as the maximum punishment for aggravated murder and do not believe that LWOP promotes the symbolic and/or practical benefits of punishment as effectively as capital punishment. The quest for alternatives, accordingly, would profitably focus on enhancements of LWOP that stop short of extinguishing life.

Systematic public opinion research would be important to supply more definitive answers about why a sentence of LWOP fails to compare to a death sentence in denouncing aggravated murder. In the absence of such research, we might speculate about the reasons. In the first place, the very language employed—one that announces "life" as the primary attribute of the sentence—is symbolically less foreboding than a pronouncement of "death." LWOP by definition is considered to be a lesser punishment than death and when returned as the sentence in a capital trial it is frequently hailed as a "victory" for the defense. Moreover, unlike a death sentence, LWOP can be and often is imposed automatically, without individualized consideration given to the offender or the offense circumstances (*Harmelin v. Michigan* 1991). It consequently lacks an expressive or ritualistic element of censure or condemnation that is unique to the offender and his or her crime.

Perhaps, as former New York Governor Mario Cuomo was wont to do in promoting LWOP as an alternative to capital punishment, a sentence of life imprisonment without parole should be conceptualized differently and described in harsher terms, such as "death by incarceration" (Blair 1994:205). Perhaps different gradations of LWOP should be recognized, with singular conditions attached through juries' or judges' individualized judgments in especially opprobrious cases. For example, the concept of "civil death" is not unknown to the law, although in this country it is now most commonly associated with convicted felons losing the right to vote. In other times and places, a verdict of "civil death" worked a forfeiture of the offender's rights of inheritance. It is not suggested that a special verdict of LWOP plus civil death should prejudice a defendant's heirs, yet other consequences could attach and the special mark of denunciation accompanying such a sentence could serve a valuable function. In terms reminiscent of Stephen's characterization of offenders dispatched to capital punishment, the concept of "civic death" once meant "the absolute loss of all civil rights; 'it sunders completely every bond between society and the man who has incurred it; he has ceased to be a citizen ... he is without country; he does not exist save as a human being; and this, by a sort of commiseration which has no source in the law'" (von Bar *et al.* 1916:272, quoted in Ewald 2002:1060 n. 44).

In principle, a sentence of life imprisonment without parole also could assume a form that more effectively promotes the social protection function of punishment. Offenders who are considered to pose a special risk of future dangerousness could be singled out for confinement under conditions of heightened security, such as in a supermax prison, to minimize the threat of violence to correctional staff and other prisoners. Where consistent with constitutional provisions, clemency authorities could be denied the power to commute LWOP sentences to eliminate the risk of an offender's eventual parole eligibility (*cf., California v. Ramos* 1983). Indeed, a strikingly similar proposal was made in an 1841 New York legislative report that recommended abolition of capital punishment. Notably, the recommendation was conjoined with the suggestion that the offender would suffer "a civil and social death."

> An essential part of the proposed reform [doing away with capital punishment] is the removal from the hands of the Executive Chief Magistracy of the State, the power of pardon. Satisfied that this power ought to be entirely abolished in all cases, ... the propriety of its abolition in the case of a punishment expressly designed to be perpetual and to operate as a civil and social death, seems to the judgment of the committee a point on which no variance of opinion can anywhere exist. (Amsterdam *et al.* 2001–2002:424 n. 89, *quoting* Report in Favor of Abolition of Capital Punishment 1841:131; *see id.*: 424 n. 91)

Available research suggests that an element of restoration is a desirable attribute of punishment for murder. Public opinion polls reflect that support for punishing murder by a sentence of life imprisonment without parole, if coupled with restitution to the murder victim's family (LWOP + R), is dramatically higher than support for either the death penalty or LWOP that lacks the "plus restitution" component (Bowers, Vandiver, and Dugan 1994; Gross 1998). "The absence of a restorative element in LWOP and the shortage of punitiveness in [life imprisonment with parole eligibility] may make these latter options insufficiently appealing to some who would otherwise prefer an alternative to the death penalty" (Bowers *et al.* 1994:111). Because victims' families may strongly desire to break ties with the offender as completely as possible, establishing a state-administered compensation fund may have distinct advantages over programs relying on restitution paid by the murderer (Kay 2006).

Proposals also are gaining increased attention that would invest cost savings that could be realized by finding alternatives to the death penalty in services designed to benefit murder victims' survivors. For example, after hearing testimony about what victims' families endure following the murder of a relative or spouse, the New Jersey Death Penalty Study Commission recommended that "[s]ufficient funds should be dedicated to ensure adequate services and advocacy for the families of murder victims" (New Jersey Death Penalty Study Commission 2007:62). It concluded "that any cost savings resulting from the abolition of the death penalty [should] be used for benefits and services for survivors of victims of homicide" (New Jersey Death Penalty Study Commission 2007:67). A bill was recently introduced in the Colorado Legislature that aimed to abolish the death penalty and divert funds to police agencies for investigating unsolved murder cases that otherwise would be used to seek and carry out capital sentences. The proposed legislation, which did not pass, was motivated largely out of consideration for the families of murder victims in cases where their loved ones' killers had not been brought to justice and presumably remained at large (Brown 2007; *cf.*, Radelet and Stanley 2006).

In short, research would be useful that precisely and comprehensively assays the functions that the public and policymakers consider important to a just and effective punishment for murder and evaluates the efficacy of alternative punishments in serving those functions. Corresponding information would have to be collected about the types and perceived importance of drawbacks or costs associated with alternative punishments. Such inquiries could suggest creative ways of maximizing benefits and minimizing costs that build on the research findings. Particular attention might be focused on variations of LWOP that enhance the denunciative, social protection, and restorative capabilities of that sentence without incurring the unique potential costs that inevitably accompany fallible systems of capital punishment. Much presumably could be learned by studying how countries that have abandoned the death penalty—including most of the Western Hemisphere—punish murderers and respond to murder victims' survivors.

A "Guillotine Effect"?

In December 1789, just months after the storming of the Bastille and the onset of the French Revolution, Dr. Joseph-Ignace Guillotin successfully advocated before the French Assembly that capital punishment should be carried out in all cases through the bladed instrument that would thereafter be associated with his name. Previously, execution methods varied in France according to the offender's rank and the type of crime committed, and included such grisly practices as breaking at the wheel, burning at the stake, and quartering. Beheading had been the method of choice to execute nobles (Applbaum 1995:459–460).

Guillotin's proposal thus was offered in a spirit of reform; the decapitation machine was intended to strike "wrongdoers competently, impartially, and (as far as possible) kindlily [sic], in the triple tradition of rationality, egalitarianism and humanitarianism" (Kershaw 1958:18). Thousands died by the guillotine in the ensuing Reign of Terror, when ruling factions ruthlessly carried out executions against political enemies (Laurence 1960:73). Dr. Guillotin reportedly was despondent about the misappropriation of his reform effort. He "bore the remarks of a profound grief" on witnessing "the exploits of his terrible offspring" (Kershaw 1958:17).

Embarking on a quest for a sanction for murder that deliberately is more punitive than life imprisonment without the possibility of parole, perhaps one marked by a special stigma such as "civil death" or characterized by confinement in a supermax facility, raises concerns that parallel Dr. Guillotin's legacy. What may be perceived in the short term as one step forward, at least by those seeking a less severe and less absolute punishment than death, could one day threaten to represent two steps backward. Such backsliding could be evident, for example, if the harsh alternative sentence were imposed with procedural indifference, indiscriminately, or in great numbers, in contrast to the largely ceremonial contemporary use of capital punishment.

Such concerns, while justifiable, would represent abuses of commendable reform efforts. Problems that eventuated with an alternative punishment's implementation would be subject to correction by policymakers. They should not discourage researchers from exploring alternative sanctions for murder that lie in the expanse between capital punishment and LWOP. The principled search for a punishment with a more advantageous benefit-cost equation than is presently offered by either the death penalty or life imprisonment without the possibility of parole should not be scuttled because of possible abuses. Nevertheless, reform efforts should be carefully monitored, mindful of a possible "guillotine effect" through which even the best intentions and most promising plans are subject to being hijacked.

Conclusion

Capital sentences are now imposed in a miniscule percentage of murder cases and carried out even less frequently. As a practical matter, the death penalty does not figure prominently in contemporary criminal justice policy. At the same time, the political and symbolic significance of capital punishment is substantial and undeniable. The discrepancy between the practice and symbolism of capital punishment is not new. Societies throughout history have infused the taking of human life with ritual, to serve social functions as diverse as appeasing the gods and affirming secular political authority (Purdum and Paredes 1989; Steele 2001; Turnbull 1978). Some have employed severe punishments to promote important social functions while nevertheless sparing life. For example, in the Dutch colony of New Netherland, the antecedent of present-day New York State, courts occasionally ordered "sham executions" in which offenders were sentenced to die with the secret understanding that the sentence would never be carried out. "An example is the case of Thomas Cornel in November, 1644. Having found Cornel guilty of desertion, the seven magistrates conferred, voted, and announced the sentence, that the prisoner be tied to a stake and shot to death. But, while the prisoner was being borne from the room, the court's secretary wrote in his record book that the executioners were to fire over the prisoner's head, 'as an example to other evil doers.'" (Mackey 1982:6).

Many Americans voice support for the death penalty. Others oppose capital punishment in principle or entertain reservations about it because of possible errors or procedural unfairness, or based on resource constraints or other practical considerations. All, presumably, would be willing to consider alternatives to the death penalty if persuaded that another sanction provided comparable or superior symbolic and practical benefits and entailed fewer risks or demonstrable costs.

Although much disagreement exists about the death penalty, considerably more agreement certainly exists about the propriety of punishing murderers. The challenge for future researchers will be to identify and measure the benefits and costs associated with alternative sanctions for aggravated murder, including punishments that may not presently be commonly used. Possibilities such as LWOP with the special demarcation of "civil death," LWOP served under conditions of heightened security, and LWOP plus restitution or compensation for murder victims' survivors—special "add-ons" that enhance the denunciative, social protection, and/or reformative functions of imprisonment, accompanied by diminished or at least less final costs than capital punishment—should actively be considered. Empirical research has raised many doubts about the efficacy and procedural regularity of capital punishment. Equivalent investment should be made in research focusing on the alternative sanctions for murder that should affirmatively be considered.

References

Abernethy, Jonathan S. 1996. "The Methodology of Death: Reexamining the Deterrence Rationale." *Columbia Human Rights Law Review* 27:379–428.

Acker, James R. 2006. "The Myth of Closure and Capital Punishment." Pp. 167–175 in *Demystifying Crime and Criminal Justice*, edited by Robert M. Bohm and Jeffery T. Walker. Los Angeles, CA: Roxbury Publishing Company.

Acker, James R. and Charles S. Lanier. 1994. "'Parsing this Lexicon of Death': Aggravating Factors in Capital Sentencing Statutes." *Criminal Law Bulletin* 30:107–152.

Acker, James R. and Jeanna Marie Mastrocinque. 2006. "Causing Death and Sustaining Life: The Law, Capital Punishment, and Criminal Homicide Victims' Survivors." Pp. 141–160 in *Wounds That Do Not Bind: Victim-Based Perspectives on the Death Penalty*, edited by James R. Acker and David R. Karp. Durham, NC: Carolina Academic Press.

Amsterdam, Anthony *et al.* 2001–2002. "Brief of Amici Curiae, Court of Appeals of the State of New York, People of the State of New York, Against Darrel K. Harris." *New York University Review of Law and Social Change* 27:399–475.

Applbaum, Arthur Isak. 1995. "Professional Detachment: The Executioner of Paris." *Harvard Law Review* 109:458–486.

Atkins v. Virginia (2002). 536 U.S. 304.

Bailey, William C. 1998. "Deterrence, Brutalization and the Death Penalty: Another Examination of Oklahoma's Return to Capital Punishment." *Criminology* 36:711–733.

Berk, Richard. 2005. "New Claims About Executions and General Deterrence: Déjà vu All Over Again?" *Journal of Empirical Legal Studies* 2:303–330.

Berns, Walter. 1979. *For Capital Punishment: Crime and the Morality of the Death Penalty.* New York, NY: Basic Books.

Beschle, Donald L. 2001. "Why Do People Support Capital Punishment? The Death Penalty as Community Ritual." *Connecticut Law Review* 33:765–790.

_____. 1997. "What's Guilt (or Deterrence) Got to Do With It? The Death Penalty, Ritual, and Mimetic Violence." *William and Mary Law Review* 38:487–538.

Bessler, John D. 1997. *Death in the Dark: Midnight Executions in America.* Boston, MA: Northeastern University Press.

Bilz, Kenworthey and John M. Darley. 2004. "What's Wrong With Harmless Theories of Punishment." *Chicago-Kent Law Review* 79:1215–1252.

Blair, Danya W. 1994. "A Matter of Life and Death: Why Life Without Parole Should Be a Sentencing Option in Texas." *American Journal of Criminal Law* 22:191–214.

Blecker, Robert. 2003. "Roots." Pp. 169–231 in *America's Experiment With Capital Punishment: Reflections On the Past, Present, and Future of the Ultimate*

Penal Sanction, edited by James R. Acker, Robert M. Bohm and Charles S. Lanier. 2nd ed. Durham, NC: Carolina Academic Press.

Blume, John H., Stephen P. Garvey and Sheri Lynn Johnson. 2001. "Future Dangerousness in Capital Cases: Always 'At Issue'." *Cornell Law Review* 86:397–410.

Booth v. Maryland (1987). 482 U.S. 496.

Bowers, William J. 1995. "The Capital Jury Project: Rationale, Design, and Preview of Early Findings." *Indiana Law Journal* 70:1043–1102.

Bowers, William J. and Glenn Pierce. 1980. "Deterrence or Brutalization: What is the Effect of Execution?" *Crime and Delinquency* 26:453–484.

Bowers, William J. and Scott Sundby. This Volume. "Why the Downturn in Death Sentences?"

Bowers, William J., Margaret Vandiver and Patricia H. Dugan. 1994. "A New Look at Public Opinion on Capital Punishment: What Citizens and Legislators Prefer." *American Journal of Criminal Law* 22:77–149.

Brown, Jennifer. 2007. "Cold-Case Pursuits vs. Death Penalty: Families of the Slain Urge Funding Shift." *Denver Post*, June 13, A1.

California v. Ramos (1983). 463 U.S. 992.

Cochran, John K. and Mitchell B. Chamlin. 2000. "Deterrence and Brutalization: The Dual Effects of Executions." *Justice Quarterly* 17:685–706.

Coker v. Georgia (1977). 433 U.S. 584.

Death Penalty Information Center. 2006. "The Death Penalty In 2006: Year End Report." (http://www.deathpenaltyinfo.org/2006YearEnd.pdf).

Dezhbakhsh, Hashem and Joanna M. Shepherd. 2006. "The Deterrent Effect of Capital Punishment: Evidence from a 'Judicial Experiment'." *Economic Inquiry* 44:512–535.

Ellsworth, Phoebe C. and Samuel R. Gross. 1994. "Hardening of the Attitudes: Americans' Views on the Death Penalty." *Journal of Social Issues* 50:19–52.

Ewald, Alec C. 2002. "'Civil Death': The Ideological Paradox of Criminal Disenfranchisement Law in the United States." *Wisconsin Law Review* 2002:1045–1137.

Fagan, Jeffrey. 2006. "Death and Deterrence Redux: Science, Law and Capital Punishment." *Ohio State Journal of Criminal Law* 4:255–321.

Foucault, Michel. 1979. *Discipline and Punish: The Birth of the Prison.* New York, NY: Vintage Books.

Furman v. Georgia (1972). 408 U.S. 208.

Galliher, James M. and John F. Galliher. 2001–2002. "A 'Commonsense' Theory of Deterrence and the 'Ideology' of Science: The New York State Death Penalty Debate." *Journal of Criminal Law and Criminology* 92:307–333.

Garland, David. This Volume. "'Symbolic' and 'Instrumental' Aspects of Capital Punishment."

Gatrell, V.A.C. 1994. *The Hanging Tree: Execution and the English People.* New York: Oxford University Press.

Godfrey v. Georgia (1980). 446 U.S. 420.

Gradess, Jonathan E. and Andrew L. B. Davies. This Volume. "The Cost of the Death Penalty in America: Directions for Future Research."

Gregg v. Georgia (1976). 428 U.S. 153.

Gross, Samuel R. 1998. "Update: American Public Opinion on the Death Penalty—It's Getting Personal." *Cornell Law Review* 83:1448–1475.

Harding, Roberta M. 2000. "Capital Punishment as Human Sacrifice: A Societal Ritual as Depicted in George Eliot's *Adam Bede*." *Buffalo Law Review* 48:175–248.

Harmelin v. Michigan (1991). 501 U.S. 957.

Hay, Douglas. 1975. "Property, Authority and the Criminal Law." Pp. 17–64 in *Albion's Fatal Tree: Crime and Society in Eighteenth Century England*, edited by Douglas Hay, Peter Linebaugh, John G. Rule, E.P. Thompson and Cal Winslow. New York, NY: Pantheon Books.

Kansas v. Marsh (2006). 126 S. Ct. 2516.

Kay, Judith W. 2006. "Is Restitution Possible for Murder?—Surviving Family Members Speak." Pp. 323–347 in *Wounds That Do Not Bind: Victim-Based Perspectives on the Death Penalty*, edited by James R. Acker and David R. Karp. Durham, NC: Carolina Academic Press.

_____. 2005. *Murdering Myths: The Story Behind the Death Penalty.* New York, NY: Rowan & Littlefield Publishers.

Kershaw, Alister. 1958. *A History of the Guillotine.* London: John Calder.

Laurence, John. 1960. *A History of Capital Punishment.* New York, NY: The Citadel Press.

Logan, Wayne A. 2006. "Victims, Survivors, and the Decisions to Seek and Impose Death." Pp. 161–177 in *Wounds That Do Not Bind: Victim-Based Perspectives on the Death Penalty*, edited by James R. Acker and David R. Karp. Durham, NC: Carolina Academic Press.

Mackey, Philip English. 1982. *Hanging in the Balance: The Anti-Capital Punishment Movement in New York State, 1776–1861.* New York, NY: Garland Publishing, Inc.

New Jersey Death Penalty Study Commission. 2007. *New Jersey Death Penalty Study Commission Report.* Trenton, NJ: State of New Jersey. (http://www.njleg.state.nj.us/committees/dpsc_final.pdf).

Pastore, Ann L. and Kathleen Maguire (eds.). 2005. *Sourcebook of Criminal Justice Statistics.* (http://www.albany.edu/sourcebook/pdf/t6792005.pdf).

Payne v. Tennessee (1991). 501 U.S. 808.
Purdum, Elizabeth D. and J. Anthony Paredes. 1989. "Rituals of Death: Capital Punishment and Human Sacrifice." Pp. 139–155 in *Facing the Death Penalty: Essays on a Cruel and Unusual Punishment*, edited by Michael L. Radelet. Philadelphia, PA: Temple University Press.
Radelet, Michael L. and Dawn Stanley. 2006. "Learning from Homicide Co-Victims: A University-Based Project." Pp. 397–409 in *Wounds That Do Not Bind: Victim-Based Perspectives on the Death Penalty*, edited by James R. Acker and David R. Karp. Durham, NC: Carolina Academic Press.
Report in Favor of the Abolition of Capital Punishment, made to the Legislature of the State of New York. 1841 (April 14). New York Assembly Doc. No. 249.
Roper v. Simmons (2005). 543 U.S. 551.
Sarat, Austin. 2001. *When the State Kills: Capital Punishment and the American Condition.* Princeton, NJ: Princeton University Press.
Shepherd, Joanna M. 2005. "Deterrence versus Brutalization: Capital Punishment's Differing Impacts Among States." *Michigan Law Review* 104:203–249.
Sorensen, Jon. This Volume. "Researching Future Dangerousness."
Steele, John. 2001. "A Seal Pressed in the Hot Wax of Vengeance: A Girardian Understanding of Expressive Punishment." *Journal of Law and Religion* 16:35–68.
Sumner v. Shuman (1987). 483 U.S. 66.
Turnbull, Colin. 1978. "Death by Decree." *Natural History* 87:50–66.
Umbreit, Mark S., Betty Vos, Robert B. Coates and Katherine A. Brown. 2003. *Facing Violence: The Path of Restorative Justice and Dialogue.* Monsey, NY: Criminal Justice Press.
van den Haag, Ernest. 2003. "Justice, Deterrence and the Death Penalty." Pp. 233–249 in *America's Experiment With Capital Punishment: Reflections On the Past, Present, and Future of the Ultimate Penal Sanction*, edited by James R. Acker, Robert M. Bohm and Charles S. Lanier. 2nd edition. Durham, NC: Carolina Academic Press.
von Bar, Carl Ludwig and Others. 1916. *A History of Continental Criminal Law.* London: John Murray.
von Hirsch, Andrew. 1976. *Doing Justice: The Choice of Punishments.* New York, NY: Hill and Wang.
Woodson v. North Carolina (1976). 428 U.S. 280.
Zant v. Stephens (1983). 462 U.S. 862.
Zimring, Franklin E. 2003. *The Contradictions of American Capital Punishment.* New York, NY: Oxford University Press.

CHAPTER 21

LIFE UNDER SENTENCE OF DEATH: SOME RESEARCH AGENDAS

*Robert Johnson, Sandra McGunigall-Smith,
Jocelyn Fontaine and Christopher Dum*

Introduction

Conditions of confinement on death row have been a topic of study for some time now; yet most of this work is exploratory and descriptive. There has been little analytical research on what it means to live and die on death row, and even less on the experiences of the correctional officials who work on death row and serve on execution teams. In light of the gaps in the extant literature, we use this chapter to identify some topics for future research on death row and the executions that culminate this confinement. In addition, we suggest some useful research strategies to guide future research.

Future Research Topics

Conditions on Death Row

The objective conditions of confinement on death row have been fairly consistent over the centuries and have always been grim (Johnson 2003). With rare exceptions, close custody and near-solitary confinement have been and remain the central characteristics of life under sentence of death. The majority of offenders are housed in SHUs (special housing units), including supermax facilities, where they spend an average of 23 hours each day in a small cell. These offenders typically have limited, if any, access to educational or vocational programs and are denied access to library facilities. Televisions and radios, where available, must be earned—and since these media must be bought or rented by prisoners whose access to paid employment is limited, many prisoners do not have these luxuries. Visits typically take place in barrier booths, which place a strain on personal relationships with family and friends. Moreover, family members often have to travel long distances and be subjected to body searches when entering prison. As a result of these inconveniences and intrusions, visits can be unrewarding and often are less common than phone calls. In sum, the conditions of confinement for death row inmates are harsh. Offenders spend an inordinate amount of time in their cell alone; they are cut off from the outside world and must live in the shadow of the executioner with extremely limited access to family, friends or, indeed, even sounds or images of the outside world.

Repressive living conditions arguably are one reason why one in ten condemned offenders drop their appeals and, in effect, "volunteer" for execution, essentially choosing death in the execution chamber over continued life on death row. A recent study of execution volunteers notes that "in virtually every state, death row inmates are 'locked down' in their cells for most of the day, have little or no access to educational or other prison programs and experience great isolation and loss of relationships" (Blume 2005). Vandiver, Giacopassi, and Turner (forthcoming) examined motives for opting out of the appeals process and found Durkheim's suicide theory to have some relevance:

> The strictness of the norms contributes to death row syndrome, and is characteristic of fatalistic suicide, where the individual finds the social conditions unbearable but has no ability to change his life situation. Interestingly, the fatalistic suicide is often over-looked because of its rareness in modern society, but it may be viewed as one of the dominant types of suicides for death row inmates. (Vandiver *et al.* forthcoming)

Conditions of confinement are affected by other factors such as the size and composition of a death row population. The experiences of those in a small death row population, for example, may not be the same as those living on a bigger death row. Furthermore, the experience of life on death row may depend on how often executions are carried out. Death row offenders in Texas, where executions occur with some regularity, may cope with confinement differently from those death row offenders in states where executions are rare.

Coping

As a general matter, prisoners on any given death row may experience the conditions of confinement in different ways. Each prisoner has his or her own personality, values, and history, which influence how that person copes on death row. Ideally, studies of death row conditions should include research on how prisoners adapt. Patterns of adaptation, in turn, should be examined in terms of such variables as gender, race, class, and mental and physical health, to name a few.

The pains of confinement as originally described by Sykes (1958) are certainly suffered by death-sentenced prisoners but the pains of life on death row are likely to be more intense than those experienced by regular prisoners and hence may require different coping strategies from those used by regular inmates (McGunigall-Smith 2004). For instance, pains arising from the deprivation of liberty are suffered in two distinct ways by condemned prisoners: death-sentenced prisoners are deprived of liberty to live in the outside world, as well as the liberty to live in the general inmate population. Sykes (1958) also talked of loss of heterosexual relations, but for those in punitive segregation there is also a loss of the opportunity for homosexual relations. This may be significant for those who are unlikely ever to leave prison and who must, therefore, develop relationships within prison if they are to have any relations at all. A significant difference between death-sentenced prisoners, most of whom live under highly restrictive conditions, and general population prisoners is the fixed conditions of imprisonment. Unlike most other prisoners, death-sentenced prisoners will rarely progress through the prison system to a more tolerable existence. Condemned offenders are not likely to be released, and as such, the concept of "doing time" is very different for them; they are never done doing time and can only escape prison by death. The pains of death row prisoners are different; it makes perfect sense to explore the ways coping may be different as well.

Much has been written about the general stresses of living on death row and whether human beings can psychologically survive intact under such regimes (Cunningham and Vigen 2002; Johnson 2003). Next to nothing has been written about specific ways specific persons experience the stresses of death row confinement. To be sure, prior research reveals, sometimes in moving detail, the enormous pressures under which condemned prisoners live, particularly during the final hours in the death house (Johnson 1998, 1981; Prejean 1993). These studies, including studies of those who drop their appeals in favor of execution, provide portraits of prisoners in decline and do not examine the active coping process by which prisoners attempt, with varying degrees of success, to adapt to their confinement.

A particular coping technique, "tripping," was described by death-sentenced prisoners to McGunigall-Smith (2004). Since there is little condemned prisoners can do to escape or lessen the effects of isolation, they engage in a deliberate and learned activity whereby they take their minds out of prison. Explained simply, tripping occurs when offenders pace their cells and induce a trancelike state which enables them to "leave" the setting on "trips" to the outside world. Prisoners talked of planning ahead for these "trips"; where they would go, which friends they would take, which brand of beer they would drink, and so on (McGunigall-Smith and Johnson forthcoming). The work of Cohen and Taylor (1981) is useful in understanding this coping technique. Their work refutes the notion of inmates slotting into describable roles (like Sykes' argot roles) as a way of adapting; the focus is on how inmates actively create meaning in their daily prison lives, a process that often moves them from adaptation (essentially going along) to resistance (fighting back, at least in existential terms). Condemned prisoners (and others in special housing) may epitomize Foucault's (1977) concept of docile bodies, but they do not necessarily have docile minds. Tripping, as a way of actively coping with repressive conditions, is a concept worthy of further research.

Guards

Few occupation groups are faced with more difficult challenges than correctional officers. Few work groups are "more maligned than that of the guards; fewer are faced with more difficult challenges and are more misunderstood, mismanaged and alienated" (Toch in Lombardo 1981:xiii). Unfortunately little attention has been given to the experiences of prison guards, though officers are key players in the prison world. Even less attention is given to those who manage death-sentenced prisoners. Existing data, though limited, suggest that managing death sentenced prisoners consumes a relatively high percentage of administrative time and energy; yet, specialized training is not offered in the majority of jurisdictions (Hudson 2000). We have already argued that the pains of imprisonment are different for death-sentenced prisoners; therefore, any examination of prison life for these prisoners must also examine correctional officers and their adjustments, adjustments that shape and are shaped by the adjustments of prisoners.

Johnson (1998, 1990) found the job of guarding death-sentenced prisoners stressful and unrewarding. Guards were there solely to "preserve the corpus of the condemned" and considered their role as one of unwanted and intrusive escorts. They were often bored and tense and harbored feelings of vulnerability, including fear of being taken hostage or making procedural mistakes. This fear, according to Johnson, produces a casualty, simple human compassion, the loss of which affects how guards and prisoners cope. McGunigall-Smith

(2004) found a similar distance between staff and inmates, with the result that there was little understanding on the part of guards about the ways in which condemned prisoners coped. For instance, even though death-sentenced inmates cited "tripping" as a significant way of coping, not a single staff member, from the Executive Director to the line staff, had ever heard of this way of coping.

Executions

Guards

The uncertainty of the appeals process means that no one knows for sure when the next execution will take place. Moreover, executions are something many staff may never have to deal with or face with any regularity. Yet one thing is certain—the management of the deaths of condemned prisoners is a far cry from the management of the lives of those prisoners. One would expect that those managing death-sentenced inmates where execution rates are high may become desensitized. However, support for the death penalty does not mean staff members are prepared to take part in an execution or can readily distance themselves emotionally from the prisoners facing death by execution (McGunigall-Smith 2004). Where prisoners have been on death row for many years, and particularly on small death rows, individual prisoners may become well-known to some staff. And while it is safe to say that prisoners and guards rarely become friends, a mutual respect may develop. In this sense, it may be painful for guards to be instrumental in the death of someone they have come to know over many years.

There may also be differences in officer-prisoner relations when an execution is "voluntary." McGunigall-Smith (2004) found that officers were unsure of their role in such situations. They were not as much carrying out the order of the court as punishment as facilitating "release" for a prisoner whose wish was to put an end to an intolerable existence. In this case, roles were to some extent reversed, with the prisoner in charge and the staff doing his bidding, which caused considerable discomfort among staff. In fact, one prisoner studied by McGunigall-Smith (2004) went to great lengths to ease this discomfort among staff by making jokes and playing down the seriousness of the situation. Research could usefully be developed to examine why officers and other officials seem to experience a sense of discomfort when a prisoner in effect helps determine the date of execution. It may be because this is the first time in many years that the condemned prisoner has exercised control of his or her destiny. Garland (2007) has suggested that public support for executions is rooted in part in the enjoyment derived from inflicting such a profound punishment on people convicted of terrible crimes. When condemned prisoners "choose" death this decision arguably helps nullify the punishment, taking away society's essential pleasure in taking their lives by force. Now it is society that, in a sense, does the prisoner's bidding (Death Penalty Roundtable, ASC 2007).

Prisoners

Prisoners in general population are almost certainly affected by an execution. The old "us and them" divide comes into much sharper focus when guards and administration ("them") are instrumental in the death of a prisoner ("us"). For other death-sentenced inmates, executions bring home the reality of the death penalty as a force in their personal lives, not merely as an exercise in power. For those who have formed friendships with the about-to-be-executed, an execution is an extremely painful time. Friends on death row are drawn from a small reserve and the loss of just a friend to execution leaves a distinct void for some survivors who must ponder both their loss and their fate. McGunigall-Smith (2004) found distress among inmates when an inmate decided to opt out of the appeals process. At the same time, inmates struggled to show support for the man's desire to hasten his execution and end his painful days on death row.

Research Strategies

Research should examine how prisoners under sentence of death cope with the conditions of confinement over time. Research should also examine how policies and procedures related to death row prisoners change over time. Since death-sentenced prisoners spend many years between imposition of sentence and execution or other dispensation, examining whether their coping mechanisms are dynamic or static over time would be consequential. For example, do offenders' coping mechanisms change significantly over time, depending on factors such as how long they live on death row and the conditions of specific death rows? McGunigall-Smith (2004) observed marked deterioration in one prisoner over a period of ten years on death row. He went from a fairly upbeat, friendly man to a mere shadow of his former self, having grown dependent on Prozac to make it through each day. She also noted the changes in another prisoner on the same death row. In eight years, this man had changed from an apprehensive newcomer to death row, anxious to be accepted by the death-row culture, to a seemingly savvy individual dealing calmly with life under sentence of death. These cases suggest that on the same death row one may find very different patterns of adaptation over time. The correlates of such change over time should be of interest to our understanding of the death penalty in action.

Taking a different tack, research might compare experiences of prisoners and staff in two large death row facilities: one with a high rate of executions (*e.g.*, Texas), and one with a low rate of execution (*e.g.*, California). Smaller death rows might be compared with each other and with larger death rows, again looking at small facilities with high rates of execution (*e.g.*, Nevada or Virginia) and low rates (*e.g.*, Utah). It would also be informative to make comparisons within jurisdictions and facilities. McGunigall-Smith (2004) compared experiences of death-sentenced prisoners locked down in isolation more than 23 hours a day with those in the same prison who were part of a reformed program which provided more out of cell time with other death-sentenced prisoners. She additionally explored differences between death-sentenced prisoners and lifers (those who were unlikely for a variety of reasons to ever be released) (McGunigall-Smith 2004; see Johnson and McGunigall-Smith forthcoming)

Appropriate ways of collecting data have to be considered and the choices largely will be determined by access and cooperation on the part of different Departments of Corrections and individual research subjects. Where direct access is not given to researchers, mailed questionnaires would be one way to attempt to gain information from prisoners. This method, however, has limitations. While prisoners often have little with which to occupy their time and so may be inclined to complete and return the document, there is no guarantee that the response rates would be high (for either guards or prisoners). In addition, prisoners' mail is censored and so data will be limited. Furthermore, prisoners are still likely to remain apprehensive even if researchers deliver and collect surveys personally. Offenders are not likely to want their responses to be seen by prison employees and since cells are subject to random searches, information about sensitive issues may not be recorded. There is also a suspicion (unfounded or otherwise) that staff listen in on interviews. Prisoners also are often suspicious of outsiders. Most do not want to discuss the offenses that brought them to prison. For a prisoner to detail personal and sensitive information to a stranger typically requires face-to-face interaction—prisoners need a chance to decide whether the researcher can be trusted. In general, then, the quality and quantity of data will be limited without access to the prison.

Provided the researchers had access to the prison, highly structured interviews made up of closed-ended questions could be conducted face to face by more than one researcher. Coding and analyzing are made simpler this way. One limitation on this method is that responses may be restricted to the questions asked and topics covered, which represents a trade-off for the quantity of data gathered. Open-ended interviews in the ethnographic tradition yield rich data, but they are extremely time-consuming. A point for consideration is that face-to-face interviews may attract more subjects because they enable prisoners to get out of their cells.

Measurement: Quality of Life

One means of exploring the experience of life on death row is to examine the quality of life such environments provide to their inhabitants. The phrase "quality of life" has an odd resonance in this context, but condemned prisoners live on death rows for years, sometimes decades, and must forge a life for themselves, one they find by and large worth living. This life, such as it is, must be built from the objectively meager resources available to condemned prisoners. A simple concern for human decency suggests that we assess the quality of life on death row with an eye toward reforms that make life on death row as bearable as possible. Condemned prisoners are meant to suffer, but surely not so much that they come to favor execution over life on death row.

Quality of life is a fluid, subjective concept. There is general agreement, however, that most individuals find satisfaction or happiness from their family and friends, their work, and their health, although the relative importance assigned to any of these aspects of life varies from person to person, presumably influenced in part by setting or context. Our focus is the prison context, and more specifically death rows. Data on quality of life can be used to compare living conditions across different death rows. We know that objective conditions vary somewhat across death rows, but we do not know whether and how those differences affect inmates' quality of life.

Quality of life research would allow us to compare the daily existence of condemned prisoners with other prisoners, notably prisoners sentenced to life without the possibility of parole (LWOP). LWOP has been called "our other death penalty" because the LWOP prisoner is sentenced to what amounts to "death by incarceration" (Johnson and McGunigall-Smith forthcoming). Comparative data on quality of life can be used to assess the severity of punishment as experienced by persons living under traditional death sentences and under life sentences without the possibility of parole. To the extent that quality of life is comparably diminished for condemned and LWOP prisoners, it bolsters the argument that LWOP is a sanction severe enough to serve as a viable alternative to the death penalty. Admittedly, the purpose of punishment is not expressly to diminish quality of life. But much support for the death penalty, if not for punishment in general, rests on retributive grounds—society both expects and wants prisoners, and especially condemned prisoners, to suffer. Any alternative to the death penalty would have to entail suffering comparable to that associated with the death penalty.

Measuring Quality of Life in Prison

Quality of life measures would offer a nuanced view of daily life on death row, a view that cannot be inferred from simple descriptions of confinement conditions but rather must be derived from an understanding of conditions as they are experienced by prisoners and as they affect daily life in prison. Quality of life is a useful perspective if for no other reason than that different people may experience the same objective environmental conditions in different ways. We hope to develop an instrument to assess quality of life on death row. Our main goal is to compare death rows as living environments. A secondary goal is to compare quality of life experiences of prisoners on death rows with the experiences of prisoners condemned to death by incarceration, or LWOP. In general, we hope to explore how inmates carve out some measure of happiness—or at least forge lives they consider worth living—from the raw materials afforded by different prison environments.

Quality of life is a concept that has been measured in a variety of ways. The United Nations uses the Human Development Index, which measures three facets of human development: a long and healthy life, knowledge or education, and standard of living (United Nations 2007). This Index, and others like it, focus on economic prosperity to determine the quality of life. The Economist Intelligence Unit's Quality of Life Index (Economist 2007) attempts to deal with the fact that "material wellbeing" is not the sole measure of quality of life. Therefore, the Economist Intelligence Unit (Economist 2007) introduced subjective life-satisfaction surveys that asked questions such as, "On the whole are you satisfied with the life you lead?" The survey uses nine quality of life factors: material wellbeing, health, political stability and security, family life, community life, climate and geography, job security, political freedom, and gender equality. Some of these factors can be readily translated into a prison quality of life measurement, while others are not entirely relevant.

Another source of information about life quality comes from The General Social Survey (National Data Program for the Sciences 2007). The General Social Survey provides a framework for how non-institutionalized Americans organize their lives. This information could be translated into the prison context with reasonable modifications. It includes several questions on religious experiences, altruism, social networks and group membership, familial relations, and personal philosophy that could reasonably form a measure of quality of life.

Alison Liebling's (2004) seminal work, *Prisons and Their Moral Performance*, has been commended for examining "the quality of life in prison as an aspect of moral performance and an evaluation of those aspects of the interpersonal and material treatment of prisoners that determines just how dehumanizing prison life is" (van Zyl Smit 2005:765). Liebling's study is a general evaluation of quality of life in prison, using a survey that measures several different dimensions of prison life. This survey builds on the idea that prisons are worlds of their own with a special morality. Liebling (2004) argues that based on the results of her study, prisons should adopt an "explicitly moral agenda" and focus on "the role of values in penal practice, policy-making and evaluation" (Preface). Her survey measures aspects of prison life that both staff and prisoners deemed important, adding validity to the measure. Liebling's instrument has been widely used in prisons in the UK and has the advantage of building on the earlier work of Toch (1992), who first mapped the ecology of prison adjustment.[1]

We are in the process of adapting Liebling's instrument to fit the conditions of prison life in America, and in particular to assess the experiences of prisoners living on death row as well as prisoners serving life without parole The dimensions of quality of life examined in Liebling's research are: Respect, Hu-

---

1. Efforts to measure quality of life in prison have been quite limited. In "Prisons and Prisoners: Some Observations, Comments and Ethical Reflections Based on a Visit to a Prison Hospital in the Ukrainian Republic," Brykczynska (2002) examines well-being and general health among prisoners. Upon a visit to a Ukrainian prison hospital, Brykczynska was appalled by the lack of funding and treatment of the prisoners in hospital care. Of course, the health and wellbeing of prisoners could be one way of measuring prison quality, and a limited one for our purposes. In the study "The Effect of Incarceration on Prisoners' Perception of Their Health," Blanc, Lauwers, Telmon and Rouge (2001) aimed to measure the quality of life using a French version of the Nottingham Health Profile. They expected to use this information to gain insight into the effect of incarceration on emotional reaction. The Nottingham Health Profile is a self-reporting survey which measures perceived health. Its validity has been established in several different types of populations. Reporting on the NHP is grouped into six scales relating to energy, pain, emotional reaction, social isolation, sleep, and physical mobility. Although this measurement is reliable, easy to administer, and well-received by the prison population, it has its faults. In particular, these scales are mainly focused on physical health, and there obviously are many other aspects of life in prison in addition to tangibles such as mobility and pain. Finally, in their article, "Prison Conditions, Capital Punishment and Deterrence," Katz, Levitt and Shustorovich (2003) assert that they lack a direct measure of prison conditions. Because of this, they decided to use the death rate among prisoners (from all causes) in a given state and year as a measure of prison conditions. The authors concluded that they were unable to find other variables with consistent data. In their words, it was "likely that prison death rates correlate with many important aspects of the relative unpleasantness of the prison experience" (*id.*:321). They raised the important question of whether poor prison conditions will lead to more or less crime, addressing the all-important issue of whether prison acts as a deterrent and if so, why? However, the authors cautioned that they do not believe that their data can be used to make any policy recommendations.

manity, Relationships, Trust, Support, Fairness, Order, Safety, Wellbeing, Personal Development, Family Contact, Decency, Power, Prisoner Social Life, and Quality of Life (an overall self-assessment). Each item is measured by several questions; we have selected (and adapted) two items for each dimension. Our work with prisoners on death row and serving LWOP sentences suggests to us that there will be variation along most if not all of these dimensions.

Another source of quality of life items is McGunigall-Smith's (2004) exploratory study of life on Utah's death row. This research included a sizable sample of life-sentenced prisoners as well. Analysis of McGunigall-Smith's interviews revealed several items that regularly came up in her discussions with prisoners. These items reflect the daily and often quite specific concerns raised by interviewees for simple creature comforts (a good night's sleep; a shower when you need it; warm food), for getting along with staff, for securing visits, and for constructive things to do with one's time (*e.g.*, programs, work). We intend to perform a factor analysis on the range of items raised by McGunigall-Smith's interviews. Her interviews suggest that the simple decency of daily conditions of life will be central to the assessments of quality of life made by American prisoners on death row and serving LWOP.

A preliminary version of our quality of life instrument will be administered to samples of prisoners on death row, and then a scoring system will be developed to allow us to assess varying degrees of quality of life. Employing such a strategy will permit an examination of variations within and across various death rows. An important next step would be to survey LWOP prisoners, to allow comparisons between condemned prisoners and LWOP prisoners. Comparisons between condemned prisoners, LWOP prisoners, and prisoners serving lesser sentences may suggest a broad range of quality of life issues that may guide prison reform efforts in the future.

Punishment is meant to be a just undertaking, not an exercise in degradation and abuse. As a practical matter, this means that conditions of confinement must meet some level of simple decency. Empirical studies using our emerging quality of life instrument may provide useful data about the nature and decency of life in prison that can guide efforts at reform.

References

American Society of Criminology. 2007. Death Penalty Round Table.
Blanc, Anthony, Valerie Lauwers, Norbert Telmon and Daniel Rouge. 2001. "The Effect of Incarceration on Prisoners' Perception of Their Health." *Journal of Community Health* 26:367–381.

Blume, John H. 2005. "Killing the Willing: "Volunteers, Suicide and Competency." *Michigan Law Review* 103:939–1009.

Brykczynska, Gosia. 2002. "Prisons and Prisoners: Some Observations, Comments and Ethical Reflections Based On a Visit to a Prison Hospital in the Ukrainian Republic." *Nursing Ethics* 9:361–372.

Cohen, Stanley and Laurie Taylor. 1981. *Psychological Survival*. London, England: Penguin Books.

Cunningham, Mark D. and Mark P. Vigen. 2002. "Death Row Inmate Characteristics, Adjustment, and Confinement: A Critical Review of the Literature." *Behavioral Sciences and the Law* 20:191–210.

Economist. 2007. "Quality of Life Index." The Economist Newspaper Limited. (http://www.economist.com/media/pdf/QUALITY_OF_LIFE.pdf).

Foucault, Michel. 1977. *Discipline and Punish*. London, England: Penguin Books.

Garland, David. 2007. Personal Communication. November.

Hudson, Major Daniel. 2000. *Managing Death-sentenced Inmates: A Survey of Practices*. MD: American Correctional Association.

Johnson, Robert. 2003. Life Under Sentence of Death: Historical and Contemporary Perspectives." Pp. 647–671 in *America's Experiment with Capital Punishment: Reflections on the Past, Present, and Future of the Ultimate Penal Sanction*. 2nd ed., edited by James R. Acker, Robert M. Bohm and Charles S. Lanier. Durham, NC: Carolina Academic Press.

_____. 1998. *Death Work: A Study of the Modern Execution Process*. 2nd ed. Belmont, CA: Wadsworth.

_____. 1990. *Death Work: A Study of the Modern Execution Process*. 1st ed. Belmont, CA: Wadsworth.

_____. 1981. *Condemned to Die: Life Under Sentence of Death*. New York, NY: Elsevier.

Katz, Lawrence, Steven D. Levitt and Ellen Shustorovich. 2003. "Prison Conditions, Capital Punishment and Deterrence." *American Law and Economics Review* 5:318–343.

Liebling, Alison and Helen Arnold. 2004. *Prisons and Their Moral Performance: A Study of Values, Quality, and Prison Life*. Oxford, England: Oxford University Press.

Lombardo, Lucien X. 1981. *Guards Imprisoned: Correction Officers at Work*. New York, NY: Elsevier.

McGunigall-Smith, Sandra. 2004. "Men of a Thousand Days: Death-Sentenced Inmates at Utah State Prison." Unpublished Ph.D thesis. University of Wales, Bangor, ME.

McGunigall-Smith, Sandra and Robert Johnson. Forthcoming. "Escape from Death Row: A Study of 'Tripping' as an Individual Adjustment Strategy Among Death Row Prisoners." *Pierce Law Review*.

National Data Program for the Sciences. 2007. "General Social Survey." Chicago, IL: National Opinion Research Center. (http://www.norc.org).

Prejean, Helen. 1993. *Dead Man Walking*. New York, NY: Vintage Books.

Sykes, Gresham M. 1958. *The Society of Captives: A Study of a Maximum Security Prison*. Princeton, NJ: Princeton University Press.

Toch, Hans. 1992. *Living in Prison: The Ecology of Survival*. Washington, DC: American Psychological Association.

United Nations. 2007. "Human Development Index." The United Nations Human Development Reports. (http://hdr.undp.org/en).

van Zyl Smit, Dirk. 2005. "A Review of *Prisons and Their Moral Performance* (2004), by Alison Liebling and Helen Arnold." *British Journal of Criminology* 45:765–792.

Vandiver, Margaret, David J. Giacopassi and K.B. Turner. Forthcoming. "'Let's Do It': An Analysis of Consensual Executions." Pp. 189–208 in *The Death Penalty Today*, edited by Robert M. Bohm. London, England: CRC Press-Taylor & Francis Group.

CHAPTER 22

THE FUTURE OF EXECUTION METHODS

Deborah W. Denno

On February 14, 2006, *Morales v. Hickman*, a federal district court opinion, rendered a ruling that would draw criticism to the intricacies of the nation's execution process like never before (Denno 2007). While *Morales* concerned California's lethal injection procedures, the case would also inspire a framework for assessing the future of all execution methods throughout the country.

For California to conduct the lethal injection execution of Michael Morales, the state had to choose one of two court-mandated options: provide qualified medical personnel who would ensure Morales was unconscious during the procedure, or alter the department of corrections' execution protocol so that only one kind of drug would be given, rather than the standard sequence of three different drugs. Evidence suggested that, of the eleven inmates lethally injected in California, six may have been conscious and tormented by the three-drug regimen, potentially creating an "unnecessary risk of unconstitutional pain or suffering" in violation of the Eighth Amendment's Cruel and Unusual Punishments Clause (*Morales v. Hickman* 2006:1039). In a captivating legal moment, the state chose to have medical experts present at Morales' execution, setting the stage for a showdown between law and medicine (Denno 2007).

Immediately, medical societies protested the *Morales* court's recommendation and the ethical quandaries it posed. Three groups—the American Medical Association, the American Society of Anesthesiologists, and the California Medical Association—united in their opposition to doctors joining executioners. Even bigger surprises from *Morales* were yet to come. It took just one day for prison officials to find two anesthesiologists willing to take part in Morales' execution, after assurances were made that they would remain anonymous. It soon became clear, however, that these doctors had not been fully informed of their roles. In a stunning blow to the *Morales* court's directive, both anesthesiologists resigned mere hours before the scheduled execution time. Because of their ethical responsibilities, the anesthesiologists would not accept the interpretation of the U.S. Court of Appeals for the Ninth Circuit that they would have to intervene personally and provide medication or medical assistance if the inmate appeared conscious or in pain (Denno 2007; *Morales v. Hickman* 2006). The doctors' reasons for refusing to participate spotlight a crucial predicament states face in the administration of lethal injection (Denno 2007).

The *Morales* case unearthed a nagging paradox. The people most knowledgeable about the process of lethal injection—doctors, particularly anesthesiologists—are often reluctant to impart their insights and skills. This very dilemma moved Judge Jeremy Fogel, who presided over Morales' hearings, to assume unprecedented involvement in an area that had been controlled primarily by legislatures and department of corrections personnel. In response to the doctor pullout and questions about lethal injection's viability, Judge Fogel organized an unusually long and thorough evidentiary hearing. The homework paid off: Examinations and testifying experts opened a window into the hidden world of executions (Denno 2007).

Given that lethal injection is this country's leading execution method, *Morales* cast a shadow over executions across the nation. By the time Judge Fogel issued a memorandum decision on December 15, 2006 holding that California's lethal injection protocol "as implemented" violated the Eighth Amendment, a Missouri district court already had reached a conclusion concerning its own state's protocol (Denno 2007; *Morales v. Hickman* 2006; *Taylor v. Crawford* 2006, 2007). Indeed, less than a year later, on September 19, 2007, a Tennessee district court would similarly find its state's revised protocol unconstitutional (*Harbison v. Little* 2007).

Constitutional challenges to lethal injection currently dominate much of the nation's death penalty litigation, with no end in sight. For example, on May 15, 2007, California released a new, even more problematic, protocol, which Judge Fogel will review again. Meanwhile, during a three-month period in 2007, five other states also issued revised protocols. These revisions included two overhauled versions for Florida—one in May 2007 and one in July 2007—neither of which adequately addressed the problems of the previous protocol, as well as the new version for Tennessee that was rendered unconstitutional in September 2007. While *Morales* served as a catalyst for this protocol-revising rush, such activity now covers the entire country (Denno 2007).

As *Morales* makes clear, medicine is the key to understanding the problems of lethal injection. Like all lethal injection states that offer information on the chemicals used, California's execution protocol provides for the intravenous administration of three drugs: sodium thiopental, a common anesthetic for surgery used to cause unconsciousness; pancuronium bromide, a total muscle relaxant that stops breathing by paralyzing the diaphragm and lungs; and potassium chloride, a toxin that induces cardiac arrest and permanently stops the inmate's heartbeat. In *Morales*, the defendants urged, and the court agreed, that under the state's protocol, the listed amount of the first drug, sodium thiopental, should cause the condemned inmate to lose consciousness in less than a minute. The parties concurred, however, that if the sodium thiopental was ineffective, it would be unconstitutional to inject the second and third drugs into a conscious person. Because of its paralytic effects, the second drug, pancuronium bromide, would mask indications that the inmate was conscious and in "excruciating pain" from feelings of suffocation as well as intense burning as the potassium chloride entered the vein (Denno 2007; *Morales v. Hickman* 2006).

Judge Fogel determined that California's process embodied too much risk of unconstitutionality due to "a number of critical deficiencies" in the protocol. These included (1) *"inconsistent and unreliable screening of execution team members"*—highlighted, for instance, by one execution team leader's smuggling of illegal drugs into the prison while also in charge of handling the sodium thiopental (a pleasurable and addictive controlled substance); (2) *"lack of meaningful training, supervision, and oversight of the execution team"*—exemplified by the court's conclusion that team members "almost uniformly have no knowledge of the nature or properties of the drugs that are used or the risks or potential problems associated with the procedure" and the shockingly indifferent reactions by team members when describing troublesome executions; (3) *"inconsistent and unreliable record-keeping"*—revealed by inadequate documentation concerning whether all of the sodium thiopental prepared for an execution actually was injected and testimony that in several executions it was not, as well as evidence that "[a] number of the execution logs are incomplete or contain illegible or overwritten entries with respect to critical data;" and (4) *"inadequate lighting, overcrowded conditions, and poorly designed facilities"*—noted by descriptions that the execution team members, who were in a separate room from the inmate, worked in conditions in which the lighting and sound were so poor and the space so constrained that team members could not effectively observe or hear the inmate—much less tell whether the inmate was unconscious (Denno 2007:56; *Morales v. Hickman* 2006:979).

Other lethal injection challenges throughout the country revealed comparably disturbing details. In Kentucky, the protocol allowed improperly trained executioners to insert catheters into an inmate's neck despite a doctor's refusal to do so and heated criticism of the procedure, a practice ultimately ruled unacceptable (*Baze v. Rees* 2005; Denno 2006, 2007). In Missouri, a doctor ("Dr. Doe") who had supervised fifty-four executions over the course of a decade had a record of more than twenty malpractice suits and revoked privileges at two hospitals (Denno 2007; Roko 2007; *Taylor v. Crawford* 2006). A nearly two-hour execution of an Ohio prisoner who appeared to be suffocated alive in May 2007 followed a comparably controversial ninety-minute execution a year earlier that had compelled the state to revise its procedures (Denno 2007). In turn, in North Carolina, a doctor present to monitor the inmate's level of consciousness—a court-ordered requirement, but one that would violate the American Medical Association's ethical guidelines—later said he had not done so (Denno 2007). In Florida in December 2006, the execution of a tormented, conscious prisoner prompted a study that resulted in two protocol revisions and an evidentiary hearing that halted all the state's executions until September 10, 2007 (Denno 2007). When, after repeated needle pokes, California inmate Stanley Tookie Williams asked his executioners—"'[y]ou guys doing that right?'"—Williams could have been addressing department of corrections personnel in every lethal injection state (Denno 2007).

Medical personnel—those individuals most likely to know whether a lethal injection is being done "right"—often avoid the procedure. In 2006, when a surge of court cases and resulting media attention began to focus on botched lethal injections, the president of the American Society of Anesthesiology (ASA) reacted defensively: "Lethal injection was not anesthesiology's idea," he insisted. Rather, the problem rested with "American society," which "decided to have capital punishment as part of our legal system and to carry it out with lethal injection." For these reasons, "the legal system has painted itself into this corner and it is not [the medical profession's] obligation to get it out" (Denno 2007). What the ASA president's statement does not acknowledge, however, is that medicine is in the same corner with law, holding the paint can and the brush.

This next phase of the examination of lethal injection in this country will prove most critical: How will states handle the perplexing medical questions that lethal injection has posed? Lethal injection is here to stay for the foreseeable future because there is little indication that states are looking for another execution method. Indeed, most courts would agree with Judge Fogel that while the system of "lethal injection is broken ... it can be fixed" (*Morales v. Tilton* 2006:974). But how?

Attempts to find the "fix" have now garnered the Supreme Court's unprecedented involvement. On September 25, 2007, the Court granted certiorari in *Baze v. Rees* (2007), the Court's first opportunity since 1878 to evaluate an execution method under the Eighth Amendment (Petition for a Writ of

Certiorari, *Baze* 2007).[1] The *Baze* petitioners have asked the Court to address three primary issues centered around the following question: Does Kentucky's lethal injection procedure lead to "an unnecessary risk of pain and suffering in violation of the Eighth Amendment" given the availability of alternative procedures that would create less risk of pain and suffering? (Petition for a Writ of Certiorari, *Baze* 2007).[2]

The answer is of unusual importance. Because lethal injection is this country's prevailing execution method, the Court's decision will impact virtually every death penalty case in the country. Indeed, the Court's grant of certiorari has led to a de facto moratorium on executions while the legality of Kentucky's formula is under review. *Baze* therefore provides a fortuitous forum for this chap-

---

1. The Supreme Court has addressed lethal injection previously, but in another doctrinal context. In *Heckler v. Chaney* (1985), inmates sentenced to death in Oklahoma and Texas claimed the drugs used for lethal injection had been approved by the Food and Drug Administration (FDA) only for the medical purposes stated on their labels—for example, animal euthanasia—and not for the executions of humans. Given this circumstance and the likelihood that the drugs would be applied by unknowledgeable prison personnel, "it was also likely that the drugs would not induce the quick and painless death intended" (*Heckler v. Chaney* 1985:823). According to the inmates, such practices constituted the "unapproved use of an approved drug" and therefore a violation of the prohibition against "misbranding" under the Federal Food, Drug, and Cosmetic Act (*Heckler v. Chaney* 1985:823–824). However, the Supreme Court steadfastly held that the FDA's discretionary authority in refusing to initiate proceedings according to the inmates' demands was not subject to judicial review. One year later, the Fifth Circuit Court of Appeals relied on *Heckler* in *Woolls v. McCotter* (1986) to deny Randy Woolls' claim that Congress failed to provide for judicial review of the FDA's refusal to evaluate the use of sodium thiopental as a lethal drug, emphasizing that the use of such a drug did not constitute cruel and unusual punishment.

2. The petition for a writ of certiorari in *Baze* originally posed four questions (Petition for a Writ of Certiorari, *Baze* 2007). On October 3, 2007, however, the Supreme Court limited the petition to the following three questions (*Baze v. Rees* 2007):

(I) Does the Eighth Amendment to the United States Constitution prohibit means for carrying out a method of execution that create an unnecessary risk of pain and suffering as opposed to only a substantial risk of the wanton infliction of pain?

(II) Do the means for carrying out an execution cause an unnecessary risk of pain and suffering in violation of the Eighth Amendment upon a showing that readily available alternatives that pose less risk of pain and suffering could be used?

(III) Does the continued use of sodium thiopental, pancuronium bromide, and potassium chloride, individually or together, violate the cruel and unusual punishment clause of the Eighth Amendment because lethal injections can be carried out by using other chemicals that pose less risk of pain and suffering?

(Petition for a Writ of Certiorari, *Baze* 2007:ii–iii).

ter's goal of assessing the future of execution methods. At the same time, such a venture requires historical context. The analysis starts with an examination of how execution methods evolved to their present dilemma before tackling what lies ahead.

The Search for a Medically Humane Execution Method

Thirty years ago, this country's centuries-long search for a medically humane method of execution landed at the doorstep of lethal injection. Currently, of the thirty-eight death penalty states, injection is the sole method of execution in twenty-eight states and is one of two methods of execution in nine. Nebraska uses only electrocution (Denno 2007).

The turn to lethal injection reflects states' growing reliance on medicine as a response to philosophical, financial, and political pressures to eliminate the death penalty. For example, New York State's increasing opposition to capital punishment in the early 1800's—a move prompted by a series of disastrous public hangings attended by crowds of thousands—led the state's governor to ask the legislature in 1885 whether the state could not find a less barbaric means to execute. The governor's appointed commission of three prominent citizens ultimately selected the electric chair, following their impressively detailed two-year study of every execution method ever used throughout history (Denno 2007).

In 1890, the murderer William Kemmler became the first person in the country to be electrocuted. New York's decision to enact electrocution spurred intense legal and scientific battles, resolved only when the United States Supreme Court decided that the Eighth Amendment did not apply to the states (*In re Kemmler* 1890). Kemmler was executed in a day of confusion and horror, suffering a slow demise of burning flesh and ashes. Such catastrophe did not dissuade states from adopting this new method of purported scientific advancement. Electrocution still was deemed superior to hanging or, at the very least, was far less visible (Denno 2007).

The problems with electrocution only worsened with the passing decades, despite (or perhaps because of) the enhanced scrutiny of the method's application. By the time Allen Lee Davis was executed in Florida in 1999, over a century after Kemmler, the tragedies of the method appeared insurmountable: Davis suffered deep burns and bleeding on his face and body, as well as partial asphyxiation from the mouth strap that belted him to the chair's head-rest. Millions of people around the world viewed virtually the results of Davis's execution through the Florida Supreme Court's website postings of Davis's post-execution color photographs—ultimately crashing and disabling the Florida court's computer system for months. While the Davis botch did not halt electrocutions, it did prompt the Florida legislature to enable inmates to choose between electrocution and lethal injection (Denno 2007).

In light of this troubling execution methods history, lethal injection's popularity is understandable. Modern hangings risked being too long and cruel, like their predecessors. Lethal gas was judged the worst of all. In 1992, for example, Donald Harding's eleven-minute execution and suffocating pain were so disturbing for witnesses that one reporter cried continuously, "two other reporters 'were rendered walking "vegetables" for days,'" the attorney general ended up vomiting, and the prison warden claimed he would resign if forced to conduct another lethal gas execution (Denno 2007:63). While the firing squad has not been systematically evaluated, and may even be the most humane of all methods, it always has carried with it the baggage of its brutal image and roots. The law turned to medicine to rescue the death penalty (Denno 2007).

Indeed, lethal injection was considered a potential execution method in the United States as early as 1888. The New York governor's appointed commission rejected it, in part because of the medical profession's belief that, with injection, the public would begin to link the practice of medicine with death (Denno 2007).

In 1953, Great Britain's Royal Commission on Capital Punishment also dismissed lethal injection, concluding after a five-year study of Great Britain's entire death penalty process that injection was no better than hanging, the country's long-standing method (Royal Commission Report 1953). Critical to the Royal Commission's investigation of lethal injection, however, was the substantial weight the commission gave to medical opinions and expertise. The commission solicited input from members of two of the country's most established medical organizations—the British Medical Association and the Association of Anaesthetists—as well as prison medical officers (Denno 2007; Royal Commission Report 1953).

The host of problems these medical experts detected with lethal injection still ring true today. For example, based on such medical contributions, the Royal Commission determined that a standard lethal injection could not be administered to individuals with certain "physical abnormalities" that make their veins impossible to locate; rather, it was likely that executioners would have to implement intramuscular (as opposed to intravenous) injection, even though the intramuscular method would be slower and more painful. Significantly, the commission emphasized that lethal injection requires medical skill. While the British medical societies made clear their opposition to participating in the process, the Royal Commission still believed that acceptable executioners could be located, even in the medical profession. Nonetheless, other obstacles to lethal injection proved determinative. In particular, the commission found a lack of "reasonable certainty" that lethal injections could be performed "quickly, painlessly and decently," at least at that time (Royal Commission Report 1953: 261). Ultimately, in 1965, the British abandoned the death penalty with a few exceptions (Denno 2007).

In 1976, the United States reexamined the lethal injection issue after the Supreme Court reinstated the death penalty following a four-year moratorium (*Gregg v. Georgia* 1976). Remarkably, during this reexamination, none of the medical opinion evidence gathered on lethal injection—either from the New York or the British commissions—was addressed in legislative discussions or debates. Seemingly oblivious to prior concerns, American lawmakers emphasized that lethal injection appeared more humane and visually palatable relative to other methods. It was also cheaper (Denno 2007).

In May 1977, Oklahoma became the first state to adopt lethal injection. Contrary to the thorough and deliberative approaches taken by the New York and British commissions, however, accounts suggest that two doctors (at most) were the sole medical contributors to the method's creation. At each step in the political process, concerns about cost, speed, aesthetics, and legislative marketability trumped any medical interest that the procedure would ensure a humane execution. A detailed investigation of lethal injection's creation and history shows that at no point was the procedure medically or scientifically studied on human beings (Denno 2007).

Given the lack of medical justification for lethal injection, a focus on physician participation in the method's implementation is critical, particularly for assessing the future of execution methods. As *Morales* (2006) indicated, states increasingly have looked to physician involvement in lethal injections in an attempt to prevent problems—ranging from California's option of including anesthesiologists, to Missouri's requirement of a physician's presence, to Georgia's recently enacted statute forbidding medical boards from reprimanding doctors who participate in executions, to Florida's inclusion of "a physician" among the possible execution team members for each aspect of the execution procedure in the state's latest July 2007 protocol. Although some physicians have indicated a willingness to engage in executions, a number of medical associations have protested. Currently, the matter is facing a medical and legal crossroad, with no clear resolution (Denno 2007).

The Search for Solutions

In *Morales*, Judge Fogel stated that the lethal injection process can be "fixed" (*Morales v. Tilton* 2006:974). Yet, it is questionable whether any of the remedies that have been proposed across the country can fix lethal injection protocols with a sufficient degree of reliability. The difficulty with identifying the "fix" is that states have not provided enough information on the problems. Recent revelations about lethal injection in this country have resulted in more questions than answers: What is the appropriate level of medical involvement? And who should decide? Are states using the correct drugs? Do less constitutionally vulnerable alternatives exist (Denno 2007)? The Supreme Court will be addressing a number of these same questions in 2008, when it decides *Baze v. Rees* (2007).

This chapter declines to join blindly the search for solutions without complete knowledge and understanding of the problems. Nor should legislatures, courts, governors, or departments of corrections fall into such a trap. Lethal injection requires some kind of medical expertise, of course, but the nature and extent of it are unknowable unless the state provides material information about how executions are performed. Until that point is reached, this country cannot justly make the necessary legal and ethical choices about what role the medical profession can or should assume in executions. This chapter's goal, then, is to avoid following the faulty roads of uninformed recommendations that states continue to create but which often lead only to inhumanity (Denno 2007).

Therefore, this part recommends a method for solving the underlying problem—the lack of accurate information—as a pre-requisite for answering the key questions. First, states should provide for adequate time to conduct an in-depth study of the proper implementation of lethal injection. Second, states should make transparent lethal injection procedures. An apt analysis of the constitutionality of lethal injections cannot succeed without states' release of all critical information on the execution process (Denno 2007).

In-Depth Study of Lethal Injection

States adopted lethal injection without medical or scientific justification for the procedure. As such, it is not surprising, for example, that Texas botched this country's first lethal injection and that states continuously have failed to prevent such debacles. From the start, however, the medical profession strongly opposed the use of lethal injection for executions, fearing that the public would associate the practice of medicine with death. Yet lethal injection's link to medicine did make executions appear more humane and palatable—a perception states encouraged. The vision of a serene inmate gently falling asleep evoked all the beneficial associations that only the medial profession could bring. Such inaccurate depictions have shielded states from careful review of their implementation of lethal injection (Denno 2007).

Within the past few years, however, growing skepticism over troublesome executions has dented this shield, as well as threatened the viability of the death penalty itself. In response, a few states attempted to review and possibly repair their lethal injection procedures. In both Florida and Ohio, for example, highly publicized botched executions served as the focal point for the states' appointed commissions (Denno 2007).

On the surface, these efforts seem like sensible solutions to lethal injection's problems. The commissions incorporate, for instance, a number of the Human Rights Watch Report's recommendations to state and federal corrections agencies on improving lethal injection procedures. These recommendations include an effort to "[r]eview lethal injection protocols by soliciting input from medical and scientific experts, and by holding public hearings and seeking public comment" (Human Rights Watch 2006:7). Florida assembled such a commission following the botched lethal injection of Angel Diaz in December 2006. But a greater amount of time would have enabled a more thorough final report which was released less than four months after the commission's creation (Denno 2007).

Other states have fared even worse than Florida. In North Carolina, for instance, officials ignored concerns of condemned inmates and their lawyers and requests to provide input, instead focusing solely on approving the new protocol quickly. Ohio's "study" of the causes of its lethal injection botch resulted in a two-and-a-half page report. In Ohio, only when a condemned inmate strapped to the gurney told the state—"'It's not working'"—did department officials acknowledge their lethal injection procedures might be "broken" (Denno 2007:119).

Neither Florida nor Ohio has fared well in the aftermath of such quick revisions. Florida released its first revision in May 2007, but a judge then harshly criticized its vagueness. While on September 10, 2007, the same judge found the July 2007 revision constitutional, the skeletal, scientifically unsupported, and contradictory composition of the judge's five-page order prompts continuing concerns over the state's lethal injection procedure (Denno 2007; *State v. Lightbourne* 2007). Likewise, in May 2007, an Ohio execution lasted nearly two hours as executioners attempt to find a suitable vein, thereby demonstrating that Ohio's protocol revision had been futile (Denno 2007).

In early 2007, Tennessee provided a ninety-day moratorium on executions and less than an hour of public hearings for its "quick fix" examination of its lethal injection procedures, which delegated all responsibility for the study to the corrections department. In the Tennessee governor's own words, the ninety-day review "would give the state time to correct 'sloppy cut and paste' execution proceedings that were 'full of deficiencies'" (Denno 2007:114). Yet the governor himself mirrored the same kind of mistakes he accused the department of corrections of making. The constrained time frame was "neither responsible nor realistic" (Denno 2007:114). Accounts also indicate that no medical personnel spoke at the public hearings and there was no clear documentation that any attended.

The U.S. Court of Appeals for the Sixth Circuit characterized the resulting Tennessee protocol as "better" despite such criticism of it and the inadequate research supporting it (Denno 2007). But continuing criticism predicted well the Tennessee protocol's constitutional vulnerability. On September 19, 2007, in a thorough and sophisticated opinion, a district court judge rendered the protocol unconstitutional; in so doing, the judge questioned many aspects of the protocol's construction, ranging from the three-drug regimen, to the qualifications of the executioners, and, most significantly, the gross disregard of those in charge of creating a humane execution procedure (Denno 2007; *Harbison v. Little* 2007).

The shortcomings in the resulting protocols exemplify the built-in failures of attempted speedy resolutions. Overall, these states' efforts at examining lethal injection have been so limited in time and expertise that their recommendations should carry no weight. Ironically, execution moratoria fuel these rushed and reckless assessments of lethal injection's problems and solutions because of the pressure to carry out the punishments. Regardless of the establishment of moratoria, states should conduct an extensive review (Denno 2007).

In contrast to recent cursory studies of lethal injection, New York's nineteenth-century approach to examining execution methods was far more thorough than any other examination subsequently attempted in this country. The state's 1885 commission spent two years evaluating every execution method ever used, while also conducting a massive review of materials to prepare for a detailed evidentiary hearing on electrocution. Given the medical complexity of lethal injection, modern attempts at studying execution methods are frivolous in comparison (Denno 2007).

There is also impressive precedent from mid-twentieth-century Great Britain. For example, the Royal Commission consisted of a group of the highest-ranking experts in the United Kingdom. Over a five-year period, these experts produced a 500-page report considering all aspects of capital punishment, including a detailed assessment of execution methods, particularly lethal injection (Denno 2007; Royal Commission Report 1953). With this perspective, the Royal Commission could make relatively informed recommendations on how the country should proceed if in fact the death penalty would continue. For instance, highly respected medical societies participated in the review, even though they opposed their participation in executions. The commission took seriously expert medical input about the hazards and impracticalities of injection, but also believed that the medical profession's unwillingness to be involved only "magnified" the "consequences" of medicine's link to capital punishment and was not a reason for rejecting a particular execution method. Indeed, the commission favored another medical take on the matter: The medical profession should view physician participation "as one of individual conscience, and not all doctors would feel debarred from giving instruction for such a purpose" (Denno 2007; Royal Commission Report 1953:259).

Of course, one key factor of current analyses of lethal injection in the United States concerns physician participation. But this area is the most immersed in paradox. While the American Medical Association's Ethics Council has derided physician involvement in executions, the Council also concedes that physicians can make executions more humane. This stance bears on the Eighth Amendment because it brings some substantive contours to the "very narrow question" of whether a "lethal-injection protocol—as actually administered in practice—creates an undue and unnecessary risk that an inmate will suffer pain so extreme that it offends the Eighth Amendment" (*Morales v. Tilton* 2006:974). Without physician participation, is any pain an inmate experiences "unnecessary" (Denno 2007)? That question is one that demands the input of medical organizations, but they are loathe to provide it. As Judge Fogel noted in *Morales*, "[T]he need for a person with medical training would appear to be inversely related to the reliability and transparency of the means for ensuring that the inmate is properly anesthetized" (Denno 2007; *Morales v. Tilton* 2006:983).

While the medical associations can—and perhaps should—protest their involvement, most doctors are not even members of these organizations. A more thorough study might reveal the willingness of a sizable number of doctors to participate—something the law does not prohibit. In turn, medical associations' participation in evaluations of lethal injection could give their arguments against it more credibility. As time has shown, the current hands-off strategy of medical associations has not worked. In addition to decrying medical participation in lethal injections, medical associations should accept the reality that some doctors do participate and work to solve the conflict, rather than contribute to it (Denno 2007).

Increased Transparency of Lethal Injection Procedures

Of course, even the most thorough and comprehensive study would prove meaningless if its recommendations were not implemented properly. As Judge Fogel emphasized in *Morales*, "the reliability and transparency" of the injection process has implications for the need to have medical personnel involved. Such a philosophy need not be limited to medical involvement. It should be applied to every aspect of lethal injection (Denno 2007).

Evidence shows that states currently do not follow even their vague protocols. Missouri's Dr. Doe altered the amount of sodium thiopental delivered. Ohio executioners failed to maintain the required dual intravenous access lines. The Florida commission acknowledged that the execution team did not heed the state's existing guidelines for the delivery of chemicals. In California, state officials misled the anesthesiologists about their role while some of those involved in executions claimed during the *Morales* hearings that they had never seen the state's protocol. And, in North Carolina, the state and participating doctor ignored a court order to monitor the inmate's level of unconsciousness (Denno 2007).

Given such blatant disregard for existing procedures, states cannot be trusted to perform executions without oversight. States have withdrawn information in the face of challenges, reinforcing the belief that they lack the ability or willingness to conduct executions in line with constitutional mandates. According to this author's study of lethal injection protocols, in 2005, a disturbingly high number of states failed to provide public protocols, thereby hiding from public scrutiny how they execute. States' agencies have the ability to change protocols without informing the public, and often information about protocols is not subject to state freedom of information laws. Even the mere delegation of execution procedures to corrections officials decreases their visibility (Denno 2007).

Judge Fogel tried to improve transparency by placing the responsibility of lethal injection where it belonged—with the governor, an elected official. Ironically, California's governor insisted in operating in complete secrecy in the state's protocol review, a request that Judge Fogel rightly denied. Likewise, the state court decisions in Maryland and Kentucky struck at the heart of this matter, with inmates arguing that implementation regulations should be subject to public review. Maryland found such review necessary; while the Kentucky court initially ruled in the same way, it then reversed the ruling, fearing that the focus of such proceedings would be the death penalty itself rather than the regulations for implementing lethal injection. On the other hand, a North Carolina administrative law judge rightly ruled that the state had to consider inmates' input or risk denying them due process (Denno 2007).

Such public availability of execution procedures is critical, however, to ensuring the constitutionality of executions. And such transparency might also help resolve the conflict between law and medicine because society will start to take responsibility for implementing executions. Devoid of the distracting need to finger-point, law and medicine can work jointly, sharing communications and expertise to better understand how to "fix" the "broken" system.

Conclusion

On February 20, 2006, Michael Morales was hours away from execution when two anesthesiologists declined to participate in the lethal injection procedure. As Judge Fogel would later explain, there had been "'a disconnect'" between the anesthesiologists' and the courts' "expectations" of what the doctors' roles should be. This disconnect, however, went beyond one execution in California. The events surrounding Morales's impending fate brought to the surface the long-running schism between law and medicine, raising the question of whether any beneficial connection between the professions ever existed at all. History shows it seldom did. Decades of botched executions prove it (Denno 2007).

Until states address this schism, instead of ignoring it, lethal injections will remain constitutionally vulnerable. Inmates will continue to challenge the implementation of the method; states will continue to make uninformed changes to ensure the death penalty survives. Only by conducting a thorough study of the method will society be able to know whether lethal injection can meet constitutional mandates (Denno 2007). And by clarifying, in *Baze v. Rees* (2007), what those mandates should be, the Supreme Court can then provide the kind of Eighth Amendment guidance states need to foster humane executions. The future of execution methods depends on it.

References

Baze v. Rees (2005). No. 04-CI-1094, slip op. (Ky. Cir. Ct. July 8), *aff'd* (2006) 217 S.W.3d 207 (Ky.), *reh'g denied* (2007) No. 2005-SC-000543-MR, 2007 Ky. LEXIS 98 (Ky. Apr. 19), *cert. granted* (2007) No. 07-5439, 2007 U.S. LEXIS 9066 (U.S. Sept. 25), *amended* (2007) No. 07-5439, 2007 U.S. LEXIS 11115 (U.S. Oct. 3).

Denno, Deborah W. 2007. "The Lethal Injection Quandary: How Medicine Has Dismantled the Death Penalty." *Fordham Law Review* 76:49–128 (reprinted with permission).

_____. 2006. "Death Bed." *TriQuarterly* 124:141–168.

Gregg v. Georgia (1976). 428 U.S. 153 (plurality opinion).

Harbison v. Little (2007). No. 3:06-01206, slip op. (M.D. Tenn. Sept. 19).

Heckler v. Chaney (1985). 330 U.S. 821.

Human Rights Watch. (2006). *So Long as They Die: Lethal Injections in the United States.* 18:1–67.

In re Kemmler (1890). 136 U.S. 436.

Morales v. Hickman (2006). 415 F. Supp. 2d 1037 (N.D. Cal.), *aff'd per curiam*, 438 F.3d 926 (9th Cir.), *cert. denied*, 126 S. Ct. 1314.

Morales v. Tilton (2006). 465 F. Supp.2d 972 (N.D. Cal.).

Petition for a Writ of Certiorari, *Baze* (2007). 2007 U.S. LEXIS 9066 (No. 07-5439).

Roko, Ellyde. 2007. "Executioner Identities: Toward Recognizing a Right to Know Who Is Hiding Beneath the Hood." *Fordham Law Review* 75:2791–2829.

Royal Commission On Capital Punishment. 1953. *1949–53 Report*. London: Her Majesty's Stationery Office.

State v. Lightbourne (2007). Nos. 1981-170 CF, SC06-2391, slip op. (Fla. Cir. Ct. Sept. 10).

Taylor v. Crawford (2006). No. 05-4173-CV-C-FJG, 2006 WL 1779035 (W.D. Mo. June 26), *rev'd* (2007) 487 F.3d 1072, 1085 (8th Cir.).

Woolls v. McCotter (1986). 798 F.2d 695 (5th Cir.).

CHAPTER 23

Conclusion—An Agenda for the Next Generation of Capital Punishment Research

*James R. Acker, William J. Bowers and
Charles S. Lanier*

Facts, Values and Capital Punishment Policies

The death penalty has long been a part of this country's history and legal culture. Records of the first government-sponsored execution date back to 1608, when George Kendall met his death by firing squad in colonial Virginia after being convicted of spying for the Spanish (Coyne and Entzeroth 2001:5). Four centuries later, more than 15,000 others have been executed on American soil as punishment for crimes (Espy and Smykla 2004). As long as capital punishment has been practiced, questions about it have been raised. Rather than being laid to rest, many of those questions have endured and still hover over legal and policy disputes regarding the death penalty. The issues are complex and sometimes overlapping. They include the essential morality and justice of the death penalty; its effectiveness in promoting utilitarian goals, such as general deterrence and social protection; whether alternative, less severe punishments are similarly capable of advancing those objectives; and whether this ultimate sanction is applied reliably and evenhandedly.

Empirical research is indispensible for answering questions about the utility of capital punishment, including its measurable benefits and costs, and for shedding light on the details of its administration. While conclusions about the justice and morality of the death penalty are essentially normative in character, they nevertheless can be informed and shaped by the empirical reality revealed by the results of scientific inquiry. Indeed, perceptions about the essential justice of capital punishment may turn in part on factual matters such as whether the death penalty saves innocent lives, by uniquely deterring prospective murderers, or conversely claims innocent lives through executions resulting from wrongful convictions; whether the race of murderers or their victims influences capital charging or sentencing decisions; or whether the alternative sentence of "life" imprisonment truly means that the offender will not be released from prison alive, to name just a few.

Even where facts are not alone determinative, they can be instrumental in helping to isolate the issues and clarifying the value judgments that ultimately drive normative decisions (Faigman 1991; Grisso and Saks 1991). For example, the NAACP Legal Defense Fund (LDF), which spearheaded the legal assault against capital punishment in the 1960s and the ensuing decades, consistently implored the justices not to evaluate the constitutionality of the death penalty in abstract terms but in the concrete ways it actually was applied in courts and communities throughout the land. In reality, the LDF argued, capital punishment was applied freakishly and plagued by racial and socioeconomic discrimination. They claimed that accused offenders were too often represented by woefully inadequate defense counsel and tried before biased and essentially lawless juries. The illusory benefits of a system thus constituted could not possibly outweigh its many infirmities, the LDF lawyers maintained (Acker 1993:18–20; Meltsner 1973).

The Supreme Court's Reception: *Furman, Gregg* and Beyond

The Supreme Court initially was receptive to these and related arguments, indulging factual assumptions that fundamentally altered the nation's capital punishment laws and policies. The justices inferred in their epochal ruling in *Furman v. Georgia* (1972) that capital sentencing decisions, made pursuant to standards no more definitive than whether mercy should prevail over death, were arbitrary and incapable of promoting legitimate punishment objectives. The 5–4 ruling by the fragmented Court meant that, as applied, the death penalty violated the Eighth Amendment's prohibition against cruel and unusual punishments. In his concurring opinion in *Furman*, Justice Thurgood Marshall famously advanced the provocative hypotheses that "American citizens know almost nothing about capital punishment" (*id*:362), and that if they understood its realities—that (in his view) it is not a more effective deterrent than life imprisonment, that it is more expensive than incarceration, that racial minorities and the poor are disproportionately subjected to capital punishment, that innocent people have been executed, and that convicted murderers can be and often are rehabilitated, to name a few—they would overwhelmingly reject it (*id*.:362–369) (*cf.*, Clarke, Lambert and Whitt 2000–2001; Vidmar and Ellsworth 1974).

Yet, neither the public nor legislatures rejected capital punishment in *Furman's* aftermath. Most states and Congress quickly enacted replacement legislation (Zimring and Hawkins 1986:38–45). And, just four years later, in *Gregg v. Georgia* (1976) and companion cases, the Court's skepticism gave way to optimism, if not the conviction that revised statutes that specified a narrower range of death penalty-eligible crimes, established criteria to guide sentencing decisions, and mandated appellate review of capital sentences, righted the earlier perceived deficiencies. In the justices' estimation, the new death penalty laws sufficiently harnessed sentencing discretion to remove the threat of arbitrary application. Legislatures were then justified in using capital punishment as retribution or to deter prospective murderers. The Constitution was no longer a barrier to capital punishment laws, either in principle or as applied (Acker and Lanier 2003; Steiker and Steiker 2003).

The revival of capital punishment laws simultaneously provoked a groundswell of empirical research that coincided with and often helped inform the legal issues that were presented to the courts in the ensuing waves of post-*Gregg* litigation. One line of research, either anticipating or inspired by the *Gregg* Court's explicit acceptance of general deterrence as a legitimate and rationally defensible end of capital punishment, scoured the few existing studies that supported the superior deterrent efficacy of the death penalty and continued to look for new evidence to corroborate or refute the deterrence hypothesis (*see* Baldus and Cole 1975; Bowers and Pierce 1975; Ehrlich 1977, 1975; Fagan and West, this volume; Klein, Forst and Filatov 1978; Peterson and Bailey 2003).

The question of racial bias in the death penalty's administration endured. On the heels of *Gregg* and companion cases, the NAACP Legal Defense Fund and the University of Pennsylvania criminology program jointly convened a conference at Howard Law School where attorneys and social scientists met to consider the kinds of research that would be relevant to the Court's decisions. At that gathering, Morris Dees, an attorney with the Southern Poverty Law Center, observed that the race of the murder victim, more so than the race of the defendant, determined whether a killing would be prosecuted capitally under Alabama's post-*Furman* statute. Fortuitously, the FBI's Supplemental

Homicide Report was revised in 1976 to identify the race of both the victim and the suspected offender. This newly available data allowed for a series of investigations of both defendant and victim racial disparities in the application of the death penalty (*see* Bowers and Pierce 1980; Gross and Mauro 1989; United States General Accounting Office 1990). Most prominent among the studies of racial bias was the litigation-related research of David Baldus and colleagues, which investigated the administration of Georgia's post-*Furman* capital punishment statute for lingering effects of racial disparities in prosecutors' charging and juries' sentencing decisions (*see* Baldus, Woodworth and Pulaski 1990). Notwithstanding the study's findings, which revealed pronounced differences in the law's application in white-victim and black-victim murder cases, a 5–4 majority of the Supreme Court perceived no constitutional infirmities in the new statute's operation (*McCleskey v. Kemp* 1987).

Another issue addressed by social science research after *Gregg* involved the death qualification of jurors in capital trials. Doubts about the impartiality of juries that had been purged of individuals harboring strong personal convictions against capital punishment had been raised in the Supreme Court as early as 1968, in *Witherspoon v. Illinois*. Although research suggesting that death-qualified juries were "conviction prone"—*i.e.*, more inclined to return guilty verdicts, and to convict defendants of more serious charges than juries that were not death-qualified—was tendered to the Court in briefs filed in *Witherspoon*, the studies were dismissed as "too tentative and fragmentary" to support a constitutional ruling condemning the challenged juries (*Witherspoon v. Illinois* 1968:517). The justices nevertheless signaled their receptivity to reconsidering the issue if more persuasive evidence could be marshaled (*id.*:518). After *Gregg*, the research community conducted numerous additional studies that supplemented and largely fortified the evidence available when *Witherspoon* was decided (*e.g.*, Cowan, Thompson and Ellsworth 1984; Haney 1984; Thompson *et al.* 1984). The justices reconsidered death-qualification issues in light of those new studies in *Lockhart v. McCree* (1986) where, dismissing both the validity of the research and its logical implications, a majority of the Court definitively laid the constitutional challenge to rest. "A more complete repudiation of social science research evidence could hardly have been accomplished" (Acker 1993:76 n. 9; *see also* Ellsworth 1988).

Predicting offenders' future dangerousness also was investigated in the post-*Gregg* era, inspired in large part by the Court's approval of Texas's reformed death penalty law, which required juries to consider the defendant's likely future dangerousness in making their sentencing decisions (*Jurek v. Texas* 1976). Psychiatrists and psychologists routinely offered their expert opinions about capital murderers' propensities to engage in future violence—frequently with great confidence—notwithstanding broad consensus among researchers that those predictions were roughly as reliable as the results of flipping a coin (*Barefoot v. Estelle* 1983:931, Blackmun, J., dissenting; Sorensen, this volume). Trusting the adversarial system to expose potential weaknesses in expert testimony, the justices approved of its admissibility in this context, an outcome in considerable tension with the Court's prior declarations that capital cases entail especially heightened demands for reliability (*Barefoot v. Estelle* 1983).

Potentially fatal miscarriages of justice were another critical research focus. In their historical investigation of potentially capital cases, Hugo Adam Bedau and Michael Radelet (1987) identified 23 individuals executed in the 20th century who, in their estimation, were innocent, and scores of other innocents who had come perilously close to execution. Their study triggered an immediate reaction (Markman and Cassell 1988) and has garnered continuing judicial attention (*Callins v. Collins* 1994:1158 n. 11, Blackmun, J., dissenting from denial of certiorari; *Herrera v. Collins* 1993:415 n. 15; *id.*:424 n. 1, Blackmun, J., dissenting; *Kansas v. Marsh* 2006:2528; *id.*:2534–39, Scalia, J., concurring); *Ring v. Arizona* 2002:617, Breyer, J., concurring in the judgment; see Steiker, this volume). The full implications of this and related research involving the risk of executing innocent persons, in policy arenas and for helping shape public attitudes, remain to be determined (Dieter, this volume).

Widespread flaws in the trial of capital cases also became the subject of empirical inquiry. Liebman, Fagan and West (2000) examined the extent to which capital convictions and death sentences were invalidated on appeal or subsequent stages of judicial review, and the reasons for such reversals. They found that two out of every three death sentences over the period 1973–1995 were invalidated and that the foremost reasons for this "broken system" were defense ineffectiveness and prosecutorial misconduct. Hence, those most responsible for the success of the system proved to be the cause of widely prevalent and extremely costly failures in its operation. Some observers argue that the invalidation of so many death sentences is a demonstration of the success of the appellate process in detecting errors (Coate, Lewis and Parker 2007; Wilson 2000), but the prevalence of such problems is not only expensive but also worrisome for what it portends about the likelihood that many other flaws will go undetected.

Additionally, advances were made in assessing public opinion about capital punishment (*see* Bohm 2003; Bowers, Vandiver and Dugan 1994), in understanding the exercise of peremptory challenges by prosecutors and defense attorneys in capital cases (Baldus *et al.* 2001; Winick 1982), and in ascertaining jurors' ability to understand (Hans 1995; Wiener *et al.* 2004) and abide by judicial instructions designed to guide their deliberations (Bowers, Fleury-Steiner and Antonio 2003; Bowers and Foglia 2003; Haney 2005). Researchers studied jurisdictions that authorized judges to override juries' advisory sentencing verdicts in capital cases (Bowers et al. 2006; Radelet and Mello 1992). They investigated the methods used and results reached by state supreme courts that engaged in comparative proportionality review of capital sentences, a process designed to help detect and correct aberrant death penalty verdicts (Baldus, Pulaski and Woodworth 1983; Bienen 1996). Trends in executive clemency decisions in capital cases were analyzed (Burnett 2002; Radelet and Zsembik 1993). Research contributed to the justices' evaluation of the constitutionality of capital punishment for juveniles (*Roper v. Simmons* 2005; *Stanford v. Kentucky* 1989; *Thompson v. Oklahoma* 1988; see Bowers et al. 2005) and for mentally retarded offenders (*Atkins v. Virginia* 2002; *Penry v. Lynaugh* 1989; see Blume, Johnson and Seeds, this volume). And, many other facets of the death penalty and its administration were subjected to critical scrutiny by empirical researchers in the generation following *Gregg's* resuscitation of capital punishment laws (see Acker, Bohm and Lanier 2003).

As the post-*Gregg* laws were upheld, refined, and occasionally invalidated by the courts, accountability for capital punishment policies and practices increasingly shifted to legislative and executive officials. Concerns mounted in many jurisdictions about several aspects of the death penalty, including wrongful convictions and the attendant risk of executing the innocent, racial disparities, the quality of defense counsel, cost, and others. Legislatures and governors in several states were besieged with calls to halt executions while study commissions examined the implementation of death penalty laws (Kirchmeir 2002; Lanier and Acker 2004). Sometimes those calls were heeded, as in Illinois, where Governor George Ryan imposed a moratorium on executions, appointed a blue-ribbon panel to study the capital punishment system in that state, and in 2003 commuted the death sentences of all condemned prisoners there based on evidence that the death penalty enterprise was "haunted by the demon of error" (Ryan 2003; see Lanier and Breslin 2006). Going even farther, a legislatively appointed study commission recommended abolishing capital punishment in New Jersey and that state repealed its death penalty law in 2007 (New Jersey Death Penalty Study Commission 2007; Peters 2007). Elsewhere, reactions were quite different. Death penalty practices essentially stayed the course in other states notwithstanding the scrutiny and recommendations of study commissions. And the jurisdictions that relied most heavily on executions, including many southern states, largely declined even to study the implementation of their capital punishment laws (Acker 2008).

At present, the nation's appetite for capital punishment appears to have abated, at least temporarily, as executions have slowed, the number of new death sentences imposed annually has begun to freefall (Bowers and Sundby, this volume), and New York (judicially) and New Jersey (legislatively) have interred their death penalty laws (*People v. LaValle* 2004; *People v. Taylor* 2007; Peters 2007). This most recent lull is not unprecedented. Support for the death penalty has waxed and waned throughout history, and abolition and retention efforts have inched forward or been arrested and reversed in irregular cycles and patterns (Banner 2002; Bowers 1984:6–41). Elsewhere in the world, however, the United States' closest political and economic allies have marched almost in lockstep to abandon the death penalty. The Supreme Court occasionally has taken note of other countries' capital punishment policies while interpreting the Eighth Amendment (*Roper v. Simmons* 2005:575–78) and international trends otherwise may influence domestic death penalty policies (Patterson 2006; Proctor 2006–2007; Trail 2002; Wilson 2003). Now, perhaps more than at any other time since the frenzied re-enactment of capital punishment laws in the vacuum created by *Furman*, the public and public policymakers appear willing not only to raise questions about the death penalty, but also to reflect meaningfully on the answers and their implications. In this atmosphere of potential receptivity, the scientific research community must anticipate, and be poised to address and analyze the issues that are most likely to be important to the future of this country's diverse capital punishment laws and policies.

Research Challenges

The Need for Data

The availability and accessibility of data—of objective and reliable information about the death penalty's implementation, benefits, costs, and related matters—are obviously a prerequisite for meaningful analysis of capital punishment laws and practices. But for many reasons, even the most elementary information often is unavailable. Some data deficiencies are deliberate and can be traced to institutional policies (for example, the law's insulating capital jurors' deliberations from public scrutiny (*see* Bowers, Brewer and Lanier, this volume)) or actors' tactical decisions (for example, prosecutors' refusal to disclose how they decide whether to pursue a capital sentence, or defense attorneys' unwillingness to reveal their reasons for exercising peremptory challenges). In other instances, difficulties in designing, carrying out, or funding research may explain why important information is lacking or difficult to obtain (for example, data on how the capital punishment process affects murder victims' survivors (*see* Vandiver, this volume)). Yet far too often, vital evidence is lacking about the death penalty and its administration for no apparent reason other than officials not considering data collection a priority and no one else having the time, resources, or initiative to compile the information (*see* Fleischaker, this volume).

The responsibility for creating and maintaining comprehensive data collection systems falls most naturally to the officials charged with administering capital punishment laws within the states, the federal jurisdiction, and the United States military. Several study commissions have arrived at this essential conclusion and have made corresponding recommendations to their respective state governments (Acker, forthcoming). In the continuing absence of governmental oversight of this vital task, research efforts will be severely compromised or limited unless analogous mechanisms for systematically collecting, analyzing, and disseminating jurisdiction-specific data are independently developed and funded. Since data analysis depends on the availability of data, concerted efforts to establish research centers or government clearinghouses to collect and distribute the information needed to help assess death penalty systems must have greater priority (Lanier, this volume).

Directions for Future Research

The contributors to this volume have identified a host of issues that will be critical to informed decision making in the capital punishment legal and policy arenas within the foreseeable future. Some of those issues have emerged prominently only recently, in the death penalty's modern era, while others have persisted for centuries. This mix of new and old is not surprising because in many respects death penalty cases provide a lens on larger social issues, both contemporary and enduring. At the same time, capital cases represent a microcosm of the criminal justice process as a whole, even though the stakes are uncommonly high. We thus encounter several questions that are not confined to the death penalty but emerge in heightened relief because human life is at stake. Recapitulating briefly, the identified research issues include:

- To obtain and make available jurisdiction-specific data that will support meaningful examination of capital punishment laws and policies (Fleischaker, this volume).
- To build a repository of information on capital punishment that contains historical and current data, both national and local in character, and that are indexed and accessible to prospective researchers, attorneys, journalists, and the public. An ongoing program of data acquisition of this nature should be informed by the research potential of prospective

acquisitions and the data needs of potential investigators (Lanier, this volume).
- To explore the courts' willingness to embrace the conclusions of empirical research in constitutional decision making in capital cases and the role that elites and other influential parties may play in bringing about change in death penalty policies and practices (Steiker, this volume).
- To isolate the factors that have contributed to the recent decline in capital sentences and to understand their broader implications for punishment policies (Bowers and Sundby, this volume).
- To conduct more extensive, refined, and exacting studies of the influence of race and ethnicity on decision making in potentially capital cases, including law enforcement officials' aggressiveness and effectiveness in investigating crimes (Radelet and Pierce, this volume), and prosecutors' charging decisions and juries' sentencing determinations (Baldus, Woodworth and Weiner, this volume; Baldus, Woodworth, Zuckerman, Weiner and Grosso, this volume).
- To continue scrutinizing how juries make the unique moral choice between capital punishment and life imprisonment, to assess jurors' receptivity to mitigation evidence, and to evaluate the degree of departure or conformity between those decisions and the legal rules designed to guide sentencing discretion (Bowers, Brewer and Lanier, this volume).
- To assess the risk that innocent parties will be convicted and punished by death, to identify and evaluate the factors that contribute to this risk, and to assess the effects of such knowledge on attitudes toward and the use of the death penalty (Dieter, this volume).
- To learn how murder victims' families are affected by capital trials, appeals, and executions, what those survivors or co-victims most urgently need in the way of supporting services and resources, and how the families of condemned offenders cope with their relatives' death sentences and execution (Vandiver, this volume).
- To determine the extent to which limits placed on the scope and authority of federal courts to review state criminal convictions and sentences have resulted in fundamental errors going uncorrected in capital cases (Dow and Freedman, this volume).
- To shed light on the decision making processes and the immediate and longer term ramifications of executive clemency decisions in capital cases (Sarat, this volume).
- To understand how the unique conditions of confinement that confront death-sentenced prisoners affect them and their custodians (Johnson, McGunnigall-Smith, Fontaine and Dum, this volume).

- To explore the ways in which the legal and medical communities might work collaboratively to address questions surrounding lethal injection as a method of execution (Denno, this volume).
- To evaluate the suitability of the litigation context for diagnosing and determining mental retardation and other facets of mental health that implicate the objectives of capital punishment (Blume, Johnson and Seeds, this volume).
- To gain more insights about the unique symbolism and symbolic importance of the death penalty, and corresponding policy implications (Acker, this volume; Garland, this volume).
- To estimate the resources required to maintain death penalty systems and pursue executions, to obtain the analogous costs for life imprisonment without parole, and to make explicit the trade-offs between investing in punishment and providing criminal justice services and supporting social programs (Gradess and Davies, this volume).
- To clarify the assumptions underlying research on the deterrent effect of the death penalty and to assess the forms such investigations might take in light of the nature and limitations of data available for this purpose (Fagan and West, this volume).
- To obtain more exacting estimates of the potential for violence among convicted murderers on death row and those serving life imprisonment without parole, and to identify the circumstances and incentives that tend to reduce the level of violence among such prisoners (Sorensen, this volume).

Other issues, not addressed at length in this volume, also promise to be important. We will want to know much more about the considerations that influence public opinion about capital punishment, the perceptions that legislators and other policymakers have about relevant public opinion, and how those perceptions influence their own attitudes and decisions (*see* Baumgartner, De Bouf and Boydstun 2008; Bowers, Vandiver and Dugan 1994; Ellsworth and Gross 1994). In this vein, determining the media's influence in helping shape public beliefs about a host of issues relevant to the death penalty, embracing race, fundamental notions of good and evil, how law enforcement and other officials function within the criminal justice system, and many others, merits careful attention (*see* Beale 2006; Brown 2004; Eberhardt *et al.* 2006; Haney 2004, 1997; Sarat 2001:209–245). Measuring and evaluating the "evolving standards of decency" that figure into the Supreme Court's Eighth Amendment jurisprudence present challenging research issues (Niven, Zilber and Miller 2006; Raeker-Jordan 1996).

Wide variations in execution and death sentencing practices exist throughout the country. The South outstrips other regions in carrying out executions (Gershowitz 2007:90–93; Steiker and Steiker 2006). Texas, of course, is far and away the country's execution leader, although its rate of sentencing murderers to death is below the national mean (Blume, Eisenberg and Wells 2004). Within states, counties vary dramatically in capital prosecution and sentencing policies. Some, such as Harris County, Texas (Houston), Philadelphia County, Pennsylvania, and Baltimore County, Maryland are renowned for their aggressive use of the death penalty. Conversely, great numbers of counties in many capital punishment states have not had a single capital trial in the post-*Furman* era (Ditchfield 2007; Gershowitz 2007:93–96; Steiker 2002:105–106). Gaining a better understanding of what underlies these significant inter- and intrastate differences in applying the death penalty should be a priority (*see* Zimring 2003). Learning more about the application of capital punishment within the unique system of the United States Military would similarly be of interest (*see Loving v. United States* 1996; Simon 2005; Sullivan 2006).

How the qualifications, training, resources, and strategic decisions of defense counsel influence the conduct and outcomes of potentially capital cases are important questions (*see* American Bar Association 2003; Wallace and Carroll 2004). The factors that influence prosecutors' decisions about whether to seek a death sentence in potentially capital cases also need to be better understood (*see* Hitchcock 2007; Paternoster 1993; Songer and Unah 2006). A related issue, with significant doctrinal and practical implications including its potential to influence estimates of the costs associated with maintaining death penalty systems (Gradess and Davies, this volume), is how the implicit threat of a capital sentence may influence plea bargaining and the entry of guilty pleas in aggravated murder cases (Ehrhard forthcoming; Kuziemko 2006; Hoffmann, Kahn and Fisher 2001).

Mental health issues in addition to those linked to implementing the Supreme Court and legislative prohibitions against executing mentally retarded offenders can be expected to figure into future death penalty policies (Blume, Johnson and Seeds, this volume). Psychological research may be especially informative as debate continues about whether offenders with serious mental illness should be death-eligible (Ryan and Berson 2006; Tabak 2006, 2005) or, if lawfully sentenced to death, are or can be rendered competent for execution (Ackerson, Brodsky and Zapf 2005; Bonnie 2005). This roster is far from exhaustive; numerous other research questions loom as potentially quite significant to the continuing evolution of capital punishment laws and policies (Bedau, this volume; Diamond and Casper 1994:188–194; Lanier and Acker 2004).

Conclusion: Looking toward the Future

A generation ago, legislatures passed and the Supreme Court approved the guided discretion death penalty statutes that remain effective today in 36 states and under federal and United States military authority. The new laws heralded change from the preceding era's permissive and largely unregulated capital punishment systems (*McGautha v. California* 1971), and were vastly different than in generations further removed, when legislation mandated punishment by death on conviction for capital crimes (*see Woodson v. North Carolina* 1976). Yet whether and to what extent the promised reforms would be evident in the operation of post-*Furman* death penalty statutes could not immediately be known.

More than three decades have now elapsed since the first execution was carried out under contemporary capital punishment laws. Now, in light of that experience, it is fair to conclude that the sanguine assumptions regarding those modern laws have in many respects fallen short or been called into serious doubt. Moreover, there are indications that in many jurisdictions concerned citizens as well as policymakers are interested in knowing more about the benefits and costs of the death penalty and the details of its administration, and are ready and willing to take stock of punishment practices. The times seem ripe for change.

The pages within this volume offer a menu of the issues that promise to be central to the continuing assessment of capital punishment laws and policies, and blueprints for conducting the research needed to allow informed decisions to be made about them. Whether the required research can and will be carried out will necessarily be affected by the availability of data about the laws and their administration, by the extent to which resources are invested to support data collection and analysis, and by researchers' own ingenuity and resourcefulness. Whether the research, once conducted, will contribute meaningfully to public policy decisions about capital punishment is beyond the control of the research community. Those decisions ultimately are entrusted to legislative, executive, and judicial officials, and to the public on whose behalf the laws are administered and the policies are implemented—those who need the answers that such research can provide.

References

Acker, James R. 2008. "Scrutinizing the Death Penalty: State Death Penalty Study Commissions and Their Recommendations." Pp. 29–59 in *The Death Penalty Today*, edited by Robert M. Bohm. London: Taylor & Francis.

_____. This volume. "Alternative Sanctions for Aggravated Murdr: Form and Function."

_____. 1996. "The Death Penalty: A 25-Year Retrospective and a Perspective on the Future." *Criminal Justice Review* 21:139–160.

_____. 1993. "A Different Agenda: The Supreme Court, Empirical Research Evidence, and Capital Punishment Decisions, 1986–1989." *Law & Society Review* 27:65–88.

_____. 1993. "Mortal Friends and Enemies: Amici Curiae in Supreme Court Death Penalty Cases." *New England Journal on Criminal and Civil Confinement* 19:1–59.

Acker, James R., Robert M. Bohm and Charles S. Lanier, eds. 2003. *America's Experiment With Capital Punishment: Reflections on the Past, Present, and Future of the Ultimate Penal Sanction*, 2d ed. Durham, NC: Carolina Academic Press.

Acker, James R. and Charles S. Lanier. 2003. "Beyond Human Ability? The Rise and Fall of Death Penalty Legislation." Pp. 85–125 in *America's Experiment With Capital Punishment: Reflections on the Past, Present, and Future of the Ultimate Penal Sanction*, edited by James R. Acker, Robert M. Bohm and Charles S. Lanier. Durham, NC: Carolina Academic Press.

Ackerson, Kimberley S., Stanley L. Brodsky and Patricia A. Zapf. 2005. "Judges' and Psychologists' Assessments of Legal and Clinical Factors in Competence for Execution." *Psychology, Public Policy, and Law* 11:164–193.

American Bar Association. 2003. "American Bar Association Guidelines for the Appointment and Performance of Defense Counsel in Capital Cases." *Hofstra Law Review* 31:913–1090.

Atkins v. Virginia (2002). 536 U.S. 304.

Baldus, David C. and James W. C. Cole. 1975. "A Comparison of the Work of Thorsten Sellin and Isaac Ehrlich on the Deterrent Effect of Capital Punishment." *Yale Law Journal* 85:170–186.

Baldus, David C., Charles Pulaski and George Woodworth. 1983. "Comparative Review of Death Sentences: An Empirical Study of the Georgia Experience." *Journal of Criminal Law & Criminology* 74:661–753.

Baldus, David C., George G. Woodworth and Charles A. Pulaski, Jr. 1990. *Equal Justice and the Death Penalty: A Legal and Empirical Analysis*. Boston, MA: Northeastern University Press.

Baldus, David, George Woodworth and Neil Alan Weiner. This volume. "Perspectives, Approaches, and Future Directions in Death Penalty Proportionality Studies."

Baldus, David C., George Woodworth, David Zuckerman, Neil Alan Weiner and Barbara Broffitt. 2001. "The Use of Peremptory Challenges in Capital Murder Trials: A Legal and Empirical Analysis." *University of Pennsylvania Journal of Constitutional Law* 3:3–170.

Baldus, David, George Woodworth, David Zuckerman, Neil Alan Weiner and Catherine M. Grosso. This volume. "Empirical Studies of Race and Geographic Discrimination in the Administration of the Death Penalty: A Primer on the Key Methodological Issues."

Banner, Stuart. 2002. *The Death Penalty: An American History.* Cambridge, MA: Harvard University Press.

Barefoot v. Estelle (1983). 463 U.S. 880.

Baumgartner, Frank R., Suzanna De Boef and Amber Boydstun. 2008. *The Decline of the Death Penalty and the Discovery of Innocence.* New York, NY: Cambridge University Press.

Beale, Sara Sun. 2006. "The News Media's Influence on Criminal Justice Policy: How Market-Driven News Promotes Punitiveness." *William and Mary Law Review* 48:397–481.

Bedau, Hugo Adam. This volume. "Death Penalty Research Today and Tomorrow."

Bedau, Hugo Adam and Michael L. Radelet. 1987. "Miscarriages of Justice in Potentially Capital Cases." *Stanford Law Review* 40:21–173.

Bienen, Leigh B. 1996. "The Proportionality Review of Capital Cases by State High Courts After *Gregg*: Only 'The Appearance of Justice'?" *Journal of Criminal Law & Criminology* 87:130–314.

Blume, John, Theodore Eisenberg and Martin T. Wells. 2004. "Explaining Death Row's Population and Racial Composition." *Journal of Empirical Legal Studies* 1:165–207.

Blume, John H., Sheri Lynn Johnson and Christopher Seeds. This volume. "Mental Retardation and the Death Penalty Five Years After *Atkins*."

Bohm, Robert M. 2003. "American Death Penalty Opinion: Past, Present, and Future." Pp. 27–54 in *America's Experiment With Capital Punishment: Reflections on the Past, Present, and Future of the Ultimate Penal Sanction*, 2d ed., edited by James R. Acker, Robert M. Bohm and Charles S. Lanier. Durham, NC: Carolina Academic Press.

Bonnie, Richard J. 2005. "Mentally Ill Prisoners on Death Row: Unsolved Puzzles for Courts and Legislatures." *Catholic University Law Review* 54:1169–1193.

Bowers, William J. 1984. *Legal Homicide: Death as Punishment in America, 1864–1982.* Boston, MA: Northeastern University Press.

Bowers, William J., Thomas E. Brewer and Charles S. Lanier. This volume. "The Capital Jury Experiment of the Supreme Court."

Bowers, William J., Benjamin D. Fleury-Steiner and Michael E. Antonio. 2003. "The Capital Sentencing Decision: Guided Discretion, Reasoned Moral Judgment, or Legal Fiction." Pp. 413–467 in *America's Experiment With Capital Punishment: Reflections on the Past, Present, and Future of the Ultimate*

Penal Sanction, 2d ed., edited by James R. Acker, Robert M. Bohm and Charles S. Lanier. Durham, NC: Carolina Academic Press.

Bowers, William J. and Wanda D. Foglia. 2003. "Still Singularly Agonizing: Law's Failure to Purge Arbitrariness from Capital Sentencing." *Criminal Law Bulletin* 39:51–86.

Bowers, William J., Wanda D. Foglia, Jean E. Giles and Michael E. Antonio. 2006. "The Decision Maker Matters: An Empirical Examination of the Way the Role of the Judge and the Jury Influence Death Penalty Decision-Making." *Washington & Lee Law Review* 63:931–1010.

Bowers, William J. and Glenn L. Pierce. 1980. "Arbitrariness and Discrimination Under Post-*Furman* Capital Statutes." *Crime and Delinquency* 26:563–635.

——————. 1975. "The Illusion of Deterrence in Isaac Ehrlich's Research on Capital Punishment." *Yale Law Journal* 85:187–208.

Bowers, William J. and Scott E. Sundby. This volume. "Why the Downturn in Death Sentences?"

Bowers, William J., Margaret Vandiver and Patricia H. Dugan. 1994. "A New Look at Public Opinion on Capital Punishment: What Citizens and Legislators Prefer." *American Journal of Criminal Law* 22:77–149.

Brown, Raymond M. 2004. "The 'American Taliban' Versus the Junior 'Beltway Sniper': Toward Understanding Death, 'Brainwashing,' 'Terror,' and Race in the Court of Public Opinion." *DePaul Law Review* 53:1663–1673.

Burnett, Cathleen. 2002. *Justice Denied: Clemency Appeals in Death Penalty Cases.* Boston, MA: Northeastern University Press.

Callins v. Collins (1994). 510 U.S. 1141.

Clarke, Alan W., Eric Lambert and Laurie Anne Whitt. 2000–2001. "Executing the Innocent: The Next Step in the Marshall Hypotheses." *New York University Review of Law and Social Change* 26:309–344.

Coate, Ben, Ryan Lewis and Paul Parker. 2007. "Miscarriages of Justice: Eye of the Beholder." *Journal of the Institute of Justice and International Studies* 2007:104–114.

Cowan, Claudia L., William C. Thompson and Phoebe C. Ellsworth. 1984. "The Effects of Death Qualification on Jurors' Predisposition to Convict and on the Quality of Deliberation." *Law and Human Behavior* 8:53–79.

Coyne, Randall and Lyn Entzeroth. 2001. *Capital Punishment and the Judicial Process.* 2d ed. Durham, NC: Carolina Academic Press.

Denno, Deborah W. This volume. "The Future of Execution Methods."

Diamond, Shari Seidman and Jonathan D. Casper. 1994. "Empirical Evidence and the Death Penalty: Past and Future." *Journal of Social Issues* 50 (2):177–197.

Dieter, Richard C. This volume. "The Future of Innocence."
Ditchfield, Andrew. 2007. "Challenging the Intrastate Disparities in the Application of Capital Punishment Statutes." *Georgetown Law Journal* 95:801–830.
Dow, David R. and Eric M. Freedman. This volume. "The Effects of AEDPA on Justice."
Eberhardt, Jennifer L., Paul G. Davies, Valerie J. Purdie-Vaughns and Sheri Lynn Johnson. "Looking Deathworthy: Stereotypicality of Black Defendants Predicts Capital-Sentencing Outcomes." *Psychological Science* 17:383–386.
Ehrhard, Susan. Forthcoming. "Plea-Bargaining and the Death Penalty: An Exploratory Study." *Justice System Journal*.
Ehrlich, Isaac. 1977. "Capital Punishment and Deterrence: Some Further Thoughts and Evidence." *Journal of Political Economy* 85:741–788.
_____. 1975. "The Deterrent Effect of Capital Punishment: A Question of Life and Death." *American Economic Review* 65:397–417.
Ellsworth, Phoebe C. 1988. "Unpleasant Facts: The Supreme Court's Response to Empirical Research Evidence on Capital Punishment." Pp. 177–211 in *Challenging Capital Punishment: Legal and Social Science Approaches*, edited by Kenneth C. Haas and James A. Inciardi. Newbury Park, CA: Sage Publications.
Ellsworth, Phoebe C. and Samuel R. Gross. 1994. "Hardening of the Attitudes: Americans' Views on the Death Penalty." *Journal of Social Issues* 50 (2):19–52.
Espy, M. Watt and John Ortiz Smykla. 2004. Executions in the United States, 1608–2002: The ESPY File. Ann Arbor, MI: Inter-university Consortium for Political and Social Research. (http://www.icpsr.umich.edu/cocoon/NACJD/STUDY/08451.xml).
Fagan, Jeffrey and Valerie West. This volume. "Death and Deferrence Redux: Science, Law, and Causal Reasoning on Capital Punishment."
Faigman, David L. 1991. "'Normative Constitutional Fact-Finding': Exploring the Empirical Component of Constitutional Interpretation." *University of Pennsylvania Law Review* 139:541–613.
Fleischaker, Deborah. This volume. "The ABA Death Penalty Moratorium Implementation Project: Setting the Stage for Further Research."
Furman v. Georgia (1972). 408 U.S. 238.
Garland, David. This volume. "'Symbolic' and 'Instrumental' Aspects of Capital Punishment."
Gershowitz, Adam M. 2007. "Imposing a Cap on Capital Punishment." *Missouri Law Review* 72:73–124.
Gradess, Jonathan E. and Andrew L. B. Davies. This volume. "The Cost of the Death Penalty in America: Directions for Future Research."
Gregg v. Georgia (1976). 428 U.S. 153.

Grisso, Thomas and Michael J. Saks. 1991. "Psychology's Influence on Constitutional Interpretation: A Comment on How to Succeed." *Law & Human Behavior* 15:205–211.
Gross, Samuel R. and Robert Mauro. 1989. *Death & Discrimination: Racial Disparities in Capital Sentencing.* Boston, MA: Northeastern University Press.
Haney, Craig. 2005. *Death by Design: Capital Punishment as a Social Psychological System.* New York, NY: Oxford University Press.
_____. 2004. "Condemning the Other in Death Penalty Trials: Biographical Racism, Structural Mitigation, and the Empathic Divide." *DePaul Law Review* 53:1557–1589.
_____. 1997. "Commensense Justice and Capital Punishment: Problematizing the 'Will of the People.'" *Psychology, Public Policy, and Law* 3:303–336.
_____.1984. "On the Selection of Capital Juries: The Biasing Effects of the Death-Qualification Process." *Law and Human Behavior* 8:121–132.
Hans, Valerie P. 1995. "How Juries Decide Death: The Contributions of the Capital Jury Project." *Indiana Law Journal* 70:1233–1240.
Herrera v. Collins (1993). 506 U.S. 390.
Hitchcock, Amanda S. 2007. "Using the Adversarial Process to Limit Arbitrariness in Capital Charging Decisions." *North Carolina Law Review* 85:931–973.
Hoffmann, Joseph L., Marcy L. Kahn and Steven W. Fisher. 2001. "Plea Bargaining in the Shadow of Death." *Fordham Law Review* 69:2313–2392.
Johnson, Robert, Sandra McGunigall-Smith, Jocelyn Fontaine and Christopher Dum. This volume. "Life Under Sentence of Death: Some Research Agendas."
Jurek v. Texas (1976). 428 U.S. 262.
Kansas v. Marsh (2006). 126 U.S. 2516.
Kirchmeier, Jeffrey L. 2002. "Another Place Beyond Here: The Death Penalty Moratorium Movement in the United States." *University of Colorado Law Review* 73:1–116.
Klein, Lawrence R., Brian Forst and Victor Filatov. 1978. "The Deterrent Effect of Capital Punishment: An Assessment of the Estimates." Pp. 336–360 in *Deterrence and Incapacitation: Estimating the Effects of Criminal Sanctions on Crime Rates,* edited by Alfred Blumstein, Jacqueline Cohen and Daniel Nagin. Washington, DC: National Academy of Sciences.
Kuziemko, Ilyana. 2006. "Does the Threat of the Death Penalty Affect Plea Bargaining in Murder Cases? Evidence from New York's 1995 Reinstatement of Capital Punishment." *American Law ands Economics Review* 8:116–141.
Lanier, Charles S. This volume. "The National Death Penalty Archive (NDPA): 'The Greatest Body of Evidence Ever Collected about the Death Penalty in the United States.'"

Lanier, Charles S. and James R. Acker. 2004. "Capital Punishment, the Moratorium Movement, and Empirical Questions: Looking Beyond Innocence, Race, and Bad Lawyering in Death Penalty Cases." *Psychology, Public Policy, and Law* 10:577–617.

Lanier, Charles S. and Beau Breslin. 2006. "Extinguishing the Victims' *Payne* or Acquiescing to the 'Demon of Error': Confronting the Role of Victims in Capital Clemency Proceedings." Pp. 179–201 in *Wounds That Do Not Bind: Victim-Based Perspectives on the Death Penalty*, edited by James R. Acker and David R. Karp. Durham, NC: Carolina Academic Press.

Liebman, James S., Jeffrey Fagan and Valerie West. 2000. *A Broken System: Error Rates in Capital Cases, 1973–1995.* (http://www2.law.columbia.edu/instructionalservices/liebman/).

Lockhart v. McCree (1986). 476 U.S. 162.

Loving v. United States (1996). 517 U.S. 748.

Markman, Stephen J. and Paul G. Cassell. 1988. "Protecting the Innocent: A Response to the Bedau-Radelet Study." *Stanford Law Review* 41:121–159.

McCleskey v. Kemp (1987). 481 U.S. 279.

McGautha v. California (1971). 402 U.S. 183.

Meltsner, Michael. 1973. *Cruel and Unusual: The Supreme Court and Capital Punishment.* New York, NY: Random House.

New Jersey Death Penalty Study Commission (2007). *New Jersey Death Penalty Study Commission Report.* Trenton, NJ: State of New Jersey. (http://www.njleg.state.nj.us/committees/dpsc_final.pdf).

Niven, David, Jeremy Zilber and Kenneth W. Miller. 2006. "A 'Feeble Effort to Fabricate National Consensus': The Supreme Court's Measurement of Current Social Attitudes Regarding the Death Penalty." *Northern Kentucky Law Review* 33:83–114.

Paternoster, Raymond. 1993. "Assessing Capriciousness in Capital Cases." *Law & Society Review* 27:111–123.

Patterson, Krista L. 2006. "Acculturation and the Development of Death Penalty Doctrine in the United States." *Duke Law Journal* 55:1217–1246.

Penry v. Lynaugh (1989). 492 U.S. 302.

People v. LaValle (2004). 3 N.Y.3d 88, 817 N.E.2d 341, 783 N.Y.S.2d 485.

People v. Taylor (2007). 878 N.E.2d 969, 9 N.Y.3d 129.

Peters, Jeremy W. (2007). "Corzine Signs Bill Ending Executions, Then Commutes Sentences of 8." *New York Times* B3 (Dec. 18, 2007).

Peterson, Ruth D. and William C. Bailey. 2003. "Is Capital Punishment an Effective Deterrent to Murder? An Examination of Social Science Research." Pp. 251–282 in *America's Experiment With Capital Punishment: Reflections on the Past, Present, and Future of the Ultimate Penal Sanction*, edited by

James R. Acker, Robert M. Bohm and Charles S. Lanier. Durham, NC: Carolina Academic Press.

Proctor, Greta. 2006–2007. "Reevaluating Capital Punishment: The Fallacy of a Foolproof System, the Focus on Reform, and the International Factor." *Gonzaga Law Review* 42:211–255.

Radelet, Michael L. and Michael Mello. 1992. "Death-to-Life Overrides: Saving the Resources of the Florida Supreme Court." *Florida State University Law Review* 20:195–228.

Radelet, Michael L. and Glenn L. Pierce. This volume. "Racial and Ethnic Disparities in Resolving Homicides."

Radelet, Michael L. and Barbara A. Zsembik. 1993. "Executive Clemency in Post-*Furman* Capital Cases." *Richmond Law Review* 27:289–314.

Raeker-Jordan, Susan. 1996. "A Pro-Death, Self-Fulfilling Constitutional Construct: The Supreme Court's Evolving Standard of Decency for the Death Penalty." *Hastings Constitutional Law Quarterly* 23:455–556.

Ring v. Arizona (2002). 536 U.S. 584.

Roper v. Simmons (2005). 543 U.S. 551.

Ryan, Eileen P. and Sarah B. Berson. 2006. "Mental Illness and the Death Penalty." *Saint Louis University Public Law Review* 25:351–381.

Ryan, George. 2003. "I Must Act" (prepared text of Gov. George Ryan's speech at Northwestern University College of Law, January 11, 2003). (http://www.deathpenaltyinfo.org/article.php?scid=13&did=551).

Sarat, Austin. This volume. "Toward a New Perspective on Clemency in the Killing State."

_____. 2001. *When the State Kills: Capital Punishment and the American Condition*. Princeton, NJ: Princeton University Press.

Simon, Douglas L. 2005. "Making Sense of Cruel and Unusual Punishment: A New Approach to Reconciling Military and Civilian Eighth Amendment Law." *Military Law Review* 184:66–128.

Songer, Michael J. and Isaac Unah. 2006. "The Effect of Race, Gender, and Location on Prosecutorial Decisions to Seek the Death Penalty in South Carolina." *South Carolina Law Review* 58:161–209.

Sorensen, Jon. This volume. "Researching Future Dangerousness."

Stanford v. Kentucky (1989). 492 U.S. 361.

Steiker, Carol S. 2002. "Capital Punishment and American Exceptionalism." *Oregon Law Review* 81:97–130.

Steiker, Jordan M. This volume. "The Role of Constitutional Facts and Social Science Research in Capital Litigation: Is 'Proof' of Arbitrariness or Inaccuracy Relevant to the Constitutional Regulations of the American Death Penalty?"

Steiker, Carol S. and Jordan M. Steiker. 2006. "A Tale of Two Nations: Implementation of the Death Penalty in 'Executing' Versus 'Symbolic' States in the United States." *Texas Law Review* 84:1869–1927.

_____. 2003. "Judicial Developments in Capital Punishment Law." Pp. 55–83 in *America's Experiment With Capital Punishment: Reflections on the Past, Present, and Future of the Ultimate Penal Sanction*, 2d ed. edited by James R. Acker, Robert M. Bohm and Charles S. Lanier. Durham, NC: Carolina Academic Press.

_____. 1995. "Sober Second Thoughts: Reflections on Two Decades of Constitutional Regulation of Capital Punishment." *Harvard Law Review* 109:355–438.

Sullivan, Dwight H. 2006. "Killing Time: Two Decades of Military Capital Litigation." *Military Law Review* 189:1–50.

Tabak, Ronald J. 2006. "Executing People with Mental Disabilities: How We Can Mitigate an Aggravating Situation." *Saint Louis University Public Law Review* 25:283–306.

_____. 2005. "Overview of Task Force Proposal on Mental Disability and the Death Penalty." *Catholic University Law Review* 54:1123–1131.

Thompson v. Oklahoma (1988). 487 U.S. 815.

Thompson, William C., Claudia L. Cowan, Phoebe C. Ellsworth and Joan C. Harrington. 1984. "Death Penalty Attitudes and Conviction Proneness: The Translation of Attitudes Into Verdicts." *Law and Human Behavior* 8:95–113.

Trail, Rebecca. 2002. "The Future of Capital Punishment in the United States: Effects of the International Trend Toward Abolition of the Death Penalty." *Suffolk Transnational Law Review* 26:105–131.

United States General Accounting Office. 1990. *Death Penalty Sentencing: Research Indicates Pattern of Racial Disparities: Report to Senate and House Committees on the Judiciary*. Washington, D.C.: General Accounting Office.

Vandiver, Margaret. This volume. "Capital Punishment and the Families of Victims and Defendants."

Vidmar, Neil and Phoebe Ellsworth. 1974. "Public Opinion and the Death Penalty." *Stanford Law Review* 26:1245–1270.

Wallace, Scott and David Carroll. 2004. "The Implementation and Impact of Indigent Defense Standards." *Southern University Law Review* 31:245–327.

Wiener, Richard L., Melanie Rogers, Ryan Winter, Linda Hurt, Amy Hackney, Karen Kadela, Hope Seib, Shannon Rauch, Laura Warren and Ben Morasco. 2004. "Guided Jury Discretion in Capital Murder Cases: The Role of Declarative and Procedural Knowledge." *Psychology, Public Policy & Law* 10:516–575.

Wilson, James Q. 2000. "What Death Penalty Errors?" *New York Times* A19, July 10.
Wilson, Richard J. 2003. "The Influence of International Law and Practice on the Death Penalty in the United States." Pp. 147–165 in *America's Experiment With Capital Punishment: Reflections on the Past, Present, and Future of the Ultimate Penal Sanction*, 2d ed. edited by James R. Acker, Robert M. Bohm and Charles S. Lanier. Durham, NC: Carolina Academic Press.
Winick, Bruce J. 1982. "Prosecutorial Peremptory Challenge Practices in Capital Cases: An Empirical Study and a Constitutional Analysis." *Michigan Law Review* 81:1–98.
Witherspoon v. Illinois (1968). 391 U.S. 510.
Woodson v. North Carolina (1976). 428 U.S. 280.
Zimring, Franklin E. 2003. *The Contradictions of American Capital Punishment*. New York, NY: Oxford University Press.
Zimring, Franklin E. and Gordon Hawkins. 1986. *Capital Punishment and the American Agenda*. New York, NY: Cambridge University Press.

About the Authors

James R. Acker is a Distinguished Teaching Professor at the University at Albany School of Criminal Justice. He earned his JD at Duke Law School and his PhD at the University at Albany. He is the co-editor of two additional volumes that address capital punishment: *America's Experiment With Capital Punishment: Reflections on the Past, Present, and Future of the Ultimate Penal Sanction* (Carolina Academic Press, 2d ed. 2003), and *Wounds That Do Not Bind: Victim-Based Perspectives on the Death Penalty* (Carolina Academic Press 2006). He has recently authored *Scottsboro and Its Legacy: The Cases That Challenged American Legal and Social Justice* (Praeger Publishers 2008).

David C. Baldus is the Joseph B. Tye Professor of Law at the University of Iowa College of Law where, among other things, he has taught courses on criminal law, capital punishment, and statistical methods for lawyers. He is co-author of *Statistical Proof of Discrimination* (1980), *Equal Justice and the Death Penalty* (1990) and numerous articles on capital punishment. He has conducted empirical studies of capital charging and sentencing in Georgia, Colorado, New Jersey, Nebraska, Maryland, and Philadelphia. His Georgia research conducted with George Woodworth, Professor of Statistics at the University of Iowa, formed the basis of petitioner's claims in *McCleskey v. Kemp* (1987). In the late 1980s and early 1990s, Professor Baldus served the New Jersey Supreme Court as a special master for proportionality review in death sentence cases. In that capacity, he helped the New Jersey court establish the empirically based system of comparative proportionality review that it uses in its review of death sentences for evidence of comparative excessiveness and race discrimination. His current research focuses on jury selection and capital charging and sentencing in Philadelphia.

Hugo Adam Bedau, PhD (Harvard, 1961) is the Austin B. Fletcher Professor of Philosophy, Emeritus, at Tufts University in Medford, Massachusetts. He is best known for his long-standing interest in issues having to do with punishment, and the death penalty in particular. He edited the standard work on capital punishment, *The Death Penalty in America* (1st edition, 1964; 4th edition, 1997), and co-edited *Capital Punishment in the United States* (1976) and *Debating the Death Penalty* (2004). He is the author of *The Courts, the*

Constitution, and Capital Punishment (1977), *Death is Different* (1987), and *Killing as Punishment* (2004), and co-author of *In Spite of Innocence* (1992). In 1997, Bedau received the August Vollmer Award of the American Society of Criminology, and in 2003 he received the Roger Baldwin Award from the ACLU of Massachusetts. A long-time (and founding) member of the National Coalition Against the Death Penalty, he has served on its board and as its chairman; he is currently on the board of the Capital Punishment Research Initiative in Albany, New York.

John H. Blume received a BA from the University of North Carolina at Chapel Hill, an MAR from Yale Divinity School, and a JD from Yale Law School. After clerking for the Honorable Tom Clark, and spending several years in private practice and almost a decade as the Executive Director of the South Carolina Death Penalty Resource Center, he joined the faculty of Cornell Law School in 1997, where he is a Professor of Law and Director of the Cornell Death Penalty Project. He teaches Criminal Procedure, Evidence, and oversees the Law School's Capital Punishment Clinics. His scholarly interests primarily are empirical in nature and involve how the death penalty "works" (or doesn't), especially when confronted with defendants with mental impairments.

William J. Bowers received a PhD in Sociology from Columbia University in 1966. He is a Senior Research Associate at the Capital Punishment Research Initiative, School of Criminal Justice, University at Albany. He was formerly Principal Research Scientist at Northeastern University's College of Criminal Justice and Founding Director of Northeastern's university-wide Center for Applied Social Research. He is author of *Executions in America* (1974) and *Legal Homicide* (1984). In 1991, he initiated the National Science Foundation funded Capital Jury Project (CJP), a fourteen state study of how capital jurors make their life or death sentencing decisions. The CJP has yielded some forty research based publications, ten doctoral dissertations, and has been cited in U. S. Supreme Court decisions. Dr. Bowers has testified on death penalty legislation before committees of the Congress and of the Massachusetts and New York legislatures. He has appeared as an expert witness in more than thirty capital cases. Professor Bowers was the recipient of the August Vollmer Award of the American Society of Criminology for his research on capital punishment and for "outstanding contributions in applied criminology" in 2000.

Thomas W. Brewer is an Assistant Professor in the Department of Justice Studies and a Research Fellow at the Institute for the Study and Prevention of Violence at Kent State University. Dr. Brewer earned a PhD from the School of Criminal Justice, University at Albany in 2003. Along with directing the Capital Jury Project research in Ohio, Dr. Brewer's research interests include capital juror decision-making, the application of social science to law and public policy, and trends in violent crime.

Andrew L. B. Davies is a doctoral student at the University at Albany and a researcher with the New York State Defenders Association. He received his MSc in criminology from Oxford University in 2004, where he was awarded the Roger Hood prize for placing first in his year. At Albany, he has held the Michael Hindelang fellowship in criminal justice from 2004 to 2007 and has developed research interests in state criminal justice policy-making, the psychology of criminal victimization, and the death penalty.

Richard C. Dieter is a graduate of the Georgetown University Law Center, where he was one of the University's first Public Interest Law Scholars. He has served as the Executive Director of the Death Penalty Information Center in Washington, D.C., since 1992, and is an Adjunct Professor at the Catholic University School of Law. Mr. Dieter has worked for many years on issues related to human rights and the death penalty. He has prepared reports for the U.S. House of Representatives and has testified at numerous state legislative hearings. He is the author of many articles and reports on the death penalty and is frequently quoted in both national and international media. He was the founder of the Alderson Hospitality House and of the Quixote Center's death penalty project.

David R. Dow is the University Distinguished Professor at the University of Houston Law Center. He is author of *Machinery of Death: The Reality of America's Death Penalty Regime* (Routledge 2002) (with M. Dow), *Executed on a Technicality: Lethal Injustice on America's Death Row* (Beacon 2005), and numerous articles in scholarly and popular journals. A frequent lecturer at professional seminars, Dow has also represented more than 75 death row inmates in appellate proceedings. He is the Director of the Texas Innocence Network and the litigation director of the Texas Defender Service. A member of the ALI, Dow graduated from Rice University, and received his MA (in history) and JD from Yale.

Christopher Dum is a Master's student studying Justice and Public Policy at American University in Washington, D.C. He is also a licensed private investigator in the State of Maryland and the District of Columbia. His research interests include prison quality of life, the correctional officer profession, violent crime, and death and dying within prison. After completing his Master's degree, Christopher hopes to pursue a doctoral degree with a focus on prison hospice programs.

Jeffrey Fagan is a Professor of Law and Public Health at Columbia University, and Director of the Center for Crime, Community and Law at Columbia Law School. His research and scholarship focuses on crime, law and social policy. His current and recent research examines capital punishment, racial profiling, social contagion of violence, legal socialization of adolescents, the social geography of domestic violence, the jurisprudence of adolescent crime, drug control policy, and perceived legitimacy of the criminal law. He is a member of the *National Consortium on Violence Research* and the *Working Group on Legitimacy and the Criminal Law* of the Russell Sage Foundation. He formerly was Vice Chair of the *Committee on Law and Justice* of the National Academy of Science, and served as the Committee's Vice Chair for the last two years. From 1996–2006, he was a member of the MacArthur Foundation's *Research Network on Adolescent Development and Juvenile Justice*. From 2002–2005, he received an Investigator Award in Health Policy Research from the Robert Wood Johnson Foundation. He was a Soros Senior Justice Fellow for 2005–06. From 1994–98, he served on the standing peer review panel (IRG) for violence research at the National Institute for Mental Health. He is past Editor of the *Journal of Research in Crime and Delinquency,* and serves on the editorial boards of several journals on criminology and law. He has served as Executive Counselor on the Boards of both the American Society of Criminology and the Crime and Deviance Section of the American Sociological Association. He received the Bruce Stone Award from the Academy of Criminal Justice Sciences. He is an elected Fellow of the American Society of Criminology.

Deborah Fleischaker is the Director of the American Bar Association Death Penalty Moratorium Implementation Project. In this position, she encourages state government leaders to establish moratoriums, pass reforms, and/or undertake detailed examinations of capital punishment laws and processes. She also encourages bar associations and others to press for moratoriums in their jurisdictions. In addition to her work at the ABA, Deborah is an adjunct professor at the University of Maryland School of Law and teaches a seminar on the death penalty. Prior to her work at the ABA, Ms. Fleischaker served as the Campaign Coordinator for a U.S. Congressional campaign and worked at the Maryland General Assembly. She has worked in private practice as an associate at the Baltimore, Maryland, firm of Brown, Goldstein & Levy LLP and as an Equal Justice Fellow at Public Citizens Congress Watch. Deborah earned her bachelor's degree from Vanderbilt University and obtained her law degree from the University of Maryland.

Jocelyn Fontaine is a PhD candidate in the Justice, Law and Society program at American University, where she also earned her Master of Science degree. During her nascent career she has examined an array of issues related to criminal justice and public policy, including procedural justice and police legitimacy, race and crime, violence against women, corrections and sentencing, and prisoner reentry. She has held positions at the National Institute of Justice,

U.S. Department of Justice in the Violence and Victimization Research Division, The Pew Charitable Trusts on the Public Safety Performance Project, and is currently working at The Urban Institute in the Justice Policy Center. Her most recent work on maternal homicide was published by the *Criminal Justice Policy Review*.

Eric M. Freedman is the Maurice A. Deane Distinguished Professor of Constitutional Law at Hofstra Law School. Professor Freedman serves as the Reporter for the American Bar Association's *Guidelines for the Appointment and Performance of Defense Counsel in Death Penalty Cases* (2d ed. 2003). He is the author of *Habeas Corpus: Rethinking the Great Writ of Liberty* (NYU Press 2002), and numerous articles for scholarly and general publications concerning capital punishment, habeas corpus and related subjects. In 2004, the American Association on Mental Retardation presented Professor Freedman with its Dybwad Humanitarian Award for his efforts on behalf of Earl Washington, Jr., a mentally retarded black man who was the first person ever released from death row in Virginia on the grounds of innocence. A graduate of Yale College and Yale Law School, Professor Freedman holds a Master's Degree in History from Victoria University of Wellington, New Zealand, is an elected member of the American Law Institute, and serves on the Advisory Board of the Capital Punishment Research Initiative of the University at Albany.

David Garland is the Arthur T. Vanderbilt Professor of Law and Professor of Sociology at New York University. The author of *Punishment and Modern Society* (1990) and *The Culture of Control* (2001), he is currently at work on a book entitled *Peculiar Institution: Capital Punishment and American Society*.

Jonathan E. Gradess is Executive Director of the New York State Defenders Association (NYSDA), a not-for-profit organization dedicated to improving the quality and scope of public legal representation in New York. The Association operates the nation's only state-funded Public Defense Backup Center, which serves New York's more than 5,000 public defense attorneys, providing training, legal research, consultation and technical assistance. Under its contract with the State of New York, NYSDA is called upon to "review, assess and analyze the public defense system in the State, identify problem areas and propose solutions in the form of specific recommendations to the Governor, the Legislature, the Judiciary and other appropriate instrumentalities." Mr. Gradess began his career as a paralegal, thereafter graduating *cum laude* in 1973 from Hofstra Law School's charter class. He has worked as a criminal defense lawyer, a private investigator, and a law school professor. Mr. Gradess is the recipient of the New York State Association of Criminal Defense Lawyers Gideon Award and the New York State Bar Association Criminal Justice Section award for Outstanding Contribution to the Delivery of Defense Services. He serves on the

Board of New Yorkers Against the Death Penalty and chairs the Restorative Justice Commission of the Roman Catholic Diocese of Albany.

Catherine Grosso has been a visiting assistant professor at the University of Illinois College of Law since September 2005. She is a member of the Illinois Program in Criminal Law and Procedure and teaches criminal procedure, evidence, death penalty law, and constitutional law. Ms. Grosso received her JD with high distinction from the University of Iowa College of Law, where she was a member of the Order of the Coif and served as an Articles Editor for the Iowa Law Review. Ms. Grosso received her BA in International Studies with a concentration in the Middle East from Earlham College in Richmond, Indiana, receiving college and departmental honors.

Robert Johnson is a Professor of Justice, Law and Society at American University in Washington, D.C. His social science books include *Culture and Crisis in Confinement, Condemned To Die, Hard Time,* and *Death Work*, which received the Outstanding Book Award of the Academy of Criminal Justice Sciences. Johnson's creative writing includes two collections of original poems, *Poetic Justice*, which received the L.I.F.E. Award from WilloTrees Press, and *Burnt Offerings*; and two collections of short stories, *Justice Follies* and *The Crying Wall*. Johnson has testified or provided expert affidavits before state and federal courts, the U.S. Congress, and the European Commission of Human Rights. He is a Distinguished Alumnus of the Nelson A. Rockefeller College of Public Affairs and Policy, University at Albany, State University of New York.

Sheri Lynn Johnson received her BA from the University of Minnesota and her JD from Yale University. After working for the public defender in New York City, she began teaching at the Cornell Law School, where she is now a professor. She teaches Constitutional Law, Criminal Procedure, and the Capital Punishment Clinic, which presently represents inmates on death rows in South Carolina, Alabama, Georgia, and the military. Her scholarly interests focus on racial issues in the criminal process, for which the Clinic's cases provide ample material. She is Co-Director of the Cornell Death Penalty Project.

Charles S. Lanier, PhD, is the Director of the Capital Punishment Research Initiative (CPRI), at the School of Criminal Justice, University at Albany. Since 1995, he has worked to develop and institutionalize both the Capital Punishment Research Initiative and the National Death Penalty Archive. His most recent published work is "Extinguishing the Victims' *Payne* or Acquiescing to the 'Demon of Error': Confronting the Role of Victims in Capital Clemency Proceedings" (with Beau Breslin), in *Wounds That Do Not Bind: Victim-Based Perspectives on the Death Penalty* (2006). He is co-editor/co-author of *America's Experiment with Capital Punishment: Reflections on the Past, Present, and Future of the Ultimate Penal Sanction* (1998; 2003) (with James R. Acker and

Robert M. Bohm). His research interests include the death penalty, terrorism, corrections/reentry, and the success narratives of former prisoners (see *Beyond Prison Walls: Personal Narratives of People Formerly Imprisoned*, forthcoming). He has conducted mitigation investigations in capital cases since 1997, at both the trial and post conviction level, in New York and Georgia. Much of his mitigation work today involves federal capital cases.

Sandra McGunigall-Smith received her PhD in Criminology at the University of Wales, Bangor, UK, in 2005. Her research interests include the effects of imprisonment on supermax and death-sentenced prisoners. She is currently Associate Professor in the Behavioral Sciences Department at Utah Valley University.

Glenn Pierce, PhD, is currently the Acting Director of the Institute for Security and Public Policy and Principal Research Scientist for the College of Criminal Justice at Northeastern University. At Northeastern University he has also served as Director of Strategic Planning and Research for Information Services, Director of Academic Computing, and Director for the Center of Applied Social Research. Dr. Pierce has conducted research on a broad range of social and economic issues and has obtained funding for his research from a variety of agencies including the National Institute of Justice, the National Institute of Mental Health, the Bureau of Alcohol, Tobacco, Firearms and Explosives, and the National Science Foundation. His most recent research has focused on crime and firearms violence and on criminal justice information and intelligence systems. As Director of Academic Computing he oversaw the implementation of Northeastern University's institution-wide 12,000 node computer network, the development of a centralized computer support service, and the university-wide delivery of software applications and other network services.

Michael L. Radelet is Professor and Chair, Department of Sociology, University of Colorado-Boulder. Dr. Radelet's research focuses on capital punishment, especially the problems of erroneous convictions and racial bias. He has testified in approximately 100 death penalty cases, worked with scores of death row inmates, and is a member of the Board of Directors of Families of Homicide Victims and Missing Persons (FOHVAMP), a Colorado group of families of homicide victims whose homicides have never been solved.

Austin Sarat is the William Nelson Cromwell Professor of Jurisprudence Political Science at Amherst College and Five College Fortieth Anniversary Professor. He is former President of the Law and Society Association, former President of the Association for the Study of Law, Culture and the Humanities, and former President of the Consortium of Undergraduate Law and Justice Programs. He is author or editor of more than sixty books including *When the State Kills: Capital Punishment in Law, Politics, and Culture; Something to*

Believe in: Politics, Professionalism, and Cause Lawyers (with Stuart Scheingold); *Cultural Analysis, Cultural Studies and the Law: Moving Beyond Legal Realism* (with Jonathan Simon); *Looking Back at Law's Century* (with Robert Kagan and Bryant Garth); *Law, Violence, and the Possibility of Justice*; *Pain, Death, and the Law*; and *The Blackwell Companion to Law and Society*. His most recent book is *Mercy on Trial: What It Means to Stop an Execution*. He is currently writing a book entitled *Hollywood's Law: What Movies Do for Democracy*. He is editor of the journal *Law, Culture and the Humanities* and of *Studies in Law, Politics, and Society*. His public writing has appeared in such places as *The Los Angeles Times* and *The American Prospect*, and he has been a guest on National Public Radio, The News Hour, Odyssey, Democracy Now, and The O'Reilly Factor. His teaching has been featured in *The New York Times* and on NPR's Fresh Air and The Today Show. He was the co-recipient of the 1997 Harry Kalven Award given by the Law and Society Association for "distinguished research on law and society" and was co-recipient of the 2004 Reginald Heber Smith Award given biennially to honor the best scholarship on "the subject of equal access to justice."

Christopher Seeds is a Visiting Fellow and Scholar to the Cornell Death Penalty Project at Cornell Law School. Mr. Seeds was previously a Deputy Capital Defender with the New York State Capital Defender Office and a Fellow and staff attorney with the Center for Capital Litigation in Columbia, South Carolina. He served as death penalty clerk for the New Jersey Supreme Court and as law clerk for former Associate Justice Alan B. Handler of the New Jersey Supreme Court.

Jon Sorensen is a Professor of Justice Studies at Prairie View A&M University. He has published articles on prison violence and capital punishment, and is coauthor of *Lethal Injection: Capital Punishment in Texas during the Modern Era* (University of Texas Press 2006). His research on deterrence and incapacitation was cited by Justice Breyer in *Ring v. Arizona* (2002). He also serves as an expert witness on future dangerousness in capital murder trials.

Jordan Steiker is the Cooper K. Ragan Regents Professor of Law at the University of Texas School of Law. He received his JD from Harvard Law School in 1988. He subsequently clerked for Hon. Louis Pollak, U.S. District Court (Eastern District of Pennsylvania) and Justice Thurgood Marshall of the United States Supreme Court. He has taught constitutional law and death penalty law at the University of Texas since 1990, where he is co-director of the law school's Capital Punishment Center. He has written extensively on federal habeas corpus and the death penalty. He has also represented numerous indigent death-sentenced inmates in state and federal court, including in the U.S. Supreme Court.

Scott Sundby is the Sydney and Frances Lewis Professor of Law at Washington & Lee School of Law. In addition to teaching courses in criminal law and procedure, he has served as Director of the Virginia Capital Case Clearinghouse, a clinic which advises lawyers appointed to represent capital defendants. Recently, much of his research has been conducted as part of the Capital Jury Project, a National Science Foundation study that has focused on interviewing jurors who have served on capital juries. His articles based on the Project have examined a variety of aspects of the death-penalty decision, including the role of the defendant's remorse in affecting the jury's decision, the impact of expert witnesses, the importance of how jurors perceive the victim, and how different trial strategies influence the jury's choice between a life and death sentence; his findings on how trial strategy affects a juror's death-penalty decision were relied upon by the United States Supreme Court in its opinion in *Florida v. Nixon* (2004). His book, *A Life and Death Decision: A Jury Weighs the Death Penalty*, relates many of the Project's findings through the telling of one jury's struggles over whether to sentence a defendant to die. *A Life and Death Decision* was selected as a 2006 Finalist for the American Bar Association's Silver Gavel Award.

Ronald J. Tabak is Special Counsel and Pro Bono Coordinator at Skadden, Arps, Slate, Meagher & Flom LLP. He has been involved in capital punishment litigation on a pro bono basis since 1983, and has won a death penalty case in the Supreme Court. Since the late 1980s, he has been Chair of the Death Penalty Committee of the American Bar Association's Section of Individual Rights and Responsibilities. He also chaired the Section's Task Force that developed proposals on Mental Illness and the Death Penalty that have become the policy of the ABA, the American Psychological Association, and the American Psychiatric Association. He has written numerous articles and chapters on capital punishment.

Margaret Vandiver is a professor in the Department of Criminology and Criminal Justice at the University of Memphis; she holds MA and PhD degrees in Criminology from Florida State University. Her principal research interest is collective violence, ranging from the use of the death penalty in America to contemporary instances of genocide. She has worked extensively with defense attorneys in capital cases as well as with condemned prisoners and their families. Much of her recent research has focused on the history of capital punishment in America. In 2006 she published *Lethal Punishment: Lynchings and Legal Executions in the South* with Rutgers University Press.

Neil Weiner is the Research Director at the Vera Institute of Justice in New York City. Neil came to Vera from the University of Pennsylvania, where he was a Senior Research Investigator at the School of Social Policy and Practice. He received his MA and PhD in Sociology from the University of Pennsylvania and was a postdoctoral fellow at the Urban Systems Institute at Carnegie

Mellon University. He was the Senior Research Associate on the National Academy of Science's Panel on Understanding and Preventing Violent Behavior and was a Visiting Fellow at the U.S. Department of Justice, National Institute of Justice. Neil's research interests include disparities in capital-case processing and sentencing; public-policy and programmatic formulation, implementation, and evaluation; social protection, justice and welfare; trajectories of individual violent-criminal careers; situations in which violence occurs and escalates; historical patterns in violent crime; the classification and management of risk; criminological theory; and research methods.

Valerie West is an Assistant Professor in the Department of Law, Police Science and Criminal Justice Administration in the John Jay College of Criminal Justice. She earned her PhD in Sociology at New York University. Her research interests include the effects of incarceration on communities, and capital punishment. She is the co-author (with James S. Liebman and Jeffrey Fagan) of *A Broken System: Error Rates in Capital Cases, 1973–1995* (2000), and she is the author of several additional scholarly articles.

George Woodworth is a Professor of Statistics and Actuarial Science at the University of Iowa. He received his BA in Mathematics from Carleton College in 1962 and his PhD in Statistics from the University of Minnesota in 1966. He is co-author of numerous articles on the death penalty, and of *Equal Justice and the Death Penalty* (Northeastern University Press 1990).

David Zuckerman has been a public defender in Philadelphia for over twenty years. He has litigated several claims alleging racial discrimination in the implementation of the death penalty in Philadelphia. For the last three years he has worked in the Defender Association of Philadelphia's federal division representing death-sentenced inmates in federal habeas corpus proceedings.

Index

Note: *f* indicates footnotes and *t* indicates tables.

A

Abdul-Kabir v. Quarterman, 44
Abramson, Brecht v., 264
activists, death penalty
   abolitionists, 445–46
   supporters, 446–47
actuarial prediction of future dangerousness, 372–73
adaptive behavior, 246–49
AEDPA. *See* Anti-terrorism and Effective Death Penalty Act of 1996 (EAEDPA)
affective action, 442
African Americans. *See also* Race; Racial disparities
   and homicide clearance rates, 118 (*See also* Homicides, racial and ethnic disparities in resolving)
   representation on juries, 54
   and symbolism of death penalty laws, 434
allocution, 440–41*f*
Alston, Charlie, 301*f*
Alternative sanctions for murder, 453–64
   benefits/cost calculus, 458–62
   future research, 464
   "Guillotine effect," 462–63
   jurors' misunderstanding of, 204

American Association on Mental Retardation (AAMR), 242, 243
   deficits in adaptive behavior, 246–47*f*
   definition of adaptive behavior, 247
   definition of intelligence, 243
American Bar Association
   Death Penalty Moratorium Implementation Project, 69–87, 145
   additional questions, 74–78
   innocence commissions, 234–35
   key findings, 72–74
   lack of data, 78–87
   methodology, 70–72
   federal habeas corpus, 269
   guidelines for defense counsel, 55
   policies on mentally retarded inmates, xix
   review of death penalty systems, 236
American Medical Association, 483, 494
American Psychiatric Association
   deficits in adaptive behavior, 246
   mental retardation, 242, 243
   policies on mentally retarded inmates, xix, 78

American Psychiatric Association *continued*
  position on future dangerousness, 29
American Psychological Association, xix, 78
American Society of Anethesiologists, 483
American Voice, 313
Amsterdam, Anthony, 144f
Angelone, Ramdass v., 35f
Anti-terrorism and Effective Death Penalty Act of 1996 (AEDPA), 226f
  criticism of, 266
  effects on federal habeas corpus, 261–93
appeals procedure, 262, 262f
Apprendi v. New Jersey, 41, 41f
arbitrariness, 24, 25–26. *See also* Proportionality reviews
archives, death penalty, 5. *See also* National Death Penalty Archive (NDPA)
  Capital Jury Project, 93, 96–97, 97f, 105
  of clemency petitions, 96, 105
  virtual, 95–96
Arizona, Clark v., 30f
Arizona, Ring v., 41–42, 503
Arizona, Tison v., 26
Arrington, Commonwealth v., 183–84, 185f
Association of Anaesthetists, 489
Atkins v. Virginia, 43, 43f, 78, 241–42, 250, 373, 504
  clinical definitions of mental retardation, 243
  culpability, 252–53
  deficits in adaptive behavior, 246, 247
  determination of mental retardation, 242, 242f
  impact of research on, xvii
  retribution, 456
At the Death House Door (documentary), xxiv

B
Babbit, Manny, 93, 103
Babbitt, Bill (collected papers), 91, 103–104
Back from the Dead, 13
Baldus study, 31–34, 61, 502
Barefoot v. Estelle
  court rejection of empirically based claims, 29–31
  future dangerousness, 359, 503
Barnett, Arnold, 179–80
Bartlett Commission, 406f
Batson v. Kentucky, 143f
Bayesian statistics, 158, 158f
Baze v. Rees, 486–87, 487f, 496
Beard, Rompilla v., 43, 55
Becker, Gary, 312
Bedau, Hugo Adam (collected papers), 93, 104
Belford, November (collected papers), 104
Belmontes v. Brown, 137f
benefit/cost calculus of alternative sanctions, 458–62
Bishop, Maxwell v., 144, 161–62
Blackmun, Harry, 41, 93, 412
Bonowitz, Abe (collected papers), 91, 104–105
Booth v. Maryland, 457
Bowers, William J. (collected papers), 93, 96, 105

Brecht v. Abramson, 264
Brennan, William, 41
Brewer v. Quarterman, 44
Breyer, Stephen, 41
Briseno, ex parte, 251
British Medical Association, 489
Brown, Belmontes v., 137f
Bush, George W., 299–300

C

Caldwell v. Mississippi, 202
California, McGautha v. See McGautha v. California
California Medical Association, 483
California v. Ramos, 461
Callins v. Collins, 41, 412, 503
Cantu, Ruben, 234
Capital Jury Project (CJP), 5, 51f, 227. *See also* Juries and jurors
  additional areas of research, 212–17
  archives, 93, 96–97, 97f, 105
  courts' rejection of empirically based claims, 34–37, 35f
  differences between African-American and white jurors, xxi–xxii
  and *McCleskey*-style research, 146–47
  overview, 202–203, 202f
  research on jurors and mitigation, 206–12
    assessing receptivity to mitigation, 207–209
    racial disparities, 210–12
    social pressures on decision making, 209–10
  and study of decline in death sentences, 59–60, 62f

Capital Losses: The Price of the Death Penalty in New York State, 400–401
capital murders
  decline in, 50
  research on prosecutorial discretion, 60–61f, 60–62
capital offenders, commuted and paroled, 360–62
capital prosecutions. *See* Prosecutions
capital punishment. *See* Death penalty
Capital Punishment Clemency Petitions collection, 105
Capital Punishment Research Initiative (CPRI). *See also* National Death Penalty Archive (NDPA)
  objectives, 4–5, 89f
  symposium, 3–4, 3–4f, 5
Capote, Truman, 39
Carey, Hugh, 431
Centers for Disease Control and Prevention homicide data, 327
certificates of appealability (COA), 267, 267f
  denied by district court, 285t–291t
  granted by district court, 278t–284t
  summary of dispositions, 292t–293t
Chaney, Heckler v., 487f
Chase v. State, 245f
Cheever, Joan, 13
Cherry v. State, 245f
Chester v. Texas, 251
Chief Justices, Conference of, 269
Christianson, Scott (collected papers), 89, 93

civil death, 460–61
claims of error, 73
Clark v. Arizona, 30f
Classification and Regression Trees (CART) approach, 172–73, 173f
clemency, 82–84, 297–305
   ABA policy recommendations, 83–84
   archives of petitions, 96, 105
   cases granted, 301f
   commutations, 298–302, 299f
   future research, 304–305
   numbers of commutations, 298–99, 299f
   problems with, 73
   research on, 298
Clinton, Bill, 300
COA grants. *See* Certificates of appealability (COA)
Coalition to Abolish the Death Penalty, National (collected papers), 108
Coker v. Georgia, 456
Coleman v. Thompson, 264–65
collections. *See* Archives; National Death Penalty Archive (NDPA)
Collins, Callins v., 41, 412, 503
Collins, Herrera v., 38, 93, 107, 298, 503
commissions
   death penalty, 4, 4f, 97f, 236–37, 406f, 504
   execution methods, 489, 493–94
   financial costs of death penalty, 404
   innocence, 231–33, 234–35
   victims' families, 462
Commonwealth v. Arrington, 183–84, 185f

commutations. *See also* Clemency; Ryan, George
   decline in, 298–302
   numbers of, 298–99, 299f
condemnation, moral, and denunciation, 437–38, 454–56
Conference of Chief Justices, 269
confessions, false, xx–xxi, 84
Connor, John, 411–12
constitutional facts, 23–24. *See also* Death penalty research
Consular Relations, 1963 Vienna Convention on, 301f
controlling fact finding (CFF) rule, 165, 165f
convictions and/or executions, erroneous
   claims of error, 73
   impact on public opinion, 227
   jurisprudential significance of, 38–44
      Herrera v. Collins, 38
      Kansas v. Marsh, 39–42
      Ring v. Arizona, 41–42
      United States v. Quinones, 38–39
   need for research on prevention, xx–xi
   research on, 503
   Supreme Court concerns about, 24
Cornel, Thomas, 464
correctional officers. *See* Death row, guards
cost-benefit calculus
   of alternatives sanctions, 458–62
   in criminal activity, 337–40
costs of death penalty. *See* Death penalty, costs of

Costs of Processing Murder Cases in North Carolina, The, 403
Counsel. *See* Defense counsel; Prosecutors
Crawford, Taylor v., 484, 486
crime
  decline in fear of, 50, 53
  fear of, in juror's decisions, 53–54
  impact of capital punishment on, xxiii–xxiv
  rates of, 50–51
crime labs, 72
Criminal Cases Review Commission, 232–33
Criminal Justice Legal Foundation, 313
culpability approach to estimate adjusted disparities, 176–78, 176f, 177f, 179–82, 181f
Cuomo, Mario, xxvi, xxvii, 431, 432, 460

D

dangerousness, future. *See* Future dangerousness
data collection instrument (DCI), 162–63, 163f
data collections, 96–100
data mining, 178–79, 179f
Davis, Allen Lee, 488–89
Davis, People v., 406f
death-eligible murders. *See* Capital murders
death notification, 391
death penalty
  alternatives (*See* Alternative sanctions for murder; Life without parole (LWOP))
  constitutionalization of, 25–37
  costs of, 14, 47, 98, 397–412
    dissemination of evidence, 403–406
    diversion of budgetary resources, 409–411
    early research period, 399–400
    future research, 406–411
    indirect, 407–408
    need for research on, xxv–xxvi
    research studies, 400–403
    saving costs through coercion, 408–409
  crime control effects of, 436–37
  effects on families of victims and defendants (*See* Families of victims and defendants)
  efforts to reinstate, 235–36
  jurors' mistaken beliefs about, 204
  justifications in support of, 114
  rarity of, 331–32, 385
  regional differences in practices, 508–509
  social meanings of, 432–33
  and status politics, 427–35
  symbolic characterization of, 422–24, 428f
  symbolic/instrumental distinction, 421–49
    balance, 444
    discounting of instrumental efficacy, 422
    discounting of symbolism, 441, 443–44
    expansion of, 442
    future research, 443–49
    meaning and purpose of, 425–27
    misuse of, 424, 436–43

death penalty *continued*
  public opinion, 422–23
  shifts in meaning of, 435–43
  symbol-of-status effect, 433–34
  symbolism of, 455
death penalty commissions, 4, 4*f*, 97*f*, 236–37, 406*f*, 504
Death Penalty Information Center
  numbers of death sentences and executions, 385
  opinion poll on innocence and death penalty, 227
  quantification of innocence cases, 228–29, 230, 230*f*
Death Penalty in New York Testimony Collection, 105–106
Death Penalty on Trial, The, 13
death penalty research, 13–21. *See also* American Bar Association, Death Penalty Moratorium Implementation Project
  areas for future study
    factors leading to erroneous convictions, xx–xxi
    impact on court decisions and possible reforms, xvii–xx
    public policy on existence of death penalty, xxiii–xxviii
    racial disparities, xxi–xxii
    same jury for guilt and sentencing phases, xxii
  challenges, 505–508
  historical analysis, 444–45, 449
  issues for future research, 506–510
  methodology of discrimination studies, 153–93
    "adjusted" race disparities, 174–82
    data collection and coding, 163–65
    modeling case flow, 166–67, 166*f*, 167*f*
    presenting results, 182–85
    race–neutral defendant culpability control variable, 186–93 (Appendix)
    research design, 156–63
    research team, 155–56
    screening for factual death-eligibility, 165–67
    unadjusted geographic disparities, 173
    unadjusted race disparities, 167–73, 167*f*
  need for, 499–500
  need for data, 505–506
  overview of, 501–505
  Paternoster-Brame Maryland study, 166–67, 166*f*, 167*f*, 171, 172, 173, 175–76, 183, 184*f*
  pilot studies, 156–57
  proportionality studies, 135–47
  recent publications (2000–2008), 13, 15–21
  role in Supreme Court jurisprudence, 23–44
    Capital Jury Project studies, 34–37, 35*f*
    death qualification of jurors, 27–29
    rejection of empirically based claims, 26–37
    future dangerousness, 29–31
    racial bias, 31–34
    reasons for, 26–27
  state histories, 13–14

studies commissioned by governmental bodies, 144–45, 144f, 402
studies of impact of race on decision making, 153–54f, 153–55
symbolism of death penalty, 444–45, 448
death qualification of jurors, 27–29, 28f, 502
death row
  conditions of, 469–70
  coping strategies, 471–72
  decline in size of, 226
  executions, 473–74
  guards, xxiv, 472–74
  measuring quality of life, 476–79, 478f
  removal from, 398, 398f, 401f
  research strategies, 474–77
death-sentenced inmates, 363–64, 369, 386
death sentences. *See also* Death penalty
  decline in
    disparities within states, 48–50
    explanations for, 47, 50–55
    fear of crime, 53–54
    improved defense counsel, 55–56, 56f
    minority representation on juries, 54–55
    need for research on, xxvii–xxviii
    option of life without parole (LWOP), 52–53
    residual doubt, 51–52
    restraints on prosecutors, 56–57, 57f
  impact of innocence on, 225–26
  research questions, 236–37
  research strategy, 57–63
  statistics, 47, 48, 49t
  number of overturned, 398, 398f
Death Without Justice: A Guide for Examining the Administration of the Death Penalty in the United States, 70
Dees, Morris, 501
defendants
  and due process, 264
  families of, 379–92 (*See also* Families of victims and defendants)
  future dangerousness of (*See* Future dangerousness)
  race of, and determination of mental retardation, 253–54
  remorse, 207f
  symbolism and status of, 429–30
defense counsel
  ABA research on, 76–77
  effectiveness of
  47
  inadequate, 55
  increased regulation of, 43
  ineffective assistance of, 55, 76–77
  professionalization of, 55–56, 56f
  research on voir dire questioning, xxii
  state policies regarding, 73
DeLuna, Carlos, 234
Dempsey, Moore v., 263
Denning, Alfred, 454–55
denunciation and moral condemnation, 437–38, 454–56
detectives, 117

deterrence, 114
  legislative debates on, 456–57
  need for research, xxiii
  and rarity of death penalty, 331–32
  research questions to consider, 14
Deterrence and Incapacitation, National Research Council Panel on Research on, 322
deterrence studies, 311–345
  acceptance of, 315–16, 342–43
  claims, 316–17, 341
  designs, 316
  Ehrlich's research, 312–13
  estimation techniques, 329–31
  implications of, 344–45
  inadequate peer review, 343–44
  introduction of priors into regression model, 343
  limitations, 317–341
  limitations of deterrence theory, 332–33
  list of studies, 357–58 (Appendix)
  measurement and specification errors, 325–29
    computation errors, 328–29
    early cutoffs in panel designs, 327–28
    missing data, 326–27
  media reception of, 313
  omission of factors
    co-morbid epidemics, 323–24
    distinction between homicides, 324–25
    life without parole (LWOP) considerations, 321–23
  overview of analysis of, 314–15
  prerequisites to link punishment and behavior, 333–341
  refutation of, 312–13
  replication of, 342
  structure of data, 318–20
  theory and specifications, 320–25
Diagnostic and Statistical Manual, 247
Diaz, Angel, 492
direct standardization of rates, 176–78, 176f, 177f, 179–82, 181f
discretion. *See* Prosecutors, discretion of; Sentencing discretion
DNA evidence
  exonerations based on, 51
  as requirement for capital conviction, 235–36
DNA testing
  public opinion on, 227
  statutes, 73
doctors and lethal injection, 483–96. *See also* Lethal injection
domestic homicides, 325
Dominquez, New Mexico v., 37
doubt of guilt, 51–52, 207f
drug epidemics and homicide rates, 323–24
due process, 264
Dukakis, Michael, xxvi–xxvii
Dunn, State v., 245

E

early release, myth of, 52–53, 52*n*
Easley, Mike, 301f
Economist Intelligence Unit's Quality of Life Index, 477
Eddings v. Oklahoma, 200
Edward, Don, 228, 230f
Ehrlich, Isaac, 14, 312–13
Ehrlich, Isaac (collected papers), 93
Ehrmann, Sara R. (collected papers), 95

Eighth Amendment, 154f
  and death penalty research, 14
  law cases citing, 456
  and lethal injection, 484, 494
  McCleskey v. Kemp, 31–34
  standardless discretion *(Furman)*, 36–37
electrocution, 488–89
empirical studies. *See* death penalty research
endowment effect, 337
Equal Protection Clause, 31–34, 135–36f
equipoise provision, 39–41
error, claims of, 73
Espy, M. Watt (collected papers), 91, 93–94, 106
Estelle, Barefoot v. See Barefoot v. Estelle
Estelle v. Smith, 29, 359
Evans, Timothy John, 234
evidence and problems of preservation, 72
evidentiary hearings, 73
executions
  decline in, 226, 385, 504–505
  erroneous, 233–35, 503
  impact on families (*See* Families of victims and defendants)
  of non-triggermen, 26
  number of, 318–19, 319f, 455
    vs. commutations, 298–99, 299f
    vs. homicides, 328
  regional differences, 508–509
  research questions to consider, 14
  search for humane methods, 488–90
  sham, 464
  voluntary, xix, 470, 473–74

Executions in America, 93
Executive Clemency Petitions collection, 96
exonerations
  based on DNA evidence, 51
  impact on public opinion, 227
expert testimony, Supreme Court rejection of, 29–31, 30f
expressive politics, 442f
eyewitness identification, 84
eyewitness testimony, Supreme Court's attitude toward, 30–31

F

factory safety legislation, 426–27
Fagan, Jeffrey, 5
fair-cross-section requirement, 27–28
false confessions, xx–xxi, 84
families of victims and defendants, 379–92
  context of research, 384–87
  current research, 380–82
  future research, 387–89
  policy implications, 390–91
Federal Bureau of Investigation (FBI)
  definition of homicide, 120
  Supplemental Homicide Reports (SHR) (*See* Supplemental Homicide Reports (SHR))
Federal Bureau of Investigation (FBI) *continued*
  Uniform Crime Reporting (UCR) data, 326
federal habeas corpus. *See* Habeas corpus, federal
Fifteenth Amendment, 263
finding aid (of archives), 92, 92f
Fitzpatrick, People v., 406f

Florida, Proffitt v., 199f
Florida Commission on Capital Cases, 232
Flynn effect (IQ testing), 245–46
Fogel, Jeremy, 484, 485, 494, 495, 496
Food and Drug Administration, 487f
Ford, Alvin (collected papers), 90, 106
Ford v. Wainwright, 90, 106
Fourteenth Amendment, 135–36f, 154f, 263
Fowler v. North Carolina, 312
Furman v. Georgia, 4, 83, 101, 199, 200, 500–501
    court rejection of empirically based claims, 26–37
    deterrence, 332
    financial cost of death penalty, 399, 399f
    standardless discretion, 36–37
    standards of decency, 405
future dangerousness, 29–31, 30f, 456
    future research, 373–75
    jurors' fear of, 53, 53f
    methodological issues in studies, 367–73
        agency records, 370–71
        comparison or control groups, 368–70
        definitions and effect on base rates, 367–68
        predictions of dangerousness, 371–73
    prior research, 360–66, 502–503
    research on, 359–75

G

Gallego, Gerald, 398, 398f
gangs and risk/benefit calculus, 339–40
General Social Survey, 477
geographic discrimination, research on, 154, 154f
Georgia, Coker v., 456
Georgia, Furman v. See *Furman v. Georgia*
Georgia v. McCollum, 143f
Gilmore, Gary, 114
Godfrey v. Georgia, 456
Godsey, State v., 75
Good, New Mexico v., 37, 212
Green, United States v., 212
Green River killer, 437
Gregg v. Georgia, 4, 26, 101, 199–200f, 217, 501
    deterrence, 312
    guided discretion, 199, 199f, 200
    retribution, 455–56
Grenander (M.E.) Department of Special Collections and Archives, 92
grief inventories, 389
Griffin, Larry, 234
gubernatorial pardons. *See* Clemency
guided discretion, 36–37, 199–202, 199f
Guillotin, Joseph-Ignace, 462–63

H

habeas corpus, federal
    act of 1867, 263
    decline in relief rates, 261–62, 267
    effects of AEDPA, 261–93
    future research, 268–69

Liebman study, 265
non-capital cases, 265–66f
possible reasons for, 268
prior to 1995, 262–65
relief rate data, 270t–277t
restrictions of, 264–65
statutory limitations on, 37–38
summary of dispositions, 292t–293t
Haenszel, Mantel, 176f
Hall, Kermit, 89, 100
Halperin, Rick (collected papers), 90, 106
Harbison v. Little, 484, 493
Harding, Donald, 489
Harlan, John
   allocution, 440–41f
   McGautha v. California, 35–36, 218
Harmelin v. Michigan, 460
Harris, Pulley v., 200
Hawkins, Steve (collected papers), 107
Hearn, In re, 245
Heckler v. Chaney, 487f
Henry, Brad, 301f
Herrera, Leonel, 93, 107
Herrera, Norma (collected papers), 93, 93f, 107
Herrera v. Collins, 38, 93, 107, 298, 503
Hickman, Morales v., 483–85, 490, 495
Hidden Victims, 380–81
Hispanic victims and homicide clearance rates, 118–19. *See also* Homicides, racial and ethnic disparities in resolving
historical analysis, 444–45, 449

Holton, State v., 75
homicide data, 98, 326, 327
homicide(s)
   clearance rates, 391
   decline in, 50
   decline in arrests, 117
   definition of, 120
   domestic, 325
   in prisons, xxiii, 362
   racial and ethnic disparities in resolving, 113–32
      additional research, 131
      findings, 120–30
      methodology in research, 119–20
   rates, 384–85
      and drug epidemics, 323–24
      and executions, 318–19, 319f, 328
   research on, 117–19
   resolution rates
      by circumstance and victim's race/ethnicity, 123–24, 124t
      by number of victims and victim's race/ethnicity, 125–26, 126t
      by race and ethnicity of victim, 121–22, 121t
      by relation and victim's race/ethnicity, 124–25, 125t
      by size of city and victim's race/ethnicity, 122–23, 122t
      combined effects of control variables, 126–130, 127t, 129t, 130t

homicide(s), *continued*
   resolved and unresolved, definition of, 120
   homicide victims, families of
      death penalty justification and, 113, 115
      difficulty of studying, 115–16
Howell v. State, 245f
Human Development Index, 477
Human Rights Watch, 492

I

identification, eyewitness, 84
Illinois, Morgan v., 54, 55, 201
Illinois, Witherspoon v., xx, 27
Illinois Death Penalty Commission, 231–32
incapacitation and deterrence, 322
incarceration and deterrence, 322–23
In Cold Blood, 39
Independent Living Scale, 249
index of receptivity to mitigation, 207
Indiana Criminal Law Study Commission, 404
ineffective assistance of counsel
   ABA research, 76–77
   Supreme Court decisions regarding, 55
inmates
   behavioral studies
      death-sentenced, 363–64, 369, 386
      life without parole (LWOP), 365–66, 367–68, 374–75
      sentenced to terms of imprisonment, 364–66
   general population, and impact of executions on, 474

innocence, 225–37
   areas of research, 226–28
   commissions, 231–33
   counting and defining cases, 228–31
   and executions, 233–35
   future research, 231–37
   impact on death penalty, 225–26
   impact on public opinion, 227
   Innocence List, 228–29
   symbolic framing of, 446–47
Innocence Inquiry Commission, 233
In Spite of Innocence, 14
intelligence, definition of, 243
intelligence tests, 244–46, 244f
International Court of Justice, 301f
international human rights law, 15
international opposition, 41–42
In the Shadow of Death, 381
Inventory of Complicated Grief, 389
IQ tests, 244–46, 244f

J

Johnson, Walton v., 245
Journey of Hope (collected papers), 107
Judicial Conference, United States. *See* United States Judicial Conference
judicial independence, 85–87
Jurek v. Texas, 199f, 359, 502
juries and jurors. *See also* Capital Jury Project (CJP); Sentencing discretion
   assessment of prospective reforms, 216
   death qualification of, 27–29, 28f, 502

failure to meet constitutional requirements, 203–206
frustration with ambiguous definition of *life*, 52–53, 52*n*
interviews for decision making studies, 59–60
minority representation, 54–55
mock, 216
problems with, 73
pro-death predisposition of, 203, 213
psychological effects on, 215, 215*f*
receptivity to mitigation, 206–12
racial disparities, 210–12
recording deliberations, 214*f*
reluctance to decide for death, 47
responsibility for punishment, 204–205, 214–15
separate juries for guilt and sentencing phases, xxii
shadow, 214–15
social pressures on decision making, 209–10, 213–14
tipping points affecting final verdict, 51–55, 52*f*
jury instructions, xix–xx, xxi, 216
Justice Department, U.S., data, 316
Justice for All, 313
juveniles, execution of
impact of research on court decisions, xviii
Roper v. Simmons, 42, 43, 78, 373, 504, 505
Stanford v. Kentucky, 26, 43, 504

K

Kansas v. Marsh
jurisprudential significance of wrongful convictions, 39–42
Scalia's concurrence, 230–31, 458, 503
Souter's dissent, 230
Kemmler, In re, 488
Kemmler, William, 488
Kemp, McCleskey v. See McCleskey v. Kemp
Kendall, George, 499
Kentucky, Batson v., 143*f*
Kentucky, Stanford v., 26, 43, 504

L

Lake, I. Beverly, 233
Lane, Teague v., 264
Latino victims and homicide clearance rates, 118. *See also* Homicides, racial and ethnic disparities in resolving
LaValle, People v., 407*f*, 505
law enforcement
ABA policy recommendations, 85
lack of data on policies, 84–85
problems with evidence preservation, 72
problems with interview procedures, 72
lawyering. *See also* Defense counsel
ABA research on, 76–77
problems with state policies, 72–73
Lawyers. *See* Defense counsel; Prosecutors
legislation, death penalty, 226*f*
New York 1995 act, 431–32, 434–35
reinstatement, 235
symbolism of, 423
lethal injection, 483–96
constitutional challenges, 484–85

lethal injection *continued*
history of, 489–90
research questions to consider, 15
search for solutions, 490–94
study of, 491–94
transparency of procedures, 494–95
life without parole (LWOP)
and deterrence theory, 321–22
and juror decision making, 52–53, 53–54, 53*f*
jurors' misunderstanding of, 204
perceptions and conceptions, 460–61
quality of life research, 476
research questions to consider, 15
and restoration, 461
study of inmates' behavior, 365–66, 367–68, 374–75
Lightbourne, State v., 492
Lindh v. Murphy, 265
Little, Harbison, v., 484, 493
Llera Plaza, United States v., 35*f*
Lockett v. Ohio, 200, 359
Lockhart v. McCree, 27–29, 28*f*, 202
Lott, State v., 246*f*
Lundy, Rose v., 297
Lynaugh, Penry v., 26, 43, 201, 201*f*, 242, 504

M

Madison, James, 263
Marsh, Kansas v. See Kansas v. Marsh
Marshall, Thurgood
costs of death penalty, 399, 399*f*
realities of death penalty, 500–501
standards of decency, 41, 405
Maryland, Booth v., 457
Maryland, Mills v., 201

Maryland (Paternoster-Brame) study, 166–67, 166*f*, 167*f*, 171, 172, 173, 175–76, 183, 184*f*
Maxwell v. Bishop, 144
Maxwell v. Bishop problem, 161–62
McCleskey-style studies, 139–40, 140*f*, 141–42, 144*f*, 146–47, 155. *See also* Death penalty research, methodology of discrimination studies
McCleskey v. Kemp, 101, 202
aftermath, 37–38
Baldus Study and, 61
conflation of odds and probabilities, 172, 172*f*
court rejection of empirically based claims, 31–34, 144
McCleskey v. Zant, 297
McCollum, Georgia v., 143*f*
McCotter, Woolls, v., 487*f*
McCree, Lockhart v., 27–29, 28*f*, 202
McGautha v. California, 218, 510
allocution, 440–41*f*
standardless discretion, 35–36, 200, 200*f*
McKoy v. North Carolina, 201
McManus, State v., 245*f*
McVeigh, Timothy, 435*f*
media influence, xxvii
medical doctors and lethal injection, 483–96. *See also* Lethal injection
Mello, Michael A. (collected papers), 107–108
mens rea, 30*f*
mental illness and/or retardation
ABA research on, 78, 79*f*
and clemency, 83
need for research, xix

mental retardation (and executions), 241–56. *See also Atkins v. Virginia*
deficits in adaptive behavior, 246–49
determination of
based on *Atkins*, 242–43
effects of race, 253–54
intelligence tests, 244–46, 244*f*
procedural issues, 251–53
states' additional criteria, 250–51
three criteria, 243–50
disproving, 247–48
future research, 255–56
impact of research on court decisions, xvii
juror conceptions of, xviii–xix
onset before age 18, 249–50, 250*f*
Penry v. Lynaugh, 26, 43, 201, 201*f*, 242, 504
shift away from executions, 241–42
state applications of clinical definitions, 243–51
subaverage intellectual functioning, 243–46
Michigan, Harmelin v., 460
Millions Misspent: What Politicians Don't Say about the High Costs of the Death Penalty, 403–404
Mills v. Maryland, 201
Milsap, Samuel, 234
minorities. *See also* Race; Racial disparities
representation on juries, 54
research on death sentences, xxi
Mississippi, Caldwell v., 202
mitigation and jurors' receptivity to, 206–12

assessing, 207–209
racial disparities, 210–12
social pressures on decision making, 209–10
mock jurors, 216
Moore v. Dempsey, 263
moral condemnation and denunciation, 437–38, 454–56
Morales, Michael, 483, 496
Morales v. Hickman, 483–85, 490, 495
Morales v. Tilton, 486, 490–91, 494
moratorium movement, 14
moratoriums on death penalty, 47–48
Illinois, 38
increased regulations following, 42–43
Morgan v. Illinois, 54, 55, 201
Murder and the Death Penalty in Massachusetts, 13
murderers, reasons for punishing, 454–58
murders, capital. *See* Capital murders
murder-suicides, 325
Murder Victims' Families for Human Rights, 115
Murder Victims' Families for Reconciliation, 115
Murphy, Lindh v., 265
Murray, Turner v., 202

N

NAACP Legal Defense Fund
challenges to death penalty, 500
conference on research, 501
data collection on race, 98
investigations of innocence claims, 234

National Academy of Sciences
  capital punishment as deterrence, xxiii
  deterrence, 313
National Center for Health Statistics (NCHS), 327, 327f
National Coalition to Abolish the Death Penalty (collected papers), 108
National Death Penalty Archive (NDPA), 5, 89–110
  background and evolution, 90–94
  contents of, 92–94
  future of, 94–101
  history, 90–91
  new collections, 99
  quantitative data collections, 96–99
  selected holdings, 103–110 (Appendix)
  users of, 100
  Virtual Archive, 95–96
National Institute of Justice, 145
National Research Council Panel on Research on Deterrence and Incapacition, 322
Netherland, O'Dell v., 35f
New Jersey, Apprendi v., 41, 41f
New Jersey Death Penalty Study Commission, 462, 504
New Mexico v. Dominquez, 37
New Mexico v. Good, 37, 212
New York State Defenders Association (NYSDA) (collected papers), 108
Nichols, Brian, 397
non-triggermen, execution of, 26
North Carolina, Fowler v., 312
North Carolina, McKoy v., 201

North Carolina, Woodson v., 200, 456, 458, 510
Nottingham Health Profile, 478f

O

O'Dell v. Netherland, 35f
offenders, commuted and paroled, 360–62
O'Hern, Daniel, 156f
Ohio, Lockett, v., 200, 359
Oklahoma, Eddings v., 200
Oklahoma, Thompson v., 504
Oklahoma City terrorist attack, 226f
online archives, 95–96
opposition, international, 41–42
Oral History of the Death Penalty in America Project (OHDPA) (collected papers), 108–109
outcome-based regulation, 34

P

Panetti v. Quarterman, 44
pardons. *See* Clemency
parole and future dangerousness, 361
Pataki, George, 432
Paternoster-Brame Maryland study, 166–67, 166f, 167f, 171, 172, 173, 175–76, 183, 184f
Payne v. Tennessee, 457
Pelke, Bill (collected papers), 91, 107
Penry v. Lynaugh, 26, 43, 201, 201f, 242, 504
People v. Davis, 406f
People v. Fitzpatrick, 406f
People v. LaValle, 407f, 505
People v. Smith, 406f
People v. Taylor, 408f, 505
perceived net cost hurdle, 337

Perkins, Ex parte, 245f
Peterson, Scott, 435f
p-hats, 280
physicians and lethal injection, 483–96. *See also* Lethal injection
pilot studies, 156–57
plea bargains, 408, 408f, 437
politics. *See also* Death penalty, symbolic/instrumental distinction
 expressive, 442f
 symbolic/status, 425–27, 426f, 427–35
 symbolic struggle in, 445–48
 value-rational, 442–43
polls. *See* Public opinion
Porter, Anthony, 228
post-conviction procedure, 262, 262f
post traumatic stress disorder, 215, 381
Powell, Lewis, 33
practice effects (IQ testing), 245
Prisoners. *See* Inmates
prison guards. *See* Death row, guards
prisons
 drop in homicides in, xxiii, 362
 supermax, 374, 469–70
Prisons and Their Moral Performance, 477–78
prison violence. *See* Future dangerousness
Proffitt v. Florida, 199f
propensity analysis, 178
proportionality. *See also* Arbitrariness
 reviews
  ABA research on, 73, 74–76
  flaws in, 75
  New Jersey review, 154f, 156f, 157f, 158f
 studies, 135–47
  analyses of case flows, 136–37, 136f
  of effects of race on decision making, 142–43, 143–43f
  future research, 145–47
  legal and policy implications of findings, 143–45
  McCleskey-style studies, 139–40, 140f, 141–42, 144f, 146–47, 155 (*See also* Death penalty research, methodology of discrimination studies)
  potential consumers of, 144–45
  pre-1990 studies, 137, 137f
  Supplemental Homicide Report (SHR) approach, 138–39, 140–41, 141f, 154–55
prosecutions
 and ability to deal with other crimes, xxiv
 expense of, 47
 stages of, 136, 136f
 subsequent to trial reversal, 157–58, 158f
prosecutors
 ABA policy recommendations, 81–82
 case selection, 60–61f, 60–62
 discretion of
  need for research on racial factors, xxi
  racial disparities and, 61, 143

prosecutors *continued*
  state policies regarding, 72
  growing restraints on, 56–57, 57f
  lack of research data on, 81–82
  training of, 73
prospect theory, 334
protection, social, 456–57
public opinion
  cost of death penalty, 398–99, 405–406, 406f
  death penalty, 226, 227, 399f
  executions of innocents, 51, 226f
  future research, 508
  influences on, xxvi–xxvii
  life without parole (LWOP), 460, 461
  motivational basis of, 427
  post-abolition, xxvii
  symbolism of death penalty and, 422–23
public policy, xxiii–xxviii
Pulley v. Harris, 200
Punishments, alternative. *See* Alternative sanctions for murder

Q

quality of life research, 476–79, 478f
quantitative data collections, 96–100
Quarterman, Abdul-Kabir v., 44
Quarterman, Brewer v., 44
Quarterman, Panetti v., 44
Quinones, United States v., 38–39

R

race
  data collection on, 98
  of defendants and determination of mental retardation, 253–54
  research questions to consider, 14
  and symbolism of death penalty laws, 434
  of victims
    and capital sentencing disparities, 31–34, 501–502
    and sentencing disparities, 77–78
racial disparities, 73–74
  ABA studies, 77–78
  in capital sentencing, 31–34
  and clemency, 83
  in considering mitigating factors, 210–12
  need for research, xxi–xxii
  in pretrial process, 142–43, 142–43f
  and prosecutorial discretion, 61, 143
  in resolving homicides (*See* Homicides, racial and ethnic disparities in resolving)
Radostitz, Rita, 300f
Ramdass v. Angelone, 35f
Ramos, California v., 461
rationality test, 333–35
Reagan, Ronald, 300f
recidivism, studies of, 360–62
redemptive constitutionalism, 302
Reed, Susan, 234
Rees, Baze v., 486–87, 487f, 496
regulation, outcome based, 34
Rehnquist, William, 38
Reign of Terror, 463
religion and retribution, 114
research, death penalty. *See* Death penalty research

resentencing cases, xxii
residual doubt of guilt, 51–52, 207f
retribution, 455–56
retributive justification, 114–16
Rhines v. Weber, 261
Richardson, Elaine, 410
Richmond, State v., 75
Ring v. Arizona, 41–42, 503
Rogers v. State, 245
Romney, Mitt, 235
Rompilla v. Beard, 43, 55
Roper v. Simmons, xviii, 42, 43, 78, 373, 504, 505
Rose v. Lundy, 297
Royal Commission on Capital Punishment, 489, 493
Ryan, George, 38, 48, 51, 83, 231, 298, 373, 504

S

Salazar, State v., 75
sampling problems, 161–62
sanctions, alternative. *See* Alternative sanctions for murder
scale-based methods to estimate adjusted disparities, 176–78, 177f, 179–82, 181f
Scalia, Antonin
  erroneous convictions, 24
  Kansas v. Marsh, 39, 40–42, 230–31, 458
  McCleskey v. Kemp, 33
Schirro v. Summerlin, 314, 315
secondary victims, 215
sentencing discretion
  guided, 36–37, 199–202
  standardless, 35–37
sentencing phase requirements and jurors, 203–206
September 11 terrorist attack, 226f

shadow juries, 214–15
Shafer v. South Carolina, 201
sham executions, 464
Shuman, Sumner v., 456
Simmons, Roper v., xviii, 42, 43, 78, 373, 504, 505
Simmons v. South Carolina, 201
Simpson, O. J., 435f
Sixth Amendment
  fair-cross-section requirement, 28
  psychiatric testimony, 29
  and recent Supreme Court death penalty jurisprudence, 37–44
Skipper v. South Carolina, 359
slavery and legal rights, 263
Smith, Estelle v., 29, 359
Smith, People v., 406f
Smith, Wiggins v., 43, 55
Smith v. Texas, 44
social protection, 456–57
social worth
  of defendants, 429–30
  of murder victims, 430–31
Souter, David, 40–42, 230
South Carolina, Shafer v., 201
South Carolina, Simmons v., 201
South Carolina, Skipper v., 359
Southern Coalition on Jails and Prisons (collected papers), 109
special housing units (SHUs), 469–70
standard error of measurement in IQ tests, 244–46
standardless discretion, 35–37
Stanford Binet test, 244
Stanford v. Kentucky, 26, 43, 504
states and death penalty research, 13–14
State v. Dunn, 245

State v. Godsey, 75
State v. Holton, 75
State v. Lightbourne, 492
State v. Lott, 246f
State v. McManus, 245f
State v. Richmond, 75
State v. Salazar, 75
State v. Williams, 245
status (symbolic) politics, 426–27, 427–35
Stephen, James Fitzjames, 429, 455
Stephens, Zant v., 200, 456
Stevens, John Paul, 39
Stewart, Potter, 199f
studies, death penalty. *See* Death penalty research
SUDAAN, 162f
Summerlin, Schirro v., 314, 315
Summerlin v. Stewart, 35f
Sumner v. Shuman, 456
supermax prisons, 374, 469–70
Supplemental Homicide Reports (SHR), 98, 119–20, 157f, 159f
   data on race, 501–502
   studies based on, 138–39, 140–41, 141f, 154–55 (*See also* Death penalty, methodology of discrimination studies)
Supreme Court, U.S. *See* United States Supreme Court
Supreme Courts, state
   New Jersey study, 144, 144f, 145, 145f
   studies commissioned by, 144
surveys. *See* public opinion
survivors of victims. *See* Victims, families of
Sykes, Wainwright v., 297

symbolic action, 427–28, 445
Symbolic Crusade: Status Politics and the American Temperance Movement, 425
symbolic (status) politics, 425–27, 426f, 427–35
symbolism, political, 435f

T

Taylor, People v., 408f, 505
Taylor, Williams v., 43, 55
Taylor v. Crawford, 484, 486
Teague v. Lane, 264
temperance movement, 426
Tennessee, Payne v., 457
testimony, eyewitness, 30–31
Texas, Chester v., 251
Texas, Jurek v., 199f, 359, 502
Texas, Smith v., 44
Texas Defender Service (TDS), 76–77
Texas Revised Inventory of Grief, 389
Thirteenth Amendment, 263
Thomas, Clarence, 39–40
Thompson, Coleman v., 264–65
Thompson v. Oklahoma, 504
Tibbs, Delbert, 230–31
Tibbs v. State, 231
Tilton, Morales v., 486, 490–91, 494
Tison v. Arizona, 26
Torres, Osvaldo, 301f
trial transcripts
   archives of, 96–97, 97f
   and assessment of jurors' receptivity to mitigation, 207–209
   and study of decline in death sentences, 58–59, 59–60
"tripping," 472

True, Walker v., 245
Turner v. Murray, 202
Turow, Scott, 13

U

Ultimate Punishment, 13
Uniform Crime Reporting (UCR) data, 326
United State Department of Justice data, 316
United States Judicial Conference
　costs of defense, 404
　federal habeas corpus, 269
United States Supreme Court. *See also* Death penalty research, role in Supreme Court jurisprudence
　and lethal injection, 486–87, 487f
　and use of historical data, 100–101
　ineffective assistance of counsel decisions, 55
　influence of research on, xvii–xviii
　initial post-*Furman* regulation of death penalty, 25–26
　reception to death penalty, 500–501
United States v. Green, 212
United States v. Llera Plaza, 35f
United States v. Quinones (2002a, 2002b), 38–39

V

value-rational politics, 442–43
van den Haag, Ernest (collected papers), 109
Vandiver, Margaret, 5
Van Tran v. State, 249

venire pools and minorities, 54. *See also* Juries and jurors
victims
　families of, 379–92 (*See also* Families of victims and defendants)
　assistance for, 391, 462
　impact of executions on, xxiv–xxv
　opinion on death penalty, 383, 390
　restoration, 457–58
　race of, and disparities in capital sentencing, 31–34 (*See also* Homicides, racial and ethnic disparities in resolving)
　symbolism and status of, 430–31
victims' rights movement, 457–58
Vienna Convention on Consular Relations, 301f
Vineland Scale, 249
Virginia, Atkins v. See Atkins v. Virginia
Virtual Archive, 95–96
voir dire, xxii
voluntary execution, xix, 470, 473–74
Von Drehle, David (collected papers), 93, 101

W

Wainwright, Ford v., 90, 106
Wainwright v. Sykes, 297
Wainwright v. Witt, 54
Walker v. True, 245
Walton v. Johnson, 245
Weber, Rhines v., 261
Wechsler Intelligence scales, 244, 244f

West, Bobby, 104
White, Edward, 332
Wiggins v. Smith, 43, 55
Williams, Stanley Tookie, 486
Williams, State v., 245
Williams v. Taylor, 43, 55
Willingham, Cameron, 234
Witherspoon-excludables, 27–28
Witherspoon v. Illinois, 502
   court rejection of empirically based claims, 27
   voir dire, xx

Witt, Wainwright v., 54
Wolfgang, Marvin, 143–44
Woodson v. North Carolina, 200, 456, 458, 510
Woolls v. McCotter, 487f
wrongful convictions. *See* Convictions and/or executions, erroneous

Z

Zant, McCleskey v., 297
Zant v. Stephens, 200, 456